MEDIEVAL UPHEAVAL
A CATALOGUE OF BLOODY EUROPEAN EVILS

AN ESSAY TO EMPOWER AFRICAN AMERICANS

MEDIEVAL UPHEAVAL
A CATALOGUE OF BLOODY EUROPEAN EVILS

AN ESSAY TO EMPOWER AFRICAN AMERICANS

Or,

CONFRONTING THE WHITEWASHING

OF

EUROPEAN HISTORY

Sheshet Kemet

COPYRIGHT © Sheshet Kemet 2015
All rights reserved. No part of this publication may be reproduced, stored in a retrieval system or transmitted in any form or by any means electronic, mechanical, recording, and photocopying or otherwise without the prior written permission of the publisher.

978-0-692-55288-9

Disclaimer: Medicinal recipes and cures included in this book are not endorsed, nor do the author, publisher, or their agents encourage their use. No one should attempt to duplicate, manufacture, ingest, or treat illness or disease using recipes and cures cited within these pages. The author, publisher and their agents are not responsible for the duplication, sale of, or for any possible harm (real or perceived) that derives from the production of, or ingestion of any enclosed recipe.

Ancient recipes are cited in these pages only for the purposes of research and awareness. Properly licensed medical professionals, their surrogates, or authorized providers only can lawfully prescribe medicines. Seek the advice of licensed medical providers for treatment of illnesses.

*Cover art: San Bartolomeo (St. Bartholomew's Day Massacre) from a faithful reproduction of a two-dimensional public domain work of 16th century artist Giorgio Vasari.

Khoekhoe Publishing

Khoekhoe Publishing
P.O. Box 3298
Southfield, MI 48037
www.medievalupheaval.wordpress.com/
khoekhoepublishing@gmail.com

Contents

IN MEMORY IX
MAAFA: MOVING ALL AFRICANS FORWARD ANEW 1
    EUROPEAN AND AFRICAN HISTORY EQUALLY IMPORTANT 8
INTRODUCTION 18
    THE BLOODY HELL ON EARTH 14TH CENTURY EUROPE CALLS AFRICANS SAVAGES 19
    MEDIA IMAGES OF SADISTIC MEDIEVAL EUROPEANS TRUER THAN FICTION 25
    WHEN MONOPOLY WAS A CRUEL MEDIEVAL SPORT 31
    CHAOS REIGNED OVER MEDIEVAL EUROPE FOR 50 GENERATIONS 38
THE CATALOGUE OF EVILS 40

1 41
THE DECLINE AND FALL OF EUROPE 41
    LONG BEFORE THE FALL, GREEKS AND ROMANS STUDIED AT THE FEET OF WISE AFRICANS 44
    IN ANCIENT ROME AND THE U.S., POLITICS OF CORRUPTION, ECONOMIC DISTRESS BESIEGE POOR 53
    AS BARBARIANS ADVANCE ON ROME "DEATH BREATHES OUT DEATH" 57

2 60
MEDIEVAL LAWS INFLUENCE OUR LEGAL SYSTEM 60
    ANCIENT EUROPEAN LAWS VALUE PROPERTY OVER HUMAN LIFE, PROMOTE INEQUALITY 61
    SUNDAY BECOMES A DAY OF REST, TAX EXEMPTIONS FOR THE CHURCH 62
    "PRETENSE OF A COURT" OF LAW: SWEARING OATHS ON BIBLES, SECRET COURTS AND JURIES 63

3 66
THE TRIBES OF EUROPE 66
    GERMANIC TRIBES RULE: SURVIVAL OF THE SADISTS 67
    MORE STILL CAME BY SEA: ASSAULTS, HUMAN SACRIFICE & CANNIBALISM 72
    ROOTS OF ROYAL ANCESTRY: EUROPE'S HIGHEST HOODS BECOME ROYAL HIGHNESSES 74
    SOME VIKING CUSTOMS AND TRADITIONS STILL PRACTICED 79
    VIKING MYTHS 80

4 82
FEUDALISM 82
    A POORLY DISGUISED SYSTEM OF SLAVERY 83
    THE MUDDLE OF MEDIEVAL LIFE 90

THE DIRT ON EUROPEANS: POOR HYGIENIC PRACTICES BRING ON PLAGUES............. 93
THE LIFESTYLE OF THE BARON WAS BARELY BETTER...................... 98
LET THE GAMING BEGIN 105

5 107

MEDIEVAL SOCIAL UPHEAVAL 107
WHAT HAPPENS WHEN PRINCES INSIST ON MAKING GAMES OF CHAOS?...........107
"SHOCK AND AWE" IN MEDIEVAL WARFARE 112
FAMINE: SKELETONS OUT OF THE CLOSET AND ONTO THE EUROPEAN DINNER TABLE:
FAMILY MEMBERS BECOME THE MAIN COURSE 114
EUROPE'S PAST HELPS EXPLAIN THE AFRICAN'S PRESENT 120

6 129

MEDIEVAL SLAVE NARRATIVES 129
EUROPE'S SLAVE INDUSTRY BEFORE THEY STOLE AFRICANS, FORCING THEM TO GROW
WHITE WEALTH 129
A PARADIGM ADJUSTMENT FOR READERS BELIEVING THAT "SLAVES WERE ONLY
BLACK FOLK" 132

7 146

MEDIEVAL ATTRACTIONS: GLADIATORS MUST "DIE BECOMINGLY" 146
"HE IS WOUNDED!" HUMAN CARNAGE THE #1 MEDIEVAL ENTERTAINMENT 147
SLAUGHTERED HUMANS AND ANIMALS SACRIFICED TO ROMAN GODS 149
POLITICS, GAMBLING IMPORTANT BEHIND THE SCENES ACTIVITIES...................... 152
DEADLY GAMES BLUR LINES BETWEEN REALITY AND FANTASY...................... 155
CHRISTIAN LEADERS DESPISE THE GAMES 156
CHILDREN GLADIATORS 158
SPECTATORS MURDER A MONK ATTEMPTING TO STOP THE DEADLY GAMES............160
MILDLY TAMER MEDIEVAL GAMES 161
DE SPECTACULA: BAWDY AND DEADLY THEATRICS...................... 161

8 165

CHRISTIAN LEADERS: SWINDLERS AND "MARVEL MONGERS" IN HIGH
PLACES 165
CHURCH CORRUPTION CLEARS THE WAY FOR 1000 YEARS OF ANARCHY AND MAGICAL
THINKING AS EUROPE BEGINS A NEW WORLD ORDER...................... 165
"PAPAL OFFICE WORTH FIGHTING FOR": CLERICS DRAW BATTLES LINES OVER
CHURCH RICHES 167
KINGS AND CHURCH LEADERS FIGHT FOR DOMINANCE...................... 169
CHURCH LEADERS INTRODUCE PURGATORY PURELY FOR PROFITS 171
THE POPE'S TEMPORAL POWERS ALLOW CHURCH CORRUPTION...................... 173
A PLUNDERING PRIEST PLUS A CERTAIN PILFERING POPE, RODRIGO BORGIA...........173
"MYTH-MAKING AND MARVEL-MONGERING": THE CHURCH BACKS SCAMS...........175
THE SAINTS PRESERVED! SHRINES SPUR PILGRIMS TO OPEN THEIR PURSES...........179

A MODERN DAY CHRISTIAN "HEALING" SCAM HAS MEDIEVAL ROOTS 182
THE FIRST RECORDED CASE TO FALSELY ACCUSE A "BLACK BOY" OF A CRIME? 182
END OF WORLD FEARS GRIP EUROPE AS THEY MARK THEIR 1ST MILLENNIUM 183
THE DEVIL'S IN THE DISEASES, ACCORDING TO THE CHURCH 184
GIROLAMO SAVONAROLA CHALLENGES THE POPE'S AUTHORITY 185
EUROPEANS DIG UP SKELETONS, BELIEVE SAINTS' BONES HOLD CURES 186
THE CHURCH USES HUMAN SKULL CUPS DURING SERVICES AND AT "HOLY" WELLS 188
EUROPEAN CHURCHES CONSTRUCTED OF HUMAN BONES 191

9 194

THE CHRISTIAN COMMUNITY EMBRACES BENT BELIEFS 194

EUROPEANS SAY, "IF EARTH IS ROUND ANTIPODES WALK ON THEIR HEADS" 195
CHRISTIANITY: A JUMBLE OF EUROPE'S PAGAN BELIEFS SHAKEN UP AND POURED OUT
TO THE MASSES: TALL TALES BECOME RELIGIOUS TRADITIONS 200
CHRISTMAS TAKES ROOT IN THE SHADOWS OF EUROPE'S TREE-WORSHIPPING
CUSTOMS 204
SON (SUN) WORSHIP, WATER BAPTISM & MUCH MORE: CUSTOMS OF CHRIST AND
MITHRA CURIOUSLY IDENTICAL 206
VIKING TRADITIONS CELEBRATED, HONORED BY MODERN CHRISTIANS 209
TALL TALES OF CHIMERA INSPIRE BLOODY TALES OF TERROR FOR TOTS 211
EUROPE'S FEAR OF CAPE NOTHING 212

10 214

INQUISITIONS OF THE CRIMINAL CHRISTIAN CHURCH 214

THE HOLY ROMAN CHURCH STRIKES OUT VIOLENTLY AT HERETICS: FREE THINKERS
BECOME TARGETS 214
WHO ARE HERETICS? THE CHURCH SAYS THEY "AVOID LIES... AND FRAUDS" 216
THE CHURCH MURDERS MILLIONS, CASUALLY BURNS VILLAGES HUNTING FOR
HERETICS 217
"HOW TO" TORTURE BOOKS: THE ODYSSEY OF TERROR BY BISHOPS 218

11 222

THE CHRISTIANS CRUSADE 222

NOT EVEN CHRISTIANS ARE SAFE FROM CHRISTIAN CRUSADERS 223
CHRISTIANS GO CANNIBAL: MAKING BANQUETS OF MEN, WOMEN AND CHILDREN.230
CRUSADERS GO ROGUE; AND GYÖRGY DÓZSA MEETS A SADIST 232

12 235

MEDIEVAL MED-INSANE 235

EARLY EUROPEAN PRACTITIONERS STUDIED IN KMT 235
FIRST, THE DOCTOR WANTS TO KNOW, "WHAT'S YOUR SIGN?" 238
DEAD HUMANS MEDICINE: EUROPEANS HARVEST THE HUMAN BODY FOR CURES &
COSMETICS 242
WASTE NOT, WANT NOT: HUMAN URINE AND SWEAT USED AS MEDICINES 245

- Human Feces used as a Medicine 247
- Human Fat used as a Medicine 248
- Human Blood in Medicines: Its Origins and Many Strange Uses 252
- In the European Paradigm, a Human Death Becomes Life 253
- Menstrual Blood Used in Medicinal Preparations Up to the 20ᵗʰ Century 258
- Europeans Bathe in Human Blood 260
- Moss from Human Skulls as a Medicine 265
- "Mummie is Become Merchandise": Pharaoh's Embalmed Body Becomes Balsam for the Living 266
- Europeans Believed Killers' Hands Could Cure 278
- European Cannibalism Older Than Methuselah, as Common as Dirt .. 280

13 282

IF WE ARE WHAT WE EAT, THEN 282
- Is Christian Communion Actually a Celebration of European Cannibalism? 282
- Ritual Sacrifices of Humans Replaced by Animals: Communion Table and Altar Historically the Same 284
- European Pre-Christian Gods Practiced Cannibalism, Too 287
- Thyestean Feasts: Centuries-Long Accusations of Christian Cannibalism 290

14 293

MEDIEVAL TERRORISTS 293
- The Mechanics of Torture 294
- The Terrorizing Torturing Punishments of the Papacy 295
- Europe's Macabre Chambers of Horrors 298
- Europeans Fine-tune Physical Torment to Elicit Confessions, True and False 300
- Europeans Use Perfected Torture Techniques on Africans 302

15 305

EUROPEANS EXPORT TERRORISM TO AFRICA 305
- Europe Kills Millions Vowing to "Serve the Well-Being of the Native" .. 306
- Egun Civil Despite Europe's Cruelties: "African Savagery" Meme is Projection of European Behavior and Traditions 308
- The Portuguese Oppress an African King and a Nation 310
- Christian Missionaries Gain Riches in Africa, Egun Lose Their Homes, Their Hope and Their Future 312
- The Past is Always Present in Our Lives 313
- Indo-Europeans Conjure Religious Theories to Overthrow African Supremacy 315

16 318

AFRICAN FIRSTS: INTRODUCING SOME AFRICAN SOCIAL CUSTOMS 318
    AFRICANS DEVELOP A STURDY CONSTITUTION: FEUDALISM IS NOT AN AFRICAN TRADITION 318
    "VALLEY OF DREAMS": EUROPEANS DESCRIBE AFRICA TO OTHER EUROPEANS 323
    LITERACY IN AFRICA LONG BEFORE WHITE EUROPE DEVELOPS 327
    MORAL CODES OF AFRICA 330
    AFRICANS USE "HONORS SYSTEM." HURT BY LACK OF TRUST ASK, "WHAT! DO YOU THINK I AM A WHITE MAN?" 332
    AFRICANS CHOOSE THEIR LEADERS, EVICT NARCISSISTS FROM VILLAGE 334
    "YOUR MONEY OR YOUR LIFE" IS NOT AN AFRICAN TRADITION: AFRICAN HEALING 335
    WESTERN PHARMACEUTICALS MAKE MILLIONS ADOPTING AFRICAN MEDICINES ... 336
    TRADITIONAL AFRICANS TAKE FROM THE LAND ONLY WHAT'S NEEDED 337
    AN INTRODUCTION TO A FEW STURDY CIVILIZATIONS EGUN DEVELOPED 338

17 342

AFRICANS FACE TROUBLE IN EUROPE'S PARADIGM 342
    OWNING OUR AFRICAN PAST 345
    WHY AFRICANS FEEL SHAME WHEN EUROPEANS FEEL NONE: EXPOSING A FEW OF EUROPE'S TRICKS OF THE TRADE 346
    A PERSON IS A PERSON BECAUSE THERE ARE PEOPLE: BUILDING AN AFRICAN FUTURE 354
    WHEN WE STAND ON TRUTH WE TRAMPLE LIES AND RISE TO MEET OUR DESTINY. 357

MEDIEVAL MASSACRES 360

APPENDIX A 361

SELECTED PASSAGES FROM THE JEW AND HUMAN SACRIFICE 361
    FROM THE BIBLIOGRAPHY OF THE JEW AND HUMAN SACRIFICE 361
    BLOOD RITUAL 362
    BLOOD OF EXECUTED PERSONS: HANGMAN'S ROPE 365
    BLOOD-SUPERSTITION AMONG CRIMINALS AND ITS CONSEQUENCES 367

APPENDIX B 369

SELECTED PASSAGES FROM THE BLOOD COVENANT 369
    THE PRIMITIVE RITE ITSELF 369
    THE ROYAL BLOOD 369
    SUPPLEMENT 371

APPENDIX C 372

SELECTED PASSAGES FROM MANNERS, CUSTOMS, AND DRESS 372
    PUNISHMENTS 372

APPENDIX D 377

SELECTED PASSAGES FROM CHRONICLES OF PHARMACY, V.2 377

x   MEDIEVAL UPHEAVAL

   ANIMALS IN PHARMACY 377
SELECTED BIBLIOGRAPHY **379**

IN MEMORY

This book is written in memory of my Mother.
Mom's love for Africa and African people everywhere inspired this work.

Dedicated To

Troy and Stephanie.
Your love, wisdom, encouragement and support helped to make this book possible.
May the Earthly journeys of you and your children
Be filled with great African knowledge and wisdom.

Special Thanks To

T.L. Pierce, your African wisdom liberated my African identity.
T. Young, you tirelessly read many versions of this manuscript
And offered invaluable critiques;
Particular thanks to Joe who read the manuscript's final version
And advised me to publish it, and SW who urged me to write again.
All things came together for good.

Egun Wole! Welcome Ancestors!

I pour libations to each ancestor, especially Jerry, Mama Love, John Lee, Eva, Dolly, Samuel, Beattie, Ora, Louvenia, Albert, George, William, Lonnie, Roberta,
I celebrate Sekhmet: Within her forces rests the essence of potential.
Finally, I honor and acknowledge my Spirit guides and protectors, Sigi Tolo and Sabu.

I write this essay on behalf of the billions of Africans whose lives and futures were shattered, their homes and families destroyed by sinister forces that harbored great greed and heartlessly used destruction to achieve their disturbing goals. These sweet African souls with their amiable sensibilities faced great cruelties that lasted fully a lifetime. However, the mortal and psychic indignities they endured were not enough for those oppressive Europeans who set about slandering the African character and sullying the exceptional achievements of an honorable people imbued with impressive natural talents and learned skills.

Europe's goal was to crush the world's memory of the collective achievements of Africans the way locusts blot out a cornfield. And their efforts nearly worked, except for the remarkable scholarly triumphs of African-descended traditionalists (and some Europeans, too) who refused to allow the deceptions to continue. From these traditionalists we have learned that thousands of years before Europe's invasion of Africa, great African minds had come together cooperatively. First they gathered in small groups, and then clustered in larger communities until the first civilization – and all that such a magnificent endeavor brought to bear – was established.

The purpose of this book is to set to right some of the unjust wrongs done unto our African forebears while attempting to offer their descendants the peace of mind and confidence that grows from knowing that Europe brutalized our African ancestors not because they were crazed and untamed, but because handfuls of Europe's own citizens were.

MAAFA:[1] MOVING ALL AFRICANS FORWARD ANEW

When I began studying African history — mostly written, and taught by African traditionalists, I kept encountering a particular phrase. And it did not matter whether the instructor had a background in psychiatry, astrophysics, anthropology, medicine, sociology, chemistry, or history these well-studied individuals appeared to draw the same conclusion about early Europeans: "They had come storming out of the hills of Europe" into the rest of the world. At the time I did not fully understand the meaning behind this phrase that had become a sort of scholastic earworm inserted into my consciousness every so often; nor did I know what these esteemed African traditionalists wanted me to learn from it. But my mind became stimulated anyway. Since I am a fairly creative thinker it was easy for me to visualize the scenes: Swarming bands of pale-skinned men, their foul-smelling bodies wrapped in equally offensive animal skins, slogging their way through the dark and misty waste lands of Europe into the rest of the world. Following behind them were their herds and flocks. In the midst of this mélange, disheveled women pulled along dozens of their scraggly-looking children.

Historians tell us that these early westerners stumbled across frigid wastelands that iced-over fully eight months of the year. In fact, so determined were these westerners that they doggedly wandered over areas so cold that the *chilled* wine they toted along with them was frozen solid, as were the rivers they crossed:

> The Rhine and the Danube were frequently frozen over, and capable of supporting the most enormous weights. The barbarians, who often chose that severe season for their inroads, transported, without apprehension or danger, their numerous armies, their cavalry, and their heavy wagons, over a vast and solid bridge of ice.[2]

In this environment of such stunning misery, locating adequate shelter and food became enormous challenges. But, the farther away they slogged from their own country the closer they advanced into territories belonging to others. I saw these wild, axe-wielding, spear-throwing men rampaging on their horses as they aggressed against civilized nations, killing, pillaging and destroying everything that lay in their path. If these bands represented turbulence, the rest of the world must have been in some measure of peace,

---

[1] Maafa is a Swahili term for disaster. Used here it indicates all Africans and their
[2] Edward Gibbon, *The Decline and Fall of the Roman Empire*, vol. 1, p. 261.

2 MEDIEVAL UPHEAVAL

I thought then. It was not much later that I learned early Europeans had, indeed, stormed civilizations. It was soon after gleaning that information that I connected my earworm with a senior high school history lesson learned years earlier.

* * * * *

"Aryan tribes journeyed far, conquering and colonizing the great stretch of country from the passes of Afghanistan to the Ganges. Those were years in which clans or families grew into nations...."[3]

The Indus Valley was one of those long-standing advanced ancient civilizations that many believe swarming bands of Indo-Europeans dismantled and replaced with one of their own design. The Rig-Veda records the toppling of this ancient empire as a struggle between light and dark forces ending in the overthrow of the darker forces, according to many African scholars who believe the saga describes the Indo-Europeans'[4] advancement on and untimely destruction of a magnificent African civilization. Book 9, Hymns 40 - 41:6 Soma Pavamana records the following about the ousting of the black-skinned Dasyu:

1. The Very Active hath assailed, while purified, all enemies:
    They deck the Sage with holy songs.
2. The Red hath mounted to his place, to India, goes the mighty juice:
    He settles in his firm abode.
3. O Indu, Soma,[5] send us now great opulence from every side,
    Pour on us treasures thousandfold.
4. O Soma Pavamana, bring, Indu all splendours [sic] hitherward:
    Find for us food in boundless store.
5. As thou art cleansed, bring hero strength and riches to thy worshipper,
    And proper thou the singer's hymns.
6. O Indu, Soma, being cleansed, bring hither riches doublypiled [sic],
    Wealth, mighty Indu, meet for lauds.

1. ACTIVE and bright have they come forth, impetuous in speed like bulls,
    Driving the black skin far away.
2. Quelling the riteless Dasyu, may we think upon the bridge of bliss,
    Leaving the bridge of woe behind.

---

[3] A. C. Clayton, *The Rig-Veda, and Vedic Religion*, p. 155.
[4] 4 Indo-European refers to the people who spoke early Indo-European languages, and are ancestors to the Greeks, Romans, Germans, Slavs, post-Aryan invasion Indians, and later Celts. Archaeologist Marija Gimbutas hypothesizes that early Indo-Europeans (battle axe cultures) overran stable, organized matrilineal farming communities. The belief is that these violent, war-mongering patriarchal tribes overran flourishing matrilineal communities, replacing female gods with male gods.
[5] Some researchers believe Soma likely was a plant-based intoxicating/hallucinogenic drink, and was a god offering. Pavamana means purified.

3. The mighty Pavamana's roar is heard as 'twere the rush of rain
    Lightnings are flashing to the sky.
4. Pour out on us abundant food, when thou art pressed, O Indu wealth
    In kine and gold and steeds and spoil.
5. Flow on thy way, Most Active, thou fill full the mighty heavens and earth,
    As Dawn, as Surya with his beams.
6. On every side, O Soma, flow round us with thy protecting stream,
    As Rasa flows around the world. – Trans., Ralph T.H. Griffith, 1896.

Ironically, the invaders to the Valley call the aboriginal people of the land, Dasyu,[6] the "destroyers and injurious," though the author of *Rig-Veda and Vedic Religion*, A. C. Clayton, clearly identifies the Indo-Europeans as the land's newcomers. Below, Clayton provides commentary on the Indo-Europeans who stumbled upon the Valley:

In the dawning time of *history*, somewhere in the lands beyond Afghanistan and north of Persia roamed bold tribes of fair-complexioned men and women with their horses and cattle. From stories that have come down to us about them, from words that they used which have still place in our speech, and from rites of worship still observed by many of their descendants to-day something can be known of their life and thoughts. *They were a rough, brave, hardy, adventurous race, of honest and simple soul.*

Some of them gradually limited their wanderings to Iran, the land of Persia…. Others of these tribes, more daring, by long marches, and through many generations approached and entered India from the north-west. These were the men who called themselves Aryas', Aryans, a word meaning ' kinsmen' as *distinct from the aboriginal tribes already dwelling in the land.* And though much concerning them is obscure, not a little is evident, and to-day it is possible to look back across the many centuries that separate us from those nomads and learn what manner of men they were.[7] (Italics added).

Clayton continues, "From [the hymn] we learn that before the Aryans came India was *sparsely* peopled by some of the races that are now often

---

[6] "There these aborigines are named 'Dasyu' 'destroyers' or '**Dāsa**' or 'injurious.' Their skins were much darker than those of the Aryans and so they were stigmatized as 'black' or 'black-skins'. From the shape of their broad noses they were called 'goat-nosed'. They possessed herds, they had strongholds called 'pur'. Those who were captured were made slaves, and the very word 'dāsa' came to mean 'slave' in later Sanskrit and cognate languages. The references to their religion describe them as offering no sacrifices, being unbelievers in the gods of the Aryans, and thus grievously impious. There are two passages in which they are called śiśna-devah, 'whose god is the phallus' (Rig-veda vii. 21.5; x. 99. 3), and it will be remembered that the phallus, as the linga, came to be the chief symbol of the god Siva in later Hinduism. From the first these Dasyus were the enemies of the Aryans, but their demon worship greatly affected the Aryans, especially in the simpler domestic religion that has always been that of the ordinary folk." Clayton, *Rig-veda*, p. 6.
[7] Ibid., pp. 3-4.

called 'jungle tribes.' Among them the majority would be Dravidians. The Gonds, Bhils and Santals[8] are modern survivors of those races."[9] (Italics added). According to Clayton's early assessment, the poems cover a period of at least 700 years describing an era full of "expeditions, warfare, and adventure."

However, reading about the advanced achievements of the egalitarian Indus Valley people who designed complex urban centers, including inventing the blueprint for water drainage,[10] and who introduced an originally black-skinned, curly-haired Buddha and his spirituality of peace to the world makes the Indo-Europeans' barbaric attack on her a crime against humanity... to say the least. Though dismantling high societies is a signature trademark of Indo-European cultures, their historians cite a lack of relevant evidence as they deny such a disturbance ever took place in the Valley. Despite that rebuttal, African scholars who trust in their studious and judicious interpretation of physical evidence,[11] in addition to data gleaned from the saga,[12] believe a violent incursion did take place and that those "jungle tribes" of the Indus Valley were probable descendants of ancient Egyptians: "Thou, thou alone, hast tamed the Dasyus; singly thou hast subdued the people for the Arya." (Book 6: Hymn 18:3 Indra). The obscene skin color-based caste system introduced by the invaders persists in India to this day.

*   *   *   *   *

Europeans called themselves barbarians long before others did so. In fact, the Greeks applied the term barbaros[13] to non-Greeks. From their perspective barbaros were foreigners, and unrefined people who the Greeks believed lacked an ability to learn, and who were less developed socially. Romans adopted the term and called the ancient German peoples who lodged their families in the dense, frigid woods of Europe barbarians; it was from within the misty shadows of those marshy lands that barbarians plotted, then launched their attacks against European-held territories inspired by "hunger for land, together with the love of fighting

---

[8] Bhils and Santals are not racially classified as Dravidians.
[9] Clayton, *Rig-veda*, pp. 4-5.
[10] Western civilization adapted the Indus Valley sewage system.
[11] See Runoko Rashidi: Distinguished Africans in the European Renaissance.
[12] From 1st century BCE historian Diodorus Siculus: Asr (Osiris) "passed through Arabia, bordering upon the Red sea as far as to India, and the utmost coasts that were inhabited; he built likewise many cities in India, one of which he called Nysa, willing to have a remembrance of that in Egypt where he was brought up. At this Nysa in India, he planted ivy.... He left likewise many other marks of his being in those parts... and took care to have statues of himself in every place, as lasting monuments of his expedition." George Booth, *The Historical Library of Diodorus the Sicilian, in Fifteen Books*, (London: M'Dowall, 1814), p. 26.
[13] The female name Barbara is an adaptation of barbarian.

and the desire for booty and adventure, which led to their migrations,"[14] according to Professor Hutton Webster who adds:

> This home land of the Germans in ancient times was cheerless and unhealthy. Dense forests or extensive marshes covered the ground. The atmosphere was heavy and humid; in summer clouds and mists brooded over the country; and in winter it was covered with snow and ice. In such a region everything was opposed to civilization. Hence the Germans, though a gifted race, had not advanced as rapidly as the Greek and Italian peoples."[15]

I first learned the definitions of medieval-era terms like barbarian, villain, and vandal in the 11th grade. It was during one early European history lesson that Mr. Kelvin[16] revealed the astonishing fact that Vandals emerged from a tribe of Germans who once upon a time ago wreaked havoc across Europe and on into North Africa:

> Putting out in their long, light vessels, they swept the seas and raided many a populous city on the Mediterranean coast. So terrible were their inroads that the word "vandalism" has come to mean the wanton destruction of property.[17]

What a revelation! In my day, the media never showed images of white people wilding — the kinds of scenes that were beginning to flood my young, and still mostly impressionable mind. Up to that point, I had a much smaller frame of reference for vandals who — the media informed me, were thieves and, oh by the way, Black! Suddenly, learning that small 'v' vandalism originated with an uppercase 'V' group of riotous, pillaging, murderous white folks filled my heart with esteem: "It wasn't just Black folks!" cutting up in the world as I learned to believe, thanks to modern media. Knowing that European savages, subduing the African Barbary coast between 429-534 of the Common Era (CE), introduced[18] vandalism

---

[14] Webster, *History*, p. 241.
[15] Webster, *History*, p. 239.
[16] This is a pseudonym.
[17] Webster, *History*, p. 248.

[18] My personal story attempts to illustrate a point. Incursions into African began very early on by Hyksos, Assyrians, Babylonians, etc. Before incursions began, Kemet (KMT) experienced thousands of years of peace. In another part of North Africa, Carthage and Rome competed over territories, resources, wealth and trade routes. In 146 BCE, the Roman Republic took Carthage and "razed it to the ground," mostly because of jealousy. Henry Francis Pelham and Henry Stuart Jones, Rome: Republic; Rome: Empire, Encyclopaedia Britannica, 11th ed. 1911. p. 631. Also, in 254 "When the exhausted country no longer supplied a variety of plunder, the Franks [Germans] seized on some vessels in the ports of Spain, and transported themselves into Mauritania. The distant province was astonished with the fury of these barbarians, who seemed to fall from a new world, as their name, manners, and complexion were equally unknown on the coast of Africa. — Aurel. Victor. Eutrop. ix. 6." Gibbon, Decline, vol. 1, p. 309.

into Africa resulted in a significant shift in my consciousness and an adjustment in the way I would view the world.

> From the pages of Salvian and Augustine we may safely infer that there was, at any rate relatively, a large amount of wealth, and culture, and prosperity in the three most important African provinces, up to the day when the first footprint of the Vandal was seen on the Numidian sands.[19]

That day's history lesson never fully faded from my youthful brain still in an early stage of drawing important conclusions about our society. After a time, though, I filed that lecture - along with far less significant moments from my adolescent years - away. However, I had come to realize that there is always *more to the story*, especially the aptly named history that puts the positive achievements of European men front and center while seeking to soften the more negative aspects of *his* story.

A people's life story, or biography - herein called history - when properly taught introduces micro concepts that allow students to expand their minds and imaginations into the macro, so that we grow excited to explore more on our own. Having an ability to broaden the micro is helpful in recognizing patterns, especially in storytelling since traditional African and European storytellers work from different models. There was something quite unique about the role played by traditional African Griots whose task was to entertain audiences, but to accurately preserve cultural and generational history at the same time. However, European storytelling focuses on creative invention, rather than veracity. Their narratives are *designed to distort reality for entertainment purposes*; they *steer the audience's attention toward a particular societal concern* or theme; and are *intended to trigger desired responses*. According to Gibbon:

> When in calm retirement we peruse the combats described by Homer or Tasso, we are insensibly seduced by the fiction, and feel a momentary glow of martial ardor. But how faint, how cold is the sensation which a peaceful mind can receive from solitary study! It was in the hour of battle, or in the feast of victory, that the bards celebrated the glory of heroes of ancient days, the ancestors of those war like chieftains who listened with transport to their artless but animated strains. The view of arms and of danger heightened the effect of the military song; and the passions which it tended to excite, the desire of fame, and the contempt of death, were the habitual sentiments of a [barbarian] German mind.[20]

In other words, European storytellers have manipulated the emotions of their audiences for a very long time. In fact, history professor Philip Van Ness Myers writes this about researches into the exploits of ancient

---

[19] Thomas Hodgkin, *Italy and Her Invaders*, vol. 2, p. 237.
[20] Gibbon, Decline, vol. 1, p. 280.

European heroes, "These were in some cases, perhaps, historical characters, but so much of myth and fable has gathered about them that it is impossible to separate that which is really historic from that which is purely fabulous."[21] The central elements to European storytelling come into play once we study the Vandals further. They were definitely a rowdy bunch that eagerly complied with the pleas of certain European leaders who enlisted their barbaric skills in disrupting politics in their specific cities. However, we soon discover that the Vandals were not the only tempestuous tribe creating havoc across the European landscape and the rest of the world known at that time to Europeans.

The Vandals partnered with some equally, or perhaps, even more vicious and cruel tribes. However, focusing the narrative on a single brutal tribe - such as the Vandals were - allows the other arrogant, uncivilized tribes of Europe to escape broad historical review. We can see this pattern (paradigm, social construct) unfold in the historical treatment of Adolf Hitler and Alexander of Macedonia. Both men envisioned themselves as rulers over vast empires. Each went to deadly lengths to reach their goal. However, Hitler's monstrous acts are severely scrutinized while historians overlook Alexander's murderous conquests in favor of drooling over his *military genius*. When we focus on Hitler's atrocities we miss Alexander's crimes cleverly hidden beneath the "great" moniker though together these psychopathic men and their followers casually killed millions of people. Europeans and Anglo-Americans routinely cling to this pattern to manipulate folklore and listener emotions so that specific social results are gained.

So, of course, the European narrative that is grounded in distorting reality and redirecting the story's focus will always approach the account of African-Americans starting with our captivity on the coastlines of the United States. While they gladly quarry the land to steal the wealth of Africa, Europeans prefer that the extensive historical achievements of Africans stay smothered beneath the sands of that great Continent. This is one stealthy way *his* story depresses the minds of Maafan children nurtured by people themselves taught to believe that our own achievements are meaningless, and/or non-existent. Indeed, African-Maafans are the only persons who learn cultures over and above our own. And that is because *we allow the very people who abused us to teach us.*

Obviously, it makes sense that the domineering population of the United States teaches history through their own paradigm and schools children in the European way of the world. But, their lessons train our African minds to accept bizarre ideas. For example, we are taught that Africans are inferior though we have the most diverse human genes.

---

[21] Phillip Van Ness Myers, *Outlines of Ancient History*, p. 131.

African genes make adaptation, survival and birthing healthy babies on this ever-changing Earth easiest for Africans; it was thousands of years ago that great African genetics gave them the ability to survive the frigid cold of the northern hemisphere. Besides all that, several prehistoric African systems remain helpful to today's world, including the math system that drove ancient Ethiopian commerce and undergirds today's computers.

Another message from Europeans is that individuality is better, yet Earth's eco-system thrives on cooperation and inter-dependence; valuable concepts of teamwork and shared responsibility acquired from the animal kingdom helped Egun navigate their environment, and aided them as they erected splendid and stable societies. What's more, Europeans tell us to accept the most immoral human behaviors as normal: greed, wars, poverty, hunger, etc., have all become tolerable situations the world over. Europe-centered schooling makes integration of an African perspective difficult. That is even if we want to learn about our pre-historical African identity after being subjected to centuries of disinformation. Sadly, such a posture causes us to miss learning important African teachings. But we miss out on hearing the simple, yet profound lessons, too. Like, for instance, that the majestic melody to the American standard, "Amazing Grace" probably derives from Africa; an inspiring kernel of knowledge taught by a popular African-American vocalist/educator.

European and African History Equally Important

This brings me to the point of this essay and my reasons for taking on such a hefty project scouring through hundreds of books, documents, and video/audio resources on European history, especially aspects of the Germanic/Scandinavian tribes: Despite centuries of inciting monstrous murders and instigating hundreds of wars, European's glorify their own history, while they eclipse the story of African cultures. And I understand why there has been all the deception: Africans were some very impressive people who engineered many wonderful achievements[22] before and during an obscenely long era when the collective European society was in a state of political decay and moral decline. The following passage on the political and civil growth of ancient Africa comes from a 1907 edition of The Church Missionary Review:

> Now that the seclusion of this vast domain has been *invaded* and exposed, one of the most surprising and interesting facts that are revealed is that *for many centuries before the fifteenth* the Soudan was the scene of *a civilization on a par with, and even in advance of, that of the greater part of Europe at the same period*... The first of the above divisions is regarded as the original home of the Fulani; the second division is the region where the Berber influence became for a time

---

[22] See the Kingdom of Kongo during the 14th century for one example.

predominant; the third division was the home of a black Mohammedan people who established the mighty Mellestine [Mali] empire, to be followed by another still more extensive, that of Songhay; the fourth division includes Hausaland and Bornu.[23] (Italics added).

A more humbled people when meeting these refined Africans for the first time might have tried to win friendships, and gain information that might improve their own miserable conditions. However, self-important people would dismiss those achievements, then set about dismantling them and exploiting their creators. Europeans were the latter. In fact, sincerely asking for the Africans' help was never an option for Europeans if the following quote represents the general attitude White men held towards Africans, as acclaimed British journalist Flora L. Shaw reveals in the upcoming passage. In it Shaw quotes the Arab traveler and chronicler Ibn Battuta who was dismayed upon seeing "white-skinned" Berbers practicing African customs when he reached Mali for the first time in 1352:

"Mohammedan as they called themselves, they had fallen into habits which scandalised [sic] him. He felt, as unfortunately many a white man since then has had sorrowful occasion to feel in similar circumstances, that these white men did not sustain the dignity of their race in the presence of the blacks by whom they were surrounded and to whose rule they bowed.

"The black viceroy who received the merchants of the caravan with which Ibn Batuta [sic] travelled remained seated while they stood before him. He spoke to them through an interpreter, not because he did not understand, or because they were not close enough for him to hear, but 'solely to indicate his disdain for them.' The experience stirred in Ibn Batuta such wrath that he regretted to have entered the country of black men who were thus ill mannered, and who treated white men with so little respect."[24]

It is well past time to confront the very passé whitewashing that reinforces Africans as *savages* while it upholds Europeans as moral, innocent, decent, and moder*n*. Inside this essay is where we begin to peel away layers and layers of lily-white paint to see the shabby European social infrastructure that lies just beneath.

I know early European societies were in a state of moral degradation and internal deterioration because their own academic historians tell us they behaved uncivilly during their self-described Dark,[25] Medieval, and Renaissance Ages when warlord leaders cloaked their cruel natures and

---

[23] G.F.S., "Ancient Kingdoms of the Soudan." *The Church Missionary Review*, vol. 58 (1907) pp. 15-16.
[24] Flora (née Shaw), Lady Lugard, *A Tropical Dependency*, pp. 130-131.
[25] According to English lawyer James M. Ludlow, "Cardinal Baronius, the historian of the church down to the year 1198, designated the period which then closed as the Dark Ages." *The Age of the Crusades*, p. 6.

enterprises in pomp and circumstance, then nurtured and exploited their *subject's* unruly behavior. For instance: "The Olympic games of the Greeks tended… to… improve them in those exercises which were useful in the warfare of the times. The *gladiatorial exhibitions of the Romans kept up that apathy to scenes of blood without which an empire rising upon the spoils of slaughter and conquest could never have been extended and preserved.*"[26] (Italics added). And now I'm telling my African, African-American and African Maafan readers that Europeans deluded us into believing our ancestors were the wretched savages in need of saving.

The Europeans' distortions of Africa's story (Afristory, or Nubistory) have led many of us to toss it aside, leaving us instead to adopt *his* story of European and African interactions. What many of us do not know is that racial (cultural) quarreling and hostilities existed early on in Europe between Europeans; in committing these acts of white on white crime, they maimed and slaughtered each other mercilessly for thousands of years. We do not hold a collective understanding that Europeans exported those hostilities around the world, targeting brown, black, and yellow populations with them. What we learned (and believed) was that their way was and is better than our African way; it encouraged many of us to set aside our own Afristory, so that we align our thoughts with the very Europeans who not only oppressed our ancestors, and, by extension, us, but whose societies lacked an ability to treat their very own members with dignity. And if they mistreated their own family members, they lacked the capacity to regard *other* families favorably. The European's premise about our African ancestors was baseless, yet it allowed their power brokers to manipulate[27] their own populations; and resulted in Africans feeling self-shame.

But, if the premise is wrong, the conclusion will be wrong, too. Still, the current[28] European social construct rests comfortably upon the myth of the African savage. African-Maafans' continued belief in the truthfulness of that myth dissuades us from discovering our real value and using reignited self-esteem as fuel to challenge the European and Anglo-American version of history that would rattle their regressive and abusive power structure. Reuniting with our ancestors (our selves) is quite possibly the European's greatest nightmare. Former Jamaican governor Sydney Olivier (d. 1943)

---

[26] Horatio Smith and Samuel Woodworth, Festivals, Games, and Amusements, Ancient and Modern, pp. 185-86.

[27] John George Godard, author of several political and social science books, states that Europeans are easily distracted by the ideology of racial supremacy. This distraction allows merchants to engage in "Emporialism." *Racial Supremacy Being Studies in Imperialism*, p. 9. Some of Godard's conclusions suggest that even as he defends social policies of equality, he was influenced by delusions of European racial superiority.

[28] Much of the wealth Europeans acquire (d) is obtained from African and indigenous people's natural resources.

speaks to the cultural bonding that formed between African men during their service to World War I: "There has grown up during the war, and there is progressively shaping itself, a greater common consciousness and determination among Africans as to the future and the rights of African races. Some white men fear this, and would seek to hold it in check... statesmanship and its ideals have to plough their way against heavy obstruction from prejudice and material interests, or rather from the short-sighted self-interest of those who would deal with Africa and the African as mere land and labour [sic] force to be employed for their own enrichment or sustenance." [29] Despite European interference and restrictive laws, African-Americans have achieved successes in dance, *art*, architecture, literature, chemistry, business, genetics, astronomy, history, computer engineering, music, sports, etc. What majesties might we introduce to the world if our brains were not shackled, our efforts unencumbered? How far into the black ether might our collective African consciousness expand if we embraced fully our African identity, and similarly, our African brothers and sisters?

If instead Europeans can keep Africans everywhere focused on the monkey they can keep us inside their zoos. The discussion will never move beyond arguing about not being monkeys. Nor will we notice ourselves perched within European-designed menageries (their feudal paradigm/prison), while they stand outside poking through the bars at us with sticks (regressive laws).

I believe that what we lack is a mini-course in European history. It is within those dusty and crumbling pages lining the shadowy shelves of the world's finest libraries and universities where lurk those gloomy, and murky vestiges of them. If after 500 years, African-Americans can still be called children of slaves, it follows, then, that Europeans are still the children of barbarians, and vandals, and villeins [sic]. And it is African Maafans tasked with reminding Europeans of that reality each time they remind us of our own. What's more, operating within that framework, our ancestors can never be accused of having perpetrated crimes against humanity. Europeans cannot make that same claim about their own ancestors. Within these pages I strive to en-blacken readers minds to the medieval conduct of the parents of the children we are fated to live with, as Anglo-Americans are so fond to remind us of our own. But, more importantly, learning European history, and maneuvering our minds along the confines of their culture helps us to draw boundaries that define our own cultural uniqueness. As matters stand today, few give due consideration to the impact of Europe on the way we self-identify. Far too few of us explore to what extent the European's have influenced our

---

[29] Sydney Olivier, preface to *Africa: Slave Or Free?* by John H. Harris, pp. ix, x.

thoughts and actions, or reflect on ways our egos express true African-ness.

Sadly, it is the case that many practices and traditions African-Americans join in have come to us by way of Medieval Ages traditions or earlier. And when African-Maafans hold on to European traditions we hold their culture above over our own, helping to maintain the current social construct. For example, Europeans inherited some of their wedding customs from the Vikings, forefathers to the Germans: "From several passages [of the Sagas] we see that the bride was (white-folded), and (enveloped in linen), which implies that the bridal dress was white.... This bridal linen was a long wide head-dress hanging down the back from the top of the head, or a kind of veil.... a head-dress, which was fastened on the head with an ornament," writes celebrated anthropologist, Paul B. Du Chaillu author of *The Viking Age*.[30] Even the word bride comes to us from the Indo-European word that references taking something without approval of the owner, aka theft: "The resemblance between the word for "bride" and the verb meaning "to steal away" in Indo-Germanic languages is taken as evidence of marriage[31] by capture[32] in early times, and another indication pointing in the same direction is the formality of prearranged abduction and mock pursuit in early German law."[33] Preeminent European historian Lynn Thorndike's description conjures all too familiar images of burly European cave dwellers[34] dragging their unfortunate women around by the roots of their hair.[35] In ancient Africa, women were not possessions, nor items for barter. The much-respected African woman was integral to classical African society conducting businesses and running the marketplace, both aspects of the intimate connection she had to farming and sustaining her growing family.

Other traditions passed on to us originated from hoary European blood

---

[30] Du Chaillu, *The Viking Age*, vol.2, p. 11.
[31] The young woman was literally kidnapped by the desirous groom-to-be who was assisted by the "best men" able to complete the task. According to J.B. Bury, in these tribes "married women and their offspring joined the family of their husband." The Cambridge Medieval History, vol. 2, p. 631.
[32] Marriage by capture is part of the mythology surrounding the founding of Rome by twins Remus and Romulus. Some people today would consider marriage-by-capture, kidnapping and rape.
[33] Lynn Thorndike, *The History of Medieval Europe*, p. 4.
[34] Ludlow informs us of one harrowing hair-pulling story: "When William of Normandy, afterwards the Conqueror of England, learned that Baldwin of Flanders had refused him his daughter Matilda in marriage, the chronicle says ' he forced his way into the countess's chamber, found the daughter, took her by her tresses, dragged her about the room, and trampled her under his feet.' The young lady does not seem to have been grieved by the violence of the wooing, but rather to have acquired a better appreciation of the lordly qualities of her future husband." *Crusades*, p. 21.
[35] Many Hollywood movies show scenes depicting European couples physically fighting before they engage in sex.

ceremonies, such as the exchange of wedding rings. H. Clay Trumbull, pastor and author of *The Blood Covenant* writes, "It would, indeed, seem, that from this root-idea of the binding force of an endless (blood) covenant, symbolized in the form, and in the primitive name, of the bracelet, the armlet, the ring, there has come down to us the use of the wedding-ring,[36] or the wedding-bracelet, and of the signet-ring as the seal of the most sacred covenants."[37] Though Egun[38] introduced the concept of exchanging wedding rings in ancient Egypt thousands of years ago, there is more to learn about blood covenants[39] that Europeans used to bind relationships. And it turns out that the wedding toast has roots in obscure European traditions of blood covenants, too. Of this practice Trumbull[40] writes:

> As the primitive and more natural method of commingling bloods, in the blood-covenant, by sucking each other's veins, or by an inter-transference of blood from the mutually opened veins, was in many regions superseded by the symbolic laving, or sprinkling, or anointing, with blood; and as the blood of the lower animals was often substituted, vicariously, for human blood; so the blood and wine which were commingled for mutual drinking in the covenant-rite, or which were together poured out in libation, when the covenant was between man and the Deity, came, it would appear, to be represented, in many cases, by the wine alone. First, we find men pledging each other in a sacred covenant, in the inter-drinking of each other's blood mingled with wine. They called their covenant-draught, "assiratum," or "vinum assira tum"; "wine, covenant-filled." By and by, apparently, they came to count simple wine "the blood of grapes" as the representative of blood and wine, in many forms of covenanting.

Trumbull continues, "This mutual drinking, as a covenant-pledge, has been continued as an element in the marriage ceremony, the world over, down to the present time."[41] And he adds:

> Among the ancient Romans, as also among the Greeks, the outpouring of sacrificial blood, and the mutual drinking of wine, were closely linked, in the marriage ceremony. When the substitute victim was ready for slaying, "the soothsayer drank wine out of an earthen, or wooden, chalice, called in Latin,

---

[36] "The wedding-covenant has commonly been attributed to the relation of that finger to the heart as the bloodcentre [sic], and as the seat of life." H. Clay Trumbull, *The Blood Covenant*, p. 72.
[37] Ibid., pp. 69-70.
[38] This is one Yoruba term for blood ancestor.
[39] Some very serious folks suggest that Africans and African-Maafans who take part in European blood rituals become bound by spell to their traditions.
[40] Though Trumbull indicates one African nations as performing a blood ritual, his information is taken from a mid 19th century missionary. European traditions have altered many classical African marriage rituals.
[41] Trumbull, *Covenant*, pp. 191-92.

simpilum, or simpuvium. It was in fashion much like our ewers, when we pour water into the basin. This chalice was afterward carried about to all the people, that they also might libare, that is, lightly taste thereof; which rite hath been called libation." The remainder of the wine from the chalice was poured on to the victim, which was then slain; its blood being carefully preserved. And these ceremonies preceded the marriage feast. The wedding wine-drinking is now, however, all that remains of them.[42]

The wedding cake is held over from the ancient Roman custom of offering sacred salted cake[43] to the supreme Roman god Jupiter during the confarreatio ceremony, a marriage custom that involved animal sacrifice, and vested women as the property of their husbands. Many other wedding rituals (flower bouquets, stag parties, etc.,) derive from Europe's medieval experiences or earlier traditions that have little to nothing to do with African customs. African Maafans engage in many other customs handed down from some of the world's most vulgar and unrefined people - as we shall read later - that support/sustain the current European paradigm. In the least, we can agree on the wisdom of adopting the most tried, truest and enlightened practices from Egun, if for no other reason than *our own ancestors* had *our best interests* in mind.

Documentation of European history is extensive and exhaustive. There have been millions upon millions of pages dedicated to the subject. I am certain to have missed more information than I am able to share with readers. Additionally, there are many more books containing far more revelations written in more languages than I can ably translate. But, hopefully this essay is full of enough surprises so that the minds of young African readers become excited in the way mine did back in high school. What's more, after reading this essay, our African youth will be better able to share with Anglo-Americans historical truths hidden from them: For Europeans have told each other that Europeans are all good for as long as they have told Africans that we are all bad. As well, this essay may serve as a type of cultural decoder for some of the images and symbols Anglo-Americans place inside their mass media communications, too, which go well beyond being insignificant by-products of a writer's or producer's wild imaginings, and may have more to do with DNA-stored memories.

I am not a historian, so in this essay distinguished early writers of European history tell their story in their own words. Additionally, beyond the fall of the Roman Empire, this essay is not organized chronologically, but by categories. For the sake of brevity, I strive to generalize the social construct of the feudal age. However, from this approach readers should not gather that events that occurred in England, took place in other

---

[42] Ibid., p, 200.
[43] Theodor Mommsen, *The History of Rome*, vol. 1, p. 88.

European territories in a similar way. Different dominions established and maintained different strategies for their medieval world though were all influenced by barbarism - to one degree or another. In the following passage, Thorndike writes:

> Feudalism existed in its most highly developed form in the north and east of what is now France, where by the fourteenth century it had come to be the rule that there was no land without its lord, where the feudal aristocracy was most sharply marked off from the rest of society, and where most of the peasants remained serfs into the thirteenth century. In some parts of Europe feudalism prevailed less universally and society was not divided so sharply into the two extremes of serfs at the bottom and feudal nobles at the top. In southern France, for instance, many landholders recognized no feudal lord and would not admit that their estates were fiefs. In Brittany serfdom had always been exceptional; in Normandy it early disappeared, and in both these provinces the word "fief" was applied to the free holdings of peasants as well as to the estates of nobles. In Germany powerful lords sometimes granted fiefs to their servile personal attendants, called *ministeriales*, and thus made knights out of serfs or slaves. Many features of feudalism were found in England before the Norman conquest, but William the Conqueror introduced it in a more developed state from the Continent.[44]
>
> We should further realize that the so-called feudal states of medieval Europe instead of being perverse and regrettable obstacles to true geographical and racial and linguistic union, instead of being ugly, fragments of a once splendid empire of Charlemagne or of an ideal France or Germany or Italy, really *often were the organic units of their age and represented local life and vigor and enterprise* and governable groups a great deal better than did the impossible empires aimed at by Charlemagne and Justinian and Otto the Great and Henry II.[45] (Italics added).

Consider that the laws of Naples allowed for family ownership of land, while in other places of Italy there were limits placed on inheritance. According to the acclaimed historian Jacob Burckhardt, "The feudal system, which from the days of the Normans had survived in the form of a territorial supremacy of the Barons, gave a distinctive colour [sic] to the political constitution of Naples; while elsewhere in Italy, excepting only in the southern part of the ecclesiastical dominion, and in a few other districts, a direct tenure of land prevailed, and no hereditary powers were permitted by the law."[46]

As well, note that many European historians view medieval history

---

[44] Thorndike, *Europe*, p. 246.
[45] Ibid., p. 260.
[46] Jacob Burckhardt, *The Civilisation of the Renaissance in Italy*, p. 35.

through their own racial, and cultural prejudicial lenses; it is not unusual to read an English historian demean the character of the people of a French or German nation, and vice versa. Nor is it unusual to detect snobbery in the attitudes of European writers toward women, so-called slaves and poorer classes. And, though it probably will not surprise some readers, I waded through some truly disgraceful comments on Africans made by some of Europe's more prestigious historians who allowed personal passions to displace their professionalism. It is easy to understand that African-Maafans pass on studying European history once European publishers allowed vulgar and demeaning language to enter *historical* treatises.

Much of the historical information witnesses, early historians, and academicians present may seem familiar to those of us living within the borders of the United States that many observers refer to as the modern Roman Empire. It is my hope that readers are able to make important connections between events of the past - when anarchy ruled, with events occurring today. There is much more to Anglo-Americans than what their movies and glossy magazines present to the world. Having the ability to distinguish reality from European supplied imagery – as well as forming relevant connections - is fundamental to shaking the African consciousness to wake.

Within these pages much is written on the European religion of Christianity because a people's collective tribal memories become their religion. Their traditions, philosophy, beliefs, hopes, dreams and fears fill their arsenal of personal stories that they, in this case, call the Bible. A culture's religion tells us much about the psyche of its people, providing valuable insight into their social organization. Of course, European cultures whose ancient gods favored pale-skinned men as heirs to their thrones, and whose men very early on yielded huge treasures from violence (sometimes at the request of their women), would carry those traditions forward.

It follows that Christianity became the engine, or, more to the point, the destructive force behind an astounding number of deadly events that occurred during and after the medieval European era. From the Christian church's endorsement of uncivilized acts that, in reality, sanctified their national (cultural) beliefs, we gain a rich understanding of its religious leaders and their *behind the scenes* motives. Despite compelling claims of piety, Christianity had little to nothing to do with reverencing the Cosmos, per se. The church's accumulation of power, vast estates, wealth - and above all - their determination to chain brown, black, and yellow people over the centuries rather lends credibility to the accusation that Christianity was agenda-driven. And by most accounts today, it still is.

Traditional African religion, or rather, the classical African's reverence (respect) for the natural world, their acknowledgement of her supremacy, and their way of relating to her was never placed inside a book. Early

Africans expressed that relationship organically within our "art," symbols, music, and dance. We were deeply attached to and understood ourselves as reflections of our mother, Nature. And so, her divine splendor was brilliantly woven into the designs of our villages and into the magnificent Kente patterns of our fabrics. Our elegant twists and sculpted braids rise in tribute to her beauty and complexity. African spirituality lives and breathes. It is life. It is Nature become manifest in thought and deed. Nature seeks balance and so traditional African teachings have not sought, nor do modern Africans seek to dominate other cultures. The same claim cannot be made about the cultural beginnings of Christianity or Europeans.

And lastly, traditional African thought[47] proclaims, "I have not" an affirmation of the awareness of personal actions, reflection and accountability. Whereas the European religion commands, "Thou shalt not" leaving plenty of room for mischief and the subsequent required repentance ad nauseam: Pointless - like refrains of old tired songs - bible commandments stunt personal growth and ethical development because they deter personal reflection. From this marked deficit African traditionalists have concluded that the European religion is not noble or meaningful enough for African-descended peoples.

Here, I acknowledge *Yurugu: An Afrikan-Centered Critique of European Cultural Thought and Behavior* by African scholar and anthropologist, Dr. Marimba Ani. *Yurugu* painstakingly deconstructs European behaviors, artfully diagramming the system that manifests those behaviors. *Yurugu* collaborated with other forces in my life nudging me awake. Surprisingly, after untold hours of university lectures the words of a senior high teacher were left to ferment in the fertile shadows of my subconscious waiting for the right moment to excite my imagination again; although, I suspect my Anglo-American teacher never intended for me to carry forward a lesson that opened the way for me to completely reject European philosophy and what I refer to as "their version of me." Still, kudos to Kelvin for instilling in me a life-long lesson that resulted in my acceptance of me as being wholly, unashamedly, unapologetically… and proudly African.

Htp[48]
-Sheshet Kemet

---

[47] From the 42 Laws of Ma'at written 2000 years before the Ten Commandments.
[48] Peace.

INTRODUCTION

No doubt, as in Asia and South America, the eventual outcome of the colonization of Africa by alien peoples will be a compromise-a dark-skinned race with a white man's brain. Sir Harry H. Johnston's depraved vision for oppressing the people of Africa in 1905.[49]

This essay takes a brief glance into some of the terrible customs and practices Europeans had during their medieval era, a historical period roughly comprising the 5th to the 15th centuries. For while medieval Europe is commonly romanticized by revised, and modernized stories — like those involving virtuous mythical King Arthur and the crusading heroes of his eminent Round Table, it is just as likely that the medieval European's exceptional cruelty and inhumanity go undisclosed and, therefore, un-discussed. Medieval Europe is synonymous with chaos, extreme violence, brutality, corruption, and backwardness. Wars, widespread murders, rapes, brigandry (highway robberies), truly horrendous types of torture, and Inquisitions were just a few of the challenges that Europeans dealt with daily when large segments of the population sank to some of their lowest social levels. However, during the early 15th century when the inventors and masters of that barbaric medieval world first trolled the lands of indigenous populations they accused Egun of being uncivilized.

The European conscience (or perhaps it was unapologetic narcissism) apparently did not entertain the possibility that their long, miserable record of turbulence and bloodshed voided their ability to appropriately judge other cultures. Rather they excused their own brutal behavior, disregarded it or, more likely, considered their cruelty normal, but not corrupt.[50] And

---

[49] Johnston was a leading figure during Europe's struggle for dominance over African resources and people. He was instrumental in developing British policies in Africa. His books make it clear that Johnston believed Africans were inferior to Europeans. He gained knighthood for his role in helping Great Britain reach certain goals that included toppling African leaders, stealing ancestral lands and redrawing long- established boundaries.

[50] The European's very own gauge of high civilization – the dinner fork - had not even come into use by the time ships sailed for West Africa. The fork came into use in Italy during the 16th century. It was exported to England during 17th century. There is controversy surrounding the fork's possible impact on good health. Additionally, researchers have stated that important digestive fluids are produced when we eat with our fingers, as vital signals are sent from the fingertips to the brain. Using the fork interferes with that communication.

even though modern Europeans claim that period of *exploration* as their Renaissance — or period of enlightenment, 15th century Europe was still no safe place for the faint of heart. Nor were 15th century Europeans much enlightened, as we shall soon read. Their long record of moral decay and recurring occurrences of chaos notwithstanding, Europeans set about unraveling stable, long-standing and advanced African civilizations.

The Bloody Hell on Earth 14th Century Europe Calls Africans Savages

According to their own historical records, by 1433 wealth and resource-starved Portuguese directed their attentions and sails toward West Africa after trial expeditions brought them gold dust, and African hostages who they forced to labor for free. Beginning with 1443 several more quickly commissioned caravels creaked, and rocked as they skimmed along the African coastline.[51] After setting anchor, scores of malodorous pale-skinned men quietly steered their rowboats toward crystalline-colored sandy beaches where they moored them. Sometimes they traveled a short distance into forests, concealing their presence on hilltops from where they patiently spied on the activities of Africans. After selecting the most vulnerable ones, these awful men ruthlessly chased down, then snatched up unsuspecting locals in the midst of doing chores, while strolling alone, or in pairs. Portuguese raided African villages in the early dawn as people slumbered. Or sometimes they snatched fishermen right off their boats. Whomever the European laid his ravenous eyes upon became a possible target for kidnapping. They seized our unfortunate Egun, claimed them as "booty," (loot, stolen goods) and then hauled them aboard ships destined for Portugal. Our forebears - innocent bystanders - suddenly became consumer products to a people making far-fetched declarations of saving[52] African souls for Christ. And despite the endless streams of tears Africans shed for families, homes, and their way of life, the caravels sailed them on to Portugal as this passage illustrates:

> On the next day, which was the 8th of the month of August, very early in the morning, by reason of the heat, the seamen began to make ready their boats, and to take out those captives, and carry them on shore, as they were commanded. And these, placed all together in that field, were a marvellous [sic] sight; for amongst them were some white enough, fair to look upon, and well

---

[51] It is unlikely that early Europeans would have encountered advanced African cultures while skimming along the coastline as classical African customs dictated that cities be built miles inland.
[52] One soulless Portuguese writer recognizes, yet dismisses the obvious despair of Africans working in chains. He remarks that it was a small price for them to pay in exchange for receiving *the gift* of Christianity.

proportioned; others were less white like mulattoes; others again were as black as Ethiops [sic], and so ugly, both in features and in body, as almost to appear (to those who saw them) the images of a lower hemisphere. But what heart could be so hard as not to be pierced with piteous feeling to see that company? For some kept their heads low and their faces bathed in tears, looking one upon another; others stood groaning very dolorously, looking up to the height of heaven, fixing their eyes upon it, crying out loudly, as if asking help of the Father of Nature; others struck their faces with the palms of their hands, throwing themselves at full length upon the ground; others made their lamentations in the manner of a dirge, after the custom of their country. And though we could not understand the words of their language, the sound of it right well accorded with the measure of their sadness. But to increase their sufferings still more, there now arrived those who had charge of the division of the captives, and who began to separate one from another, in order to make an equal partition of the fifths; and then was it needful to part fathers from sons, husbands from wives, brothers from brothers. No respect was shewn [sic] either to friends or relations, but each fell where his lot took him....
And you who are so busy in making that division of the captives, look with pity upon so much misery; and see how they cling one to the other, so that you can hardly separate them. And who could finish that partition without very great toil? for as often as they had placed them in one part the sons, seeing their fathers in another, rose with great energy and rushed over to them; the mothers clasped their other children in their arms, and threw themselves flat on the ground with them; receiving blows with little pity for their own flesh, if only they might not be torn from them.[53]

Not only did the Christianized Portuguese ignore the suffering of Egun, who Portuguese further separated from loved ones, but we witness Europe's early injection of the poisonous seeds of Colorism into our psyches - a disgusting social disease that plagues our community today.

The Portuguese chronicler who penned the above narrative writes that he believes this was the African's fate for "not having knowledge of bread or wine and they were without the covering of clothes, or the lodgment of houses; and worse than all, through the great ignorance that was in them, in that they had no understanding of good, but only knew how to live in bestial sloth."[54] The chronicler highlights his apparent ignorance of both what is "good" and "humane." However, he does shamelessly acknowledge that already the Portuguese had seen the wealth of their country grow from the hard labor of Africans:

When [Portuguese] saw the first Moorish captives brought home, and the

---

[53] Charles Raymond Beazley and Edgar Prestage, trans., *The Chronicle Of The Discovery and Conquest of Guinea*, vol. 1, Gomes Eannes de Azurara, (London: The Hakluyt. Society, 1896), pp. 81-82.
[54] Ibid., p. 85.

second cargo that followed these, they became already somewhat doubtful about the opinion they had at first expressed; and altogether renounced it when they saw the third consignment that Nuno Tristão brought home, captured in so short a time, and with so little trouble; and constrained by necessity, they confessed their mistake, considering themselves foolish for not having known it before. *And so they were forced to turn their blame into public praise; for they said it was plain the [Henry] Infant [sic] was another Alexander; and their covetousness now began to wax greater. And, as they saw the houses of others full to overflowing of male and female slaves, and their property increasing, they thought about the whole matter, and began to talk among themselves.*[55] (Italics added).

There are great discrepancies in the stories told by 15th century (and later) invading Europeans who accused African Egun of lacking development and needing salvation, yet, whom –not so coincidentally - greatly increased their own personal estates and fortunes by "delivering pagan[56] souls to Jesus." However, there are a few Europeans who felt it necessary to be a bit more forthcoming about Africa. Enter Shaw who most surely has personal quibbles with certain African social customs, but still manages to supply the following quote:

The civilisation [sic] represented by these empires was no doubt, if judged by a modern and still more by a Western standard, exceedingly imperfect... Yet the fact that civilisation, far in excess of anything which the nations of Northern Europe possessed at the earlier period of Soudanese history, existed with stability enough to maintain empire after empire through a known period of about 1500 years, in a portion of the world which *mysteriously disappeared in the sixteenth century from the comity of modern nations*, is interesting enough to merit recognition....[57] (Italics added).

Additionally, impressive evidence exists of European on European violence during the Middle Ages. Were the people who (bafflingly) violated their own mothers, fathers, daughters and sons qualified to judge what constituted civilization? Consider that in 1438 Portugal, citizens revolted against an unpopular successor to the throne, Eleanor of Aragon, Queen of Portugal. So angry were they over an edict that allowed royal favorites to have full access to the public treasury protestors "rose up indignantly, and violently assailed these bearers [of the edict], one of which was cast out of the window, and by a miracle was not killed, and the other was saved by some of his friends, who were able to defend him. The city was in such a disturbed state, that it was impossible to calm it."[58] Decades

---

[55] Ibid., pp. 60-61.
[56] Non-Christian.
[57] Shaw, *Tropical*, p. 217.
[58] Edward McMurdo, *Portugal*, vol. 2, p. 419.

22 MEDIEVAL UPHEAVAL

later Portugal introduced the Inquisitions, a strangely popular feature of medieval life, to its citizenry. Nineteenth century minister and author William Harris Rule describes the Inquisitors of Portugal thusly, "Not content to burn his heretic out of the way, he preferred to roast him [the victim] for hours over a slow fire, that he might treat himself and the public with a sight of long-protracted human anguish in its several degrees of horror."[59]

Jews who had earlier sought refuge in Portugal from the "hot, vengeful, improvident" [60] Spanish [61] inquisitors were forcibly converted to Christianity, or deported. The Portuguese removed Jewish children below the age of 14 years from their families to educate them in the Catholic faith. According to historians, some Jews killed their own children to shield them from forced conversion. Furthermore, after the papal bulls of the mid-15th century supposedly made it *legal* for "pagans" to not only be kidnapped, but to have their land and wealth of resources stolen, too, this heartbreaking event unfolded in 1506 Portugal:

> Sismondi states, "On the occasion of a newly-converted Jew, in 1506, who had appeared to disbelieve, in some miracle, the people of Lisbon rose, and "having assassinated him, burnt his dead body in the public square. A [Dominican] monk, in the midst of the tumult, addressed the populace, exhorting them not to rest satisfied with so slight a vengeance, in return for such an insult offered to our Lord. Two other [Dominican] monks, raising the crucifix, then placed themselves at the head of the seditious mob, crying aloud only these words, 'Heresy! heresy! Exterminate! Exterminate! And during the three following days, two thousand of the newly converted, men, women, and children, were put to the sword, and their reeking limbs, yet warm and palpitating, burnt in the public places of the city. The same fanaticism extending to the armies, converted Portuguese soldiers into the executioners of infidels and the tyrants

---

[59] William Harris Rule, *History of the Inquisition*, p. vi.
[60] Ibid., p. vi.
[61] "Not to speak of Spain, that classic land of the faggot [bundled sticks and twigs used for fuel], where Moor and Jew are always accompanied by the Witch, there were burnt at Treves seven thousand, and I know not how many at Toulouse; five hundred at Geneva in three months of 1513; at Wurtzburg eight hundred, almost in one batch, and fifteen hundred at Bamberg; these two latter being very small bishoprics! Even Ferdinand II., the savage Emperor of the Thirty Years' War, was driven, bigot as he was, to keep a watch on these worthy bishops, else they would have burned all their subjects. In the Wurtzburg list I find one Wizard a schoolboy, eleven years old; a Witch of fifteen: and at Bayonne two, infernally beautiful, of seventeen years. Mark how, at certain seasons, hatred wields this one word Witch, as a means of murdering whom [he] will. Woman's jealousy, man's greed, take ready hold of so handy a weapon. Is such a one wealthy? She is a Witch. Is that girl pretty? She is a Witch." La Socière: *The Witch of the Middle Ages*, L.J. Trotter, pp. 5-6.

of the east."[62]

Imagine being forcefully taken from the serenity and tranquility of the tropics and plunged into the midst of such medieval madness. Just imagine. Indeed, if any souls needed saving surely they belonged to the Portuguese and the other nationals who participated in this massacre. There is no question that 15th century Portugal entertained a surplus of insanely vicious brutes. Unfortunately for the rest of Africa, by 1448 the greedy and eager for profits Portuguese *royals* completed construction of its fort and *trading post* at Arguin (also spelled Arguim) Island off the coast of Mauritania that allowed them to increase their theft of natural resources, and people. Meanwhile, this is what eminent German historian of medieval history Ferdinand Gregorovius reveals about 15th century Rome. In 1443, Pope Eugenius upon seeing:

> The barbarous and deserted state of Rome, [he] must have shuddered in horror. His biographer, speaking of the condition of Rome at the time, says: " Owing to the absence of the Pope, the city had become like a village of cow-herds; sheep and cattle wandered through the streets, to the very spot now occupied by the merchants' stalls." The daily sight of heads or limbs of men who had been quartered nailed to the doors, left in cages, or exhibited on spears, or the daily spectacle of criminals led to prison or the place of execution, must have shocked even the hardened nerves of contemporaries.[63]

Author William W. Story who spent his later years living in Italy further elaborates on the crudeness of Rome of the 15th century:

> [In 1447] Rome was now in a state of complete desolation —fire and war, famine and pestilence, tempest and inundation, had ruined and depopulated it. The once splendid and crowded city had shrunken to a village with a handful of inhabitants. The herdsman drove his flock on the Capitol, which had now become the Monte Caprino, the Hill of Goats; or pastured his cattle in the Forum, which had degenerated into the Campo Vaccino, the Field of Cows. There was no pavement anywhere. Cattle and beasts of every kind roamed at will through the dismal and deserted streets. From San Silvestro to the Porta del Popolo, all was either marsh, haunted by flocks of wild duck and overgrown with rustling canes, or garden given over to the rearing of vegetables. The ancient tombs alone were alive, for they were fortresses for the oppression of

---

[62] Thomas Timpson, *The Inquisition Revealed; Its Origins, Policy, Cruelties and History With Memoirs Of Its Victims in France, Spain, Portugal, Italy, England, India, and Other Countries*, pp. 91-92.
[63] Ferdinand Gregorovius, *History of the City of Rome in the Middle Ages*, vol. 7, pp. 88-89.

the people. The stars alone lighted the streets. Such was the condition of Rome when Nicholas V. succeeded Eugenius IV.[64]

Savage behavior played a glaring role in 15th century Italian *civil* society. This is how Story describes Rome's condition mere decades later:

> [By 1484]... The condition of Rome continued to be dreadful. There were daily tumults; the soldiers now entering the city by night, and carrying off with violence the most respectable maidens and young married women, — taking the latter from the side of their husbands in bed—at which the Pope only smiled and winked; now pouring in and attacking Castle St. Angelo, plundering it, killing the defenders, and carrying off bodies of labourers [sic] employed upon it; now soldiers issuing from the Castle to battle, and returning with prisoners taken in fight, or prisoners seized on suspicion, and tortured then and there. There is no crime with which the annals of the time do not abound. The record is of perpetual violence, murder, rape, battle [sic]. "The whole city," says Infessura, "is filled with villains, who, after committing homicide, betake themselves for refuge to the houses of the cardinals, and do not issue therefrom; and the homicides of which they are guilty are considered as nothing (pro nihil aestimantur)." On the Tor di Nona, close by the Castle, bodies of persons are constantly found suspended, of whom nobody knows, or cares to know, the names. Executions within the Castle are of constant occurrence, and they occasion neither surprise nor remark. [65]

It is quite interesting that 1000 years earlier, prominent rhetorician Minucius Felix (2nd-3rd CE) comments on a similar type of barbaric behavior that occurred very early on in European history, seeding the state of Rome:

> The original Romans gathered together in an asylum, to which had flocked numbers of desperate men, criminals, lewd fellows, cut-throats, and traitors; and Romulus himself, their leader and commander, to surpass his people in crime, killed his own brother. Such were the first beginnings of this religious state! Soon afterwards, they carried off, ridiculed, and violated young women from other states, already betrothed and promised to a husband, and even married women an unparalleled insult. To crown all, they made war upon their own fathers-in-law and shed the blood of relatives. What could have been more impious, more audacious, more disgraceful than this shameless crime? The result was, that the other kings and later rulers, like Romulus, made it their common practice to drive out their neighbours from their territory, to overthrow the states nearest to them together with their temples and altars, to drive them into captivity, to grow greater by robbing others and by their own crimes.

---

[64] William W. Story, "Castle St. Angelo and The Evil Eye," Blackwood's Edinburgh Magazine, vol. 110, no. 669 (1871), p. 604.
[65] Ibid., p. 607.

Thus, all the territory that the Romans now hold, cultivate, and occupy, has been acquired by barefaced theft; the temples have all been built with the proceeds of the spoils of war, the destruction of cities, the murder of priests, the plundering of the gods.[66]

Clearly, over the centuries the European cultural construct has passed on some truly vulgar customs to its children. It was the unscrupulous tactics of cold-hearted Italian and Portuguese citizens that initially devised[67] Egun's subjugation. Despite the nearly endless pandemonium characteristic of their home countries, these and other conceited Europeans judged Egun as wild and savage. Their skewed lessons — filled with guile and deceit, disoriented many Africans, placing us in an unsustainable condition of severing emotional and physical ties with our home Continent; and induced us to abandon beneficial wisdom obtained by Egun over the millennia that helped them overcome challenges, and could help us with ones we face right now. Today, as we look around at the endless waves of devastation that devour our people and communities, some of us are convinced that Egun must have done something terribly wrong for us to reap such whirlwinds of madness. Yet, closer to the truth is that Egun encountered a European culture that thrives on destruction, mayhem, chaos, death, and disorder, the way a newborn thrives best on her mother's breast milk.

Media Images of Sadistic Medieval Europeans Truer Than Fiction

Some African Maafans may care very little about historical Europe, its customs, or how cultures developed there. Consequently, many do not know what life was like for them before they sailed to and invaded the shores of Egun. We do not know, nor do we understand whom those self-described *enlightened* and *sophisticated* Europeans of the 14th - 20th centuries were who claimed they were bringing *civilization*, not only to Africans, but to other people of color, too. The following account summarizes Europe's own political and social struggles during that time:

The nations of Europe were formed before 1500, *spent the sixteenth century in turmoil,* each to assert its independence, *and now with the seventeenth century they are beginning to appear in a group with definite federal rules.* Thus Henry [IV] fights

---

[66] J.H. Freese, trans., *The Octavius of Minucius Felix,* (New York: Macmillan & Co. 1919), p. 72.

[67] Arabs have a much longer history of imprisoning and selling Africans having dedicated specific land trade routes for those purposes. Their treatment of Africans could be as brutal as the European's. Arab imprisonment of Africans lasted well into the 20th century. There is some evidence that it continues to this day.

the [dominance] of Spain and retakes the French town of Amiens [1597]. The signal result of that act was the treaty of Vervins.

But to hold France thus as a watch-dog in Europe was but one side of Henry's policy. If he desired her independence and her power it was, in his practical mind, but one aspect of a general well-being which was his chief object.... He... saw the supreme importance of recognizing the unity of the country in the equality of its citizens. The policy was doomed to fail, and that unity was not achieved by a compromise, but by the fierce armies of the ideal nearly two hundred years after Henry's time. It was this common sense, and this practical but patriotic policy which made Henry so dear to the people. The peasants understood him and he them; so that *in the Revolution [1789-1799]* his name survived and his grave was spared.[68] (Italics added).

Because of social upheavals that plagued their own "Renaissance" era societies, clearly Europeans were not the wise, bearded scholars as they professed when they first approached Egun. Yet, many have believed them when they told us that their way of life was far better than Egun's lifestyle. Having an ability to describe the 14th or 15th century European mentality is crucial. Ignorance of their state of mind centuries ago puts African-Maafans at a disadvantage; important events are placed behind a veil with us standing without. We have nothing to compare their current practices and behaviors to, nor can we place current world events into proper context. As is often said, "the past is present" so if we are unable to see Europeans and Anglo-Americans clearly before, we are not able to see them clearly now. It is precisely for these reasons why we must study their history, so that their version of events that took place in Africa does not become the acceptable default history. For as conquerors, European storytellers of African life will deliberately skew events and accounts in favor of Europeans, giving them far too much power over what ought to be our narrative. (What's more, it is prudent to be wary of storytellers who begin their own tales by resetting the world clock, thereby wiping out the histories of other cultures, as Europeans did).

Readers should prepare [69] to have the conventional perception of Europeans challenged, shaken, disturbed, upended, etc., because as one European historian puts it: "No people[70] were so much addicted to robbery, to riotous frays, and to feuds arising out of family revenge, as the Anglo-

---

[68] Hilaire Belloc, *Paris*, p. 361.
[69] One book I was psychologically unprepared to read is *The Jew and Human Sacrifice*. It is well-researched response by German theologian, Hermann L. Strack, to Christian charges of cannibalism leveled against Jewish people. Readers desiring further information can access that publication.
[70] Descendants of the Anglo-Saxon tribes reside mostly in the United States, Britain, Canada, Europe, Australia, New Zealand and South Africa.

Saxons."[71] The stories of the grandfathers and grandmothers of Europeans and Anglo-Americans presented here are stunning. Violent behavior was standard for the Middle Ages; even murder was inconsequential and routine: "The massacre of countless people of less consequence, the plunder of the rest, and all the horrors of torture and traffic in human life, show clearly enough what was possible...."[72] And when the goal was to murder an individual, disposing of him (or her) by slow poisoning was a preferred method. Europeans have used lethal liquids and potent powders against enemies for thousands of years. I did not exhaustively research this topic, but one historian traces poisoning activity to early Finns and their altar rituals. Indeed, these stories are everywhere found in Europe's historical accounts: Poisoning a foe happened as often as handing a person a goblet of water, and was a source of scourge among Europe's self-described "genteel" classes. Roman philosopher Lucius Annaeus Seneca (d. ca. 65 CE) writes:

> The greatest hullabaloo is about money: this it is which wearies out the law-courts, sows strife between father and son, concocts poisons, and gives swords to murderers just as to soldiers: it is stained with our blood: on account of it husbands and wives wrangle all night long, crowds press round the bench of magistrates, kings rage and plunder, and overthrow communities which it has taken the labour of centuries to build, that they may seek for gold and silver in the ashes of their cities.[73]

Greek and Roman citizens eagerly employed "poison-makers and poison-mongers," according to the poet Juvenal. The "high society" employed treacherous concoctions to kill opponents, some of whom were their relations:

> Now you are confronted by a lady of position, who, when her husband is thirsty, just before she hands him the mild Calenian, puts in a dash of poison, and, like a superior Lucusta, teaches her unsophisticated kinswomen to carry their livid husbands to burial right through the Town and all its gossip."[74]

Because "getting away with murder was so easy" it is not surprising that slow poisoning became a popular technique for silencing enemies during the Middle Ages. Newly introduced crops of potent potions that were odorless, and tasteless caused the victim's demise over time thereby concealing the true cause of death. Once the use of toxins became stealthy,

---
[71] Henry Hallam, *View of the State of Europe During the Middle Ages*, vol. 2, p. 82.
[72] Burckhardt, *Renaissance*, pp. 122-23. (Regarding the 1526 sack of Rome by solders).
[73] Lucius Annaeus Seneca, *L. Annaeus Seneca Minor Dialogues Together With The Dialogue On Clemency*, trans. Aubrey Stewart (London: George Bell and Sons, 1889), pp. 151-52.
[74] Alexander Leeper, trans., *Thirteen Satires of Juvenal* (London: Macmillan & Co., 1902), p. 4.

they grew in demand as a justifiable means to deal with adversaries. According to anthologists and historians lethal potions gained popularity during the 16th and 17th centuries; they compare their spread to natural plagues that often overtook, and devoured the medieval populace. These historians point to both France and Italy as centers of major poisoning activity where the upper classes and nobility became particularly fond of their permanent effects. Denis Arthur Bingham, author of *The Bastille* remarks: "It may be said that half France either poisoned, or was suspected of having poisoned, the other half":

> In 1673 the confessors of Notre Dame informed the authorities that several women had confessed having poisoned their husbands. There were gangs of poisoners all through the country. It is supposed that the Man in the Iron Mask about whom so many conjectures have been made, was the chief of one of these gangs. In 1676, the Marquise de Brinvilliers, who wished to marry her lover, a Gascon officer called St. Croix, was arrested on the charge of having poisoned her husband, her brothers, sisters, father, etc., etc., and we are assured that "she was devout and visited the hospitals," but then, " it is said that she tried her poisons on the sick." She was condemned to death to her great astonishment; she heard mass, was decapitated and burned; the crowd squabbled for her ashes, and the executioner was so struck with her piety, that he had six masses said for the repose of her soul.[75]

Burckhardt informs us about the poisonings of Italy:

> The worst example of all was set by princes and governments, who without the faintest scruple reckoned murder as one of the instruments of their power. And this, without being in the same category with Caesar Borgia. The Sforzas, the Aragonese monarchs, the Republic of Venice, and later on, the agents of Charles V. resorted to it whenever it suited their purpose. The imagination of the people at last became so accustomed to facts of this kind, that the death of any powerful man was seldom or never attributed to natural causes."[76]

Merck's Archives reports that interested persons took "how to" courses for making these toxins: "Some of our most powerful and useful modern vegetable drugs were introduced by the skilled professional poisoners of the Dark and Middle Ages, as belladonna, stramonium, and hemlock. As is known, there were a number of colleges in Italy where poisoning was taught scientifically by notorious adepts."[77]

While murder by poison is quite loathsome, it hardly ranks as the most wicked ever concoction distilled by Europeans and delivered to Europeans.

---

[75] Denis Arthur Bingham, *The Bastille*, vol. 1, p. 299.
[76] Burckhardt, *Renaissance*, p. 451.
[77] Albert Schneider, "Some Ancient Therapeutics." Merck's Archives 3 (1901): 258.

For instance, respected 20th century German theologian Hermann L. Strack, author of *The Jew and Human Sacrifice*, mentions the following pharmaceutical recipe[78] recorded from the 1600's: "The Dresden taxation of apothecaries in 1652 contains 51 animal fats, amongst them human and monkey fat. *Human fat was said to strengthen, disperse, alleviate pains, soften hardened scars, and dispel small-pox scars....*' 'Even human after-birth and the umbilical cord did not escape our ancestors' pharmacological art. The former was applied externally, and given internally for epilepsy [a neurological disorder] and for the endurance of labour-pains. Secundinae (placenta) occurred in German drugstores right up to the middle of last century....' 'Even the great Friedrich Hoffmann recommended in the previous century the following prescription for epilepsy: The whole ashes of a young crow still in the nest, and of a turtle dove, *2 lot (a lot is .5 oz.) of burnt human skull*, 2 lot lime-tree buds, 1 lot lion's excrement; all these substances were separately digested with brandy, after which the fluids were poured together."[79] (Italics added). However, Europeans intended that these specific concoctions not cause harm, but provoke healing.

In this essay we will learn much, much more about human body parts used extensively in European prescriptions including ones for ensuring a strong building[80] foundation: "The so-called 'Bauopfer,' building sacrifices (the [imprisoning] of a human being, later also of an animal or other 'rudiments'), in order to assure the foundation of a house, a dam, etc., are really only a special kind of human sacrifice."[81] Strack shares a few instances of building sacrifices recorded in European history. I have included his citations in the following passages:

Bologna, 1864, 12Q.— Pater Hieronymus Saucken relates that *in 1685 the inhabitants of Brunsbüttel, when a dam burst, wanted to bury a child alive, as he heard from its mother herself; it was, however, rescued.* At Delve, in Dithmarschen, as is reported in the chronicles of the Pastor Neocorus, after a dam burst in 1597, as the elders declared, " animam quaeri " ("a soul was required "), a dog was drowned in the breach of the dam, v. Urds-Brunnen V. (1887-8), 165 sq.[82] In the Poschechon district of the Government of Jaroslaw *runs the saying that in former times the millers in order to protect the mill-dam against the rushing spring flood, used to drown any belated pedestrian* in the mill pond in propitiation of the water-sprite

---

[78] I have included many ancient recipes in these pages. I neither endorse, nor encourage their use or manufacture.
[79] Hermann L. Strack, *The Jew and Human Sacrifice*, p. 29.
[80] "Lemery explains how to make a plaster from the blood of a healthy young man, after drying it, which was useful in old ulcers." A.C. Wootton, *Chronicles of Pharmacy*, vol. 2, p. 7. See Chapter 12 for more on the use of blood.
[81] Strack, *Sacrifice*, p. 31.
[82] "Cf. the legends according to which the soul, which first enters an edifice, falls a victim to the devil, v. UrQuell, 1893, 206-8. " Strack, p. 32.

(Löwenstimm 16). — Immuring of a hen in order to make a quarry secure, Salzburg, middle of the nineteenth century, Ur-Quell, 1898, 230. In the foundation of old houses in Schleswig-Holstein may at times be found horse skulls, horse bones, or even the leg of a wild fowl. Ur-Quell, 1894, 157 sq. — In order to lend stability to a building, a corpse-bone or an animal skull is buried in the ground (Transylvania, V. Ur-Quell, 1898, 98).

Among the Szeklers in Transylvania the ballad of the wife of the builder Kelemen is widely known. (Contents: The master builders are alarmed to observe that their buildings are continually falling to ruins. So they have taken an oath to sacrifice the wife of the builder among them who should be the first to see his wife, and they act accordingly. — In the "Märkisches Museum" *in Berlin are remains of building structures, in which the bones of human beings or animals and birds' eggs are to be seen immured.*[83] (Italics added).

Positive messaging, known as propaganda[84], message manipulation and an "evil genius" ability to "flip the script," has been an important and successful tool for Europeans to cover over some of their most shameful actions. It is clear that message manipulation has been an important technique of Europeans as far back as 1700 BCE the approximate date for Rig-Veda[85] when Indo-Europeans claimed their god destroyed the Dasyu. However, once we pull back the millennia-old curtain of chicanery with its elaborately decorated sign marked *"Good White Folks"* and step into their darkened closet, we see that the skeletons within are of the real kind. It is there that historicity looms large, opening up European behavior to scrutiny and criticism; but only when analyzed from an African holistic point of view. As the twist to the old African proverb goes, "Paul Revere's ride takes on an entirely new dimension once his horse has her say." And though Revere's mount becomes the hero in the story told from the horse's mouth, Europeans become abusers and mischief-makers when we tell our version; colonialism morphs into foreign invasions, slavery becomes kidnapping, African-Maafans become hostages. And then we can see the method to the madness within their social constructs: slavery becomes feudalism becomes slavery becomes Jim Crow becomes the prison industrial complex. And that shift in perspective happens because we have familiarized ourselves with medieval scenes rife with torture, mass confusion, social upheaval, and other unenlightened behaviors. And we glean, too, that the European story overflows with sadism and wanton acts

---

[83] Ibid., pp. 32-33.
[84] Propaganda is a church creation. Sacred Congregation for the Propagation of the Faith, originally Sacra Congregatio de Propaganda Fide, began in 1622 by Gregory XV to push self-serving religious messages onto unwitting populations.
[85] As cited earlier, invading Indo-Europeans label the indigenous population as "destroyers and injurious" while the native religion is rejected as demonic.

of violence — so much so, in fact, that we begin to understand that when Europeans spoke of savagery and backwardness in Africa, they were projecting Europe's own societal unsteadiness and insecurities,[86] flaws, and bizarre realities onto Africans.

When Monopoly was a Cruel Medieval Sport

Some of us living within this European paradigm have come to trust and accept that the way in which we live is the correct way (meaning the "godly or modern way"), the normal way, or even the only way to live. The truth is that we are living within a social construct (i.e., pattern, paradigm) developed from the European's personal experiences; his interpretation and reactions to those experiences, taught him certain lessons and informed him on how his world must work so that he succeeds economically, socially and politically. Unfortunately, he has learned that he prospers materially from social chaos, human suffering, and environmental degradation; and he likely learned those lessons during those early frigid days and nights in the inhospitable bosom of ancient Europe. For instance, European historians tell us that ancient merchants caused famine and food shortages by "cornering" the food (corn) supplies, artificially raising prices until very few people could afford to eat:

> Although the rich had every luxury that desire could suggest and wealth afford, the great need of the common people was food. The city [Augustus' Rome] had to rely mainly on imported corn, and the price of this at times became prohibitive owing to scarcity— sometimes the result of piracy and the dangers of the sea, but often caused by artificial means owing to the merchants "cornering" the supply— and it was necessary for the State, through the Emperor, to intervene to make regulations and to distribute the grain free or below its market value. It has been computed that about 50,000 strangers lived in Rome, many of whom were adventurers.[87]

Monopolizing supplies was common, too, according to Burckhardt:

> In time of famine [5th century Italy] corn was brought from a distance and seems to have been distributed gratuitously; but in ordinary times it compensated itself by the monopoly, if not of corn, of many other of the necessaries of life—fish, salt meat, fruit, and vegetables, which last were carefully planted on and near the walls of the city.[88]

---

[86] A societal insecurity that the majority people of color have bought into is the notion that Europeans are the world's majority population. Statistics suggest that Europeans make up between 8-12% of the world's population, making them the true minorities.
[87] James Sands Elliot, *Outlines of Greek and Roman Medicine*, p. 58.
[88] Burckhardt, Renaissance, p. 47.

The following tales on capitalistic intrigues comes to us from Gibbon:

Constantinople did not escape the rapacious despotism of Justinian.[89] Till his reign, the Straits of the Bosphorus and Hellespont were open to the freedom of trade, and nothing was prohibited except the exportation of arms for service of the Barbarians. At each of these gates of the city, a praetor was stationed, the minister of Imperial avarice; heavy customs were imposed on the vessels and their merchandise; the oppression was retaliated on the helpless consumer; the poor were afflicted by the artificial scarcity, and exorbitant price of the market; and a people, accustomed to depend on the liberality of their prince, might sometimes complain of the deficiency of water and bread.[90] The aerial tribute, without a name, a law, or a definite object, was an annual gift of one hundred and twenty thousand pounds, which the emperor accepted from his Praetorian prefect; and the means of payment were abandoned to the discretion of that powerful magistrate. IV. Even such a tax was less tolerable than the privilege of monopolies, which checked the fair competition of industry, and, for the sake of a small and dishonest gain, imposed an arbitrary burden on the wants and luxury of the subject. "As soon" (I transcribe the Anecdotes) "as the exclusive sale of silk was usurped by the Imperial treasurer, a whole people, the manufacturers of Tyre and Berytus, was reduced to extreme misery, and either perished with hunger, or fled to the hostile dominions of Persia."[91]

H. H. Milman notes that state-sponsored monopolies of corn, wine, and oil were in force during the First Crusade, something to keep in mind as we read the chapter on *The Christians Crusade*. "Cornering" life-sustaining supplies and market manipulation through monopolies are unscrupulous tactics still practiced within the capitalistic system that governs billions of lives. They strangle our collective natural resources allowing a few hoarders to grow rich. Indeed, presently there are Europeans seeking to patent seeds and genes, in addition to privatizing water resources. Roger Bacon, a 13th century philosopher and Franciscan Friar, had this to say about the merchants of his day, "Of merchants and craftsmen there is no question, since fraud and deceit and guile reign beyond all measure in all their words and deeds…. Certainly if men had faith, reverence, and

---

[89] Justinian is described by historian Procopius (d. ca. 560 CE) as "a demon in human shape." Then adds, "It would be easier for a man to count the grains of sand on the seashore than the number of his victims. Considering generally the extent of country which was depopulated by him, I assert that more than two millions of people perished. He so devastated the vast tract of Libya that a traveller, during a long journey, considered it a remarkable thing to meet a single man…." See The Athenian Society, *The Secret History of the Court of Justinian*, p. 149.
[90] H. H. Milman notes: "Leaden pipes, which Justinian, or his servants, stole from the aqueducts."
[91] Gibbon, *Decline*, vol. 4, p. 78.

devotion to this sacrament as they are in duty bound, then they would not corrupt themselves with so many errors and sins and wickednesses, but would know all wisdom and wholesome truth in this life...."[92] At the turn of the 20th century, Godard attempted to awaken the European populace to the crass commercialism of his day:

> Industry thus organized by two evils, wrong production and mal-distribution; it results in an insufficiency of necessaries on the one hand, and a plethora of luxuries on the other; the healthy wants of some remain unsatisfied, because the unhealthy wants of others are gratified. There is something rotten in the State when large numbers live from hand to mouth, with intervals of starvation, and yet as much can be expended in a fashionable entertainment as would keep a hundred families in comfort for a year. And this rottenness is the natural outcome of our commercial system... concerned only with accumulating riches, without regard to their cost, their nature.... It results in a waste of energy.... It is promoting, not life, but death. [93]

By all appearances today, Goddard's alert proved a vain one. It is dismaying that 800 years later Bacon's criticism of fellow European's unwillingness to adhere to loftier principles, and Godard's condemnations of capitalism stand as valid criticisms. Beyond that, however, far too many non-European cultures have bought into ridiculous Christian precepts that pronounce the White man as Supreme Being over humans and animals alike. Our belief in such foolishness has made us all unwitting co-conspirators to the sufferings of millions of people worldwide, in addition to endless wars, and a despoiled environment — all manufactured for material gain. Egun Nelson Mandela remarked that poverty is [European] man-made. Of course wars are European man-made, too. The European paradigm is a fool's paradigm, and all is not well. The good news is that there are better more productive ways to live on this planet; there are constructive systems that Egun embraced after living, learning and surviving for hundreds of thousands of years. I supply an overview on some African traditions in a later chapter.

So, those African Maafans who fuss about reading ancient European history can study it with the goal of dissecting, analyzing and understanding a culture that used aggression as a source of energy to push themselves across the world into Africa with the specific purpose[94] of subjugating Egun, and who thought that it was unnecessary to bargain honestly for what they wanted or needed. When we study European

---

[92] G. G. Coulton, trans, *A Medieval Garner: Human Documents from the Four Centuries preceding the Reformation*, (London: Constable & Co. 1910), pp. 340-41.
[93] Godard, *Racial Supremacy*, pp. 108-09.
[94] Papal Bulls issued in 1452 and 1454 authorize Europeans to commit crimes against Africans.

history we learn that their infliction of cruelties on Africans was not the first time Europeans used aggressive energy to satisfy their bloodlust - and by all current accounts, nor was it their last. They often released similarly aggressive energy during Europe's early ages when their enterprises took on the shapes of "neighborhood wars," circuses, Inquisitions, Crusades and mob violence. The early European years were viciously insane and terrifying times when barbarians — led by even more vicious barbarian kings, roamed the lands literally slaughtering all whom they came upon. Europeans took the lives of at least tens of millions[95] of Europeans through wars, acts of torture, and other brutalities — seemingly executed with precise cruelty, and without an ounce of earnest remorse.

One particularly macabre, but authentic account[96] concerns a 15th century king of Naples, Ferrante. He supposedly delighted in a morbid type of dining with his enemies: "Besides hunting, which he practised [sic] regardless of all rights of property, his pleasures were of two kinds: he liked to have his opponents near him, either alive in well-guarded prisons, or dead and embalmed, dressed in the costume which they wore in their lifetime. He would chuckle in talking of the captives with his friends, and made no secret whatever of the museum of mummies. His victims were mostly men whom he had got into his power by treachery; some were even seized while guests at the royal table." Ferrante filled his dining room chairs with mummified remains of his opponents who were the Barons of the land, and his own relatives who had made the unfortunate mistake of forging treaties with the king's foreign enemies. Ferrante's eldest son seemed inclined toward the same dementia. Of him historian Jacob Burckhardt writes, "The elder of the King's sons, Alfonso, Duke of Calabria, enjoyed in later years a kind of co-regency with his father. He was a savage, brutal profligate—described by Comines as 'the cruelest, worst, most vicious and basest man ever seen'—who in point of frankness alone had the advantage of Ferrante, and who openly avowed his contempt for religion and its usages."[97]

Europeans signal their indifference to barbarity in this much earlier account of a mob killing a soldier of Roman Emperor Theodosius (d. 395 CE): "When the barbarian leader [Botherich], imprisoned a charioteer [for gross immorality] who was a great favorite in the races of the circus, the mob of the city [Thessalonica] rose in rebellion and killed the commandant.

---

[95] David A. Plaisted, *Estimates of the Number Killed by the Papacy in the Middle Ages and Later.* These figures reflect only the murders conducted by the church.

[96] There is an account of Pope Stephen VI who disinterred the body of the previous pope, Formosus. He then dressed it in vestments, and put it on trial for committing crimes during the "Council of the Cadaver."

[97] Burckhardt, *Renaissance*, p. 37.

The news of this riot threw Theodosius into a terrible rage...."[98]

In response, Theodosius ordered his troops into the stadium where thousands of spectators waited excitedly for the games to begin: "Upon the people crowded in the circus the soldiers poured and an indiscriminate slaughter ensued."[99] After three hours at least seven thousand[100] spectators inside the stadium were mercilessly slain. There is nothing in written accounts to suggest that the rioters and slaughtered spectators were one in the same, though that matters not at all. Later, after the pope and others complained about his actions, Emperor Theodosius repented. But, as the saying goes: "the deed was done." It is troubling that one man felt he had moral authority to take the lives of others; just as distressing is that soldiers eagerly carried out monstrous orders against fathers, mothers, sons, and daughters. Undeterred by his immoral behavior, European history honors him as Theodosius "the Great," a devout Christian who was instrumental in making the Nicene sect of Christianity the official state[101] religion of Rome.

But, far more alarming than Theodosius' esteemed[102] status within the annals of Christendom is that slaughtering citizens was a typical response of Medieval Ages leaders to challengers of their authority, real or imagined. Behaving narcissistically was a typical response, too: Tacitus' vivid depiction of the Roman emperor Aulus Vitellius' (d. 69 CE) indifference as he wades through thousands of corpses after the 69 CE battle for the Roman crown is fodder ripe for the psychiatrist's sofa:

> Vitellius... conceived a desire to visit the field of Bedriacum, and behold with his own eyes the traces of his recent victory. It was a horrible and ghastly spectacle. Not forty days had elapsed since the battle. The mangled bodies, the severed limbs, the rotting corpses of men and horses: the blood-stained ground, the levelled [sic] trees and trampled crops, made up a scene of hideous desolation. Not less revolting was that part of the road which the people of Cremona had strewn with laurels and with roses, building up altars and slaying victims as if for an Oriental monarch tokens of joy for the moment, soon to turn to their destruction.... Vitellius never turned his eyes away; he felt no horror at those thousands of unburied citizens; he even revelled [sic] in the sight, and ignorant of his approaching doom offered sacrifice to the deities of the place.[103]

There is more information about Cremona and the battles for Rome later

---

[98] Thorndike, *Europe*, p. 77.
[99] Bury, *Cambridge*, vol. 1, p. 244.
[100] Ibid.
[101] Theodosius made Christianity the state religion. He forbade sacrifices, closed temples, and confiscated their property.
[102] Theodosius slaughtered supporters of Arianism, while elevating the Nicene doctrine.
[103] George Gilbert Ramsay, trans., *The Histories of Tacitus*, (London: John Murray, 1915), pp. 177-78.

in this essay. An added insight gained from reading the account of Theodosius is that enraged sports fans felt justified in murdering a soldier after their favorite contestant was jailed. That mindset is worthy of discussion, especially since riotous behavior is still connected with games in this modern era. So, we will learn in Chapter 7 how the games were crucial diversions for medieval Europeans — a sort of gallery of terror that helped them to escape mentally (and placed them at a relatively safe distance physically) from the other horrors filling their world. Fifth century Christian writer and priest Salvian (b. ca. 400 CE) summarizes the passion Europeans held for their games, "In these the greatest pleasure is to have men die, or, what is worse and more cruel than death, to have them torn in pieces, to have the bellies of wild beasts gorged with human flesh; to have men eaten, to the great joy of the bystanders and the delight of onlookers, so that the victims seem devoured almost as much by the eyes of the audience as by the teeth of beasts. That such things may take place the whole world is ransacked; great is the care with which the search is carried on and perfected. Hidden retreats are entered, pathless ravines are searched, impenetrable forests traversed, the cloud-bearing Alps are climbed, the depths of valleys plumbed, and in order that the flesh of men may be devoured by wild beasts...."[104] Romans went to great lengths to supply entertainment for its citizens. After reading what other ancient observers say about the *amusements* of their day, readers may have questions about the role modern sporting events and other amusements play in today's society.

Reading and processing a variety of sordid accounts like the ones about poisoners; the use of human body parts in medicinal cures; and vengeful emperors, in addition to learning pre-medieval European history will, hopefully, encourage Africans living within the European social construct to begin asking important questions. For example, Black psychiatrists have correctly diagnosed the African-American people as being collectively traumatized by the ill effects of racism (European patriarchy), and suffering from post-traumatic slave disorder (PTSD). In one aspect of this complex psychological disease the victims of brutality share the feelings with ones who inflict their pain. In the African-American culture PTSD manifests itself in certain behaviors. For instance, psychiatrists believe spanking our children carried over from when European and Anglo-American kidnappers beat Egun.

But, where is the western psychiatrists' report on the European culture? What do they say about a culture that devises a dysfunctional system centered on violating themselves and others? Where can analyses be found

---

[104] Eva M. Sanford, trans., *Salvian, Presbyter of Marseilles, On The Government of God*, (New York: Columbia University Press, 1930), p. 160.

on a social system that builds its own cultural esteem from the devaluation of other cultures? And what of persons - who claim displeasure for the European social system of violence, yet have their hands positioned snuggly inside that system's collective cookie jar? What are that culture's diagnoses? Which western psychologists will publicly issue the findings on such a report?

A rather limited assessment of the European's self-inflicted psychological harm from their embrace of brutality comes to us from an 18th century slave ship captain turned minister and also author of the lyrics to the classic American hymn, *Amazing Grace*, John Newton. Newton, who participated in dismantling African lives for 9 years, adds that his "experience and observation" qualify him as a "competent witness upon this subject" as he writes of the moral decay that befell slave traders and holders:

> There is a second which either is, or ought to be, deemed of importance, considered in a political light: I mean the dreadful effects of this trade upon the minds of those who are engaged in it. There are, doubtless, exceptions; and I would willingly except myself. But in general, I know of no method of getting money, not even that of robbing for it upon the highway, which has so direct a tendency to efface the moral sense, to rob the heart of every gentle and humane disposition, and to harden it, like steel, against all impressions of sensibility.[105]

Keep in mind that Europe's inhumane slavery system has existed for thousands of years, as I detail in Chapter 6. How has slavery affected Europeans? Of course, discussing these and other fitting questions only begin that journey into awakening the African consciousness to what probably is a greatly damaged European psyche. But, at least the journey will have begun.

However, Europeans have damaged the African psyche, too. So, to help that damaged African heal, it is imperative that we embrace the truth that European's manifested chaos and barbarism upon their own people first... long before they turned their cruel enterprises toward Africans. Being African did not push Europeans to do what they did to Egun. Being European[106] did.

It is fortunate that we know a great deal about what occurred during the European Dark Ages. Western vanity has incited them to write volumes[107] on subjects that a more introspective and humane people might have dared only to discuss in soft whispers; however, delusions of superiority, and a

---

[105] John Newton, *The Posthumous Works of the Late John Newton*, p. 235.
[106] History confirms that Europeans have been attackers of Africans, both on the African continent and off.
[107] European texts are presented in their original form. Minor adjustments to spelling and punctuation are made to ease comprehension.

demented embrace of destruction conspire against better judgment.[108]

While there are a multitude of sources from which to collect data this essay is not comprehensive. Its main goal is to skim around the edges of European history to highlight some rarely revealed aspects of their culture before, during, and after it collided with African Egun living on the Continent. Because the European social construct is so directly opposite the classical African's — as *Yurugu* so clearly demonstrates, knowing who Europeans are will help us realize we are not just people who "happen" to be black. To the contrary African history is long and complex. The classical African society is a formidable social system sensitive to the demands of Nature and humans alike.

Furthermore, generally researchers do not plot out their course in advance, but allow the material to escort them to proper conclusions. And so this essay demonstrates, too, that the medieval mentality and vices remain contemporaneous in our society today. In any event, if I successfully reach my goal readers who struggle with their African identity because of centuries of malignant, and malicious propaganda directed toward Africa and Africans will begin to take a fresh approach when thinking of their history and of Egun. I am confident that many African Maafan readers will weigh the compelling evidence presented here and ultimately choose to reject western philosophy along with its unhealthy social paradigm. Or, at least, we will begin to ask ourselves, and each other, some very serious questions.

As I escort readers along the pathway to confronting the whitewashing of European history, it is instructive for African-Maafans to remain mindful that as medieval and Renaissance era Europe engaged in many of the perverse activities documented here their barbarians were raiding Africa of people and resources and calling Egun savages.

Chaos Reigned Over Medieval Europe for 50 Generations

The word anarchy derives from Greek /anarkhos/, according to etymology dictionaries. Anarchy means no law, no social order and no organized government. In other words, anarchy is chaos. Because chaos quickly became the norm socially, physically, psychologically and lawfully for European families, the dystopian horror raged on for *at least fifty* generations. Historians call this era of ubiquitous death and destruction, the Middle Ages. Its system was feudalism and its tight grip across Europe and European-held lands resulted in blood soaked valleys and mass graves.

---

[108] I do not suggest that European history be hidden, but placed into context of a comprehensive world record.

Then... *As Europe welcomed their 15th and 16th centuries, enlightenment spread across their lands.... Europeans lay to rest the last vestiges of feudalism and its attending violence, choosing instead to grab hold the reins to world leadership.* Or so the story goes. Informed skeptics question whether European feudalism and barbarism ever stopped, insisting that it remains alive and well today - though some of its more outlandish features have been softened. The facts can be sorted out as we flip through Europe's "Catalogue of Evils."

For the purposes of this essay, the medieval era includes the Dark and Middle Ages. This work includes all three terms.

THE CATALOGUE OF EVILS

1

THE DECLINE AND FALL OF EUROPE

Classical civilization suffered a great shock when the Germans descended on the empire and from its provinces carved out their kingdoms. These barbarians were rude in manners, were very ignorant, and had little taste for anything except fighting and bodily enjoyments. They were unlike the Romans in dress and habits of life. They lived under different laws, spoke different languages, obeyed different rulers. Their invasions naturally ushered in a long period of confusion and disorder... large parts of western Europe, particularly Gaul, Spain, and Britain, fell backward into a condition of ignorance, superstition, and even barbarism.[109]

The night grows darker and darker, and we seem to get ever deeper into the mire.[110]

Every story has its beginning. Europe's story begins much earlier than the rise and fall of the Roman Empire, used here simply as a point of demarcation. It is as good a place as any to begin cataloguing the medieval evils.

"The Roman[111] Empire included all the lands bordering upon the Mediterranean Sea, which was for long the great thoroughfare of civilization," writes esteemed historian Lynn Thorndike.[112] It included eastern and western lands. Under the command of their emperors, Roman soldiers marched to foreign soils. They subdued[113] nations, imposed high taxes, seized the most scenic and prosperous lands for senators and patricians, and subjected native peoples to the laws of Empire. For nearly 1000 years, the western Empire held a tight grip over broad swaths of the Old World. Roman citizens and subordinates numbered into the millions. Romans paved streets and built a system of sewers. The arts and education[114] flourished, but so did slavery. In fact, slavery was widespread;

---

[109] Webster, *History*, p. 251.
[110] Hodgkin, *Italy*, vol. 2, pp. 536-37.
[111] It is important to note that some of Europe's early emperors and popes were of African descent. The story of two Black men battling for Rome is here: Mark Hyman, "Blacks Fought To Rule Rome," The Afro-American, March 3, 1984, 8, accessed 2014.
<https://news.google.com/newspapersnid=2211&dat=19840303&id=eC0mAAAAIBAJ&sjid=gf4FAAAAIBAJ&pg=1282,825791&hl=en>. Also see the Severan dynasty, begun by Emperor Septimius Severus, 193 CE.
[112] Thorndike, *Europe*, p. 19.
[113] "The whole tendency of the incessant wars of the Republic was to make the rich richer and the poor poorer...." Hodgkin, vol. 2, p. 565.
[114] Sources differ on the type of education provided. Some maintain education was extensive and included seven liberal arts. Other sources state that only Latin, rhetoric, and literature

it was a sanctioned, and regulated institution. Besides slavery, "corruption reigned through the empire with little check..."[115] so writes noted medieval historian John Bagnell Bury. Still, as their own propaganda of the time states, imperial Rome was a beloved civilizing authority that brought about a Pax Romana: A Roman Peace: "They celebrate the increasing splendor of the cities, the beautiful face of the country, cultivated and adorned like an immense garden; and the long festival of peace, which was enjoyed by so many nations, forgetful of their ancient animosities, and delivered from the apprehension of future danger,"[116] Gibbon tells us. Hutton Webster author of *Early European History* adds, "Every municipality was a Rome in miniature. It had its forum and senate-house, its temples, theaters, and baths, its circus for racing, and its amphitheater for gladiatorial combats."[117]

Though as great as historians tell us Roman life was, it had an underbelly of cultural problems, including some rather putrid conditions that contributed to soaring suicide and infanticide[118] rates resulting in: "the Roman Empire [being] stained with the blood of infants."[119] And according to Roman historian Gaius Cornelius Tacitus (ca. 56 – 117 CE) Rome was, "where all things hideous and shameful from every part of the world find their centre [sic] and become popular."[120] Cultural problems, in addition to the barbarian invasions, made that underbelly sag until it finally exploded from the weight of its burdens. And that is because imperialism - a policy whereby one country exerts control over another - fails to create paradises, instead it triggers pandemoniums[121] that *deify brute force,*[122] John George Godard informs us as he writes about another swollen European empire that came into existence a little over a thousand years after the fall of Rome.

Satirists Horace and Juvenal,[123] who lived just prior to and after European year zero, respectively, pass along stinging analyses of early Roman life. Both men seem uneasy with living in Rome City proper, but offer valuable insight into daily activities of a vibrant metropolis where a

---

were taught, and that soldiers doubled as teachers. See Mommsen, *Rome*, vol. 4, p. 216.
[115] Bury, *Cambridge*, vol. 1, p. 51.
[116] Gibbon, *Decline*, vol. 1, p. 81.
[117] Webster, *History*, p. 209.
[118] Murdering children - even babies - by leaving them outdoors in freezing weather is an ancient Indo-European practice.
[119] Gibbon, *Decline*, vol. 4, p. 345.
[120] Alfred John Church and William Jackson Brodribb, trans., *The Annals of Tacitus*, (London: Macmillan & Co., 1906), pp. 304-05.
[121] Godard, *Racial Supremacy*, p. 15.
[122] Ibid., p. 10.
[123] Some of Juvenal's complaints concerned ancient Egyptians and his completely mistaken notions of their relationship to nature. But, even then, though they were Rome's major supplier of the food staple, corn, Africa to Europeans was 3rd world: "In the division of the earth's surface is regarded as the 3rd part of the world...." See Charles Christopher Mierow, *The Gothic History of Jordanes*, p. 99.

Romans' irrational craving for high fashion[124] might ultimately lead him to financial ruin. Horace grumbles over the sweeping commotion filling Roman streets, and the Roman millionaire's endless cycle of ostentatious banquets served by "hosts of slaves ministering to luxury,"[125] even as Roman soldiers were poorly paid and housed. (Mistreatment of soldiers escalated during Justinian's rule after he abolished military pensions, forcing veterans to beg for bread).

I use Juvenal's complaints of murders, knife robberies and certain types of men who do not rest unless they have assaulted another man first, to signal the opening warning that ancient Romans and folks living in our so-called modern world stressed over similar concerns like high rent, shoddy architecture, and noise pollution that caused sleepless nights. But more glaring similarities between the past and present are forthcoming. Meanwhile, the satirist complains that throngs of slaves and herds of cattle contributed to already bustling crowds clogging Rome's narrow, winding streets. Road rage incidents between wagon drivers were common. Wealthy citizens reclining on luxurious lecticas (portable loungers) hoisted by sextets of burly men jostled pedestrians as they pushed forward, heightening the street tensions. But so did building residents; crowded into tight spaces, it was common for them to callously toss debris — including buckets of feces and urine — through their windows and onto the heads of passers-by.

Thorndike remarks on the unredeemable enterprises ordinary Roman citizens engaged in during the empire's declining years: "Lawlessness and brigandage[126] were a natural result of the invasions and disorder. Tombs were robbed, parents sold their children[127] into slavery, slaves ran away from their masters and were probably guilty of worse acts of rapine and cruelty than the barbarians."[128]

However, the more influential citizens behaved no better. Eminent historian Thomas Hodgkin, author of *Italy and Her Invaders* writes, "The spirit of injustice, and hard, unpitying selfishness, according to Salvian, pervaded all classes. The prefect looked upon his prefecture as a mere source of plunder. The life of the merchant was one long tissue of fraud and perjury, that of [magistrate] of injustice, that of the officials of [defamation],

---

[124] "Gauze fabrics, Dress [sic], which displayed rather than concealed the figure, and silken clothing began to displace the old woollen [sic] dresses among women and even among men." Mommsen, vol. 4, p. 185. According to Hodgkin, "silk was then worth its weight in gold" vol. 2, p. 571.
[125] Mommsen, *Rome*, vol. 4, p. 185.
[126] Ambushing, robbery, and murders were common occurrences in the hills and forests of Europe.
[127] Tertullian laments over children murdered by parents via drowning, exposure to cold, hunger or wild dogs. Dodgson, p. 22.
[128] Thorndike, *Europe*, p. 91.

that of the soldiers of plunder."[129] Quintus Septimius Florens Tertullianus known as Tertullian (ca. 160 – ca. 225) a prominent Christian author of his time mourns the Romans' lack of dedication to their ancestral foundations. He scolds them for ignoring ancient laws against greed and corruption and criticizes the Senate for surrendering to extravagance and ambition. Unsurprisingly, the social ills of the Empire glossed over by modern storytellers were traditions carried forward from centuries earlier when a man's unwavering craving for wealth and extravagance offered him two ways to get them: usury and "agriculture by slave labor," both despicable remedies. And much like today's societies, yet centuries before Rome's fall: "Corruption readily found its way into the senate; the votes of that body, not less than the votes of the poorer citizens, were a merchantable commodity. Venalis Curia patrum.[130] The wisdom and the decrees of the senate were for sale to the highest bidder."[131]

Wealth disparity was clearly illustrated by the towering palaces of the patricians and the peasant hovels: "Poverty was extreme," writes William O. Blake in *The History of Slavery and the Slave Trade*.[132] It is rarely mentioned that invading barbarian warlords simply rubber-stamped Rome's obscenities, adding fresh ones of their own as citizens suffered limitless miserable conditions throughout the centuries whomever reigned supreme.

The fall of the Empire coincided roughly with their disposal of the Ancient Egyptian (Kemetan) Mystery[133] and philosophical schools on edicts issued by Roman Emperors. Bury informs us that, "Theodosius II forbade private teachers to give public lectures under pain of banishment. Justinian, determined to crush the last remains of paganism,[134] confiscated the funds which furnished the salaries of the professors, seized on the endowments of the Academy of Plato, and closed the schools. The persecuted philosophers fled to Persia to avoid imprisonment or death...."[135]

Long Before the fall, Greeks and Romans Studied at the Feet of Wise Africans

And the Genius proceeded to enumerate and point out the objects to me: Those

---

[129] Hodgkin, Italy, vol. 1, p. 929.
[130] The familiar Latin phrase is: Venalis populus venalis curia patrum: People are venal, and the senate is equally venal; every one has a price.
[131] William O. Blake, comp., *The History of Slavery and the Slave Trade. Ancient and Modern* (Columbus: H. Miller, 1859) p. 63.
[132] Blake, *Slavery*, p. 47.
[133] There is no suggestion that one event influenced the other.
[134] Pagan is a term used to describe teachings outside of Christianity. It is a term intentionally used to slander, cause shame, and provoke hostility toward knowledge and belief systems that directly oppose Christianity.
[135] Bury, *Cambridge*, vol. 1, pp. 113-14.

piles of ruins, said he, which you see in that narrow valley watered by the Nile, are the remains of opulent cities, the pride of the ancient kingdom of Ethiopia. the wrecks of her metropolis, of Thebes with her hundred palaces, the parent of cities, and monument of the caprice of destiny. There a people, now forgotten, discovered, while others were yet barbarians, the elements of the arts and sciences. A race of men now rejected from society for their sable skin and frizzled hair, founded on the study of the laws of nature, those civil and religious systems which still govern the universe....[136]

Long before the births of the Roman emperors Theodosius and Justinian, Kemet (KMT)[137] was the enlightened holy land to where Greeks made religious journeys, scholar George G. M. James tells us.[138] Superficial evidence of this is found in the name Greeks bestowed upon the ancient Medu Neter (Mdu Ntr) script that still remains exquisitely etched onto buildings and monuments throughout KMT, including their every conceivable nook and cranny. Hieroglyph, the Greek word for the ancient writing, translates into sacred carvings, or words of god. That the Greeks chose to honor the ancient African script with such a laudable term suggests how quite impressed they were with the knowledge and wisdom distributed in Africa. Despite that, it was during the 4th and 6th centuries when edicts of Theodosius and Justinian closed the ancient Kemetan philosophical schools and temples in cities and villages beyond KMT. Their closings stood at odds with events only hundreds of years earlier when Greek foreigners clamored for access to KMT, the "Black land." According to Greek historian Diodorus Siculus, who lived during the 1st century before the common era (BCE): "The former [Kemetan] kings allowed no strangers to come into Egypt, and if any did arrive, they either put them to death, or made them slaves."[139] That all changed after Psamtik [140] (Psammetichus) overthrew the 100 year reign of the 25th Dynasty Nubian kings. It was Psamtik who allowed the Greeks their first full-throated[141] taste of African high society.

Indeed, KMT had long been a great influence on the thinking of ancient Europeans. Thorndike writes of a Kemetan population in Crete long before

---

[136] C. F. Volney, *The Ruins, Or Meditation on the Revolutions of Empires: And The Law of Nature*, pp. 15-17.
[137] Kemet is also known as Ancient Egypt.
[138] George G.M. James, *Stolen Legacy: Greek Philosophy Is Stolen Egyptian Philosophy*, p. 38.
[139] Booth, *Diodorus*, pp. 70-71.
[140] A. H. Sayce, trans., *The Ancient Empires of the East, Herodotus*, p. 337.
[141] Pharaoh "Amasis [Ahmose II (570-525 BCE)] was partial to the Greeks, and, among other favours [sic] which he granted them, gave to such as liked to settle in Egypt the city of Naucratis for their residence. To those who only wished to trade upon the coast, and did not want to fix their abode in the country, he granted certain lands where they might set up altars and erect temples to the gods." George Rawlinson, trans., The History of Herodotus, vol. 2 (New York: The Tandy-Thomas Co., 1909), pp. 47-48.

there was Rome.[142] African Scholar Cheikh Anta Diop informs us that KMT had planted colonies in Greece: Africans soothed the savage beasts (proto-Greeks) by teaching them how to raise crops and to do metal working. Even Greek mythology speaks of the African Cecrops introducing African learning and becoming Greek's first king: "From Egypt came Cecrops, bringing with him the arts and learning and priestly wisdom of the Nile Valley."[143]

It was later, writes Siculus who lived just decades before European year zero CE, that early western thinkers like Pythagoras, Solon, and Plato journeyed into KMT for their studies. He states that the proof of their Kemetan education is found in their literature, religious rites, and fables:

> We shall now give a brief account of those laws and customs of the Egyptians that are most to be admired and may especially delight and profit the reader. For many of the ancient customs of the Egyptians were not only allowed by the natural inhabitants, but were greatly admired by the Grecians so that every learned man earnestly coveted to travel into Egypt to learn the knowledge of their laws and customs, as things of great weight and moment: and though the country anciently forbade all reception of strangers, (for the reasons before alleged), yet some of the ancients, as Orpheus and Homer, and many of later times as Pythagoras the Samian, and Solon the lawgiver, ventured to travel hither. And therefore the Egyptians affirm that letters, astronomy, geometry, and many other arts were first found out by them; and that the best laws were made and instituted by them. To confirm which, they allege-this as an undeniable argument, that the native kings of Egypt have reigned there for the space of above four thousand and seven hundred years, and that their country, for all that time has been the most prosperous and flourishing kingdom in the world, which could never have been so, if the inhabitants had not been civilized, and brought up under good laws, and liberal education in all sorts of arts and sciences.[144]

Benjamin Jowett's 1871 translation of Plato's dialogue, "Phaedrus," affirms that the Kemetans *invented many* arts such as "arithmetic, calculation, geometry, astronomy, draughts, and dice," but adds that their greatest invention was writing. Myers provides us with a glimpse into the African world of literature with a surprising result:

> We have now read the Ritual of the Dead, which tells us what the Egyptians thought about the future life; romances and fairy tales, among which is "Cinderella and the Glass Slipper," and a story written for the amusement of the little son of Rameses II.; treatises on medicine, astronomy, and various scientific

---
[142] Thorndike, *Europe*, pp. 20-21.
[143] Myers, p. 130.
[144] Booth, *Diodorus*, p. 72.

subjects; and books on history—in prose and verse—which fully justify the declaration of the Egyptian priests to Solon: "You Greeks are mere children, talkative and vain: you know nothing at all of the past."[145] [146]

Thorndike writes that the Roman world borrowed its knowledge from the Greeks.[147] So, it is not surprising to learn that the early Roman world was full of schools and universities for their early culture came by way of imitating the traditions and practices that Greeks adopted from African Egun.

So to be clear, once invaders of KMT lifted the protective barriers that kept foreigners from its major cities, early mainline Greeks studied African knowledge and wisdom with African priests — sometimes for decades, in the temples where the mysteries of the universe were held. Later Romans borrowed their knowledge from them: "It cannot be too strongly emphasized that Roman philosophy and Roman medicine were borrowed from the Greeks, and it is certain also that the Greeks were indebted to the [ancient] Egyptians for part of their medical knowledge."[148] Note, too, that the process to become a Kemetan priest required solemn dedication and a several years cerebral journey intended to *en-blacken* the consciousness through education and virtuous living. Otherwise, "they would not be called wise men or magi.[149] But following Pythagoras, they assumed the name of philosophy: yet they gathered no more than a few gleams like shadows from the magic of the Persians and the Egyptians.... Of this art and wisdom the Greeks knew very little or nothing at all; and therefore we shall leave this philosophical wisdom of the Greeks as being a mere speculation utterly distinct and separate from other true arts and

---

[145] Myers, *Outlines*, p. 41. For the Kemetan version of the story of Cinderella, known as Rhodopis, see Olive Beaupré Miller, "Rhodopis and Her Little Gilded Sandals: The First Cinderella Story," in *Through Fairy Halls of My BookHouse*, ed. Olive Beaupré Miller. (Chicago: The BookHouse For Children, 1920), pp. 262-67. See Strabo, *Geography*, 17.1.33 for his mention of Rhodopis in KMT. Cinderella was not the only fairy-tale the West *borrowed* without properly crediting the original Kemetan authors. For a partial list of those stories and to learn how KMT influenced western thinking, see: G.H. Richardson, "The World's Debt to Egypt," *The Open Court*, vol. 28, no, 692 (1914) pp. 303-17.

[146] More of the passage reads: "'You know nothing at all of the past. Being destitute of letters,' continued the priest, 'you forget all and have to begin over again as children, and know nothing of what happened in ancient times. As for the things you have been recounting, they are like children's tales. You remember one deluge only; there have been many....'" James H. Anderson, *Riddles of Prehistoric Times*, p. 132.

[147] Thorndike, *Europe*, pp. 32-34.

[148] Elliot, *Outlines*, p. 12.

[149] The author Paracelsus, who we will hear more from later, writes, "Magic, indeed, is an art and faculty whereby the elementary bodies, their fruits, properties, virtues, and hidden operations are comprehended.... Magic is full of natural secrets." Arthur Edward Waite, trans., *The Hermetic and Alchemical Writings of Aureolus Philippus Theophrastus Bombast in Two Volumes*, vol. 1, (London: James Elliot & Co., 1894), p. 51.

sciences."[150] So while a few Greeks gained some African knowledge, very few gained it all. Historians believe Pythagoras studied the longest in KMT. James points to Pythagoras and Thales of Miletus (ca. 624 – ca. 546 BCE), the Greek philosopher who planted the African philosophical trees in Europe from which later Greek thinkers munched, as initiates. Albert Churchward and other European researchers state that no Greek ever progressed beyond the African mystery system's first two degrees. They point to the writings of church father Clement of Alexandria (ca. 150 - ca. 215 ACE) found in his descriptions of KMT's mystery system:

> Whence also the Egyptians did not entrust the mysteries they possessed to all and sundry, and did not divulge the knowledge of divine things to the profane; but only to those destined to ascend the throne, and those of the priests that were judged the worthiest, from their nurture, culture and birth.[151]

African-Maafans are not trained to think of us as the former leaders of the First World. Yet, it is impossible to ponder ancient societies unless we toss African brilliance into the mix for some of the Indo-European world's earliest concepts came to them from Kemetans, Ethiopians, and Nubians. (As nothing is new under the Sun, today African-Americans popularize practices that are hungrily consumed by the world's cultures; a close look behind the scenes at technological advances in North America reveals African-American men and women in key roles. See NASA, computing, medicine, etc.). Even early European writers from ancient Greek historian Herodotus (d. ca. 5th c. BCE) to Plutarch (d. 2nd c.) recognize the African contributions. They readily admit to Greek and Roman gods being interpretations of African gods; and that some celebrated practices still in use in our day, such as wearing the royal purple[152] and crowns, developed from ancient Kemetan practices: "Wherefore the purple, and the gold, the ornaments of the neck, were marks of dignity among the Egyptians and Babylonians, in the same manner as in these days, the bordered, and the striped, and the palm embroidered robes, and the golden crowns of the provincial priests; but not under the same conditions."[153] From the Tekken (obelisk) that worshipped the Sun[154] in Rome to Asr's[155] (Osiris) Kemetan

---

[150] Ibid.
[151] William Wilson, *The Writings of Clement of Alexandria*, p. 245.
[152] The royal purple, which is actually a burnt-orange color, may have connections to Asr and to red-ochre used early by Africans that European archeologists believe had some connection to menses. The bases to red ochre, hematite, can be found as early as 1600 BCE in the Perneb tomb.
[153] Dodgson, *Tertullian*, p. 245.
[154] Tertullian mentions that an old Egyptian superstition remained etched into the side of the obelisk during his time.
[155] In KMT custom, Asr represents rebirth. Asr (Osiris) is described by Diodorus Siculus as being cheerful and happy. He loved to sing and dance. Asr was disinterested in making

ivy, African influence was plainly seen in the lands of early Europeans.

The Olympiads[156] started in 776 BCE. Chiefly organized to celebrate gods in the Greek pantheon, including Dionysus, games, according to Webster, were exercises that prepared the population for war: "The Olympian feast was a dedication to the gods because *display of manly strength was thought to be a spectacle most pleasing to the gods.*"[157] (Italics added).

Even the raucous ancient Phallephoria festival finding favor among today's modern Greeks is an ancient, though distorted, custom borrowed from KMT. During this feast the penis of Dionysus is prominently displayed through the streets. Phallephoria is an inaccurate interpretation of KMT's celebration of the legends of Ast (Isis) and Asr. According to Herodotus:

> Melampus, the son of Amytheon, cannot (I think) have been ignorant of this ceremony - nay, he must, I should conceive, have been well acquainted with it. He it was who introduced into Greece the name of Bacchus, the ceremonial of his worship, and the procession of the phallus. He did not, however, so completely apprehend the whole doctrine as to be able to communicate it entirely; but various sages since his time have carried out his teaching to greater perfection. Still it is certain that Melampus introduced the phallus, and that the Greeks learnt from him the ceremonies which they now practise [sic]. I therefore maintain that Melampus, who was a wise man, and had acquired the art of divination, having become acquainted with the worship of Bacchus through knowledge derived from Egypt, introduced it into Greece, with a few slight changes, at the same time that he brought in various other practices. For I can by no means allow that it is by mere coincidence that the Bacchic ceremonies in Greece are so nearly the same as the Egyptian - they would then have been more Greek in their character, and less recent in their origin. Much less can I admit that the Egyptians borrowed these customs, or any other, from the Greeks. My belief is that Melampus got his knowledge of them from Cadmus the Tyrian, and the followers whom he brought from Phoenicia into the country which is now called Boeotia. Almost all the names of the gods came into Greece from Egypt.[158]

Plutarch presents impressive evidence that the Roman god Bacchus, and by extension Dionysus, were odd manifestations of Asr. Additionally, it is noteworthy that Christianity metaphorically expresses overthrowing ancient African beliefs through infamous actions of the vilified, but

---

war, and went about training the world in horticulture and husbandry. He taught humans to become civilized. For these attributes, he was honored as a god.
[156] Olympic games abolished by the Emperor Theodosius I in 394 CE.
[157] Webster, *History*, p. 80.
[158] Rawlinson, *Herodotus*, vol. 1, pp. 250-51.

nameless pharaoh who — according to the myth, tried to stop the flight of the Jews: "First indeed when the people being at large and set free from Egypt, escaped the violence of the king of Egypt by passing over the water, the water utterly destroyed the king with all his armies. What figure more manifest in the Sacrament of Baptism? The nations are delivered from the world, to wit by water, and leave the devil [Africans], their former master, overwhelmed in the water,"[159] writes Tertullian.[160] The African's custom of showing appreciation for (anthropomorphizing) natural forces and the animal world, or, as Tertullian puts it: "the consecration of birds and beasts," would not be tolerated in the new world religion of Christianity, where the European god places White men in dominion over animals; although in Roman mythology, Roman history begins with orphaned twin brothers being suckled by a she-wolf, and fed by a woodpecker.[161]

But, while borrowings took place, so did cultural selection. Greeks and Romans closely modeled their gods, goddesses, and temples, etc., after those in KMT, but James agrees with Herodotus that the Greeks and Romans neglected to fully adopt the philosophical and ethereal practices of KMT.[162] Indeed, the Indo-Europeans had their own ideas of the world and reckoned for themselves what was possible and permissible. Webster proposes that neither Greeks, nor Romans were fully committed to their borrowed gods: "The ancient religion came gradually to lose their meaning. The worship of the Roman gods had never appealed to the emotions. Now it tended to pass into the mere mechanical repetition of prayers and sacrifices." [163] For a while stoicism's preaching of brotherhood and forgiveness became important among the educated classes of Greeks and Romans, according to Webster. But, after its introduction Christianity grew in popularity because its message was simple and clear for poor people to understand. Spreading the gospel between countries became less burdensome than it might have been otherwise had not Alexander's[164] earlier conquests resulted in Greek and Latin becoming common languages in the conquered countries.

So, Europeans set about overthrowing an ancient world dominated by African philosophy, figuratively and literally. To zealous Christians an

---

[159] Dodgson, *Tertullian*, pp. 265-66.
[160] Clement of Alexandria writes that the gods of KMT were neither lewd nor adulterous, and never sought pleasures "contrary to its own nature."
[161] According to the 1910 Encyclopedia Britannica, Romulus committed fratricide. He is the founder of the military and political institutions of Rome. In Roman mythology, he is the son of Mars.
[162] James, *Stolen*, p. 37.
[163] Webster, *History*, p. 226.
[164] "The work of Christianity would have been infinitely hampered if the Greek language had not been ready at hand, understood by Jew and Gentile alike, for the use of the Evangelists and of St. Paul." William Stearns Davis, *Readings in Ancient History*, p. 298.

official clerical order to close temples meant leveling them to the ground. If zealots failed to destroy the temples entirely they made unsuccessful, but violent attempts to chisel away the etched-in-stone ancient knowledge in hopes of blighting out the Afristory of the "Black Land" our Egun intended to last forever. To this day sharp, deep gashes remain clearly visible on portions of temple walls as stark reminders of the irrationality and frenzy that gripped early Europeans and Europeanized Christians.[165] Temple wall scarring conjures memories of the intense hostilities that once raged between followers of ancient KMT gods and those worshipping the Christian triumvirate that sought to replace them. During the 3rd century:

> Worshippers of Serapis, of Jehovah, or of Jesus, sceptics [sic] and illuminati, philosophers in search of the absolute, and neophytes who believed they had found it, all detested and despised one another. Hatred brought about riots, and riots became revolt. As soon as one man had struck, all came to blows; the streets were full of dead bodies, and in the harbor the sea was red with blood.... Diocletian set out for Egypt, arriving there in the middle of the year 295. Alexandria resisted all his efforts for eight months, and he only entered the city after having cut the aqueducts which brought the water of the Canopic branch of the Nile. To end these perpetual revolts, which were a dangerous example, he gave the city up to a military execution; it was sacked, and blood flowed in torrents. Coptos and Busiris shared the same fate." Note: " Malalas (xii. 309) relates one of those stories so dear to the Oriental mind: Diocletian had given orders to kill until the blood should come to his horse's knees; but the horse having stumbled over a corpse, got up with his knees bloody. It was a sign sent by the gods; the Emperor comprehended it, and stopped the massacre.[166]

In locations where temples remained undestroyed, Christians dedicated them to their own religious personalities.[167] In other places, Christian missionaries went to work. The European religion spread like wildfire aided by another unintended consequence of Alexander's conquests that smoothed border crossings. Christian successes prompted church leaders, like Tertullian, to brag of their strength in numbers and resourcefulness. He writes, "We are but of yesterday, and by to-day are grown up, and overspread your empire; your cities, your islands, your forts, towns, assemblies, and your very camps, wards, companies, palace, senate, forum, all swarm with Christians. Your temples indeed we leave to yourselves, and they are the only places you can name without Christians. What war

---

[165] Gerald Massey informs us that Christian zealots attempts to plaster over Mdu Ntr in some cases resulted in perfectly preserving the holy script. *The Historical Jesus and Mythical Christ*, p. 23.
[166] Victor Duruy, *The History of Rome and the Roman People*, vol. 7, pp. 374-75.
[167] St. Peter's Basilica sits on the site of the original Sibylline (Cybele) Temple. See Acts: 19:27.

can we now be unprepared for?"[168] Professor Asa G. Hilliard tells us that one function of 4th century Councils of Nicaea (Nicea) was to usher in the new world order by terminating African teachings.[169] To make their intentions known, religious leaders pleaded with the people to renounce the old religions by telling them that the old world needed the light from candles[170] because their souls were dark. Tertullian implored Christians wobbly in their faith to break away completely from the old world lessons telling them: "Thou art the light of the world and a tree that ever flourisheth; if thou hast renounced temples, make not thine own house-door a temple."[171] As noted earlier, overthrowing the teachings of KMT in the minds of the people was crucial before Christianity could settle comfortably within. From writer Dionysius bar Salibi (d. 1171) we have the following interpretation of Revelation that, once again, equates KMT[172] and her citizens with wickedness:

> Hippolytus of Rome answered [Caius], and said that, in like manner as God wrought signs such as these... that [were wrought] in Egypt were partial, inasmuch as a part of the people was subjected there.... The text, that *the day of the Lord cometh as a thief*, signifies as regards the unbelieving that they are darkness, inasmuch as the faithful are *children of light*, who *walk not in the night* [St. John xi. 10; xii. 35, 36; Eph. v. 8]. Accordingly, in Egypt this type was completed; for the Egyptians had *darkness*, but *the Hebrews had light* [Exod. x. 22, 23].' (Rev. 8:8).[173]

Beginning with Constantine in 326 CE, Rome accepted this so-called new[174] religion on behalf of the state and its people. Everyone had to

---

[168] William Reeve, trans., *The Apology of Tertullian*, (London: Griffith, Farran, Okeden, and Welsh, 1907), p. 104.
[169] Asa G. Hilliard III, *The Meaning of KMT (Ancient Egyptian): History for Contemporary African American Experience*, vol. 49 (1992) p. 11.
[170] According to W. Robertson Smith, in ancient Semitic traditions lighted candles substituted burnt offerings. Candle-shaped temple pillars replaced large displays of candles (the candelabra). In ancient times, offerings to deities were placed between the temple pillars.
[171] Dodgson, *Tertullian*, p. 243.
[172] The light (Europeans) versus the dark (African-Americans) analogy continues today. It is portrayed in the media as white hats (good) vs. black hats (evil). White as purity, and cleanliness while black means filth, vulgarity, etc. appears in everyday language. What is left unsaid is that all life begins in darkness. There can be no tree, no food, no flower, no star, no planet, no animal, nor man unless there is blackness first.
[173] John Gwynn. "Commentary on the Apocalypse, Acts, and Epistles, of Dionysius Barsalibi: Hippolytus and His Heads Against Caius," The Tertullian Project. 2005. Web. 7 Oct. 2013.
[174] Many books have been written over the years that proclaim Christianity, Judaism and Islam as fringe religions, offspring of African spirituality. See John Henrik Clarke's *Christianity Before Christ*, et al.

practice Christianity. But, traditions linger long within the hearts of people. Husbands converted while their wives did not, and vice versa. What did not last long was the church's tolerance for rivals or for disobedience. Church leaders turned their hand wringing and pleadings into strict commands and the state began to legally persecute those holding on to their outlawed, ancient religious beliefs. The punishment for these holdouts was severe: confiscations, banishments, and death were dispensed in measurable dosages. Rule reports that Christian leaders hunted down and slaughtered heretics, ordering their soldiers "to [wipeout] heresy with fire[175] and sword, and magistrates enforced the laws of Justinian and his successors, or other laws like them, in open court...."[176] These chilling persecutions of non-believers were in stark contrast to an era little more than 300 years earlier when Pliny the Younger - who in his official capacity as magistrate - wrote of torturing women slaves to gain information on Christian activities banned by Rome;[177] and it was certainly at odds with emperors who hanged priests[178] alive in view of the public:[179] "Each day are we beset, each day betrayed; in our very meetings and assemblies are we mostly surprised,"[180] writes Tertullian of the challenges Christians once faced at the hands of the state.

Though it must be added that it was a twisted and sad aftermath that allowed tyranny to befall believers whose opinions of Christ differed from the narrow interpretations of church leaders whose own beliefs became undisputable church edicts. Despite the heretics who openly worshipped Christ, yet secreted ancient altars inside their hearts; and despite that Christians themselves remained deeply divided over doctrinal interpretations - the resolutions of Councils Nicene notwithstanding - Rome had granted Christianity status as an unerring institution before the Empire fell. Because Christianity cranked the engines of the medieval world, it is discussed more in the latter half of this essay.

In Ancient Rome and the U.S., Politics of Corruption, Economic Distress Besiege Poor

> But the condition of Roman subjects in time of peace is far more grievous than the evils of war, for the exaction of the taxes is very severe, and unprincipled men inflict injuries on others because the-laws-are-practically not valid against

---

[175] Tens of thousands of unbelievers were burned alive, according Rule, *Inquisition*.
[176] Rule, *Inquisition*, p. 4.
[177] Alfred Church and William Jackson Brodribb, trans., *Pliny's Letters* (Edinburgh: William Blackwood and Sons, 1872), p. 153.
[178] Human sacrifice: Dodgson notes that priests were hanged as "offerings, on the trees, whereon they hung the offerings of their God." p. 21.
[179] Dodgson, *Tertullian*, p. 21.
[180] Ibid., p. 17.

all classes. — A transgressor who belongs to the wealthy classes is not punished for his injustice, while a poor man, who does not understand business, undergoes the legal penalty, — that is, if he does not depart this life before the trial, so long is the course of lawsuits protracted, and so much money is expended on them. The climax of misery is to have to pay in order to obtain justice. For no one will give a hearing to the injured man except he pay a sum of money to the judge and the judge's clerks. - Salvian quotes a disenchanted former Roman citizen.[181]

With the African philosophical schools closing, and with unenlightened, roaming barbarian hordes literally banging at the gates of Rome, the levers of control became too unwieldy. The author of *Essentials in Early European History*, Samuel Burnett Howe, informs us that Rome began its collapse assisted by population declination brought on by economic distress. Rome needed men who normally labored in the fields to support the army instead. There was not enough food to feed the population, and the cost of living increased. Men who could not afford to feed their family stopped having children.

Additionally, disease, taxation, a workless city population, and dwindling numbers of Roman citizens abetted the process. About taxes, British historian Henry William Carless Davis (d. 1928) writes in *Medieval Europe*, "Barbarous methods of taxation and corrupt practices among the ruling classes had aggravated the burden to such a degree that the municipalities of the provinces were bankrupt, and the middle-class capitalist was taxed out of existence."[182]

In French historian Victor Duruy's (d. 1894) criticism of Roman taxation, he provides details of policies that haunt modern middle class taxpayers in the United States: "Above its head and weighing upon it with all the weight of its privileges and its insolence, a mass of functionaries and titled persons who drew largely from the public treasury, while many of them paid but little into it. We can scarcely exaggerate the number of these privileged persons. Titles were sought with all the eagerness that has been shown in the countries of modern Europe in seeking patents of nobility. As early as the time of which we speak they were bought, and the number of taxpayers had diminished, while that of parasites increased.... Hence the language of Lactantius, which is alarming with its evident exaggeration: 'Those who live upon the taxes are more numerous than those who pay them.'"[183]

The economic distress was so high, according to Howe, that thousands of men experienced financial ruin. Webster adds: "These two forces - the

---

[181] James Harvey Robinson, *Readings in European History*, pp. 31-32.
[182] Henry William Carless Davis, *Medieval Europe*, p. 17.
[183] Duruy, *Rome*, vol. 8, pt. 1, p. 27.

decline in population and the decline in wealth - worked together to produce economic ruin. It is no wonder, therefore, that in province after province large tracts of land went out of cultivation, that the towns decayed, and that commerce and manufactures suffered appalling decline. 'Hard times' settled on the Roman world." Davis continues the discussion on the cultural divisions that plagued Rome:

> The Western Empire, on the eve of dissolution, had already assumed the appearance of a semi-barbarian state. In those districts which had been lately settled with Teutonic [German] colonists the phenomenon may be explained as resulting from over-sanguine attempts to civilise [sic] an intractable stock. But even in the heart of the oldest provinces the conditions were little better. Law and custom had conspired to sap the ideas and principles that we regard as essentially Roman. The civil was now subjected to the military power. The authority of the state was impaired by the growth of private jurisdictions and defied by the quasi-feudal retinues of the great. For civic equality had been substituted an irrational system of class-privileges and class-burdens. Law was ceasing to be the orderly development of general principles, and was becoming an accumulation of ill-considered, inconsistent edicts. So far had decay advanced through the negligence of those most vitally concerned that, if Europe was ever to learn again the highest lessons which Rome had existed to teach, the first step must be to sweep away the hybrid government which still claimed allegiance in the name of Rome.[184]

So, according to these writers of early European history, Rome endured a host of problems that included low birthrate, high taxation, a dwindling middle class, and disease. Additionally, laws[185] became tilted in favor of the wealthy, whereas the poor suffered Rome's economic burdens. But, Reeve presents another cause for Rome's downfall by way of Tertullian who confronts the Empire with a notable threat to passively resist the state's brutality by staging economic boycotts and threatening a mass exodus of citizens: "We could also make a terrible war upon you without arms, or fighting a stroke, by being so passively revengeful as only to leave you; for if such a numerous host of Christians should but retire from the empire into some remote region of the world, the loss of so many men of all ranks and degrees would leave a hideous gap, and a shameful scar upon the government; and the very evacuation would be abundant revenge. You would stand aghast as your desolation, and be struck dumb at the general silence and horror of nature, as if the whole world was departed. You would be at a loss for men to govern, and in the pitiful remains you would

---

[184] Davis, *Medieval Europe*, pp. 21-22.
[185] Laws favoring the rich, unfair taxation of the poor, and a dwindling middle class seriously undermine the social stability of the United States today.

find more enemies than citizens...."[186]

Webster opines that Christians refused to sustain the social and economic Roman pagan society that persecuted them.[187] In fact, some historians boldly conclude that the Christian's withdrawal from Roman society weakened it and was quite a significant element to its collapse, as was slavery.

Mostly unspoken in modern discussions as a possible cause of Rome's fall, Blake writes about the devastating effects slavery had on Rome:

> The barbarians did not ruin Italy. The Romans themselves ruined it. Slavery had made it a waste and depopulated land, before a Scythian or a Scandinavian had crossed the Alps.
>
> When Alaric led the Goths into Italy, even after the conquest of Rome, he saw that he could not sustain his army in the beautiful but desert territory, unless he could also conquer Sicily and Africa, whence alone daily bread could be obtained. His successor was, therefore, easily persuaded to abandon the unproductive region, and invade the happier France.
>
> Attila had no other object than a roving pilgrimage after plunder; and as his cupidity was little excited, and the climate was ungenial, the wild, unlettered Calmuck was easily overawed by the Roman priesthood, and diverted from the indigent Italy to the more prosperous North. Rome still remained an object for plunderers, but none of the barbarians were tempted to make Italy the seat of empire, or Rome a metropolis. Slavery had destroyed the democracy, had destroyed the aristocracy, had destroyed the empire; and now at last it left the traces of its ruinous power deeply furrowed on the face of nature herself.'[188]

Additionally, reviewers of history note that empires require soldiers to guard over their great expanse of conquered territory (though they fail to mention why guards are necessary for "happy and peaceful" conquered peoples). And ancient Rome's vast empire comprised the lands of many conquered nations that needed multitudes of troops. Davis explains more in this passage:

> Evidently the original error of the Romans was the undue extension of their power.... Embracing the whole of the Mediterranean [shoreline] and a large part of the territories to the south, east, and north, the Empire was encumbered with three land frontiers of enormous length. Two of these, the European and the Asiatic, were perpetual sources of anxiety, and called for separate military establishments.

In desperation, the Roman army reached out to surrounding barbarian

---

[186] Reeve, p. 105.
[187] Webster, *History*, p. 225.
[188] Blake, *Slavery*, p. 68.

tribes to protect many of those areas. Ironically, those same barbarian tribesmen who acted as mercenary protectors eventually directed their finely honed, bloody fangs toward the gates of ancient Rome. According to Duruy Rome hired upwards of 40,000 Goths hoping to seize the booty from provinces and believing barbarians desired fully to live "within the bosom of Roman felicity... [Instead] we shall see these dangerous auxiliaries warning their fellow countrymen, left behind in German forests, of the designs of the Romans against them, and deserters from their ranks guiding bands of Germans or Persian plunderers to the pillage of the provinces."[189]

The [Roman] armies were now largely recruited with barbarians, who numbered more than half the fighting strength and were esteemed the flower of the Roman soldiery. Many of these hirelings showed an open contempt for their employers, and sympathised [sic] with the enemies whom they were paid to fight.... But it was aggravated under the successors of Diocletian [Roman Emperor 245-31]), as the barbarian element in the armies increased and the Roman element diminished. Its worst effects appeared in the years 406-407.[190]

As Barbarians Advance on Rome "Death Breathes Out Death"

Professor Davis continues, "The immediate and obvious causes which ruined the Western Empire were military and political-the shortcomings of a professional army and professional administrators.... The beginning and the end of the disaster were successful raids on Italy. [Visigoth king] Alaric and his Visigoths (401-410 A.D.) shattered the prestige and destroyed the efficiency of the government...."[191] The resources of western Roman Empire stretched to their fullest, in 452 CE Attila (the Hun) invaded Italy's northern provinces. Then in 455: " [King of the Vandals, Gaiseric] fitted out his piratical fleet, and soon from mouth to mouth in Rome flitted the awful tidings, 'The Vandals are coming.' Many of the nobles fled."[192] The Vandals "attacked and ravaged Rome in such a frightful manner that their name has ever since been a term of reproach,"[193] For fourteen days they stripped "Rome of her wealth. Besides shiploads of booty the Vandals took away thousands of Romans as slaves, including the widow and two daughters of an emperor."[194] In 476 Arian Flavius Odoacer, upset the emperor rejected his demand for land, stormed Rome's gates. He deposed Romulus Augustulus, crowning himself the first barbarian king of Italy. In 489

---

[189] Duruy, *Rome*, vol. 8, pt. 1, pp. 44-45.
[190] Davis, *Medieval Europe*, pp. 15-16.
[191] Ibid., pp. 10-11.
[192] Hodgkin, vol. 2, p. 204.
[193] Webster, *History*, p. 125.
[194] Ibid., p. 249.

another barbarian German, Theodoric, overthrew Odoacer. Between 489-493 CE:

> The Ostrogoths under Theodoric[195] destroyed the last [representation] of an imperial power rooted in Italy.... All three of the invading hordes came from the Danube. The Roman bank of the great river was inadequately garrisoned, and a mistaken policy had colonised [sic] the Danubian provinces with Teutonic peoples....[196]

Treves (Trier), with a population that numbered in the tens of thousands, was one of the largest cities sacked. Salvian lived there before barbarians burned and pillaged it. After the barbarian's advance he provides an eyewitness account on the smoldering waste of the once vibrant city whose gates went unprotected and whose destruction severely affected other towns: "The greatest city of Gaul, three times destroyed by successive captures, yet when the whole city had been burned to the ground, its wickedness increased even after its destruction. Those whom the enemy had not killed when they pillaged the city were overwhelmed by disaster after the sack; those who had escaped death in capture did not survive the ruin that followed. Some died lingering deaths from deep wounds, others were burned by the enemy's fires and suffered tortures even after the flames were extinguished. Some perished of hunger, others of nakedness, some wasting away, others paralyzed with cold, and so all alike by diverse deaths hastened to the common goal.

"Worse than all this," remarks the highly regarded Salvian about Treves, "other cities suffered from the destruction of this single town. There lay all about the torn and naked bodies of both sexes, a sight that I myself endured. These were a pollution to the eyes of the city, as they lay there lacerated by birds and dogs. The stench of the dead brought pestilence on the living: death breathed out death. Thus even those who escaped the destruction of the city suffered the evils that sprang from the fate of the rest."[197] By the end of the fifth century: "the northern tribes had overrun the Western Empire, and on its ruins had raised the six kingdoms of the English, Franks, Burgundians, Visigoths, Vandals, and Ostrogoths."[198] Davis informs us that:

---

[195] "Theodoric, the most famous of the Ostrogoth kings in Italy, could not write his name, and is said to have restrained his countrymen from attending those schools of learning.... Scarcely one of the barbarians, so long as they continued unconfused with the native inhabitants, acquired the slightest tincture of letters; and the praise of equal ignorance was soon aspired to and attained by the entire mass of the Roman laity." Hallam, *View*, vol. 2, p 468.
[196] Davis, *Medieval Europe*, pp. 11-12.
[197] Sanford, *Government*, pp. 182-83.
[198] W. H. Barker and William Rees, *The Making of Europe*, p. 22.

The barbarian states which arose on the ruins of the Western Empire were founded, under widely different circumstances of time and place, by tribes and federations of tribes drawn from every part of Germany.... From a broader point of view they may be grouped in two classes, not according to affinities of race, but according to their relations with the social order which they had invaded. One group of kingdoms was founded under cover of a legal fiction; the Visigoths, the Ostrogoths, and the Burgundians claimed to be the allies of the Empire.[199]

By the sixth century the lights were going out all over Europe. Charles Martel (688-741) belonged to the Carolingian House in Frankish territory Gaul, a family that had feuded and splintered. Davis writes that though Martel did not start feudalism, he did very much like the idea of it and salivated at the "possibility of basing royal power on the support of vassals pledged to support their lord, in every quarrel, with life and limb and earthly substance. To provide his vassals with fiefs [feudal estates] he stripped the churches of many rich estates."[200] In the year 768 Charlemagne came on the scene. By the year 800 he sat on the throne as the Holy Roman Emperor being crowned on December 25: "The ninth century in western Europe was... a period of violence, disorder, and even anarchy. Charlemagne for a time had arrested the disintegration of society which resulted from the invasions of the Germans, and had united their warring tribes under something like a centralized government. But his work, it has been well said, was only a desperate rally in the midst of confusion."[201] As well, it is important to note that Charlemagne united these warring tribes and disciplined their embattled lands by using terror and brute force, defining trademarks of this fierce dictator.

---

[199] Davis, *Medieval Europe*, pp. 23-24.
[200] Ibid., p. 44.
[201] Webster, *History*, p. 415.

2

MEDIEVAL LAWS INFLUENCE OUR LEGAL SYSTEM

For skeptical readers who are thinking that that was then and this is now, much has been written about the legal and judicial contributions of Europe's Medieval life to today's western society: "That the feudal system is an important branch of historical knowledge will not be disputed, when we consider not only its influence [202] upon our [British] constitution,"[203] British historian Henry Hallam tells us. While Bury writes, "Roman Law is not merely the law of an Italian Community which existed two thousand years ago, nor even the law of the Roman Empire. It was, with more or less modification from local customs and ecclesiastical authority, the only system of law throughout the Middle Ages, and was the foundation of the modern law of nearly all Europe; one cannot but perceive that certain principles and institutions have had a guiding influence in this checkered Society, that there is a continuous development from Roman or barbaric roots, and that there is no other way to explain the course of events during our period but to trace the working of both these elements of social life."[204]

Medieval life provides the outlines for modern European and Anglo-American culture. It is why we lack deep existential knowledge of the sciences[205] and education. Medieval Europe is why scientists *experiment* and why doctors *practice* medicine, even though humans have been aware of themselves and their environment for millennia.[206] In fact, in the United States at least, western science is still establishing proper dietary guidelines for their citizens. And there are still no set, clearly identifiable successful standards for educating[207] western children.

And while life in ancient Rome may have been rather dicey, the people who overthrew policies and traditions - adapted from African conventions

---

[202] Of course, the United States' political system is based on the British system.
[203] Hallam, *History*, vol. 1, p. xiii.
[204] Bury, *Cambridge*, vol. 2, p. 53; p. 630.
[205] Some Europeans have scrutinized Dogon science. See Paul Griaule, *The Pale Fox* and Laird Scranton, *The Science of the Dogon*.
[206] Sound judgment was present when an author in July 1901 writes: "Leading authorities unreservedly admit that it [pharmacology] is a science still in its infancy, though it is as old as the history of man."
[207] It is stated often that education began in the U.S. only because businessmen needed people who could help them maintain their accounts. Thusly learning the 3 R's of reading, writing, and doing arithmetic became the fundamental features of education.

- had nothing of value to replace them with except for backwards practices that surfaced from the way warlord kings organized their fiefdoms. (Note: Barbarian practices were very much endemic to some European sensibilities, that is to say, they were acceptable both aesthetically and psychologically). Western society is shackled by regressive cultural practices that intersect our daily lives: political corruption and assassinations, [208] dishonest trade practices, [209] market manipulation, misogyny (The European cultural paradigm sacrifices daughters, wives, mothers and sisters on the altar of patriarchy for the sake of European male dominance), child slavery, sex slavery, Christian rituals, entertainment (from the theatre to the circus),[210] ancient superstitions reworked into *mystical* sacred rituals,[211] warmongering, and authoritarianism - to name a few - represent the Europeans' code of conduct, rooted in manipulating and dominating, but not necessarily concerned with obtaining the best results possible. Modern European institutions and philosophy bare roots from Europe's Middle Ages or from ages well before then. Medieval European practices are of particular concern to African readers who are as affected by them now as European's have been always.

Ancient European Laws Value Property Over Human Life, Promote Inequality

The edicts of Rome serve as a sterling example of the continued influence of ancient laws on western societies.[212] Originally named the Laws of the Twelve Tables, Europeans codified them in 450 BCE after, Gibbons writes, the rich "yielded with reluctance to the just demands of the people." Originally inscribed on "brass, or wood, or ivory," the Twelve Tables give important insight into the European man's thinking, then and now: Laws mirror the culture, and the early European culture honored neither, children nor women. For example, laws looked on children as things and not people; s/he could be sold by her/his owner to repay debt, etc.;'[213] and

---

[208] The term assassin comes to us by way of Arabs who were followers of Hassan-i Sabbah. Loyal followers of Hassan, the Haschichini, murdered many of his enemies. Assassinating key figures is a long-standing tradition in European politics.

[209] Caveat Emptor translates to "Let the buyer beware." It is standard western philosophy that approves of deception and fraud in the market place.

[210] The barbarians are said to have only tolerated the games.

[211] Europeans utilize many blood rituals that include slaying children, and fetuses. These rituals, outlines of which have been included in games, books, movies, etc. for mass consumption, supposedly convey magic powers on the perpetrators of those crimes against children and others. Their rituals are far too numerous to be included in this essay. However, African-American acquiring knowledge of these rituals protects us from becoming victim to the mentally ill who value them.

[212] Thorndike, *Europe*, p. 30.

[213] See also The Declaration of the Rights of the Child and the Convention on the Rights of

women became chattel and possessions.[214] Other aspects of the Twelve Tables are recognizable aspects of the American judicial system, such as using deadly force to protect property, noted as declarations of Moses and Solon. (Should the value of material objects be equal to or greater than the value of human life?). Additionally, being a debtor could certainly be a ruinous affair for the poor;[215] fathers or husbands could kill adulterous women; and being a slave oftentimes brought one serious injury or death.

According to Thorndike, Roman law gave great consideration to equity and humanity.[216] Though Bury informs us that the laws of Justinian acknowledged three classes of people: "honestiores, humiliores or tenuiores, servi." The honestiores were senators, soldiers and their sons, high officers, titled persons, landholders and merchants. This class was never subjected to capital punishment except for committing parricide or treason; or by imperial order. Instead, laws stripped honestiores of citizenship and banished them. The humiliores were given capital punishment, or sent to the mines.[217] On the other hand, Roman laws beheaded, crucified, and burned[218] servis. Duruy remarks that honestiores could not be compelled to a court of law by humilores described as "all persons who had inscribed upon the city registers as branded with infamy on account of their employment; also, all the poor...."[219] Indeed, social class had rank privileges as it now does: "From this time, whoever had municipal honors, any official position in the city, or a certain fortune in the system, was no longer of the people: 'Let the judge,' says Constantine, 'especially consider the testimony of the honestior.'"[220]

Sunday Becomes a Day of Rest, Tax Exemptions for the Church

Some ancient western religious laws are active today, too. Constantine passed an edict that required "magistrates, city people, and artisans" to rest on Sunday: "This was the first "Sunday law," though Webster notes: "It is highly doubtful, however, whether this legislation had any reference to Christianity. More probably, Constantine was only adding the day of the

---

the Child, UN General Assembly.
[214] See Laws of the Twelve Tables; Table VI, Law V.
[215] If unable to pay debt after a period of time, the debtor with more than one creditor was divided (literally) into pieces; Laws of the Twelve Tables; Table III, Law X.
[216] Thorndike, *Europe*, p. 31.
[217] "There is nothing more absurd than to cause countless numbers of men to perish in extracting from the bowels of the earth gold and silver, metals in themselves absolutely useless, and which constitute wealth only because they have been chosen as the symbols of it." Charles Montesquieu, *The Persian Letters*, (London: Atehneum Publishing), Letter 119, p. 265.
[218] Bury, *Cambridge*, vol. 2, pp. 106-07.
[219] Duruy, *Rome*, vol. 8, pt. 1, p. 33.
[220] Ibid., pp. 32-33.

Sun, the worship of which was then firmly established in the empire to the other holy days of the Roman calendar."[221] Considering Constantine's other religious laws, Webster's explanation is unlikely. Tax exemption of churches is a holdover from the Middle Ages with Constantine being the first to free the clergy, and their families, from taxation:

> The clergy were given many privileges by the Christian successors of Constantine, as their edicts in the Theodosian Code show. They were in large measure personally exempted from state duties and taxes; and in most criminal and some civil cases were to be tried by their own bishops rather than by the imperial courts.[222]

"Pretense of a Court" of Law: Swearing Oaths on Bibles, Secret Courts and Juries

The Theodosian Code first approved bequests whereby a person leaves all his worldly goods to the church. Also, the Code states that only bishops can hear charges against clerics; it sanctioned religious intolerance in the form of book burning and other means; and restricted the right to assembly to Christians. Swearing an oath on the bible is a practice in Roman law: "No judge was to commence the hearing until he had the Scriptures placed before the tribunal, and they were to remain there until judgment. All advocates had to take an oath, touching the Gospels, that they would do what they could do for their clients in truth and justice, and resign their case if they found it dishonest."[223] Oath taking was a custom of Europe's barbarian tribes, too.

According to historian Paul Lacroix, "As early as the time of the invasion, the Franks, Bavarians, and Visigoths, when investigating cases, began by an inquiry, and, previously to having recourse to trials before a judge, they examined witnesses on oath. Then, he who swore to the matter was believed, and acquitted accordingly. This system was no doubt flattering to human veracity, but, unfortunately, it gave rise to abuses; which it was thought would be avoided by calling the family and friends of the accused to take an oath, and it was then administered by requiring them to place their hands on the crucifix, on some relics, or on the consecrated Host."[224] In other cases, trial by combat was an accepted way of settling disputes. No one was exempt from these ordeals, according to Lacroix, including old men, women, children, and the disabled. These judicial duels followed the Franks use of red-hot iron, and of scalding

---

[221] Webster, *History*, p. 235.
[222] Thorndike, *Europe*, p. 105.
[223] Bury, *Cambridge*, vol. 2, p. 102.
[224] Paul Lacroix, *Manners, Customs and Dress During the Middle Ages and During the Renaissance Period*, pp. 351-52.

water, to settle disputes. Lacroix writes, "Christianity established common ties between these different legislations, and imperceptibly softened their native coarseness, although they retained the elements of their pagan and barbaric origin."[225]

Additionally, medieval secret tribunals that conducted private trials and sentencing were recently reintroduced into the United States. Lacroix writes this about the secret tribunals that surged throughout the medieval world. The free judges who oversaw this institution went about the country "seeking out crimes, denouncing them, and inflicting immediate punishment on any *evil doer* caught." Lacroix adds:

> "During the Middle Ages, human life was generally held in small respect various judicial institutions—if not altogether secret, at least more or less enveloped in mystery—were remarkable for being founded on the monstrous right of issuing the most severe sentences with closed doors, and of executing these sentences with inflexible rigour [sic] on individuals who had not been allowed the slightest chance of defending themselves. While passing judgment in secret, they often openly dealt blows as unexpected and terrible as they were fatal. Therefore, the most innocent and the most daring trembled at the very name of the Free Judges of the Terre-Rouge, an institution which adopted Westphalia as the special, or rather as the central, region of its authority; the Council of Ten exercised their power in Venice and the states of the republic; and the Assassins of Syria, in the time of St. Louis, made more than one invasion into Christian Europe."[226]

For the most part western laws are for show as they are often ignored or modified to accommodate whatever resource, or institution, or people Europeans and Anglo-Americans plan to exploit.[227] In this way, Europeans do not have to actually change their behavior; yet can still present their heinous actions as lawful. The cloak of legality is important to Europeans and Anglo-Americans, despite actions that are clearly morally and ethically illegal. In *The Age of the Crusades*, a book that focuses on 11th and 12th centuries Europe, English lawyer James M. Ludlow (d. 1911) puts it this

---

[225] Ibid., p. 353.
[226] Ibid., p. 381.
[227] In the United States bribing elected officials is supposedly illegal. However, in a recent 5-4 ruling, the Supreme Court essentially ruled that a duck is not a duck even if it walks or quacks like one, or was once an egg laid by a duck. The Court's opinion on campaign financing also displays their lack of skill in fortune telling. It reads in part: "This Court now concludes that independent expenditures, including those made by corporations, do not give rise to corruption or the appearance of corruption. That speakers may have influence over or access to elected officials does not mean that those officials are corrupt. And *the appearance of influence or access will not cause the electorate to lose faith in this democracy."(Italics added). Citizens United v. Federal Election Commission.* Decided January 21, 2010.

way:

> This ethical degradation was reflected in the low state of the laws, if the changeable wills or whims of a host of petty lords can be dignified with the title of legislation. Power claimed possession with little regard for the method of acquisition. Disputes, when relegated to the pretense of a court, were tried not by weighing evidence, but by counting the number of compurgators, that is, of those persons who would swear that they believed the oath of one or the other party.... If further evidence be needed that the very sense of justice had become largely extinguished, it is found in the prevalence of judicial perjury, allowed, and even prompted, by legalized custom.[228]

So, it seems times have changed - as has the name of the system that governs us, though not much else is different. The flawed practice of swearing oaths on bibles remains. And today, as in the past, a person's perceived status gives him great influence over the courts and the laws of the land. Many researchers have documented this reality, including those from Princeton whose data concludes that United States' policies are greatly/mostly influenced by the wealthiest people.[229]

We will read later in Chapter 14 of the medieval world's extraordinary torture techniques, some of which have been recently re-introduced by the United States government.

---

[228] Ludlow, *Crusades*, pp.16-18.
[229] Martin Gilens and Benjamin I. Page, *Testing Theories of American Politics*, (Princeton University), September 2014, accessed October 2014.
<http://scholar.princeton.edu/sites/default/files/mgilens/files/gilens_and_page_2014_-testing_theories_of_american_politics.doc.pdf>

3

THE TRIBES OF EUROPE

> *The most civilized nations of modern Europe issued from the woods of Germany, and in the rude institutions of those barbarians we may still distinguish the original principles of our present laws and manners.*[230]

Some westerners view tribes as a concept that is exclusively inherent to Africa. In fact, when Europeans want to ridicule Africans, they classify us as *tribesmen, natives and primitives* (sic); of course, the implied connotation is that tribesmen, natives, and primitive people are ignorant, savage, and unsophisticated. The truth is that learned Europeans acknowledge their own historical affiliation with tribes: "Individual tribes, or in other words, races or stocks, are the constituent elements of the earliest history,"[231] Nobel Laureate Theodor Mommsen informs us. Tribe itself derives from old Latin *tribus* meaning three (or a third, according to Mommsen) and is a reference to the three original families of Rome: the Ramnes, Tities, and Luceres,[232] who in uniting agreed to divide resources by thirds. Duruy writes, "Italy became the country where the greatest number of foreign races have met together. All the surrounding nations contributed their share in forming the population: and each revolution that which disturbed them produced a new people.... Italy was, therefore, a common asylum for all the wanderers of the ancient world. All brought in with them their language and their customs; many preserved their native character and their independence, until from the midst of them there should arise a city which formed at their cost her population, her laws, and her religion, — Rome herself, the asylum of all races and of all Italian civilizations!"[233]

So, tribes consist of members who share common ancestry, language, culture, sensibilities, etc. Other words substituted for tribe include: family, clan, house, nation, group, kindred, dynasty, etc. Being a tribe member is normal and natural; but for the purposes of this essay, and unless I am quoting source material, European nations only carry that title of Latin origin. Furthermore, natives are original citizens of lands. In the context of this essay being a native means that neither you, nor your ancestors have

---

[230] Gibbon, *Decline*, vol. 1, p. 260.
[231] Mommsen, *Rome*, vol. 1, p. 30.
[232] Ibid., p. 70.
[233] Duruy, *Rome*, vol. 1. pp. 44-45.

stolen another nation's land. There is no shame in being native.

Different historians applaud or criticize European tribes for the collapse of the Roman Empire. Historians who praise the barbarian invasions point to the customs eventually put into place by the roughened warlords that began to show their effect by the year 1000. One of them writes that the social and political life was regenerated by Germanic and Scandinavian people's; that new nations were beginning to show highly developed political consciousness and energy; that new languages had come into use; that the Christian church, its philosophy and literature began to dominate "nearly every phase of European life"; and that church was helping to improve social and economic conditions.

Other historians blame barbarism and its lack of refined organization for the eventual collapse of an *ordered* society, and for the illiteracy that sprang up and choked life's essence out of the living. Thorndike finds the proverbial silver lining in the gray clouds of barbarism: "The lack of strong central government had been one cause of that feudalism which fills the political gap between the break-up of Charlemagne's empire and the central development of the national European states of modern times. The various kingdoms founded by the German invaders, even including the Prankish Empire and the administrative efforts of Charlemagne, had not proved successful experiments in the political art. Their efforts to combine the last embers of Roman administration with their primitive institutions, imported like green wood from German forests, had resulted in failure — in a steady decrease in the amount of government and a constant development in the direction of feudalism, which was only partially interrupted by the energy of the first Carolingians. But along with such division came the feudal bond, which united men and united territory, though primarily only in a personal and private way. It gradually led, however, to the growth of political units and to new forms of government. The great lord, who had many vassals, could by means of their military service command a small army...."[234]

Germanic Tribes Rule: Survival of the Sadists

To be sure, barbarism spread the germs of dysfunction Western civilization lounges on now. Historians have written much about Europe's barbarian tribes such as the Goths (Germanic; lived inside holes, dug out of the ground), Vandals (Germanic; came from the forests), Franks (Germanic) and Saxons (Germanic), all predecessors to many Europeans, including North Americans. Ancient and modern writers describe Germanic tribes as barbaric and merciless to their foes that included basically anyone outside their own clan. The Goths settled near the Black Sea and may have

---

[234] Thorndike, *Europe*, pp. 256-57.

originally journeyed to their adopted land by boat from Scandinavian lands. Jordanes, a Goth who wrote their history in his controversial[235] *Getica: The Origins and Deeds of the Goths*, identifies them as ancestors to (Gog and) Magog.[236] Their family sub-groupings include Visigoths, Ostrogoths, and Scythians. Prominent church figure, then and now, and primary historian Isidore of Seville who lived during the 6th and 7th centuries writes that the Goths' name came from Magog, too. Isidore described the tribes of Europe thusly:[237]

> The nations of Germany are so-called because their bodies are of monstrous size, and their tribes are terrible, being inured [adjusted] to the fiercest cold, and they have derived their characteristics from the rigor of the climate, of fierce spirit and always unconquerable, living on plunder and hunting.... The frightfulness of their barbarism contributes a certain fearfulness of sound to their very names. The tribe of Saxons, dwelling on the shores of the Ocean [sic] and among pathless marshes, brave and active. And from this they get their name, because they are a hardy and very strong race of men, and one that surpasses other tribes in piracy. It is believed that the Francs [sic] were so-called from a certain leader. Others think that their names comes from the savagery of their character. For their customs are uncouth, and they have a natural fierceness of spirit.

Tacitus' records state that these Germanic tribes believed peaceful people were shiftless (lazy) people. During their "times of sloth" youths sought to join other chiefs waging wars so they could gain infamy; for their part, chiefs could not "maintain a numerous following except by violence and war."[238] An unsuccessful chief in wartime, or in capturing booty during raids soon found his youth leaving, "home... to flock abroad around warriors who achieve fame and obtain booty."[239] However, during "the laziness of peace" Tacitus writes, "Whenever they are not fighting, they pass much of their time in the chase, and still more in idleness, giving themselves up to sleep and to feasting, the bravest and the most warlike doing nothing, and surrendering the management of the household, of the home, and of the land, to the women, the old men, and all the weakest members of the family. They themselves lie buried in sloth, a strange combination in their nature that the same men should be so fond of

---

[235] Historian Jordanes is said to have mixed fact with fancy leaving later historians with the weighty job of discerning the truth.
[236] According to biblical prophecy Gog and his Magog followers attack the church in a final battle.
[237] Ernest Brehaut, *An Encyclopedist of the Dark Ages: Isidore of Seville*, pp. 211-12.
[238] John Alfred Church and William Jackson Brodribb, trans., *The Agricola and Germany of Tacitus, and the Dialogue on Oratory* (London: Macmillan & Co., 1885), p. 98.
[239] Bury, *Cambridge*, vol. 2, p. 639.

idleness, so averse to peace. It is the custom of the states to bestow by voluntary and individual contribution on the chiefs a present of cattle or of grain, which, while accepted as a compliment, supplies their wants. They are particularly delighted by gifts from neighbouring [sic] tribes, which are sent not only by individuals but also by the state, such as choice steeds, heavy armour [sic], trappings, and neck- chains. We have now taught them to accept money also."[240]

In the next few paragraphs Herodotus describes a few barbaric tribes of Europe beginning with the Scythians who drank the blood of their victims. According to him, Scythians descend from the tribes of three brothers. Their 4th century dress includes a tall cone-shaped headpiece and draped cape that look eerily similar to modern costumes worn by a certain race-centered group today. About the Scythians, Herodotus tells us:

> The Scythian soldier drinks the blood of the first man he overthrows in battle. Whatever number he slays, he cuts off all their heads, and carries them to the king; since he is thus entitled to a share of the booty, whereto he forfeits all claim if he does not produce a head. In order to strip the skull of its covering, he makes a cut round the head above the ears,[241] and, laying hold of the scalp, shakes the skull out; then with the rib of an ox he scrapes the scalp clean of flesh, and softening it by rubbing between the hands, uses it thenceforth as a napkin. The Scyth is proud of these scalps, and hangs them from his bridle-rein; the greater the number of such napkins that a man can show, the more highly is he esteemed among them. Many make themselves cloaks, like the capotes of our peasants, by sewing a quantity of these scalps together. Others flay the right arms of their dead enemies, and make of the skin, which is stripped off with the nails hanging to it, a covering for their quivers. Now the skin of a man is thick and glossy, and would in whiteness surpass almost all other hides. Some even flay the entire body of their enemy, and stretching it upon a frame, carry it about with them wherever they ride. Such are the Scythian customs with respect to scalps and skins. [242]

Tertullian comments on these practices, "Touching [on] the eating of blood,[243] and such like tragic dishes… certain nations have ordained for the making of a treaty[244] the shedding of blood from their arms, and the

---

[240] Church and Brodribb, *Agricola*, pp. 98-99.
[241] It is common knowledge that during the Indian wars in the United States Anglo-Americans offered rewards for collecting American Indian scalps. See Howard Zinn, *A People's History of the United States*, p. 72. In Africa, Europeans required severed hands and genitals of Africans as proof that spent cartridges had been used to kill Africans: See Edmund D. Morel, *King Leopold's Rule in Africa*, pp. 58 & 187.
[242] Rawlinson, *Herodotus*, vol. 2, pp. 224-25.
[243] This practice is recorded: Rawlinson, vol.1, p. 87.
[244] This practice is recorded at least as far back as 500 years before the European year zero: Trumbull, p. 61.

drinking it the one from the other." The scarring that remained on the skin from the blood covenant ceremony became an important symbol. Historian and bible scholar Lewis Bayles Paton (d. 1932) informs us that: "Tattooing, which often accompanied the letting of blood, was designed to mark one as a permanent worshipper of the spirit to which the blood was offered."[245] "Under [L. Sergius Catilina] Catiline[246] also there was some drinking of the same sort. They say too that among some tribes of the Scythians every one that dieth is eaten by his relations."[247] [248]Strack writes that these and other blood rituals were common practices for Europeans: "The drinking of human blood, or of wine mixed with such blood when friendship was sworn, and alliances were concluded, was the custom of many nations, in antiquity and in the middle ages."[249]

Indeed, Europeans have a long tradition of making blood covenants. Bury informs us, "A common practice for starting it was to exchange weapons; sometimes each of the would-be brothers made a cut on his arm or chest and mixed the blood flowing from it with that of his comrade. The newly created tie of brotherhood was usually confirmed by an oath; a historical instance of this variety is presented by the arrangement between Canute and Eadmund Ironside. This kind of artificial relationship lent itself readily to the formation of fresh associations not engrafted on existing kindreds, but carrying the idea of close alliance into the sphere of voluntary unions."[250] Of this ceremony minister H. Clay Trumbull, author of *The Blood Covenant* writes that it "has been recognized as the closet, the holiest, and the most indissoluble, compact conceivable."[251] The tribal deity is always party to these covenants, according to bible scholar and professor W. Robertson Smith.

---

[245] Lewis Bayles Paton, *Spiritism and the Cult of the Dead in Antiquity*, p. 11.
[246] "A report prevailed at that time, and was received by many, that Catiline, at the close of his harangue, proceeded to bind his accomplices by an oath of fidelity; and, to give it the most solemn sanction, sent round the room bowls of human blood mixed with wine. When, after dreadful imprecations, all had swallowed the unnatural beverage, as if it was a libation used in religious sacrifices, he took the opportunity to open the secrets of his heart. He gave the assembly to understand, that by the ceremony he had introduced, his intention was to bind them to each other by the most sacred obligation, in the presence of numbers engaged in a great and glorious enterprise." Arthur Murray, trans., *The Works of Sallust*, (London: James Carpenter and J. Cuthelll and P. Martin. 1807), p. 34. In taking an oath of partnership against the Roman Republic, it is suggested that the blood came from slaughtered humans whose bodies became a part of the ritual meal, too.
[247] Dodgson, *Tertullian*, p. 22.
[248] "In certain cases it is the duty of the survivors to eat up their dead, just as in Nilus's sacrifice. This was the use of the Issedones, according to Herodotus (iv. 26)."W. Robertson Smith, *Lectures on the Religion of the Semites*, p. 370.
[249] Strack, *Sacrifice*, p. 43.
[250] Bury, *Cambridge*, vol. 2, p. 636.
[251] Trumbull, *Covenant*, p. 204.

We will read more on Europe's bloody practices throughout this essay. In the meantime Trumbull asserts that blood covenants have historical precedence with Indo-Europeans: "Another item of evidence that the blood-covenant in its primitive form was a well-known rite in primitive Europe, is a citation by Athenseus [sic] (3rd c.) from Poseidonios (d. 51 BCE) to this effect: 'Concerning the Germans, Poseidonios says, that they, embracing each other in their banquets, open the veins upon their foreheads, and mixing the flowing blood with their drink, they present it to each other; esteeming it the farthest attainment of friendship to taste each other's blood.' As Poseidonios was earlier than our Christian era, this testimony shows that the custom with our ancestors was in no sense an outgrowth, nor yet a perversion, of Christian practices."[252] As Strack mentions briefly above, Europeans have a long tradition of mixing blood with wine, too. And as a reminder of an earlier citation, the Latin word for that blood-wine mixture is assiratum. Assir means blood. Renderings of assir mean to bind, to tie, covenant, compact, and bracelet. According to some historians, blood covenants were essential to the European wedding ceremony, and the exchanging of rings grew out of the custom of binding relationships by blood.

Slavic people are likely descendants of the Scythians, according to some sources. There were other tribes whose kings formed allegiance to the Scythians. Of them the Tauri and the Androphagi stand out - in regards to violence - from the rest, but not by much. We turn to Herodotus once more for information on these ancient tribes, "The manners of the Androphagi are more savage than those of any other race. They neither observe justice, nor are governed by any laws. They are nomads, and their dress is Scythian; but the language which they speak is peculiar to themselves. Unlike any other nation in these parts, *they are cannibals.*"[253] (Italics added).

According to Isidore, the Anthropophagi, also written variously as Andropophagi, and Androphagi were a fierce people whose name comes from eating human flesh. Finns or Siberians are probable descendants of Androphagi. Herodotus explains the customs of other tribes in league with the Scythians:

> The Tauri... offer in sacrifice to the Virgin all ship wrecked persons, and all Greeks compelled to put into their ports by stress of weather. The mode of sacrifice is this. After the preparatory ceremonies, *they strike the victim on the head with a club.* Then, according to some accounts, they *hurl the trunk from the precipice whereon the temple stands, and nail the head to a cross.* Others grant that the head is treated in this way, but deny that the body is thrown down the cliff— on the contrary, they say, it is buried.... When they take prisoners in war

---

[252] Ibid., p. 320.
[253] Rawlinson, *Herodotus*, vol. 2, p. 253.

they treat them in the following way. *The man who has taken a captive cuts off his head, and carrying it to his home, fixes it upon a tall pole, which he elevates above his house,* most commonly over the chimney. The reason that the heads are set up so high, is (it is said) in order that the whole house may be under their protection. These people live entirely by war and plundering. The *Agathyrsi* are a race of men very luxurious, and very fond of wearing gold on their persons. They have wives in common, that so they may be all brothers, and, as members of one family, may neither envy nor hate one another…. The Neurian customs are like the Scythian. The Melanchlseni wear, all of them, black cloaks, and from this derive the name which they bear. Their customs are Scythic.[254] (Italics added).

Throughout this essay, we will learn how the unsettling practices of these bloodthirsty tribes were not dissimilar from the disturbing practices of the later general European populations.

More Still Came by Sea: Assaults, Human Sacrifice & Cannibalism

Note Before delving into the topic of the Vikings, I wish to acknowledge that the 19th and early 20th centuries resources used here have derived much of their information about these people from Scandinavian Sagas (sayings) and medieval chroniclers. Since the 19th century, archaeologists and anthropologists have uncovered Scandinavian artifacts that are leading them to fresh interpretations. They are developing new theories about the lives of early northern Europeans. Some historians say medieval Muslim chroniclers provide them with a more favorable impression of the Vikings, also.

So now, researchers are able to report that these particular Scandinavian people were gentle farmers who lived in snug little cottages, while the upper classes provided the warriors. Even if this restrained view of Vikings is partly correct, the leaders needed thousands of men with whom to war. Whatever the case, regions that Vikings eventually settled in either were handed over peaceably or became victims to bloody sieges. I find it troubling that some modern historians attempt to reject Viking accounts simply because they are written by medieval Christian chroniclers who critics claim may have had their own axe to grind against Vikings. In the face of Europeans proclaiming the accuracy of interpretations of historical Africans, perhaps we can agree on one fundamental point: It is critically important for people to document their own history.

Probably Europe's most admired barbarians for the sheer unrepentant ferocity of their uncivilized behavior are the north men (Norsemen, Normans) also called Vikings:[255] "In the ninth century their marauding and

---

[254] Ibid., pp. 251-53.
[255] "The term ' Viking ' is derived from the Old Norse vik, a bay, and means one who haunts a bay, creek or fjord. In the 9th and 10th centuries it came to be used more especially of those warriors who left their homes in Scandinavia and made raids on the chief European

conquering expeditions filled the European world with terror... even at the very sound of their name. They subdued England, seized on Normandy, laid siege to Paris, conquered a considerable portion of Belgium, made extensive inroads into Spain."[256] The word berserk comes to the English language from a tribe of Norsemen – Berserkers,[257] who were extreme in their cruelty: "They were often seized with a kind of frenzy, either arising from an excited imagination, or from the use of stimulating liquors[258] – committing then the wildest extravagances, and striking indiscriminately at friends and foes."[259] Berserkers tossed children with the point of their spear, according to *The Vikings*. A brief description of the Vikings' warring nature follows: [260]

> Tranquil occupations did not enjoy any reputation among the ancient Norsemen, while war and fighting were a sure way of acquiring an eminent name with contemporaries, glorious fame with succeeding generations, and means and riches in abundance.... Life was of little value, and had to be risked at any cost for honor; and an old warrior, when unable to wield his sword, often caused one of his friends to kill him, to avoid a natural death, which was an exclusion from the privileges of Valhalla."[261] Women encouraged their men to seek loot; who a young girl married depended much on the man's ability to procure goods: "Young men went into warlike expeditions to attain great fame, so that their acts of bravery could be known or extolled, and that they might become worthy of the maiden they wished to woo.[262]

Historians note that the Vikings' reputation preceded them and are stuff of legends. They designed ships for speed and agility that allowed them to quickly enter or exit foreign ports where they warred and looted: "They were constantly at war with their neighbours, by sea and by land, murder and rapine were so prevalent as ordinarily to excite little beyond a passing local interest, and men held their property and lives by virtue only of the strength of their own right hands and the uncertain tenure of the loyalty of greedy relations and jealous friends."[263]

Vikings plundered churches and monasteries of gold, silver and other fineries in France, Germany, Italy, Spain, England, Scotland, and Ireland.

---

countries." Allen Mawer, *The Vikings*, p. 1.
[256] Charles Young, *Harald: First of the Vikings*, p. 12.
[257] Berserker mercenaries became the private police force to the Byzantine Empire. They provided security to the emperor and other wealthy citizens. They were called Varangian Guard. Modern day mercenaries play similar roles.
[258] Some historians say hallucinogens were used.
[259] Paul C. Sinding, *History of Scandinavia*, (2nd ed), p. 46.
[260] Mawer, *Vikings*, p. 84.
[261] Sinding, *Scandinavia*, p. 29.
[262] Du Chaillu, *Viking*, vol. 2, p. 2.
[263] Young, *Harald*, p. 15.

Their savage behavior invited potential victims to pay them tribute; however, payment only encouraged far more menacing assaults from them and increased the number of raids. During the 10th century Arab chronicler Ibn Fadlan[264] met the Vikings in an area today known as Russia. He describes a violent and filthy[265] band of drunken men, who treated women in an entirely vulgar manner.

According to Du Chaillu, human sacrifice was widely practiced by the Vikings to ward off famine or in exchange for victory against an enemy: "'Every ninth year, nine animals of every species (without excepting the human) were sacrificed, and their bleeding bodies suspended in the sacred grove adjacent to the temple,'" Gibbon informs us.[266] The leader's son was sometimes chosen to carry this burden for everyone. Mythical (?) King Aun desired longevity. He sacrificed nine of his sons in exchange for a long life: "Men, particularly the slain after a battle, were sometimes given to Odin for victory, the largest number ever given being those who fell at the famous battle of Bravalla. It seems to have been customary to redden the altars with the blood of the fallen chiefs. Prisoners of war, no matter what their rank, were called thralls [slaves], and were sacrificed; sometimes they were slaughtered like animals, their blood put into bowls, and their bodies thrown into bogs or a spring outside the door of the temple called Uotkelda (sacrificing spring), or their backs broken on sharp stones; sometimes they were thrown from high cliffs."[267]

Some Vikings blended sacrificial rituals with a horrific torture technique: "Among the human sacrifices were those called Nodorn (blood eagle), so called on account of the skin or flesh being cut down the whole back to the ribs, from both sides of the spine, in the shape of an eagle, and of the lungs being drawn through the wound. This special mode of sacrifice seems to have been practised [sic] on the slayer of a man's father."[268] According to *History of Scandinavia*, Vikings sacrificed animals every 9th month. They divided meat among the community while the priests used the entrails and blood for divination: "Sometimes even men were offered—mostly slaves and prisoners of war—for the Norsemen, in their uncultivated state, were, to a certain extent, cannibals,"[269] Paul Sinding observes. Thusly are the customs of a few of Europe's male-dominated tribes.

Roots of Royal Ancestry: Europe's Highest Hoods Become Royal

---

[264] James E. Montgomery, "Ibn Fadlan and the Rusiyyah." *Universitetet I Bergen*. Web. 26 Aug. 2014.
[265] The men of the north were said to be mindful of cleanliness when it came to dating.
[266] Gibbon, *Decline*, vol. 1, p. 291.
[267] Du Chaillu, *Viking*, vol.1, p. 368.
[268] Ibid., p. 372.
[269] Sinding, *Scandinavia*, p. 26.

Highnesses

Charles Young remarks on Norman ancestry: *"If ever the child is father of the man, the Scandinavians were the fathers of the English. They have bequeathed to them their love of war, their pioneering instincts, their passion for the sea. The Englishman has the same love as they for martial daring and fame, for the Ocean that girdles his island home, for discovery, for colonising, for subduing savage peoples. And these tall, blonde men, with their defiant blue eyes, who obeyed their kings while they had confidence in them, and slew them when they had forfeited their respect, were the ancestors, too, of the Normans who, under William the Conqueror, invaded and founded the only European State which has since reached the highest civilisation, combined with the widest liberty, through slow and even stages of orderly development."*[270] (Italics added). The highly esteemed, yet terribly brutal Norman, William the Conqueror (aka William the Bastard), was illiterate. He invaded and defeated the original inhabitants of England with the help of thousands of other men seeking to "to receive the spoils of the island kingdom if the enterprise went well." Thusly, William became England's first Norman king reigning from 1066-1087. His ongoing battles with the Anglo-Saxons led to their eventual replacement with Norman aristocracy. Queen Elizabeth II is a descendant to William as are an estimated quarter of the English population. Many North Americans are distantly related, too. Northmen are, "Teutonic [Germanic] ancestors of the modern Danes, Swedes, and Norwegians, and inhabited the Scandinavian peninsula, where there was good hunting Influence and fishing, but a rather barren soil."[271]

Unfortunately, European history is stained by its capitulation to the order of male dominance at the exclusion of all else: "In the ordinary course of affairs, the father's authority was fully recognised [sic] and the families and kindreds of the host must have been chiefly composed of [patrilineal] groups bearing distinctive names from real or supposed ancestors and tracing their descent from him through a succession of males."[272] Tribal warlord chiefs, the strongest and most violent of the lot during what Bury tells us was: "a time when the social co-operation and defensive alliance of a group of strong men was recognised as a most efficient means of getting on in the world and of meeting possible aggression,"[273] exalted themselves to kingship and prince hood, bathed themselves in mythos of sacred royal blood: *"The pretensions of* [Saxon founders] *Hengist and Horsa to be immediate descendants of Woden [Odin] would seem to imply their mythical origin. But many Saxon chiefs of undoubted reality rested their pretentions [sic] upon a*

---

[270] Young, *Harald*, pp. 12-13.
[271] Thorndike, *The Europe*, p. 217.
[272] Bury, *Cambridge*, vol.2, p. 631.
[273] Ibid., p. 635.

similar genealogy,"[274] and then lorded over the lands and people of Europe. (Italics added). "In this way the kindreds did not disappear from the history of Western Europe without leaving many traces, and such traces were most noticeable in the case of noble families keenly interested in tracing their pedigrees and able to keep their cohesion and privileges,[275] writes Bury.

Hengist and Horsa (their names translate as stallion and horse, respectively), mentioned above, were but two of these haughty warlords who seized power and kept it by employing unscrupulous, but Europe-honored methods, including, as mentioned above, linking their heritage to highly regarded Indo-European gods. The brother's expedition to England and resultant battles there with a beleaguered king laid the foundation for modern England. Their tale follows:

> At this and other times came over a mixed multitude from three of the German nations; that is to say, the Angles, Saxons, and Jutes.... Hence the men of this country have made a *virtue of necessity,* and, when driven from their native soil, *they have gained foreign settlements by force of arms.* The Vandals, for instance, who formerly over-ran Africa; the Goths, who made themselves masters of Spain; the Lombards [Germanic tribe], who, even at the present time, are settled in Italy; and the Normans, who have given their own name to that part of Gaul which they subdued. From Germany, then, there first came into Britain, an inconsiderable number indeed, but well able to make up for their paucity by their courage. These were under the conduct of *Hengist and Horsa,*[276] two brothers of *suitable disposition, and of noble race in their own country.* They were great-grandsons of the celebrated Woden,[277] *from whom almost all the royal families of these barbarous nations deduce their origin; and to whom the nations of the Angles, fondly deifying him, have consecrated by immemorial superstition the fourth day of the week....*[278] (Italics added).

The tale of the beleaguered warlord king belongs to King Vortigern. During the fifth century, after the Romans quit the land, he sought outside assistance once his sovereignty fell under siege from Picts and Scots. Noted English historian William of Malmesbury recounts the following about

---

[274] Charles Knight, *History of England,* vol. 1, p. 61.
[275] Bury, *Cambridge,* vol. 2, p. 634.
[276] These brothers, who successfully helped the king of Briton defend against foreign invaders, later overthrew the king.
[277] In Norse literature he is called Odin, "Father of gods and men, and rules the whole world, which he by his wise and judicious eye, contemplates and views from his high... heavenly seat," his gold radiating palace. Paul Sinding, *The Scandinavian Races: The Northmen; The Sea-Kings and Vikings,* pp. 22-23.
[278] J. A. Giles, *William of Malmesbury's Chronicle of the Kings of England From the Earliest Period to the Reign of King Stephen,* p. 8.

Vortigern:

At this time Vortigern was King of Britain; a man calculated neither for the field nor the council, but wholly given up to the lusts of the flesh, the slave of every vice: a character of insatiable avarice, ungovernable pride, and polluted by his lusts. To complete the picture, as we read in the History of the Britons, he had defiled his own daughter, who was lured to the participation of such a crime by the hope of sharing his kingdom, and she had borne him a son. Regardless of his treasures at this dreadful juncture, and wasting the resources of the kingdom in riotous living, he was awake only to the blandishments of abandoned women. Roused at length, however, by the clamors of the people, he summoned a council, to take the sense of his nobility on the state of public affairs. To be brief, it was unanimously resolved to invite over from Germany the Angles and Saxons, nations powerful in arms, but of a roving life. [279]

Vortigern hoped that the fierce mercenaries who came to his country's aid would accept land in exchange for fighting at his side. The brothers desired more than a few plots of land, so Horsa's daughter, Rowena, deceived [280] the king into allowing even more of the fierce Saxon mercenaries ashore: "And then they sent for the Angles, and told them of the worthlessness of the people and the excellences of the land. This is the Saxon narrative."[281] Vortigern was outmaneuvered and outnumbered. In 455, six years following their landing in Britain, Horsa died battling Vortigern, and Hengist "obtained the kingdom." An uneasy truce existed for several years until the aggressions of Vortigern's son dissolved it. Hengist and Horsa are founders of the Saxon heptarchy[282] established in Britain that divided the land into seven kingdoms: "They were the sons of Wihtgils; Wihtgils son of Witta, Witta of Wecta, Wecta of Woden: from this Woden sprang all our royal families, and those of the South-humbrians also."[283]

The struggle between King Vortigern and brothers Hengist and Horsa illustrates one of uncountable blood-drenched competitions that took place during the Dark Ages. Acts of intrigue,[284] deceit, treachery, theft, incest, murder, and manipulation emerge as the core elements of an unimaginable number of real-life medieval dramas. The Anglo-Saxon Chronicle, an ancient record of European history beginning from European year zero[285] to

---

[279] Ibid., p. 7.
[280] This ploy of swooning by seduction of love and wine is "an embellishment of British traditions." Knight *History*, p. 61.
[281] Ibid.
[282] Sinding, *Scandinavia*, p. 20.
[283] John Allen Giles, *The Anglo-Saxon Chronicle*, p. 7.
[284] See Niccolo Machiavelli's *Of Conspiracies*.
[285] One translation of the chronicle explains that European history places the beginning of

the 12th century highlights the medieval struggles of Europeans as they fought each other for supremacy. For example, the powerful Anglo-Saxon king, Edwin of Northumbria, gained the throne after a rival was killed in battle. Years later, Edwin's throne was usurped after he was killed in battle. The king who overthrew Edwin was subsequently killed, too. And so the story went all over Europe, year after year for 1000 plus years.

Of course it follows that a barbaric political system that honored mythical royal blood, and granted enormous privileges to certain titleholders had to allow others to share in the gross benefits that system produced over time. Quite naturally a superficial social system such as this one would eventually pit kinsmen against kinsmen. "But even of the nobility the greater part of them arose through the success of new men and especially through service [rewarded] by kings and other potentates. As for the rest of the people it became more and more difficult to keep up the neatly framed groups of kinsmen. From being definite organizations the kindreds were diverted into the position of aggregates of persons claiming certain rights and obligations in regard to each other,"[286] Bury informs us. To this point Hallam adds, "The original nobility of the continent were, what we may call self created, and did not derive their rank from any such concessions of their respective sovereigns, as have been necessary in subsequent ages."[287] Duruy writes similarly of Rome, "'Constantine,' says Eusebius, "devised a large number of titles in order to be able to honor a larger number of citizens,"[288] and that Augustine sought to "distribute all the citizens into well marked classes."[289]

As is presently customary, materialism ranked high for early Europeans who awarded those with greater material wealth leadership duties: "Above the peasants ranked the chiefs or leaders, not on account of peculiar privileges, but of the greater credit and influence they enjoyed, because they were in possession of larger property, and descended from distinguished families."[290] The poisonous political system the warlords manifested is called feudalism, a fitting reference to property (fief, feudum),[291] and cattle (wealth) over which thousands of battles were fought. In Roman society and later during the feudalistic structure that followed, people having neither of these commodities suffered greatly. We will read about them momentarily.

---

the European world to 5226 years before the European year 0.
[286] Bury, *Cambridge*, vol. 2, p. 634.
[287] Henry Hallam, *View*, vol.1, p 192.
[288] Duruy, *Rome*, vol. 8, pt. 1, p. 2.
[289] Ibid.
[290] Sinding, *Scandinavia*, p. 38.
[291] Ibid., pp. 305-06.

Some Viking Customs and Traditions Still Practiced

Note *'Habits of some African-Americans, like other folks, come from watching and imitating our parents. Some of us rarely think of why we do things the way we do them. We rarely focus on the root of a tradition, though understanding why we do what we do is important in avoiding societal confusions and awakening our Black conscious. Cultures provide cues to its people. Those cues help to decode the larger social environment. With those cues, it is fairly easy to navigate society – without them, we can become lost. Some African-Americans do not receive the same social cues as Anglo-Americans, unless one or both of our parents are Anglos, or we have friends who can help us understand and adapt. I grew up not understanding much of what I was seeing and hearing from the domineering culture, because my relatives provided me with African cues. Because I received African cues, it was more difficult for me to understand the Anglo-American world in which I was maturing.*

For example, egalitarianism was a fundamental principle of my family. I never knew the workings of hierarchy, and so experienced culture shock as a university freshman when a male Anglo sociology professor told my class that Black women were on the bottom of some European/Anglo-American created social ladder that conveniently placed all European and Anglo-American men on its top rung. Actually, I was doubly shocked because I had grown up watching the men in my family reverence their women. Before the professor's lecture, it had never occurred to me that the domineering culture saw me perched on some lower rung upon which their adolescent boys and girls stepped as they advanced to take over positions held by their mothers and fathers. I found myself instinctively rejecting the professor's scholarship in favor of more humanitarian lessons learned from my family that embraced equality and fairness.

Below are a few Viking customs that linger within our current European paradigm. Following them are examples of Viking mythos that may be familiar to many of us. Many more familiar Viking myths are found in Chapter 9.

-Class-based social order: "From very early times the people of the North were divided into classes. Men and women were educated from their childhood to believe in the superiority or inferiority of their own being, of the position inherited by them at their birth, and consequently to think themselves superior or inferior to other people of the commonwealth. This belief was intensified by the education they received, their surroundings and their mode of life, as seen throughout from the day of their birth to the time when they were buried. The class that governed held that they were born to rule, and the slave to remain a slave. The lot of each had been hereditary, fate had so decreed. This demarcation into classes was acquiesced in by the people of the land, for *it could not have existed a single moment without their will*, and formed an integral part of the social and political fabric throughout the whole history of the people."[292]

---

[292] Du Chaillu, *Viking*, vol.1, p. 486.

(Italics added).

-Individual land ownership was practiced. Additionally, leasing land and paying rent were established customs. It was possible for a king to own all the land and water rights as was the case with eleventh century King Harald. "King Harald became the owner of all odals,[293] and of all the land cultivated and uncultivated in every Fylki,[294] and even of the sea and the rivers and lakes. All boendr[295] were to be his tenants, both those who cultivated the field and the salt makers; and all fishermen, hunters and trappers, both on sea and on land, were his men " (Egil's Saga, c. 4)."[296]

-Days of the week: "The month was subdivided into six weeks; each week contained five days. The days were called Tysdag (Tuesday); Odinsdag (Wednesday); Thorsdag (Thursday); Frjadag (Friday); Laugardag (bath-day) or Thvattdag (washing-day, Saturday)."[297]

Viking Myths

- Svafrlami, son of Sigrlami and grandson to Odin attempted to sacrifice on the altar to gods two Dvergar, but "on their begging to be allowed to give a ransom for their lives, Svafrlami asked their names."[298] Svafrlami relents for a time asking the Dvergar for a sword with which he later attempted to kill them. But, instead of stabbing the Dvergar, Svafrlami lodged the sword into the stone. Tyrfing (the name given the sword), according to Svafrlami's directions to the Dvergar, was to have a "hilt to be of gold, and the scabbard to be ornamented and inlaid with gold. The sword was never to fail, and never to rust; to cut iron and stone as well as cloth; and it was to bring victory in all battles and duels (einvigi) to every one who carried it."[299]

- Odin often appeared in dreams on the eve of battles.

- A strange man enters the wedding of King Völsung's daughter Signey to King Siggeir: "He had a sword in his hand, and wore a hood low down over his face; he was very grey-haired, and looked old, and was one-eyed. He went to the tree, and drew the sword, and stuck it into the trunk so that it sank up to the hilt. No man dared to speak to him. He said: 'He who pulls this sword out of the trunk shall get it as a gift from me, and will find that he never had a better sword in his hand than this one.' The old man then went out, and no one knew

---

[293] Family titled land that was absolute.
[294] This is a division of land.
[295] These are the head chiefs of the country.
[296] Du Chaillu, *Viking*, vol. 1, p. 484.
[297] Ibid., pp. 37-38.
[298] Ibid., p. 54.
[299] Ibid., p. 54.

who he was, or where he went. Then all the foremost men tried to pull out the sword, and could not. Sigmund, the son of King Volsung, pulled it out as easily as if it had been quite loose. No man had seen so good a sword, and Siggeir offered three times its weight in gold for it. Sigmund answered that he should have pulled it out ; now he should never get it, though he offered all the gold he owned. (Volsunga, c. 3X1."[300]

- Hell: "A different lot or fate fell to the cowards who feared the battle and dangers of war, and allowed themselves to be cut off by disease. Cast down to Helheim (hell) they had to continue their life there, as silent, trembling shadows, without pleasure and exploits, and under the perpetual suffering of anguish, remorse, and famine."[301]

Thus the tribes of Europe marched into the world: "There were at the north and south of Europe two great nations who knew the earliest arts, and commenced this struggle against physical nature which our modern civilization continues with so much success. Both were subdued and cursed after their defeat by the warlike tribes who looked upon work as servile labor, and made slavery the law of the ancient world."[302]

---

[300] Ibid., pp. 60-61.
[301] Sinding, *Northmen*, p. 24.
[302] Duruy, *Rome*, vol. 1, p. 46.

4

FEUDALISM

These were times of great misery to the people, and the worst, perhaps, that Europe has ever known. Even under Charlemagne, we have abundant proofs of the calamities which the people suffered. The light which shone around him, was that of a consuming fire.[303]

No political institution can endure, which does not rivet itself to the hearts of men, by ancient prejudice, or acknowledged interest. The feudal compact had originally much of this character. Its principle of vitality was warm and active. In fulfilling the obligations of mutual assistance and fidelity by military service, the energies of friendship were awakened, and the ties of moral sympathy superadded to those of positive compact.[304]

Until recently, modern media outlets did not come close to supplying adequate representations of the Middle Ages. Most often stories of medieval life appeared as backdrops to love stories and war, or they made sport of chaos. However, today's narratives still fall short as they center on the lives of wealthy citizens. It is understandable then that so few Americans can relate our current social construct to practices originating during Europe's medieval period and earlier. Writing to us from the 19th century is James Ludlow. He presents readers with an eloquent summation of medieval life during the 11th and 12th centuries. His narrative sincerely conveys the types of despair Europeans confronted:

"The once luxuriant civilization of Rome had been swept away by the Northern invaders as completely as a freshet despoils the fields when it not only destroys standing vegetation, but carries with the debris the soil itself. The most primitive arts, those associated with agriculture, were forgotten, and the rudiments of modern industries were not thought of.

"Much of the once cultivated land had, as has elsewhere been noted, reverted to native forest and marsh, and in places was still being purchased by strangers on titles secured by occupancy and first improvement, as now in the new territories of America.[305] But even nature's pity for man was outraged; the bounty she gave

---

[303] Hallam, *History*, p. 18.
[304] Hallam, *View*, p. 255.
[305] See The Homestead Act of 1862. Early in U.S. history many "pull yourself up by your own bootstraps Americans" were given land grants by the U.S. and foreign governments to encourage colonization. The Homestead Act of 1862 allowed for mostly White Americans to acquire a 160-acre parcel of land from the government so that they could settle it. For an $18 filing fee, they could build on the land. Their only requirement was to improve it over 5

from half-tilled acres was despoiled by men themselves, as hungry children snatch the morsels of charity from one another's hands. What was hoarded for personal possession became the spoil of petty robbers, and what was left by the neighborhood marauder was destroyed in the incessant baronial strife.

"To these devouring forces must be added the desolating wars between the papal and imperial powers, the conquest and reconquest of Spain by Moors and Christians, and the despoiling of Saxon England by the Normans. Throughout Europe, fields, cottages, castles, oftentimes churches, were stripped by the vandalism which had seemingly become a racial disposition. To this ordinary impoverished condition was added the especial misery, about 1195, of several years' failure of crops. Famine stalked through France and middle Europe; villages were depopulated. Cruel as they were, men grew weary of raiding one another's possessions when there was nothing to bring back but wounds. Even hatred palled when unsupported by envy and cupidity."[306]

A Poorly Disguised System of Slavery

Feudalism is a vulgar system of individuals who have it all and others who have absolutely nothing. It is an oppressive social framework that allows the "have it alls" to suck out all available oxygen (wealth and resources) leaving most of the population gasping for breath (housing, nourishment, healthiness, and clothing). Feudalism is brutal and socially regressive. It consciously and deliberately justifies human degradation, further encouraging human injustice; feudalism trivializes humanity by pitting one person against another:

> The feudal principle was essentially aristocratic, and tended to enhance every unsocial and unchristian sentiment involved in the exclusive respect for birth. It had, of course, its countervailing virtues, which writers of M. Thierry's school do not enough remember. But a rural aristocracy in the meridian of feudal usages was insulated in the midst of the other classes of society far more than could ever happen in cities, or in any period of an advanced civilization. "Never," says Guizot," had the primary social molecule been so separated from other similar molecules; never had the distance been so great between the simple and essential elements of society.[307]

As mentioned earlier, Europeans manifested feudalism - in one form or another - in certain of their territories long before the era known as the Medieval Ages suggesting just how deeply rooted social inequality is in

---

years. These land grants helped the government expand its hold on territories. Likewise, colonizing European governments handed out similar land grants in African countries to their citizens.

[306] Ludlow, *Crusades*, pp. 40-41.
[307] Hallam, *History*, vol. 1. p. 260.

European cultural DNA. Military historian Charles Oman in *A History of the Art of War* writes of the type of feudalism that existed in England by 700 CE:

> We find not merely slaves and Welshmen, but English ceorls [socially classified as the lowest order of peasants] under a hlaford or lord, to whom they owe suit and service. If they try to shirk their duty to him, heavy fines are imposed on them. We are tempted to infer that a large proportion of ceorls were now either the vassals of lords or the tribute-paying tenants on royal demesne land.[308]

Feudalism is, quite simply, a social system of subordination, wherein one person pledges loyalty to a (perceived) more powerful person, and rival tribes stay in constant war with each other. British historian C. Raymond Beazley writes the following about feudalism in France:

> Feudalism may be understood as a social and political organization based upon land-ownership, and upon the personal relations created by that land-ownership. Its theory required (i) that he who held land of another was his immediate subordinate and owed him the service of a vassal to a lord; (ii) that every free man under the King should have a lord; (iii) that any man, not holding land at all, was in a state of dependence or serfage; (iv) that all land was ultimately held of the King, who was the apex of the social and political pyramid.[309]

Europeans supported feudalism and sustained it, though most of them languished in excruciating poverty. Largely, they accepted the impositions of unfair laws that disadvantaged them and their own children for at least a millennium.[310] The civilian revolts to this abhorrent system register as insignificant once compared to the length of time "official" feudalism existed. And while serfs may have gained slight advantages here and there, the system's structure continued uninterrupted.[311] In contrast, far fewer numbers of so-called noble families acquired sizable wealth. Status gained from that wealth gave families access to powerbrokers that granted them excessive privileges. Ultimately, their children inherited those privileges and perpetuated the unfair, degenerate system. Concerning the social

---

[308] Charles Oman, *A History of the Art of War, The Middle Ages From the Fourth Through the Fourteenth Century*, p. 67.
[309] Beazley, *Notebook*, p. 68.
[310] There were revolts against the system. About the year 1000 a well-organized one "was quelled with the severest punishments." Hallam, *History of Europe During the Middle Ages*, p. 265.
[311] The Peasant's Revolt of 1381, in addition to famines and plagues that had wrecked Europe, finally began to lead to some changes in the feudal structure. Though there was another popular uprising in the 19th century to end feudalism. It was put down within a year. See Revolutions of 1848: Springtime of the Peoples.

classifications of feudal Europeans, Hallam writes:

> The classes below the gentry may be divided into freemen and villeins. Of the first were the inhabitants of chartered towns, the citizens and burghers.... As to those who dwelt in the country, we can have no difficulty in recognizing, so far as England is concerned, the socagers, whose tenure was free, though not so noble as knights service, and a numerous body of *tenants for term of life*, who formed that ancient basis of our strength, the English yeomanry. But the mere freemen are not at first sight so distinguishable in other countries.[312] (Italics added).

In this badly disguised system of slavery, feudalism offered different levels of servitude for those who relied on others for their livelihood. According to Lacroix, "During the tenth century, indeed, if not impossible, it was at least difficult to find a single inhabitant of the kingdom of France who was not 'the man' of some one, and who was either tied by rules of a liberal order, or else was under the most servile obligations."[313] Known as *dependents*, these citizens included villeins* [sic] (bound to the land; given more freedom); serfs (bound to land); slaves; vassals (bondsmen, servants); laeti (serfs, half-free); or colons (tenant farmers tied to the land; technically free, could be hunted down for leaving the land). On the subject of runaway colons Constantine says, "'Let him be pursued like the fugitive slave.'"[314]

> The characteristic distinction of a villein was his obligation to remain upon his lord's estate. He was not only precluded from selling the lands upon which he dwelt; but his person was bound, and the lord might reclaim him at any time, by suit in a court of justice, if he ventured to stray. But, equally liable to this confinement, there were two classes of villeins, whose condition was exceedingly different. In England, at least from the reign of Henry II., one only, and that the inferior species, existed; incapable of property, and destitute of redress, except against the most outrageous injuries. The lord could seize whatever they acquired or inherited, or convey them, apart from the land, to a stranger. Their tenure bound them to what were called villein services, ignoble in their nature, and indeterminate in their degree....'[315]

Over the course of the Middle Ages, the titles and/or duties of dependents could change. In any event, the rules tied most people to the land or to the landowner in one way or another; they had few rights and different degrees of freedom. For example, according to their rules, colons

---

[312] Hallam, *History*, vol.1, p. 164.
[313] Lacroix, *Manners*, p. 18.
[314] Duruy, *Rome*, vol. 8, pt. 1, p. 37.
[315] Hallam, *History*, vol.1, p. 167.

were *free* people. Yet, landowners sold colons along with their estates because their lives remained attached to the soil. It was not unheard of for smaller landowners to turn over their land to a larger landowner and succumb to membership in one of the lowest classes of medieval European society:

> The poor Provincial, who could not fly to the Goths because his whole property was in land, hunted to despair by the tax-gatherer, would transfer that land to some wealthy neighbour [sic], apparently on condition of receiving a small life annuity out of it. He was then called dedititius (or surrenderer) of the new owner, towards whom he stood in a position of a certain degree of dependence. Not yet, however, were his sorrows or those of his family at an end, for the tax-gatherer still regarded him as responsible for his hands. From the life-rent for which he had covenanted he might possibly be able to satisfy this demand, but on his death his sons, who had utterly lost their paternal inheritance, and still found themselves confronted with the claim for taxes, were obviously without resource. The next stage of the process accordingly was that they abdicated the position of free citizens and implored the great man to accept them as *coloni*, a class of labourers [sic], half-free, half-enslaved, who may perhaps with sufficient accuracy be compared to the serfs *adscripti glebae* of the middle ages.[316]

Generally, a lord (baron, prince, nobleman, etc.) or the church owned the land, but serfs worked it. According to Thorndike, during the Carolingian era one-third of Gaul belonged to the church, a fact he claims would have amazed Julius Caesar. And during Charlemagne's (d. 814 CE) reign, in exchange for prayers, some nobles turned their land over to the church. For example, the lands of Abbot St. Germain "consisted partly of seigniorial[317] domains possessed by nobles, in their own right, but for various reasons decided to become vassals of the abbey, and paid tribute..."[318] and partly of the abbey's own property that the church divided into fiscs or manors, each administered by a steward. Each fisc consisted of a number of mansi (manors) or farms worked by tenants. Household members residing on these privately-owned lands were not only responsible for tending the estate, they had to share with the lord a percentage of whatever produce they reaped from their harvest. "Even of wheat and oats and barley, and even of his sheep, pigs, hens, and eggs, he had to hand over a part,"[319] Thorndike tells us. Author and educator Eva March Tappan, who wrote *When Knights Were Bold* adds, "They must pay for letting their pigs run in

---

[316] Hodgkin, *Italy*, vol. 1, pp. 927-28.
[317] Land belonging to the Lord, or "old man."
[318] Canon Brownlow, "Roman Slavery and Medieval Serfdom," *The Month, A Catholic Magazine and Review*, vol. 68, no. 307 (1890) 203-04.
[319] Thorndike, *Europe*, p. 234.

the forest, for cutting wood, and often for catching fish, and for the use of their lord's weights and measures."[320] Additionally, serfs had to use the lord's tools and pay for their use as well:

> The tenants were obliged to grind their grain in the lord's mill, bake their bread in his oven, press their grapes in his winepress, and of course pay a good price for the privileges.[321]

Speaking of their medieval tools, the kinds used during this era were, of course, bulky and burdensome: "The scythes were short and straight, and the sickles small and heavy. The great wooden ploughs were so big and cumbersome that even with eight oxen to pull them they cut into the ground only a little way, and a second ploughing was usually necessary."[322]

Exhaustive work was a main feature of serfs who sometimes had their own personal plots of land to tend to as well. For these so-called dependents the workdays were long, tedious and back-breaking: "[In England] The felling of timber, the carrying of manure, the repairing of roads for their lord, who seems to have possessed an equally unbounded right over their labour and its fruits. For the serfs indebted to these estates, the disadvantages were many, but the rewards were few. But by the customs of France and Germany, persons in this abject state seem to have been called serfs, and distinguished from villeins, who were only bound to fixed payments and duties in respect of their lord, though, as it seems, without any legal redress,[323] if injured by him."[324] Serfs were bound by other obligations, too, like tithing "one tenth of their income to the Church besides fees at every birth, baptism, marriage, and death. Even what was left of their produce they were forbidden to sell until the produce of their lord's land had been sold. This land, or the 'demesne' they were obliged to cultivate, each villein doing an amount of work in proportion to the area which he held."[325]

Tappan informs us of the English system whereby the free tenants under that system were not obligated to push the plow. On the other hand:

> Some of the villein tenants, however, had to do so many kinds of work that it is a wonder how they knew when it was finished. One poor man had to work for

---

[320] Tappan, *When Knights Were Bold*, p. 112.
[321] Ibid., pp. 111-12.
[322] Ibid., p. 117.
[323] To decide legal matters a court was held. "It can hardly have been invariably just, for the lord or his agent was the judge, and he generally had a personal interest in the cases. Moreover, the various fines and fees went straight into his own purse, and that must have made it a temptation to inflict as heavy ones as would be borne." Tappan, p. 115.
[324] Hallam, *View*, vol. 1, p. 198.
[325] Tappan, *Knights*, p. 112.

his land three days a week for eleven months of the year, save for a week at Christmas, Easter, and Whitsuntide [vacation week following Pentecost], and find his own food. He must weed, help plough and mow, carry in hay, reap, and haul grain. It was carefully stated just when the lord would provide food for him and how much and what kind. When this man and the other villeins were mowing, they were allowed three bushels of wheat, one ram worth eighteen pence, one jar of butter, and one cheese "next to the best from the dairy of the lord," and salt and oatmeal for their porridge, and all the morning milk. They had also several definite perquisites while they were doing this work; for instance, at the close of each day every man might have as much green grass as he could carry on the point of his scythe [sic]; and when the hay was in, he might have a cartful. At harvest time, each worker might have three handfuls for every load of grain that he brought in. Besides the weekly work during the greater part of the year, there were also "boon-works" in time of ploughing, planting, and harvest. For these, the tenant must leave his own land, often when it needed him most, and give his time to that of his lord. In short, more than one half of the time of the average villein had to be given to the lord of the manor.[326]

As we read in the above passage, abuse of workers was another distinctive trait of the medieval style of living that Europeans carried forward into our current world. While Lacroix observes that over the course of the Middle Ages a few slaves became landowners, that transition occurred over a long and slow progression of time.[327] In the meanwhile, the only possession a slave owned was his life - though his very existence relied on the ungovernable whims (and mercy) of his owner, and thus offered no real sense of security:[328] "Some are so subject to their lord, that he may take all they have, alive or dead, and imprison him whenever he pleases, being accountable to none but God; while others are treated more gently, from whom the lord can take nothing but customary payments, though at their death all they have [is legally returned] to him."[329]

While the serfs worked very hard to eke out a puny existence, the wealthier citizens engaged themselves in what at times appears to be a type of recreational turmoil: "The destructive work of war and the productive toil of agriculture were the chief occupations in the early Middle Ages and the basis of feudal society,"[330] Thorndike informs us. And in a disorderly atmosphere of ever-changing rules - and relations, it is probably safe to say

---

[326] Ibid., pp. 112-15.
[327] Serfs were allowed to pay for their freedom. The Peasants' Revolt of 1381, and the loss of labor following the Black Plague influenced changes.
[328] Lacroix, *Manners*, p. 12.
[329] Hallam, *History*, vol. 1, p. 167.
[330] Thorndike, *Europe*, p. 327.

that vassals were closer in rank to the lord than other medieval servants, though there was certainly a hierarchy among their class. He tells us, too that, "Vassal and lord alike belonged to the noble class and passed their lives in the same round of warlike occupations and amusements."[331] According to Thorndike, during a special ceremony the vassal pledged his loyalty to the lord. Part of the vassal's responsibilities included attending the court of his lord, and perhaps advising him. The vassal's presence at court bestowed upon the lord "social prestige" and political power. It was normally agreed that military service be rendered to the lord, but servile and menial labor were forbidden:

> He might also have some ceremonial function to perform, such as waiting upon his lord at table, lighting his way with a candle as he went to bed, or counting his chessmen on Christmas Day. Such services were not considered humiliating and seldom involved much work. We even hear of a vassal of the King of England whose privilege and duty it was to support the royal head during a rough passage of the [English] Channel.[332]

It seems the barons took the rights of their vassals rather seriously. A vassal whose lord ignored his rights could withdraw his oath and make war against him. In this medieval system of cronyism lords awarded vassals with land divisions, called benefices, or fiefs (fees or pay) in exchange for his services. According to Davis, "In days when law and morality availed little as the sanctions of contracts, the landlord naturally desired to bind his tenant to him by a personal obligation; and there were obvious advantages in providing that every tenant should be liable to aid his lord with arms."[333] Hallam informs us of other duties the vassals supplied: "In some places, the vassal was not bound to go beyond the lord's territory, or only so far as he might return the same day. Other customs compelled him to follow his chief upon all his expeditions! These inconvenient and varying usages betray the origin of the feudal obligations, not founded upon any national policy, but springing from the chaos of anarchy and intestine war, which they were well calculated to perpetuate."[334] After all, the point of instilling massive amounts of fear and confusion was to accumulate wealth and power. It was essential to protect greatly sought after assets. So, it was common for a lord with vassals of his own to himself become a vassal; this lord with smaller holdings gained added protection from a wealthier lord with greater resources for defense. Thorndike writes:

---

[331] Ibid., p. 251.
[332] Ibid., pp. 242-43.
[333] Davis, *Medieval Europe*, pp. 98-99.
[334] Hallam, *History*, vol. 1, p. 142.

The owner of only one or two villas, who was not strong enough to stand alone with his handful of peasants against the storm of invasion or the cupidity of some great neighbor with a large band of vassals, would be forced to become the vassal of the lord who otherwise might take his land from him entirely, or else the vassal of some other lord who would protect him from that lord.[335]

There was any number of combinations of *subinfeudation* established to satisfy a lord's appetite for material wealth. Thorndike tells us that even, "The peaceful bishop or abbot, who had many church estates under his care, granted part of them to some powerful warrior who would defend the rest."[336] Subinfeudation - that may have begun as an earnest attempt to shield territory from invading barbarians - soon turned into a thrill-seeking, cannibalistic hunt for blood and treasures. Thorndike writes that, "This situation, however, can be paralleled in the modern business world, where one may buy stocks in any number of different companies, may be both a stockholder and a bondholder, may be the president of one corporation and a director in another and a mere stockholder in a third."[337] [338]

The Muddle of Medieval Life

By the 11th century, most people lived in the country, according to Ludlow: "Or they were huddled together in rude hamlets under the walls of the castles, whose lords enslaved while they protected them."[339] The barbarian invasions opened many wounds in civil life. One of them was the city itself: "Cities there were, crowded with dense masses of humanity, the breeding-places of all sorts of vice and social disorder."[340] Instead, of folks gathering there for trade, the occasional fair and market served as the business districts, Thorndike tells us. Following the barbarian invasions, people who fled the cities for the countryside did not find their lives better off there:

> Life in a medieval village was rude and rough. The peasants labored from sunrise to sunset, ate coarse fare... and suffered from frequent pestilences. They were often the helpless prey of the feudal nobles. If their lord happened to be a quarrelsome man, given to fighting with his neighbors, they might see their lands ravaged, their cattle driven off, their village burned, and might

---

[335] Thorndike, *Europe*, p. 244.
[336] Ibid.
[337] Ibid., p. 245.
[338] To carry Thorndike's analogy further, the stock market encourages despoilment of lands, and promotes the enslavement and slaughter of millions of people all for the sake of ever-larger profits; the market, in and of itself, produces nothing. Its structure is a fitting illustration of the feudal relationship between the masses and the lords of the land.
[339] Ludlow, *Crusades*, p. 11.
[340] Ibid., p. 12.

themselves be slain.[341]

Thorndike tells us, "The serfs did not live together in slave barracks, but were allowed to build separate huts of their own.... The rude walls were made of crossed or interwoven laths with the interstices stuffed with straw or grass, and with a thatched roof. There was only one floor to the hut, and it was the ground floor, and usually there was but one room inside with a fire in the center."[342] The medieval living arrangement was *untidy* and sparse, indeed. According to Ludlow, country people lived in huts and hovels. Tappan refers to the English versions as, "miserable little one-room sheds of clay."[343] Family members slept on the ground, and shared their living space with their farm animals: "they actually 'kept the pig in the parlor,'"[344] writes Howe. Europeans lined the bottom of their hovels with straw,[345] also called rushes. One historian notes that as the straw wilted and wore away, fresher straw was simply piled atop the worn straw. There was no glass in the windows and a hole poked through the roof helped rid smoke created from indoor hearths. Ludlow reveals in some detail the pitiable lifestyle of the poor put-upon peasants:

> Homes were almost as dreary in their outward appointments as the nests of eagles or the caves of beasts. In the city were narrow apartments of stone or the shanty with its mud-built walls, often as contracted as the cells of the monastery and as damp and fetid as the vaults of the prison; so that the monk lost little of this world's comfort in entering his religious retreat, and the prisoner might think himself happy at times in being better housed than he would have been had he made his home with honest toil. If one lived in the country the habitation was a hut but little better than the shelter provided for cattle. Indeed, in many cases the "ox knew his owner" from having slept on the same straw, and the "ass his master's crib" from its proximity to the family table. The floor of the rude domicile was of earth or stone, the windows unglazed, so that to exclude the winter weather was to shut out the light also. A hole in the roof scarcely sufficed to carry off the smoke from the stoveless [sic] fires.[346]

Dining utensils were rare, too, according to Howe: "The furniture and tools of a peasant consisted of a few pots and pans, two or three dishes and cups, a three-legged stool or so, and an axe. Even as late as the 16th century (long after Europeans complained of Africa's lack of development) a foreigner observed that 'the peasants live in small huts and pile up their

---

[341] Webster, *History*, p. 434
[342] Thorndike, *Europe*, p. 234.
[343] Tappan, *Knights*, p. 110.
[344] Howe, *Essentials In Early European History*, p. 251.
[345] Stitched floor mats replaced straws and rushes.
[346] Ludlow, *Crusades*, pp. 13-14.

refuse out of doors in heaps so high that you cannot see their houses.' It is no wonder that plagues were frequent and 'slew the people like flies.'"[347] The tremendous number of deadly plagues during Europe's early history ushers in questions about medieval hygiene that is discussed more fully in the next section.

Medieval amusements were mundane. People were illiterate, so pleasure reading was not a leisure activity. Serfs rarely strayed from their Lord's territory, nor did they have to since serfs produced most of life's necessities on the estate:

> Food, with the exception of salt and the delicacies brought for the use of the lord, grew on the land. Hemp and wool were raised, spun into yarn, woven, and made into clothes on the spot. Sandals could be made by any one, and rough shoes could be put together by the shoemaker of the manor. There was also a carpenter, who could easily put up the wattled huts of the tenants. If anything more elaborate was to be undertaken, like the building of a church, builders were sent for from away.[348]

Apparently, barbaric repercussions discouraged frivolous pursuits such as merely meandering about the land anyway. After all, this being feudalism meant that if the city was not safe, the country was certainly not safe, either. According historians hospitality was not a feature of medieval life: "The country people were disposed to murder any stranger who fell into their hands. This was especially the case in the more remote parts of the Kingdom of Naples, where the barbarism dated probably from the days of the Roman 'latifundia,'[349] and when the stranger and the enemy ('hospes' and 'hostis') were in all good faith held to be one and the same."[350] Apart from that, chance encounters with laborers from other estates might cause disputes that could turn into dangerous, sometimes prolonged neighborhood wars. Additionally, the countryside might contain camouflaged booby traps. It was not unusual for advancing armies planning to invade an area to dig out pits and fill them with sharpened stakes; so, the open country was no safe place to travel. But, if all that potential danger was not enough to deter wandering, then there was this: Strolling innocently into forested areas could result in trespassing charges. Punishment was harsh, to say the least. And anyway until the 13th century, hunting was a recreation reserved for nobility; and forests were private property. Ludlow fills in the details:

---

[347] Howe, *Essentials*, p. 240.
[348] Tappan, *Knights*, p. 117.
[349] Roman plantation.
[350] Burckhardt, *Renaissance*, pp. 449-50.

Even the peasant's liberty of his own solitude was denied him; he could not range the woods nor float upon the streams at his pleasure. We are told of certain instances where the rustics rebelled against these restrictions imposed upon them. "They took short cuts through the woods, or used the fords and rivers at will;" but they were punished by the knights, who "cut off the hands and feet of the trespassers."[351]

Still, Howe opines about the life of the serf: "It must not be supposed that he was entirely unhappy. Much amusement was gained from the rude merrymakings which occasionally brought the people of the manor together, and it must be remembered that a man cannot miss a happiness of whose existence he has never dreamed."[352]

The Dirt on Europeans: Poor Hygienic Practices Bring on Plagues

Widespread diseases and plagues were a contributing factor to the misery of medieval life and affected the poor and the rich, too, as we will soon discover. As mentioned before, it was normal for animals to cohabit with their human owners. Europeans living in close proximity of their farm animals eased the transmission of deadly diseases. Poor nutrition and diet made the populace an easy target, too. Additionally, Europeans carelessly dumped their body wastes on streets and into rivers and streams. Those same waters were then used for drinking and in food preparation. Because of these and other unhealthy practices, plagues in the west happened often during their history and account for the deaths of millions of Europeans: "In the Middle Ages they raged from time to time throughout Europe: such plagues as the Black Death and the sweating sickness [disease marked by shivers, pain, sweat] swept off vast multitudes...."[353] history professor Andrew Dickson White tells us. The death toll from the infamous Black Death itself is between 100-200 million, on the high side. All told, that means that over the centuries, hundreds of millions of Europeans died because of plagues. White blames Europe's substandard sanitary conditions on the church:

> The main cause of this immense sacrifice of life is now known to have been the want of hygienic precaution, both in the Eastern centres [sic], where various plagues were developed, and in European towns through which they spread. And here certain theological reasonings came in to resist the evolution of a proper sanitary theory. Out of the Orient had been poured into the thinking western Europe the theological idea that the abasement of man adds to the glory of God; that indignity to the body may secure salvation to the soul; hence,

---

[351] Ludlow, *Crusades*, p. 14.
[352] Howe, *Essentials*, p. 242.
[353] Andrew Dickson White, *A History of the Warfare of Science with Theology*, vol.2, p. 67.

that cleanliness betokens pride and filthiness humility. Living in filth was regarded by great numbers of holy men, who set an example to the Church and to a society, as an evidence of sanctity.[354]

It is generally known that Europe's crowned heads boasted of not taking baths. Historians tells us that King Louis XIV (1643-1715) made vain attempts to mask months-old body odors with perfumes; and that the Queens Elizabeth (1558-1603) and Isabella (1474-1504) rarely soaked in a tub they liked. To that list White adds several church authorities, including certain Carmelite monks who suffered greatly from pestilences, he says, from being especially filthy. Others listed include: St. Hilarion (unclean his entire life); St. Anthony who never washed his feet; St. Abraham washed neither his hands, nor feet; St. Sylvia washed only her fingers; and St. Simon Stylites who "lived in ordure and stench intolerable to his visitors." White adds, "For century after century the idea prevailed that filthiness was akin to holiness...."[355] Unfortunately for Europeans their medical community was for a long time in shambles and of little assistance when it came to consulting Europeans on proper hygiene and determining the causes of diseases. Thorndike remarks:

> As for health, medical practice was vastly inferior to that of our time, and was full of magic, and as a result disease was more rife. Society was, however, exceedingly susceptible to the ravages of plagues and pestilences. In estimating both ancient and medieval callousness to cruel customs like torture and gladiatorial combats we must take somewhat into account the fact that men were then more accustomed to physical pain, since they lacked many modern preventives, such as dentistry and anaesthetics [sic].[356]

Medical practitioners were supremely enchanted by the supposed workings of magic, a topic covered more fully later. No matter, the medical community mattered little to a church that had early on declared itself as an infallible authority. Its official capacity was that of intercessor between their god and men, so clergymen took the lead when plagues gripped their populaces. Again regrettably for Christians, the church believed that plagues were mystical workings and approached pestilences by casting blame on two specific agencies. White observes, "In the principle towns of Europe, as well as in the country at large, down to a recent period, the most ordinary sanitary precautions were neglected, and pestilences continued to be attributed to the wrath of God or the malice of Satan,"[357] as is discussed

---

[354] White, *Warfare*, vol. 2, p. 69.
[355] Ibid.
[356] Thorndike, *Europe*, p.38.
[357] White, *Warfare*, vol. 2, p. 70.

later. As a way of addressing these devastating plagues, it was quite common for the church to make a show of penance in the form of public demonstrations. These penitential performances, designed to appease the gods and quell public fear, became popular in the 6th century after Pope Gregory claimed to witness the angel Michael in a vision. Gregory pronounced Michael's visitation as a sign of the plague's demise. Although the epidemic did not necessarily end quickly, for believers its eventual demise confirmed the pope's prediction. Thereafter, religious street parades became a prominent way to attack diseases. However, it is important to add that there were far more unscrupulous motivations for penitential promenades as White explains in the following passage:

> First among these agencies [methods by which the Divine wrath might be averted], naturally, were evidences of devotion, especially gifts of land, money, or privileges to churches, monasteries, and shrines-the seats of fetiches which it was supposed had wrought cures or might work them. The whole evolution of modern history, not only ecclesiastical but civil, has been largely affected by the wealth transferred to the clergy at such periods. It was noted that in the fourteenth century, after the great plague, the Black Death, had passed, an immensely increased proportion of the landed and personal property of every European country was in the hands of the Church.
>
> Other methods of propitiating the higher powers were penitential processions, the parading of images of the Virgin or of saints through plague-stricken towns, and fetiches innumerable. Very noted in the thirteenth and fourteenth centuries were the processions of the flagellants, trooping through various parts of Europe, scourging their naked bodies, shrieking the penitential psalms, and often running from wild excesses of devotion to the maddest orgies.[358]

It was not unusual for grateful survivors of epidemics to turn over all their worldly possessions to church officials who seemed to have a great talent for jumping to the front of the line when it came to moneymaking opportunities. The clergy graciously accepted these gifts as tokens of the layman's religious devotion. But, far more important is that somehow these shady saints of sin, the church clergymen, whom we shall learn more about in upcoming chapters, had managed to make disease a profitable proposition. A popular saying of those times, according to White, was, "pestilences are the harvest of the ministers of God."[359] It can hardly be surprising that despite the "spiritual" interventions of clergy the deadly plagues continued:

> "Down to the sixteenth and seventeenth centuries the filthiness in the ordinary mode of life in England was such as we can hardly conceive; fermenting

---

[358] Ibid., p. 71.
[359] Ibid., p. 71.

organic material was allowed to accumulate and become a part of the earthen floors of rural dwellings; and this undoubtedly developed the germs of many diseases. In his noted letter to the physician of Cardinal Wolsey, Erasmus describes the filth thus incorporated into the floors of English houses, and, what is of far more importance he shows an inkling of the true cause of wasting diseases of the period. He says, 'If I entered into a chamber which had been uninhabited for months, I was immediately seized with a fever.' He described the fearful plague of the sweating sickness to this cause. So, too, the noted Dr. Caius advised sanitary precautions against the plague, and in after-generations, Mead, Pringle, and others urged them; but the prevailing thought was too strong, and little was done. Even the floor of the presence chamber of Queen Elizabeth in Greenwich Palace was 'covered with hay, after the English fashion,' as one of the chroniclers tells us."[360]

The noxious European plagues continued unabated. Some people believe the microscope's discovery helped convince Europeans of the need to look to natural causes, instead of Satan, as reasons for plagues. Whatever the case, White points to several communities that resisted implementing sanitary conditions, including London, Spain, and Scotland. In a dumb kind of luck, large fires that destroyed European cities also destroyed areas that were breeding hotspots for diseases. By the 19th century European cities began to embrace sanitation standards that resulted in a decrease of deaths attributed to pestilences. England's Public Health Act of 1875 saw a marked decrease in mortality:

The recent history of hygiene in all countries shows a long series of victories, and these may well be studied in G. Britain and the United States.... It was only in the year 1838 that a systematic sanitary effort was begun in England by the public authorities.... In many other parts of the British Islands the sanitary condition was no better.[361]

Forty years later, in 1914, British missionary to Africa John H. Weeks published his book, *Among The Primitive BaKongo*, after claiming to spend thirty years collecting local data. His book, written nearly five hundred years following Europe's first invasion of West Africa, notes that bathing was an essential institution for Egun who avoided people who did not bathe daily. The following passage presents an exchange between a *traveling* European and some African villagers. The villagers watch the traveler "strip off his jacket, turn down the collar round his neck, and roll up his shirt-sleeve" in preparation for his bath:[362]

---

[360] Ibid., p. 82.
[361] Ibid., pp. 90-91.
[362] John H. Weeks, *Among the Primitive BaKongo*, pp. 29-30.

The ablutions[363] are finished and the white man is now drying himself, and while two or three spectators are passing remarks on the using of so good a cloth (towel) for such a purpose, a woman on the outskirts of the crowd asks, "Is that all he is going to wash? Why, we wash all over." And there is disdain mingled with disappointment as she puts the question, and a suggestion that the white man is not so clean as he might be. The white man's boy does not like the query in the tone, and as his honor is bound up with his master's, he informs the crowd generally that his master *baths regularly in his own town.* (Italics added).

Meanwhile, in the United States Anglo-Americans became aware of the necessity of good hygienic practices and the health benefits that arise from using them, too. Here, the Sanitary Commission, formed in 1861, took the lead. They trained government officials and layperson's to use proper sanitary techniques during the Civil War. Merck's Archive from 1901 records the shift in attitudes toward proper sanitary habits: "Preventive medicine or hygiene is beginning to be recognized as of prime importance, and the future physician will be valued as much for his advice to the healthy as for his treatment of disease."[364] Indeed, hygiene was an important issue to turn of the 20th century United States. Medical professionals, along with the government, issued dozens of books and pamphlets on proper sanitation. And in Upton Sinclair's 1921 publication of the wisdom-filled, *Book of Life: Mind and Body,* he counsels Europeans and Americans on proper bathing techniques:

> We need to bathe with soap to remove the grease, and we need to rub with a towel to brush away the dead cells of the skin, so that the pores may be kept open. No one is taking care of his body who does not wash and rub it once every twenty-four hours, and once or twice a week with warm water and soap. It is often stated that hot baths are weakening, but I have never found it so; however, I think it is a bad practice to pamper the body, which should be accustomed to the shock of cold water. The rule as to bathing, both as to temperature and time, is simple. If, after the bath and rub-down, your body has reacted and you feel vigorous and fresh, that bath has done you good. If, on the other hand, you feel chilled and depressed, then you have been too long in the water, or its temperature was too low. Every person has to find his own rules in such matters. The only general rule is that as one grows older the body reacts less quickly.[365]

White notes that the attitude of Americans toward hygiene changed once North American pastors stopped making a false connection between

---

[363] Ritual bathing.
[364] Schneider, "Ancient Therapeutics," p. 258.
[365] Upton Sinclair, *The Book of Life,* pp. 161-62.

sin and disease: "This development of sanitary science and hygiene in the United States has also been coincident with a marked change in the attitude of the American pulpit as regards the theory of disease. In this country, as in others, down to a period with living memory, deaths due to want of sanitary precautions were instantly dwelt upon in funeral sermons as 'results of national sin,' or as 'inscrutable Providences.'"[366] But, while some turn of the century pastors taught parishioners not to blame Satan[367] for man's sins, that has not stopped certain 21st century pastors from reaching back into the medieval time machine to pull out some of the church's other dirty old tricks.

The Lifestyle of the Baron was Barely Better

The medieval rich folks were better off materially, but according to one historian, not by much. They lived in poorly appointed stone houses and castles, that one historian calls medieval templates for modern warships. Historians write a lot about the feudal manses of the wealthy. Cold, damp and dark are three distinct features of this type of housing. Comfort was far less of a concern than protection. And though built among the rolling hills of the green countryside, the great views could only be appreciated by standing outdoors:

> Unless the castle was large enough to comprise inner courts, upon which windows might safely open and where decorative stone carving and sculpture could be indulged in without fear of its being damaged by stones hurled from catapults — unless this was the case, the rooms of the interior were of necessity dark and cold, since they were enclosed by walls several feet thick with only a rare aperture. Often an entire floor of the castle or of the donjon [dungeon; the lord's residence] would be used as the great hall, where the lord and his followers ate their meals, drank their ale or wine, held court, talked together, or warmed themselves before the fire in the huge open chimney-place. When we read of horrible, damp, underground dungeons where prisoners languished, we must remember that even the lord and lady in their apartments of state were none too comfortable. The fireplace, however, represented a great improvement in domestic life, for chimney flues were a medieval invention. If the Greeks and Romans wished to avoid filling the house with smoke, they had to cook outdoors, although the Romans had hypocausts to warm their floors from underneath. Although the castle was poorly lighted and heated and dreary enough within, from its lofty battlements a wonderful view often could be

---

[366] White, *Warfare*, vol. 2, p. 94.
[367] Exorcisms are back in style inside the Roman Catholic Church. Critics claim these unscientific procedures increase the church's political power.

obtained of the countryside for miles around."³⁶⁸

Ludlow adds: "If the rich were better conditioned, their residences were unfurnished with that which the middle classes in our day regard as necessary to comfort and decency. The bounty of the table was without variety. Apparel, however gay, was such as could be wrought by the women of the household. The tapestries which excite our admiration were the product of untold toil or purchased at vast expense. Within the castle was spacious monotony, relieved too generally by the grossness of private debauch; without was the wilderness, threaded by roads that were unfit for wheeled vehicles, menaced by wild beasts and more dangerous men.³⁶⁹ And, according to Howe, there was no heating, lighting, or plumbing. And because glass was expensive to make, windows were but narrow slots: "tiny panes of glass set in lead...."³⁷⁰ *Manners, Customs and Dress During the Middle Ages* reports that French kings lived rather bleak lives, too. Between the years 1202-1203: "the children of the King [Philip Augustus] slept in sheets of serge" (a heavy-duty twilled woolen or worsted fabric); and "kings and princes changed their apparel three times" during a given year. On the other hand, Philip Augustus was among the kings who spared no expense for war.

Hallam cites the work of Italian historian Ludovico Antonio Muratori (d. 1750) on the years of Frederic II (1194-1250): "'In those times the manners of the Italians were rude. A man and his wife ate off the same plate. There was no wooden-handled knives, nor more than one or two drinking cups in a house. Candles of wax or tallow were unknown; a servant held a torch during supper. The clothes of men were of leather unlined: scarcely any gold or silver was seen on their dress. The common people ate flesh but three times a week, and kept their cold meat for supper. Many did not drink wine in summer. A small stock of corn seemed riches. The portions of women were small; their dress, even after marriage, was simple. The pride of men was to be well provided with arms and horses; that of the nobility to have lofty towers, of which all the cities in Italy were full.'"³⁷¹

Despite their modest lifestyle — by today's western standards — an individual's wealth and power made him *independent*, and therefore free. Of course, the rich maintained their own hierarchy, too. In the days when money was scarce, land became the standard for determining the means of production, and, therefore, defined wealth. The "only class in society who remained at all prosperous were the wealthy aristocrats, the great landowners, who had enough influence with the government to secure

---

³⁶⁸ Thorndike, *Europe*, p. 248.
³⁶⁹ Ludlow, *Crusades*, p. 14.
³⁷⁰ Howe, *Essentials*, p. 250.
³⁷¹ Hallam, *View*, vol. 2, p. 531.

themselves from oppression or even to oppress others with impunity, whose large estates only a large band of invaders could venture to attack, and whose retinue of servile tenants and dependents was now being constantly reinforced by poor citizens, who in these hard, disturbed, and cruel times found it impossible to maintain their independence either in town or country. In this landed aristocracy the barbarian invaders formed an increasing element, since they everywhere demanded and took lands for themselves."[372]

Not surprisingly the less wealthy were often taken advantage of by far wealthier landowners: "Albere, or right of shelter, was the principal charge imposed upon the noble. When a great baron visited his lands, his tenants were not obliged only to give him and his followers shelter, but also provisions and food, the nature and quality of which were all arranged beforehand with the most extraordinary minuteness. The lesser nobles took advantage sometimes of the power they possessed to repurchase this obligation; but the rich, on the contrary, were most anxious to seize the occasion of proudly displaying before their sovereign all the pomp in their power, at the risk even of mortgaging their revenues for several years, and of ruining their vassals. History is full of stories bearing witness to the extravagant prodigalities of certain nobles on such occasions,"[373] writes Lacroix.

Entertaining with grand feasts was the traditional way to please guests. Nothing else in the European world compared to the opulence of the medieval banquet! Handmade goblets of gold or silver and inlaid with precious stones seem to have been table centerpieces. Dinner plates - on the other hand, were of secondary concern: "People ate from trenchers [mortarboards], or rude plates. At first, thick slices of stale bread were used; then trenchers were made of wood and were kept measurably clean by being scoured with ashes."[374] During these formal affairs, it was customary to serve several courses: "What would a modern caterer say to a bill of fare that began boldly with venison, a quarter of bear, and the shoulder of a wild boar, and worked its way valiantly onward through a course of roasted peacocks and swans, a second of poultry, and a third of waterfowl and small game to venison and pheasant pasties and pigeon pie?[375] Feasters eagerly gorged on their meal; apparently, gluttony at the banquet table was a medieval tradition, too. Following the main course were "trifles as shad, salmon, mullet, and eel pie, the last a special favorite."[376] Lords served wine flavored with honey or spice, too.

---

[372] Thorndike, *Europe*, p. 92.
[373] Lacroix, *Manners*, p. 39.
[374] Tappan, *Knights*, p. 90.
[375] Ibid., pp. 86-88.
[376] Ibid., p. 88.

But - despite the opulent feasts - conditions within medieval manors beyond the banquet table were less than sanitary: "The table linen was clean and plentiful; but the floor was covered with rushes, with bones and other refuse, and perhaps had not been swept for twenty years.[377] A feast in a nobleman's castle was a grotesque medley of splendor and filth."[378] As we have learned, poor hygiene was yet another dismal theme of medieval life. Poor and wealthy alike were quite unconcerned with properly disposing their waste products. The conditions at the manor seem quite awful as Tappan tells us that the lords of multiple estates — along with their families, routinely rotated between them. And not so much because he needed to keep a watchful eye on his prized possessions:

> He and his family and servants went from one manor to another, partly to use up what they could of produce on the spot, and partly, it is whispered, because so little attention was paid to cleanliness that it was the part of comfort as well as wisdom to allow a house to "sweeten" after it had been occupied for some weeks.[379]

Aside from being always ready for Albere duties, lords were their own masters; their land was theirs to do with as they pleased. They levied tolls on roads and bridges that ran through their land, and on merchants passing thorough them with merchandise. Wealthy travelers were often robbed (highway robbery), or kidnapped and held for ransom when passing through the lands of the lords. Sometimes lords sold travelers into slavery. Ludlow tells us, "Every petty lord exacted toll of those who passed the border of his estate. Many of the occupants of the castles lived by open robbery, and kept men-at-arms, as they kept their falcons, to pounce upon their prey. Not only the goods, the persons also of travellers [sic] were regarded as legitimate booty, the victims being held for ransom and often sold as slaves. So enterprising were these robber knights that it is said to have been dangerous for the king to go from Paris to St. -Denis without an army at his back. The armed merchantman rode generally with lance in rest. In towns, says Thierry [of Chartres, d. 1150], 'nobles, sword in hand, committed robbery on the burghers, and in turn the burghers committed violence upon the peasants who came to buy or sell at the market of the town.'"[380]

Another way the wealthy classes filled their treasure chests was through taxation. No matter the capitalist society, ever-increasing taxes are likely a cause of social distress: "The people of the Middle Ages and the

---

[377] Lacroix writes of a French king whose household disposed of the odiferous floor straw daily.
[378] Tappan, *Knights*, p. 92.
[379] Ibid., p. 116.
[380] Ludlow, *Crusades*, p. 12.

Renaissance period were literally tied down with taxes and dues of all sorts," says [author, and journalist] M. Mary-Lafon, "If a few gleams of liberty reached them, it was only from a distance, and more in the hope of the future than as regarded the present."[381] Lord's collected taxes from vassals who "owed him occasional feudal aids and reliefs; he could also fill his treasury by exercise of the rights of wardship and marriage; thus feudalism had its equivalents for state taxation and revenue."[382]

Churches collected taxes from their clergy. And in the cities and towns merchants formed restrictive trade gilds with medieval chambers of commerce that heavily taxed items imported into their towns. Heavy taxes even became a cause of medieval social unrest. One medieval tale of taxes comes to us from Flanders, an important trading center whose international commerce brought them national prestige and beautiful houses made of stones:

> Flanders with its large towns and flourishing industries and trade, was of great economic value and was naturally coveted by the French king. But the Flemish towns had close economic relations with England, whence they obtained much of the raw wool for their weaving industries, and whose import trade too they largely controlled. Flanders, however, was divided within itself. Besides its count there were rival parties in the communes themselves. As elsewhere in northern France, toward the close of the thirteenth century there were uprisings of the artisans against the few rich burghers who had secured control of the machinery of municipal government and distributed all the offices and favors among themselves, while they not only taxed the masses heavily, but kept wages down to starvation rates. This caused risings against the ruling class in 1280 and 1281 in Bruges, Ghent, Tournai, Ypres, and Douai in Flanders, as well as in some towns of northern France.[383]

Flanders was as an example of the type of wealth that was possible for other Europeans. Up to the 10th century "very little oriental commerce could have existed in these western countries of Europe. Destitute as they have been created, speaking comparatively, of natural productions fit for exportation, their invention and industry are the great resources from which they can supply the demands of the East. Before any manufactures were established in Europe, her commercial intercourse with Egypt and Asia must of necessity have been very trifling; because, whatever inclination she might feel to enjoy the luxuries of those genial regions, she wanted the means of obtaining them."[384]

Concerning the 11th and 12th centuries Ludlow informs us that "there

---

[381] Lacroix, *Manners*, p. 42.
[382] Thorndike, *Europe*, p. 257.
[383] Ibid., p. 498.
[384] Hallam, *View*, vol. 2, p. 506.

was no importation of things for common use; the labor and danger of transportation limited the articles of trade to those of rarest value, which became the spoil of the powerful or the purchase of the rich."[385] In Italy, the foreign luxury items obtained by the (Marco) Polos from their travels to an exotic China helped to excite the masses and shopkeepers to the possibilities that commerce and trade with the East could advance "and it may be asserted that the *luxury* which was displayed in the dwellings of the nobility *was the evidence*, if not the result, *of a great social revolution in the manners* and customs of private life."[386] (Italics added).

By the 13th century, Europeans were beginning to crave the fineries of life; importers eased luxury items into the lives of a lucky few feudal society people. In 1294 and again in 1306 a king issued orders that controlled and limited the classes of people purchasing certain luxury products. Gold and precious stones were items the rich only could have. The king reserved chariots for the very wealthy, too.[387] By 1307 the kings and queens of Europe had acquired a taste for "gold, diamonds, pearls and precious stones."[388] The all too visible sparseness that had defined castle living was changing. Elaborate tapestries began to cover cold and clammy bare stonewalls and ornate furniture filled large cavernous rooms. Additionally, carpets and worked linen were growing in demand; by the 14th and 15th centuries luxury items such as silk, satin and gold embroiders decorated castles. Still, writes Tappan, the English attempted to limit certain classes from wearing fashionable clothing: "Parliament decreed that no one but the king, queen, and their children should be allowed to wear imported cloth, and that no one should wear foreign furs or silks unless he had a yearly rent of £100... a man had to be very well to do before the law would permit him and his family to dress as they chose."[389]

Muratori, mentioned earlier, references the 13th century chronicles of Rico Baldus de Ferrare who observed the following changes taking place: "'But now frugality has been changed for sumptuousness; everything exquisite is sought after in dress; gold, silver, pearls, silks, and rich furs. Foreign wine and rich meats are required. Hence usury, rapine, fraud, tyranny, etc.' This passage is supported by other testimonies nearly of the same time. The conquest of Naples by Charles of Anjou in 1266 seems to have been the epoch of increasing luxury throughout Italy. His Provencal knights with their plumed helmets and golden collars, the chariot of his queen covered with blue velvet and sprinkled with lilies of gold, astonished the citizens of Naples. Provence had enjoyed a long tranquillity,

---

[385] Ludlow, *Crusades*, p. 13.
[386] Lacroix, *Manners*, p. 76.
[387] Ibid., p. 85.
[388] Ibid., p. 72.
[389] Tappan, *Knights*, p. 79.

the natural source of luxurious magnificence; and Italy, now liberated from the yoke of the empire, soon reaped the same fruit of a condition more easy and peaceful than had been her lot for several ages. Dante [d. 1321] speaks of the change of manners at Florence from simplicity and virtue to refinement and dissoluteness, in terms very nearly similar to those quoted above."[390]

Mistakenly believing that material wealth equated with accomplishments, modernity, and high civilization, the medieval European's materialistic inclinations reached out toward Africa as their appetite for sumptuousness expanded; Prince Henry Infante, known as The Navigator, commissioned voyages for the first time to explore the world beyond latitude 29: In Henry "the spirit of medieval faith and the spirit of material, even of commercial, ambition, were united... he was the central representative of a general expansive and exploring movement; and... he took up and carried on the labors of various predecessors,"[391] writes Portuguese chronicler Gomes Eannes de Azurara. But, more on Dom Henry's exploits in Chapter 9.

In the 15th century, Europeans began trading expeditions with West African nations south of the Sahara. The free labor of Africans forcefully removed from their homes to Portugal was making the Portuguese very wealthy men. And typical of the type of arrogance that was symbolic of medieval Europe, the Portuguese laid legal claim for African territories that did not belong to them. As early traders with Great Benin, the Portuguese[392] boasts of exchanging cheap European goods for palm oil, elephant's teeth (tusks) and the much desired "peppers with a taile."[393] This new enterprise of the Portuguese was raising eyebrows and interest in other European countries. So, they kept secret many of their trading locations. In 1551, despite Portugal's protests and using the force of a papal bull, English navigator Thomas Wyndham sailed to Morocco. There he gathered sugar, molasses, dates, and almonds — all luxury items in scarce supply in England.[394] That country had been in the midst of a depression, according to James A. Williamson, author of *The Foundation and Growth of the British Empire*, who writes that, "oceanic enterprise was stimulated by

---

[390] Hallam, *View*, vol. 2, pp. 531-32.
[391] Beazley and Prestage, *Guinea*, vol. 2, pp. vi, vii.
[392] The Portuguese were not benevolent travelers to West Africa. On their first trips to the coastal islands they kidnapped Africans, returning to Portugal with them. By 1446 an estimated 927 Africans had been forcefully taken from Africa to Portugal. They became interpreters, guides and slaves and were used as assets to reveal intelligence on other Africans and their resources.
[393] These peppers produced in Benin are described as being hot and having a sharper taste than black pepper. They were very popular with early European traders.
[394] Williamson, *The Foundation and Growth of the British Empire*, p. 31.

misfortunes in Europe." The stimulus came when "enterprising Englishmen" realized "that there was no need for [them] to confine their activities to the waters of Europe. In two different directions, therefore, we find a beginning of better things."[395]

A couple of years later, Wyndham and some British merchants sailed farther south to Benin where they acquired 150 pounds of gold dust "in exchange for beads and metal basins and other goods of very slight value,"[396] and the spicy pepper. In 1588, "Queen Elizabeth granted a charter to an all African Company of English merchants who thereupon started trading all over the West Coast of Africa, much to the annoyance of the Dutch and the Portuguese."[397] Needless to say, the wealth the British received from Africa was enormous.[398] And according to Felix Dubois, the "English coin, the guinea, [is] so called because the first pieces were struck from gold coming from there."[399]

Lacroix reminds us that despite the luxuries that were making social life more pleasant for the nobility, the lower classes continued to suffer: "Many centuries elapsed before the dawn of liberty could penetrate the social strata of this multitude... development was slow, painful, and dearly bought...."[400]

Let the Gaming Begin

Neither the castle's cold, clammy environment, nor its paltry furnishings lessened the urge for nobles to engage in exciting hunting expeditions. Hawking and falconry were favorite pastimes for the idle (not at war) wealthy. This outdoors sport that trains large birds of prey to pursue and catch game dates back to the 4th century. By the 12th century sporting a hawk upon one's wrist became fashionable and suggested nobility. Hawking and falconry became so important that king's passed laws to prevent their theft. Probably because noblemen spent a lot of time and money training birds to land on the hawking glove, their birds became pampered pets. At least one medieval doctor wrote a book on treating them properly. In it he advises owners to stay fond of their birds and to show them patience. Also, he suggests a healthy meal for hawks that I include in Chapter 12. Other meals fed to these birds clarify the social hierarchy of this strange medieval world of Europe: historians write that bird owners gave their predator birds meats and foods unavailable to destitute serfs

---

[395] Ibid.
[396] Ibid., p. 32.
[397] Alan Boisragon, *The Benin Massacre*, pp. 1-2.
[398] In the 1560's Queen Elizabeth granted permission for the first English slave ship "Jesus" to transport kidnapped West Africans to the Americas.
[399] Felix Dubois, *Timbuctoo The Mysterious*, p. 172.
[400] Lacroix, *Manners*, p. 83.

living on the same estate.

Regarding other medieval recreations Webster adds, "Outside castle walls a common sport was hunting in the forests and game preserves attached to every estate. Deer, bears, and wild boars were hunted with hounds...."[401] Ludlow explains that these activities replaced intellectual pursuits that left a lasting mark: "Such a limitation of the more generous and worthy interests of mankind, which stimulate and enlarge the mind, left the common intelligence in an almost infantile condition. Sismondi says that even the nobles came to count it a duty not to think. One can readily believe this on recalling the titles given at court to the various royal personages who graced it: Pepin the Short, Charles the Bald, William the Red, Louis the Fat, etc."[402] According to Ludlow, the low intellect of European men along with their belief in superstitions was responsible for their lack of morality: "Such a condition of the mental faculties could have only a deleterious influence on the moral sense. We are not, therefore, surprised to find the conscience of the age correspondingly crude:"[403] Webster adds the following about the crude consciences of the lords and barons, "The nobles... found in fighting their chief outdoor occupation and pastime. 'To play a great game' was their description of a battle."[404]

Despite the incredibly high human toll involved, war making was just another medieval pastime and the citizens became the fuel that fed the medieval war beast.

---

[401] Webster, *History*, p. 428.
[402] Ludlow, *Crusades*, p. 15.
[403] Ibid., p. 16.
[404] Webster, *History*, p. 428.

5

MEDIEVAL SOCIAL UPHEAVAL

What Happens When Princes Insist on Making Games of Chaos?

As we read earlier, for a time Charlemagne managed to unite wide swaths of western Europe under a central government: "For the first time since the fall of the West-Roman Empire the same organisation [sic] was imposed on all the peoples from the Ebro [Iberian Peninsula] to the Danube."[405] His armies remained on the offensive to squelch all disturbances. And though Charlemagne is a highly esteemed historical figure — Germany and France developed from his conquests — he was no less barbaric than the other warlords of his time: "Unsparing of blood... he beheaded in one day [782 CE] four thousand Saxons—an act of atrocious butchery, after which his persecuting edicts, pronouncing the pain of death against those who refused baptism, or even who ate flesh during Lent, seem scarcely worthy of notice,"[406] writes Hallam. Within 50 years of Charlemagne's death civil wars tore at his empire, before finally dismembering it. No longer was there a central authority to quell the chaos as the once great empire came to its end. As territories split along racial lines barons and great landholders in their own territories became a law unto themselves. With their immunity they began "waging war at their pleasure, administering justice to their military tenants and other subjects... free from all control beyond the conditions of the feudal compact."[407] The social chaos held in unsteady abeyance by Charlemagne soon gave way to another bloody free-for-all:

> "But far worse must have been their state under the lax government of succeeding times, when the dukes and counts, no longer checked by the vigorous administration of Charlemagne, were at liberty to play the tyrants in their several territories, of which they now became almost the sovereigns. The poorer landholders accordingly were forced to bow their necks to the yoke; and either by compulsion, or through hope of being better protected, submitted their independent patrimonies to the feudal tenure.... Each frontier of the

---

[405] Oman, *War*, p. 75.
[406] Hallam, *History*, vol. 1, p. 13.
[407] Ibid., p. 23.

empire had to dread the attack of an enemy."[408]

Medieval Europe was divided into a patchwork of fiefdoms. Noblemen craving bigger lands, ever-changing loyalties, and men jockeying for loftier positions, plus rules that allowed only the eldest son to inherit his father's fortunes strongly contributed to the medieval upheaval. Younger sons who had no inheritance rights waged war to gain property of their own, sometimes even challenging their own fathers and older brothers, according to Thorndike. Roger Bacon railed against private warfare during the 13th century by writing:

> Princes and barons and knights oppress and rob each other, and trouble their subjects with infinite wars and exactions, wherein each striveth to despoil the other even of duchies and kingdoms, as we see in these days. For it is notorious that the King of France hath most unjustly despoiled the King of England of that great territory; and Charles [of Anjou] hath even now crushed the heirs of Frederick [II.] in mighty battles. Men care not what is done nor how, whether by right or wrong, if only each may have his own will; meanwhile they are slaves to gluttony and lechery and the wickedness of other sins. The people, harassed by their princes, hate them and keep no fealty save under compulsion; more over, corrupted by the evil examples of their betters, they oppress and circumvent and defraud one another, as we see everywhere with our own eyes; and they are utterly given over to lechery and gluttony, and are more debased than tongue can tell.[409]

It was the turbulence created from war that brought them acquisitions in what Thorndike calls the "natural state of the feudal world." No different from war profiteers of our day, medieval warlords hungered to fill their personal treasury from war booty: "and every man who owned a castle to shelter him in case of defeat, and a sufficient number of dependents to take the field, was at liberty to retaliate upon his neighbors whenever he thought himself injured. It must be kept in mind, that there was, frequently, either no jurisdiction to which he could appeal, or no power to enforce its awards...."[410] Webster suggests that: "Fighting became almost a form of business enterprise, which enriched the prevalence lords and their retainers through the sack of castles, of private the plunder of villages, and the ransom of prisoners. Every hill became a stronghold and every plain a battlefield."[411] It is little surprise then that Europeans had many wars.[412]

---

[408] Ibid., p.18.
[409] Coulton, *Garner*, p. 340.
[410] Hallam, *History*, vol. 1, p. 174.
[411] Webster, *History*, p. 423.
[412] According to online sources, from 400 CE until the early decades of the 20th century, Europeans conducted well over 300 wars on their land alone; this amounts to roughly 5

Certain princes argued for the right to war with whom they wanted, whenever they pleased. After all, these wars expanded territories and amassed treasures of silver, gold, and plenty of fine linen. Oftentimes private wars lasted for years. Fighters were not only killed, but they slaughtered large populations of people. Raging battles despoiled natural resources, too, as armies fueled by the swinging scythes of feudal tenants and sub-tenants sieged manors (castles), leaving vast tracts of land littered with body parts, and drenched with blood. The following passage from Jordanes centers on an earlier clash, but illustrates the type of damage that intense conflicts inflicted on people and land:

> A battle was fought and the party of the Goths was found to be so much the stronger that the plain was drenched in the blood of their fallen foes and looked like a crimson sea. Weapons and corpses, piled up like hills, covered the plain for more than ten miles. When the Goths saw this, they rejoiced with joy unspeakable, because by this great slaughter of their foes they had avenged the blood of Valamir their king and the injury done themselves.[413]

Interestingly, wars may have been the one time servants gained any amount of respect from the lords of the land: "While private wars were at their height, the connexion [sic] of lord and vassal grew close and cordial, in proportion to the keenness of their enmity towards others. It was not the object of a baron to disgust and impoverish his vavassors [vassals] by enhancing the profits of seigniory; for there was no rent of such price as blood, nor any labour so serviceable as that of the sword."[414]

While smaller manses were drawn often into wars, larger territories were subject to invasions by menacing warlord princes. As brutal as any war will certainly be, the "in your face with a battle-axe" style of medieval clashes were not for the skittish. Protection was of greatest importance. Of course, landowners with tremendous holdings acquired better security. Devising reinforcements for castles with interior hideaways that would not be penetrated by enemies became an essential element to surviving prolonged sieges. Castles, those bulky, gray-stoned fortified edifices situated among the green rolling hills of Europe packaged to today's honeymooners and tourists as idyllic escapes are actually medieval battle stations. It was not that long ago that splattered blood and decaying bones of European men fertilized surrounding landscapes. Today's charming descriptions of these rocky quarters notwithstanding, once upon a time, massive man-built slab walls punctuated by ominous-looking turrets (corner towers) and battlements (walls) surrounded castles, blighting out

---

wars/uprisings per year.
[413] Mierow, *Jordanes*, pp. 131-32.
[414] Hallam, *History*, vol. 1, p. 222.

bucolic settings. The presence of such mammoth structures provides evidence that former residents were properly concerned with maintaining adequate protection. Thorndike provides details of some features common to castles:

> One is the prominence of towers, square, round, or pentagonal, with pyramidical, conical, or flat roofs. Some of these towers line the outer circuit of walls.... Oldest and chief of the towers are the donjon, or residence of the lord, and the keep, or central and most strongly fortified part of the castle where the garrison makes its last stand. Normally the defenders of the castle fight from the tops of its walls and towers, where they will be farthest away from the range of the missiles of the enemy below, and whence their own missiles will carry farthest and fall with most force. For this purpose a walk is built behind a parapet [protective wall] all along the top of the wall. The battlements of the parapet are usually crenelated; that is, openings through which the defenders may shoot alternate with sections of solid wall behind which they may stand protected from the enemy's arrows. Sometimes, especially around the tops of towers, are found machicolations [openings]. In this case the battlement is built out beyond the walls of the tower below upon projections called corbels, and the floor of the encircling walk behind the parapet is pierced with numerous openings or trapdoors through which such things as boiling pitch and molten lead may be poured directly upon those trying to enter the tower below or to scale its walls. The walls of the castle are also pierced with many narrow slits through which arrows may be shot at the foe. These walls are very thick, especially at the base in order to withstand battering-rams and support the weight above. Indeed, the castle was something like a modern battleship[415] with its heavy armor plate, its portholes and gun shields, and its turrets.[416]

Private wars that marshaled enormous private[417] armies are why lords built castles, dug moats and then filled them with water. Just glancing at the type of weapons used in besieging castles gives a small hint of the fear that most likely filled the hearts of dwellers whose estates fell under attack:

> The development of more powerful hurling engines for both stones and arrows became a necessity. These were of two kinds: the [catapult], used to shoot large arrows or bolts with great force, and the Petraria, which hurled large stones. The motive power was provided by the torsion of twisted ropes or the sudden release of a heavy counter-poise, and great ingenuity was exercised to increase their force.... They were chiefly effective in clearing the walls of defenders, which facilitated other siege operations. Battering rams of various kinds were

---

[415] A guided tour through the Smithsonian confirms for visitors that battleships are simply floating castles.
[416] Thorndike, *Europe*, pp. 247-48.
[417] Mercenaries have been utilized by the United States more often since the Iraq invasion.

also used, and, as a protection for the manipulators, [shields] made of wattled stakes were constructed.... The most effective devices in overcoming strongly fortified towns were the great movable towers and the blockade.... Scaling ladders of wood were of subsidiary value....[418]

Particularly striking was the way princes conducted warfare. In battles that lasted for months and years, it was not unusual for advancing armies to camp just outside perimeter walls carrying out sustained attacks, hurling stones and using other means to weaken the structure. The end goal, or success was not measured by taking possession of the fortress. A victorious battle was one that left no witnesses to speak on events that had transpired. Ludlow opines, "Victory was measured by the heaps of the slain, not by the progress of the cause. No quarter was ordinarily given or expected on the capture of strongholds; and not infrequently the entire surviving population of conquered cities paid with their lives the penalty for having permitted themselves to be defended by the vanquished."[419]

Thorndike presents a slightly different picture of the type and amount of violence employed during these conflicts, "We must remember for one thing that *war had been incessant before feudalism and that it has not ceased yet.* Then feudal warfare was in the main conducted on a small scale; it was local or neighborhood war and the numbers of men engaged were never very large nor the number killed very great. Their armor protected the knights fairly well, and they were more often captured, imprisoned, and ransomed than they were slain. One reads of bitter strife between lord and vassal or father and son drawn out over many years, and finds both contestants as hale and hearty at the end as they had been at the beginning."[420] (Italics added). However, that was not necessarily the case for many of the fighters who picked up arms in their defense.

In any event, feudal armies had to adopt new techniques for obtaining fighters given that tenants were not necessarily the best fighters; they were likely more skilled at swinging a scythe than a sword; plus an adversary's use of more advanced equipment required better defenses. By the 13th century: "Mercenary troops were substituted for the feudal militia.... It now became manifest that the probabilities of war inclined to the party, who could take the field with selected and experienced soldiers. The command of money was the command of armed hirelings, more sure and steady in battle, as we must confess with shame, than the patriot citizen."[421] Princes filled armies with men, granted them knighthood and then allowed

---

[418] August C. Krey, *The First Crusade: The Accounts of Eyewitnesses and Participants*, p. 21.
[419] Ludlow, *Crusades*, p. 22.
[420] Thorndike, *Europe*, p. 250.
[421] Hallam, *History*, vol. 1, p. 225.

112 MEDIEVAL UPHEAVAL

them to plunder[422] cities. This was a significant arrangement because it allowed armies to obtain booty, and the payment that soldiers expected in return for services, though it was not unusual for knights to gain land or salaries for their service, either. In any event: "by the end of the thirteenth century we find the condottiere[423] system coming into existence—noted mercenary chiefs[424] have collected huge bodies of men numbered by the thousand, and hawk their services about from court to court."[425] In a nod to feudalism, mercenary armies have been reintroduced in the United States. They presently hawk their services from court to court.

"Shock and Awe" in Medieval Warfare

By the 14th century, Europeans advanced their military arsenal: "In the first part of the fourteenth century cannon, or rather mortars, were invented, and the applicability of gunpowder to purposes of war was understood. Edward III employed some pieces of artillery with considerable effect at Crécy [a *Hundred Years War* battle]. But its use was still not very frequent; a circumstance which will surprise us less when we consider the unscientific construction of artillery; the slowness with which it could be loaded; its stone balls, of uncertain aim and imperfect force, being commonly fired at a considerable elevation; and especially the difficulty of removing it from place to place during an action...." Still, the English use of this artillery was particularly effective. French writer Jean Froissart (d. 1405), a reliable source to events at the Battle of Crécy, mentions that the English remained motionless while cannons pummeled the stunned and frightened Genoese.[426] A later account describes the awesome effect the cannons had on the Genoese. According to Hallam, "It was as though god thundered with a great killing of people and... of horses."[427]

This new weapon of mass destruction that lay at the fingertips of European warlords saw improvements fairly quickly: "The French made the principal improvements. They cast their cannon smaller, placed them on lighter carriages, and used balls of iron. They invented portable arms for a single soldier, which, though clumsy in comparison with their present state, gave an augury of a prodigious revolution in the military art."[428]

---

[422] Il Sacco di Roma (The Sack of Rome) occurred in 1526 when troops sought payment for services rendered to Charles V. Soldiers killed thousands of citizens, plundered the estates of nobility.
[423] This is a chief or leader of mercenaries.
[424] In recent times, mercenary armies were used in the invasion of Iraq. Today they hawk their services to political figures, and foreign countries.
[425] Oman, *War*, p. 374.
[426] G.C. Macaulay, *The Chronicles of Froissart*, p. 104.
[427] Hallam, *History*, vol. 1, p. 396.
[428] Ibid., pp. 396-97.

These improvements by the French are said to have made their arms superior to the Italians who are credited, too, with revolutionizing war weaponry and techniques: "Italy ... was the first country to adopt the system of mercenary troops, which demanded a wholly different organisation [sic]; and the early introduction of fire-arms did its part in making war a democratic pursuit, not only because the strongest castles were unable to withstand a bombardment, but because the skill of the engineer, of the gun-founder, and of the artillerist—men belonging to another class than the nobility—was now of the first importance in a campaign."[429]

In the late 1400's Vasco Da Gama became the first European to sail around the Cape of Africa to India. Along the way he used the intimidating thundering sound of cannon fire to announce his ship's arrival into foreign ports, and to terrorize and pacify the citizens within. The Europeans' love affair with gunpowder had certainly begun.

Another striking feature of medieval clashes was the use of biological weapons. Most of us are aware of biological warfare as a mostly recent development. However, researchers have found that biological warfare was a feature of Hittite fighting as far back as 1500 BCE. Catapults employed by medieval Europeans hurled rotting and/or diseased corpses, diseased animals, plus human and animal feces over besieged walls in hopes of infecting the inhabitants sheltering within. From the Crusader's siege and capture of Nicaea in 1097 comes the following disturbing story of biological warfare: "Coming gladly, moreover, [the Turks] began to descend from the crest of the mountain a short distance. As many as descended remained there with their heads cut off at the hands of our men; moreover, our men hurled the heads of the killed far into the city, that they (the Turks) might be the more terrified [there after]."[430] Later in 1346, notary Gabriele De' Mussi witnessed Black Plague-laden bodies being catapulted over the walls of Caffa as the Tartars sieged on Christians sheltering within, "At first the Tartars were paralysed [sic] with fear at the ravages of the disease, and at the prospect that sooner or later all must fall victims to it. Then they turned their vengeance on the besieged, and in the hope of communicating the infection to their Christian enemies, by the aid of the engines of war [trebuchet], they projected the bodies of the dead over the walls into the city. The Christian defenders, however, held their ground, and committed as many of these plague-infected bodies as possible to the waters of the sea. Soon, as might be supposed, the air became tainted and the wells of water poisoned, and in this way the disease spread so rapidly in the city that few

---

[429] Burckhardt, *Renaissance*, p. 98.
[430] Krey, *Crusade*, p. 102.

of the inhabitants had strength sufficient to fly from it."[431]

Famine: Skeletons out of the Closet and onto the European Dinner Table: Family Members Become the Main Course

Wars never occur in a vacuum. They are always accompanied by the depressing consequences of the loss of innocent life, environmental degradation, and eventually, famine. Famines were common throughout the Middle Ages in Europe: "Evil indeed were those days in France, when out of seventy-three years, the reigns of Hugh Capet and his two successors, forty-eight were years of famine. Evil were the days for five years from 1015, in the whole western world, when not a country could be named that was not destitute of bread."[432] The madness of William the Conqueror was responsible for one such famine during his pursuit of his enemy, Danes, challengers to his authority, who had sieged York with the help of local nobility:

> While he himself continued his march through an almost inaccessible country, overgrown with wood, in the full intention of pursuing the enemy, without relaxation, into the fastness in which they lurked. His camps were scattered over a surface of one hundred miles; numbers of the insurgents fell beneath his vengeful sword, he levelled [sic] their places of shelter to the ground, wasted their lands, and burnt their dwellings with all they contained. Never did William commit so much cruelty; to his lasting disgrace, he yielded to his worst impulse, and set no bounds to his fury, condemning the innocent and the guilty to a common fate. In the fulness of his wrath he ordered the corn and cattle, with the implements of husbandry and every sort of provisions, to be collected in heaps and set on fire till the whole was consumed, and thus destroyed at once all that could serve for the support of life in the whole country lying beyond the Humber. There followed, consequently, so great a scarcity in England in the ensuing years, and severe famine involved the innocent and unarmed population in so much misery, that, in a Christian nation, more than a hundred thousand souls, of both sexes and all ages, perished of want.[433]

The burning of the land and slaughter of the people and husbandry caused devastation and hardship for nine years, but especially between the years 1068-1070, according to the historian.[434] The endless cycle of warfare

---

[431] Francis Aidan Gasquet, *The Great Pestilence (A.D. 1348-9) Now Commonly Known As The Black Death*, pp. 5-6.
[432] Hallam, *History*, vol. 1, notes xv, p. 264.
[433] Ordericus Vitalis, *The Ecclesiastical History of England and Normandy*, vol. 2, trans., Thomas Forester, (London: Henry G. Bohn, 1854), p. 28.
[434] On his deathbed, William confessed to his sadism for posterity: "I did not attain that high honour by hereditary right, but I wrested it from the perjured king Harold in a desperate battle, with much effusion of human blood, and it was by the slaughter and banishment of

placed a great burden on the people and the environment, so much so that clergymen demanded pledges from the narcissistic warlords:

> The peasants, whose crops were destroyed and homes burned, and who had neither armor nor the prospect of large ransom to protect their lives, were the ones to suffer most from these neighborhood wars and from the ravages of robber knights who got their living largely by plundering raids. A French bishop, intent upon reforming this evil of feudalism, proposed in 1023 that feudal nobles should take the following oath: "I will not take away ox nor cow other beast of burden. I will not seize the peasant nor the peasant's wife nor the merchants. I will not take their money, nor will I force them to ransom themselves. I do not want them to lose their property through a war that their lord wages, and I won't whip them to get their nourishment away from them. From the first of March to All Saints' Day I will seize neither horse nor mare nor colt from the pasture. I will not destroy and burn houses; I will not uproot and devastate vineyards under pretext of war; I will not destroy mills nor steal the flour." A measure more generally adopted by the clergy was the Truce of God, by which bishops forbade fighting in their dioceses over the week-end and on a number of church holidays. It can readily be imagined that this ecclesiastical prohibition was not easy to enforce.[435]

The *Truce of God* originated from hoary ceremonies of warring German tribes honoring their deity Ertha: "The unknown symbol of the Earth, covered with a thick veil, was placed on a carriage drawn by cows; and in this manner the goddess, whose common residence was in the isle of Rugen, visited several adjacent tribes of her worshippers. During her progress the sound of war was hushed, quarrels were suspended, arms laid aside, and the restless Germans had an opportunity of tasting the blessings of peace and harmony."[436] According to Webster had the truce been observed by the warring Christian factions it, "would have given Christendom peace for about two hundred and forty days each year; but it seems never to have been strictly observed except in limited areas."[437] However, the oath that the bishop sought for the princes sadly suggests that much of the destruction attached to warfare was unprovoked.

---

his adherents, that I subjugated England to my rule. I have persecuted its native inhabitants beyond all reason. Whether nobles or commons.... I fell on the English of the northern counties like a raving lion. I commanded their houses and corn, with all their implements and furniture, to be burnt without distinction, and large herds of cattle and beasts of burden, to be butchered wherever they were found. It was thus that I took revenge on multitudes of both sexes by subjecting them to the calamity of a cruel famine; and by so doing, alas me! became the barbarous murderer of many thousands, both young and old, of that fine race of people." Vitalis, *Ecclesiastical*, vol. 2, p. 413.

[435] Thorndike, *Europe*, pp. 250-51.
[436] Gibbon, *Decline*, vol. 1, pp. 278-79.
[437] Webster, *History*, p. 423.

As noted above, sometimes famine fell on populations as a result of intense battles. However, Lacroix suggests that beyond Charlemagne's reign, vegetables[438] "were never considered as being capable of forming solid nutriment, since they were almost exclusively used by monastic communities when under vows of extreme abstinence."[439] [440] Still, it is likely that lands ruined by warfare, plus a lack of rain[441] and poor soil conditions from improper crop rotation were all causes[442] of famine: "Enriching the land and draining the soil were rarely practiced during the earlier part of the Middle Ages. Crops at best were small, often not more than one third of what the same amount of land would produce to-day. Frequently they failed almost altogether, because so little was known of agriculture; and even when there was a year of plenty, it was hardly safe to sell the surplus, for it might all be needed during the following year," Tappan tells us. Thorndike confirms that harsh conditions resulted from the medieval Europeans' dismal agricultural knowledge:

> In those days they did not raise nearly so many different things from the soil as we do to-day. Clover, beets, potatoes, and many other agricultural products were unknown. Scientific farming, irrigation, and fertilizing were little known or practiced. Therefore the lack of variety in the crops soon impoverished the soil, and a very general custom was to let a field lie fallow every other or every third year, in order that it might recover its fertility. Consequently each peasant needed to have several strips of arable land scattered through the large fields which the peasants ploughed [sic] together, in order that while some of his land remained untilled he might get his subsistence from the rest. The land reserved for the lord was sometimes scattered in strips among the holdings of the peasants, and sometimes consisted of separate fields. Then there were common lands where serfs and lord alike might pasture their cattle or send forth their pigs to feed on acorns under the charge of the swineherd of the villa, to whom every one had to give a loaf of bread for his support.[443]

To make matters worse medieval farm tools were substandard for the job: "Farm implements were few and clumsy. The wooden ploughs only scratched the ground. Harrowing was done with a hand implement little better than a large rake. Grain was cut with a sickle, and grass was mown with a scythe. It took five men a day to reap and bind the harvest of two

---

[438] Charlemagne's botanical garden grew healing herbs, according to White, p. 34.
[439] Lacroix, *Manners*, p. 111.
[440] This attitude changed sometime after the 14th century, according to Lacroix.
[441] Tappan, *Knights*, pp. 117-18.
[442] The mini Ice Age experienced by Europe between 1300-1900 is considered a contributing factor, too.
[443] Thorndike, *Europe*, pp. 236-37.

acres."[444]

Whatever the reason, western history books contain hundreds of stories of starving citizens. And as for those acorns that supplied nourishment for pigs, Lacroix reports that during the 16th century reign of Francis I, poor conditions reduced the population in many places to eating acorn bread. So, from times very early on it became common for families unable to feed their children to sell them into slavery. Jordanes informs us about the types of deals struck to avoid starvation as the German tribes entered Rome:

> Soon famine and want came upon them, as often happens to a people not yet well settled in a country. Their princes and the leaders who ruled them in place of kings, that is Fritigern, Alatheus and Safrac, began to lament the plight of their army and begged Lupicinus and Maximus, the Roman commanders, to open a market. But to what will not the "cursed lust for gold" compel men to assent? The generals, swayed by avarice, sold them at a high price not only the flesh of sheep and oxen, but even the carcasses of dogs and unclean animals, so that a slave would be bartered for a loaf of bread or ten pounds of meat. When their goods and chattels failed, the greedy trader demanded their sons in return for the- necessities of life. And the parents consented even to this, in order to provide for the safety of their children, arguing that it was better to lose liberty than life; and indeed it is better than one be sold, if he will be mercifully fed, than that he should be kept free only to die.[445]

In scenarios such as this the gut-wrenching reality is that a parent's only guarantee was the receipt of a loaf of bread. And according to Bury, a child's age was no barrier to a sale: "In those times when terrible need and famines were frequent, parents had the legal right to sell their children directly after their birth and *a person who had taken care of a foundling was considered its owner*. It is to ecclesiastical authorities that the emperors turn in order to *prevent these rights from degenerating into a ruthless kidnapping of children*."[446] Hallam writes, "'The poor[447] early felt the necessity of selling themselves for subsistence in times of famine...' says Gregory of Tours, A.D. 585. This long continued to be the practice: and probably the remarkable number of famines which are recorded, especially in the ninth and eleventh centuries, swelled the sad list of those unhappy poor who

---

[444] Webster, *History*, p. 433.
[445] Mierow, *Jordanes*, pp. 88-89.
[446] Bury, *Cambridge*, vol. 1, p. 567.
[447] The wives, sons and daughters of Russian nobility were fair game, too: "The Parents, although they bee [sic] of the more Noble [sic] or of the Rustickes [sic], sell their owne [sic] Children [sic], their Sonnes [sic] for Slaves, their Daughters [sic] or Wives [sic] to the Turkes [sic] and Tartars, also to many Christians, and those which they are wont to steale [sic] secretly among themselves, they sell closely beyond the Sea [sic] to barbarous strangers after a more then [sic] barbarous manner." Samuel Purchas, *Hakluytus Posthumus or Purchas His Pilgrimes*, vol.13, pp. 472-73.

were reduced to barter liberty for bread."[448]

Norsemen who likely experienced some of the severest temperatures had a rather unseemly remedy for dealing with the lack of food: They exposed youngsters to the outdoor elements when a family was too poor to raise it. And though they seemed to have many reasons for exposing boys and girls: "No violent hand was ever laid upon children that were to be exposed. Only one case is mentioned of a child which was to be thrown into the water. One custom was to put the child in a covered grave; but the most common was to leave the death or life of the child to fate, by exposing it in an out of-the-way place; for instance, between heaped-up stones, or in a hollow under the root of a tree, but making it tolerably secure against wild animals. Sometimes nourishment, mostly pork to suck, was given, in order to prolong its life, in case any one might possibly find it and take pity on it."[449]

So, harsh conditions resulting from famines forced families to make some difficult choices. Those choices included selling children or even exposing them to the skin-blistering cold that eventually killed them. However there is abundant evidence that all too often during times of famine, Europeans committed acts of cannibalism against their family, neighbors, and strangers, too. Contemporary historians document the following stories:

> Meanwhile, the Goths elected Totila king, and soon afterwards laid siege to Rome. During the continuance of the siege the famine in the city was so severe that mothers were ready to feed on their own children.[450]

> In 1068 England [mentioned earlier] during a famine: in consequence of the ravages of the Normans, first, in Northumbria the preceding year, and again in the present and following year, throughout nearly the whole of England, so severe a famine prevailed in most parts of the kingdom, but chiefly in Northumbria and the adjacent provinces, that men were driven to feed on the flesh of horses, dogs, cats, and even of human beings.[451]

> Procopius and other historians... tell us that in the province of Picenum alone 50,000 victims succumbed; and, still more shocking, when they relate deeds of cannibalism which excite both horror and pity. For instance, we hear of two women who kept themselves alive by killing and eating the travelers who came to their house; several were dispatched in this way, when at last one came who awoke in time to avert the deadly weapon, and after hearing from the women's

---

[448] Hallam, *History*, vol. 1, notes xv, p. 264.
[449] Du Chaillu, *Viking*, vol.2, pp. 41-42.
[450] Vitalis, *Ecclesiastical*, vol. 1, p. 343.
[451] Thomas Forester, *The Chronicles of Florence of Worcester*, pp. 173-74.

own lips the avowal of their crime he murdered them both.[452]

Mr. Wright, in the thirtieth volume of the Archaeologia (p. 223), has extracted an entry from an Anglo-Saxon manuscript, where a lady, about the time of the Conquest, manumits some slaves, " whose heads," as it is simply and forcibly expressed, 'she had taken for their meat in the evil days'....[453]

From 1015 -1020 there were famines, as Radulfus Glaber and other contemporary writers tell us, in which mothers ate their children, and children their parents.[454]

Moreover, about the same time, a most mighty famine raged for five years throughout the Roman world, so that no region could be heard of which was not hunger stricken for lack of bread, and many of the people were starved to death. In those days also, in many regions, the horrible famine compelled men to make their food not only of unclean beasts and creeping things, but even of men's, women's, and children's flesh, without regard even of kindred; for so fierce waxed this hunger that grown-up sons devoured their mothers, and mothers, forgetting their maternal love, ate their babes.[455]

In 414, five years after the Vandals had entered Spain, the Visigothic chieftain followed them thither. There he and his successors carried on a long and bloody struggle with their fellow-Teutons, during part of which time the Goths professed to fight as champions of Rome, and for the remainder on their own account. The provinces, lately fertile and flourishing, were so harried by friend and foe that the Vandal soldiery were fain to buy wheat at thirty-six shillings a pint, and a mother slew and ate her own children.[456]

The Barbarians exercised their indiscriminate cruelty on the fortunes of the Romans and the Spaniards, and ravaged with equal fury the cities and the open country. The progress of famine reduced the miserable inhabitants to feed on the flesh of their fellow creatures; and even the wild beasts, who multiplied, without control, in the desert, were exasperated, by the taste of blood and the impatience of hunger, boldly to attack and devour their human prey. Pestilence soon appeared, the inseparable companion of famine; a large proportion of the people was swept away; and the groans of the dying excited only the envy of their surviving friends. At length the Barbarians, satiated with carnage and rapine, and afflicted by the contagious evils which they themselves had introduced, fixed their permanent seats in the depopulated country. The ancient Gallicia, whose limits included the kingdom of Old Castille, was divided

---

[452] P. Peter Lechner, *The Life and Times of St. Benedict: Patriarch of the Monks of the West*, p. 190.
[453] Hallam, *History*, vol. 1, notes xv, p. 264.
[454] Ibid.
[455] Coulton, *Garner*, p. 6.
[456] Hodgkin, vol. 2, p. 221.

between the Suevi and the Vandals.[457]

Cannibalism was such an acceptable practice that vendors put human body parts up for sale in market stalls. Of this horror Hallam writes, "Human flesh was sold, with some pretense of concealment, in the markets. It is probable that England suffered less than France; but so long and frequent a scarcity of necessary food must have affected, in the latter country, the whole organic frame of society."[458] Cannibalism forms a grotesque missing piece of the puzzle of early Europe's white washed history, as we shall see in upcoming chapters. Even European historians admit cannibalism became an acceptable practice for many Dark Ages (and earlier and later) Europeans who had run out of food and options, but not their singular will to live. The feudal world was a rapidly changing world. And either a person changed with the times or they, quite literally, became food and fodder to it. Thorndike writes about the unsettled system that bedeviled Europeans in his book published in 1917:

> Confused conditions were due not merely to war and violence and anarchy, nor further to the complicated network of feudal relationships at any given time, but also to the continual change and shifting and reshaping of those relations with passing years, making society assume new forms as when one shakes up the bits of glass in a kaleidoscope. Death, inheritance, forfeiture, escheat, vassals' changing lords, partition of fiefs, subinfeudation [sic], union of fiefs by marriage, conquests in war — all these changes kept the feudal world in almost as fluctuating a condition as the modern stock market.[459]

Europe's Past Helps Explain the African's Present

There is consensus that the European feudal system of the Middle Ages grew out of the need for protection from barbarian invaders. In exchange for (the illusion of) security, medieval people surrendered much of their personal freedom, as so many of us are willing to do today. However, the high number of wars during the medieval era proves that despite enhanced fortifications, and the people's acquiescence to brutal authority tens of millions of people died anyway. In exchange for that false sense of security, people labored on the land for free and then handed their children over to the same fate. The act of condemning the children to the parents' fate perpetuated the brutal system and allowed the feudal wars to continue for tens of generations. The lords of the land had great control over the lives of their workers. They even compelled marriages so that children born to those unions worked the land, too. Indeed, the children were just as

---

[457] Gibbon, *Decline*, vol. 3, p. 309.
[458] Hallam, *History*, vol. 1, notes xv, p. 264.
[459] Thorndike, *Europe*, p. 253.

attached to the land, as were their parents.

Hallam writes the following passage about feudalism's effects on Europe:

> So far as the sphere of feudality extended, it diffused the spirit of liberty, and the limitations of private right. The bulk of the people, it is true, were degraded by servitude.... The peace and good order of society were not promoted by this system. Though private wars did not originate in the feudal customs, it is impossible to doubt... they were perpetuated by so convenient an institution.... And as predominant habits of warfare are totally irreconcilable with those of industry, not merely by the immediate works of destruction which render its efforts unavailing, but through that contempt of peaceful occupations which they produce, the feudal system must have been intrinsically adverse to the accumulation of wealth, and the improvement of those arts....
>
> But as a school of moral discipline, the feudal institutions were perhaps most to be valued. Society had sunk, for several centuries after the dissolution of the Roman empire, into a condition of utter depravity; where... vices... were falsehood, treachery and ingratitude. In slowly purging off the [refuse] of this extreme corruption, the feudal spirit exerted its [reforming] influence.[460]

So despite the writer's admission that feudalism muzzled civil rights, and inflamed warfare he proclaims that its institutions had a *reforming* influence on society. There are a multitude of examples of the inhumanity that raged throughout feudal society. During the Crusades, which I cover in Chapter 11, inhumanity reached some fairly low levels in Europe as religious zealots, psychopaths, manipulators, and other wily individuals took great advantage of some risky ventures. Crusader stories are infamously vicious. Ludlow expounds on a few of them here: "Foulques the Black, the greatest of the counts of Anjou (987-1040), was pious enough to go on a pilgrimage to Jerusalem, but not sufficiently humane to refrain from burning his young wife at the stake, decked for her doom in her gayest attire. He was so humble that he paraded the streets of the Holy City with a halter about his neck, while the blood streamed from the scourge-wounds on his shoulders, yet he forced his own son to be bridled and saddled like an ass and to crouch on all fours at his feet. Of the whole line of Anjou at this period the historian Green remarks that 'their shameless wickedness degraded them below the level of man....'

"William Rufus (1056-1100) is thus described by one who knew him: 'The outrager [sic] of humanity, of law, and of nature; beastly in his pleasures, a murderer and blasphemous scoffer.' Henry I. of England (1068-1135) put out the eyes of his brother Robert and of his two grandchildren,

---

[460] Hallam, *History*, vol. 1, p. 230.

and forced his daughter to cross a frozen fosse, stripped half naked.... Raymond of Toulouse we shall learn to admire as our story advances. He was one of the most self-restrained and chivalric of the early crusaders; yet he put out the eyes and cut off the noses of his captives, and sent them thus mutilated to their homes, as a warning to their neighbors not to molest the march of the 'soldiers of the cross.' Of this act of atrocity the chronicler of the day remarks: 'It is not easy to do justice to the bravery and wisdom conspicuously displayed by the count here.' Too commonly the innocence of childhood, the venerableness of age, and the sacredness of sex were indiscriminately outraged by the license of conquest."[461]

Speaking of innocent children, in 1212 a scheme known as the Children's Crusade began. Boys and girls below the age of 12 years were encouraged to join Crusaders in Jerusalem, albeit, without weapons. From the reports of various accounts it appears that possibly 100,000 children heeded the call. But, instead of fighting for Jesus they found themselves in a fight for their lives. Lured aboard Arab ships with the promise of safe passage to Jerusalem, most of these crusading children were kidnapped to foreign lands and sold into slavery. In all, seven ships were used to ferry these unwitting children who, according to accounts, were never heard from again.[462]

The social instability of that era — that Thorndike likens to the ever-fluctuating stock market, accompanied by ceaseless *neighborhood wars*, whereby at any given time the gates to Lord's estate fell under siege to pillaging men heaving ramming rods, flinging fire and boiling tar, (not to mention the human corpses) had to play havoc on their central nervous system. According to Ludlow, the neighborhood wars could easily spread to nearby districts: "The love of war for its own sake was the dominant passion of such people. When no plausible pretext could be urged for declaration of hostilities, it burst out between neighborhoods as by spontaneous combustion. Raids and counter-raids took the place of the commercial rivalries of later times."[463]

Individuals living during that era probably employed mental self-defense mechanisms to shut out as much chaos and horror as possible, or either accepted such terrorism as the norm. It is partly understandable then that early on many remained fixated on circus events to blot out the screams of torment coming from neighbors, friends and family being slaughtered all around. Unimaginable terrors must have filled their daily lives during and especially after the barbarian's savage sack of cities. As mentioned earlier, Salvian saw nude corpses of men and women lying

---

[461] Ludlow, *Crusades*, pp. 20-22.
[462] Tappan, *Knights*, pp. 143-146.
[463] Ludlow, *Crusades*, pp. 22-23.

about everywhere, shredded by birds and dogs. Ludlow writes that the private combats, or duels, which spread easily to other neighborhoods, provide evidence that "stifling of the sense of justice was quite naturally attended by the suppression of the gentler emotions of kindness and humanity. This was an age of almost incredible cruelty.... But, beyond the fascination of the individual and the obligations of kinship, the sentiment of love seemed unknown to the masses." [464] Victims of intra-family cannibalism might disagree that "obligations of kinship" were present in their circumstances.

What happens to the DNA of a people subjected to thousands of years of harsh climatic conditions, and unyielding violence?[465] Since psychologists say that trauma impacts genes forever, one can argue that the horrific experiences of terror-filled days have negatively affected European DNA and are quite possibly heavily ingrained on their collective psyche adversely affecting their cultural construct, too. Sociopathy might explain the emotional detachment toward victims of the mindless, brutal beyond words hangings in the United States. Psychopathy might explain mobs of celebratory Anglo-American men, women, and children gathered on Sunday afternoons after church to inhumanely cheer on the genital mutilation of African-American men moments before swinging their tormented persons from trees.

Trees[466] play an important role in the European's culture of sacrifices. According to the Encyclopaedia Britannica:

Tree-worship again is a constantly recurring feature, seen, for instance, in the permanently sacred character of the ficus Ruminalis [fig-tree [467] intimately connected to the Romulus and Remus legend of the founding of Rome] and the caprificus [fig-tree] of the Campus Martius,[468] and above all in the oak of

---

[464] Ibid., p. 19.
[465] Not to mention the regular occurrences of famine, and disease.
[466] In Italy, "Oscilla masks of human faces... were suspended on fruit trees and vines. The old antiquaries of Rome explained these masks as substitutes for heads of human victims, which the Dodona oracle bade the Pelasgians offer to Saturn (Kronos)." A. Lang, "Method and Minotaur." *Folk-Lore: A Quarterly Review Myth, Tradition, Institution, & Custom*, vol. 21, no. 1 (1910) p. 142. Another source says masks symbolized animal skins worn by predecessors. Masks allowed them to enter communion with their deities.
[467] In KMT, the Tree of Life was an attribute of the mother cow goddess Hathor. This tree, represented by the Sycamore (nehat) fig tree, was important for its ability to sustain itself and humans under some rather harsh conditions. From its fruit a divine drink was distilled and offered.
[468] The altar to Mars, Roman god of war, was built on Campus Martius. Early in Roman history, Martius was a training field for the military. According to Jordanes: "Mars was always worshipped by the Goths with cruel rites, and captives were slain as his victims. They thought that he who is lord of war ought to be appeased by the shedding of human blood. To him they devoted the first share of the spoil, and in his honor arms stripped from the foe were suspended from trees. And they had more than all other races a deep spirit of

Juppiter (sic) Feretrius, on which the spolia opima were hung after a victory.[469]

Shrouded in mysticism is the fig tree that sheltered the twin male infants Romulus and Remus before their foster parents discovered them, according to the myth. Beneath the tree a she-wolf suckled the infants, and when he was older the adult Romulus offered spolia opima, the spoils of war, to Roman god Jupiter there – starting a fresh tradition. Thereafter, following triumphant battles soldiers placed spoils taken from the corpses of defeated men on fig trees as sacrificial offerings to Rome's supreme god. These spoils ranged from parts of body armor to parts of human bodies:

> A tribune of the soldiers named Aulus Cornelius Cossus.... Having struck and unhorsed his man [Tolumnius], he himself leaped quickly to the ground by the help of his lance, and as the king struggled to his feet flung him back with the boss of his shield, and plunging the spear again and again into his body, pinned him to earth. Then stripping the spoils from the corpse and cutting off the head, he bore it victoriously on the point of his spear and drove the enemy before him, panic-stricken at the sight of their slain king....
>
> Having been everywhere victorious, the dictator, as decreed by the senate and ratified by the people, returned to the City in triumphal procession. By far the greatest spectacle in the triumph was Cossus, bearing the spoils of honour of the slain king, while the soldiers sang rude verses about him, comparing him to Romulus. The spoils he fastened up as an offering, with solemn dedication, in the temple of Jupiter Feretrius, near the spoils of Romulus, which had been the first to be called opima, and were at that time the only ones.[470]

Soldiers decorated temples, public places and homes with their spoils. According to historians, the mystical trees grew on Capitoline hill (one of Rome's seven hills). Their orientation marked the parameters for Jupiter's future temple near Campus Martius.

Very early on Romans hanged criminals from trees as sacrificial offerings; in time the cross took the place of the tree as the sacrificial vehicle:

> The ancient practice of execution by hanging criminals on trees apparently led to the adoption of crosses constructed for a similar purpose. Hence, hanging from some part of a tree and the being fixed to a cross appear to have conveyed to the Romans the same import; accordingly the expressions infelix arbor and infelix lignum, each of which may consistently be rendered "the accursed tree,"

---

religion, since the worship of this god seemed really to be bestowed upon their ancestor." Mierow, *Jordanes*, p. 61.
[469] Cyril Bailey, "Roman Religion." *Encyclopaedia Britannica*. 11th ed. 1911. p. 577.
[470] Titus Livius, *Livy*, vol. 2, trans., B.O. Foster, (London: William Heinemann, 1919), pp. 319-21.

alike denoted crucifixion.[471]

Two methods were followed in the infliction of the punishment of crucifixion. In both of these the criminal was first of all usually stripped naked, and bound to an upright stake, where he was so cruelly scourged with an implement, formed of strips of leather having pieces of iron, or some other hard material, at their ends, that not merely was the flesh often stripped from the bones, but even the entrails partly protruded, and the anatomy of the body was disclosed.[472]

Robertson Smith writes the following passage on ritual hangings in ancient Greece:

The execution of criminals constantly assumes sacrificial forms, for the tribesman's life is sacred even if he be a criminal, and he must not be killed in a common way. This principle is finally extended to all religious executions, in which, as the Hebrews and Moabites say, the victim is devoted, as a herem, to the god. In one peculiar sacrifice at Hierapolis [a holy city said to have been founded by Apollo] the victims were suspended alive from trees, and the trees were then set on fire. The fire is perhaps a later addition, and the original rite may have consisted in suspension alone. The story of a human victim hung up in the temple at Carrhae by the Emperor Julian, and the similar stories in the Syriac Julian-romances, are too apocryphal to be used, though they probably reflect some obsolete popular superstition.[473]

The subject of ritual [474] hangings in European cultures, and its insinuation into other cultures around the world is worthy of more research by interested African-American scholars. However, it is undeniable that the marks of the medieval world are indelibly etched into the (sub) conscious thoughts and actions of those Anglo-American citizens who carried snippets of the condemned African-American's penis, hair,[475]

---

[471] Charles Boutell. "Cross." *Encyclopaedia Britannica*. 9th ed. 1888. p. 610.
[472] Thomas Macall Fallow. "Cross, and Crucifixion." *Encyclopaedia Britannica*. 11th ed. 1910. p. 506.
[473] Smith, *Lectures*, p. 371.
[474] "Mars, whom the fables of poets call the god of war, was reputed to have been born among [Goths]. Hence Vergil says: 'Father Gradivus rules the Getic fields.' Now Mars has always been worshipped by the Goths with cruel rites, and captives were slain as his victims. They thought that he who is lord of war ought to be appeased by the shedding of human blood. To him they devoted the first share of the spoil, and in his honor arms stripped from the foe were suspended from trees. And they had more than all other races a deep spirit of religion, since the worship of this god seemed to be really bestowed upon their ancestor." Mierow, *Jordanes*, p. 61.
[475] Pliny informs us that early Europeans credited human hair with magic: "The hair of a man torn down from the cross, is good for quartan fevers [fever from malaria which appears every 3rd day]. Ashes, too, of burnt human hair are curative of carcinomata." John Bostock and H. T. Riley, trans., *Pliny's Natural History Remedies Derived From Man, vol. 5*, (London: Henry G. Bohn, 1856), p. 291. Also, "Hair left hanging on the tree as a votive offering," C. F.

ears, fingers, etc., home as trophies,[476] once we learn how medieval crowds often fought over the warm blood of newly executed persons believing it held curative powers; or once we discover Europeans kept corpse hands, toes, ears, and fingers[477] as amulets, and believed that the freshly used hangman's rope[478] brought wealth. Tappan informs us:

> Of the manner of life and habits of thought of the [Europeans] who lived between the eighth and fifteenth centuries. Our writings and our everyday conversation are full of their phrases and of allusions to their ideas. Many of our thoughts and feelings and instincts, of our very follies and superstitions, have descended to us from them. To become better acquainted with them is to explain ourselves.[479]

Hair clippings carry their own significance in the Indo-European world of rituals. Early Europeans placed hair clippings inside boxes, and dedicated them to gods. According to Paton, mentioned earlier, "Hair-offerings to deities are... analogous to blood-offerings, the strength being supposed to reside in the hair."[480] He adds, "At the cremation of Patroclus, Achilles and his friends cut off their hair and laid it upon the bier."[481]

There is abundant proof that Christianized Anglo-Americans carried "souvenirs" home from some very ghastly scenes where African-Americans were brutally tortured; many times Anglo spectators picked ritual areas clean of the deceased's remains. But instead of hundreds of thousands collecting together at the amphitheater as they did in the not too distant past, Anglo-Americans gathered around mass-produced postcards of unseemly deeds, whereas today media outlets mass distribute images of "lynched-by-gun" Black men... the scenes of lifeless Black bodies sprawled on the ground stoke long ago medieval memories, sparking adrenaline rushes in some viewers, while disgusting others. On the surface it seems that the torture and murder of African-American men, women and

---

Gordon Cumming.
[476] Perhaps used as magical amulets and fetiches (fetishes). Hair, according to Smith, was a "special seat of life."
[477] Europeans believed that hands and fingers from corpses warded off diseases such as herpes, and goitre; healed toothaches; faded freckles, and warts. There were many more gruesome uses for hands and fingers as cited by Strack. Regarding the tooth Pliny writes: "A human tooth, reduced to powder, is a cure, they say, for the sting of a serpent.... Some persons recommend the tooth to be fumigated with the smoke of a burnt tooth, which has belonged to another person of the same sex; or else to attach to the person a dogtooth, as it is called, which has been extracted from a body before burial. Bostock and Riley, trans., *Pliny's*, vol. 5, pp. 291-93.
[478] Strack, *Sacrifice*, pp. 70-76.
[479] Tappan, *Knights*, p. v.
[480] Paton, *Spiritism*, p. 11.
[481] Ibid., p. 131.

children closely follows established patterns[482] for European blood rituals. It appears, too, that African-Americans have become convenient substitutes for European intra-familial tensions.

Roots of western sociopathy grow deep and long if early eminent European philosophers, such as Cicero and Hecaton are any indication. These wise men seem inclined toward a similar sociopathy, or individualism, that ignores the humanness of "others." Individualism is a central theme of the theories of many African scholars (and some Europeans, too) who argue convincingly that the tendency to disconnect from humanity arose while Europeans survived against the odds through the darkened, blistering cold, harsh and infertile climate of the Eurasian steppes. The singular focus on survival that developed allows certain of them to disengage from the broader humankind opening the way to dehumanizing other people.

Let's turn back to Cicero and Hecaton who ponder over serious questions such as: Who is worth more, a beast of labor or a slave? Or they even wonder whether owners must feed slaves in times of famine.[483] The humanity of Cicero and Hecaton seems compromised by the material world and by the same lack of empathy many sociopaths experience that are unable to feel or relate on an emotional level with others. In fact, one can envision the nostrils on Cicero's big pointy nose bulge as he writes that, "There is no injustice in making slaves of those who know not self-government." [484] And Hecaton, according to the 1910 edition of the Encyclopaedia Britannica, believes that *self-interest* is "the best criterion."[485] Centuries of witnessing the perils of the poor, and the misery and degradation of disenfranchised people failed to change that attitude among Europeans as Ludlow writes, "Dean Stanley [486] remarks of even the thirteenth century that 'the age had no sense of obligation to the poor and middle class.' It was still needful that rulers should repeat the dying counsel of Charlemagne to his sons, 'not to deprive widows and orphans of their remaining estates.'"[487] Many modern Christians bristle at having to use tax dollars to ease the burdens of the poor, yet rally behind war and violence that strips native people of their lives, homes and resources. And, of course, sociopathy is sometimes expressed in the psychopathy of violence. And if the European culture is assessed by the standards of the

---

[482] Read the horrific stories of the torture and murders of Jessie Washington of Waco, Texas; Sam Hose of Georgia; Henry Smith, of Paris Texas.
[483] A. Frédéric Ozanam, *History of Civilization in the Fifth Century*, p. 148.
[484] Ibid., p. 148.
[485] "Hecato of Rhodes." *Encyclopaedia Britannica*. 11th ed. 1910. p. 194.
[486] Perhaps this is a reference to Arthur Stanley (d. 1881), Dean of Westminster, biblical scholar, and priest.
[487] Ludlow, *Crusades*, p. 19.

psychopathy checklist, it could easily score 18/20 traits listed.

So, when evaluating the emotional intelligence of the European culture, one must consider sociopathy, and psychopathy (as well as narcissism) as likely cultural diseases. A sociopathic person is one who lacks a conscience. A psychopath suffers from mental disorder and displays a tendency toward being anti-social, or violent. Narcissism places the ego (the self) at the center of the world. Many non-Europeans believe that the western man's lack of conscience feeds his decisions to wreak havoc on nature, and to create war machines capable of the instantaneous annihilation of millions of people with each powerful blow.

6

MEDIEVAL SLAVE NARRATIVES

Europe's Slave Industry Before They Stole Africans, Forcing Them to Grow White Wealth

It was asserted even then, that the human race in that quarter* was pre-eminently fitted for slavery by its especial power of endurance Plautus {Trin. 542) commends the Syrians: genus quod patientissimum est hominum [What breed of patient men.].[488]

The abyss of misery and woe, which opens before our eyes in this most miserable of all proletariates, we leave to be fathomed by those who venture to gaze into such depths; it is very possible that, compared with the sufferings of the Roman slaves, the sum of all Negro suffering is but a drop.[489]

Note I include a separate chapter on slavery in Europe after the top results from a quick internet search on slavery for another project returned articles discussing only Black people as slaves. It was after clicking through several pages that results revealed information on so-called "white slavery." And then those articles had some fairly twisted titles that they alone managed to distort the history of slavery simply by labeling it as "white slavery." The mere thought of being perceived negatively causes enough collective angst and distress that many Europeans and Anglo-Americans turn to "whitewashing" and "down-playing" their awful reality. In this case, they have whitewashed slavery, a brutal, insane, and inhumane system that has been integral to the European class structure for a very, very long time. At the outset they distinguish the system that brutalized them as "white slavery" because, they reason, slaves are Black. By adding the adjective "white" their audience is informed right away they are referring to a *different type of institution* than the harsh one endured by Africans. Two points here: the type of slavery endured by Indo-Europeans was as brutal as what Africans endured; and calling a system of Europe's own creation "white slavery" is redundant since their concept of slavery developed from the subjugation of Slavic (Eastern European) people. Slavics – Slavs - became slaves. So, originally slaves were White. Slavs mean Slaves; Slavs are White. These historical bullet points alone make the "Blacks were the only slaves" meme patently untrue. *Note 2* I agree with those who insist that African-Americans reject using slave as a term to define

---

[488] Mommsen, *Rome*, vol. 3, p. 100.
[489] Ibid., p. 103.

Egun imprisoned and forced to labor in the hoary European system of degradation and torture.

At the end of this chapter, German historian Mommsen elaborates on the similarities between slavery of the Americas with the ancient Roman system. He reveals the location of "Negroland" of that period — a particular area where Romans acquired their slaves.

To begin, it must be made clear that this chapter does not concern who endured the worst treatment, or suffered the most pain, Africans or Europeans. Its intent is to push back against an emotionally and psychologically damaging narrative intended to demean African-Maafans who are told that "Blacks were the only slaves" in history. Secondly, kidnapped Africans forced to work for free are still owed reparations from those who gained their wealth from that free labor, despite that Europeans once were slaves. Finally, the next few pages address an ancient inhumane system of punishment, that has negatively affected millions upon millions of innocent people, and by some estimates "was the chief and most direct cause of the ruin of the Roman Empire...."[490] [491]Yet, this vile institution that has caused so much damage over the centuries remains a plague in this so-called modern world. In the following passage, Hodgkin's presents a few pointed facts about an institution that is "peculiar" only to those who do not know European history:

> The life of the Roman's slave, especially of him who was engaged in agriculture, seems to have been hard and dismal beyond even the hardness and dismalness of ordinary negro slavery....
>
> In the fifth century the conscience of the whole civilised (sic) world acquiesced in the fact of slavery....
>
> The Roman legislator said that this abrogation of the natural rights of man was an institution of the universal law of nations, and his saying was confirmed by the fact that there was in all probability not one nation[492] then existing, civilised (sic) or barbarian, wherein Slavery, in one form or another, did not exist. And so the bondsman of those days submitted to his servile condition, as men now

---

[490] Blake, *Slavery*, p. xv.
[491] In the United States prisons are becoming privately owned institutions where prisoners are required to work for slave wages.
[492] This, of course, is wrong. The servant system in Africa was very unlike the brutal system put in place by Europeans. Some Africans were forced into servitude because of offenses committed against certain groups. In their case, they worked land that after a time became theirs to inhabit. Additionally, servants attained all group privileges; they became family members and intermarried, if they so desired. I am told that slavery has no corresponding word in traditional African languages.

submit to poverty or disease, grumbling indeed that they have drawn a bad number in the lottery of life, but without any intolerable feeling of injustice, without any indignant questioning, 'Why was this horrible fate ever placed for me or for any one among the possible conditions of existence?'

But in Rome it had been working through twelve centuries....

Slavery had aided in the massing together of those 'wide farms' which were the ruin of Italy. Slavery had emptied the fields and villages of the hardy rustics who had once been the backbone of Roman power. Slavery had filled the cities with idle and profligate babblers. Slavery had indoctrinated these men, themselves often freedmen or the sons of freedmen, with the pestilent notion that manual labour was beneath the dignity of a citizen....

Slavery was to be softened into Serfdom, and Serfdom was slowly to disappear....[493]

Historical revisionisms and omissions attempt to make Dark Ages slavery far less violent and not nearly as emotionally crippling as the type of institution inflicted upon stolen Africans. However, as stated earlier, slaves in Europe were vulnerable to serious injury or death, depending on the locale and era. Additionally, it is ludicrous for someone to suggest that while even in the midst of all the destruction and terrorism that occurred during the Dark Ages, slaves holders treated European slaves agreeably. In fact, the Scythians regularly blinded their slaves,[494] according to Herodotus who writes that Scythian slaves produced milk. Rawlinson, who translated Herodotus, explains that eyesight was not necessary for slaves to do certain pastoral work; and blinding them prevented slaves from running away, or revolting. Indeed, before Europeans reached along the Aethiopian Sea (Atlantic Ocean) to snatch away the hopeful futures of Egun, they captured, and then abused one another. Or they bought slaves outright, and then abused them.

As pointed out earlier, when crop yield was poor in the dark, dreary, cold landscape of Europe it was normal for hungry family members to sell their children into slavery. Slavery in Europe was a customary practice. Mommsen writes thusly, "It was in Italy alone that moral subjection became transformed into legal slavery. In the same way the principle of the slave being completely destitute of legal rights—a principle involved in the very nature of slavery—was maintained by the Romans with merciless rigour [sic] and carried out to all its consequences."[495] Still, it was surprising to learn that Roman law allowed fathers to sell sons (children)

---

[493] Hodgkin, vol. 2, pp. 560-65.
[494] Rawlinson, *Herodotus*, vol. 2, p. 184.
[495] Mommsen, *Rome*, vol. 1, p. 49.

simply because the sons displeased them: "The father of the household not only maintained the strictest discipline over its members, but he had the right and duty of exercising judicial authority over them and of punishing them as he deemed fit in life and limb.... Indeed a father might convey his son as well as his slave in property to a third person: if the purchaser was a foreigner, the son became his slave; if he was a Roman, the son, while as a Roman he could not become a Roman's slave, stood at least to his purchaser in a slave's stead,"[496] Mommsen tells us. According to Greek Historian, Dionysius of Halicarnassus (ca. 1st c. BCE), Romulus passed this law forward.[497]

It is rarely, if ever, mentioned that Vikings routinely enslaved other Europeans captured through warfare. Recall that Vikings turned prisoners of war into slaves, and then offered them up as sacrificial blood gifts to their gods. And if they did not kill slaves, they treated them dreadfully: "The ancient Norsemen hardly acknowledged slaves to be men. A slave might be beaten, starved, and otherwise tormented, or be killed by his master's order, and the abuser might go unpunished. They could not buy, sell, nor inherit—not take oath, not marry—but were sold and bought as other wares. Slaves never carried arms, except when expressly armed for military service.... Slaves were even sometimes let out to serve other citizens, and in that case they were permitted to have a part of their wages, and the money thus earned was often saved to purchase the liberty of the slaves."[498]

A Paradigm Adjustment for Readers Believing that "Slaves were only Black Folk"

> [During the Middle Ages] ...the "common folk," the many thousand people who were neither clergy nor nobles. They were the ones who did the work of the manors. They were of various ranks. A few were slaves, and were looked upon as having no more rights than a horse or a cow.[499]

So, despite claims made during a recently televised supposed *documentary* on African-Americans, Europeans did indeed enslave other Europeans. Early Europeans acquired slaves for the same reasons the *filthy rich* today buy expensive luxury cars: slaves were an indication of one's social status. The more slaves, the wealthier the owner. Before the western empire fell, its citizens imported multitudes of slaves as: "Domestic servants, farm

---

[496] Ibid., p. 91.
[497] Earnest Cary, trans., *The Roman Antiquities of Dionysius of Halicarnassus*, vol. 1, (Cambridge: Harvard University Press, 1937), p. 391.
[498] Sinding, *Scandinavia*, pp. 39-40.
[499] Tappan, *Knights*, pp. 107-08.

laborers, miners, artisans,[500] factory hands, and even shopkeepers."[501] A landowner with great acreage leased it to contractors who sublet it to tenants or used slave labor to cultivate the soil. The landowner never tilled his own land, according to historians. Greece is well known for its large slave population, and accounted for more slaves than citizens. The same might be said about Rome.[502] According to Webster, "Every victorious battle swelled the troops of captives sent to the slave markets at Rome. Ordinary slaves became as cheap as beasts of burden are now. The Roman poet Horace tells us that at least ten slaves were necessary for a gentleman in even moderate circumstances. Wealthy individuals, given to excessive luxury, might number their city slaves by the hundreds, besides many more on their country estates."[503] Blake remarks, "The statement of Athenasus that very many Romans possessed 10,000 and 20,000 slaves, and even more, is probably an exaggeration; but a freedman under Augustus, who had lost much property (including slaves) in the civil wars, left at his death as many as 4,116 [excluding the number who died in the war]. Two hundred was no uncommon number for a person to keep."[504] Church historian and theologian Johann Joseph Ignaz Döllinger (d. 1890) in *The Gentile and the Jew in the Courts of the Temple of Christ* remarks that it was normal for a single household to have 500 males. In *The Decline and Fall of the Roman Empire*, Edward Gibbon ups the ante with an "imperfect" analysis of the census during the reign of Claudius (first c. CE), putting the slave number at 60 million, or half the Roman world population.

Tacitus confirms the large slave population: "Rome, where men already trembled at the vast scale of the slave-establishments, in which there was

---

[500] "The greater part of economic labor, as performed by the artisan and the colonus, became, therefore, very nearly servile. The feudal system used no harsher language towards the artisan than that employed by the sons of Constantine in a rescript: 'Let them not dare to aspire to any honor, even if they might deserve it, the men who are covered with the filth of labor and let them remain in their own condition.'" Duruy, *Rome*, vol. 8, pt. 1, pp. 37-38.
[501] Webster, *History*, p . 269.
[502] "Blair supposes the number of freemen, and slaves to hare been nearly equal, between the expulsion of the kings and the destruction of Carthage, but that from the fall of Corinth to Alexander Severus (146 B.C. to 222 A.D.), the slaves were three to one. On the other hand, Bureau de la Malle maintains the proportion of slaves to free men to have been as one to twenty-five in 476 B.C.., and in 225 B.C. to have been as twenty-two to twenty-seven, counting in peregrini. Zumpt holds Bunsen's numbers to be far too low, when he puts the slave population of Rome in the year 5 B.C. at 650,000, and would himself count two slaves for one freeman. With greater certainty it may be affirmed, that male slaves exceeded female four to one; and as no slave could intermarry with a free citizen, it is evident that to at least four-fifths of the males a contubernium even with a female slave was rendered an impossibility." John J. I. Döllinger, *The Gentile and The Jew in The Courts of the Temple Of Christ: An Introduction to the History of Christianity*, vol. 2, p. 267.
[503] Webster, *History*, p. 269.
[504] Blake, *Slavery*, pp. 47-48.

an immense growth, while the freeborn populace daily decreased...."[505] Blake adds, "Down to the age of Theodosius, wealthy persons still continued to keep as many as two or three thousand.

As their class size grew in numbers, so did their burdens." Duruy tells us: "Cato's frightful language as to the slave (instrumentum vocale [speaking tool]) was used in respect to them. In the time of [3rd c. Roman jurist] Ulpian they were reckoned with the ox, the plough, and agricultural implements, - attached to the soil, the instrumentum fundi [non-persons; agricultural property]."[506] Justinian did much to promote the ultimate extinction of slavery; but the number of slaves was again increased by the invasion of the northern barbarians, who not only brought with them their own slaves, who were chiefly Sclavonians [Slavonians, Slavics], but also reduced many of the inhabitants of the conquered provinces to the condition of slaves. But all the various classes of slaves became merged in the course of time into the serfs of the Middle Ages."[507] Döllinger adds, "Slavery was spread over the whole face of heathendom, and found in Gaul and Germany as well as in Rome."[508]

The Romans kidnapped slaves from wherever they found them, but of course they came from client states, too. Wherever Romans planted colonies the slave population was large there. Gibbon informs us that, "The slaves consisted, for the most part, of barbarian captives, taken in thousands by the chance of war, purchased at a vile price...."[509] "The slave-merchant made his purchases from armies after battle, pirates, or even in the slave's own country and home. He then exposed them for sale in the cities upon a wooden scaffold,"[510] Döllinger remarks. Slavery was a lucrative business. It was common for European pirate crews to skulk their ships along coastlines in search of potential kidnap victims: "In the time of the Heptarchy [7th and 8th centuries Anglo-Saxon kingdoms of Britain], slaves were an article of export. Great numbers were exported, like cattle, from the British coasts. The Roman market was partially supplied with slaves from the shores of Britain. Pope Gregory the Great, struck with the blooming complexions and fair hair of some Saxon [boys] in the slave market, sent over St. Augustine from Rome to convert the islanders to Christianity. In the time of Alfred [9th c. CE], slaves were so numerous that

---

[505] Church and Brodribb, *Annals*, p. 125.
[506] Duruy, *Rome*, vol. 8, pt. 1, p. 37.
[507] Blake, *Slavery*, p. 49.
[508] John J. I. Döllinger, *The Gentile and The Jew in The Courts of the Temple Of Christ: An Introduction to the History of Christianity*, vol. 2, trans., N. Darnell, (London: Longman, Green, Longman, Roberts, & Green, 1862), p. 265.
[509] Edward Gibbon, *The Decline and Fall of the Roman Empire*, vol. 1. p. 61.
[510] Döllinger, *Gentile*, p. 261.

their sale was regulated by law."[511]

> The slave merchant gets his cargoes from kidnappers, and the first cost, therefore, is inconsiderable. The great centres [sic] of this traffic were in the harbors bordering on the Euxine [Black Sea]; and Scythians were often stolen.... Blacks were in high value; they were somewhat rare, and therefore both male and female negroes were favorite articles of luxury among the opulent Romans. At one period, Delos was most remarkable as the emporium for slavers. It had its harbors, chains, prisons, every thing so amply arranged to favor a brisk traffic, that ten thousand slaves could change hands and be shipped in a single day."[512]

It was not unusual for a person to volunteer to become a slave, or to become enslaved to a creditor. Breaking the law, such as avoiding military service or the census could subject a person to slavery, too. And depending on the era, children born to female slaves themselves became slaves. Though, according to Blake, in early Rome breeding slaves was costlier than kidnapping and selling them. That may not have been the case each time as Döllinger tells us that the elder Cato[513] coupled his slaves so they could breed more.

A slave's subjection to the auction block is a telling feature of a cruel system that thrives on the complete degradation of humans: "Slaves were usually sold by auction at Rome; and, as we have observed of the Greek auctions, they were conducted very much like those of our southern cities. They were placed on a raised stone, or table, so that every one might see and handle them, even if they did not wish to buy them. Purchasers took care to have them stripped, for slave-dealers had recourse to as many tricks to hide personal defects, as a horse-jockey of modem times. Sometimes purchasers called in the advice of medical men. Slaves of great beauty and rarity were not exhibited to public gaze in the slave market, but were shown to purchasers in private. Newly imported slaves had their feet whitened with paint; and those that came from the East had their ears bored which was a sign of slavery among many eastern nations.... The character of the slave to be sold, was set forth on a scroll, hanging abound his neck, which was a warranty to the purchaser; the vendor was bound to announce fairly all his defects, and if he gave a false account, had to take him back, any time within six months after he was sold, or make up to the purchaser what the latter had lost by obtaining an inferior article to what had been warranted. The vendor might, however, use general terms of

---

[511] Blake, *Slavery*, p. xv.
[512] Ibid., p. 64.
[513] "The same Cato made a traffic of his fellow-men under a disguised name. His slaves were ordered to buy and train boys, whom he sold again." Döllinger, Gentile, p. 261.

commendation without being obliged to make them good,"⁵¹⁴ Blake tells us. Döllinger adds, "The fairest and finest slaves were to be found at the taberna of the merchant., where they had to strip themselves at the request of purchasers. Asia was the great supplier of slaves: Syrians, Lydians, Carians, Mysians, Phrygians, and, above all, the vigorous, large-limbed Cappadocians, were purchased in troops at Rome."⁵¹⁵

In the European narcissistic, inhumane social system that depends on hierarchy to elevate the egos of its members the laws confined slaves to a class structure, too. They became publicly or privately-owned. Employed as custodians of public facilities, or tasked with caring for the needs of magistrates and priests, publicly owned slaves had slightly better social circumstances, and did not face the daily threat of being sold. Private slaves were sub-divided between urban and rural with their duties sub-dividing them further still: ordinarii tended to supervisory duties; vulgares attended to the personal needs of their master, and were the cooks, etc.

The Romans' abuse and mistreatment of slaves is well known. For example, in the following passage Tacitus reminds us that early Germans lived beneath the ground:

> They also dig subterranean caves and cover them over with a great quantity of dung". These they use as winter-retreats, and granaries; for the severity of the cold is mitigated in them: and upon an invasion, when the open country is plundered, these recesses remain undiscovered, either because the enemy is ignorant of them, or because he will not trouble himself with the search.⁵¹⁶

Although the supposedly more socially advanced Romans scoffed at the savage behaviors of early Germans, the ergastula, an underground prison, was a sadistic tool Romans used to prevent their slaves from escaping: "The dungeons, where slaves in chains were forced to work, were common all over Italy. [Lucius Junius Moderatus] Columella [1ˢᵗ c. CE] advises that they be built under ground; and recommends the duty of having a careful overseer to call over the names of the slaves, in order to know when any of them had deserted. Sicily was full of these dungeons, and the soil was cultivated by laborers in chains,"⁵¹⁷ Blake tells us. Tacitus relates many great abuses endured by slaves who arrogant, unfeeling Romans classified as chattel. The term chattel evolved from cattle, an important staple of the early world, and originally referred to property, goods, profit, and wealth.

---

⁵¹⁴ Blake, *Slavery*, pp. 49-50.
⁵¹⁵ Döllinger, *Gentile*, p. 262.
⁵¹⁶ C. Cornelius Tacitus, *A Treatise on the Situation, Manners, and Inhabitants of Germany and the Life of Agricola*, trans., John Aiken (Cambridge: W. Grant, 1823), pp. 44-45. ("Large bodies ', powerful in sudden exertions, but less firm under toil and labour...." pp. 10-11).
⁵¹⁷ Blake, *Slavery*, p. 20.

Though Roman cattle were likely treated better than Roman slaves as we learn here:

> As to their housing, Columella prescribed 'ergastula subterranea Underground prison.' in which openings were to be contrived out of reach of the hand, either for the purpose of preventing escape, or of cutting off the sight of the world, which was denied them. Those employed at the mill carried a large wheel round their necks to prevent their raising to the mouth a handful of the flour that they spent the day in grinding. This deprives the Chinese of the honor of having invented their peculiar mode of torture, and it was the *mildest method of treatment*, as the law of Antonine had not taken away the *right of making eunuchs of slaves*, and they were to be counted by troops... as well as crowds of gladiator-slaves who assembled... and *took the terrible oath to let themselves be burnt, fettered, scourged, and slaughtered... if not men at least merchandise, subject matter for contracts of sale and purchase, and therefore obliging, in some manner, the attention of the jurisconsults.*[518] (Italics added).

In addition to working in Roman households, slaves served as prostitutes and fought in wars. They were the "artisans... bakers, cooks, confectioners, porters, bed-chamber slaves and litter bearers. The literati, or literary slaves, were used for various purposes by their masters, either as readers, copyists or amanuenses."[519] According to Döllinger, Roman slaves from Germany and Gaul worked the fields. And physicians, who could be enslaved along with other skilled workers,[520] routinely mutilated the slaves.[521] In the eyes of Romans, slaves were lifeless objects; after a master's death, his heirs assumed his slaves along with other household furniture. Clearly then for Romans, slaves, who did everything from working the farms to plucking the hairs[522] from their masters' bodies, were appropriate fodder for games of the bloody amphitheater,[523] as noted in the passage above: "The games of the amphitheatre required an immense number of slaves trained for the purpose,"[524] writes Blake. Döllinger informs us that out of desperation slaves often volunteered for the brutal games as an escape from the even more brutal treatment of owners. Though if they somehow managed to survive the games, slaves went back to their masters. Ozanam reveals the level of insensitivity the general populace directed towards

---

[518] Ozanam, *Fifth Century*, p. 150.
[519] Blake, *Slavery*, p. 51.
[520] Gibbon, *Decline*, vol. 1. p. 64.
[521] Ozanam, *Fifth Century*, p. 151.
[522] Elliot, *Outlines*, p. 60.
[523] Bear and bull baiting began in England in the 1500's. Bears, and other animals, were raised specifically for the purpose of fighting against dogs to the amusement of the royal families and their courts. It was blood sport for the *royal* court that cheered on dogs ripping apart bears' throats.
[524] Blake, *Slavery*, p. 48.

slave participation in the violent games: "Fear was expressed lest oxen fail, but no one seemed to fear a scarcity of gladiators."[525] Indeed. Slaves were as plentiful as people.

Tacitus recounts a Roman law that was once used to execute four hundred slaves after one of them murdered the master of the house, and the others failed to leak the murderer's plot.[526] Evidently this law protected vastly outnumbered household members and discouraged slave revolts. Tacitus relates multiple tales of slaves being tortured, even stating that provinces erected special areas for punishing slaves. In one case he writes: "As a consequence, her slave girls were examined under torture, and though some were forced by the intensity of agony into admitting falsehoods, most of them persisted in upholding the virtue of their mistress."[527] Tacitus is referring to a mistress accused of having an affair with a slave, an intolerable indiscretion that must have been common considering that Roman law proposed to lower the status of women having affairs with slaves. (Apparently, a man sexually engaging slaves was permissible). In any event, it was customary to compel testimony from slaves:

> Slaves were tortured, to get a favourable testimony out of them for a master on his trial and the same was done to stranger slaves, to obtain evidence from them against an accused person, whose property they were not. If it were the case of misdemeanour, a crime committed by a slave himself, torture was ordinarily in requisition. In the time of the emperors, however, slaves were frequently tortured for evidence against their masters.[528]

Also, there was the infamous cruelty of Vedius Pollio.[529] Pollio, the elder Pliny tells us, "was a Roman knight, one of Augustus's friends, who distinguished himself by making a practice of throwing his slaves, when they deserved punishment, to [man-eating] lampreys [muraena] in his fishponds."[530] The fiendish punishment this Roman equestrian and former slave delivered is notorious and repeated often by his contemporaries. The next passage from Seneca supplies the details:

> It was a notable story that of Vedius Pallio [sic], upon his inviting of Augustus to supper. One of his boys happened to break a glass: and his master, in a rage,

---

[525] Ozanam, *Fifth Century*, p. 151.
[526] Church and Brodribb, *Annals*, p. 275.
[527] Ibid., p. 282.
[528] Döllinger, *Gentile*, p. 263.
[529] "[Pollio] was a freedman by birth, and remarkable for nothing except his riches and his cruelty. Cf. Dion Cassius, liv. 23 ; Pliny, H. N.ix. 23 ; and Seneca, "On Anger," iii. 40. 2." Seneca, *Seneca*, p. 404.
[530] Church and Brodribb, *Annals*, p. 337.

commanded him to be thrown in a pond to feed his lampreys. This action of his might be taken for luxury, though, in truth, it was cruelty. The boy was seized, but brake loose and threw himself at Augustus' feet, only desiring that he might not die that death. Caesar, in abhorence [sic] of the barbarity, presently ordered all the rest of the glasses to be broken, the boy to be released, and the pond to be filled up, that there might be no further occasion for an inhumanity of that nature. This was an authority well employed. Shall the breaking of a glass cost a man his life? Nothing but a predominant fear could ever have mastered his choleric and sanguinary disposition. This man deserved to die a thousand deaths, either for eating human flesh at second-hand in his lampreys, or for keeping of his fish to be so fed.[531]

And though Augustus makes himself out to be a hero of his own story, Döllinger points out Augustus' inability to recognize his own vile inhumanity: "Augustus, who had himself saved a slave of Vedius Pollio from this punishment, ordered Eros, his steward, to be crucified on the mast of his ship, for having roasted and eaten a quail of his that had been trained for the quail-pit, and had won many mains."[532] Döllinger adds other dehumanizing indignities suffered by Roman slaves:[533]

'The unhappy slave (in his master's presence) is not free to move his lips, even for speaking. Whispering is silenced with the rod: even accidental acts, like coughing, sneezing, or hiccuping, meet with the same retribution. Every sound to break the silence has a heavy penance attached to it: they have to continue the whole night through fasting and dumb; we abuse them, in fact, not as if they were men, but beasts of burden....'

As it seldom happened any crime was committed without the aid or privity of slaves, their masters had often urgent grounds for putting such dangerous witnesses out of the way, or making them incapable of doing harm. Cicero mentions the case of a slave being crucified, but not till he had had his tongue cut out to prevent his betraying his mistress. Martial records a similar case of a master cutting his slaveys tongue out, and alleging it had been done by others....

There were instances of masters having their slaves hands cut off....

Many European storytellers place the punishing lives European slaves endured roughly on the same level as a nagging hangnail. There are anecdotes of slaves having to amuse their owners by hopping on one foot, or having to beat the waters surrounding castles to quiet down croaking

---

[531] Roger L'Estrange, trans., *Seneca's Morals A Happy Life, Benefits, Anger and Clemency* (Chicago: Belford, Clarke, & Co., 1882), pp. 315-16.
[532] Döllinger, *Gentile*, p. 261.
[533] Ibid., p. 261.

frogs. This trivialization of European slavery may have much to do with cultural narcissism that constrains members to whitewashing over harsh realities. Besides that, stories of slaves forced to do menial tasks make everyone laugh, so they feel comfortable about their status. Others, like Döllinger, are more forthright in their observations of this regressive system that victimizes all participants (willing and unwilling) psychologically: "It is in vain one looks for any thing like common human feeling in the Roman slave-law of republican times and that of the earlier empire. The breaking-up of slave families was entirely in the hands of the merchant or the owner; husband might be separated from wife, and mother from children, all dispersed and sold off into the houses of strangers and foreign towns. Slavery is equivalent to death in the eye of the civil law, which does not admit the existence of the slave; which entirely avoids and annuls the contract of a master with his slave; gives the slave no action at law against him; admits not of adultery being committed by or with one of them; makes over all a slave's earnings to his master; and compels female slaves to surrender themselves to their master's lust against their will."[534]

Slaves endured many humiliations and abuses. Because slaves lacked standing as human beings, they were given no civil protections. Depending on the era, they were at the complete mercy of the slave owner who controlled how they lived and, indeed, whether they lived, or died.[535] In the following passage, Salvian paints an interesting picture of the slavery in his day: "Insufficiently supplied by their avaricious masters with the bare necessaries of life, they were almost compelled to rob in order to keep soul and body together, and the masters, however they might affect to blame their thievish habits, knew in their secret hearts that no other resource was left to them.... The common herd of slaves suffered torment from the fellow-slaves who were set over them. The steward, the driver, the confidential valet, were so many petty tyrants who made the life of the poor drudge, whether in the house or in the field, well-nigh unendurable. Sometimes, in desperation, a slave would fly from his fellow-slaves to their common master, and would find a shade more of compassion from him than from them."[536]

Though slaves seeking relief from their slave owner may have been a pointless exercise. Döllinger informs us that owners holding lots of slaves knew only a few of them. Anyway, considering the times they lived, it is doubtful there were very many of those compassionate masters idling about.

Escaping from their masters' estates was the only remedy for some

---

[534] Ibid., pp. 263-64.
[535] One punishment was to send slaves to fight against the wild beasts in the arena.
[536] Hodgkin, *Italy*, vol. 1, pp. 928-29.

slaves desperate for relief. But, as was the case during the antebellum South, capturing runaways spawned an entire industry of slave-catchers, though captured escapees reaped some serious penalties:

> Terrible was the fate of such as endeavoured to escape ill-treatment, either in city or country, by flight. The tracking and recapture of runaway slaves formed a trade of its own, that of the fugitivarii. Recovered slaves were branded on the forehead, and their sum of ill-treatment and labour doubled; or, in case the master was indifferent to the life of his slave, he was thrown to the wild-beasts in the amphitheatre.[537]

And as if all that violence was not enough to deter future escapees, returned slaves were crucified, too. Europeans may not have been all that helpful to runaways; harboring such people was against Roman law, and anyone offering refuge to a runaway became a slave. In the following passage Seneca chastises slave owners, but appears to lack an understanding of human equality, as he (in line with the times) refers to humans as chattel and classifies them as being of a lower status:

> It is creditable to a man to keep within reasonable bounds in his treatment of his slaves. Even in the case of a human chattel one ought to consider, not how much one can torture him with impunity, but how far such treatment is permitted by natural goodness and justice, which prompts us to act kindly towards even prisoners of war and slaves bought for a price (how much more towards free-born, respectable gentlemen?), and not to treat them with scornful brutality as human chattels, but as persons somewhat below ourselves in station, who have been placed under our protection rather than assigned to us as servants. Slaves are allowed to run and take sanctuary at the statue of a god, though the laws allows a slave to be ill-treated to any extent, there are nevertheless some things which the common laws of life forbid us to do to a human being. Who does not hate Vedius Pollio more even than his own slaves did, because he used to fatten his lampreys with human blood, and ordered those who had offended him in any way to be cast into his fish-pond, or rather snake-pond? That man deserved to die a thousand deaths, both for throwing his slaves to be devoured by the lampreys which he himself meant to eat, and for keeping lampreys that he might feed them in such a fashion. Cruel masters are pointed at with disgust in all parts of the city, and are hated and loathed; the wrong-doings of kings are enacted on a wider theatre: their shame and unpopularity endures for ages: yet how far better it would have been never to have been born than to be numbered among those who have been born to do their country harm![538]

---

[537] Döllinger, *Gentile*, p. 260.
[538] Seneca, *Seneca*, pp. 404-05.

The following accounts of Roman slavery from Bury sounds ominously and perilously close to a narrative on the antebellum South:

> The economical position of slaves requires some notice also. In theory they were simply instruments of their master; what they acquired passed at once to him; they were not capable of having property of their own, he was responsible for them as he was for any other domestic animal that he kept. But in practice slaves were usually allowed to accumulate property out of their savings or from gifts, and the law by a fiction allowed them to use it in purchasing their own freedom. Such quasi-property was called their *peculium* ("petty stock"): it existed only so long as their master chose; he could withdraw it, but rarely did so, except for grave offences [sic]. But so long as it existed and his master gave him a free hand, a slave could trade with it and enter into all kinds of business transactions ostensibly for himself, but in the eye of the law for the master's account. He could not however give away anything, and he had no *locus standi* in court: he could sue and be sued only in the name of his master. If he was freed by his master when living, the *peculium* was deemed to accompany him, unless expressly withdrawn. But if he was freed by will or alienated, it did not pass with him unless expressly granted."[539]

Revisionists like to mention the church influence in decreasing slavery. The 15th century papal bulls authorizing the conquest and subjugation of Africans sets the record straight: any African forcefully removed from her homeland, then forced to labor for free is proof enough of the whitewashing of that particular part of history. Duruy writes the following on the church's complicity in the slave trade: "The great evil of the ancient civilization had been slavery. The church mitigated it in a fatherly spirit, for the reason that of which Julian speaks with envy. In his will Saint Gregory bequeaths 'to the Russian virgin' two maid-servants, who, after her, shall belong to the church Nazianen. When, in the fifth century, the body of the clergy became the greatest land-owners in the Empire, they had, as such, multitudes of slaves, whom they treated mildly; but while they favored enfranchisements by private individuals, they did not enfranchise themselves for they needed all these laborers to cultivate their vast domains. Softened in character, but still preserved by the Church, slavery was maintained by Constantine, who in certain cases increased the rigor of the penal laws applicable to slaves as such; and this severity of the first Christian Emperor was not likely to inspire more pity in the hearts of those masters who had not learned compassion from the teaching of the gospel."[540] Cristoforo Colombo's (aka Columbus) first *gifts* to the church from his voyage were slaves (as though gifts can be made of humans).

---

[539] Bury, *Cambridge*, vol. 2, p. 63.
[540] Duruy, *Rome*, vol. 8, pt. 1, pp. 38-40.

Perhaps the most revealing information comes from the writings of Mommsen from which I quote liberally:

> While the captives taken in war and the hereditary transmission of slavery sufficed to keep up the stock of slaves during the earlier period, this system of slavery was, just like that of America, based on the methodically prosecuted hunting of man; for, owing to the manner in which slaves were used with little regard to their life or propagation, the slave population was constantly on the wane, and even the wars which were always furnishing fresh masses to the slave market were not sufficient to cover the deficit. No country where this species of game could be hunted remained exempt from visitation; even in Italy it was a thing by no means unheard of, that the poor freeman was placed by his employer among the slaves.
>
> But the Negroland of that period was *western Asia, where the Cretan and Cilician corsairs [pirates], the real professional slave hunters and slave-dealers, robbed the coasts of Syria and the Greek islands; and where, emulating their feats, the Roman revenue-farmers instituted human hunts in the client states and incorporated those whom they captured among their slaves. This was done to such an extent, that about 650 the king[541] of Bithynia [northwestern modern Turkey; once a province of Rome] declared himself unable to furnish the required contingent, because all the people capable of labour [sic] had been dragged off from his kingdom by the revenue-farmers. At the great slave market in Delos, where the slave-dealers of Asia Minor disposed of their wares to Italian speculators, on one day as many as 10,000 slaves are said to have been disembarked in the morning and to have been all sold before evening—a proof at once how enormous was the number of slaves delivered, and how, notwithstanding, the demand still exceeded the supply. It was no wonder.
>
> Already in describing the Roman economy of the sixth century we have explained that it was based, like all the great dealings of antiquity generally, on the employment of slaves (ii. 434 et seq. 451). In whatever direction speculation applied itself, its instrument was invariably man reduced in law to the status of a beast of burden. Trades were in great part carried on by slaves, so that the proceeds belonged to the master. The levying of the public revenues in the lower departments was regularly conducted by the slaves of the associations that leased them. Servile hands performed the operations of mining, making pitch, and others of a similar kind; it became early the custom to send herds of slaves to the Spanish mines, whose superintendents readily received them and

---

[541] "When Marius, at the command of the senate, required Nicomedes, king of Bithynia, to supply his contingent of auxiliary troops, the king replied he had no subjects fit for service, for nearly all his able-bodied men had been carried off by Roman collectors of customs, converted into slaves, and dispersed among the different provinces." John J. I. Döllinger, *The Gentile and The Jew in The Courts of the Temple Of Christ: An Introduction to the History of Christianity*, vol. 2, p. 262.

paid a high rent for them.

The vine and olive harvest in Italy was not conducted by the people on the estate, but was contracted for by a slave-owner. The tending of cattle was universally performed by slaves. We have already mentioned the armed, and frequently mounted, slave-herdsmen in the great pastoral districts of Italy (ii. 441); and the same, sort of pastoral husbandry soon became in the provinces also a favourite [sic] object of Roman speculation—Dalmatia, for instance, was hardly acquired (599) when the Roman capitalists began to prosecute the rearing of cattle there on a great scale after the Italian fashion.

But far worse in every respect was the plantation-system proper—the cultivation of the fields by a band of slaves not unfrequently [sic] branded with iron, who with shackles on their legs performed the labours [sic] of the field under overseers during the day, and were locked up together by night in the common, frequently subterranean, labourers' [sic] prison [ergastula]. This plantation-system had migrated from the East to Carthage (ii. 16), and seems to have been brought by the Carthaginians to Sicily, where, probably for this reason, it appears developed earlier and more fully than in any other part of the Roman dominions.[542]

Döllinger summarizes the centuries-long industry of Roman slavery similar in so very ways to the system instituted hundreds of years later in the United States and the Americas:[543]

The slave in Rome was a chattel and a possession, had no individuality or "caput;" whatever he earned belonged to his master, and he might be made a present of, lent, pawned, or exchanged. His union with a wife was no marriage, that is, was devoid of all its privileges and effects, and only a contubernium, or cohabitation. A master might torture or kill his slave at will; there was no one to prevent his doing so, or to bring him to account. The modes of torture and punishment were various and cruel, and the ordinary punishment of death was crucifixion [hanging]. Every thing was allowable and privileged as against a slave. There was nothing a master could not do, and a great deal that any freeman could....

The numerous female slaves in personal attendance on their mistresses were often obliged to perform their various services with shoulders and bosom bare, that their nudity might intensify their feelings of pain. One cruel infliction, and not unfrequently [sic] resorted to; was chaining to a block of wood, which served the poor sufferer for a seat, and "which she had to drag about with her day and night. This was the ordinary meed of such as had provoked the

---

[542] Mommsen, *Rome*, vol. 3, pp. 100-02.
[543] Döllinger, *Gentile*, pp. 259-60.

jealousy of their mistress.

Duruy is here given the last words on an ancient European institution that still plagues "modern" societies, including the United States: "A society in which existed so many forms of servitude, and in which so many men were striving to escape from the condition into which they had been born, was, indeed, sick unto death."[544]

---

[544] Duruy, *Rome*, vol. 8, pt. 1, p. 40.

7

MEDIEVAL ATTRACTIONS: GLADIATORS MUST "DIE BECOMINGLY"

(Attraction [ə' trak SH ən] noun
Entertainment or diversions that *bring pleasure*)[545]

"Let it not be imagined that these spectators were the refuse of the people; the most distinguished orders of the state delighted in these cruel amusements, even the Vestal virgins [pre-Christian priestesses] being placed with great ceremony in the front rows in the amphitheatre...."[546]

Many modern critics describe the ancient games of Rome as absurd distractions for the masses. In fact, gladiator games were the violent video games of their day. Juvenal called them panem et circenses, bread and circuses. He laments the crazed obsession for pleasure presented to Romans willfully manipulated by handfuls of pathological and monomaniacal tyrants who kept subjugated citizens distracted from their awful plight. For as long as the state provided grain and games people remained content. And while games certainly distracted citizens from their own pain-filled lives, strictly speaking, they were hardly silly. In fact, gladiatorial games were utterly bloody. Visualizing the types of weaponry used in these competitive amusements is critical to appreciating just how ferocious they were. Horatio Smith and Samuel Woodworth reveals the lengths event promoters went to assure blood-soaked contests: "Not only was art exhausted, and every incentive applied to perfect the skill and animate the courage of the unhappy victims so that they might die becomingly: but the utmost ingenuity was employed in varying and rendering more terrible the murderous weapons with which they were to butcher one another."[547]

According to Smith and Woodworth, authors of *Festivals, Games and Amusements, Ancient and Modern*, there were several classes of gladiators characterized entirely by their attire and weaponry. Gladiators fought in pairs, on chariots, and on horseback. There were even female and blindfolded gladiators, too. The weapons of choice for them included: long

---

[545] There were exhibitions of "racing, in the Circus; plays, in the Theatre; gymnastics, in the Stadium; gladiators and fighting with beasts, in the Amphitheatre."
[546] Smith and Woodworth *Festivals*, p. 85.
[547] Ibid., p 85.

and short-bladed swords; lead-bearing clubs; short swords with curved blades, called scimitars; three-pronged spears called tridents; weighted nets, and concealed leaded daggers. Another weapon was the caestus (battle glove). It originated from a Greek sport called pankration (no-holds-barred mixed boxing-wrestling). Gladiators filled these *boxing gloves* with sharp, metal objects – such as blades and spikes, and used them to bludgeon opponents to death. It was not unusual for some gladiators to be armed from head to toe. A round shield held by the handle, called a buckler, was both a defensive and offensive weapon.

Though the games' out-and-out brutality was an issue now and then, as long as people remained entertained by them emperors delighted in keeping them in operation. Starting out at first as a way to honor the gods[548] of Rome, the games grew to become the number one entertainment for Dark Ages people, rich, poor, young, and old. The game's motto might easily have been "when gladiators bleed, gladiators please" as Smith and Woodworth report that: "By varying the arms it was proposed to diversify the mode of their death...."[549] Apparently in these spectacularly bloody exhibitions, variety was the spice of death: How gladiators died was far more important than how they lived, as the lyrics of William Shakespeare eloquently affirm:

> Let us be sacrificers, but no butchers, Caius.
> Let's kill him boldly, but not wrathfully;
> Let's carve him as a dish lit for the gods,
> Not hew him as a carcass for hounds!
> - William Shakespeare[550]

"He Is Wounded!" Human Carnage the #1 Medieval Entertainment

> Nor can men be familiarized to the sight of violence and blood, without being tempted to imitate that which they see a whole people applaud.[551]

There was a shameless type of entertainment during early Europe that citizens delighted in and secular leaders encouraged them to attend. They were known simply as games and were held in amphitheaters of the circuses Maximus (Circo Massimo), Flaminius, [552] Caligula, Neronis, Maxentius, etc.[553] Christian author, Tertullian, blames[554] the genesis of the

---

[548] Eventually both secular and non-secular games were held.
[549] Smith and Woodworth *Festivals*, p. 85.
[550] Charles Badham, trans., *Juvenal* (New York: Harper & Bros., 1837), p. 153.
[551] Ibid., p. 86.
[552] The Circus Flaminius in the Campus Martius was built in 221 B.C. by the C. Flaminius Nepos who was killed at the Trasimene Lake in 217 BCE; remains of the structure existed until the 16th century. Middleton and Jones, "Rome, Places of Amusement," p. 605.
[553] Gregorovius, *Rome*, vol. 1, pp. 22-30.

games on Lydians who migrated to Etruria, in present-day central Italy. A few historians believe it was there that Etruscans[555] produced public shows to honor ancient gods: "They are said to have been first exhibited by the Etruscans, and to have had their origin in the custom of killing slaves and captives at the funeral pyres of the deceased,"[556] writes Blake. The Romans watched the games, and then transported the performers to Rome, thereby instituting games of their own. Also, according to Blake, initially exhibitions served a funereal function:

> Gladiators were first exhibited at Rome in B. C. 264, in the Forum Boarium, by Marcus and Decimus Brutus, at the funeral of their father. They were at first confined to public funerals, but afterwards fought at the funerals of most persons of consequence, and even at those of women. Private persons sometimes left a sum of money in their will to pay the expenses of such an exhibition at their funerals. Combats of gladiators were also exhibited at entertainments, and especially at public festivals by the aediles and other magistrates, who sometimes exhibited immense numbers with a view of pleasing the people. Under the empire the passions of the Romans for this amusement rose to its greatest height, and the number of gladiators who fought on some occasions appears almost incredible. After Trajan's triumph over the Dacians, there were more than 10,000 exhibited.[557]

Döllinger adds: "Compulsory combats of these unfortunates [slaves]

---

[554] Dodgson, *Tertullian*, p. 194.
[555] The origin of Etruscans is a hotly debated topic amongst professionals and laypersons alike despite that the current Tuscan population was DNA-tested. Should Etruscans (they called themselves Ras or Rasena) prove to be of African ancestry it upsets the European narrative on the foundation of Rome. At least two of three founding families of Rome have Etruscan names: The Ramnes and Luceres: "'The Etruscans,' Dionysius said long ago, 'are like no other nation in language and manners.'" Mommsen, *Rome*, vol. 1, p. 109; "From the coasts of Syria and Africa, the more certain colonies which Tyre and Carthage established in the two great Italian islands. And if we were to trust to the patriotic pride of one of her historians, Etruria would owe to Egypt and the distant East her religious creeds, her arts, and her sacerdotal government." Duruy, vol. 1, pp. 44-45. Roman civilization grew from the foundation laid by Etruscans: "Rome received from Etruria, — the division into tribes, curiae, and centuries [sic], the order of battle, the dress of the magistrates, the laticlave, the praetexta, the toga, the apex, the curule chair, the lictors, all the display of the triumphs and public games, the nundinae, the sacred character of property, and the science of the augur, — that is to say, the state religion." Duruy, vol. 1, p. 134. As so often happens when Europeans conquer nations, the Etruscan's own history is blighted out; their literature destroyed. Finally, the Etruscans, "the most civilized of the Italian nations," had its own version of the Valley of the Kings, and incorporated KMT ancient symbol of rebirth, the scarab, into their artwork: "The Etruscans dug funereal chambers underground, or in the rocky sides of their hills. Some of these, as, for instance, in the valley of Castel d'Asso, have a singular likeness to those which are seen at Thebes in Egypt." Duruy, vol. 1, p. 82.
[556] Blake, *Slavery*, p. 53.
[557] Ibid.

were first established by private persons, as mortuary games; but in the last century of the republic became public amusements, forming part of the state expenditure, and therefore under the care of the aediles, which made their celebration periodical and fixed. Rich and distinguished individuals still indeed kept them up in honour of their dead at their private charges, but principally with a view to win popular favour [sic]. The number of combatants went on increasing."[558] However they began and by whomever, Romans dedicated games to patron[559] (sponsors) gods in much the same way sports teams today dedicate games to corporations (patrons) that sponsor them. Christian writer Tertullian (ca. 160-225 CE) tells us:

> For the amphitheatre is consecrated to deities more numerous and more barbarous than the Capitol. It is the temple of all daemons. As many unclean spirits there sit together as the place containeth [sic] men. To speak finally of the performances also, we know that Mars and Diana are the presiding deities of each game.[560]

Slaughtered Humans and Animals Sacrificed to Roman Gods

Tertullian complains much about Christians observing games "chiefly dedicated to the Sun."[561] Even their venue - the circus - identifies the deity worshippers dedicated games to: Circe, daughter of the Sun. In tribute to Circe, Romans designed their arenas in the shape of a circle, or ring. *Circle* comes to the Latin language from Circe.

Games became a national pastime. Attendance throughout their duration stayed high. Emperors controlled the games, and used them tactically to inflame soldiers marching to war and to excite citizens upon the warring victors' return home. Third century Roman Emperor Aurelian Augustus commanded that his Roman citizens enjoy the games, but demanded, too, that they leave state business to him: "Let me be concerned with the needs of the state, and do you busy yourselves with your pleasures."[562] He addressed the citizens without a hint of humor. Later Roman Emperor Marcus Aurelius Probus (d.ca. 282 CE) made the amphitheater so elaborate that designers duplicated forests and filled them with thousands of animals. Afterwards they let spectators hunt and take home what they managed to kill. Döllinger informs us that, "Caesar once brought 320 pair of gladiators into the arena; but Trajan on one occasion had 10,000 slaves engaged together, and prolonged the massacre 123 days.

---

[558] Döllinger, *Gentile*, p. 265.
[559] The root for patron is /patr/, father or protector.
[560] Dodgson, *Tertullian*, p. 203.
[561] Ibid., p. 197.
[562] David Magie, trans., *The Scriptores Historiae Augustae*, vol. 3 (Massachusetts: Harvard University Press), p. 395.

For a change, the Roman people enjoyed the baiting of wild-beasts, in which the bestiarii, for the most part condemned slaves, engaged lions, leopards, tigers, and other animals, which they had to face naked and weaponless, and sometimes actually chained together."[563]

Over the course of the games that lasted more than a thousand years, men slaughtered hundreds of thousands, or more likely, millions of animals - many of them tamed - to the delight of spectators. At other times, they flooded the arena with water so that naval battles consisting of thousands of men at a time took place. During these water spectacles, only the slaughter of an entire team ended the contests. And the teams were quite large:

> There were naval combats (naumachise), for which great reservoirs had to be excavated, and in these thousands were killed, or perished in the water, at a time, in one sham fight. Gladiators were selected from the strongest prisoners or slaves, Thracians, Gauls, Germans, or Sarmatians. At the leading schools of Ravenna, and in Campania, they were practised in different modes of fighting, and by that, as well as by variety of armour, a kind of relief to the monotony of carnage was obtained. In return for the abundant food which the lanista provided them with, they swore to suffer themselves to be burnt, fettered, and killed by the sword; and after living months and years in daily intercourse, they were necessitated to murder one another, like mortal foes, to please the spectators.[564]

Typically, the gladiators were prisoners, criminals, or, as we just learned, slaves; readers are probably familiar with stories of Romans feeding Christians to the lions. It was Emperor Nero who put on those infamously bloody displays in 64 CE after a fire destroyed much of Rome. He accused Christians of that devastation, then convicted them for "hatred of mankind":

> Accordingly, an arrest was first made of all who pleaded guilty; then, upon their information, an immense multitude was convicted, not so much of the crime of firing the city, as of hatred against mankind. Mockery of every sort was added to their deaths. Covered with the skins of beasts, they were torn by dogs and perished, or were nailed to crosses, or were doomed to the flames and burnt, to serve as a nightly illumination, when daylight had expired. Nero offered his gardens for the spectacle, and was exhibiting a show in the circus, while he mingled with the people in the dress of a charioteer or stood aloft on a car. Hence, even for criminals who deserved extreme and exemplary punishment, there arose a feeling of compassion; for it was not, as it seemed, for

---

[563] Döllinger, *Gentile*, p. 265-66.
[564] Ibid., p. 266.

the public good, but to glut one man's cruelty, that they were being destroyed.[565]

And, "Constantine, in the year before his acceptance of Christianity, gave a multitude of prisoners as prey to the wild beasts of the arena."[566] (There is the infamous tale, too, of Caligula throwing spectators into the arena to feed the wild beats after all the slaves and criminals had been defeated).

Though typically gladiators fell into one of the three earlier mentioned classes women and freeborn citizens became gladiators, too. Also, according to Blake, equites and senators fought in the arena. The typical lifespan of a gladiator was brief, as gladiatorial fights oftentimes ended only after an opponent had been mercilessly and brutally slain.

Apparently, the timing of a gladiator's death was a crucial feature of the *games*; audiences wanted to view a challenging battle, but craved bloodshed, too. Seneca complains of crowds that turned against gladiators unable to take the pains of injuries. Crowds expected severely wounded, but not yet dead gladiators to put on brave faces and continue the battle: "There are some motions that look like anger, which cannot properly be called so; as the passion of the people against the gladiators, when they hang off, and will not make so quick a dispatch as the spectators would have them.... They take it for a contempt, if the gladiators do not immediately cast themselves upon the sword's point. They look presently about them from one to another, as who should say, 'Do but see, my masters, how these rogues abuse us."[567] Romans further degraded gladiators by dragging their bodies from the arena floor with hooks. The Spanish picked up this degrading custom, dragging away dead bulls with hooks following bullfights.

Volunteers to the games took an oath to the lanistae (fight owners/managers) whose schools trained gladiators in fighting techniques. In fact, an entirely new moneymaking enterprise erupted from this degenerate industry that developed from what supposedly began as a somber ceremony: "A lucrative trade was pursued by the lanistae, who had the training of the slaves as gladiators, let them out to hire, and otherwise trafficked with them. Most of the powerful Romans maintained troops of gladiators, who at the same time served them as a body-guard in several instances. The fashion set by Rome now grew contagious. Schools (ludi) for gladiators arose in many places, and a passion for the sanguinary scenes of the arena possessed the inhabitants of all the cities of importance. Perseus had introduced them betimes into Macedonia; and Herod Agrippa, in

---

[565] Church and Brodribb, *Annals*, p. 305.
[566] Elliot, *Outlines*, p. 131.
[567] L'Estrange, *Seneca*, p. 309.

Judaea, made seven hundred couple fight in one day. The people of Pollentia, in Liguria, would not allow the body of a centurion to be buried until his heirs paid down a certain sum for a combat of gladiators."[568] Gladiators who fulfilled their contract were sometimes freed after three years, became famous, and usually handsomely rewarded.

The games sometimes continued from sun-up to sundown: "For which the day no longer sufficed, the combat being prolonged by torchlight,"[569] or lasted for days on end. Gibbon tells us:

> The impatient crowd rushed at the dawn of day to secure their places, and there were many who passed a sleepless and anxious night in the adjacent porticos. From morning to the evening, careless of the sun, or rain, the spectators, who sometimes amounted to the number of four hundred thousand, remained in eager attention; their eyes fixed on the horses and charioteers, their minds agitated with hope and fear, for the success of the *colors* which they espoused: and the happiness of Rome appeared to hang on the event of a race.[570]

Politics, Gambling Important Behind the Scenes Activities

Because there was competition, there was plenty of betting and gambling taking place, too. In fact, the 1910 Encyclopaedia Britannica records that the circus venue was a "political club, and fashionable lounge, a rendezvous of gallantry, a betting ring, and a playground for the million,"[571] containing restricted areas perhaps similar to today's luxurious owner's suites where the rich and politically-connected mingle and forge deals. Game contestants divided into factions. Rivalries developed between factions and led to teams and colors. Added to the original team colors of red (for the summer Sun), and white (for the ripe harvest), green (for Spring) and blue (for the sky)[572] were purple and gold, worn only for a short time.

Rowdy crowds identified with their favorite teams and players oftentimes to the point of bloodshed, as we read earlier with the murder of Theodosius' soldier. Color-coded emperors driving high-speed chariots further embroiled the passions of the masses to outrageous feuds, according to Gregorovius:

> (In 501, more than 3000 men were slain on the occasion of a combat between the Greens and Blues), still Rome also witnessed many a bloody scene." It is surprising," says Cassiodorus, "how, more than in any other game, the mind is carried away by unreasonable passion. A Green conquers, immediately half of

---

[568] Döllinger, *Gentile*, p. 265.
[569] Ibid., p. 265.
[570] Gibbon, *Decline*, vol. 3, pp. 263.
[571] Francis Store, "Games, Classical." *Encyclopaedia Britannica.* 11th ed. 1910. p. 445.
[572] Dodgson, *Tertullian*, p. 199.

the people lament; a Blue excels in running and the greater part of the city complains; do they win nothing, their insults increase; while if they lose nothing they feel themselves deeply aggrieved, and the unimportant strife occupies them as much as if the safety of their country depended on it."[573]

Nearly every man, woman and child, regardless of social station, is said to have taken pleasure in viewing their favorite competitors. Tertullian laments, "He, who guardeth the ears of his virgin daughter from every lewd word, doth himself carry her to the theatre to such words and actions: and the very man, who in the streets restraineth or protesteth against one that carrieth on a quarrel by blows, doth in the race-course give his voice in favour of more serious battles: and he who shuddereth at the corpse of a man that hath died in common course, doth in the amphitheatre bend down most enduring eyes upon bodies mangled and torn in pieces and begrimed with their own blood."[574] The largest venue, Circus Maximus, could seat 240,000 spectators, though there are estimates of its capacity being closer to 350,000[575]- 400,000.

Chariot racing, car racing's probable predecessor, was a choice sport. Spectators watched from wooden[576] seats as their most prized players sped wildly around the arena in war engines drawn by either two or four horses. Apparently outrageous speeds were essential in building excitement: "Chariots with two horse [sic] or four were common, but sometimes also they had three and exceptionally more than four horses. Occasionally there was combined with the chariots a race of riders (desultores), each rider having two horses and leaping from one to the other during the race."[577] The races started after a magistrate tossed a white flag. Racing chariots could be an extremely brutal activity as chariot-drivers attacked each other as they nudged their vehicles against the other rigs attempting to overturn them. The barbarity of the races spilled over into the stands as spectators attacked each other, too. The rivalry between color-coded spectators was fierce with Emperors joining in backing their favorite teams:

> The exciting four horse chariot-races of the circus, which were held, usually on Sunday, in the great Hippodrome seating thirty thousand men — for women did not attend. The spectators took sides according to the colors worn by their favorite charioteers, and occupied blocks of seats reserved for their respective colors. Thus arose the two great parties of Greens and Blues, who divided the city and who often carried their rivalry to the point of animosity and blows. These two factions could, at least on occasion, become political parties.

---

[573] Gregorovius, *Rome*, vol.1, p. 306.
[574] Dodgson, *Tertullian*, p. 211.
[575] Smith and Woodworth cite Pliny as the source for this number, p. 94.
[576] The moneyed folks had reserved seating on concrete benches on the lower decks.
[577] "Circus." *Encyclopaedia Britannica*. 11th ed. 1910. p. 390.

Anastasius had favored the Greens. Justinian and Theodora adhered to the Blues.[578]

Foot races, horse races, and animal combats were held, also. But, seemingly the most popular games involved blood sport that resulted in the loss of limbs and plenty of lives. It is disquieting to learn that games that focused on bloodletting and humans being torn to shreds by men and beasts[579] alike lasted for a thousand years, yet reveals the prolonged stagnation of early European societies. Smith and Woodworth report that the public's fascination with seeing fresh blood spilled on the arena floor affected the gladiator's diet: "They were fed upon barley cakes and other fattening aliments, in order that the blood might flow slowly from their wounds, and that the spectators might enjoy as long as possible the sight of their dying agonies."[580] We will learn much more on Europe's ritual use of gladiator blood in Chapter 12.

Tertullian appealed in earnest to the citizens of his day to reject the games that highlighted the lack of humanity of its spectators. He writes plainly about what apparently had become a celebrated blood ritual:

> They too, who in the games, in the theatre have drunk with greedy thirst the fresh blood streaming from the neck of the butchered criminals to cure the falling sickness, where are they? They too, who from the stage sup on the meat of wild beasts, who fetch it from the boar, from the stag? That boar hath from the man, whom he hath covered with blood, in struggling with him, wiped it off. That stag hath lain in the blood of a gladiator. The paunches of the very bears are in request, reeking yet with undigested human entrails. The flesh which hath been fed on a man forthwith riseth in the stomach of a man.
>
> Ye that eat these things, how far removed are ye from the feasts of the Christians? And they too, who with brutal appetite seize on human bodies, do they do the less because they devour the living? Are they the less consecrated to filthiness by human blood, because what they take up hath yet to become blood? They feed not indeed on infants, but on those of riper age.... Moreover what manner of thing is it to believe that they, who ye are assured abhor the blood of beasts, pant for human blood? unless perchance ye have found it sweeter![581]

---

[578] Thorndike, *Europe*, p. 132.
[579] During his reign Emperor Probus let loose 600 lionesses, bears and leopards against 600 gladiators. Magie, *Scriptores*, vol. 3, p. 377.
[580] Smith and Woodworth *Festivals*, p. 85.
[581] Dodgson, *Tertullian*, pp. 22-23.

Deadly Games Blur Lines Between Reality and Fantasy

Tertullian knew of what he spoke. The pleasure Europeans received from bloodlust events blurred the line between fantasy and reality, as was the case during the fall-winter of 69 CE. The following terrifying scenes take place after soldiers enter the gates of the city in the midst of one of the many ancient battles for the throne of Rome:

> The populace looked on at the fighting as at a [circus] spectacle, cheering and encouraging, now one side, now the other. Whenever either side gave way, they would tell of some who were hiding in taverns, or had taken refuge in private houses, and suggest that they should be dragged out and butchered, securing thereby most of the plunder for themselves; for while the soldiers were intent on blood and slaughter, the spoils fell to the mob. The city everywhere presented a hideous and monstrous aspect: bloody fights at one place, baths and cookshops at another pools of blood and piles of dead bodies, with prostitutes and their like standing by; all the lusts of luxurious ease, with all the crimes and cruelties usual at the capture of cities, till one felt that the whole community had gone mad, at one and the same time, both with rage and lust. Battles, indeed, between armed hosts had been fought in the city before, and with no less cruelty - twice when Lucius Sulla, once when Cinna, was the victor. But on this occasion there was an inhuman indifference; not for one moment were pleasures intermitted. Men triumphed and enjoyed themselves as if a new zest had been added to that holiday season, caring nothing for either cause, and exulting in the calamities of their country.[582]

Viewing combatants slaughter each other is another startling tradition carried forward by Anglo-Americans who gathered close by to watch U.S. civil war battles. More recently cameras went live when the U.S. bombed Iraq, and Israelis picnicked on nearby hills while Israeli armed forces dropped bombs on Palestinian neighborhoods.

In the ancient days of Europe, the punishment for spectators cheering on eventual losers of battles was lavish. In Cremona, mentioned earlier in the essay, supporters of Vitellius and others who happened to be in the city attending a winter festival soon lost their own lives:

> Forty thousand armed men now burst into the city, together with sutlers and camp followers in greater number-a crowd still more prone to acts of lust and violence. *No age, no dignity, was a protection.* Ravishing was mixed up with slaughter; and slaughter followed upon outrage. *Old men and women, well stricken in years and of no value for plunder, were maltreated by way of sport. Grown-up maidens or comely youths that came in the way were violently torn to pieces by ravishers, who ended by falling in murderous conflict upon each other. Men carrying off*

---

[582] George Gilbert Ramsay, *Histories*, pp. 289-90.

for themselves money or offerings of solid gold from the temples, were hewn down by others stronger than themselves. Others, not satisfied with the plunder ready to their hand, plied owners with lash and torture in their hunt for hidden or buried treasure; bearing torches in their hands, they threw them by way of sport into the vacant houses and temples as soon as they had emptied them of their valuables. In an army so varied in character and in tongue, made up of citizens, allies, and foreigners, every man had his own cupidities, each was a rule unto himself, and nothing was unlawful.

Cremona lasted them for four whole days. And when every other building, sacred and profane, had sunk into the flames, the temple of Mefitis alone, outside the walls, survived: protected, perhaps, by its situation-perhaps by the divinity. Such was the end of Cremona, in the 286th year from its foundation....[583](Italics added).

Christian Leaders Despise the Games

Returning to the subject of the games, Smith and Woodworth write that the people willingly exchanged their freedom for these public spectacles:

During the republic it was... the interest of the emperors to pacify and keep in subjection... a people avowedly desiring nothing but bread and the public spectacles... The wealth of a conquered world enabled the imperial despots to gratify this propensity on the most magnificent scale; and their subjects, therefore, had probably in exchange for their loss of liberty a greater share of festivals, exhibitions, and holidays than any nation that ever existed. Truly they [the people] had sold their birthright for a mess of pottage.[584]

While there are notable similarities in the *bread and circus* politics of the past and present, today few Americans in dire need receive an adequate amount of food from the government and some games have been shifted to pay-per-view audiences. Yet, it is important to know the political motives for public games. Smith and Woodworth elaborate on a few behind the scenes motives for the early games in Athens:

In the time of Homer [8th century BCE], when murders were so common that they scarcely left a stain upon the character of the perpetrator, and human sacrifices were still offered to the gods, and to the manes of the dead, we cannot expect to discover any thing refined, still less intellectual, in the amusements or recreations. These were groveling and sensual, while the public games, being simply calculated to exercise and strengthen the bodily powers, were but personal struggles, scarcely amicable in their nature, and evidently intended as

---

[583] *Ibid.*, p. 240.
[584] Smith and Woodworth, *Festivals*, p. 76.

preparations for war.[585]

In modern times, sporting events are accompanied by overt militaristic jingoism providing evidence for two basic points: Anglo-Americans, like their forefathers in Europe, find it profitable to connect games with war and the minds of the American public are being manipulated. According to Smith and Woodworth: "War was considered the paramount business of life"[586] and the games were imitations of military exercises. Despite the games' popularity and militaristic overtones, Christian leadership often berated citizens for reveling in them. Constantine sought the games' end:

> [He], by a constitution of a.d. 325... had, indeed, forbidden those games of bloodshed; but the passions of the populace, stronger than law, had not only protected their pleasures, but insisted on making the princes accomplices in them, so that the victories of Theodosius still provided gladiators for the amphitheatres of Borne. Vainly did the eloquence of the Fathers ring against these bloody amusements; vainly did the poet Prudentius, in pathetic verse, press Honorius to command that death should cease to be a sport, and murder a public pleasure. But charity accomplished what no earthly power had dared commence.[587]

Salvian, an outspoken critic of the times, rebuked Christians whose special fondness for the circus games rivaled their love for the church. Salvian seems at his wits ends as he describes atrocities taking place as city after city falls to barbarian invaders. He describes the drunkenness and raucous revelry that attended the breeching of city walls, mournfully reminding his readers that barbarians sacked Gaul on several occasions. Salvian writes the following concerning a calamity happening at the same time games were underway:

> Outside the walls, as I have said, and inside them too, was heard the din of battle and of the games; the voices of dying men mingled with the voices of revellers [sic]; the outcry of the people slain in the war could scarcely be distinguished from the clamor of those who shouted in the circus....[588] The whole Roman world is at once wretched and voluptuous. What poor man is also wanton? What man awaiting captivity thinks of the circus? Who laughs in the shadow of death? Yet we, in the fear of captivity, continue to frequent the games, and shadowed by the fear of death, we laugh. You would think the whole Roman people had been steeped in Sardonic[589] herbs: they are dying, yet

---

[585] Ibid., pp. 32-33.
[586] Ibid., p. 17.
[587] Ozanam, *Fifth Century*, p. 121.
[588] Sanford, *Government*, p. 179.
[589] Sanford notes this is an ancient proverbial expression used by Isidore, et al: "The herb recalled by many writers and poets, which contracts men's jaws and kills them while they

they laugh.⁵⁹⁰

He was just as perplexed that in Treves blood sports fans cried out for the circuses to continue even as the city lay in a pile of rubble, as we learned earlier: "'Citizens of Trier, do you ask for games? And that, when your country had been laid waste, when your city has been taken, after the bloodshed, the tortures, the captivity and all the calamities of your ruined town? What can be the folly? I confess I thought you of all men most miserable when I heard of the destruction of your city? But I think you more miserable now when you are begging for games.... So then, oh man of Trier! Thou askest for public amusements. Where, pray, shall they be celebrated? Over the tombs, over ashes, over the bones and the blood of the slain? What part of the city is free from these dread sights? Everywhere there is the appearance of a sacked city, everywhere the horror of captivity, everywhere the image of death.... The city is black with her burning, and wilt thou put on the sleek face of the merry-maker? All around thee mourns, and wilt thou rejoice? Nay, more, wilt thou with thy flagitious delights provoke the Most High, and draw the wrath of God upon thee by the vilest idolatries? I do not wonder now, I do not wonder that all these evils have befallen thee. For if three catastrophes failed to correct thee, though deserveth to perish by the fourth.'"⁵⁹¹

Children Gladiators

"The butcheries of the Coliseum" continued in one form or another across Europe preserved by a feudal system that reinforced the worst imagined human behaviors. Most often the butcheries occurred during bloody neighborhood and civil wars. Of course, the greedy barons instigated these catastrophes. However, there were occasions when Europe's appetite for bloody delights turned their average moms and dads into formidable aggressors. They became part of the crazed mobs; and mob mentality ruled Europe. Ozanam explains below:

> If the Italy of the Middle Ages did not actually revive the gladiatorial conflicts, she did not renounce bloody spectacles. At Ravenna, at Orvieto, and at Sienna, *custom had fixed certain days upon which two bands of their citizens took up arms and slaughtered each other for the amusement of the mob.* ⁵⁹²

It is likely (or not, considering the times) that these *mob meet-ups* involve adults only. More perplexing are the maddened mobs that flex their *no*

---

seem to laugh."
⁵⁹⁰ Ibid., p. 190.
⁵⁹¹ Hodgkin, *Italy*, vol. 1, pp. 930-31.
⁵⁹² Ozanam, *Fifth Century*, p. 130.

holds barred types of mentalities during the 14th century. These moms and pops look on in amusement as their own children are butchered. The Italian poet Petrarch provides the backstory in 1346 by writing of "armed noble youth" roaming the streets of Naples terrorizing the population. Petrarch blames their actions on "a curious survival of the cruel classic days."[593] He is speaking of the continuation of the hellish gladiatorial games in that part of the country, but in this instance the games involve the noble youths. Petrarch gasps as parents and other onlookers gather in a wide circle to watch calmly as their children engage in ferocious combats for their life. Ozanam informs us that it is on these occasions that the father's glory comes "in the coolness with which [sons] receive the death-blow." The poet was so disturbed by the sight of children doing bloody battle that he fled from the sight and the city. His account of events follows:

> "But can it be astonishing," Petrarch remarks," that such disgraceful scenes should pass in the night, when the Neapolitans celebrate, even in the face of day, games similar to those of the gladiators, and *with more than barbarian cruelty?* Human blood is shed here with as little remorse as that of brute animals; and, *while the people join madly in applause, sons expire in the very sight of their parents*; and it is considered the utmost disgrace not to die with becoming fortitude, as if they were dying in the defence [sic] of their religion and country. I myself, ignorant of these customs, was once carried to the Carbonara, the destined place of butchery. The queen and her husband, Andrew, were present; the soldiery of Naples were present, and the people flocked thither in crowds. I was kept in suspense by the appearance of so large and brilliant an assembly, and expected some spectacle worthy of my attention, when I suddenly heard a loud shout of applause, as for some joyous incident. *What was my surprise when I beheld a beautiful young man pierced through with a sword, and ready to expire at my feet!* Struck with horror, I put spurs to my horse, and fled from the barbarous sight, uttering execrations on the cruel spectators.
>
> "*This inhuman custom has been derived from their ancestors, and is now so sanctioned by inveterate habit, that their very licentiousness is dignified with the name of liberty.*
>
> "You will cease to wonder at the imprisonment of your friends in this city, where *the death of a young man is considered as an innocent pastime*. As to myself, I will quit this inhuman country before three days are past...."[594] (Italics added).

This particular narrative informs us that these types of spectacularly bloody spectacles had become customary. It sounds an alarm regarding recent movies that threaten to desensitize us to children waging bloody battles against other children. It is shocking to learn that medieval youth engaged in blood sports during the Middle Ages. Smith and Woodworth describe Sunday evening entertainment in Spain: "In many towns bulls are lent to form the Sunday-evening amusement of the children of the place....

---

[593] Marie-Louise Egerton Castle, "Petrarch at Naples," *The Treasury*, vol. 11 (1908) p. 555.
[594] Thomas Campbell, *Life and Times of Petrarch*, pp. 265-66.

where he is subjected for some hours to all the ingenuity of his young tormentors."[595] A similar type of sociopathy was on display centuries earlier during the Paris massacre of 1418 when children played games with corpses. Spartans first devised military dances for children to engage them in blood sports and war games:

> [For] ...*early excitation of the courage of their children, and to lead them on insensibly to the exercise of the armed dance...This warlike people exercised their children, at it from the age of five years* to the accompaniment of hymns and songs... three choirs—one of children, another of young men, and the third of old. The latter opened the dance, saying, "In time past we were valiant." The young men answered, "We are so at present." To which the chorus of children replied, "We shall be still more so when our time comes." The Spartans never danced but with real arms.[596] (Italics added).

War dances, called pyrrhic dances, were patterned after ancient German youth who "stripped themselves and danced along the edges of sword and spears."[597] Tacitus writes, "Naked youths who practise [sic] the sport bound in the dance amid swords and lances that threaten their lives. Experience gives them skill, and skill again gives grace; profit or pay are out of the question; however reckless their pastime, its reward is the pleasure of the spectators. Strangely enough they make games of hazard a serious occupation even when sober, and so venturesome are they about gaining or losing, that, when every other resource has failed, on the last and final throw they stake the freedom of their own persons."[598]

Spectators Murder a Monk Attempting to Stop the Deadly Games

Ultimately, a lack of funds and ruined cities made sponsoring games impractical. The games, which began in the sixth century BCE, began to subside a thousand years later. (Though as we have read in the previous paragraphs the games did not completely disappear). It was at that time that spectators pelted the monk Telemachus to death with stones. The brave Telemachus, a fierce challenger to the games, placed his immortal soul between raging spectators and the games they adored:

> An Eastern monk, named Telemachus... took up his staff one day and journeyed to Borne, to put down the gladiatorial combats.... The arena had already been reddened with the blood of several pairs of gladiators, when suddenly... a monk appeared, rushed forward with outstretched arms, and

---

[595] Smith and Woodworth, *Festivals*, p. 185.
[596] Ibid. pp. 196-97.
[597] Ibid. p. 198.
[598] Church and Brodribb, *Agricola*, p. 105.

forced the swords asunder... the astonished audience rose as one man... then curses, threats, and finally stones, rained from every circle. Telemachus fell dead.[599]

Mildly Tamer Medieval Games

Other medieval games enjoyed by players included gambling, dice, ("So addicted to dice were the Germans and other barbarians of the north, that, according to Tacitus, after having lost every thing else, they would frequently stake their freedom upon the hazard of a die.");[600] chess, backgammon, ("After dice, chess and backgammon appear to have been the most favourite [sic] sedentary amusements of the Saxons and Danes, and to have occasionally occupied a large portion of the night.");[601] cards, cock-throwing, and cock-fighting ("The common account of it is, that the crowing of a cock prevented our Saxon ancestors from massacring their conquerors the Danes, on the morning of a Shrove Tuesday, while asleep in their beds.");[602] and running of the bulls, bull-baiting, and bear-baiting ("Of a bear-baiting exhibited before Queen Elizabeth in 1575... thirteen bears were provided for the occasion.... They were baited with a great sort of [specially bred for fighting] bandogs...."[603] Bear-baiting comes with this awful afterword: "To this entertainment there often follows that of whipping a blinded bear, which is performed by five or six men standing circularly with whips, which they exercise on him without mercy, as he cannot escape from them because of his chain."[604]

Smith and Woodworth properly sum up the cruelty inherent to many of their games, "I wish I knew how to answer this reproach which is cast upon us, and excuse the death of so many innocent cocks, bulls, dogs, and bears, as have been set together by the ears, or died an untimely death only to make us sport."[605] However, this statement neglects to mention the great number of human lives taken away for sport.

De Spectacula: Bawdy and Deadly Theatrics

The Roman taste for bloodshed was sometimes gratified by mimes given in the amphitheatre, and designed to introduce the actual execution of a criminal.[606]

In the so-called post-medieval era we find ourselves living in today, social

---

[599] Ozanam, *Fifth Century*, pp. 121-22.
[600] Smith and Woodworth *Festivals*, p. 34.
[601] Ibid., p 98.
[602] Ibid., p 118.
[603] Smith and Woodworth *Festivals*, p. 188.
[604] Ibid., p 108.
[605] Ibid., p 189.
[606] Edmund Kerchever Chambers, *The Mediaeval Stage*, vol. 1, p. 5.

commentators pointing out the moral degradation of our society tell us that before long American audiences will be entertained by televised scenes of live executions. Who could have guessed that the theatre of the past actually featured death as a part of the show? We have read how important the games and circuses were to medieval Europeans, but just how important was the theatre to the medieval world? Shakespearean scholar Edmund Kerchever Chambers reminds us that, "The citizens of Tréves, three[607] times destroyed, still called upon their rulers for... theatre."[608] On the stages of theaters actors performed plays; nobles disgraced themselves; and scenes of wars were reenacted[609] before the riveted gaze of the public. Gregorovius tells us:

> The actors deferred to the brutal tastes of the populace, and with the actors were numbered the very drivers of the chariots. In the Odeum of Domitian, which contained more than ten thousand seats, perhaps also in the theatres of Balbus, of Marcellus and of Pompeius, singers, organ-players, or dancers gratified the corrupt senses of the Romans. Recited comedies or mimes encouraged sensuality by indecency of language; while the pantomimes, with their choruses and dumb gesticulations, surpassed all else in the unbridled representation of obscenity... the mimes had sunk to absurdity., that the refined ideas of pleasure of the ancient Romans had degenerated in their corrupt descendants into the lowest vice, and that what had formerly been decorous enjoyments had become perverted into scenes of sensuality and licence [sic]. The Roman populace would not relinquish these spectacles: its last passion was pleasure, — it would die laughing.[610]

Chambers, author of *The Mediaeval Stage*, traces early European theatre to 6th century Athenians who were fond of spoofing daily life. The Greek's passion for theatrical entertainment made its way to Rome, whose own audiences delighted in mocking their country's officials: "*Palladius, Vita Chrysostomi, 8*, records how the stage of Antioch in the fifth century rang with the scandals caused by the patriarch Severus and other Monophysite heretics."[611]

Scaenici were performers. They included musicians, dancers, jugglers, ropewalkers, tumblers, buffoons, stilt-walkers, beast-tamers, and strong men. As the needs of the public were often immaterial to the desires of the senators' the stage was where players challenged authorities and official policy; at the same time the theatre provided diversions for citizens grown

---

[607] Tréves has been destroyed and rebuilt several times over the course of history.
[608] Chambers, *Stage*, vol. 1, p. 19.
[609] Church and Brodribb, *Annals*, p. 186.
[610] Gregorovius, *Rome*, vol. 1, pp. 298-300.
[611] Chambers, *Stage*, vol. 1, p. 11.

weary from their miserable situation. It was in Rome where Caligula is said to have "burnt a [cheeky] playwright alive in an amphitheater."[612]

Stage antics were rude and perverse, according to Chambers who writes that crowds demanded women play their scenes in the nude. And the sexually arousing mythological stories written by poets gained popularity after erotic satyric dancers joined musicians and singers on the stage. Just as with the games, theatre spectators brawled and rioted over their beloved actors, drawing blood and the wrath of city officials. The disturbances resulted in actors being thrown from the country, at least for a time.

Scaenici were freedmen or slaves and their profession was a dishonorable one. They had no civil rights, could not vote or hold public office and could not bring criminal charges. And women could not appoint attorneys to represent them in civil suits. Sons of state officials were forbidden to marry actors or those whose parents were actors. Augustus was first to relax the laws. But, as the church had condemned the games and circuses, it had condemned the theatre too. According to Chambers:

> Moreover, they had their special reasons for hostility to the stage. That the actors should mock as the pagan religion, with whose *ludi* their own performances were intimately connected, made a good dialectical point. But the connection itself was unpardonable, and still more so the part taken by the mimes during the war of creeds, in parodying and holding up to ridicule the most sacred symbols and mysteries of the church. This feeling is reflected in the legends of St. Genesius, St. Pelagia and other holy folk, who are represented as turning from the scenic profession to embrace Christianity, the conversion in some cases taking place on the very boards of the theatre itself.[613]

The medieval church that never developed a good mood for games cared not at all for the antics on the stage. Undoubtedly, church leaders lacked a sense of humor, so there would be no forgiveness for those who openly mocked, and ridiculed the pious ones. When Genesius, a prolific stage crafter and comedian, refused to renounce his staged baptism, the church beheaded him in 303 CE, so goes the mythos. The European fondness for mixing fact with fiction makes it is impossible to discern whether Genesius was real or fictional. Chamber notes that the "*Passio of St. Genesius* represents him as a magister… converted while he was mimicking a baptism before Diocletian, and martyred. It professes to give part of the dialogue of the mime."[614] In any case, whether the events took place literally or figuratively, Genesius' prosecution set an example. New rules followed his execution.

---

[612] Ibid., p. 5.
[613] Ibid., p. 10.
[614] Ibid., p. 10.

The Canons of Hippolytus and the councils of Elvira (306), Arles[615] (314) and Carthage (397-398) condemned the theatre. The church forbade the clergy from engaging in the stage altogether, but forbade Christian laity from attending performances on Sundays and during holy festivals. Excommunication waited in the wings for transgressors. Of course, Christians could neither be actors, nor marry them. And church laws locked female actors and their daughters in their chosen career for life. Performers who professed devotion to Christ had to renounce their profession and then quit.

Still, Tertullian felt the need to bring in the church's heavy artillery. He warns Christians that actors would regret their profession after death when their bodies "are licked by the fires" of hell. He tells them, "To worldly pleasures Christians have no claim. If they need spectacula they can find them in the exercises of their Church. Here are nobler poetry, sweeter voices, maxims more sage, melodies more dulcet, than any comedy can boast, and withal, here is truth instead of fiction."[616]

The theatre's popularity was so widespread that Chambers writes: "After the edict of Milan (313), and still more after the end of the pagan reaction with the death of Julian (363), Christian influences began to make themselves felt in the civil legislation of the Empire.... The emperors were, indeed, in a difficult position. They stood between bishops pleading for decency and humanity and populaces now traditionally entitled to their panem et spectacula."[617]

Eventually though, the church's influence over the stage and all of Europe took hold and cemented; Employing pious words, yet deploying dastardly deeds, the shady saints of sin were ready to flex their hulking holy muscles. And did they ever.

---

[615] "The first council of Arles, in its fourth canon, declared that those members of the church who drove chariots at the public games should, so long as they continued in that employment, be denied communion." Alfred Edward Thomas Watson, *Horse-Racing (Great Britain)*, Encyclopaedia Britannica. 11th ed. 1910. p. 727.
[616] Chambers, *Stage*, vol. 1, p. 11.
[617] Ibid., p. 13.

8

CHRISTIAN LEADERS: SWINDLERS AND "MARVEL MONGERS" IN HIGH PLACES

Church Corruption Clears the Way for 1000 Years of Anarchy and Magical Thinking as Europe Begins a New World Order

I am able to assure you that there never has been a kingdom in which there have been so many civil wars as in that of Christ.[618]

The church, in hopeless inability to check the universal passion for fight, sought only to direct it to the suppression of ecclesiastical enemies. Pope Paschal (1099) exhorted Count Robert of Flanders to persecute to the utmost the Emperor Henry, saying, "By such battles you shall obtain a place in the heavenly Jerusalem." Bernard, without dispute the holiest man of the next century, offered no excuse or palliation for his harangue to the faithful: "Let them kill the enemy or die. To submit to die for Christ, or to cause one of His enemies to die, is naught but glory."[619]

In the wars of this period a common sight was that of bishops and archbishops, clad in coats of mail, riding through the streets of their episcopal towns on fierce chargers, and returning to their palaces clotted with dirt and blood. That was a deserved rebuke, as well as a fine sarcasm, with which Richard Coeur de Lion sent the blood-stained armor of the Bishop of Beauvais to the Pope, as the garment of Joseph to Jacob, asking the Holy Father if he recognized his son's coat.[620]

The Roman Empire had raised its own emperors to godhood status by associating them with the Unconquered Sun;[621] however, those Emperors tolerated other religions as long as citizens continued to recognize their lofty standing. However, winds of chaos were blowing Christianity clear across the land. With the help of Constantine, who gave "Christians equal privileges with other religions in the Empire, then favored them...."[622] the empire eventually adopted Christianity as its state religion.[623] The Theodosius Code outlawed ancient world religions and their teachers, and set the framework upon which the Inquisitions were

---

[618] Montesquieu, *Letters*, p. 56.
[619] Ludlow, *Crusades,*, p 23.
[620] Ibid., p. 24.
[621] Thorndike, *Europe*, p. 70.
[622] Ibid., p. 72.
[623] Ibid., p. 72.

later built.[624] Though Constantine waited until the time of his death before being baptized,[625] his successors (in imperial offices) were nearly all Christians.[626] Even the barbarian Goths, described originally as Arians, believers who denied Christ's divinity, accepted church teachings during the 4th century CE.[627] The barbarians' reluctant embrace of Christianity and later the Vikings' was probably crucial to its survival as a major European institution.

However, it is divine irony that brought a thousand years of anarchy, terrorism and hand wringing to Europe instead of the Book of Revelation's predicted millennium of peace and hope.[628] After all, Rome had fully embraced Christianity, so understandably there was great gnashing of teeth as its buildings and institutions began to tumble. As barbarians sieged city walls murdering and/or raping everyone and looting everything within, Christian laity questioned their god's judgment and his lack of personal involvement in the daily lives of his children. On the other hand, church father Augustine thought that the barbarian sacking of Rome was compatible with established customs of war: "All the spoiling, then, which Rome was exposed to in the recent calamity—all the slaughter, plundering, burning, and misery—was the result of the custom of war."[629] Augustine seemed rather satisfied that the barbarous hordes stopped their plundering just short of his church roost, reminding critics that those seeking shelter within church walls remained unharmed by barbarians. In line with Augustine, Salvian excused the actions of conquering barbarians as exploits of heretics and unbelievers who were too ignorant to know any better, "I have long lamented that we are much worse than the barbarian, for ignorance of the law excuses them, whereas our knowledge of it accuses us."[630] Instead, he blamed the moral failings on Christians who, he said, were more beguiled by their games and wicked behaviors than they cared about the actions of barbarians.[631] Because Christians were so enchanted by games, Salvian advocated that Christians renounce them in their baptismal vows.[632]

The church clearly saw own their fortunes rise along with each success of the barbarians. And in an early effort at establishing the church as an

---

[624] Rule, *Inquisition*, p. 2.
[625] It was thought best to wait until all sins committed during one's life could be confessed before death.
[626] Thorndike, *Europe*, p. 72.
[627] Ibid., p. 55.
[628] The Book of Revelation was written sometime between 60 and 95 CE.
[629] Marcus Dods, trans., *The City of God*, vol. 1, (Edinburgh: T. & T. Clark, 1872), p. 9.
[630] Sanford, *Government*, p.159.
[631] Chambers, *Stage*, vol. 1, p. 19.
[632] Sanford, *Government*, pp. 167-68.

authority, the Bishop of Rome, Leo the Great (440-461 CE), claimed the seat as sole head of the church.[633] Later, nearly 400 years after the death of Constantine, Charlemagne came on the scene. A highly respected figure in medieval history, historians acknowledge that he did much to hold onto the political instruments developed by the Roman Empire. During his reign, Charlemagne succeeded in using his bloodied sword to protect the church from outside assault.

"Papal Office Worth Fighting For": Clerics Draw Battles Lines over Church Riches

Yet for all its triumph over the masses during the early Middle Ages, Christianity, with its vengeance-seeking, nations-smiting god on the throne failed to bring peace to Europe. On top of the still smoldering piles of rubble of the ancient Roman Empire secular and non-secular disputes between the church authority, and the barbarian kings were brewing. The power void created by the fall of the Roman emperors, along with the Old Testament bible cry for war, encouraged the Christians to do battle and conquer. And so the wars began as the surviving powers of the medieval upheaval - the Christian church and the barbarian warlords- waged prolonged wars: "While the idea of the universal empire still held sway, secular princes, pursuing purely separatist ambitions, made war one upon another and the nations of Europe were in the throes of [childbirth]."[634]

This fighting endured for centuries as European authoritarians, and their minions, hoped to gain not only the sole right to rule over the European people, but more importantly, seize its vast lands and treasures. In the 4th century, we witness how consequential ruling Europe was to the church in this passage:

> The pagan historian, Ammianus Marcellinus, tells of a fight at a papal election in 366 as a result of which one hundred and thirty-seven persons were killed; but adds that the office was *worth fighting for, since it brought with it a large income which enabled the bishop to dress elegantly and to ride in a carriage and to give banquets that outshone those of the emperor,* Damasus (d. 384), the very pope elected on that occasion, is the first to give us a definite statement of the papal claims and of the doctrine of the Roman Church.[635] (Italics added).

Civil governments and church authorities striking a cooperative balance "through the long centuries since Christianity began to play a leading part upon the political stage [has been] the worthy task of philosophers and statesmen. That one scale should outweigh the other was perhaps

---

[633] Thorndike, *Europe*, p. 107.
[634] Arthur Stanley Turberville, *Mediaeval Heresy & the Inquisition*, p. 3.
[635] Thorndike, *Europe*, p. 107.

inevitable in the first attempts...."[636] writes Bury.

Despite behind the scenes murders and manipulations, Christians endeavored for perfection in the eyes of their Christian god. Self-flagellation,[637] fasting, renouncing riches, isolation and self-denial through desert wanderings, and other extreme measures became popular attempts at growing closer to their god. Monasticism became so popular that both the morally pure and the morally corrupt souls sought secular solitude:

> The motives of those becoming monks soon ceased to be entirely religious. The chaotic conditions of the period of barbarian invasion, loss of property, friends, and entering a home, the impossibility of earning a livelihood... the comparative quiet, security, and perhaps even comfort of a monastery — all these conditions might impel one to withdraw from the world which had become so unattractive. Jerome (d.420) wrote to one of his female friends at the time of the sack of Rome by Alaric, 'Dearest daughter in Christ, will you marry amid such scenes as these?'[638]

Despite the attempts at moral purity clerical abuses are well documented:

> Though their extent is certainly a matter of dispute, there is no doubt about the fact of serious clerical abuses in the twelfth and thirteenth centuries. There was extraordinary greatness in a church that could produce a St. Bernard, a St. Francis, an Anselm, a Grosseteste. Yet even if we leave out of account the invectives of professed enemies altogether and only rely upon the unimpeachable authority of the Church's leaders themselves, we are left with rather a dark picture.[639]

The lowly monks were not alone in having their ranks infiltrated by opportunity seekers wanting to thrust off menacing medieval rules and the sadistic shackles that accompanied them. Where ever fame, riches, and glory were found seigneur saints of sin preyed (sic) within distance. A. S. Turberville writes:

> We know too of many bishops who neglected their spiritual duties and were nothing more than feudal barons, sometimes fattening upon riches amassed by extortion. It cannot be denied that there were numerous instances of absenteeism and pluralities; while for the sexual immorality to be found among both regular and secular clergy we have the excellent authority of great men who were scandalized by it and sought to produce amendment, such as

---

[636] Bury, *Cambridge*, vol. 1, pp. 169-70.
[637] Turberville, *Heresy*, pp. 5, 51-52.
[638] Thorndike, *Europe*, p. 112.
[639] Turberville, *Heresy*, p. 8.

Honorius III, St. Bernard and Bishop Grosseteste. Monastic reforms had been tried, the Cluniac being followed by the Cistercian and others of a like severity.[640]

Kings and Church Leaders Fight for Dominance

Competing authorities committed abuses and battled for dominance over the hearts, minds, fears and wallets of their people. One famous struggle occurred between Pope Gregory VII, intent on papal supremacy, and German King Henry IV who aspired to hold the final authority over his own lands and people. Henry placed church offices on the auction block, meanwhile, Gregory made some outrageous proposals in his quest for papal power: (i) the pope never errs; (ii) he is above criticism; (iii) he is Head of State. Henry who was busily building his empire and building up allies saw his ability to maneuver against the pope constrained somewhat by the pope's machinations: "Gregory is distinguished by the violent and extreme methods which he did not hesitate to adopt in the effort to enforce his ideals.... He not only excommunicated worldly rulers with whom he had differences, but deposed them and encouraged their vassals and subjects to revolt, thus inciting sedition and civil war."[641] Henry had made enemies of some nobles, and had serious concerns of being overthrown. He decided to make amends with the pope:

> Since in 1073 the Saxons had got the better of Henry [IV] and there was danger that another king might be set up in his place, he wrote a very humble letter to the pope, Henry's first admitting that he had sold church offices and submission named unworthy bishops, and promising henceforth to cooperate with the pope in the cause of church reform.[642]

Wars of the Middle Ages, whether waged with the might of arms or with weapons of wicked words, were more often than not taken to maniacal medieval brinkmanship. Generally, wars ended only once a victor claimed his reward and his opponent became his casualty. And in the struggle between Gregory and Henry, the argument boiled down to who would appoint church officials, the church or the state. It was an important argument for the church princes and crowned heads who used church appointments as political instruments to strike alliances and seal truces, even if only for a short time. Peace between Gregory and Henry would have to wait until they had settled the question of supremacy.

As Gregory and Henry drew battle lines, these embittered foes deposed and excommunicated each other. Gregory with the backing of nobles, and

---

[640] Ibid., p. 8.
[641] Thorndike, *Europe*, p. 288.
[642] Ibid., p. 289.

Henry with the support of his bishops appointed a replacement king and an anti-pope, respectively. At one point, Henry famously waited in the snow barefoot for three days to apologize to Gregory. Eventually, though he marched to Rome to overthrow the king and to have the anti-pope crown him emperor. Things became really messy when Gregory's vassal stormed Rome to release him from imprisonment. In addition to securing Gregory's release, his soldiers resorted to burning the city and killing thousands of citizens.

Though Henry outlived Gregory - and kept his crown - the church was the victor of that lengthy engagement: "in a general way the Church and the Papacy had shown vast strength and endurance; as a whole their power and prestige had greatly increased, and were to continue to do so for another century. For another century, too, the popes and emperors were to be at bitter strife."[643]

The 11th century saw another contentious skirmish waged between Henry II, ruler over England and parts of France, and Thomas Beckett. According to Thorndike, Beckett was a friend of Henry's who he promoted to archbishop. Still, widespread corruption of "criminous [sic] clerks" unsettled Henry. He fumed at the clergy's overt misconduct. And complained that clergymen accused of murder and robbery received light sentences, if, indeed, they were not let off entirely by ecclesiastical judges. To remedy this abuse, Henry wanted secular judges present during ecclesiastical hearings. This idea was firmly rejected by Beckett who said it, "would be bringing Christ again before Pontius Pilate."[644] However they finally agreed that clergymen would yield to the Constitutions of Clarendon, a set of laws that restricted the church's rights to excommunication, and gave Henry the ability to hold court hearings, instead of the church; the Constitutions implemented other restrictions, too. Immediately after agreeing to the Constitutions, the church rejected them; one of its more objectionable laws supported ending papal appeals. From this disagreement, years-long bickering began between Henry and Beckett with the latter excommunicating some of Henry's people, and even threatening Henry similarly. Henry responded by having Beckett assassinated. That decision had the unfortunate consequences of turning Beckett into a martyr, and transforming his burial site into a popular destination for pilgrims. Henry did penance at Beckett's tomb where he was so roundly "scourged" that he fell ill the next day, writes Thorndike. Still, his decisions "laid the foundations in England of the common law and its courts, destined in the end to prevail throughout all England...."[645]

---

[643] Ibid., p. 292.
[644] Ibid., pp. 292-96.
[645] Ibid., p 298.

Church Leaders Introduce Purgatory Purely for Profits

But in the end, Henry had to allow ecclesiastical courts, and papal appeals. The church experienced later wins, too, so that by the 13th century, by one historian's estimation, the church declared itself the eventual winner,[646] though skirmishes continued. Still, from kings to popes to clergy and laity, the church had unleashed corruption in the realm and beyond:

> A fine attempt had been made to assist the endeavor of the parish priest to strive after personal holiness by the institution of the orders of the Praemonstratensians and the Austin Friars. And much good was unquestionably accomplished; yet order after order eventually fell away from its pristine purity and the seed of corruption remained un-eradicated. At the very least, we can say that most men must have had from personal experience knowledge of some glaring contrast between clerical profession and accomplishment. That some such contrast should at all times in greater or less degree exist is only the inevitable result of the weaknesses of human nature.[647]

Before the Roman Empire toppled over, the church had begun planting seeds of corruption. According to Hallam, "At the eruption of the northern invaders into the Roman empire, they found the clergy already endowed with extensive possessions. Besides the spontaneous [offerings] upon which the ministers of the Christian church had originally subsisted, they had obtained, even under the pagan emperors, by concealment or connivance, for the Roman law did not permit a tenure of lands in mortmain,[648] certain immoveable estates, the revenues of which were applicable to their own maintenance, and that of the poor."[649]

Roman law permitted confiscation of church land, especially during times of persecution. However, that changed once Constantine "gave not only a security, but a legal sanction to the territorial acquisitions of the church." Because clerical robes conceal a man's covetousness only for a time, the men of the clergy wasted little in turning heavenly petitions into earthly treasure chests: "Passing rapidly from a condition of distress and persecution to the summit of prosperity, the church degenerated as rapidly from her ancient purity, and forfeited the respect of future ages in the same proportion as she acquired the blind veneration of her own. Covetousness,

---

[646] Another dispute centered on the marital status and celibacy of priests. One reason for concern was that sons could inherit their father's religious offices and church property. There was a danger, too, of church officials becoming feudal barons, neglectful of church duties. Other historians say celibacy was important so that the king could hold onto his land.
[647] Turberville, *Heresy*, p. 9.
[648] This is a law that allows churches to hold land in perpetuity.
[649] Hallam, *View*, vol. 1, p. 614.

especially, became almost a characteristic vice," writes Hallam.[650] Although Hallam lists several church creeds manufactured for what he calls "the purpose of sordid fraud," he specifically points to the introduction of purgatory[651] as a ruse "operating upon the minds of barbarians [that]... naturally caused a torrent of opulence to pour in upon the church."[652] According to Hallam, each church owned seven or eight thousand mansi. (Thorndike informs us that by the 5th century, "the Church is estimated to have become the greatest landholder in the Empire.").[653] Hallam, however, does point out that good management helped the church's wealth grow. Nevertheless, the church acquired a great deal of its wealth immorally. Hallam writes that the church received funds when they convinced wealthy Christians that atonement came in the form of large donations to the church, both before and after death; and that penance was given in exchange for money. The clergy misrepresented land ownership to help laymen escape taxes; and forged documents:

> To die without allotting a portion of worldly wealth to pious uses, was accounted almost like suicide, or a refusal of the last sacraments; and hence [dying without a will] passed for a sort of fraud upon the church, which she punished by taking the administration of the deceased's effects into her own hands. This however was peculiar to England, and seems to have been the case there only between the reigns of Henry III. and Edward III when the bishop took a portion of the intestate's personal estate... instead of distributing it among his next of kin. The canonical penances imposed upon repentant offenders... were commuted for money or for immoveable possessions; a fertile though scandalous source of monastic wealth, which the popes afterwards diverted into their own coffers, by the usage of dispensations and indulgences....
>
> It became a customary fraud of lay proprietors to grant estates to the church which they received again by way of fief or lease, exempted from public [taxes]. And as if all these means of accumulating what they could not legitimately enjoy were insufficient, the monks prostituted their knowledge of writing to the purpose of forging charters in their own favor, which might easily impose upon an ignorant age, since it has required a peculiar science to detect them in modern times.... As an additional source of revenue, and in imitation of the Jewish law, the payment of tithes was recommended or enjoined.[654]

---

[650] Ibid., p. 615.
[651] Today churches peddle the so-called "prosperity gospel" to collect other people's wealth.
[652] Hallam, *View*, vol. 1, p. 615.
[653] Thorndike, *Europe*, p. 105.
[654] Hallam, *View*, vol. 1, pp. 617-18.

The Pope's Temporal Powers Allow Church Corruption

Rule writes that the church gave itself "divine right over estates which they had acquired by any means."[655] The pope's assumption of the church's divine rights became known as the Temporal Power of the Pope. Rule describes the sumptuousness of those powers: "Lands in many parts of the world, every where held in mortmain: asylum; ecclesiastical immunity; Papal supremacy over kings, bishops, clergy, laity of all degrees; an assumption of power on earth to forgive sins, or to punish sinners, and power beyond the grave to bind in pain, or to release imprisoned spirits; these were the real possessions and the monstrous claims which constituted a temporal power vast beyond calculation."[656] Of course the church fathers exempted their own corrupt practices and the church from their own rules.

Roger Bacon sums up church corruption in the 13th century, a mere two hundred years before the Papal Bulls authorized enslavement of all non-Christians and theft of their natural resources, by writing:

> Yet the truth is that there hath never been so great ignorance and such deep error, as I will most clearly prove later on in this present treatise, and as is already manifestly shown by facts. For more sins reign in these days than in any past age; and sin is incompatible with wisdom. Let us look upon all conditions in the world, and consider them diligently; everywhere we shall find boundless corruption, and first of all in the Head. For the Court of Rome, which once was ruled by God's wisdom, and should always be so ruled, is now debased by the constitutions of lay Emperors, made for the governance of lay-folk and contained in the code of civil law The Holy See is " torn by the deceit and fraud of unjust men. Justice perisheth, all peace is broken, infinite scandals are aroused. This beareth its fruit in utterly perverse manners; pride reigneth, covetousness burneth, envy gnaweth upon all, the whole [Papal] Court is defamed of lechery, and gluttony is lord of all.... If this be so in the Head, what then is done among the members? Let us see the prelates; how they run after money, neglect the cure of souls, promote their nephews, and other carnal friends, and crafty lawyers who ruin all by their counsels.... The whole clergy is intent upon pride, lechery, and avarice; and wheresoever clerks are gathered together, as at Paris and Oxford, they scandalize the whole laity with their wars and quarrels and other vices.[657]

A Plundering Priest Plus a Certain Pilfering Pope, Rodrigo Borgia

Bacon's complaints went unheeded. By the 16th century laity and clergy

---

[655] Rule, *Inquisition*, p. 15.
[656] Ibid.
[657] Coulton, *Garner*, pp. 339-40.

alike were overcome by acts of brigandage. Clerics conducted raids on towns and cities that resulted in massive human carnage. One particular case stands out for its obvious boldness: "It would be hard, for instance, to find elsewhere the case of a priest, gradually driven by passion from one excess to another, till at last he came to head a band of robbers. That age offers us this example among others. On August 12, 1405, the priest Don Niccolo de' Pelegati of Figarolo was shut up in an iron cage outside the tower of San Giuliano at Ferrara. He had twice celebrated his first mass; the first time he had the same day committed murder, but afterwards received absolution at Rome; he then killed four people and married two wives, with whom he travelled about. He afterwards took part in many assassinations, violated women, carried others away by force, plundered far and wide, and infested the territory of Ferrara with a band of followers in uniform, extorting food and shelter by every sort of violence. When we think of what all this implies, the mass of guilt on the head of this one man is something tremendous;"[658] But, the misdeeds of Don Niccolo were hardly exceptional. Burckhardt informs us that the lack of supervision and obscene privileges were the causes of abuses acted out by monks and clergy. Murderers and malefactors within the church were many because, Burckhardt tells us, "Ruined characters sheltered themselves in the cowl in order to escape the arm of the law, like the corsair whom Massuccio knew in a convent at Naples."[659] However, the arm of the law was more like the probing tentacle of an octopus directed by recklessly manipulative religious authorities.

And then there was the corrupt practices of certain of the principle clergy, too, like Cardinal Rodrigo Borgia (d. 1503) who acted in the most unholy fashion to gain the Roman papacy and then used his powers to torment his foes. The tale of one such foe, Girolamo Savonarola, is dealt with in the next few pages. Story narrates Rodrigo's ascendancy to the office of Pope Alexander VI, "His wealth was immense, and he bribed the whole college of cardinals, with the exception of five, who refused to sell their votes; and even [Cardinal] Ascanio sold himself at last to his rival, finding that there was no chance of his own election. The scandalous life of Alexander is only too well known. He was weak, irresolute, cowardly in character, and destitute of morals and decency; and the condition of Rome, far from improving under his guidance, sank, if possible, into more complete degradation. There was no safety anywhere from assassination and debauchery, and the state was tormented by constant war. Over the battlements of the Castle [St. Angelo] are seen the faces of prisoners led forth to be beheaded or quartered, and its prisons and halls of examination

---

[658] Burckhardt, *Renaissance*, pp. 448-49.
[659] Ibid., p. 449.

echo to the shrieks of those who are there tortured, strangled, or poisoned. It is the scene of treachery and wickedness within; and without it the clamour [sic] of battle rages at intervals."660

A growing dissatisfaction with clerical corruption that angered the devoted,661 plus competing religious interpretations, and doctrines were challenges that greatly influenced the decision to begin Inquisitions, and is discussed in Chapter 10. However, it was unfortunate for both the laity, and sincere clergymen wanting true reform that it would be the ecclesiastics' tentacles seeking out the remedy. Grievous, too, for sincere Christians likely confused by clerical antics and abuse that were in direct opposition to biblical instructions from the pulpits.

And at this delicate time when Christians endeavored to perfect their walk with god, different sects had wildly different interpretations of scripture. Some of the early Christian interpretations the church deemed heretical included: the earth is the domain of the devil, who is the father of the material world and humans; if the devil is the father of the earth, marriage, then, is the work of the devil; an attachment to family was a depravity in light of scriptures that encouraged renouncing all material goods; Christian groups sanctioned suicides for members with long-term illnesses; and John the Baptist was an evil demon. Other Christians questioned Christ's divinity, or believed that their god had two divine sons, Christ and Satan. Still, it is apparent that this doctrinal free-for-all gave Christians room to discover which beliefs were most comfortable to embrace wherein they could practice their spiritual preferences, in most cases, with the blessings of church leaders.

"Myth-Making and Marvel-Mongering": the Church Backs Scams

> If Catholics took advantage of the tendency to superstition abroad in the world to conquer the unbeliever, it was but natural that heretics often took advantage of this thirst for the marvelous to dupe the Catholics. The Cathari [believed in dual gods – one good, one evil] of Monceval made a portrait of the Virgin, representing her as one-eyed and toothless, saying that, in His humility, Christ had chosen a very ugly woman for mother. They had no difficulty in healing several cases of disease by its means; the image became famous, was venerated almost everywhere, and accomplished many miracles, until the day when the heretics divulged the deception, to the great scandal of the faithful."662

> It is undeniable that the ministers of religion, influenced probably not so much by personal covetousness, as by zeal for the interests of their order, took advantage. Many of the peculiar and prominent characteristics in the faith and

---

660 Story, "Castle St. Angelo and The Evil Eye," 608.
661 Turberville, *Heresy*, p. 11.
662 Benjamin B. Warfield, *Counterfeit Miracles*, pp. 67-68.

discipline of those ages appear to have been either introduced, or sedulously promoted, for the purpose of sordid fraud. To those purposes conspired the veneration for relics, the worship of images, the idolatry of saints and martyrs, the religious inviolability of sanctuaries, the consecration of cemeteries, but above all, the doctrine of purgatory, and masses for the relief of the dead."[663]

Christendom, both East and West, was crowded with sacred places and holy wells in the Middle Ages; and there was hardly a cathedral or great abbey church that had not its shrine, crowded with pilgrims who came for the healing of sickness as well as for other boons.[664]

It is amazing to learn that Europeans have a long history of believing in fantastical creatures and events considering how often they have mocked other cultures for their fantastical beliefs. Minucius Felix, a contemporary of Tertullian, remarks:

Our [European] ancestors were so ready to believe in fictions, that they accepted on trust all kind of wild and monstrous marvels and miracles: Scylla with serpent coils, a hybrid Chimaera, a Hydra replenishing its life from vivifying wounds, Centaurs half-horse half-man, or any other fiction of folklore fell upon willing ears. Why recall old wives' tales of human beings changed into birds and beasts, or into trees and flowers? Had such things happened in the past, they would happen now; as they cannot happen now, they did not happen then. So with our ancestors' attitude to the gods: blind and credulous they yielded simpleminded credence.[665]

When we speak of corruption that was both widespread and acceptable during Medieval Europe, we must include many stories that supposedly showcase miracles and healing. Stories of saints walking on water (or drying up river beds); raising people from the dead; changing males into females (or vice versa); and of finding gold in the bellies of fish were as numerous as the celestial signs (blood rain, shooting stars, and comets),[666] volcanoes, and earthquakes that supposedly foretold of wars, assassinations, princely deaths, famines, victories... and defeat.

It is unsurprising, then, that a people with a long tradition of mysticism include it within the pages of their high holy book of knowledge and wisdom. Healing and miracle stories are standard biblical sustenance. Bread and fish multiply to feed the masses. People heal from their afflictions, or return from the dead. The apostle Paul, according to biblical

---

[663] Hallam, *View*, vol. 1, p. 615.
[664] Percy Dearmer, "Faith and Healing," *The Treasury*, vol. 11 (1908) pp. 155-56.
[665] Freese, *Minucius*, pp. 61-62.
[666] "Lord save us from the Devil, the Turk, and the Comet" was a familiar prayer of the mid-15th century. Tappan, p. 314.

lore, lost his sight though gained powers to heal: "God wrought special miracles by the hands of Paul: So that from his body were brought unto the sick handkerchiefs or aprons, and the diseases departed from them, and the evil spirits went out of them."[667] Historians claim that the handkerchiefs and aprons supposedly taken from this apostle later became props in healing rituals. White tells us, "As a rule, the miracles of the sacred books were taken as models, and each of those given by the sacred chroniclers was repeated during the early ages of the Church and through the medieval period with endless variations of circumstance, but still with curious fidelity to the original type."[668]

According to celebrated 12th century theologian Benjamin B. Warfield, one source of miracle stories may have been monk-legends - *monkish belletristic*,[669] fictional and fanciful stories written on the harsh lives monks supposedly endured because of their vows of abstinence. Popular among medieval people, these true confession-type stories aroused imaginations and excited dulled senses the way amorous love stories do today: "Sin was fought as if it had been sickness, with diligence in ascetic practices," writes Warfield. Without fail "a harvest of visions, demoniacal assaults and miracles which followed in its wake" replaced the austere life that centered around disavowal of material goods: "The miraculous was in this literature a matter of course; and the ever-swelling accounts of miracles in that age of excited superstition transferred themselves with immense facility to life."[670] Every man, woman, and child possessed the wherewithal to weave a personal story, so many did:

> Marvellous stories, the innocent exaggerations of weak minds or the designed invention of less conscionable shrewdness, fed the credulity of the people. Bishop Arculf told of having seen the three tabernacles still standing upon the Mount of Transfiguration. Bernard of Brittany as an eye-witness described the angel who came from heaven each Easter morn to light the lamp above the Holy Sepulchre.[671]

Officious clergymen and Christian laity intoxicated by their faith offered up personal visions or dreams of Mary, the infant Jesus, and subordinate biblical characters. These miraculous manifestations made declarations, issued edicts, or chastised *the elect* for their poor spiritual performances. When the Crusading centuries incited many of the most zealous Christians to march to Jerusalem, prophets (profits!) duped believers with stories of

---

[667] *The Holy Bible Containing The Old And New Testaments*, trans. Francis Nathan Peloubet, Acts 19:11-12, p. 1143.
[668] White, *Warfare*, vol. 2, p. 24.
[669] Warfield, *Counterfeit*, p. 63.
[670] Ibid., p. 63.
[671] Ludlow, *Crusades*, p. 67.

signs and warnings. Medieval miracles, marvels and visions were merely exploitive tools used by religious leaders to sway opinions; to pursue a certain course of action, as directed by the vision; or to punish idolaters. Some particularly disturbing visions come to us from the 11th century. That was when Thietmar of Merseburg, unhappy that fake Christians overwhelmed the German church, recorded some haunting visions of dead people murdering living people and setting destructive fires. Thietmar - and church worshippers who recalled their ghostly sightings to him - was clearly more than a bit intoxicated by scripture; seemingly he and many other fellow believers feared the "torments of the grave."[672]

Miracle stories and testimonies of healing were both sanctioned and endorsed by the early church leaders: "The greatest preacher of the day, Chrysostom; the greatest ecclesiastic, Ambrose; the greatest thinker, Augustine, —all describe for us miraculous occurrences of the most incredible kind as having taken place within their own knowledge."[673] Augustine himself reports witnessing the incurably sick become healthy, the blind gaining sight, successful exorcisms, and people being raised from the dead. Apparently, the critics of his day challenged his farfetched claims. Augustine addresses their attacks in the *City of God*, "Why, they say, are those miracles, which you affirm were wrought formerly, wrought no longer? I might, indeed, reply that miracles were necessary before the world believed, in order that it might believe. And whoever now-a-days demands to see prodigies that he may believe, is himself a great prodigy, because he does not believe, though the whole world does. But they make these objections for the sole purpose of insinuating that even those former miracles were never wrought."[674]

However, Benjamin Warfield writes in *Counterfeit Miracles* that a few years before writing those words, Augustine was just as certain that miracles were no longer needed:

In his treatises, On the True Religion, which was written about 390, and On the Usefullness [sic] of Believing, written in 391 or 392, we find him speaking on the hypothesis that miracles no longer happened. "We perceive," he writes in the former of these treatises, "that our ancestors, by that measure of faith by which the ascent is made from temporal things to eternal, obtained visible miracles (for thus only could they do it); and through them it has been brought about that these should no longer be necessary for their descendants. For when the Catholic Church had been diffused and established through the whole world, these miracles were no longer permitted to continue in our time, lest the mind

---

[672] Friedrich Kurze and Johann Martin Lappenberg. trans., *Thietmari Merseburgensis Episcopi Chronicon*. (Hannoverae: Impensis Bibliopolii Hahniani, 1889) pp. 8-10.
[673] Warfield, *Counterfeit*, p. 38.
[674] Dods, *God*, p. 484.

should always seek visible things, and the human race should be chilled by the customariness of the very things whose novelty had inflamed them.[675]

Warfield notes that Augustine later clarifies his remarks by writing: "What he meant was not that no miracles were still wrought in his own day, but only that none were wrought which were as great as those our Lord wrought, and that not all the kinds our Lord wrought continued to be wrought."[676]

The Saints Preserved! Shrines Spur Pilgrims to Open Their Purses

I doubt that Augustine's original statement and politically calculating retraction mattered much at all. The Christian community was duly enthralled, anyway; their cultural paradigm energized and fully engaged.[677] They erected shrines on soon-to-be hallowed grounds across Europe and North Africa: "The bodies of St. Andrew, St. Luke, and St. Timothy, had reposed near three hundred years in the obscure graves, from whence they were transported, in solemn pomp, to the church of the apostles, which the magnificence of Constantine had founded on the banks of the Thracian Bosphorus. About fifty years afterwards, the same banks were honored by the presence of Samuel, the judge and prophet of the people of Israel. His ashes, deposited in a golden vase, and covered with a silken veil, were delivered by the bishops into each other's hands. The relics of Samuel were received by the people with the same joy and reverence which they would have shown to the living prophet; the highways, from Palestine to the gates of Constantinople, were filled with an uninterrupted procession; and the [5th c. Byzantine] emperor Arcadius himself, at the head of the most illustrious members of the clergy and senate, advanced to meet his extraordinary guest, who had always deserved and claimed the homage of kings," Gibbon tells us.[678] And when church leaders found the supposed skeletal remains of St. Stephen[679] they divvied him into portions and sent them off to different Christianized regions, including Africa.

According to Warfield, by 424 CE several sites had enshrined the saint's bones; and wherever they traveled, people reported miracles. Stories of magical healing began to spread far and wide with Augustine testifying to "even the dead [being] raised" at Stephen's shrines. Church leaders knew a good thing when they saw it. Apparently, the saints of sin delighted in

---

[675] Warfield, *Counterfeit*, pp. 40-41.
[676] Ibid., p. 41.
[677] Consider pet rocks, lines for sports shoes, phones, stuffed toys, "Black Friday mania," beanie babies, cubes, etc., which drive citizens into frenzies.
[678] Gibbon, *Decline*, vol. 3, p. 156.
[679] Stephen is Christianity's original martyr whose death by stoning was witnessed by Paul. The location of his bones was supposedly revealed to a priest during a dream.

taking advantage of their very naïve laity.

> The satisfactory experience, that the relics of saints were more valuable than gold or precious stones, stimulated the clergy to multiply the treasures of the church. Without much regard for truth or probability, they invented names for skeletons, and actions for names. The fame of the apostles, and of the holy men who had imitated their virtues, was darkened by religious fiction. To the invincible band of genuine and primitive martyrs, they added myriads of imaginary heroes, who had never existed, except in the fancy of crafty or credulous legendaries: and there is reason to suspect, that Tours might not be the only diocese in which the bones of a malefactor were adored, instead of those of a saint. A superstitious practice, which tended to increase the temptations of fraud, and credulity, insensibly extinguished the light of history, and of reason, in the Christian world.[680]

As this passage indicates, the Christian's attachment to the super silly disguised as the super natural was (and still is) quite powerful. Church laity believed miracles served as a kind of spiritual receptacle that contained spiritual instructions, and blessings. And so sightings of blood oozing from crosses, and tears dripping from images of the infant Jesus became common. Supposed miraculous events propelled masses of devotees to holy land pilgrimages where they believed that "'heaven [was] always [suspended] lowest' over these spots;"[681] The hope was that some mysterious spiritual essence of the dead be transferred to the living. Ludlow tells us:

> These ideas are set forth by Cyril of Jerusalem. He taught that a certain power dwelt in the body of the saint, even when the soul had departed from it; just as it was the instrument of the soul during life, so the power passed permanently into it (Cat. xviii. 16). This was coming very near to a belief that objects which the saints had used during their life had also a share in their miraculous powers.[682]

Throngs of worshippers imitated examples set by emperors and princes who showed their devotion by journeying to the holy land: "The pilgrimage of [Constantine's] mother, Helena, to Palestine, the alleged re-identification of sacred sites and relics by miraculous agencies, and their adornment with lavish magnificence, were the natural efflorescence of the hybrid religion that sprang up."[683] And in addition to atoning for whatever unspeakable wrong sinners committed, pilgrims returned to their homes

---

[680] Gibbon, *Decline*, vol. 3, p. 157.
[681] Ludlow, *Crusades*, p. 65.
[682] Albert Hauck, "Relics." *Encyclopaedia Britannica*. 11th ed. 1911. p. 60.
[683] Ludlow, *Crusades*, pp. 65-66.

joyfully bearing the tears of Christ. Others showed off tiny caskets supposedly containing bits of the Virgin Mary. The chance to become eyewitness to miraculous events must have caused many believers to make the demanding journey, too. But, moneymaking played the biggest role in these religious enterprises. Pilgrims paid large sums of money for those Jesus tears, Virgin Mary caskets and other religious relics. And in 1008 when Archbishop Leoteric reported finding Moses' rod in Gaul, hundreds of pilgrims who gathered there for a glimpse of it brought a financial boon to local enterprises.[684] Wherever pilgrims traveled their purses followed and church coffers grew:

> Pilgrimage was often a lucrative business as well as a pious performance. In the intervals of his visits to the sacred places the European sojourner plied his calling as a tradesman; the Franks held a market before the Church of St. Mary; the Venetians, Genoese, and Pisans had stores in Jerusalem and the coast cities of Phenicia.... A great traffic was done in relics. The pilgrim returned having in his wallet the credited bones of martyrs, bits of stone from sacred sites, splinters from furniture and shreds of garments made holy by association with the saints. These were sold to the wealthy and to churches, and their value augmented from year to year by reason of the fables which grew about them.[685]

White treads further into popular religious schemes that transferred assets from the poorest people to the ever-richer church. The following passage is astonishing for the details revealed about the business of relics:

> Enormous revenues flowed into monasteries and churches in all parts of Europe from relics noted for their healing powers. Every cathedral, every great abbey, and nearly every parish church claimed possession of healing relics. While undoubtedly, a childlike faith was at the bottom of this belief, there came out of it unquestionably a great development of mercantile spirit. The commercial value of sundry relics was often very high. In the year 1056 a French ruler pledged securities to the amount of ten thousand solidi for the production of the relics of St. Just and St. Pastor.... The body of St. Sebastian brought enormous to the Abbey of Soissons; Rome, Canterbury, Treves, Marburg, every great city, drew large revenues from similar sources, and the Venetian Republic ventured very considerable sums in the purchase of relics...
>
> Naturally, then, corporations whether lay or ecclesiastical, which drew large revenue from relics looked with little favour [sic] on a science which tended to discredit their investments.

Nowhere, perhaps, in Europe can the philosophy of this development of

---

[684] Coulton, *Garner*, p. 8.
[685] Ludlow, *Crusades*, p. 68.

fetichism be better studied today than at Cologne. At the cathedral, preserved in a magnificent shrine since about the twelfth century, are the skulls of the Three Kings, or Wise Men of the East, who, guided by the star of Bethlehem, brought gifts to the Saviour [sic]. These relics were an enormous source of wealth to the cathedral chapter during many centuries... at the neighboring church of St. Ursula, we have the later spoils of another cemetery, covering the interior walls of the church as the bones of St. Ursula and her eleven thousand virgin martyrs: the fact that many of them, as anatomists now declare, are the bones of *men* does not appear in the Middle Ages to have diminished their power of competing with the relics at the other shrines in healing efficiency.

No error in the choice of these healing means seems to have diminished their efficacy. When Prof. Buckland, the eminent osteologist and geologist, discovered that the relics of St. Rosalia at Palermo, which had for ages cured diseases and warded off epidemics, were the bones of a goat, this fact caused not the slightest diminution in their miraculous power."[686]

A Modern Day Christian "Healing" Scam has Medieval Roots

A startling narrative that illustrates people's gullibility in the face of religion comes to us by way of a ruse that is as ancient as medieval history itself and is found in *A Medieval Garner, Human Documents From Four Centuries Before the Reformation,* by G.G. Coulton. Readers may recognize the scheme as one employed by many of today's Christian leaders: "Some priest, to bring up a pilgrimage in his parish, may devise some false fellow feigning himself to come seek a saint in his church, and there suddenly say, that he hath gotten his sight. Then shall he have the bells rung for a miracle, and the fond folk of the country soon made fools, then women coming thither with their candles. And the person buying some lame beggar, three or four pairs of their old crutches with twelve pence spent in men and women of wax thrust through divers places some with arrows, and some with rusty knives, will make his offerings for one seven years worth twice his tithes."[687]

The First Recorded Case to Falsely Accuse a "Black Boy" of a Crime?

In 1138, John of Worcester relates to us what is possibly the earliest story[688] that falsely accuses a "Black boy" of a crime. In this tall tale, on three occasions a cellarer discovers the altar wine missing from casks stored in the cellar. One morning a watchful monk, alerted to the thefts, discovers a

---

[686] White, *Warfare*, vol. 2, pp. 28-29.
[687] Coulton, *Garner*, p. 703.
[688] Ibid., pp. 105-08.

little "Black boy" with his hand on the spigot. The monk takes the boy into the monastery. He gives him clothing as well as food and drink, but the boy refuses to take the nourishment. After a visiting Abbot hears the mysterious story of the boy, he accuses him of being the devil in disguise. When the boy hears the Abbot's charges, he vanishes "like smoke from between their hands." The mystery solved, the Abbot departs from the monastery. However, there was no word on whether the wine thefts disappeared along with the boy: It should be noted that cellarers and monks were notorious for sneaking their fair share of wine.

End of World Fears Grip Europe as They Mark Their 1st Millennium

Usually wherever visions appeared, testimonies of healing miracles followed closely behind. This was especially the case at the close of Europe's first millennium when believers attested to being cured of all manner of diseases and ailments. Other devotees formed long lines in front of churches, hoping to receive healing that could be shared with the world, too.

The closing of Europe's first millennium produced dread and hope. Though, truthfully, it represented just another time in Europe's history when biblical prophecy and interpretation strangled the minds of the masses: "An opinion prevailed everywhere that the end of the world was approaching many charters begin with these words, 'As the world is now drawing to its close.' An army marching under the emperor Otho I was so terrified by an eclipse of the sun, which it conceived to announce this consummation, as to disperse hastily on all sides."[689] Prophets obligingly cosigned first Millennianals' expectations of catastrophes and miracles with hair-raising details of future events. Believers' fears sent them to the churches where clergymen welcomed them with open arms:

> Then were innumerable sick folk healed in those conclaves of Holy men; and, lest men should think lightly of mere bursten skin or rent flesh in the straightening of arms and legs, much blood flowed forth also when the crooked limbs were restored; which gave faith to the rest who might have doubted. At this all were inflamed with such ardor that through the hands of their bishops they raised the pastoral staff to heaven, while themselves with outspread palms and with one voice cried to God: Peace, peace, peace![690]

Alas, the world did not conclude as predicted. Though, according to Ludlow, prophets extended the Earth's doom day prolonging "the gruesome foreboding" for 33 more years. He reports, too, that the world-ending near-miss was instructive for energizing the faithful: "The dreaded

---

[689] Hallam, *View*, vol. 2, p. 486.
[690] Coulton, *Garner*, p. 9.

year 1000 having safely passed without the anticipated destruction of the world, faith reinspired [sic] art to build temples on earth. New monasteries appeared, palatial in structure, to accommodate the people who sought in seclusion escape from the hardness or the dreariness of life in the world."[691]

The Devil's in the Diseases, According to the Church

So, hope restored - conditions returned to normal. However, miracle workers were still subject to church law. Even when tens of people at a time came forward with healing claims, the church decided which miracles to endorse. Because, the church said, demons had wings; like angels, they could copy their appearance and produce blessings that deceived the laity. On the other hand, people could only detect the deception of these malefactors in the consequences of their actions: the production of pestilences and unhealthy crops.

The list of esteemed clergymen who believed "the devil did it" is long and impressive. Following are quotes from a few: "[3rd century Theologian and scholar] Origen [Adamantius] said, 'It is demons which produce famine, unfruitfulness, corruptions of the air, pestilences; they hover concealed in the clouds in the lower atmosphere, and are attracted by the blood and incense which the heathen offer to them as gods.' St. Augustine said: 'All diseases of Christians are to be ascribed to these demons; chiefly do they torment fresh-baptized Christians, yea, even the guiltless, newborn infants....' Gregory of Nazianzus declared that bodily pains are provoked by demons, and that medicines are useless, but that they are often *cured by the laying on of consecrated hands*.... St. Bernard, in a letter to certain monks, warned them that to seek relief from disease in medicine was in harmony neither with their religion nor with the honour [sic] and purity of their order. This view even found its way into the canon law, which declared the precepts of medicine contrary to Divine knowledge. As a rule, the leaders of the Church discouraged the theory that diseases are due to natural causes...." [692] (Italics added). Of course, with fictitious healing claims replacing practical medicinal cures, sometimes the miraculously healed only became sick again. Tertullian, who lived during the 2nd and 3rd centuries, had earlier warned Christians of carrying forward primal beliefs that could lead to confusing friends with foes, but according to White, "insisted that a malevolent angel is in constant attendance upon every person."[693] Of demons Tertullian writes:

"If sorcerers call forth ghosts, and even make what seem the souls of the dead

---

[691] Ludlow, *Crusades*, p. 9.
[692] White, *Warfare*, vol. 2, pp. 27-28.
[693] Ibid., p. 27.

appear; if they put boys to death, in order to get a response from the oracle; if, with their juggling illusions, they make a pretence [sic] of doing various miracles; if they put dreams into people's minds by the power of the angels and demons whose aid they have invited.... Or if both angles and demons do just what your gods do, where in that case is the pre-eminence of deity...?[694]

Girolamo Savonarola Challenges the Pope's Authority

The church was playing it fast and loose in encouraging belief in the supernatural that could not be contained, nor controlled. Still, leaders insisted that solely church-approved clergymen be allowed to discern devilish activities from angelic ones. The threat of excommunication, or worse, hung over believers who refused to abide by church laws. Girolamo Savonarola serves as an example of what happened to miracle workers whose claims of supernatural communication from god materialized without the blessings of church leaders. Savonarola's contemporaries record that he foretold France's Charles VIII invasion of Italy; and he supposedly predicted the deaths of some of Italy's leading families, including Pope Innocent VIII, and the King of Naples. But, also, his sermons ridiculed and attacked "the wise of the world"[695] or anyone who rejected reforms he insisted that the church needed. Pope Alexander VI (Borgia) demanded that Savonarola stop his sermons. Communication between the two bore no fruit; Savonarola refused to yield to Borgia's authority, and, as we have learned, bore no scruples:

In this epistle, the Pope begins by lamenting that "new dogmas had sprung up under covers of a feigned simplicity, leading frequently, with the people and schismatic clergy, to heresies and subversions of morals, which have been combated by the church for the sake of the growth of the evil that had arisen.

"That Jerome Savonarola of Ferrera, of the order of preachers, had yielded to the delectation of this perversity of novel dogmas, and had given way to the insane idea of changing the affairs of Italy, declaring himself sent by God, and one whom God had spoken to, and, without any canonical authorizations, had set himself publicly against canonical sanctions. It is not sufficient for any person to assert such things point blank, as that he had been sent by God as an heretical person would assert; but it is essential that the person should exhibit the proofs of a manifest mission by the operation of miracles, or the special testimony of scripture...." His holiness goes on to say, he had hoped that Savonarola would have seen the sinfulness of the course he had taken, and

---

[694] Alexander Roberts and James Donaldson, trans., *The Writings of Tertullian*, vol.1 (Edinburgh: T & T. Clark, 1869), pp. 98-99.
[695] Niccoló Machiavelli, *Discourses on the First Decade of Titus Livius*, trans. Ninian Hill Thomson (London: Kegan Paul, Trench & Co, 1883), p. 440.

abandoned it of his own accord, but he had been mistaken.

"That he had sent letters to him, calling on him, in virtue of holy obedience, to come to Rome, and give an account of the matters laid to his charge, but that he had refused to come. He had been again summoned under penalty of excommunication, and had refused obedience, with many equivocations and excuses. That, finally, after consulting with the vicar-general of the Dominican order, Fra Sebastian de Madiis de Brixia, of the Lombard Congregation, he, Fra Girolamo Savonarola, had been suspended from all his functions; and that Fra Domenico de Pescia, Fra Toomas Bussino, and Fra Sylvester of Florence, would be included in the same sentence of suspension, if within nine days from that date they did not yield holy obedience to the orders given them, and proceed to Bologna to a convent of their order, &c. Given at Rome, &c., &c., &c." There is no date to this epistle.[696]

In 1498, for committing the crime of heresy, the pope imprisoned, tortured, and hanged Savonarola from a cross; then afterward, the executioner burned his body at the stake and tossed his ashes into the river so that his followers would not have access to his remains. A contemporary historian recorded that, "'While any part of his body was visible, a multitude of children and grown-up lads kept throwing stones at the remains hanging over the fire, and dropping away piece by piece, as the fury of the flames destroyed each part. The cinders and unconsumed remains of the executed friars were carefully separated from the charred wood and other scoriae of the combustible materials, put in carts, and thrown into the Arno. Some supposed fragments of the hand and arms of Savonarola were secreted either on the scaffold, or when the remains and their ashes were being conveyed to the Arno; and some portions even were said to have been taken from the river, and were eagerly sought after by the faithful friends and followers of the renowned and martyred friar San Marco.'"[697] It is noteworthy that Europeans sought after the remains of Savonarola. In a previous chapter I discussed the importance of *human trophies* to Europeans. The upcoming paragraphs divulge much, much more about just how important the remains of the dead, sainted and otherwise, were to medieval Europeans.

Europeans Dig Up Skeletons, Believe Saints' Bones Hold Cures

As we read earlier in the passage from *Acts*, Christians in search of healing especially valued the supposed mystical essence extracted from bones and other personal effects touched by saints. Paton informs us of Europe's long

---

[696] R. R. Madden, *The Life and Martyrdom of Savonarola the Christian Hero of the Fifteenth Century*, vol. 2, pp. 28-29.
[697] Ibid., p. 105.

history honoring bones: "The bones of heroes received the greatest reverence, and were frequently transported from one place to another in order to secure the presence of their owner. In 476 B.C. the Athenians brought the reputed bones of Theseus from Scyrus and deposited them in the Theseum at Athens. From that time onward the spirit of Theseus dwelt in the Theseum. Similarly in 437 B.C. the Athenians under Hagnon brought the bones of Rhesus from the Troad to Amphipolis."[698] Europeans firmly believed that qualities of the dead could be transferred to the living, improving their circumstances.

Human bones, also called *relics*, were dug up by medieval Europeans desperate for relief from pain or whatever else ailed them: "They implored the preservation of their health, or the cure of their infirmities; the fruitfulness of their barren wives, or the safety and happiness of their children.... The walls were hung round with symbols of the favors, which they had received; eyes and hands, and feet, of gold and silver.... The ministers of the Catholic Church imitated the profane model, which they were impatient to destroy. The most respectable bishops had persuaded themselves, that the ignorant rustics would more cheerfully renounce the superstitions of Paganism, if they found some resemblance, some compensation, in the bosom of Christianity."[699]

Relying on relics for physical and spiritual relief is codified in the bible providing some evidence that worshipping bones is an ancient European practice: 2 Kings: 13:20-21 (ca. 590-560 BCE) mentions the supposed healing power of bones: "And Eli'sha died, and they buried him. And in the bands of the Mo'abites invaded the land at the coming in of the year. And it came to pass, as they were burying a man, that, behold, they spied a band of men; and they cast the man into the sepulchre [sic] of Eli'sha: and when the man was let down, and touched the bones of Eli'sha, he 'revived, and stood up on his feet.' Relics were "preserved in great abundance in the Lateran,[700] which, for that reason, was of special importance for pilgrims."[701]

In fact, relics were in great demand in all of Christendom: "Chief of all their sacred possessions the Romans boasted the remains of the Apostles Peter and Paul, and would have surrendered to the Lombards their city itself rather than any portion of these relics. The Empress Constantina ingenuously implored Gregory to send her the head of the Apostle Paul, or, at any rate, a part of his remains, for the shrine of a church she was building in her palace at Byzantium, and Gregory's answer betrays the difficulty he had in mastering the irritation roused by the request. He replies that it would be a sin worthy of death to touch the sacred bodies, or

---

[698] Paton, *Spiritism*, p. 103.
[699] Gibbon, *Decline*, vol. 3, pp. 162-63.
[700] Apostolic palace.
[701] Burckhardt, *Renaissance*, p. 483.

even to approach them by a glance."[702] Indeed. To dry the persistent Empress' thirst, Gregory told her that even St. Lawrence's remains had caused the deaths of everyone who had looked upon them; they both agreed that a piece of the saint's tomb cloth, or else a link in St. Peter's chain was sufficient. But, that was only one pope's response to one empress. The demand for saints' bones was so great that it provoked body-snatching expeditions to grave yards by "Men travelling [sic] for their own ends, or in the commission of foreign bishops."[703]

Encyclopaedia Britannica informs us, "Nobody hesitated to divide up the bodies of the saints in order to afford as many portions of them as possible. They were shared among the inhabitants of cities and villages, Theodoret tells us, and cherished by everybody as healers and physicians for both body and soul."[704] And when no dead saints were available? European folklorists say worshippers murdered holy people to give to themselves an "object of devotion!"[705] The Catholic Church possesses literally hundreds of thousands of bones all over Europe. The *two heads* belonging to John the Baptist, and the fingers of saints John and Andrew[706] are mentioned, too. What's more, the remains of Charlemagne and the Magi have been given as presents to eager religious audiences. Additional relics collected over the centuries include locks of hair from the Virgin Mary and Mary Magdalene; a nail from the crucifixion; rays from the star that guided the wise men; and the hem from Jesus' garment.[707] Though without a doubt skeletal remains were the most treasured relics. Worshippers believed that over time liquid seeped from them to form pools of healing waters. These pools of waters and streams, White informs us, became popular for curing leprosy and restoring vision to the blind. Even the grounds where both the pious and pitiable persons drew in their last breaths became reverential sites where manic crowds fought over dead men's garments, hair, or other items considered valuable because believers thought that their spiritual power seeped into the surrounding grounds.

The Church uses Human Skull Cups During Services and at "Holy" Wells

Folklorist Mabel Peacock (d. 1920) writes in *Folk-Lore: A Quarterly Review*

---

[702] Gregorovius, *Rome*, vol. 2, pp. 73-74.
[703] Ibid., p. 74.
[704] Hauck, Relics, *Encyclopaedia Britannica*. 11th ed. 1911. pp. 59-60.
[705] E. Sidney Hartland, "The Cult of Executed Criminals at Palermo," *Folk-Lore: A Quarterly Review Myth, Tradition, Institution, & Custom*, vol. 21, no. 1 (1910) p. 176.
[706] William Henry P. Phyfe, Five Thousand Facts and Fancies: A Cyclopaedia of Important, Curious, Quaint And Unique Information in History, Literature, Science, Art, and Nature, p. 636.
[707] Ibid.

that the church used saints' bones for healing in religious ceremonies. However, the medieval Christian's fascination for saintly relics was not limited to human teeth, hair, or torso bones; the human skull had mystical properties conferred on it, too. Paton asserts, "The skull was regarded as particularly the seat of the spirit, hence apparently in earliest times it was preserved in the home as a means of communicating with an ancestor. This is the origin of the os resectum, or bone cut off before cremation. Originally the head was removed for preservation, later a finger, or some other part of the body was substituted."[708] The saints' corpses were laid out in coffins; their skulls decorated and provided to congregants as festive-looking drinking vessels. Strack remarks, "The monks at Treves had S. Theodulf's skull set in silver and gave fever patients to drink out of it ("Acta Sanctorum" May I, 99a). Leo von Rozmital came to Neuss in 1465: There we saw in the church a costly coffin; therein lay the dear holy Saint Quirinus, and we saw his skull, therefrom they gave us to drink."[709]

In fact skull cups were so much in vogue that medieval Europeans attached them[710] to wells where they were put into casual use as drinking vessels throughout Europe. Peacock observes the following regarding these *holy* wells:

> At St. Teilo's well, near the church of Llandeilo Llwydarth, in the Welsh half of Pembrokeshire, a skull is used as a cup. The water, according to Professor Rhys, must be lifted out of the well and given to the patient to drink by somebody born in the farmhouse close by. It is given in a skull—St. Teilo's skull—which Teilo Professor Rhys is unable to decide. This instance, in all likelihood, does not stand alone. I have, indeed, heard that a skull is similarly used at one of the Irish holy-wells, but the name of the spring has escaped my memory. Among the "remèdes extérieurs" condemned by Thiers in his Traité des Superstitions, 1777, vol. i., p. 339, he mentions that of drinking spring-water by night from the head "d'un homme mort ou brulé," to free oneself from epilepsy....[711]

According to Peacock, Europeans have a long history of using human skull cups as drinking vessels, naming the Vikings as most likely participants while ensuring readers that Celtics, and Teutonics were definite practitioners. Herodotus testifies that the Scythians were avid users

---

[708] Paton, *Spiritism*, p. 103.
[709] Strack, *Sacrifice*, p. 79.
[710] Many influential Anglo-Saxons living in the United States are members of Skull & Bones, a secretive fraternal organization whose roots course through England and extend into Germany. The group maintains close ties to established universities. Its critics allege that members - so-called "bones men" - have stolen bones of Indian warrior Geronimo, et al. A quick Internet search reveals the names of alleged members, past and present.
[711] Mabel Peacock, "Executed Criminals and Folk-Medicine," *Folk-Lore: A Quarterly Review Myth, Tradition, Institution, & Custom*, vol. 7, no. 1 (1896) pp. 276-77.

of human skulls of enemy and family alike:

> The skulls of their enemies, not indeed of all, but of those whom they most detest, they treat as follows. Having sawn off the portion below the eyebrows, and cleaned out the inside, they cover the outside with leather. When a man is poor, this is all that he does; but if he is rich, he also lines the inside with gold: in either case the skull is used as a drinking-cup. They do the same with the skulls of their own kith and kiri if they have been at feud with them, and have vanquished them in the presence of the king. When strangers whom they deem of any account come to visit them, these skulls are handed round, and the host tells how that these were his relations who made war upon him, and how that he got the better of them; all this being looked upon as proof of bravery.[712]

As readers will discover later in Chapter 12, the practice of Europeans using human skulls as cups, or for other sordid reasons, reaches back into their distant past. Strack recounts the personal story of a man after his pilgrimage to Jerusalem around 570-580 CE, "There is a nunnery there. I saw there enclosed in a gold casket adorned with jewels a human skull, of which they say, it is that of the martyr Theodota. Many drank water out of it for a blessing ('pro benedictione,') and I also drank."[713]

Peacock informs readers that pouring libations into the skulls of saints for good health is clearly a Christian practice. She writes that Christians continued to use the crania of their saints, and their malefactors, as cups from which to imbibe health- securing draughts throughout Europe:

> He who drinks out of the skull of an executed malefactor thereby aids himself against epilepsy," says Rochholz; and he furnishes instances of the barbaric observance as connected with church ceremonial in his account of the bone worship of pagan and superficially Christian Germany. Among other examples he quotes the silver-enchased brain-pan of St. Theodul at Trier, which served in the cure of fever cases, and that of the similarly ornamented skull of St. Sebastian at Ebersperg in Upper Bavaria, which secured the neighbourhood [sic] against the pest, in consequence of the pilgrims visiting the place drinking from it wine which had been blessed. The Rev. R. Polwhele, author of that quaint collection of information, the Enthusiasm of Methodists and Papists Considered, 1820, (p. 291), tells the story of a girl, who, being deemed epileptic, "was sent to the monastery of Nonhert to drink out of St. Cornelius's scull; whereby the nuns told about, but falsely, that she was better.[714]

Strack relates a seamy detail concerning St. Sebastian's remains, "As

---

[712] Rawlinson, *Herodotus*, vol. 2, p. 225.
[713] Strack, *Sacrifice*, p. 79.
[714] Peacock, "Executed Criminals and Folk-Medicine," *Folk-Lore: A Quarterly Review Myth, Tradition, Institution, & Custom*, vol. 7, no. 1 (1896) p. 276.

long as S. Sebastian's skull set in silver is kept at Ebersperg in Upper Bavaria, and the consecrated wine is given those pilgrimaging thither to drink out of the skull, the plague has never more dared to take its seat in these parts."[715]

If the perverse act of drinking wine and water from a human skull is not macabre enough for readers, the quite wealthy and well-traveled author C. F. Gordon-Cumming (d. 1924) writing for *The Nineteenth Century* relates how the Nestorians, a Syrian sect of Christians, mixed powdered bone of saints with wine, "while they eschew all veneration for relics, yet believe the remains of saints and martyrs to be endowed with such supernatural virtues, that at their wedding-feasts the dust of some reputed saint is invariably mixed with the wine in the marriage-cup a custom which would seem to require numerous additions to their saintly calendar. Doubtless, however, the holy dust multiplies, that the supply may be equal to the demand."[716]

Because they were routinely disturbed, the locations of many burial sites were kept secret or bodies were entombed beneath the floors of churches. Apparently unfazed by the grave robberies throughout the centuries, the 16th century Council of Trent Decalogue states:

> But what incredulity so obstinate but must yield to the evidence in support of the honor and invocation of the saints, which the wonders wrought at their tombs flash upon the mind? The blind see, the lame walk, the paralyzed are invigorated, the dead raised to life, and the evil demons are expelled from the bodies of men! These are authentic facts, attested not, as frequently happens, by very grave persons who have heard them form others; they are facts which rest on the ocular attestation of witnesses, whose veracity is beyond all question, of an Ambrose, and an Augustine. But why multiply the proofs on this head? If the clothes, the kerchiefs, and even the very shadows of the saints, whilst yet on earth, banished disease and restored health and vigor, who will have the hardihood to deny that God can still work the same wonders by the holy ashes, the bones and other relics of his saints who are in glory? Of this we have proof in the resuscitation of the dead body which was let down into the grave of Eliseus, and which, on touching the body of the prophet, was instantly restored to life.[717]

European Churches Constructed of Human Bones

St. Ambrose, according to White, "declared that 'the precepts of

---

[715] Strack, *Sacrifice*, p. 79.
[716] Constance Frederica Gordon-Cumming, "Strange Medicines." *The Nineteenth Century*, vol. 21, no. 119 (1887) p. 908.
[717] J. Donovan, trans., *The Catechism of the Council of Trent* (Baltimore: Lucas Brothers, 1829), p. 248.

medicine are contrary to celestial science, watching, and prayer.'"[718] In fact, Encyclopaedia Britannica notes, "The veneration of relics also received a strong impulse from the fact that the Church required that a relic should be deposited in every altar. Among the first of those whom we know to have attached importance to the placing of relics in churches is Ambrose of Milan (Ep. 22), and the seventh general council of Nicaea (787) forbade the consecration of churches in which relics were not present, under pain of excommunication. This has remained part of the law of the Roman Catholic Church."[719]

The human bone-decor of European ossuaries, also called bone churches, showcases the lure of human bones on medieval Europeans. These *bone churches* harbor skeletal remains of monks and other medieval corpses in caverns that run beneath the ground where the church stands, though there are many bones churches constructed of actual human skeletal remains. Within these *hallowed* settings, human skulls and skeletons dangle, line, or poke out from walls and ceilings in what accounts for some of the strangest "attractions" in Europe. Europeans probably erected bone churches because medieval tribulations ushered in wars, famines, plagues, etc., that killed more people than graveyards could hold, and because they liked the bones of saints to fill their churches.

Ignoring the obvious ghoulishness involved in building churches from human remains, some Europeans insist that bone churches are merely literal reminders of the fate all humans face. Of these ossuaries Strack writes: "[Christians] scarcely liked to build a church in which mouldering bones and old rags of clothes were not deposited; these saints, whose altars rose up next that of the Deity, whose festivals filled the whole year, were also lords of justice and of diseases; for all oaths were sworn on their relics, all incurables besought cure on their knees before their graves and relics."[720]

Peacock notes the special uses for human skulls still being practiced during her time by devoted Christians: "A writer in the Atlantic Monthly ixxiv, pp. 480-493, gives an account of the miraculous, chrism-dripping skulls still preserved at Kieff, and describes how a Russian pilgrim visiting that holy city knelt, crossed himself devoutly, and received from a priest the sign of the cross on his brow, administered with a soft small brush dipped in the oil from a skull."[721]

As late as 1896, "oil-exuding bones from saints"[722] continued to intrigue post-medieval Europeans. Cumming hints at the odd use of skulls in

---

[718] White, *Warfare*, vol. 2, p. 26.
[719] Hauck, *Relics, Encyclopaedia Britannica*. 11th ed. 1911. p. 60.
[720] Strack, *Sacrifice*, pp. 78-79.
[721] Peacock, "Executed Criminals and Folk-Medicine," *Folk-Lore: A Quarterly Review Myth, Tradition, Institution, & Custom*, vol. 7, no. 1 (1896) p. 277.
[722] Ibid.

medieval European medicinal remedies, a topic explored more fully later in Chapter 12: "It is certainly startling to realise [sic] how exactly they describe the medicine-lore of our [European] ancestors, of which traces survive amongst us even to this day. We know of several cases within recent years when in the north of Scotland the skull of a suicide was with great difficulty procured, and used as a drinking-cup for an epileptic patient. Still surer was it deemed to reduce part of the skull to powder and swallow it. Even the moss which grew on such skulls was deemed a certain cure for divers diseases. In the official prescription of the London College of Physicians, a.d. 1678, the skull of a man who has died violent death, and the horn of a unicorn, appear as highly approved medicines. In 1724 all human skulls are declared useful, and multitudes were exported... to Germany for the manufacture of a famous ointment."[723]

"Naturally," writes White, "the belief thus sanctioned by successive heads of the Church, infallible in all teaching regarding faith and morals, create a demand for amulets and charms of all kinds: and under this influence we find a reversion to old pagan fetiches."[724]

Probably the most horrendous detail regarding European skull worshipping that I did not need to learn is that: "The head of S. Makarius in the Marienkapelle at Würzburg is laid every year [2 January] on believers; it is a security against headache."[725]

---

[723] Gordon Cumming, *Memories*, p. 472.
[724] White, *Warfare*, vol. 2, p. 30.
[725] Strack, *Sacrifice*, p. 79.

9

THE CHRISTIAN COMMUNITY EMBRACES BENT BELIEFS

As the old pagan faith decayed, they tended to become in a literal sense superstition....[726]

The Middle Ages church leaders, who ruled medieval minds with their closed fists, seemed most at ease when it selected who was taught and what was taught. Likewise, they schooled the clerical community in patristic literature, books concerned exclusively with the religious views of the early church fathers. Augustine once said, "The authority of Scripture is higher than all the efforts of the human intelligence."[727]

Besides Augustine's apparent lack of appetite for science, there was general disinterest in the church community for knowledge outside of scriptures. Indeed, the church strongly rejected science that was not scripturally based. They labeled independent thinkers as heretics and punished them accordingly. When it came to science, early church leaders shoved their heads in the sand the way church descendants do today. Yet, it is true that the church preserved the Latin language in the face of barbarism, and it cleverly integrated local old world rituals with its own to keep the church relevant. I will discuss the marriage between old world religions and Christianity shortly. But for now, Thorndike states that the proof of their lack of refinement and sophistication is visible in Christian works:

> For a long time Christians who had any education had a classical one, because that was the only one to be had. The early Christians did not excel in art and literature, as the lack of literary style in the Greek New Testament and the rude frescoes of the Roman catacombs show.[728]

As church father, Augustine was instrumental in directing its course, and hundreds of years after his death men still feared having thoughts contrary to his centuries-old dogma. Even today, he is very greatly

---

[726] Clement A. Miles, "Christmas Eve and Twelve Days," in *Christmas in Ritual and Tradition Christian and Pagan*, (London: T. Fisher Unwin, 1912).
[727] Thorndike, *Europe*, p. 113.
[728] Ibid., p. 112

esteemed by the church. Ernest Brehaut writes the following passage on Augustine's intentions for the church:

> Men like Augustine were occupied in de-secularizing the knowledge of their times; that is, in reshaping it so that it should fill a subordinate place in the religious scheme and so support that scheme, or at least not be in opposition to it. Orosius'[729] [d.418] feat of *reshaping history* so that it was going on in every field. Such secular knowledge as was allowed to exist was brought into more or less close relation to the religious ideas that dominated thinkers, and *whatever could not be thus reshaped tended to be rejected* and forgotten.[730] (Italics added).

Ancient Africans were certainly aware that great forces existed beyond the Earth. The ancient Kemetans devised the first zodiac found at Dendera temple, while older stone circular astronomical observatories are in southern Africa. Besides all that, one look at Dogon Science is all one needs to understand that Egun demonstrated advanced knowledge of our Universe. However, the Roman world was a non-scientific world: "Among the Romans no scientists arose to assimilate the results of the work of the Greeks, and sound ideas as to the form of the universe were rare even in the most intelligent circles. Since systematic observation was not practiced, and a knowledge of the higher mathematics did not exist among the Romans, their astronomy was a matter of tradition and authority. Therefore upon the acceptance of Christianity and the realization that there was a conflict between the Greek and the Hebrew cosmologies, it was a comparatively easy matter to accept the Scriptures instead of the secular writers as the source of authority."[731] As for the barbarians, needless to say, when it came to science, they did a lot of navel-gazing.

Europeans Say, "If Earth is Round Antipodes Walk on Their Heads"

Modern European historians like to refute the idea that early ancestors believed in a flat earth. And from a moon-walker's point of view, it seems silly to believe that a (white) man once fretted over skimming his sails *close to the horizon's edge*. However, the church dominated the feudal world and church leaders led all its discussions. Clergymen based church policies on literal biblical interpretations. Interestingly, when it came to the Earth's shape, church authorities had plenty of descriptions to choose from. Pliny the Elder describes the debate, and introduces a reason that leaders believed round earth speculation was ridiculous: hand-standing creatures called "antipodes" would have to exist:

---

[729] Historian and theologian.
[730] Brehaut, *Encyclopedist*, p. 37.
[731] Ibid., p. 140.

There is here great debate between learned men; and contrariwise of the ignorant multitude: for they hold, that men are overspread on all parts upon the earth, and stand one against another, foot to foot: also that the summit of the heaven is alike unto all: and in what part soever men be, they still tread after the same manner in the midst. But, the common sort ask, how, then, it happeneth, that they who are opposite against us, do not fall into heaven? As if there were not a reason also ready, that the antipodes again should wonder why we also fell not off?[732]

Some clergymen ridiculed the idea of a spherical earth, because it meant antipodes lived there: if such creatures existed, debaters speculated, they walked on their heads and hung in the air by their feet, as Pliny mentions above. More information on these antipodes in the next few paragraphs, but first the shape of our Earth. Questions about Earth's form turned into a centuries-long debate with theorists assigning her all manners of appearances and constitutions. According to White, eminent church fathers such as Theophilus of Antioch [2nd c. CE] and Clement of Alexandria [3rd c. CE], "With others in centuries following, were not content with merely opposing what they stigmatized as an old heathen theory; they drew from their bibles a new Christian theory, to which one church authority added one idea and another, until it was fully developed. Taking the survival of various early traditions, given in the seventh verse of the first chapter of Genesis, they insisted on the clear declarations of Scripture that the earth was, at creation, arched over with a solid vault, 'a firmament' and to this they added the passages from Isaiah and the Psalms, in which it declared that the heavens stretched out 'like a curtain,' and again 'like a tent to dwell in.'"[733]

"Others," according to E.O. Winstedt, "Diodorus of Tarsus, for instance, Severianus of Gabala and Eusebius, regarded earth and heaven as a kind of two-storied house."[734] Perhaps by applying the principle "as above, so below" these early Christians envisioned the heavens shaped like homes. In this scenario the floor of this house represented Earth and the ceiling was its firmament. At the same time, the firmament was the floor to the apartment above. In it was a bathing-tank that held the waters of the firmament. God's angels released these waters upon the Earth through "windows of heaven." The Sun, Moon and Stars were just below the firmament. White adds: "As to the movement of the sun, there was a

---

[732] Philemon Holland, trans., *Pliny The Elder Natural History*, (London: George Barclay, 1847), p. 104.
[733] White, *Warfare*, vol.1, p. 92.
[734] Cosmas Indicopleustes, *The Christian Topography of Cosmas Indicopleustes*, ed. E.O. Winstedt (Cambridge: University Press, 1909), p. 7.

citation of various passages in Genesis, mixed with metaphysics in various proportions, and this was thought to give ample proofs from the Bible that the earth could not be a sphere."[735]

This may have been Augustine's position, too. In his famous *City of God* he writes:

> But as to the fable that there are Antipodes, that is to say, men on the opposite side of the earth, where the sun rises when it sets to us, men who walk with their feet opposite ours, that is on no ground credible. And, indeed, it is not affirmed that this has been learned by historical knowledge, but by scientific conjecture, on the ground that the earth is suspended within the concavity of the sky, and that it has as much room on the one side of it as on the other: hence they say that the part which is beneath must also be inhabited. But they do not remark that, although it be supposed or scientifically demonstrated that the world is of a round and spherical form, yet it does not follow that the other side of the earth is bare of water; nor even, though it be bare, does it immediately follow that it is peopled. For Scripture, which proves the truth of its historical statements by the accomplishment of its prophecies, gives no false information; and it is too absurd to say, that some men might have taken ship and traversed the whole wide ocean, and crossed from this side of the world to the other, and that thus even the inhabitants of that distant region are descended from that one first man. Wherefore let us seek if we can find the city of God that sojourns on earth among those human races who are catalogued as having been divided into seventy-two nations and as many languages.[736]

Though Augustine's passage is plainly in opposition to a round earth, apologists claim his meaning is unclear, leaving open to interpretation whether or not Augustine was a flat earth believer. White states that Augustine "seemed inclined to yield a little" on the sphericity doctrine. To this he adds, "[Augustine's] most cogent appeal, one which we find echoed from theologian to theologian during a thousand years afterward, is to the nineteenth Psalm, and to its confirmation in the Epistle to the Romans; to the words, 'Their line is gone out through all the earth, and their words to the end of the world....' The great Bishop of Hippo taught the whole world for over a thousand years that, as there was no preaching of the gospel on the opposite side of the earth, there could be no human beings there."[737] Lucius Caelilius Firmianus Lactantius (ca.240–ca.320) is probably little known today, but during his own time he was a well-respected Christian author and advisor to Constantine. On the subjects of antipodes and a round earth, he writes:

---

[735] White, *Warfare*, vol.1, p. 92.
[736] Dods, *God*, pp. 118-19.
[737] White, *Warfare*, vol. 1, pp. 103-04.

About the antipodes also one can neither hear nor speak without laughter. It is asserted as something serious, that we should believe that there are men who have their feet opposite to ours....[738]

How is it with those who imagine that there are antipodes opposite to our footsteps? Do they say anything to the purpose? Or is there any one so senseless as to believe that there are men whose footsteps are higher than their heads? or that the things which with us are in a recumbent position, with them hang in an inverted direction? that the crops and trees grow downwards? that the rains, and snow, and hail fall upwards to the earth? And does any one wonder that hanging gardens are mentioned among the seven wonders of the world, when philosophers make hanging fields, and seas, and cities, and mountains?

What course of argument, therefore, led them to the idea of the antipode? They saw the courses of the stars traveling towards the west; they saw that the sun and the moon always set towards the same quarter, and rise from the same. But since they did not perceive what contrivance regulated their courses, nor how they returned from the west to the east, but supposed that the heaven itself sloped downwards in every direction, which appearance it must present on account of its immense breadth, they thought that the world is round like a ball, and they fancied that the heaven revolves in accordance with the motion of the heavenly bodies.... But if the earth also were round.... there would be no part of the earth uninhabited by men and the other animals. Thus the rotundity of the earth leads, in addition, to the invention of those suspended antipodes. I sometimes imagine that they either discuss philosophy for the sake of a jest, or purposely and knowingly undertake to defend falsehoods, as if to exercise or display their talents on false subjects....[739]

Severian of Gabala, mentioned earlier, belonged to so-called Antiochian interpreters who rejected arguments of a spherical earth. "Among Christian scholars from the beginning there had been a desire to bring the traditional ideas of pagan cosmography into subordination to the Christian scheme," writes Brehaut.[740]

Constantine of Antiochia also called Cosmas (Indicopleustes) the monk lived during the 6th century. He wrote a Christian topography (c. 550 AD), with intentions "to refute the theory that the earth was round, and to prove that Moses' tabernacle in the wilderness was a model of the universe. The earth he reiterates is a flat surface, its length twice its breadth... supported by walls at the end of the earth and 'glued' to it."[741]

---

[738] William D. Fletcher, trans. *The Works of Lactantius*, vol. 2. (Edinburgh: T. &. T. Clark, 1871), p. 122.
[739] White, *Warfare*, vol.1, pp. 196-97.
[740] Brehaut, *Encyclopedist* p. 30.
[741] Indicopleustes, *Topography*, p. 6.

White tells us, "According to Cosmas, the earth is a parallelogram, flat, and surrounded by four seas. It is four hundred days' journey long and two hundred broad. At the outer edges of these four seas arise massive walls closing in the whole structure and supporting the firmament or vault of the heavens whose edges are cemented to the walls. These walls inclose [sic] the earth and all the heavenly bodies."[742] To understand the earth's surface Cosmas looked at the "table of shew-bread in the Jewish tabernacle. The surface of this table proves that the earth is flat, and its dimensions prove that the earth is twice as long as broad; its four corners symbolize the four seasons; the twelve loaves of bread, the twelve months; the hollow about the table proves that the ocean surrounds the earth. To account for the movement of the sun, Cosmas suggests that at the north of the earth is a great mountain, and that at night the sun is carried behind this; but some of the commentators ventured to express a doubt here: they thought that the sun was pushed into a pit at night and pulled out in the morning."[743] White sums up Cosmas' theory thusly: "'We say therefore with Isaiah that the heaven embracing the universe is a vault, with Job that it is joined to the earth, and with Moses that the length of the earth is greater than its breadth.'"[744]

And though modern revisionists claim that authorities ridiculed Cosmas' theory White observes, "Some of the foremost men in the Church devoted themselves to buttressing it with new texts and throwing about it new outworks of theological reasoning; the great body of the faithful considered it a direct gift from the Almighty. Even in the later centuries of the Middle Ages John of San Geminiano made a desperate attempt to save it."[745] White alludes to the myriad of mythologies that point to belief in upper and lower parts to our universe, including the biblical story of the building of the Tower of Babel. Cosmas and other interpreters of his time looked to "the ninth chapter of Hebrews to the tabernacle in the desert... that it gives the key to the whole construction of the world. The universe is, therefore, made on the plan of the Jewish tabernacle-boxlike and oblong,"[746] writes White. Many biblical verses mention a flat earth, including Revelation 7:1, that describes angels standing on the four corners of the Earth; Isaiah 40:22 describes "him" as sitting on the "circle of the earth" making it flat, much like a CD; in Job 26:7, the earth hangs upon nothing; and in Luke 4:5 and Matthew 4:8, Jesus sees the earth from a very high mountain, leaving one with the impression that it is flat and Isaiah 40:22: "he sitteth upon the earth... that stretcheth out the heavens as a

---

[742] White, *Warfare*, vol. 1, p. 92.
[743] Ibid., p. 94.
[744] Ibid., p. 94.
[745] Ibid., p. 95.
[746] Ibid., p. 93.

curtain, and spreadeth them out as a tent to dwell in."

Archbishop Isidore of Seville, described by Brehaut as, "the leading representative of the intellect of the dark ages, and the only important writer on secular subjects in two centuries of western European history"[747] believed that the universe was geocentric, bounded by a revolving sphere made of fire with fixed stars, according to the author. Isidore in describing his view of the world placed circular zones (northern, solstitial, equnioctial, winter, southern) of land upon a flat circle. "He evidently thought that zona and circulus were interchangeable terms, and his "circles" did not run around the circumference of a spherical earth, but lay on a flat earth...."[748] writes the author. Further proof that Isidore believed in a flat earth is found in this passage on astronomy, according to Brehaut, "The size of the sun is greater than that of the earth and so from the moment when it rises it appears equally to east and west at the same time."[749]

Brehaut suggests that Isidore's theories seem unsettled either because of confusion, or because he placated certain people. Brehaut sums it up by remarking, "In Isidore's ideas on cosmology a curious inconsistency appears. On the one hand, he shows that he regards the words of the Scripture as the final authority, and he frequently gives expression to primitive notions in accord with the Hebrew cosmology. On the other hand, he displays a greater liberality than is shown by his predecessor, Cassiodorus, or by any other Christian writer in the Latin language up to his time, in borrowing from the pagan writers on astronomy."[750] And though the opinions of Isidore of the sphericity of the earth may have confused some, he was much clearer in his disbelief in antipodes declaring, "men can not and ought not to exist on opposite sides of the earth."[751]

Christianity: A Jumble of Europe's Pagan Beliefs Shaken Up and Poured Out to the Masses: Tall Tales Become Religious Traditions

The triumph of Christianity hastened the decline of classical art, literature, philosophy, and science, which it was eventually to replace by a theology, and an art of its own. Many Christians, especially ascetics, felt that ancient art and poetry were dangerous, closely connected as they were with pagan mythology, and appealing as they did to the sense of beauty and the passion of love.[752]

As I mention in an earlier chapter, along with Christianity came the drive

---

[747] Brehaut, *Encyclopedist* p. 50.
[748] Ibid., p 53.
[749] Ibid., p 147.
[750] Ibid., p 141.
[751] White, *Warfare*, vol. 1, p. 105.
[752] Thorndike, *Europe*, p. 112.

to stifle all old world competitors for the hearts and minds of Europeans. With the edicts of Justinian and Theodosius firmly in place, Christians denounced ancient African philosophical teachings as pagan customs, and sternly forbade them. Church leaders criminalized the worship of African deities inside temples, many of which had become Europeanized. Early Greek and the Roman civilizations desired education for their citizenry, a practice originally modeled after African cultures. However, the barbarian warlords who stormed the lands and marshaled in feudal rule were a wild and uneducated lot who trended more toward mimicking Roman aesthetics in "food, clothing and love-making,"[753] according to Thorndike. Leaders reserved education for the children of the wealthy, according to Brehaut, although the overall influence of nobility was flimsy when weighted against the might of the church.

Additionally, the Fourth Council of Carthage (398 CE) banned[754] books. The Council "prohibited the reading of secular books by bishops. Jerome plainly condemns the study of them except for pious ends. All physical science especially was held in avowed contempt, as inconsistent with revealed truths. Nor do there appear to have been any canons made in favor of learning, or any restriction on the ordination of persons absolutely illiterate,"[755] writes Hallam. During the 5th and 6th centuries the church closed the books on all secular education:

> Upon their disappearance the whole burden of maintaining education fell upon the church.... There was no system established by a central authority and enforced by public opinion to guide the efforts made by these bodies, and it is plain that in each case educational facilities for the training of priests would be provided in accordance with the intelligence and character of the different bishops and abbots. Where the ecclesiastical authorities were ignorant or careless, the training of the priest or monk must have degenerated to a sort of apprenticeship. The evidence which we possess of the illiteracy of the clergy would lead us to infer that in the dark ages education, in any sense worthy of the name, was sporadic....[756]

By the 11th and 12th centuries, the wretched classes of the *dumbed-down*[757] included church leaders. Ludlow remarks, "The intellectuality of this

---

[753] Ibid., p. 126.
[754] There are differing interpretations. Another interpretation holds that the ban applied to the reading of non-scriptural books during service.
[755] Hallam, *View*, vol. 2, p. 467.
[756] Brehaut, *Encyclopedist* p. 82.
[757] In the United States, Act 3 (or 4?) of *Christianity Takes Pride In Stupidity* is under way, as many church leaders encourage their flocks to use the bible as a science reference, as vetted scientific evidence is ignored. U. S. science students routinely place well below many other countries on international tests.

period exercised itself almost entirely with theological and religious subjects. Men in seclusion elaborated and defended existing church doctrines, and gave pious flight to their imaginations. But of literature as such there was none.... One of their contemporaries gives this tribute to the ecclesiastics of the time, 'They were given rather to the gullet than to the tongue. They preferred to be schooled in salmon rather than in Solomon.' Few priests could translate the breviary they recited with parrot tongues. Of the history of the grand civilization just behind them the people knew nothing; even the laws which had so long preserved the state and society, those of Justinian, were forgotten except in some cloisters, where they were studied as classic lore.... But in the time we are studying there was no real scientific thought that was not instantly suppressed by the authorities of the church as the suggestion of heretics or of the Saracens. Roger Bacon, who flourished so late as the close of the crusades, paid with fourteen years' imprisonment for his temerity in proposing the more rational methods of viewing the world, which his great namesake, Francis Bacon, three hundred and fifty years later, more completely formulated for general acceptance."[758]

Thusly, during feudal Europe most people became uneducated, and illiterate. And what little education there was came by way of the church whose leaders had goals of overthrowing ancient knowledge and increasing church powers. Even Charlemagne, credited with holding on to some Roman structure, neglected education in favor of keeping the church intact. Charlemagne: "Himself is said to have spoken Latin and understood Greek, although he could scarcely write his name.[759] But there is no record[760] of his encouraging classical learning and literature for their own sake, nor of any great proficiency in either in his time."[761] White writes, "In the cathedral schools established by Charlemagne and others provision was generally made for medical teaching; but all this instruction, whether in convents or schools, was wretchedly poor. It consisted not in developing by individual thought and experiment the gifts of Hippocrates, Aristotle, and Galen, but almost entirely in the parrot-like repetition of their writings."[762]

---

[758] Ludlow, *Crusades*, pp. 8-11.
[759] Charlemagne's illiteracy is confirmed by Brehaut, p. 19: 'The "sixty-one correct hexameters" [verse] of the Visigothic King Sisebutus (612-620), compared, for instance, with the absolutely hopeless attempts of Charlemagne two centuries later to learn the art of tracing letters, show plainly that Spanish culture had not sunk to the level of that of other parts of the western empire. (The author references Einhard, Vita Caroli Magni in Monumenta Germaniac Historica Scriptors (Pertz ed) vol. ii, p. 456)'.
[760] According to Howe, Charlemagne issued a 789 order to clergyman to open schools for boys. Other historians note that education was reserved for Charlemagne's inner circle of advisors or for boys taken in and trained by monks as future clerks.
[761] Thorndike, *Europe*, p. 211.
[762] White, *Warfare*, vol. 2, p. 34.

Between feudalism and civilization lay superstition, and it poured through all the ideological crevices religious doctrines were unable to logically seal. According to Ludlow:

> Men become the easy prey of superstition. All sorts of stories of things supernatural, the invention of designing priests or born of the surprise of ignorance at the unusual in nature, were believed without question. The winds that rustled the leaves of the forest were supposed to be the voices of saintly ghosts, and when with wintry weight they moaned through the branches or screeched along the icy rocks, it was believed that the damned were groaning in their pains or that demons were threatening men. Every flash or shadow that could not readily be explained was regarded as a hopeful or vengeful apparition from the unseen world. This credulity was not confined to the illiterate and boorish. The chroniclers of that age, upon whose learning we depend for the facts of our history, relate with equal gravity the deeds of demons and men, connect the doings of courts and the course comets, and intermingle in relation of cause and effect the storms of nature and the wars of nations. Thus superstition completed the work of mental inoccupancy [sic], as vermin and bats inhabit an unfurnished cell.[763]

Overthrowing long-held traditional beliefs of Europeans was not as easy a task as dismantling education had been: "Christians were themselves but baptized heathen and brought their heathen conceptions into the church with them, little changed in all that was not obviously at variance with their Christian confession.... But he that was superstitious remained superstitious still; and he who lived in a world of marvels looked for and found marvels happening all about him still," opines Warfield.[764] Eventually the church grew weary from centuries of pushing for change and settled for blending old world festivities with Christian rites to make Christianity more palatable to the multitudes who took comfort in practicing age-old ceremonies. Warfield continues, "In this sense the conquering church was conquered by the world which it conquered."[765] Thorndike informs us that:

> In short, while Christianity turned its back upon much in classical civilization, it also retained a considerable amount of ancient culture into the Middle Ages. This residue has well been called 'the classical heritage.' We must keep in mind, however, that it was the last and most threadbare and decaying stage of classical culture that most influenced early medieval Christian society.... Greek philosophy had greatly influenced Christian theology already, and there were survivals from pagan mythology and festivals in the legends and ceremonies of

---

[763] Ludlow, *Crusades*, pp. 15-16.
[764] Warfield, *Counterfeit*, p. 74.
[765] Ibid., p. 74.

the Church.[766]

Christmas Takes Root in the Shadows of Europe's Tree-Worshipping Customs

Modern Christmas customs brim with Europe's old world rituals that originally took place between early November and late January. It was during these months that Europeans worshipped their agricultural and pastoral Spirits. To honor these Spirits believers burned candles, and scattered ash and straw; revelers drank alcohol liberally, making themselves into festive fools, and partygoers dressed in animal costumes with some men even dressing[767] as women.

Central to these Roman winter festivities was the tree. As part of their festivities pagan (non-Christian) worshippers dragged freshly harvested trees inside their homes in time for Christmas Eve. The early Roman's belief that Christmas eve trees bore fruit contributed to their certainty that another fruit bearing plant, the mistletoe, housed the Spirit of fertility. They garnished their home shrines with these and other seasonal fruit-bearing plants and spruce pines as reverential offerings to the harvest Spirits. This annual gesture had the added benefit of revitalizing their seemingly dead Earth temporarily turning her green, vibrant, and lively looking. Fanciful stories of trees producing fruit in winter make up English folktales, too. There in England, worshippers decorated church interiors with bundles of holly until they had transformed them into Spirit-filled miniature forests.

For believers in the old ways, the tree symbolized fertility and offered the promise of life-sustaining vegetation for famished Europeans suffering through long, bitterly cold, bleak winter days. Sacred and regenerative, tree branches – green beacons of spring and prosperity - represented hope for Europeans weary from struggling through their gray, darkened world. And depending on the local custom and era, *holy* day revelers laced their tree branches with candles, cheeses, and colored paper to imitate fruits, flowers, etc.

Perhaps their customs were holdovers from the ancient days when groves of trees stood as sanctuaries, scared places where deities ruled from inside their wooded shrines or communed with worshippers. It was along the tree branches that worshippers placed offerings to their deities, Tertullian told us earlier in this essay. Pliny provides more insight into this ancient custom in *Natural History*: "The trees formed the first temples of the gods, and even at the present day, the country people, preserving in all their simplicity their ancient rites, *consecrate the finest among their trees to some divinity;* indeed, we feel ourselves inspired to adoration, not less by

---

[766] Thorndike, *Europe*, p. 114.
[767] It seems men dressing as women occurred during other early European celebrations, too.

the sacred groves and their very stillness, than by the statues of the gods, resplendent as they are with gold and ivory."[768] Worshippers believed deities dwelled inside trees growing in *sacred groves*, as Pliny calls them. The presence of deities inside trees made those sites holy: "The statues, even, of the deities were formed of the wood of trees, in the days when no value had been set as yet on the dead [carcass] of a wild beast, and when, luxury not yet deriving its sanction from the gods themselves, we had not to behold, resplendent with the same ivory, the heads of the divinities and the feet of our tables."[769]

And just who were some of those gods? Pliny writes of them, "Each kind of tree remains immutably consecrated to its own peculiar divinity, the beech to Jupiter, the laurel to Apollo, the olive to Minerva, the myrtle to Venus, and the poplar to Hercules: besides which, it is our belief that the Sylvans, the Fauns, and various kinds of goddess Nymphs, have the tutelage of the woods, and we look upon those deities as especially appointed to preside over them by the will of heaven."[770]

One historian writes that during the early days, leaders planted trees at the front doors to churches, a tradition that lingered well into the 16th century and suggests an ancient connection to the sacred groves. Obviously, trees form an important arc in the European cultural construct: they served as temporary shelters for abandoned babies; and it was inside the trunk of a tree that a king placed the blade of his sword for safekeeping. Furthermore, Roman leaders hanged priests, and others, from trees as public offerings; and many Europeans believed humans metamorphosed into trees.

According to Robertson Smith, the candle plays a similarly weighty role in ancient Semitic traditions transforming from their use at altars where burnt[771]offerings were made to becoming those elegantly decorated candle-shaped temple pillars, or candelabras. Temple pillars, according to Smith, are symbolic of sacred trees. In ancient Europe, offerings to deities were placed between temple pillars: "In the more advanced rituals the use of fire corresponds with the conception of the gods as subtle beings, moving in the air, whose proper nourishment is the fragrant smoke of the burning flesh, so that the *burnt-offering, like the fat of the vitals in ordinary victims, is the food of the gods*, and falls under the head of sacrificial gifts," Smith writes. (Italics added). Ashes, then, represents the remains of that offering that extend blessings to worshippers. Straw symbolizes the harvest, or bread. Revelers who dressed in animal costumes were likely presenting

---

[768] Bostock and Riley, *Pliny's*, vol. 3, p. 102.
[769] Ibid.
[770] Ibid.
[771] It may be relevant that Charlemagne and early church fathers attempted to put a stop to cremation burials.

their bodies as sacrificial offerings. Ancient worshippers believed that making offerings, or sacrifices, to their deities were crucial elements to their survival, and aided in atonement.

Warfield notes that in the Roman Empire, "The gods, conceived as protecting beings, as undoubted powers in the world, but as easily offended, were, by the honor brought to them in their worship, to be made and kept disposed to interpose in the course of nature for the benefit of their worshippers, in protecting, helping, succoring, rescuing them; that is to say, were to work miracles. Belief in miracles was involved in belief in the gods; only denial of the gods could produce denial of miracles."[772]

Son (Sun) Worship, Water Baptism & Much More: Customs of Christ and Mithra Curiously Identical

Rome was no stranger to venerating gods that had come to its citizens by way of Greece. Recall, too, that before it fell the Roman emperor associated himself with the Unconquered Sun (Sol Invictus), though he tolerated the worship of other gods. Warfield remarks, "The whole population of the Roman Empire was caught in a gigantic net of superstition, the product of the combined work of East and West."[773] Sun worshipping traditions filled the days leading up to winter solstice. Brumalia was one such feast that began on November 24 and lasted until the first light of the solstice. Brumalia was a festival month that honored the god Saturn. Romans celebrated the month well into the 7th century.

The Christian's seizure of Zoroastrian[774] mythology is one of the most blatant cultural rip-offs of all time. Researcher Gerald Massey traces its presence in Rome to 70 BCE. Central to the Zoroastrian myth is the ancient Persian Sun god Mithra. Gibbon observes that in Zoroastrian belief, "The Elements and more, particularly Fire, Light, and *the Sun, whom they called Mithra*, were the objects of their religious reverence, because they considered them as the purest symbols, the noblest productions, and the most powerful agents of the Divine Power and Nature."[775] (Italics added). Mithra's birthday, celebrated on December 25, honored the *rebirth* of the Sun's light following winter solstice. Festivities surrounding Mithra must have been spectacular because the Romans borrowed the Persian customs, marking the celebrated date in gold letters. Soon, the Rome headquartered

---

[772] Warfield, *Counterfeit*, p. 75.
[773] Ibid., p. 76.
[774] See Gerald Massey's controversial book, *The Historical Jesus and Mythical Christ*. In it he traces major aspects of the Christian foundation to the Kemetan Horus mythology that preceded it by thousands of years. Additionally, Albert Churchward elaborates on the African symbols that the Christian church "borrowed" e.g., the Ark of the Covenant, the babe in the manger and the cross. See *Signs and Symbols of Primordial Man*.
[775] Gibbon, *Decline*, vol. 1. pp. 244-245.

Catholic Church adopted their customs, too, including observing December 25 as the birthday of the son (sun) of their god:

> "Factors which tended to support the feast on Dec. 25. — There can be little doubt that the Church was anxious to distract the attention of Christians from the old heathen feast days by celebrating Christian festivals on the same days. On Dec. 25 was the dies natalis solis invicti or the sol novus, especially cultivated by the votaries of Mithraism. Moreover, the Saturnalia closed on Dec. 24. The feast of the ' sol invictus.' — It is not, in the absence of direct evidence, probable that the date was chosen in order to compete with this feast, though as soon as an equation began to be made between Christ and the sun, it was natural to celebrate a Christian feast on the day previously consecrated to the sun."[776]

Despite this and an earlier writer's mental gymnastics to disassociate "Sun" day worship from so-called heathen traditions, the church clearly stole that day for their own purposes. According to the Roman Philocalian Calendar Romans celebrated Jesus' birth on December 25th as far back as either 354 or 336 CE. Franz Cumont opines: "In adopting this date, which was universally distinguished by sacred festivities, the ecclesiastical authority purified in some measure the profane usages which it could not suppress."[777] Yes, there were good reasons for selecting this date: Mithra[778] and the Christ figure have much in common: they both had virgin births (though Mithra proceeded from a rock with a knife in his hand); shepherds watched as Mithra came into the world, and offered him gifts. Mithra, born naked, clothed himself with the leaves from a fig[779] tree. The same tree provided his first meals. Constantin Volney elaborates on more profound similarities:

> Then passing on to the details of his religion, quoting from the Zadder and the Zendavesta, recounted, in the same order as they are found in the book of Genesis, the creation of the world in six gahans[780] the formation of a first man and a first woman, in a divine place, under the reign of perfect good; the introduction of evil into the world by the great snake, emblem of Ahrimanes; the revolt and battles of the Genius of evil and darkness against Ormuzd, God of good and of light; *the division of the angels into white and black, or good and bad;*

---

[776] Kirsopp Lake, "Christmas," *Encyclopaedia of Religion and Ethics*, 1910. pp. 607-08.
[777] Franz Cumont, "The Doctrine of the Mithraic Mysteries," in *The Mysteries of Mithra*, trans. Thomas J. McCormack (Chicago: Open Court Publishing, 1903), p. 196.
[778] Cumont, *Mithra*, p. 104.
[779] Plutarch informs us "figleaf [sic] is interpreted to mean the watering and fructifying of the universe, for it seems to bear some resemblance in its make to the virilities of a man." William W, Goodwin, ed., *Plutarch's Morals* (Boston: Little, Brown, and Co, 1878), p. 96. In KMT, the Sycamore is associated with Hathor.
[780] This is perhaps 6,000 years or six months, Volney.

their hierarchal orders, cherubim, seraphim, thrones, dominions, etc.; the end of the world at the close of six thousand years; the coming of the lamb, the regenerator of nature; the new world; the future life, and the regions of happiness and misery; the passage of souls over the bridge of the bottomless pit; the celebration of the mysteries of Mithra; the unleavened bread which the initiated eat; the baptism of new-born children; the unction of the dead; the confession of sins; and, in a word, he recited so many things analogous to those of the three preceding religions, that his discourse seemed like a commentary or a continuation of the Koran or the Apocalypse.[781] (Italics added).

Baptism by water; the "sacrificial meal of bread and wine;"[782] plus a Noah character (he has an Ark stocked with cattle before a flood depopulates the world) are themes central to both Mithraism and Christianity. And at a last supper Mithra dines with his companions before he ascends to heaven. Finally, in Mithraism Sunday was a holy day ruled over by the Sun. According to Webster: Mithraism "appealed to the emotions. They helped to satisfy the spiritual wants of men and women, by dwelling on the need of purification from sin and by holding forth the prospect of a happier life beyond the tomb.... They penetrated every province of the Roman Empire and flourished as late as the fourth century CE."[783] In the end Christianity borrowed the doctrines of Mithra, boldly kicking his name and history to the curb.

But the progress of the conquering religion was checked when it came in contact with Christianity. The two adversaries discovered with amazement, but with no inkling of their origin, [some believe the Jews absorbed and embraced knowledge of Mithraism while living in Persia BCE] the similarities which united them; and they severally accused the Spirit of Deception of having endeavored to caricature the sacredness of their religious rites. The conflict between the two was inevitable, a ferocious and implacable duel: *for the stake was the dominion of the world.... Mithraism was vanquished, as without doubt it should have been.... Its theology had retained too much of its Asiatic coloring to be accepted by the Latin spirit* without repugnance.[784] (Italics added).

Some rather unpleasant similarities are noted in the conduct of the priests of Mithra and Christ. Both religions demand tithes; and priests of both religions wallow in riches, while their congregants languish in poverty.

December 24 has a special history, too. Called Modranicht or Modranicht, this *night of the mothers* honored the humanity of the Virgin

---

[781] Volney, *Ruins*, pp. 98-99.
[782] Webster, *History*, p. 228.
[783] Ibid., p. 229.
[784] Cumont, *Mithra*, pp. iv-v.

Mother by baking cakes. The cakes represented the placenta,[785] according to Chambers. Pagan Anglo-Saxons celebrated this day, some say, by making blood sacrifices during the night.

Lavish stories, even supposed personal encounters with Spirit entities, fill books on medieval superstition. Despite the Europeans' supposed concerns over the rituals of Egun (read: Vodun), Europeans were drowning in their own sea of superstitions even as they cloaked themselves in clerical attire. Many of our habits today, like tossing salt over our shoulder; divining the future using the bible: "One might fast and pray and then open a Bible. The verse upon which his eye first lighted would be significant;"[786] and even Halloween customs come to us out the experiences of the Middle Ages Celtic harvest festivities. Called All Hallows' Eve or All Saints' Eve by the church, its celebration was intended to pacify converted pagans accustomed to observing their dead relatives during this time. A hallow is a saint or devout person.

The introduction of a new religion meant the dismemberment of ancient celebrated personalities. Christian leaders preferred to recognize and honor their own set of sanctified superstars, who they called saints: "Every cathedral or monastery had its tutelar saint, and every saint his legend, fabricated in order to enrich the churches under his protection, by exaggerating his virtues, his miracles, and consequently his power of serving those who paid liberally for his patronage. *Many of those saints were imaginary persons*; sometimes a blundered inscription added a name to the calendar, and sometimes, it is said, a heathen god was surprised at the company to which he was introduced, and the rites with which he was honored."[787] (Italics added).

Viking Traditions Celebrated, Honored by Modern Christians

In an earlier chapter, I introduced readers to a couple of Viking myths. Following are a few more Viking traditions that may seem familiar to practicing Christians:

Water was sprinkled on infants when given its name. There was a (Urd's) well which contained with holy water.

Vikings celebrated Geóhel, Géol (pronounced Yool (Yule)). This autumnal festival celebrated during winter solstice was symbolized by the fiery wheel representing the year at its lowest point in the sky before it begins to rise again, "In order to honor the gods several great annual feasts were established, among

---

[785] Placentas, or afterbirth, were sometimes eaten by Europeans and used in religious ceremonies.
[786] Tappan, *Knights*, p. 333.
[787] Hallam, *View*, vol. 2, p. 491.

which Géol (Christmas) was most remarkable as the most joyous and festival season to the Norsemen... friends and relatives presented one another with gifts, and many days were spent in feasts and gay [social drinking]."[788] The winter solstice festivities lasted for twelve days of celebration beginning on December 20. [The Wheel (Yule) was used as a representation of the return or rebirth of the sun].

"In the *spring* there was a *sacrificial offering*, to ensure luck in war and in Viking expeditions (piracies) usually beginning at that season."[789]

"Men worshipped Odin and the twelve chiefs (höfdingi) and called them their gods, and believed in them long afterwards" (Ynglinga Saga, ch. 7.)"[790]

Baptism by water: "The newly-born infant was placed on the floor, and remained there without being touched by any one, until taken up and put in the folds of his cloak, by his father.... If the child was to live, a religious or sacred rite called Ausa Vatni,[791] which seems to have consisted either in pouring or sprinkling water over the child, was performed, a custom so common that we are not told how the water was poured or sprinkled over, though it may have been with the hand. This ceremony was considered a most sacred rite, and was an integral part of the Asa creed, and consequently of great antiquity, [predating] Christian baptism, and most binding among the ancestors of the English-speaking peoples: to *expose* a child after this ceremony was considered murder. It was once, no doubt, practised [sic] by the Franks who belonged to the Northern tribes; and certain forms of Christian baptism of the present day may be based upon this earlier form, which was only changed in name by the earlier Christian missionaries [to the north]...."[792]

"It was his [Odin's] custom, when he sent his men into fight or on other errands, first to lay his hands on their heads and give them bjanak; they believed that luck would then be with them. Also it happened that whenever his men were in need on land or at sea they called on his name, and always felt relieved by it; for every kind of help they looked to him."[793]

Odin had temple-priests who knew Odin's wisdom and magic. Sacrificing-priests taught others this magic; and witchcraft spread far and wide. Odin

---

[788] Sinding, *Scandinavia*, p. 26.
[789] Ibid., p. 26.
[790] Du Chaillu, *Viking*, vol. 1, p. 61.
[791] Author's Note: "The words ansa moldu mean 'to pour mould on' (to bury). In Ynglingatal the expression ausinn (another form of the verb) haugi is used of a man buried in a mound." Du Chaillu, *Viking*, vol.2, p. 30.
[792] Du Chaillu, *Viking*, vol. 2, p. 21.
[793] Ibid., vol. 1. p. 55.

raised men from the dead.[794]

Tall Tales of Chimera Inspire Bloody Tales of Terror for Tots

Most people are familiar with the violent, and blood-soaked tale of Beowulf set in Denmark and Sweden. The story centers on the activities of mythical creatures. The medieval Europeans' beliefs[795] in Chimera, Centaurs, Scylla, Hydras, large dragons, unicorns, witches, faeries, vampires, werewolves,[796] etc., influenced their world of literature yesterday and influence the minds of African-Maafan children today. The danger is in their stories teaching our children that questionable behaviors are normal and acceptable. It should surprise us not at all, given what we have learned so far in this essay, that many early European fairytales include cannibals. Moreover, these grim medieval folk tales have talking blood drops, and talking severed horse heads as characters. In fact, blood is a central theme in many of their children's fables as are images of murder, mayhem, and slaughter. In one story a king beheads his children to turn a statue back into a man. These children regain their lives once their father smears them with their own blood. Other stories impart the strange medieval wisdom that blood sprinkling provides strength, and restores life. Ludlow shares a few medieval stores, two of which I present below:

> The popular stories which mothers taught their children were in praise of heroes whom we would regard as butchers and bruisers. A favorite legend was of Renoart, the flower of early Chivalry—he of the ugly visage and gigantic frame, whose mace laid open the brains of his antagonists, and who broke the skull of the monk who refused to indulge his whim of exchanging clothes with him. What child of that age had not heard of Roland, the hero of Roncesvalles, whose unstinted praises went far to form the manly habits of many generations? He was an enfant terrible, who tore his swaddling-clothes in pieces, belabored his mother furiously, and gave early promise of his prowess by beating lifeless the porter of the castle who would not let him go out to play.[797]

In another medieval story that involves a character named Roland, a foster daughter tricks her witch-mother into cutting off the head of her own daughter who lusts after the foster sister's beautiful apron. In tricking the

---

[794] Ibid., vol. 1. p. 61.
[795] Tappan informs us that Europeans were "taught that there were satyrs with horns and the feet of goats, Cyclops with one eye in the middle of their foreheads, and people with eyes in their shoulders and neither nose nor head." p 331.
[796] Medieval Europe's witch trials accused men and women of being werewolves. Additionally, Herodotus mentions Neurian tribesmen (maintained Scythian customs) who turned into wolves once a year for a few days. Rawlinson, vol. 2, pp. 252-53.
[797] Ludlow, *Crusades*, p. 20.

mother, the foster daughter ruins her witch-mother's plan to murder her and present her apron to her foster sister. Modern fables are not nearly as violent, but their images are still too traumatic for children's stories. Because fairytales grow from the myths that mirror a culture's beliefs and traditions, this essay touches on a few European god myths in an upcoming chapter.

Europe's Fear of Cape Nothing

> Quem passar o Cabo de Não Ou tornará, ou não." (Whoever passes Cape Non will turn back or never return). As beyond it was believed there was no return possible.

One amusing superstition of the Middle Ages that prevented Europeans from venturing too far along the Atlantic, and benefitted West Africans at the same time - for a while at least, was Mare Tenebroso or the Sea of Darkness. According to several sources, medieval Europeans believed that great sea creatures haunted the great depths of these waters; it was here that sirens led mariners into rocks, and great monsters dwelled in shadows beneath the sea. The presence of scary beasts in those waters made it far too dangerous to sail beyond the Canary Islands,[798] or Cape de Non (Cape No), south of Morocco.[799] Even after the state ordered sailors to break the 29°-latitude barrier and sail past Cape Bojador, they got spooked and turned back. That decision caused considerable irritation for Dom Henry the Navigator and prince who was commissioning those voyages:[800]

> Although he sent out many times, not only ordinary men, but such as by their experience in great deeds of war were of foremost name in the profession of arms, yet there was not one who dared to pass that Cape of Bojador and learn about the land beyond it, as the Infant wished.... There was great doubt as to who would be the first to risk his life in such a venture. How are we, men said, to pass the bounds that our fathers set up, or what profit can result to the Infant from the perdition of our souls as well as of our bodies — for of a truth by daring any further we shall become willful murderers of ourselves? Have there not been in Spain other princes and lords as covetous perchance of this honor as the Infant...? This much is clear, that beyond this Cape there is no race of men nor place of inhabitants: nor is the land less sandy than the deserts of Libya, where there is no water, no tree, no green herb — and the sea so shallow that a whole league from land it is only a fathom deep, while the currents are so terrible that

---

[798] Mare Tenebroso: The Sea of Darkness.
[799] António Galvao, *The Discoveries Of The World, From Their First Original Unto The Year Of Our Lord 1555*, ed., Richard Hakluyt (London: Hakluyt Society,1862), p. 61.
[800] Ibid., p. 61.

no ship having once passed the Cape, will ever be able to return.[801]

The legend of the angry black seas is recounted below:

> The poetic legend of the Black Sea (Mar Tenebrosa) was to the effect that a certain King of Portugal ordered ships to be prepared and fitted and provisioned for a long voyage, which was to last fourteen years. In effect the ships departed, and at the end of two years they arrive to a darksome region, and to the shores of an unknown and deserted island, where, in subterranean habitation, the seamen found enormous riches. This wealth, however, they dared not touch, owing to some superstitious fear which assailed them. On returning to their ships and embarking to continue their voyage, the sea became so agitated that the dread of the Portuguese navigators was greatly increased. What were they to do? Continue their voyage, or retreat back from whence the came? After some discussion, they decided in council that two of these ships should attack the place, and the third ship to await them up to a fixed time. The term of time expired and no news of the ships, and then the commander of the third ship decided to return to Portugal. When the ship arrived to Portugal and the crew disembarked, they had become so altered and had aged so in the space of twenty-four months, that neither the king nor their relatives recognised [sic] them.
>
> All manner of terrifying legends rose up and clustered over the whole expanse of that ocean. The dark sea, whose waves were black as pitch, rose up far beyond the horizon where the sun sank. This was the ancient legend, the pagan legend transmitted from generation to generation, which had prevented for a long time the most daring investigations of the Atlantic Ocean from being carried out. Whoever entered it was everlastingly lost; whoever attempted to approach it, should have the good fortune to return, came back decrepit, and having departed in manhood, would find to his sorrow that the voyage he had thought was only a few days, had really lasted long years.[802]

Unfortunately, Henry soon found a sailor brave enough to venture below the Cape. Upon his return home, Portugal honored him for bringing to them a special type of "booty" from the islands: stolen Africans.

---

[801] Beazley and Prestage, *Guinea,* vol. 1, pp. 30-31.
[802] McMurdo, *Portugal,* vol. 2, p. 445.

10

INQUISITIONS OF THE CRIMINAL CHRISTIAN CHURCH

For as the humor of Melancholic in the selfe is blacke, heauie and terrene, so are the symptomes thereof, in any persones; that are subject therevnto, leannes, palenes, desire of solitude: and if they come to the highest degree therof, mere folie and Manie: where as by the contrarie, a great number of them that euer haue bene convict or confessors of Witchcraft, as may be presently scene by manie that haue at this time confessed: they are by the contrarie, I say, some of them rich and worldly-wise, some of them fatte or corpulent in their bodies, and most part of them altogether giuen ouer to the pleasures of the flesh, continual haunting of companie, and all kind of merrines, both lawfull and vnlawfull, which are thinges directly contrary to the symptomes of Melancholie, whereof I spake, and further experience daylie proues how loath they are to confesse without torture, which witnesseth their guiltines, where by the contrary, the Melancholicques neuer spares to bewray themselues, by their continuall discourses, feeding therby their humor in that which they thinke no crime. As to your third reason, it scarselie merites an answere.[803] King James I opinion on effects of torture.

The Holy Roman Church Strikes Out Violently at Heretics: Free Thinkers Become Targets

When Christianity had become predominant throughout Europe, torture was developed with a cruelty never before known... a very simple and logical process of theological reasoning it was held that Satan would give supernatural strength to his special devotees-that is, to heretics and witches-and therefore that, in dealing with them, there should be no limit to the torture. [804]

The Inquisitions began earlier than the much-cited 12th century. According to Henry Charles Lea in *A History of the Inquisition of the Middle Ages*, state punishment for heretical thinking and practices dates to 385 CE. At that time, the state put to death wealthy nobleman Priscillian and six of his followers for teaching asceticism, a religious discipline that encourages abstention from worldly indulgences. By 447, Lea writes, "It was only sixty-two years after the slaughter of Priscillian and his followers had excited so much horror, that Leo. I., when the heresy seemed to be reviving, in 447, not only justified the act, but declared that if

---

[803] King James I, "The description of Sorcerie an Witch-craft in speciall," in *Daemonologie*, (Edinburgh, 1597) p. 30.
[804] White, *Warfare*, vol. 2, p. 77.

the followers of heresy so damnable were allowed to live there would be an end of human and divine law. The final step had been taken, and the church was definitely pledged to the suppression of heresy at whatever cost."[805]

If European citizens had somehow managed to adjust to the terroristic wild whims of feudalistic overlords, the 12th century came with an even more exhausting challenge for them. The smoldering anger of religious fanatics towards free thinkers before the 11th century became wildfires by the 12th as Inquisitions by the thousands began to take place throughout Europe instigated by both church authorities and monarchs. The church readily reestablished Inquisitions, though historians tell us that oftentimes mobs of lay Christians boldly assaulted heretics, and then mostly by fire. The church did not frown upon these actions. Its own punishments included deporting and confiscating idolater's possessions; however burning heretics alive was the church's preferred method of execution. Each feudal country conducted its own inquisitions. Reasons for them are many: they checked church dissension and heretical teachings; they silenced public dissent of monarchs and church leaders; and they became unethical, and immoral ruses to legally acquire a person's land and valuables. The fact is that Inquisitions opposed any and all resistance to church authority. (Modern revisionists challenge the traditional view of Inquisitions, saying they saved lives and brought equity in punishments).

In France, one religious group who became a target of the church because they objected to its outrageous antics was the Arnoldists. Its members thought the church was too connected to riches it had acquired in immoral ways.[806] By the 13th century the church captured and burned Franciscans, another heretical sect. In addition to rejecting the formal habit of the church, Franciscans believed, too, that the church's possession of wealth was improper.[807] Inquisitions continued well into the 17th century. During that long period, the church confined, tortured or killed hundreds of thousands of people. Some historians put the estimate of the tortured and dead into the millions.

This long era of Inquisitions revealed the church's deep hatred for the women who births and nurtures its own leaders. Pope Innocent VIII's papal bull gave Inquisitors authority to persecute women accused of rejecting church teachings. And in its rush to demonize them, the church condemned anyone who questioned its role in "witch-hunting." The church's disdain for women reaches as far back as Eve, who, according to church leaders, had a wicked ability to corrupt men. Later on, the church

---

[805] Henry Charles Lea, *A History of the Inquisition of the Middle Ages*, p 215.
[806] Frans Christiaan Günst, *The Martyrs of the Spanish Inquisition*, p. 11.
[807] Turberville, *Heresy*, p. 44.

accused women of performing abortions, making crops fail, and for inflicting suffering on animals. But, these represent only a very few of the crazy charges leveled by church authorities. Women unable to pass many of the outrageous, superstitious tests designed to trap so-called witches into confessions died horrible deaths. And while women became main targets of Inquisitors, no one else was safe, either. This includes Galileo Galilei who the church persecuted in the 17th century for his scientific belief that the Sun, rather than the Earth, was the center of the solar system. The Inquisitions, a microcosmic manifestation of the broader construct, were all about power, greed and control: "Corruption in the Church was, then, one of the contributory causes of mediaeval [sic] heresy, and anti-sacerdotalism was one of its features."[808]

Who are Heretics? The Church Says They "Avoid Lies... and Frauds"

Inquisitors wielded the power vested in them to rattle and unnerve nearly every European-held land far and wide by one tortuous method or another. The irony that Inquisitors, men who administered these sham trials, were church bishops is not lost:

> Every bishop shall visit, once or twice every year, himself, or by his archdeacon, or by other qualified persons, those parts of his diocese where it is commonly reported that heretics are living; and shall swear in three or four men of good character, and even, if he thinks it desirable, all the people of the neighborhood, binding them, if they can discover where there are any heretics or persons who hold private meetings, or that lead a different life from the faithful in general, to denounce such persons to the archbishop or the archdeacon. The bishop or the archdeacon shall then call the accused before him; and if they do not clear themselves, and follow the custom of the country, or if they relapse, they shall be punished by the judgment of the bishops. But if they refuse to swear, they shall at once be judged heretics.[809]

And just what constituted a heretic? Here is one Inquisitor's disturbing description:

> Heretics,' he goes so far as to say,' are recognized by their customs and speech, for *they are modest and well regulated. They take no pride in their garments*, which are neither costly nor vile. *They do not engage in trade, to avoid lies and oaths and frauds*, but live by their labors as mechanics — their teachers are cobblers. *They do not accumulate wealth, but are content with necessaries.* They are *chaste and temperate in meat and drink.* They do not frequent taverns or dances or other vanities. *They restrain themselves from anger.* They are always at work; *they teach*

---

[808] Ibid., p. 10.
[809] Rule, *Inquisition*, p. 13.

and learn and consequently pray but little. They are to be *known by their modesty* and precision of speech, *avoiding scurrility and detraction, light words and lies and oaths.*[810] (Italics added).

The Church Murders Millions, Casually Burns Villages Hunting for Heretics

The Inquisitor here is describing Waldenses. They believed their own righteous behavior absolved them from sin more so than could any prayer from a corrupt priest: "According to others, the original Waldenses were a race of uncorrupted shepherds, who in the valleys of the Alps had shaken off, or perhaps never learned, the system of superstition on which the Catholic church depended for its ascendency."[811] The Waldenses were against capital punishment, too. So, it is possible the church recognized that the Waldenses true goodness in words and deeds shined the light of ugly on their corrupt clergy. For instance, the Popes Innocent were anything, but innocent. Their own impious behaviors over the centuries pronounce them guilty of committing unforgiveable mortal sins.

Hallam writes this concerning Pope Innocent III, "But the epoch when the spirit of papal usurpation was most strikingly displayed was the pontificate of Innocent III. In each of the three leading objects which Rome has pursued, independent sovereignty, supremacy over the Christian church, control over the princes of the earth, it was the fortune of this pontiff to conquer."[812] Historians write that Pope Innocent III was diligent in persecuting heretics in the remotest of places. He ruthlessly tracked down already banished (to foreign lands) heretics, then threatened barbarian kings with war for providing them shelter. Apparently in a league of his very own, Rule opines that Pope Innocent III be called "patron saint of Inquisitions,"[813] as he shamelessly "besieged, stormed, and sacked" cities he suspected of harboring heretics.

The Inquisitions were bloody and savage undertakings: soldiers uprooted entire populations; they burned people alive, or dismembered them; they stole their possessions; and, finally, they burned whole cities to the ground. They committed these offensive acts supposedly in the pursuit of heretics: "After the siege of Beziers[814] [Southern France], Arnold, [a Cistercian abbot], wrote to [Pope] Innocentius: 'Sparing neither sex nor age, we have killed nearly 20,000 human beings, and afterwards pillaged and

---

[810] Turberville, *Heresy*, p. 21.
[811] Hallam, *View*, vol. 2, pp. 568-69.
[812] Ibid., vol. 1, pp. 665-66.
[813] Rule, *Inquisition*, p. 17.
[814] Although Crusaders carried out this bloody siege their charge was vs. heretics, specifically the Waldenses.

burnt the city....'"[815] And almost anyone could be accused of heresy: "An imprudent word or thoughtless utterance was sufficient to make a person suspected of heresy and to be imprisoned; a large field was thereby opened for spies and informers: whereas to be suspected was enough to be punished like a heretic."[816] Inquisitors prosecuted men, women, children and even whole families:

> Every one was subject to the inquisitorial tribunal, even kings and princes; only the following were excepted: the Popes, their delegates, nuncios, officers and familiars, and, during the first inquisition, the bishops. As soon as any of these were accused or suspected of heresy, they had to answer for this to the Pope. The respect for the kings was so much diminished that they had to obey a simple monk as soon as he was nominated inquisitor.[817]

Inquisitors even permitted heresy charges against dead people. And if (when) he was found guilty, officials disinterred him to administer the preferred punishment, burning. Next, the church removed all the victim's belongings from his family and took possession of them. Surviving members not only grieved for the soul of their loved one, but were left destitute, as well.

"How To" Torture Books: The Odyssey of Terror by Bishops

According to one source, Inquisitors had manuals that not only set forth punishments for perceived crimes, but also instructed them in ways of obtaining confessions. Two of them are Libro Necro (Book of the Dead),[818] and Directorium Inquisitorium (Guide for Inquisitors).[819] According to Frans Christiaan Günst, the Inquisitors were known for their "insensibility, ignorance, and cruelty, as well as for their hypocrisy and dissimulation."[820] Inquisitions continued despite the poor reputations earned by Inquisitors. And once an Inquisitor received the accused's name, his traumatic odyssey began. Bands of men stalked, surprised and kidnapped him. Afterwards, they removed him to a cold, damp, dark cell. Once imprisoned, the church confiscated all of his possessions. The accused might languish in the dungeon for weeks before the Inquisitor became obligated to hold a trial. Witnesses at the trials did not have to present proof, and wore masks; the accused never saw the accuser without his mask. To exact a confession

---

[815] Günst, *Martyrs*, p. 13.
[816] Ibid., pp. 17-18.
[817] Ibid., p. 20.
[818] Giacinto Achilli, *Dealings With The Inquisition; or, Papal Rome, Her Priests, and Her Jesuits, With Important Disclosures*, p. 109.
[819] Günst, *Martyrs*, p. 22.
[820] Ibid. p. 22.

from the accused, the bishop started his odyssey of torture. Any number of bone breaking, flesh peeling methods were used to bring about a guilty plea:

> There had been discovered many deep dungeons in this Palace [of the Inquisition], where prisoners were confined without light or free access to air; and the other was, that an oubliette [forgotten chamber: an underground dungeon cell with an opening on top. Aside from the trap door, there is no entrance or exit] existed at the door of the Chancery, in an upper story; the chancery being a sort of chapel where the sentences were pronounced. It may, perhaps, be necessary to observe that an oubliette was an awful mode of execution invented in the Dark Ages. The victim was directed to walk along a passage, in which there was a trap-door turning on a pivot, so that when he stepped upon it, his weight opened in chasm, down which he was precipitated to a very great depth, falling upon spikes and sharp instruments, where he was left to die. One of these horrible inventions may be seen in the Castle of Chillon, and another in the old Castle at Baden.[821]

That particular scene describes the horror chambers within the Palace of Rome. However, oubliettes were widely distributed throughout Europe and have since become sensational tourist attractions. Oubliettes are variously described as dungeons not large enough for one to sit or stand; places where raw sewage flowed; and places where one shared quarters with rats. The unfortunate victims subjected to this terror never felt the warming rays of the Sun upon their cheeks again.

Blasphemy against church saints, e.g. god, the pope or the Virgin Mary brought its own unique type of torture:

> In the list of punishments I read concerning the bit, or, as it is called by us, the mordacchia, which is a very simple contrivance to confine the tongue, and compress it between two cylinders composed of iron and wood, and furnished with spikes. This horrible instrument not only wounds the tongue and occasions excessive pain, but also, from the swelling it produces, frequently places the sufferer in danger of suffocation.... Be that as it may, this torture has been in use till the present period....[822]

Speaking of the Virgin Mary, medieval torturers gave her saintly celebrated name to a mechanical device that "'surpassed all others in fiendish ingenuity.'" Molded in the shape of a young woman's body, *The Kiss of The Virgin Mary* torture machine "annihilated" a person's body. Torturers used the Virgin Mary throughout Europe. It dates at least to the

---

[821] Alex R. C. Dallas, "A Day In The Dungeons Of The Inquisition At Rome," *The Gospel Magazine and Protestant Beacon*, no. 13 (1858) p. 163.
[822] Achilli, *Dealings*, pp. 109-10.

early 16th century, possibly originating in Spain in time for its Inquisitions. Although there were many different versions of the murdering Mary, the following passage describes one model:

> "The construction of the figure," says Mr. Pearsall, "was simple enough. A skeleton, formed of bars and hoops, was coated over with sheet iron, which was laid on and painted, so as to represent a Nuremberg citizen's wife of the sixteenth century. The front of the machine opened like folding doors, the two halves of the front part of it being connected by hinges with the back part. On the inside of its right breast are thirteen quadrangular poniards [thin daggers]. There are eight of these on the inside of the left, and two on the inside of the face. These last were clearly intended for the eyes of the victim, who must have, therefore, gone backwards into it, and have received, in an upright position, in his breast and head, the blades to which he was exposed. That this machine had been formerly used cannot be doubted; because there are evident blood-stains yet visible on its breast, and on the upper part of its pedestal. How it was worked is not known, for the mechanism which caused it to open and shut is no longer attached to it; but that there was some such mechanism, is clear from the holes and sockets which have been cut out on the surface of the pedestal, showing the points where parts of the apparatus intended to work it must have been inserted."[823]

Castle St. Angelo became one of the church's more infamous torture chambers. Blake describes the Castle as, "by turns a tomb and a fortress, a prison and a palace, a chapel and a treasure-chamber; now threatening the liberty of Rome, now defending its very existence; now the refuge of the Republic, now the hiding-place of the popes; through war and peace, from the Imperial days of Rome, through all the Gothic and medieval epochs down to the present hour, - has never ceased to be a living part of the history of Rome."[824] In those days, the bleak walls of St. Angelo reflected the obvious schizophrenia that eclipsed medieval European humanity. St Angelo was where the church celebrated life, yet they allocated space for tormenting the living. Popes and cardinals celebrated mass inside the castle; yet at other times they sought refuge from advancing foes there. St. Angelo is where church leadership displayed their unflinching reluctance to settle disputes honorably; where popes[825] drew in their last breaths; and where chains bound the beleaguered bodies of obstinate cardinals to the Castle's dark, and dank cellar walls:

In its secret cells popes have been strangled, starved, and sent to a bloody end;

---

[823] Timpson, *Inquisition*, p. 379.
[824] Story, "Castle St. Angelo and The Evil Eye," 756.
[825] At least 5 popes drew their last breath within the walls of St. Angelo.

philosophers and thinkers have perished, vainly struggling against bigotry and superstition; patriots have fought and died for liberty. On the foul walls of its dungeons artists and poets have scrawled their names, their verses, and their pictures, longing for the light of day; beauty and youth have perished in the dark, vainly praying for help; innocent men have falsely confessed crimes under the torture of the rack. In its frescoed halls emperors and popes have held their courts, and banqueted and trampled on the rights of man; and the ashes of emperors have filled the vases of its sepulchral chamber. [826]

Christians as targets of fellow Christians is a common feature of the Middle Ages, as the misconduct of Inquisitions and Crusades prove repeatedly.

---

[826] Story, "Castle St. Angelo and The Evil Eye," 755.

11

THE CHRISTIANS CRUSADE

Never before or since was there such exalted faith combined with such grotesque superstition, such splendid self-sacrifice mingled with cruel and unrestrained selfishness, such holy purpose with its wings entangled, torn, and besmeared in vicious environments.[827]

To a people such as we have described the appeal for the crusades, in which the imagined cause of heaven marched in step with their own tastes and habits, was irresistible.[828]

Crusader stories are generally romanticized and glamorized by western storytellers: Brave knights journey far and wide in total dedication to the cross to honor the one who was once hanged upon it, so goes the mythos. The truth is that the Crusades, much like the Inquisitions and most church *spiritual enterprises*, were politically motivated. Popes, kings and others used Crusades covertly to secure trade routes, root out heresy (read: control the population), and to steal land, money and valuables, as well:

The crusades gave promise of opening a new world to greed. The stories that were told of Eastern riches grew, as repeated from tongue to tongue, until fable seemed poor in comparison with what was believed to be fact. All the wealth of antiquity was presumed to be still stored in treasure-vaults, which the magic key of the cross would unlock. The impoverished baron might exchange his half-ruined castle for some splendid estate beyond the Aegean, and the vulgar crowd, if they did not find Jerusalem paved with gold like the heavenly city, would assuredly tread the veins of rich mines or rest among the flowers of an earthly paradise.[829]

In fact, after a city or town had been successfully taken, the first act of Crusaders was to *lay claim* to the bounty within, "It was a custom among us that if any one came to a castle or villa first and placed his standard there with a guard, it was touched by no one else afterward... Because of this ambition they arose at midnight and, without waiting for companions, gained all those mountains and villas which are in the meadows of the Jordan."[830] By the way, claim in the Latin /clamare/ means to declare

---

[827] Ludlow, *Crusades*, p. 2.
[828] Ibid., p. 25.
[829] Ibid., p. 41.
[830] Krey, Crusade, p. 248.

ownership.

Not Even Christians are Safe from Christian Crusaders

There were multiple Crusades; the number of them varies depending on who is doing the counting. Historians tend to count 7-8 main Crusades and several smaller ones. The first Crusade began in 1096 and Crusaders waged the last ones into the 16th century, well after Europeans had accused Africans of being savage. On one level the Crusades united warring factions of Europeans against a common Muslim enemy. Europeans interpreted Muslim territorial raids in Eurasia as approaching threats to European homelands. (However, note that during the long crusading era, Europeans never stopped warring with each other). To be sure, Crusaders pursued heretics of all stripes, even those of the European persuasion, "And thus the men of our race, zealous, doubtless, for God, though not according to the knowledge of God, began to persecute other Christians while yet upon the expedition which Christ had provided for freeing Christians."[831] It was the Albigensian Crusade of 1209, instigated by Pope Innocent III, where Crusaders destroyed an entire French city, Languedoc, murdering all of its inhabitants, estimated to number 60,000. Hallam notes: "It was here that a Cistercian monk, who led on the crusaders, answered the inquiry of how Catholics were to be distinguished from heretics: Kill them all! God will know his own;"[832] an apparent medieval version of the Anglo-American expression, "Kill them all, and let god sort out the rest." Yet, the fundamental point is clear: no one was safe from rampaging Crusaders.

In light of this information, Ludlow presents "seven conditions of life and thought in the eleventh century which facilitated or prompted the great movement:"

> 1.The intellectual and moral state of society in the eleventh century, especially its rudeness and warlike spirit. 2. The institution of chivalry, the awakening of better ideals of heroism. 3. The feudal system, which provided for the easy mobilization of men in war or adventure. 4. The impoverished condition of Europe, which forced enterprise to seek its reward in foreign countries. 5. The papal policy to consolidate and universalize the ecclesiastical empire. 6. The menace of Mohammedanism under the Saracenic and Turkish powers. 7. The prevailing superstition, which credited to pilgrimage the virtues of piety, and substituted exploits in the Holy Land for the plainer duties of holy life.[833]

In the face of dissimilar motivations, and backgrounds, Christianity was

---

[831] Ibid., p. 54.
[832] Hallam, *View*, vol. 1, p. 41.
[833] Ludlow, *Crusades*, p. 5.

the glue that held the motley crews together under a single standard. "But the chief incentive to pilgrimage was doubtless the supposed merit of treading the very footprints of our Lord."[834] Says Ludlow, "The summons for the crusades thus furnished the lacking sentiment of patriotism; but it was a patriotism that could not be bounded by the Rhine or the Danube, by the Channel or the Pyrenees. Europe was country; Christendom was fatherland."[835]

The first Crusade began only months after Pope Urban II called[836] Christians to arms during the winter of 1095, "When Urban II addressed the multitude from a lofty scaffold in the market-place of Clermont, inciting the people to undertake the crusade, he was frequently interrupted by the shout of thousands in their rustic idiom exclaiming 'Deus lo vult!' 'It is indeed the will of God!' replied the pope; and let those words, the inspiration surely of the Holy Spirit, be for ever adopted as your war cry.'"[837] For some fanaticism and love of battle encouraged them to crusade. Multitudes of other people besieged by civil war, famine, disease and high mortality dropped what they were doing to heed the zealous call to war:

> So great was the misery of the common people in medieval Europe that for them it seemed not a hardship, but rather a relief, to leave their homes in order to better them selves abroad. Famine and pestilence, poverty and oppression, drove them to emigrate hopefully to the golden East. The Church, in order to foster the crusades, promised both religious and secular benefits to those who took part in them. A warrior of the Cross was to enjoy forgiveness of his past sins. If he died fighting for the faith, he was assured of an immediate entrance to the joys of Paradise. The Church also freed him from paying interest on his debts and threatened with excommunication anyone who molested his wife, his children, or his property.[838]

Cheering on the pope's message was one thing, following through on it became an ordeal: Crusading proved to be an expensive undertaking. Extremely poor men, women, and children sold their meager possessions to heed the pope's call. Some even mortgaged their land to the church to collect funds for the long, harsh journey. After accepting the vow clerics

---

[834] Ibid., p. 69.
[835] Ibid., p 38.
[836] "Bearing a letter from the patriarch, he went to Rome and summoned Pope Urban II as the Vicegerent of Jesus, to listen to this new evangel from the ascended Lord. Urban perceived in the monk's fervor the signs of the will of Heaven, and commissioned him to proclaim it to the nations of Europe." Though the papal desire "to make itself the world monarchy had a direct bearing upon the crusades and facilitated the enterprise," according to Ludlow, p. 72.
[837] Giles, *Malmesbury*, p. 377.
[838] Webster, *History*, p. 468.

handed men their crosses: "Whether of silk, or of woven gold" which were "sewed on the shoulders of their mantles, or cassocks, or tunics, once they made the vow to go."

The nobleman compelled to march to Jerusalem for the sake of greed or piety meant those under his charge went, also: "If the baron was inclined to obey the call of his ghostly superior, the successor of St. Peter, his retainers were ready to march. And the most brawling of the barons was superstitious enough to think that the voice of the Pope might be the voice of God. If he did not, his retainers did, and disobedience to the papal will might cost him the obedience of those subject to him. Besides, many of the feudal lords were themselves in clerical orders, with their oath of fealty lying at the feet of the Holy Father."[839] So, when the Lord of the land chose to crusade, his servants had little choice, but to join him.

Crusaders were not only impressed by the charge put to them by their pope, but there were promising signs that convinced many of them that their mission came from their god. False prophets (as opposed to the real ones!) got into the act by seeing and interpreting signs. They interpreted comets and shooting stars as clear signals of their god's will: "There was another detestable crime in this assemblage of wayfaring people, who were foolish and insanely fickle. That the crime was hateful to the Lord and incredible to the faithful is not to be doubted. They asserted that a certain goose was inspired by the Holy Spirit, and that a she-goat was not less filled by the same Spirit. These they made their guides on this holy journey to Jerusalem; these they worshipped excessively; and most of the people following them, like beasts, believed with their whole minds that this was the true course."[840] Ludlow informs us that this superstition came from, "Egyptian symbol for the divine sonship, and the goat represented the devil-the opposing principles of good and evil as conceived by this Eastern sect."[841]

Crusade chronicler and German historian Ekkehard, who lived in the land the Crusaders passed through, became a witness to multiple signs and wonders visible in the heavens that many Europeans interpreted as portents from god:

> We... saw a comet in the southern sky, its radiance extending out obliquely, like a sword; and two years later, on the sixth day before the Kalends of March, 1099, we saw another star in the east changing its position by leaps at long intervals. There were also blood-red clouds rising in the east, as well as in the west, and darting up into the zenith to meet each other; and, again, about midnight, fiery splendors rushed up in the north; and frequently we even saw

---

[839] Ludlow, *Crusades*, p. 38.
[840] Krey, *Crusade*, p. 56.
[841] Ludlow, *Crusades*, pp. 78-79.

torches of fire flying through the air, as we proved by many witnesses. About three o'clock one day some years before this, Sigger, a certain priest of exemplary life, saw two knights rushing at each other in the air, and after they had fought for a long time, the one who bore a large cross, with which he seemed to strike the other, emerged as victor. At the same time, the priest, G—, who now belongs to the monastic profession with us, having paid the sheep which is owed to Christ in place of the first born of the ass, was walking one day at the noon hour in a wood, with two companions, when he saw a sword of wondrous length (which came, he knew not whence) carried up on high by a whirlwind. Until the great height hid it from his eyes, he not only saw the metal, but heard the crashing of the weapon. Some men who were keeping watch in a horse pasture also reported that they saw the semblance of a city in the air, and that they saw divers companies, both on horseback and on foot, hastening to it from different directions. Some even showed the sign of the cross stamped by divine power upon their foreheads, or clothes, or upon some part of the body; and by this sign they believed that they had been predestined for the same army of the Lord. Again, others, pricked by a sudden change of heart, or taught by visions of the night, resolved to sell their lands and goods, and to sew upon their clothes the sign of the cross. To all these people, who flocked to the churches in incredible numbers, the priests, in a new rite, distributed swords along with a blessing and pilgrims' staves and bags.[842]

The first Crusaders departed from Cologne (France) and Worm (Germany) in the spring of 1096. It is their recorded activities that have gained them notoriety as they traveled to Jerusalem via Constantinople. A monk called Peter the Hermit led these first Crusaders. We learn of Peter from chronicler Guibert of Nogent who writes:

Now then, while the princes who felt the need of large funds and the support of numerous followers were making preparations carefully and slowly, the common people, who were poor in substance but abundant in numbers, attached themselves to a certain Peter the Hermit who appeared as a master while we were as yet still considering the project. He was from the city of Amiens, if I am not mistaken, and we learned that he had lived as a hermit in the garb of a monk somewhere in Northern Gaul, I know not where. We beheld him leaving there, with what intent I do not know, and going about through cities and towns under the pretext of preaching. He was surrounded by such great throngs, received such enormous gifts, and was lauded with such fame for holiness that I do not remember anyone to have been held in like honor. He was very generous to the poor from the wealth that had been given him.[843]

Chronicler Albert Aix shares his own views on Peter's pre-Crusading

---

[842] Krey, *Crusade*, p. 46.
[843] Ibid., p. 47.

activities:

> There was a priest, Peter by name, formerly a hermit. He was born in the city of Amiens, which is in the western part of the kingdom of the Franks, and he was appointed preacher in Berri in the aforesaid kingdom. In every admonition and sermon, with all the persuasion of which he was capable, he urged setting out on the journey as soon as possible. In response to his constant admonition and call, bishops, abbots, clerics, and monks set out; next, most noble laymen, and princes of the different kingdoms; then, all the common people, the chaste as well as the sinful, adulterers, homicides, thieves, perjurers, and robbers; indeed, every class of the Christian profession, nay, also, women and those influenced by the spirit of penance—all joyfully entered upon this expedition....[844]

These chroniclers offer differing perceptions of Peter's character. But, apparently he was first to heed the pope's call and was charismatic enough to persuade thousands upon thousands of Europeans to follow him to Jerusalem. Walter the Pennyless was another leader who started out early. It was with his much smaller contingent that troubles started to brew:

> Walter, surnamed the Penniless, a well known soldier, set out, as a result of the preaching of Peter the Hermit, with a great company of Frankish foot-soldiers and only about eight knights. On the beginning of the journey to Jerusalem he entered into the kingdom of Hungary. When his intention, and the reason for his taking this journey became known to Lord Coloman, most Christian king of Hungary, he was kindly received and was given peaceful transit across the entire realm, with permission to trade. And so without giving offence [sic], and without being attacked, he set out even to Belgrade, a Bulgarian city, passing over to *Malevilla*, where the realm of the king of Hungary ends. Thence he peacefully crossed the Morava river.[845]

All was well with Walter and his small group until they reached Zemun (nicknamed Malevilla, or evil town) where men in his troop became separated. Historians tell us that a band of Hungarians robbed them of their gear. The Bulgarians denied Walter's attempts to buy goods to replace the men's stolen equipment. He retaliated by stealing herds of livestock. The Bulgarians responded to that attack by burning down a chapel where some of Walter's Crusaders had fled for safety. Ultimately, Walter appealed to the prince of the land. Afterward, he and his crew were given clear passage the rest of the way to Constantinople where he waited for Peter to rejoin him.

Later, Peter and his Crusaders, who chronicler Albert describes as

---

[844] Ibid., p. 48.
[845] Ibid., p. 48.

"innumerable as the sands of the sea,"[846] crossed through Hungary. There he heard stories of the perils of Walter and his much smaller band of believers. At first, disbelieving that Christians could harm other Christians, Peter discounted the stories until he crossed into Zemun and saw the men's stolen belongings hanging on the gates. Peter ordered the Crusaders to avenge the theft by attacking the Hungarians. His men killed four thousand people. Afterwards, Peter emptied goods and livestock from the city, then fled once he heard that the prince was gathering his forces together.

The groups' troubles did not end there. Two other leaders of smaller groups of First Crusaders were Count Emico, a nobleman, and Gottschalk, a Teuton priest. Chronicler Ekkehard describes Gottschalk as "a false servant of god." History remembers both men for leading their groups in attacks against Jewish communities in the Rhineland (communities along the Rhine river). It appears that Crusaders harbored a great deal of hostility toward Jews - who Christians viewed as their natural enemy - though some nobles had mortgaged their property to Jews[847] in return for cash that allowed them to Crusade. In the Rhineland, Crusaders plundered Christian lands; they slaughtered thousands of Jews, and buried some of them alive after they resisted forced conversion. Chronicler Albert tells us that:

> A large and innumerable host of Christians from diverse kingdoms and lands; namely, from the realms of France, England, Flanders, and Lorraine.... I know not whether by a judgment of the Lord, or by some error of mind, they rose in a spirit of cruelty against the Jewish people scattered throughout these cities and slaughtered them without mercy, especially in the Kingdom of Lorraine, asserting it to be the beginning of their expedition and their duty against the enemies of the Christian faith. This slaughter of Jews was done first by citizens of Cologne. These suddenly fell upon a small band of Jews and severely wounded and killed many; they destroyed the houses and synagogues of the Jews and divided among themselves a very large amount of money. When the Jews saw this cruelty, about two hundred in the silence of the night began flight by boat to Neuss. The pilgrims and crusaders discovered them, and after taking away all their possessions, inflicted on them similar slaughter, leaving not even one alive.[848]

As the Crusaders approached Mainz, the Jews having heard of the slaughter of other Jews looked to the safety of the church for protection. These Jews:

---

[846] Ibid., p. 50.
[847] Christians borrowed from Jews to finance the "holy enterprise," according to Ludlow. During the 2nd crusade "The people to whom the Jews had loaned money, the bonds of which were kept in the cathedral, seized these evidences of debt and burned them in pious offering before the altar." pp. 204-05.
[848] Krey, *Crusade*, p. 54.

Fled in hope of safety to Bishop Rothard. They put an infinite treasure in his guard and trust, having much faith in his protection, because he was Bishop of the city. Then that excellent Bishop of the city cautiously set aside the incredible amount of money received from them. He placed the Jews in the very spacious hall of his own house, away from the sight of Count Emico and his followers, that they might remain safe and sound in a very secure and strong place.

But Emico and the rest of his band held a council and, after sunrise, attacked the Jews in the hall with arrows and lances. Breaking the bolts and doors, they killed the Jews, about seven hundred in number, who in vain resisted the force and attack of so many thousands. They killed the women, also, and with their swords pierced tender children of whatever age and sex. The Jews, seeing that their Christian enemies were attacking them and their children, and that they were sparing no age, likewise fell upon one another, brother, children, wives, and sisters, and thus they perished at each other's hands. Horrible to say, mothers cut the throats of nursing children with knives and stabbed others, preferring them to perish thus by their own hands rather than to be killed by the weapons of the uncircumcised.

From this cruel slaughter of the Jews a few escaped; and a few because of fear, rather than because of love of the Christian faith, were baptized. With very great spoils taken from these people, Count Emico, Clarebold, Thomas, and all that intolerable company of men and women then continued on their way to Jerusalem....[849]

Multiple cities and towns fell under the sword of the First Crusaders as they made their way to Jerusalem. It is certain that tens of thousands of innocent people living within those communities were either murdered or captured and sold into slavery. (We read earlier from Ludlow that winning a battle meant that all the inhabitants within the fortress had been murdered). There are narratives that speak of rivers flowing with blood. Once the Crusaders arrived to Jerusalem:

Some of our men (and this was more merciful) cut off the heads of their enemies; others shot them with arrows, so that they fell from the towers; others tortured them longer by casting them into the flames. Piles of heads, hands, and feet were to be seen in the streets of the city. It was necessary to pick one's way over the bodies of men and horses.[850]

Chronicler Raymond writes:

In the Temple and porch of Solomon, men rode in blood up to their knees and bridle reins. Indeed, it was a just and splendid judgment of God that this place

---
[849] Ibid., p. 55.
[850] Ibid., p. 261.

should be filled with the blood of the unbelievers, since it had suffered so long from their blasphemies. The city was filled with corpses and blood.[851]

Between 40,000 and 300,000 Europeans participated in what has become known as the Peasants' Crusade or People's Crusade. And as troublesome as the news was of the Crusaders' infamous rioting and rampaging across Europe, even more disturbing news was still to come. As I mentioned earlier, besides the wealthy noblemen, average men and women of modest to little means flocked to answer Urban II's call. Many sold all of their meager belongings to finance the long, arduous journey to Jerusalem. Apparently, few understood how long the journey was, nor considered in advance what they might do once their provisions ran out. It was that lack of foresight that caused starvation to become a growing challenge that soon plagued the very lives of the poorest of the Crusaders.

Christians Go Cannibal: Making Banquets of Men, Women and Children

The path to Jerusalem crossed through Antioch and Ma'arra. Ancient historian William of Malmesbury eloquently relates the events, conquests, and challenges of that First Crusade. Of the famine that seized Frankish Crusaders in Antioch, he writes:

> And now, everything which could be procured for food being destroyed around the city, a sudden famine, which usually makes even fortresses give way, began to oppress the army; so much so, that the harvest not having yet attained to maturity, some persons seized the pods of beans before they were ripe, as the greatest delicacy: others fed on carrion, or hides soaked in water; others passed parboiled thistles through their bleeding jaws into their stomachs. Others sold mice, or such like dainties, to those who required them; content to suffer hunger themselves, so that they could procure money. Some, too, there were, who even fed their corpse-like bodies with other corpses, eating human flesh; but at a distance, and on the mountains, lest others should be offended at the smell of their cookery.[852]

And from the Gesta Francorum is written:

> These profane enemies of God held us so inclosed in the city of Antioch that many died of hunger because a little loaf of bread sold for a besant [gold coin]. Of wine I won't speak. They sold and ate horse and ass-flesh ; they also sold a cock for fifteen solidi, an egg for two solidi, and a nut for a denarius. Thus everything was very dear. They cooked and ate the leaves of the fig tree,

---

[851] Ibid.
[852] Giles, *Malmesbury*, p. 380.

grapevine, and thistle, and of all trees, so tremendous was their hunger. Others cooked the dry hides of horses, camels, asses, cattle or buffalos and ate them. These and many such troubles and straits which I cannot name, we suffered for the name of Christ, and to free the way to the Holy Sepulchre [sic]. Such tribulation, famine, and fears we endured for twenty-six days."[853]

Again from the Gesta Francorum is this recording of the siege on Maarrat al-Nu'man (modern Syria), December 12, 1098, that proved successful, except for what came afterwards: "There were some of our men who did not find it there to their taste, not only because of the long stay, but also because of the pressure of hunger, since they could find nothing outside to take. But they burned the bodies of the dead because they found gold besants [gold coins] hidden in their stomachs, while others cut the flesh of the bodies to pieces and cooked them for food."[854]

Another chronicler, Raymond, writes: "Meanwhile, there was such famine in the army that the people ate most greedily the already fetid bodies of the Saracens which they had cast into the swamp of the city two weeks and more ago. These events frightened many of our people, as well as others. On this account very many of our men turned back, despairing of the journey without the help of the Frankish people. But the Saracens and the Turks said on the contrary: 'And who can resist these people, who are so obstinate and cruel that for a whole year they could not be turned from the siege of Antioch by famine, sword, or any other dangers, and who now live on human flesh?'"[855] Daimbert writes: "Setting out into Syria, we took by storm the Saracen cities, Barra and Marra [Ma'arra], and acquired all the fortresses of the region. While we were delaying here and there, there was so great a famine in the army that the already fetid bodies of Saracens were eaten by Christian people."[856]

Billed by the pope as a religious calling and a campaign to save Christian lands, the Crusades became just another moneymaking enterprise for many folks, especially merchants. And when vendors along the way realized that starvation had overcome Crusaders, they took great advantage of their predicament by raising their prices: "Hunger was great beyond measure, and they sold a single ass-load for eight perpre, which is worth one hundred and twenty solidi of denarii. There, indeed, many of our men died because they did not have the means wherewith to buy at such a dear price."[857] Thusly, unprincipled merchants gouging the market priced desperate Crusaders out of it. As a result "famine grew so

---

[853] Krey, *Crusade*, p. 171.
[854] Ibid., p. 207.
[855] Ibid., p. 213-214.
[856] Ibid., p. 276
[857] Ibid., p. 136.

powerful... that some could scarcely restrain themselves from eating human flesh. It is a long story to recount all the misery which was present in the city."[858] And Raymond writes:

> The consciences of the soldiers, troubled with crimes, were bereft of courage. Moreover, they plucked unripe figs from the trees, cooked them, and sold them very dearly. Indeed, the hides of cattle and horses and other things which they had disregarded for a long time they now slowly cooked and sold so dearly that any one could eat the worth of two solidi. Most of the knights lived on the blood of their own horses; awaiting the mercy of God, they did not yet want to kill them. Moreover, these and many other evils difficult to enumerate threatened and besieged.[859]

Crusaders Go Rogue; and György Dózsa Meets a Sadist

The Fourth Crusade was waged during the years 1202-1204. Crusaders who had originally set out to challenge Muslims in control of Jerusalem, turned their gaze toward Christian-controlled Constantinople instead:

> Fourth Crusade, organized by Innocent III; led by Baldwin, Count of Flanders, by Boniface, Marquis of Montferrat, by other northern barons, and later by Henry (Enrico) Dandolo, Doge of Venice. The original purpose was attack upon Egypt and deliverance of Holy Land thereby. But Venice, which furnishes fleet and transports for the northern crusaders, and joins in the Crusade, turns the expedition away from crusading purposes, and makes it the instrument of her aggrandizement. Zara in Dalmatia, a revolted vassal-city of Venice, is taken. Then the crusaders proceed to Constantinople, and restore the exiled Emperor Isaac Angelos, who is to act as their ally and agent (1203). A popular rising breaks out in the city, and Angelos is murdered. A nationalist emperor is set up. Constantinople is besieged and taken by the crusaders.[860]

Europe's crown jewel, Constantinople, held vast wealth and great amenities other parts of Europe had lost to barbarian raiders. After Crusaders entered the city, they caused great havoc as they rampaged through the streets raping, murdering and setting fires. Eventually, Crusaders plundered gold, jewelry and other valuables from the city:

> The conquerors set up a Latin, or Frankish, Empire (which lasts till 1261) on the ruins of the East Roman or Byzantine. Baldwin of Flanders first Latin emperor. The Venetians secure a large share of the spoil—a quarter in Constantinople; a dominant position in the trade of the Byzantine world, especially in the Aegaean [sic] Sea and Black Sea; the island of Euboea or Negropont; the Ionian

---

[858] Ibid., p. 276.
[859] Ibid., p. 173.
[860] Beazley, *Notebook*, p. 132.

Islands—Corfu, &c.; the coast of Albania; a great part of the Peloponnesos or Morea; Crete, &c.[861]

The attack on Constantinople "marks the end of the Eastern Empire as a great Christian state." Constantinople remained in the hands of the Italians for the next 50 years. In 2000, the pope apologized for events that occurred during the Fourth Crusade.

Unlike the distorted Crusader pictures distributed by modern European storytellers, real life medieval Crusader dramas present clear, contrary images of Christian Crusaders murdering and looting their way across foreign lands, despite the billowing Christian banner, or more likely, because of it. English lawyer Ludlow shares a few true Crusader horror stories in Chapter 5.

Although filed under "Crusades," the following story depicts a Crusading story gone awry. In the early 16th century Pope Leo X authorized a crusade against the Ottomans. As soon as these peasants heard the pope's call, they set up camp; however they lacked a leader. György Dózsa, the newly heralded warrior soldier from Székel, had killed the leader of a band of Turks. The king tasked him with leading a motley group of country-folks, peasants, fugitive criminals, beggars, and vagrants on the latest Crusade. Dózsa came from a poor background. His appointment excited the peasants who immediately identified with his humble beginnings. Within days, 40,000 people gathered in Pest. Ten of thousands more gathered in nearby surrounding cities. Field laborers who volunteered for this crusade stopped working the fields. Rent and tithes went unpaid.

Additionally, throngs of volunteers lacked sufficient provisions; they began to plunder and rob. The nobility, who grew furious when laborers refused to return to their work and chores, physically assaulted the men, and imprisoned their families. One priest leader, Laurentius, who joined the crusade along with Dózsa's brother, Gerö, spoke out against the abuses. He preached against the nobility and their evil ways, urging the flock to rise up against them. Inspired by the sermon, these Crusaders murdered hundreds of nobles. The pillage was so great that the night sky glowed with fires from the burning estates of nobles. A call to arms went out across the land. Soon mercenaries captured Dózsa and other leaders. The king beheaded Dózsa's brother, a reluctant warrior, despite Dózsa's plea for a show of mercy. The following account reveals the horrors the sadist king made Dózsa endure:

> Dózsa and some forty leaders were thrown into prison, where they were left to starve until most of them had perished. The wretched survivors were then brought out to be the witnesses of an awful spectacle. On a throne of glowing

---

[861] Ibid., p. 132.

iron sat the miserable 'King of the Crusaders;' a crown of red-hot iron was on his head, and the gypsy-executioners were pouring boiling oil over him, and tearing his flesh with red-hot pincers. Zápola ordered the famished prisoners to satisfy their hunger with the roasted flesh of their late leader. Three refused, and were impaled for their disobedience; and the rest complied with the loathsome order. Dózsa still lived; but not a cry nor a groan escaped his lips through all the dreadful torture. Silent he sat on the burning throne, only once opening his mouth to say, with a ghastly smile, 'I see I have been rearing dogs, not warriors.' Death came at last; but even then his enemies were not satisfied without quartering his mutilated body, and affixing it to the gates of Buda, Pest, Stuhlweissenburg, and Nagy-Várad....

It was September before the insurrection was entirely stamped out; and, during the months it had lasted, it had cost the nation seventy thousand souls....[862]

---

[862] Selina Gaye, "Sketches From Hungarian History," *The Monthly Packet of Evening Readings*, vol. 19 (1875) pp. 323-24.

12

MEDIEVAL MED-INSANE

Up to a recent period our knowledge of Egyptian medicine was gathered solely from scattered passages from great writers. Praxagora[s] [340 BCE] (thought from Cos) [Kos], the town where Hippocrates was born, and where the temple of Esculspius [sic] was built, lived in Egypt of whom Galen speaks as the greatest symptomologist [sic] and diagnostician, and quotes his treatment for acute diseases, and especially gymnastics, was the teacher of Herophilus (400 B.C.), the first anatomist who made postmortems of cadavers. The former went to Egypt for his medical learning, and established a school for Greek physicians. The latter went for the same purpose and founded a system of pathology.

We have a continuous history of Egypt to the extent of about 5,000 years B.C., and a prehistoric account of 2,000 and a continuous culture known to us to cover about 2,000 years more, hence our continuous knowledge probably extends back to about 9000 B.C.

The Ebers Papyrus [circa 3400 B.C.E], therefore, opens a new era for the history of medicine and pharmacology. The work discloses an astonishing knowledge of a great variety of remedies, and shows that four or five thousand years before Christ there were learned men in Egypt who could make intelligent observations of disease, combine complicated prescriptions and use them with judgment. It is hardly possible to exaggerate the literary, scientific and historical importance of this wonderful papyrus, the most complete compendium of Egyptian medical science that is left to us, and we must acknowledge the fact that the copy of the Ebers Papyrus is the genesis of medicine.[863]

Note Please be advised that remedies contained throughout this and other chapters are included for research purposes alone. This author does not advise, instruct, nor recommend readers duplicate, sell, or ingest the ancient so-called cures contained within this or other chapters of this book, as they may prove harmful to ones health.

Early European Practitioners Studied in KMT

Medicinal treatments in Europe date back to at least 700 BCE. They valued herbs and used them in healing. Europeans most likely gained herbal knowledge from more ancient cultures. Around 400 BCE, Greek medical practitioner Polybus records the four humors in *On The Nature of Man*. Polybus founded dogmatism, one of several medical

---

[863] Carl H. Von Klein, *The Medical Features of the Papyrus Ebers*, p. 18.

sects that divided the beliefs and practices of the ancient European medical community - such as one existed. Dogmatics upheld the principles of medicine as practiced by Hippocrates, noted father of western medicine. Polybus not only studied under Hippocrates, but was his son-in-law, too.

The four humors[864] of the medical dogmatists corresponded with the four elements of Earth (black bile), water (phlegm), air (blood) and fire (yellow bile). Europe's medical men strongly believed that humors influenced the moods, and health of humans: "Earth has the humor of being cold and dry; water of being cold and moist; air of being hot and moist; and fire of being hot and dry. It went on further to say that earth corresponded to autumn and the melancholic temperament; water to winter and the phlegmatic; air to spring and the sanguine; and fire to summer and the choleric. If these humors were perfectly balanced, the person was well and to this day we keep the phrase 'good-humored' but if there chanced to be too much of any one of them, illness was the result; and it was the business of the doctor to decide which humor was in excess."[865] Though early European medical practitioners believed there were only four humors, Praxagora, mentioned above, believed there were eleven such humors. Despite that difference, practitioners of humor medicine believed that keeping them balanced was the key to healthy living. Humor medicine and treatment remained important areas of study in the European medical community for centuries.

Medieval physician extraordinaire, Galen (Claudius Galenus), who we will hear from shortly, "like his predecessors... asserted that there were four humors...." Born in Greece circa 130 CE, Galen lived for eight years in Alexandria where he studied medicine. Later on he acquired fame and large monetary rewards for effectively treating illnesses becoming the "chief physician to the gladiators" and "imperial physician to Marcus Aurelius, Commodus and Severus besides others." But, at least one of the cures Galen prescribed raises modern eyebrows of those who believe he recommended parts of human bodies in his medical treatments.

Galen, feted during his lifetime and long after his death for his understanding of human anatomy, is Europe's medical hero. Historians regularly cite his sizable knowledge in accounts that explore Europe's history of medicine. Galen practiced medicine in his place of birth, Pergamum, a center for the Aesculapius[866] temple where Greeks honored their god of health. Greek mythology states that Aesculapius taught healing arts, treated the wounded and sick, and restored life to the dead.

---

[864] The humors remained relevant in western medicine well into the 19th century, according to several sources.
[865] Tappan, *Knights*, p. 322.
[866] Researchers believe the Greeks adapted the Aesculapius myth from the life of Kemetan I-em-htp (Imhotep).

Within his temple walls the sick sought comfort from their ailments. The main temple to Aesculapius was in Epidaurus. Elliot describes it here:

> One of the most important structures of the lower city was the Asclepion or health resort dedicated to the god Asclepius. Dating back to Hellenistic times, Pergamum was at its height during the second century A.D. when the physician Galen practiced there and when the orator and rhetorician Aelius Aristides lectured in its theater. Here the sick, who often came from great distances, underwent treatment by suggestion, sun and water baths, music, prayer, and interpretation of dreams." Splendid temples were built to him in lovely and healthy places, usually on a hill or near a spring; they were visited by the sick, and the priests of the temples not only attended to the worship of Aesculapius, but took pains to acquire knowledge of the healing art. The chief temple was at Epidaurus, and here the patients were well provided with amusements, for close to the temple was a theatre capable of seating 12,000 people, and a stadium built to accommodate 20,000 spectators.
>
> A serpent entwined round a knotted staff is the symbol of Aesculapius. A humorist of the present day has suggested that the knots on the staff indicate the numerous "knotty" questions which a doctor is asked to solve! Tradition states that when Aesculapius was in the house of his patient, Glaucus, and deep in thought, a serpent coiled itself around his staff, Aesculapius killed it, and then another serpent appeared with a herb leaf in its mouth, and restored the dead reptile to life. It seems probable that disease was looked upon as a poison. Serpents produced poison, and had a reputation in the most ancient times for wisdom, and for the power of renovation, and it was thought that a creature which could produce poison and disease might probably be capable of curing as well as killing. Serpents were kept in the Temples of Aesculapius, and were non-poisonous and harmless. They were given their liberty in the precincts of the temple, but were provided with a serpent-house or den near to the altar. They were worshipped as the incarnation of the god, and were fed by the sick at the altar with 'popana,' or sacrificial cakes.[867]

Albert Schneider mentions other features of the Aesculapius temples, "The ancients had some very practical notions regarding hygiene[868] and preventive medicine, as is evidenced by the fact that these temples were erected in the most salutary places, surrounded by beautiful trees and supplied with fountains of pure sparkling water."[869] White writes, "Just as formerly the patients were cured in the temples of Aesculapius temples, so they were cured in the Middle Ages, and so they are cured now at the

---

[867] Elliot, *Outlines*, pp. 14-15.
[868] "The Jews... inherited many useful sanitary and hygienic ideas, which had probably been first evolved by the [ancient] Egyptians, and from them transmitted to the modern world mainly through sacred books attributed to Moses." White, *Warfare*, vol.2, p. 33.
[869] Schneider, "*Ancient Therapeutics*," 255.

shrines of saints."[870]

The temples or houses of KMT, called Per, have an even more distant history. Per served as healing centers. Patients sought rest there and received treatment for illnesses. (Per served other major roles, too). Greeks and Romans adopted this concept and then adapted healing centers to their medical and spiritual needs. It was within those Greek and Roman temples that supposed supernatural cures, some of which may have emerged from misinterpreting, and misapplying ancient African healing practices, merged with more practical treatments. These superstitious treatments gathered strength in Europe resulting in remedies bordering on and crossing into the metaphysical.[871]

Galen's anatomical studies heavily influenced early European medical practitioners. His death choked European advancement in medical theory and methodology, and according to one historian, coincided with the fall of the Roman Empire.[872] Christianity's rise allowed church fathers to exercise tremendous influence on the methods and therapies applied by medical practitioners. According to Schneider, medicine and religion had commingled for some time: "Priests[873] had a complete monopoly of the practice of medicine; they established the rules of health and hygiene, and enforced them by making them part and parcel of religious worship and ceremony.... After the advent of Christianity the ancient Greek and Roman gods and goddesses were replaced by Christian saints. In Christian Greece the Virgin Mary was now invoked to cure disease and relieve suffering.... Cosmos and Damian, took the place of Aesculapius in popular worship, and their portraits were frequently found upon the title-pages of medical books. Medicine as a science made very slow progress. Fetishism, symbolism, and superstition continued to be the main factors in medical practice for many centuries."[874]

First, the Doctor Wants to Know, "What's Your Sign?"

As we read in Chapter 8, superstitious beliefs developed into a powerful entity within the Christian community. The church held the reins of medical practitioners and guided all medical discourse. Church leaders believed that committing sins caused disease and illness, and so believed

---

[870] White, *Warfare*, vol. 2, p. 24.
[871] It should be noted here that though some Greek philosophers and physicians studied with ancient priests of KMT, none became priests. That means that Europeans received only a few degrees of what they considered to be "mysterious" knowledge.
[872] Elliot, *Outlines*, p. 111.
[873] Pliny informs us of the virtues of reciting healing prayers, adding that playing music was essential in keeping out unwanted sounds. He gives great credit to the healing powers of Vestal Virgins. Bostock and Riley, *Pliny's*, vol. 5, pp. 278-80.
[874] Schneider, "*Ancient Therapeutics*," 255-56.

that renouncing sin and moderation in living were effective treatments. They doled out useless, concocted therapies to sick patients that opened the doors for treatments containing measurably unhealthy doses of superstitious beliefs. And many medieval medical kooks strolled straight through. Tappan informs us that owing to their strong belief in astrology, medieval medical practitioners treated patients according to their birthdate:

> When a doctor was sent for, he came on horseback with the bells on his bridle rein jingling[875] so merrily that he could be heard a long way off. An assistant followed him and as many servants as his purse would permit, bearing five or six instruments and numerous sorts of ointment. When he reached the home of the sick man, his first business was not to count his pulse or note his temperature, but to inquire under what constellation he was born. With this knowledge he would set to work to ascertain what remedy would be of service. But, however valuable the medicine might be and however much it might be needed, it must not be taken when the moon was in an unfavorable sign; for then it would do harm rather than good.[876]

Some medieval alchemists, apparently refined in disguising their craft within the rigid borders of church doctrine, were behind much of the use of charms in medicinal practice. From the Encyclopedia of Religion and Ethics we learn: "Through such new interpretations and new colouring [sic], and through the addition of Christian symbols and formulae, the old charms were supposed to be sanctified, and their heathen origin was quickly forgotten. Christian and un-Christian are often so interwoven that it is difficult to trace the true source of the single threads. Moreover, in spite of all ecclesiastical prohibitions, many purely heathen charms remained, and formed the principal component of the whole extensive apparatus of the antagonistic black magic and witchcraft."[877]

According to Tappan alchemist administered charms in many of their potions: "With the chanting of charms and the drawing of magic circles an alchemist would prepare a draught warranted to heal a sick man, give pleasant dreams, or make one invulnerable. To the common folk, their work was so mysterious and the sights and sounds from their laboratories so strange and awe-inspiring that whenever they passed the house of an alchemist, they crossed themselves and prayed to be delivered from the power of the Devil."[878] It was especially surprising to learn that medieval Europeans used effigy charms. Most of us know effigy charms by its more

---

[875] These were medieval emergency sirens.
[876] Tappan, *Knights*, pp. 316-17.
[877] E. Von Dobschütz, "Charms and Amulets (Christian)," *Encyclopaedia of Religion and Ethics*. 1908. p. 422.

[878] Tappan, *Knights*, p. 322.

popular, demonized name: Voodoo dolls. Tappan informs us that:

> Another method of ridding one's self of a foe was to make an image of him in wax. Under the right arm of the image one must place the heart of a swallow, and under the left arm its liver. Whatever injury was done to the figure was supposed to be felt by the person whom it represented. If a needle was pushed into its side, the person was expected to feel a sharp pain in the side. In case of sudden death, people thought first of witchcraft, and it was sometimes dangerous to the safety of even an innocent man if his enemy died too unexpectedly. It was far safer to build a fire of wood and vervain, set the waxen image before it, and let it melt. Then the person would slowly but surely waste away. This belief in the waxen image was so firmly fixed that if a man had a hawk which he could not succeed in managing, he would sometimes send a waxen image of it to the *shrine of some saint* that he might have better success.[879](Italics added).

Beyond the use of charms were biblical remedies owing to the belief that illnesses entered the body as a result of sins: "Medicines were hardly expected to do much good of themselves. To make a dose powerful, the sick man must repeat a certain Psalm twelve times together with several Paternosters while the medicine was being prepared. It was far more likely to effect a cure if he could take it at the shrine of some saint. With some remedies one should always repeat a charm."[880]

Next to using charms came the practice of "disgusting the demon" whereby the person's body is tormented. This treatment requires that the patient swallow or apply to himself various "unspeakable ordures" with witchy ingredients such as "the livers of toads, the blood of frogs and rats, fibres [sic] of the hangman's rope, and ointment made from the body of gibbeted criminals. Many of these were survivals of heathen superstitions, but theologic reasoning wrought into them an orthodox significance,"[881] White informs us seemingly certain as to the origins of this type of practice. Other witchy ingredients included: hop-plant, wormwood, bishop wort and viper's bugloss. Instructions called for ingredients to sometimes be placed beneath altars and required patients to look out for temptations or night goblins.

Schneider includes other peculiar medical practices of the medieval church: "Instead of giving a fever patient a dose of quinine, he was given a verse from the Bible written upon paper. Or, the paper to be swallowed contained merely some hocus-pocus signs, or some meaningless jumble of letters, as 'Ahracadabra....' The popular belief that the earth and all it

---

[879] Ibid., p. 321.
[880] Ibid., pp. 317-18.
[881] White, *Warfare*, vol.2, pp. 38-39.

contains — nay, the entire universe — was created for the exclusive benefit of man has left its imprint upon the practice of medicine and has led it into queer channels. Substances were employed not because of their physiological action, but because of an imaginary sympathetic relationship to the disease, as indicated by structural or other characteristics. For example, it was concluded that liverwort (Hepatica triloba) was specially created for the cure of liver disorders, because the leaves have the shape and color of that organ. Viper's bugloss or blue weed (Echium vulgare), whose flowers show some resemblance to a snake's head, was a sure cure for snake-bite."[882] White calls this hallowed healing practice, "the doctrine of *signatures*" which seems fitting since the doctrine rested on the belief that god left his personal mark upon objects meant to cure: "Hence it was the held that bloodroot, on account of its red juice, is good for the blood; liverwort, having a leaf like the liver, cures diseases of the liver; eyebright, being marked with a spot like an eye, cures diseases of the eyes; celandine, having a yellow juice, cures jaundice; bugloss, resembling a snake's head, cures snakebite; red flannel, looking like blood, cures blood-taints, and therefore rheumatism; bear's grease, being taken from an animal thickly covered with hair, is recommended to persons fearing baldness."[883]

During the days when all of this medieval hocus-pocus was fluttering about monasteries became repositories[884] for some ancient wisdom while the monks became the practicing physicians[885] for the Middle Ages. "The places where medicine, such as it thus became, could be applied, were at first mainly the infirmaries of various monasteries, especially the larger ones of the Benedictine order: these were frequently developed into hospitals. Many monks devoted themselves to such medical studies as were permitted, and sundry churchmen and lay men did much to secure and preserve copies of ancient medical treatises... the Emperor Frederick II, though under the ban of the Pope, brought together in his various journeys, and especially in his crusading expeditions, many Greek and Arabic manuscripts, and took special pains to have those which concerned medicine preserved and studied...."[886] White informs us. Albertus (the Great) Magnus was a church bishop canonized in 1622. He was a highly esteemed character of the medieval world whose interests included alchemy and physiology. The passage of time seems not to have disturbed

---

[882] Schneider, "*Ancient Therapeutics*," 257.
[883] White, *Warfare*, vol. 2, pp. 38-39.
[884] English lawyer Ludlow informs us that: "The few manuscripts which existed were the property of monasteries or of the nobility, who kept them as articles of furniture rather than for their practical use. We have a verbal monument to the ignorance of these times in the expression we still use when we speak of 'signing,' or making a mark to signify, one's name." See p. 10. A mark, such an "X" was made in place of writing one's name.
[885] Executioners, and barbers take on that role, too.
[886] White *Warfare*, vol. 2, pp. 33-35.

his respected place in European history. *Egyptian Secrets: White and Black Art For Man and Beast* is a book attributed to Magnus that some say has old world medicinal recipes for treating humans and animals alike. Additionally, the book includes pleas for divine intercession. One disease mentioned in the book - a neurological disorder - is treated with an ingredient that, as it turns out, was not so unique for its time. And while some historians doubt that Magnus authored *Egyptian Secrets*, or that he added the human body as an essential ingredient for treating the disorder, there are many medieval physicians whose prescriptions did include dead humans' body parts.

> And ye shall eat the flesh of your sons, and the flesh of your daughters shall ye eat. - Leviticus 26:29 (A curse leveled against those worshiping foreign idols, or making graven images, 538-332 BCE)

Dead Humans Medicine: Europeans Harvest the Human Body for Cures & Cosmetics

> For the life of the flesh *is* in the blood, and I have given it you upon the altar, to make an atonement for your soul; for it *is* the blood *that* maketh an atonement for the soul. - Leviticus 17:11

> Therapeutical powers have been vulgarly ascribed to nearly every part or excretion of the human body, and a poetical German apothecary of the eighteenth century has enumerated twenty-two different remedies derived from this source. [887]

A well-kept secret in European medical history is the use of human body parts in treating illnesses. Very few people are aware that from Great Britain to central, eastern, and northern Europe, historical evidence reveals medieval Europeans consumed by their undeniable appetite for human corpses. Whether because of famine, a medicinal cure, or for beauty treatments, early Europeans harvested human body parts and human blood as they tried to sustain their own lives and/or improve their health, and beauty. In fact, there are a few European historians and scholars who have stepped forward with impressive documented evidence of European cannibalism as the following passage shows:

> It is recorded that, in 1483, King Louis XL, of France, struggled for life by drinking the blood of young children, as a means of his revivifying. 'Every day he grew worse,' it is said; 'and the medicines profited him nothing, though of a strange character; for he vehemently hoped to recover by the human blood

---

[887] M.A. Von Andel, "Adeps Hominis: A Relic of Prehistoric Therapy," *American Journal of Pharmacy*, 94 (1922).: 669.

which he took and swallowed from certain children.¹ Again there is a disputed claim, that, in 1492, a Jewish physician endeavored to save the life of Pope Innocent VIII, by giving him in transfusion the blood of three young men[888] successively. The Pope was not recovered, but the three young men lost their lives in the experiment. Yet blood transfusion as a means of new life to the dying was not always a failure, even in former centuries; for the record stands, that 'at Frankfort, on the Oder, the surgeons Balthazar, Kaufman, and Purmann, healed a leper, in 1683, by passing the blood of a lamb into his veins.'"[889]

From Italian novelist Rafael Sabatini we learn that this same pope, Innocent VIII, on the brink of death drank a woman's breast milk. Regarding the use of breast milk Pliny suggests that in addition to its abilities to heal a host of sicknesses such as fevers and stomach upsets: "It is generally agreed that it is the sweetest and the most delicate of all, and that it is the best of remedies for chronic fevers and coeliac affections, when the woman has just weaned her infant more particularly."[890] Apparently Pliny had personally experienced drinking breast milk as a cure. He continues: "Woman's milk is also a cure for affections [sic] of the lungs; and, mixed with the urine of a youth who has not arrived at puberty, and Attic honey, in the proportion of one spoonful of each, it removes singing in the ears, I find."[891]

As peculiar as the idea is of using human body fluids and corpses in medical treatments, bold European researchers candidly acknowledge what some African Maafans have known all along: When Europeans accused Africans and other brown people of cannibalism, in reality, they were projecting their own medieval perversions onto the rest of the world. In Chapter 7 we read how seeing blood-gushing gladiators thrilled ancient spectators. In the next few pages we discover reasons behind that excitement: Ancient cures recommended by Dark Ages European physicians included drinking the warm blood of fallen gladiators, as well as devouring fresh gladiator liver. Additionally, the blood of young boys was highly valued by medieval European medical practitioners as the narratives above illustrate. But, "less abominable," in Strack's opinion, "is the outward application of excrement [892] or of sperma. [893] Xenocrates

---

[888] For donating their blood and for the loss of their lives the ten-year-old youngsters were each paid a ducat. The Jewish doctor is said to have fled for his life after the pope died July 1492. *The Life of Cesare Borgia*, Rafael Sabatini, pp. 59-60.
[889] Trumbull, *Covenant*, pp. 124-25.
[890] Bostock and Riley, *Pliny's*, vol. 5, p. 302.
[891] Ibid. p. 303.
[892] Pliny writes: "In the case too, of women afflicted with sterility, they recommend the application of a pessary, made of the first excrement that is voided by an infant at the moment of its birth; the name they give it is 'meconium.'" Ibid., p. 295.
[893] Pliny states: "The shameless and disgusting researches that have been made will quite

distinguishes with great nicety the potential effects of sperma by itself, or of the sperma which flows out of the vagina after coitus."[894]

Medieval apothecaries logged many medicinal remedies that include human bodies in not easily accessible (to the public at large) pharmacy books. Additionally, apothecaries wrote recipes in languages other than English. However, I successfully obtained a few of what are possibly hundreds, or perhaps even thousands of recipes, considering dead humans medicines were fashionable in medieval Europe – and later during their supposedly more enlightened Renaissance phase - lasting well over a thousand years. Medieval and Renaissance era luminaries partook of these curious cures seemingly without fluttering their royal eyes.

Mentioned already is France's King Louis XL. Other noted Europeans whose names I ran across during my research include eminent chemist Robert Boyle (wore moss from a dead man's skull),[895] and Catherine de Medici ("wore a piece of an infant's skin as a charm").[896] During the 17th century, Theodore Turquet De Mayerne who A.C. Wootton reports, "exercised considerable influence on English pharmacy,"[897] was physician to the French King Henry IV, England's kings James I, Charles I,[898] Charles II, and Queen Henrietta.[899] Regarding Charles II, Wootton cites Sir H. Halford: "In a paper 'On the Deaths of some Eminent Persons,' printed by Sir H. Halford in 1835, it is stated that in the last illness of Charles II, when he was suffering from a stroke of apoplexy, one of the prescriptions, signed by four physicians, ordered among other ingredients 25 drops of the spirit drawn from human skulls."[900] According to A.C. Wootton, Mayerne used unburied human skull in a gout powder, and made mummy powder from the "lungs of a man who had died a violent death."[901] The following passage summarizes a few more ways Europeans used dead humans body parts:

> Bechler, in "Parnassus Medicinalis," 1663, quoted in Peter's " History of Pharmacy," says: —" Powdered human bone, in red wine, will cure dysentery. The marrow[902] and oil distilled from bone is good for rheumatism. Prepared

---

transcend all belief, when we find authors of the very highest repute proclaiming aloud that the male seminal fluid is a sovereign remedy for the sting of the scorpion." Ibid., p. 295.
[894] Strack, *Sacrifice*, p. 25.
[895] Wootton, *Pharmacy*, vol.1, p. 172.
[896] Ibid., p. 173.
[897] Ibid., p. 256.
[898] Ibid., pp. 256, 418.
[899] Ibid., p 146.
[900] Ibid., vol. 2, p. 6.
[901] Wootton, *Pharmacy*, vol. 1, p. 257.
[902] Pliny's translator records that even as late as 1856 a certain French practitioner, Guettard, recommended human marrow as an emollient liniment. Bostock and Riley, *Pliny's*, vol. 5, p.

human skull is a sure cure for the falling sickness (epilepsy). Moss grown on a skull is a hemostatic. Mummy dissolves coagulated blood, relieves cough and pain in the spleen, and is very beneficial in flatulency and delayed menstruation. Human fat properly rubbed into the skin restores weak limbs. The wearing of a belt of human skin facilitates labour and mitigates its pain. Water distilled from human hair and mixed with honey promotes the growth of hair.[903]

In the following pages, readers will view some ancient prescriptions recommended by medieval European physicians that required freshly dead human bodies, as medieval healers believed the best bodies (to use in medicines) were freshly dead ones. Moreover, there was a preference for executed bodies,[904] for practitioners saw them as most healthy, and without disease. Besides, the medieval upheaval left many dead humans scattered all about the landscape. Ages ago, Europeans had established the human body as a valuable commodity and product - *no part* of it went unsold - including urine, fat, the skull (as we learned earlier about the skull cups), and especially the blood: "The commencement of Book 28 of the important Natural History of C. Plinius Secundus, who perished in 79 a.d. at the eruption of Vesuvius. A contemporary of his was the physician Xenocrates of Aphrodisias, about whom the renowned Claudius Galenus [Galen] of Pergamos (131-200 a.d.) gives the following account: — 'He described, as from personal experience, with much boldness, what ills could be cured by the use of human brain,[905] flesh and liver; or, again, the bones of the human skull, fibula, and fingers, some burnt, some unburnt; or, lastly, by the use of blood.... He writes also what effect dung may have, if it is smeared on wounds and into the oesophagus, and is swallowed. He speaks also of the internal use of ear-wax.... The most nauseous, however, is the dung and the drinking of the menses...."

Waste Not, Want Not: Human Urine and Sweat used as Medicines

First, we will learn how urine and fat were prepared as therapeutic cures. Pliny elaborates on the effectiveness of urine in religious ceremonies, as well as its healthful benefits. Children's urine was the best, according to him, in fighting off the poisons of asps (perhaps these were Egyptian cobras):

276.
[903] Wootton, *Pharmacy*, vol. 2, p. 5.
[904] "Presumably in health and strength, with the warm red tide of life beating vigorously in every vein," writes Mabel Peacock, p. 274.
[905] Professor of medicine, alchemist Crollius "gives a recipe for an eye salve, which was to divide a human brain into half; mix one half with honey and apply it at night; dry and powder the other half and apply it in the morning." Wootton, *Pharmacy*, vol. 2, p. 7.

Thus, for instance, the urine of eunuchs, they say, is highly beneficial as a promoter of fruitfulness in females. But to turn to those remedies which we may be allowed to name without impropriety—the urine of children who have not arrived at puberty is a sovereign remedy for the poisonous secretions of the asp known as the "ptyas," from the fact that it spits its venom into the eyes of human beings. It is good, too, for the cure of albugo, films and marks upon the eyes, white specks (Argema) upon the pupils, and maladies of the eyelids. In combination with meal of fitches, it is used for the cure of burns, and, with a head of bulbed leek, it is boiled down to one half, in a new earthen vessel, for the treatment of suppurations of the ears, or the extermination of worms breeding in those organs: the vapour [sic], too, of this decoction acts as an emmenagogue. Salpe recommends that the eyes should be fomented with it, as a means of strengthening the sight; and that it should be used as a liniment for sun scorches, in combination with white of egg, that of the ostrich being the most effectual, the application being kept on for a couple of hours.[906]

Pliny continues adding that midwives use male urine extensively; it is effective at curing gout, "and all kinds of running ulcers: it is used, too, as a liniment for corrosive sores, burns, diseases of the rectum, chaps upon the body, and stings inflicted by scorpions. The most celebrated midwives have pronounced that there is no lotion which removes itching sensations more effectually; and, with the addition of nitre, they prescribe it for the cure of ulcers of the head, porrigo, and cancerous sores, those of the generative organs in particular."[907] Pliny closes by informing readers to drink their own urine, but also advises them to take care in doing so.

It seems medicinal urine was well received by patients. One example follows: "Human excrement and human urine were strongly recommended by many of the chief authorities. Mme. de Sévigné, writing to her daughter on June 13, 1685, says: —'For my vapours I take 8 drops of essence of urine, and contrary to its usual action it has prevented me from sleeping.' There are other references to this delicate remedy in some other of her letters. Apparently she took a special combination of the essence with the Baume Tranquille."[908]

One pope's ophthalmologist recommended infant's urine: "The Pope [sic] ophthalmologist... recommended the urine of infants as an eye-wash, experience having evidently shown that this fluid, which is usually bland and unirritating [sic], a solution of salts of a specific gravity such that it would not set up osmotic processes in the eye, was empirically of value."[909]

Written in an old, but still easy to understand style of English Lean's

---

[906] Bostock and Riley, *Pliny's*, *vol. 5*, p. 300.
[907] Ibid., p. 300.
[908] Wootton, *Pharmacy*, vol. 2, p. 7.
[909] James J. Walsh, *Medicine*, p. 152.

Collectanea has this suggestion for bad breath: "Creythes. The urine of a child under 14 years of age doth cure the toughnes of breath if it be dronken. If it be sodde in a brasen vessel with honey, it healeth creythes and also the webbe and the tey in the eye. There is made of it and copper good soulder for gold. It clenseth the eyelids and the creythes in the eyes. Recorde, Urinal of Physic, J. 1567."[910] And, finally, Galen approved of using saliva, according to White.

Human Feces used as a Medicine

> "Wherefore human dung has great virtue in it, because it contains in itself noble essences, as of the food and the drink, concerning which wonderful things might be written. For the body receives from it nothing save nutriment, but not the essence, as we write in our treatise on Nutriments."[911]

Earlier, I cited instances of Europeans preparing human feces for prescriptions. Pliny adds the name of a famous doctor of his time who treated illnesses with human excrement in cures: "Aeschines of Athens used to cure quinzy, carcinoma, and affections of the tonsillary glands and uvula, with the ashes of burnt excrements, a medicament to which he gave the name of " botryon" (cluster of grapes)."[912]

Regarding the prescription of medicinal human dung: [German chemist John Rudolph] "Glauber states that he had known of wonderful cures effected by these remedies. But the reason was simple. Human dung, for example, is nothing but bread and flesh reduced into their first matters, all their bonds being loosened and rendered fit for the exercise of their virtues. The essential constituent is a salt not unlike the sal enixon of Paracelsus. The mention of this great teacher leads Glauber to relate that once some physicians and noblemen asked Paracelsus to tell them some great secret of medicine. In reply he told them that incredible virtues were hidden in human dung. Whereupon they were very angry and departed, considering that he was mocking them. Paracelsus made a remedy which he called *Zebethum Occidentale* from human dung, dried and powdered. He also recommended a child's excrement to be distilled twice, and to use the oily distillate for fistulas, canker, and as an application for premature baldness."[913]

We will learn more about the highly esteemed German alchemist and physician Paracelsus shortly. Now, I turn to Pliny once more to describe human sweat use in ancient Greece. Note the indifference to this commodified extract from humans he casually refers to as, "scrapings:"

---

[910] Vincent Stuckey Lean, *Lean's Collectanea*, vol. 3, p. 4.
[911] Waite, *Hermetic*, p. 45.
[912] Bostock and Riley, *Pliny's*, vol. 5, p. 292.
[913] Wootton, *Pharmacy*, vol. 2, pp. 9-10.

In Greece, where everything is turned to account, the owners of the gymnasia have introduced the very excretions even of the human body among the most efficient remedies so much so, indeed, that the scrapings from the bodies of the athletes are looked upon as possessed of certain properties of an emollient, calorific, resolvent, and expletive nature, resulting from the compound of human sweat and oil. These scrapings are used, in the form of a pessary, for inflammations and contractions of the uterus: similarly employed, they act as an emmenagogue, and are useful for reducing condylomata and inflammations of the rectum, as also for assuaging pains in the sinews, sprains, and nodosities of the joints. The scrapings obtained from the baths are still more efficacious for these purposes, and hence it is that they form an ingredient in maturative preparations. Such scrapings as are impregnated with wrestlers' oil, [a mixture of oil and wax] used in combination with mud, have a mollifying effect upon the joints, and are more particularly efficacious as a calorific and resolvent; but in other respects their properties are not so strongly developed.[914]

Pliny informs us that Greeks collected "wall scrapings" from the gymnasia walls. They promoted them as a cure for inflamed tumors, ulcers, and burns. And finally, as late as 1901, Merck's Archives records that Anglo-American medical doctors recommended urea as a diuretic and antitubercular.[915]

Human Fat used as a Medicine

Besides the Fat, we sell the fix'd [sic] and volatile Salts of the Blood, Scull, [sic] Hair, and Urine, and other Chymical [sic] Preparations, to be found in Mr. Charas' Royal Pharmacopoeia, etc. which those who desire to know further about these Preparations, may have recourse to.[916] (A 17th century druggist's list of human body parts sold in French apothecaries).

Indo-Europeans prepared the fat of animals (including humans) for ritual sacrifices. We have learned from Smith already that altar fat was the "food of the gods," and that Europeans placed human fat in charms. Smith notes, "The reason of this is that the fat, as a special seat of life, is a vehicle of the living virtue of the being from which it is taken...."[917] The fat of the intestines was also from ancient times reserved for the deity (1 Sam. ii. 16), and therefore it also was forbidden food (Lev. iii. 17). The prohibition did not extend to the fat distributed through other parts of the body."[918]

Indo-Europeans saw fat and blood as being of equal vitality, and fat

---

[914] Bostock and Riley, *Pliny's*, vol. 5, p. 294-95.
[915] Schneider, "Ancient Therapeutics," 258.
[916] Pierre Pomet, *A Compleat History of Druggs*, p. 229.
[917] Smith, *Lectures,*, p. 383.
[918] Ibid., p. 238.

became an acceptable substitute for blood, according to Smith. In time, he informs us, fat became "an integral part" of the altar offering. Indeed, the Old Testament deity requests fat offerings, and Smith points out that worshippers burned fat upon the altar while they set aside rest of the flesh. There was a definite long time mystical quality given to human fat, as we will read shortly, that is important to keep in mind. For the American Journal of Pharmacy records that as late as 1922 Denmark sold human fat salve in a potion called "Hangman's Salve" or "Poor Sinner's Fat."

Poor Sinner's Fat was a tonic that was found in pharmacies along with oil from human brain. Merck's Archives mentions both as consumer products. Hangman's Salve and Poor Sinner's Fat reference the fat accumulated by executioners at their hangman's gallows, packaged as ointments and then sold in apothecaries. Europeans believed human fat healed wounds, and applied it "to restore the functions of tendon and nerves,"[919] among other uses. According to the 17th century chief druggist to King Louis XIV, Pierre Pomet: "Man's Grease (fat) is emollient, discussive, anodyne, and antiparalytick [sic]. It is good against the Gout, and contracted Nerves, made into an Ointment, as follows: Man's Grease, two Pounds; Gum Elemi, half a Pound; Bees-Wax and Turpentine, of each one Pound; Balm of Gilead or Peru, four Ounces; mix, and make an Ointment, by melting all together.[920] The following passage explains the extremes to which Europeans ventured to acquire human fat:

> It was also obtained from the corpses of healthy, vigorous persons who had come to a violent end, that being [absolutely necessary] for the medicinal value of the fat. Cabanes records that in 1572, during the massacre of St. Bartholomew at Lyons, the bodies of the fattest victims were delivered to the apothecaries, who extracted the fat from them, and a similar incident occurred in the history of my native town, Gorinchem, in South Holland. About the date of the massacre of St. Bartholomew the insurgents, or water-beggars as they called themselves, having raided the town, which up to that time had been loyal to the King of Spain, captured about twenty monks, and carried them off to Brielle, where the prisoners were tortured and put to death. The mob treated the corpses of the victims in the most hideous manner. The bodies were cut open, hung on ladders, like the carcases of pigs, and the fat collected and afterwards sold at Gorinchem presumably because that was the place of origin of the commodity. Apart from these special cases, other sources of supply were provided by military operations. In Motley's "History of the United Netherlands," we read that during the siege of Ostende (1601), after each engagement, the Dutch surgeons sallied forth over the stricken field and brought back well-filled bags of human fat," and Johann Dietz, a surgeon who

---

[919] Von Andel, "*Adeps Hominis: A Relic of Prehistoric Therapy*," 667.
[920] Pomet, *Druggs*, p. 229.

took part in the battle of Ofen (1686) tells us in his Reminiscences that the bodies of the Turks slain in the battle were flayed, the fat boiled out, collected in big bags, and conveyed to the camp of the conqueror.[921]

Von Andel remarks, "This curious conjunction of surgeon-executioner was by no means uncommon in the Netherlands, and with the connivance of the authorities, the dual function survived until the middle of the eighteenth century. In other countries the repute of the executioner and his marvelous salves seems to have been no less prevalent and persistent.... as late as the end of the 18th century, during the French Revolution, the fat of the victims of the guillotine was in demand, and Cabanes states, on the authority of de Balzac, that in his time the aristocrats of Sanson sold little boxes of suet[922] to the applicants for 'graisse de supplicie' [fat from tortured/crucified person]."[923] And during the full of contradictions and ironies medieval upheaval, the executioner's role as a sort of gate-keeper between the *now* and *hereafter* granted to him a distorted type of sainthood, similar to that conferred on the king for his perceived ability to vanquish illnesses with the touch of his hand. According to Peacock, "J. Collin de Plancy states in his Dictionnaire Infernal, under the heading Bourreau, that 'le maitre des hautes oeuvres'.[924] In the French province of Berry, Laisnel de la Salle relates in his Croyances et Legendes du Centre de la France [Beliefs and Legends from Central France], 1875, vol. i., p. 165, that... the peasants consider the fat of an executed criminal a specific against scrofula[925] and rheumatism.[926] Executioners collected fat from their victims, and then sold it for large sums of money from their apothecary shops:

> At least, we have authority for supposing this, when, for instance, in 1418, we see the Paris executioner, who was then captain of the bourgeois militia, coming

---

[921] Von Andel, "*Adeps Hominis: A Relic of Prehistoric Therapy*," 667-68.
[922] Suet is the hard, white fatty substance taken from animals that is used to make puddings, pastries, etc.
[923] Ibid., 668-69.
[924] "Master of advanced works had the privilege of curing certain forms of illness by touching the sick with his hand when returning from carrying out an execution... the old French custom of the monarch touching for the king's-evil with a sign of the cross, dates, in essence, from a period long anterior to the reign of the pious king Robert...." Peacock, "Executed Criminals and Folk-Medicine," *Folk-Lore: A Quarterly Review Myth, Tradition, Institution, & Custom*, vol. 7, no. 1 (1896) p. 270.
[925] Pliny speaks of the treatment of scrofula in his day: "Scrofula, imposthumes of the parotid glands, and throat diseases, they say, may be cured by the contact of the hand of a person who has been carried off by an early death: indeed there are some who assert that any dead body will produce the same effect, provided it is of the same sex as the patient, and that the part affected is touched with the back of the left hand." Translator confirms the existence of the treatment in his own time (1856).
[926] Peacock, "Executed Criminals and Folk-Medicine," *Folk-Lore: A Quarterly Review Myth, Tradition, Institution, & Custom*, vol. 7, no. 1 (1896) p. 270.

in that capacity to touch the hand of the Duke of Burgundy, on the occasion of his solemn entry into Paris with Queen Isabel of Bavaria. We may add that popular belief generally ascribed to the executioner a certain practical knowledge of medicine, which was supposed inherent in the profession itself; and the acquaintance with certain methods of cure unknown to doctors, was attributed to him; people went to buy from him the fat of culprits who had been hung, which was supposed to be a marvellous [sic] panacea. We may also remark that, in our day, the proficiency of the executioner in setting dislocated limbs is still proverbial in many countries.[927]

The high value Europeans placed on human fat is rather obvious. And as with every commodity sold in the western world, there was steep competition for acquiring it. The hangman's access to fresh human fat seriously interfered with the druggists' ability to acquire and sell it. So, although the 17th century druggist, Pomet, agrees that human fat was a great cure for rheumatism, he did not think that the executioner's shop was the best setting for obtaining it. To stifle the hangman's business, apothecaries included aromatic herbs in their potion that Pomet insists made them a superior product, "we sell human Fat or Grease, which is brought us from several Parts; but, as every Body knows in Paris, the publick Executioner sells it to those that want it; so that the Druggists and Apothecaries sell very little: Nevertheless they vend a Sort that is prepar'd [sic] with aromatical Herbs, and which is without Comparison much better than that which comes from the Hands of the Hang-Man. This Adeps or Axungia is reckon'd [sic] very good for Rheumatisms, and other Diseases proceeding from a cold Cause."[928]

Human fat was not only used as salve for wounds, nor was it acquired exclusively from state executioners and apothecaries. According to Strack, Europeans turned human fat into candles. They did this because they believed human fat candles made them invisible. It sounds quite incomprehensible, but human fat was such a valuable product that Europeans casually murdered men, women and children to obtain an essential ingredient – human fat - for candle making. The following alarming story documents in the fullest detail the gist of the human fat candlestick delusion:

"Mannhardt, 21 sq. : 'On New Year's Eve, 1864, a fearful murder with robbery was perpetrated at Ellerwald, near Elbing, on Elizabeth Zernickel, 23 years old A piece of flesh, nine inches long, and the same in breadth, had been cut out of her belly. For a considerable time there was no trace of the criminal, till on the evening of 16th February, 1865, during the committal of a thief.... A working

---

[927] Lacroix, *Manners*, pp. 413-14.
[928] Pomet, *Druggs*, p. 229.

man, Gottfried Dallian, of Neukirch, in the Niederung, was caught, and there was found on him a strange candle, consisting of a tolerably firm mass of fat, poured round a wick, and contained in a leaden cylinder…. The murderer made a frank confession at the trial. He had intended merely thieving on 31st December, but Z.'s loud screams for help had caused him to strike her senseless by blows on the head with his knotty stick. After he had packed everything together…. He cut out of the body… a piece of bellyflesh, which he roasted at home. He had made the thieves' candle out of the roasted human fat by the addition of beef tallow, but had eaten the residuum. At the Elbing Assizes he was condemned to death on 23rd June, 1865. The motive of the . . . deed was the delusion instilled into Dallian by hearsay, that a candle or small lamp prepared from the fat of a murdered person would not be extinguished by any draught, and the flame could only be put out with milk; the person who carried it would be invisible whilst all living people round about would be held in a deep slumber. In that way the thief was ensured against any interference in his business. And if the murderer cut a piece out of his victim's belly, roasted and consumed it, he would have peace in his conscience, he would never again think of the crime.'"[929]

Human Blood in Medicines: Its Origins and Many Strange Uses

Verily, verily, I say unto you, Except [sic] ye eat the flesh of the Son of man, and drink his blood, ye have no life in you. John 6: 53 (ca. 1 CE)

The Greeks and Romans poured the sacrificial wine over the flesh, but the Hebrews treated it like the blood, pouring it out at the base of the altar. In Ecclesiasticus the wine so treated is even called " the blood of the grape," from which one is tempted to conclude that here also blood is the typical form of libation, and that wine is a surrogate for it, as fruit-juice seems to have been in certain Arabian rites.[930]

Medieval and Renaissance pharmaceutical books contain recipes that call for animal blood, from the bull, goat, etc., in treating human illnesses, though Europeans still chose to use human blood in treatments. Because Europe's high *holy* book gives insight into the thought processes of the culture, it is important to look at how their cultural customs manifested as biblical edicts. Emperors and nobility oftentimes used biblical passages to justify their terroristic undertakings against the population. In a quite literal sense, streets flowed red with blood and so, too, did rivers during the frenzy-filled Dark Ages:

Hand to hand they clashed in battle, and the fight grew fierce, confused,

---

[929] Strack, *Sacrifice*, pp. 115-16.
[930] Smith, *Lectures*, p. 230.

monstrous, unrelenting—a fight whose like no ancient time has ever recorded. There such deeds were done that a brave man who missed this marvellous [sic] spectacle could not hope to see anything so wonderful all his life long. For, if we may believe our elders, a brook flowing between low banks through the plain was greatly increased by blood from the wounds of the slain. It was not flooded by showers, as brooks usually rise, but was swollen by a strange stream and turned into a torrent by the increase of blood. Those whose wounds drove them to slake their parching thirst drank water mingled with gore. In their wretched plight they were forced to drink what they thought was the blood they had poured from their own wounds.[931]

In the European Paradigm, a Human Death Becomes Life

Despite psychopathic warlords' willingness to spill, and then coldly wade through life's essential essence – blood - the European's reverence for it held fast. European's made that outcome a certainty with the help of each precious drop of blood shed by the mythical martyred Jesus of Nazareth: "That unfailing wellspring of religious emotion supplied by the teachings and the passion of the God sacrificed on the cross:"[932] His death eternally enshrined blood's role as a supernatural substance, and erected a (religious) legal structure for blood sacrifices. But, his death did not only establish the foundation to modern Christianity, it showcased a classic Indo-European tradition. Before there was even a Jesus of Nazareth, blood rituals were important among Indo-Europeans. In fact, they were so important that deities authorized their use in early Indo-European scriptures: "There were indications of the blood covenant and its involvings [sic] in the sacred writing of the Zoroastrians, and in the writings of Herodotus with reference to the Persian invasion, of Egypt, and now, as the last pages of this volume go to press [1871], there comes an illustration of the existence of this rite in Persia in its primitive form at the present time."[933]

Indo-Europeans' belief in "blood as a vehicle of vital energy" is an ancient one. And sacrificing humans or animals to receive the benefits of salvation is ancient, too. One blood ritual performed as early as 133 CE gained favor among Romans, according to Döllinger. In this ceremony of taurobolium priests place a victim on a latticed platform. Once the priest slaughters the victim, its blood showers on the *mystic* lying below in a pit. He moistens his tongue with the victim's blood becoming "endowed with the courage and strength of the slaughtered animal,"[934] Cumont tells us. While Cumont observes that the mystic "moistens his tongue," with the

---

[931] Mierow, *Jordanes*, p. 109.
[932] Cumont, *Mithra*, p. 195.
[933] Trumbull, *Covenant*, p. 369.
[934] Cumont, *Mithra*, p. 180.

victim's blood, Döllinger observes that the blood "dropped like rain" covering his whole body. The mystic took care to wet his "cheeks, ears, lips, eyes, nose and tongue" with blood. Afterwards, witnesses to this blood-bathing rite greeted the blood-soaked mystic on their knees. He wears his bloodied clothes as a badge of honor until they become ragged and fall from his body. Worshippers believed the taurobolium sacrifice aided individuals or an entire city by regenerating them and proving them "pleasing to the gods" for twenty years.

Cumont agrees that worshippers changed the meaning attached to the ancient ceremony. He remarks that in *blood bathing*, "The efficacy which was attributed to this bloody purification, the eternal new birth that was expected of it, resembled the hopes which the mystics of Mithra attached to the immolation of the mythical bull…. It was no longer a renewal of physical strength that the life-sustaining liquid was now thought to communicate, but a renovation, temporary or even perpetual, of the human souls."[935]

This ceremony's Christian symbology and foreshadowing are clear: In Mithraism, the reluctant Mithra battles and successfully slaughters a bull. The Earth receives enormous bounty following the bull's death:[936]

> According to the Mithraic theory, wheat and the vine sprang from the spinal cord and the blood of the sacrificed animal….
>
> From the body of the moribund victim sprang all the useful herbs and plants that cover the earth with their verdure. From the spinal cord of the animal sprang the wheat that gives us our bread, and from its blood the vine that produces the sacred drink of the Mysteries….
>
> From the death which he had caused, was born a new life, more rich and more [fertile] than the old.

Worshippers used rams (criobolium) in addition to bulls and other "victims" in these ceremonies. Cumont observes the importance of this symbology: "Cattle, the source of all wealth, had become an object of religious veneration. In the eyes of such a people, the capture of a wild bull was an achievement so highly fraught with honor as to be apparently no derogation even for a god."[937] And the sacrificed bull represents the gift sent from heaven for the benefit of humankind. In this scenario, the latticed platform is heaven, the blood represents regeneration of life and the mystic lying in the pit is the humbled, beseeching human seeking his blessing.

Cumont's comments on the history of taurobolium: "Like many rites of

---

[935] Ibid., pp. 181-82.
[936] Ibid., pp. 39; 136-37.
[937] Ibid., pp. 134-35.

the Oriental cults, is a survival of a savage past which a spiritualistic theology had adapted to moral ends. It is a characteristic fact that the first immolations of this kind that we know to have been performed by the clergy of the Phrygian goddess took place at Ostia, where the *metroon*... adjoined a Mithraic crypt." [938] Blood rituals run throughout the Old Testament bible. Probably, most readers know the myths of Abraham's aborted blood sacrifice of his son, and of the freshly slaughtered lamb's blood placed on the doors of the soon-departing Jews from ancient Egypt. There are many, many other examples of ritualistic blood sacrifices in European history. So, it is not unexpected that blood comes shrouded with much symbolism in their culture. For example, blood unites two lives into one, or *transfers life from one human to another*. Over the years, it shows up symbolically through "blood-bathing, by blood-anointing, and by blood-sprinkling," [939] according to H. Clay Trumbull who continues, "In its transfer from one organism to another the blood retains its life, and so carries with it a vivifying power."[940] He adds that blood sacrifice was a method of *transferring life even though it resulted in the death* of the blood-giver. However, the benefits from sacrifices, the blissful union with the deity, triumph in battle, etc., lasted only *temporarily*. That important condition, of course, required that future sacrifices be performed.

So, then in European sacrifices human death became life. Jesus of Nazareth finished what began with Abraham:[941] "The pierced hands and feet of the Divine Friend yielded their lifegiving [sic] streams."[942] In this way, the mysticism and the belief in blood's ability to restore life, from death, continued long after his martyrdom because, "It was not the death of the victim, nor yet its broken body, but it was the blood, the life, the soul, that was made the means of a soul's ransom, of its rescue, of its redemption." [943] In a startling distortion of sound reasoning and an unsettling full on slap against reality, European's successfully made the act of murdering innocents a spiritually transformative affair: human death became life.[944]

Peacock remarks, "Among the early Christians the blood of their martyrs was carefully wiped up on cloths, collected in vials, or otherwise

---

[938] Ibid., pp. 181-82.
[939] Trumbull, *Covenant*, p. 203.
[940] Ibid., p. 110.
[941] "Proofs of the existence of this rite of blood-covenanting have been found among primitive peoples of all quarters of the globe; and its antiquity is carried back to a date long prior to the days of Abraham." Trumbull, p. 206.
[942] Trumbull, *Covenant*, p. 285.
[943] Ibid., pp. 286-87.
[944] The ideas surrounding regeneration may have sprouted from some early people's lack of scientific knowledge of agriculture and plant life. They may have believed that sacrifice was necessary to ensure crop growth.

preserved, to be used as relics; and even to the present time the 'standing miracle' of the blood of St. Januarius liquefying and boiling up when the head of the martyr is brought near it on days of grand ceremonial, or of danger to the community, is one of the marvellous [sic] sights afforded to the world by the Latin Church."

Historians have documented the European's disturbing taste for blood. They report occurrences of Roman gladiators falling to their death, only to have excited spectators rush the grounds so they can guzzle their "still warm, still bubbling"[945] fresh blood: "The blood of the gladiators who fell in the circus at Rome was drunk to cure the falling-sickness; epilepsy, it would appear, being the disease most favourably [sic] influenced by this gruesome antidote, probably from its demoniacal character," [946] writes Peacock. Medieval medical authorities believed that the human liver healed epilepsy, one of many diseases whose treatment required dead humans. Utilizing human body parts in therapies began very early in European medical history. Pliny the Elder (23-79 CE) voices his discontent with the practice at the end of this section. His comments verify that not only did no part of the human body go unused; he confirms that cannibalism has deep roots in ancient Europe.

When it came to blood drinking, the best blood was the freshest blood - the warmer, the better. As mentioned earlier, the blood of young boys was highly valued. Peacock writes: "In Sweden and Denmark the blood of an offender who has been beheaded — the legal form of capital punishment — is invaluable for the treatment of a variety of disorders, if the culprit has granted the sick person leave to drink it while yet warm."[947] Peacock cites many eyewitness accounts of blood drinking up to the mid-19th century. From the following passage we gain an understanding of just how normal the act of blood drinking was for Europeans, as well as gather insight into its long lifespan:

> According to Mr. Horace Marryat, who mentions this fact in Jutland, the Danish Isles and Copenhagen, 1860, vol. i., pp. 266, 267, 'even in the present century [19th], when an execution takes place, either in the island of Amak or Moen, *the epileptic stand around the scaffold in crowds, cup in hand, ready to quaff the red blood as it flows from the still quivering body.*' Warm blood as a preservative against the usual loathing for water in cases of hydrophobia, 'is mentioned by a medical correspondent of the third volume of the Transactions of the Moscow Physico-Medical Society (see the Athenxum, 1829, p. 30), and another authority attests that a similar restorative of health is used in China.' Dr. Rennie states, 'says Mr.

---

[945] Strack, *Sacrifice*, p. 50.
[946] Peacock, "Executed Criminals and Folk-Medicine," *Folk-Lore: A Quarterly Review Myth, Tradition, Institution, & Custom*, vol. 7, no. 1 (1896) p. 271.
[947] Ibid., p. 270.

Dennys in the Folk-lore of China, p. 67, ' and I can myself confirm the assertion, that after an execution at Peking certain large pith-balls are steeped in the blood of the defunct criminal, and under the name of 'blood-bread' are sold as a medicine for consumption. It is only to the blood of decapitated criminals that any such healing power is attributed.' (Italics added).[948]

As long as there were public executions in Europe young and old alike had access to fresh blood. Strack's documentation of Europeans drinking "warm, bubbly" human blood oozes into the late 19th century. Following is one of his several citations: "'I was a pupil of the famous Prof. Herrmann at Göttingen. At his suggestion, at the beginning of January, 1859, I attended the public execution of a female poisoner at Göttingen. It was done with a sword. When the head was severed from the body, and the fountain of blood sprang up about 1½ feet high, the populace broke through the square formed by the Hanover Schiitzen, rushed upon the scaffold, and possessed itself of the blood of the dead woman, collecting it and dipping white cloths in it. It was positively a gruesome impression. To my horrified question I got answer that the blood was applied for the cure of epilepsy.'"[949]

Given the European's cultural affinity toward blood offerings — as expressed in the pages of their holy book, it is little wonder that perverted images of blood-consuming beasts, and men saturate their culture. Blood drinking takes an ominous place in medieval European history when one learns just how central it was to their existence. To medieval Europeans, blood was their way to connect to the spiritual/sacred world: "For the life of the flesh is in the blood." One particular story that expresses blood's sanctity surrounds Constantine inflicted with the skin deformity of leprosy: "The emperor, in despair at such a calamity, inquired anxiously for some cure for his disorder, and by the abominable counsel of the priests of the Capitol, ordered a crowd of infants, to the number of three thousand, to be massacred, that a bath might be prepared of their blood, in which, plunging while it was yet reeking, he was told his leprosy would be cured."[950] Constantine emerges the hero in this story. He spares the life of the children at the pleadings of their parents, and others. Soon after, the story goes, a bright light shines round his head for nearly a half hour, whereupon he submits to baptism. According to *The Blood Covenant*, leprosy cures required a "purging out the old blood, by means of an inflowing current of new blood-which was new life.... The giver must die; but it was his blood, his life, not his death, that was to be the means of cure."[951] The act of blood transference as life giving is foundational to European blood covenants,

---

[948] Ibid., pp. 270-71.
[949] Strack, *Sacrifice*, p. 72.
[950] Vitalis, *Ecclesiastical*, vol. 1, p. 326.
[951] Trumbull, *Covenant*, p. 287.

and their cultural construct.

Menstrual Blood Used in Medicinal Preparations Up to the 20th Century

However at odds with blood's sacred depiction was the menstrual blood flow from women that the church said was unclean and impure. According to the bible not only is a menstruating woman contaminated, but anyone or anything that comes in contact with her during that time is impure and must be isolated, too.

On the other hand, menstrual blood had a place in blood rituals and in a surprising number of medicinal cures. According to Strack as of 1905 "medical folk-belief" in the use of menstrual blood remained strong:

> Warm uterine blood of a virgin, applied to gouty limbs, would alleviate the violent pain. A shirt stained with this blood would ensure against blow and stab, and would quench outbreaks of fire, when thrown into the flames.

> In the "Cosmography " of the Arabian, Zakarija ben Muhammed al-Qazwmi (ob. 1283 a.d.), Edtn. of F. Wüstenfeld, Göttingen 1848 sq., it is observed I. 366: "The blood of menstruation, if the bite of the mad dog is smeared with it, cures it, and likewise tubercular (knotig) leprosy and black scab (Räude)... (In regard to these names of diseases, Cf. /. M. Honigberger, " Früchte aus dem Morgenlande," Vienna, 1853, 542 sq.); 367: "The blood of the menstruation of a virgin helps against the white spots on the pupil, if it is applied as an eye-salve."

> Birthmarks, red moles, and freckles vanish if they are smeared with warm menstrual blood, the placenta, or with blood from the umbilical cord...of a woman bearing her first child. (Unter- und Oberfranken)," Lammert, 184 sq. (ibid, original documents). "Moles . . . are cured by smearing with the blood of a fresh umbilical cord, by rubbing with a fresh afterbirth. . . The red mole is covered with a linen clout [cloth] which is moistened with fresh menstrual blood (Ennsthal)," Fossel 134. 56. "The freckles, especially of women, are sought to be dispelled by smearing...with warm menstrual blood (Oberland and neighbourhood of Graz)," Fossel 135. – "The smearing of warts with fresh menstrual blood... is universally practised [sic]," Fossel 140. Slightly different is the practice in Oldenburg: "To dispel warts, they are smeared with the blood of another person's warts; the blood of one's own warts generates more of them." Strackerjan I.

> For itch, wear a shirt, in which a woman has menstruated, during three days on the belly (Hieflau)," Fossel 135.–" Hauss-Apothec," 45: "Above all, the first virgin menses, preserved on the shift or a piece of linen, is held in high esteem, and when steeped in vinegar or rose-water, and, according to the greatness of the disease, laid and repeatedly laid on diseased glands, small-pox, apostemes, is prized as an excellent remedy."

In the Franche-Comté a good table-spoon of a woman's menstrual blood, or better still a young virgin's, in a glass of hot wine with sugar, is recommended for corrupt blood (sang gate). ("Melusine" I., C. 402).

Love-potion. " In the Oberpfalz . . . sweat, a few drops of menstrual blood . . . are mixed in the drink of the person, whose liking it is desired to win," Lammert, 151 sq.[952]

Regarding the curative properties of menstrual fluid Pliny tells us: "It is a well known fact, too, that the menstruous discharge, reduced to ashes, and applied with furnace soot and wax, is a cure for ulcers upon all kinds of beasts of burden; and that stains made upon a garment with it can only be removed by the agency of the urine of the same female. Equally certain it is, too, that this fluid, reduced to ashes and mixed with oil of roses, is very useful, applied to the forehead, for allaying head-ache, in women more particularly; as also that the nature of the discharge is most virulent in females whose virginity has been destroyed solely by the lapse of time." [953] Pliny adds some rather surprising theories on the mystical influences of a woman's monthly flow:

Over and above these particulars, there is no limit to the marvellous [sic] powers attributed to females. For, in the first place, hailstorms, they say, whirlwinds, and lightning even, will be scared away by a woman uncovering her body while her monthly courses are upon her. The same, too, with all other kinds of tempestuous weather; and out at sea, a storm may be lulled by a woman uncovering her body merely, even though not menstruating at the time. As to the menstrual discharge itself, a thing that in other respects, as already stated on a more appropriate occasion, is productive of the most monstrous effects, there are some ravings about it of a most dreadful and unutterable nature. Of these particulars, however, I do not feel so much shocked at mentioning the following. If the menstrual discharge coincides with an eclipse of the moon or sun, the evils resulting from it are irremediable; and no less so, when it happens while the moon is in conjunction with the sun; the congress with a woman at such a period being noxious, and attended with fatal effects to the man. At this period also, the lustre [sic] of purple is tarnished by the touch of a woman: so much more baneful is her influence at this time than at any other. At any other time, also, if a woman strips herself naked while she is menstruating, and walks round a field of wheat, the caterpillars, worms, beetles, and other vermin, will fall from off the ears of corn.[954]

The above discourse provides a short preview of Pliny's ideas on the

---

[952] Strack, *Sacrifice*, pp. 52-54.
[953] Bostock and Riley, *Pliny's*, vol. 5, p. 307.
[954] Ibid., p. 304.

power of menses. He also informs us that the delicate hand of a woman on her period repels bees from their hives; blunts a razor's edge; and turns linen boiling in water black. Even a raging fire is no match for these menstruating females. And pregnant women are equally vulnerable if touched by a woman at that *time of the month* - she will miscarry, according to Pliny in his chapter titled: *Facts Connected With The Menstrual Discharge*. This leaves one to wonder how European women were given slave-like status over the years considering the awesome powers attributed to them.

Europeans Bathe in Human Blood

Early Europeans certainly held some schizophrenic notions concerning blood that are confirmed by their contradictory beliefs over its significance and the mysticism attached to it. And let us not forget the blood drinking ghoulish characters that have become standards of European storytelling traditions including the werewolves, vampires and the less popular screech owls, crafty creatures regularly accused of drinking the blood of babies before devouring them. Blood-slurpers saturate Dark Ages myths. One narrative, *Nibelung Story*, gives an account of blood-drinking Burgundians who used the blood of their Hun opponents to restore their strength:

> Then the queen commanded to make fast the door, and burn down the hall. The Huns kindled it on all sides; a fresh wind rose and wrapped the house in fire. Loud roared the flames; billows of smoke all flecked with fire went rolling up to the sky. The heat was terrible; but Hagan said, 'There is blood enough within to quench the burning timbers as they drop. Stand close against the walls and get what air there is. If we can only bear the heat and tread the fire-flakes out, we may escapes.' The smoke grew stifling hot, and parched their tongues so that they hung from their mouths with drought. They knew not what to do, till they saw one stoop down to a corpse yet warm and draw the blood. Then drank they all the self-same draught, and the blood new strung their sinews, quenched their thirst, and made them fierce.[955]

It is certain that victory in battle after imbibing an opponent's blood added legitimacy to the practice: "The notion that, by eating the flesh, or particularly by drinking the blood, of another living being, a man absorbs its nature or life into his own, is one which appears among primitive peoples in many forms. It lies at the root of the widespread practice of drinking the fresh blood of enemies—a practice which was familiar to certain tribes of the Arabs before Mohammed...."[956]

Trumbull observes the following on Europe's fascination with these

---

[955] George Cox and Eustace Hinton Jones, *Popular Romances of the Middle Ages*, p. 310.
[956] Smith, *Lectures*, p. 313.

legends:

> The wide-spread popular superstition of the vampire and of the ghoul seems to be an outgrowth of this universal belief that transfused blood is re-vivification. The bloodless shades, leaving their graves at night, seek renewed life by drawing out the blood of those who sleep; taking of the life of the living, to supply temporary life to the dead. This idea was prevalent in ancient Babylon and Assyria. It has shown itself in the Old World and in the New, in all the ages; and even within a little more than a century, it has caused an epidemic of fear in Hungary, "resulting in a general disinterment, and the burning or staking of the suspected bodies."[957]

Probably early Europeans concocted blood legends as they struggled to make sense of, and create balance between contradictory interpretations on the role blood played in their cultures. Or, perhaps, they came from the Indo-European's experiences with drinking human blood. And as we read here already, recommendations from medical practitioners to drink blood for good health added to its legitimacy as an effective cure. One such practitioner was Roger Bacon, mentioned earlier; he was by some accounts a somewhat eccentric metaphysician who believed in the effectiveness of charms and incantations. He endorsed a blood recipe for restoring vitality and youthfulness to the aged and feeble and writes that many prominent medieval Europeans perished early for lack of his esoteric knowledge. The key to his recipe lay in increasing body heat.[958] He believed body heat was greatest when born, then gradually diminished with age. So, he advocated increasing heat naturally. While Bacons cloaks ancient recipes found in his book, *The Cure of Old Age, and the Preservation of Youth*, in medieval alchemists' jargon, E. Withington shares the ingredients supposedly included in Bacon's formula to slow old age:

> These secrets, with one exception, are well-known substances often named openly by Roger's predecessors, viz. gold, pearls, ambergris, viper's flesh, bone of stag's heart, rosemary and lign-aloes. The exception is the *minera nobilis animalis* or *fumus juventutis*, terms referring to the contagiousness of health by the close application of the body of a healthy adolescent, preferably with crisp [curly] yellow hair (the Galenic mark of a good temperament) to the sick or aged. Though this forms his most novel contribution to the medicine of the age, he is unusually anxious to disclaim originality, bringing in Solomon (apparently Eccles. iv. ii), as well as Damascenus and Galen, to his support. But, as he admits, they mention the subject obscurely, and the next plain and emphatic reference to the restorative value of balsamic exhalations *a sano et*

---

[957] Trumbull, *Covenant*, pp. 114-15.
[958] E. Withington, "Roger Bacon and Medicine," in *Roger Bacon Essays*, ed., A. G. Little (Oxford: Clarendon, 1914), p. 352.

athletico corpore seems to be that by our English Hippocrates, Sydenham, whose language closely resembles Bacon's, except that he fears ridicule rather than scandal [Obs. Med., i. 4. 40].[959]

Bacon was between 72-78 years old when he died circa 1292. Like Bacon, physician Marsilio Ficino advocates drinking the blood of young people as an elixir of life for remaining youthful, but with a chaser of wine and sugar; however he advises first cooking the blood for those with problems digesting it raw. Among his many studies, Paracelsus (1493-1541) investigated metals and their relationships to human physiology. According to one source the controversial scientist, whose birth name was Phillip von Hohenheim, claimed an ability to make gold and to heal all diseases. His book, *The Hermetical and Chemical Writings*, mentions his belief in nymphs and wood-sprites in addition to what he calls homonculi: tiny humans medieval scientists believed lived inside human sperm and required human blood: "If now, after this, it be every day nourished and fed cautiously and prudently with the arcanum [secret] of human blood, and kept for forty weeks in the perpetual and equal heat of a venter equinus,[960] it becomes, thenceforth a true living infant...."[961] "Paracelsus had a 'Primum Ens Sanguinis,' which was fresh blood from a healthy young person,"[962] writes Wootton. Aulus Cornelius Celsus (ca. 25 BCE- ca. 50 CE) was a physician who compiled a medical encyclopedia on surgery, diseases anatomy, orthopedics, etc. He offers the following cure for epilepsy:

> If the patient should not be cured even by these means, let his head be shaved, anointed with old oil, adding to it vinegar and nitre, and salt water poured upon it; when he is fasting, let him drink castor and water; make use of no water for drink, unless it has been boiled. Some have cured themselves of such a disorder by drinking the warm blood of a gladiator slain.[963]

Among the more shocking, eye-popping revelations in a chapter filled with disturbing ones, is that Europeans indulged in taking human bloodbaths, supplying readers with a fresh definition of a phrase that for many people singularly meant the mass slaughter of humans. The story surrounding Constantine, even if partly mythologized, verifies that taking human bloodbaths is least as old as the 3rd and 4th centuries. Additionally, the story signals to readers that children were the means for obtaining

---

[959] Ibid., pp. 351-52.
[960] Horse manure.
[961] Waite, p. 124.
[962] Wootton, *Pharmacy*, vol. 2, p. 7.
[963] James Greive, trans., *A. Corn. Celsus Of Medicine*. (Edinburgh: Dickinson & Co.,1814), pp. 134-35.

blood. Furthermore, the research of Strack confirms that the church endorsed blood-bathing: "Hildegarde Abbess of the convent on the Rupertsberg, near Bingen, d. 1179, in her 'Libri subtilitatum diversarum natur. Creatur' (Ed. Migne, Paris, 1855), the oldest work of monastic medicine composed in Germany, which also gives experiences of popular therapeutics, praises baths of menstrual blood for leprosy."[964]

One of the more sensational stories of human blood drinking and bathing involves Elizabeth Báthory (1560-1614). Báthory was a Hungarian *noble* woman. The court accused her of murdering a countless number of young girls. A film based on the sensationalism of Báthory's alleged deeds, *The Countess* (2009), suggests that the noblewoman used girls as her personal blood donors, even filling a tub full of their blood so she could keep her youthful appearance. There is more truth than fiction to Europeans filling bathtubs full of human blood. Trumbull writes of this ancient practice citing Pliny as an authority: "There certainly is ample evidence that baths of human blood were anciently prescribed as a cure for the death-representing leprosy; as if in recognition of this root idea of the re-vivifying power of transferred blood. Pliny, writing 18 centuries ago concerning leprosy, or elephantiasis, says: 'This was the peculiar disease of Egypt; and when it fell upon princes, woe to the people; for, in the bathing chambers, tubs were prepared, with human blood, for the cure of it.' Nor was this mode of life-seeking confined to the Egyptians.[965] It is said that the Emperor Constantine was restrained from it only in consequence of a vision from heaven." [966] Indeed, Pliny's translator notes that his contemporaries accused Louis XV[967] (d. 1774) of taking baths with infants' blood "to repair his premature decrepitude."[968]

Returning to the story on Báthory, Strack writes extensively from legal documents surrounding the case that appear to support the allegations made in the film:

> Elizabeth (Bathori) [sic] was excessively fond of making herself up to please her husband, and spent as much as the half of a day at her toilette. It happened, as Thurotz relates, that one day one of her chamber-maids once made some mistake in her coiffure, and received for it such a violent box on the ears, that the blood spurted on her mistress's face. When the latter washed the drops of blood off her face, the skin on the place appeared to her to be much more beautiful, whiter and more delicate. She at once came to the inhuman decision

---

[964] Strack, *Sacrifice*, pp. 52.
[965] This is a biblical reference. In the Midrash Rabboth (Shemoth, Beth, 92, col. 2) there is this comment by the Rabbis on Exodus 2:2." Trumbull, p. 324. These would not have been original Kemetans.
[966] Trumbull, *Covenant*, pp. 116-17.
[967] Several books allege that Louis XV took bloodbaths.
[968] Bostock and Riley, *Pliny's*, vol. 5, p. 276.

to bathe her face, nay her whole body, in human blood, so as thereby to increase her beauty and attractions. With this horrible intention, she took counsel of two old women, who accorded her their entire sympathy, and promised to assist her in the ghastly project.

A certain Fitzko, a pupil of Elizabeth, was also made a member of this bloodthirsty society. This madman usually killed the unfortunate victims, and the old women collected the blood, in which that monster of a woman was wont to bathe in a trough about four o'clock in the morning. She appeared to herself always more beautiful after the bath. She therefore continued her operations even after her husband's death in 1604, in order to win new worshippers and lovers. The wretched girls who were allured into Elizabeth's house by the old women under the pretence [sic] of going into service, were taken into the cellar on various pretexts. Here they were seized and beaten until their bodies swelled. Not infrequently Elizabeth tortured them herself, and very often she changed her blood-dripping clothes and then began her cruelties anew. The swollen bodies of the poor girls were then cut open with a razor. It was not uncommon for this monster to have the girls burnt and then flayed; most of them were beaten to death. She herself beat her accomplices when they did not wish to help her in her torturings [sic]; whilst, on the other hand, she abundantly rewarded the women who brought the girls to her and let themselves be used as tools for the execution of her cruelties. She was also given to supposed magic, and had a peculiar magic mirror in the shape of a cracknel, before which she used to pray for hours at a time.

Finally her cruelty reached such a pitch that she pinched her servants and stuck pins into them, especially the girls who drove with her in her carriage. She had one of her serving-maids stripped naked and smeared with honey, in order that she might be eaten up by flies. When she became ill and could not practise [sic] her usual cruelties, she had a person come to her sick bed, and bit her like a wild cat. About 650 girls lost their lives through her in the way described, partly in Cseita (in the County of Neutrau, in Hungary), where she had a cellar specially arranged for the purpose, partly in other places; for murder and bloodshed had become a necessity to her. When so many girls from the neighbourhood [sic], who were brought into the castle on the pretext of entering service or of receiving further education, disappeared, and the parents never received satisfactory, but generally ambiguous, answers to their enquiries, the matter became suspicious.... At last, by bribing the servants, it was discovered that the missing girls went hale and hearty into the cellar, and never made their appearance any more. A denunciation followed both at Court and to the then Count Palatine Thurzo. The Count had the castle of Cseita surprised, commenced the strictest investigations, and discovered the horrible murders. The monster was condemned[969] to life long incarceration for the terrible crimes, but her accomplices were executed."[970]

The malevolent behavior of another medieval European forms the basis for the vampire character. Vlad the Impaler (1431-1476) was such a ferocious and crazed psychopath that is it difficult to summarize his villainy in a few sentences. However, historians record that Vlad's favorite form of torture was impaling his victims. He killed an estimated ten's of thousands of people and, like Ferrante of Naples, enjoyed having his dead victims in the room with him while he dined and supped.

Moss from Human Skulls as a Medicine

As we have learned already, up until very recently Europeans prepared prescriptions from human skull. Seventeenth century druggist Pomet describes what usnea is, verifies its popularity, and explains a method used for getting and selling it: "The English Druggists, especially those of London, sell the Heads or Skulls of the Dead, upon which there is a little greenish Moss, which is call'd [sic] Usnea, because of its near Resemblance to the Moss that grows upon Oaks; and as Mr. Charas stay'd [sic] a considerable Time in England, and saw a great Plenty of 'em [sic], I have only related what he told me on this Subject. This Moss is an Excrescence that grows two or three Lines high, on the top of and round Mens Skulls who have died violent Deaths, and lain some Time on the Ground, or hung on Gibbets, [gallows] or the like. It only begins to grow when the fleshy Substance about the Skull is wasted away. The English Druggists generally brings these Heads from Ireland; that Country having been remarkable for them ever since the Irish Massacre."[971]

In the following passage, Pomet relates the supposed medicinal benefits that come from the scrapings of human skulls, and shares a recipe made with alcohol: "Man's Skull is a Specifick [sic] Medicine in the Cure of the Falling-Sickness, and indeed of most Diseases of the Head, taking of the crude Powder, rasp'd [sic] from the fresh Bone of the Skull, one Scruple or two, in any proper spirituous Liquor. The Oil and volatile Salt are for the same Purposes, but in less Quantities."[972] During the same time period demand for human skulls was so great that skulls showing Usnea were clearly displayed by druggists: "You may see in the Druggists Shops of London, these Heads entirely cover'd [sic] with Moss, and some that only have the Moss growing on some Parts; and we ought not to be surpris'd

---

[969] The court condemned Elizabeth Báthory to solitary imprisonment and sealed her inside a room of her castle. The court provided slots for food and air.
[970] Strack, *Sacrifice*, pp. 89-91.
[971] Pomet, *Druggs*, p. 229.
[972] Ibid.

[sic] at the Growth of this Moss on the Skulls of dead Men unburied...."[973] One can assume that since skulls were on display, customers could choose which human head to use in his medicine.

Schneider tells us of an amulet containing human skull moss (usnea) used as a cure for nosebleeds: "An amulet for epistaxis (nose-bleed) consisted of a small bag of red silk filled with frog's ash, moss from a human skull, sea-beans (some sort of snail shell), etc. Moss from the human skull figured very extensively in the medicine of the Middle Ages. During these periods it was customary in Europe to leave executed criminals hanging from trees along the roadside to serve as horrible examples to others. In time the clothing and tissues fell away, leaving only the skeleton, and in the course of several years a species of lichen (Usnea barbata) would develop upon the skull, which was known as Usnea cranii humani. This was largely imported from Ireland, as that country evidently yielded the largest tree-crop of executed criminals."[974] There are many journals and books that confirm Ireland was once a major supplier of usnea:

> "The London druggists sell skulls of the dead upon which there has grown a little greenish moss called Usnea, because it resembles the moss which grows on the oak. These skulls mostly come from Ireland, where they frequently let the bodies of criminals hang on the gibbet till they fall to pieces." The market price of skulls at that time varied in London from 8s. to 11s. each, according to size, but those with plenty of moss made fancy prices. They were largely used for compounding the "Sympathetic Ointment," described by Crollius in his 'Royal Chemist,' and were recommended in epilepsy. Germany was the principal market. The pharmaceutical authorities of that day were very decided about the superior virtue of the skulls of persons who had died violent deaths. Lemery (1738) orders: 'To make the Magistry of human skull. Calcine the skull and powder finely.' But he adds the useful comment, 'This Magistry is only a dead-head of no virtue unless you employ the skull of a young man who died a violent death.'"[975]

"Mummie is Become Merchandise": Pharaoh's Embalmed Body Becomes Balsam for the Living

Unfortunately during medieval Europe, corpses of ancient Africans became a critical ingredient [976] in a ghoulish medical potion called mummy medicine. Popularized by the so-called noble folks of Europe mummy medicine was a supposed remedy that grew in demand after rich folks

---

[973] Ibid.
[974] Schneider, "Ancient Therapeutics," 256.
[975] Wootton, *Pharmacy*, vol. 2, p. 6.
[976] There are those who believe that Europeans were seeking the mystical essence of African peoples that is thought to reside in the skull, the place from where the Spirit exits the body.

started using it. Medieval medical practitioners believed that Kemetans embalmed their ancient mummies with bitumen,[977] an ingredient - reportedly - when added to other natural ingredients[978] became an alleged mystical cure-all. Bitumen, a type of asphalt, is a smelly substance found in large deposits in the ground, and floating on water. In ancient times it had many uses, including as a building mortar, water repellant (sealant), and in charms. Cited by Pliny, bitumen had an early use as a healing agent, too. Variously written as mumia and mummia, mummy comes from the Arab word for "embalmed body" and from the Persian word "for wax." According to an ancient visitor to a site in Persia where nature produces bitumen: "Mummy is a blackish bituminous matter, which oozes from the rock, and is considered by the Persians as far more precious than gold...."[979] The Arabs and Persians were familiar with bitumen. Researchers believe that Arabs - themselves consumers of mummy medicine - were first to mistake the preparation used for embalming ancient Egyptians for bitumen.[980] *A Compleat History of Drugges* lists bitumen as an embalming ingredient.

Accordingly, mummy was used to describe the entire embalmed body, rather than the single element: bitumen, believed used as an ingredient in the process. Early practitioners explained mummy simply as being "man himself." And as the term mummy implies, mummified ancient Egyptian bodies were disinterred, and stolen. Their remains were pulverized into powder and mixed together with other ingredients, such as *unicorn's* horn,[981] and made into "wonder" elixirs. The process (obtaining and shipping the mummy, plus preparation of the potion) required a great deal of money, and so royal, noble, and merchant classes only could afford to indulge in this alarming exotic treatment. Cumming writes: "The mummy-trade was supported by various classes of the community, for artists declared that mummy-powder beaten up with oil, gave richer tones of brown than any other substance, and modern perfumers found means of preparing the perfumes and spices found inside the bodies, so as to make them exceedingly attractive to the ladies. Paper-manufacturers found that

---

[977] Bostock and Riley, *Pliny's*, vol. 5, p. 222. See note 32.
[978] "It is prescribed to be taken in decoctions of marjoram, thyme, elder, barley, roses, lentils, jujubes, cummin, seed, caraway, saffron, cassia, parsley, with oxymel, wine, milk, butter, castor, syrup of mulberries, & c." Thomas Joseph Pettigrew, *A History of Egyptian Mummies*, p. 9.
[979] Ibid., p. 5.
[980] I found conflicting information on whether bitumen was ever used in the ancient Egyptian embalming process. It is possible that if bitumen was used, it was applied sparingly, and during the latter dynasties.
[981] The supposed effectiveness of *unicorn* horns was cited by European medical authorities and placed in many "English medical works of the highest authority" according to Cumming.

the wrappings of the mummies could be converted into coarse paper for the use of grocers, and the cloth and rags were sometimes used as clothing...."[982]

Thomas Joseph Pettigrew in *A History of Egyptian Mummies* writes that mummy medicine began as a treatment when Arabic-Jewish[983] physician El Magar prescribed it for Christians and Muslims during the Crusades. Very quickly mummy became an essential salve that supposedly "consolidated and healed the broken and lacerated veins, and... it was said to have the power of throwing off from the stomach collections of congealed blood."[984]

> It is true that after the Crusades mummy was a favorite pharmacon, sometimes even in the hands of regular physicians; and Usnea, the moss from the skulls of the bodies of criminals that had been hanged and exposed in chains, was declared by many to be a sovereign remedy for many different ills; but it must not be forgotten that both of these substances continued to be used long after the medieval period, mummy even down to the middle of the eighteenth century, and Usnea almost as late.[985]

Europeans had an entire arsenal of uses for mummies, as we will learn shortly. The first mummies were stolen from the sands of Cairo. Pomet tells us which mummies were fair game: "A Mummy is a dead Body of a Man, Woman, or Child, which is embalm'd [sic] and dried. The first Mummies were taken from the Burying-Places of the antient [sic] Egyptians' near the Pyramids, where the finest were to be seen a few Leagues from Grand Cairo."[986] We may never know the actual number of ancient mummies that were disinterred, powdered and sold to satisfy the ghoulish appetites of Europeans. Though the assumption is that hundreds upon hundreds of African corpses fell victim to their sickening cures.

Regarding this, Cumming writes: "Our ancestors chiefly prize[d] a preparation of long-deceased Egyptians, or, as they were described among the standard medicines quoted in the medical books.... The learned doctors of France, Germany, Italy, and Britain all made great use of mummy, which was pronounced to be an infallible remedy for many diseases." [987] Europeans were not alone in procuring mummies. Arabs, ancient invaders of the Kemetan holy lands, raided city tombs for mummies - a rather curious activity for those who claim ancient Egyptians for their ancestors. And according to several European authors, including Pettigrew, Jewish

---

[982] Gordon-Cumming, "Strange Medicines." *The Nineteenth Century*, vol. 21, no. 119 (1887) p. 909.
[983] According to sources.
[984] Pettigrew, *Mummies*, p. 7-8.
[985] Walsh, *Medicine*, p. 22.
[986] Pomet, *Druggs*, p. 230.
[987] Gordon-Cumming, *Memories*, pp. 472-73.

merchants made a lucrative trade in trafficking mummies, even going to extremes to get them: "They took all the executed criminals, and bodies of all descriptions that could be obtained, filled the head and inside of the bodies with simple asphaltum, an article of very small price, made incisions into the muscular parts of the limbs, inserted into them also the asphaltum and then bound them up tightly. This being done, the bodies were exposed to the heat of the sun; they dried quickly, and resembled in appearance the truly prepared mummies. These were sold to the Christians."[988] It might be expected that medieval Europeans grown accustomed to paranormal healing stories credited to the saintly relics, believed there were sensational healing powers connected to embalmed ancient Egyptian pharaohs.

As was the case with saints' bones, authentic mummies were hard to come by. And as we will read momentarily, traders sold faked mummies – hinted at above - only after Europeans had managed to buy up[989] the readily available authentic mummies. Cumming writes in *The Nineteenth Century* writes of the difficulties involved in procuring them: "Among the standard medicines quoted in the medical books of Nuremberg of two hundred years ago are 'portions of the embalmed bodies of man's flesh, brought from the neighborhood of Memphis, where there are many bodies that have been buried for more than a thousand years, called mumia, which have been embalmed with costly salves and balsams, and smell strongly of myrrh, aloes, and other fragrant things.' The writer further tells how, "'when the sailors do reach the place where the mumia are, they fetch them out secretly by night, then carry them to the ship and conceal them, that they may not be seized, because certainly the Egyptians[990] would not suffer their removal.' Nevertheless, the sailors had no great liking for their cargo, believing it to be connected with unholy magic, and that ships having mummies on board would assuredly meet with terrible storms, and very likely be compelled to throw them as an offering to the angry waves."[991]

Because acquiring mummies was an expensive endeavor, buyers could afford to be choosy. According to the opinion of one medical expert of the 17th century, the best mummies were found in Libya:

Nicasius Le Febre, F.R.S., Professor of Chemistry to Charles II, in his "Compleat Body of Chymistry," 1670, says the best mummies for medical use were those of bodies dried up in the hot sands of Lybia [sic], where sometimes whole caravans were overwhelmed by simooms and suffocated. "This sudden

---

[988] Pettigrew, *Mummies*, p. 8.
[989] Europeans were apathetic toward the remains of African men, women, and children. Some Europeans even carelessly displayed precious ancient corpses in their homes.
[990] This is likely a reference to Egyptian authorities.
[991] Gordon-Cumming, "Strange Medicines." *The Nineteenth Century*, vol. 21, no. 119 (1887) p. 908.

suffocation doth concentrate the spirits in all the parts by reason of the fear and sudden surprisal which seizes on the travellers [sic]"[992]

Youthfulness was a valuable asset when it came to harvesting human blood. The same significance was applied toward mummies. The following passage represents one recipe for properly preparing mummy:

> Next to these Lybian mummies Le Febre recommends the dried corpse of a young lusty man of about 25 to 30 years of age who has been suffocated or hanged. He gives directions for drying the flesh, smoking it for a philosophical month, and then it is to be given in doses of 1 to 3 grains with some old treacle (theriaca) and vipers' flesh made into an electuary with spirit of wine. It was specially good against pestilential diseases.[993]

The particulars of the practices involved in concocting the best mummy medicine are bizarre, to say the least. Still, writers agree that by the 16th and 17th centuries: "Mummy formed one of the ordinary drugs, and was to be found in the shops of all apothecaries, and considerable sums of money were expended in the purchase of it, principally from the Jews in the East."[994] The demand for mummy was great. Pettigrew cites a few instances when mummy was in use:[995]

> The demand for mummy was greater in France than in any other country, and Francois I. is stated by Belon to have been in the habit of always carrying about with him a little packet containing some mummy mixed with pulverised [sic] rhubarb, ready to take upon receiving any injury from falls, or other accidents that might happen to him. Armed with this universal remedy, Francois I. thought himself secure against all danger.

> Avicenna, one of the most celebrated physicians of antiquity, treats of the use of mummy in medicine.... He says it is subtle and resolutive, useful in cases of abscesses and eruptions, fractures, concussions, paralysis, hemicrania, epilepsy, vertigo, spitting of blood from the lungs, affections of the throat, coughs, palpitation of the heart, debility of the stomach, nausea, disorders of the liver and spleen, internal ulcers, also in cases of poisons. For contusions he speaks of it as the best of all remedies.

> Lord Bacon says, "Mummy hath great force in staunching of blood; which, as it may be ascribed to the mixture of balmes [sic] that are glutinous, so it may also partake of a secret propriety, in that the blood draweth man's flesh."

---

[992] Wootton, *Pharmacy*, vol. 2, p. 25.
[993] Ibid., p. 25.
[994] Pettigrew, *Mummies*, p. 7.
[995] Ibid., p. 9-10.

"Mummy," says Boyle, "is one of the useful medicines commended and given by our physicians for falls and bruises, and in other cases too."

Olaus Wormius speaks of mummy as beneficial in contusions, clodded [sic] blood, hard labour, &c. But the sagacious Grew says, "Let them see to it, that dare trust to old gums, which have long since lost their virtue."

Lemeryll describes mummy as "capable of resisting gangrene, good for contusions, and preventing the blood from coagulating in the body. He was alive to the deceptions practised [sic] in this article during his time, and gives directions for the choice of the 'veritable mumie d'Egypte."

In the Pharmacopoeia Schrodero-Hofimanniana are several formulae of mummy as a drug....

In fact, a brief glance through the shop window of an 18th century apothecary reveals a rather curious mixture of ingredients added to potions: "These quaint druggists' shops were indeed a strangely vivid illustration of what must have been the general appearance of the laboratory of the learned leeches of Britain from olden times until really quite recent days—literally until the eighteenth century—as we know from the official pharmacopoeia of the College of Surgeons of London, published in a.d. 1724, that unicorn's horn, human fat, human skulls, dog's dung, toads, vipers, worms, and all manner of animal substances, either dried, seethed, or calcined, were accounted valuable medical stores. In the same medical directory for a.d. 1724, centipedes, vipers, and lizards are especially enumerated as possessing valued properties,"[996] according to Cumming.

Paracelsus, mentioned earlier, like most of the medical folks of his day understood the tangible value of the properly prepared dead human as a marketable commodity. He writes: "Examine the case of a man who has died by natural and predestined death. What further good or use is there in him? None. Let him be cast to the worms. But the case is not the same with the man who has been slain with a sword or has died some violent death. The whole of his body is useful and good, and can be fashioned into the most valuable mumia. For though the spirit of life has gone forth from such a body, still the balsam remains, in which is latent, which also, indeed, as a balsam conserves other human bodies."[997]

Mumia is the liquor diffused through the whole body, the limbs, etc., with the strength that is required. It is divided as follows: in flesh, according to the nature of the flesh; in bone, according to the nature of the bone; in the arteries

---

[996] Gordon-Cumming, *Memories*, p. 468.
[997] Waite, *Hermetic*, p. 147.

and ligaments, according to their nature; and so also in the marrow, the veins, and the skin. Hence it follows that the mumia of the flesh cures wounds of the flesh. the mumia of the ligaments cures wounds of the ligaments, etc. Thus the body which has sustained an injury carries its own cure with it; the mumia of the aged, however, is deficient in virtue and strength. The corruption of the mumia, which is often occasioned by the mistakes of ignorant physicians, impedes the cure of wounds.... The nobler the animal organism is, by so much is the mumia of the organism enhanced in power and efficacy. The medicaments which benefit wounds perform this operation by attracting the mumia to the place where its office is required.[998]

Authentic mummies[999] were ingredients in the cures of Paracelsus, as were magnets [1000] that he believed contained magical qualities: "[He] boasted of being able to transplant diseases from the human frame into the earth, by means of the magnet. He said there were six ways by which this might be effected [sic]. One of them will be quite sufficient as a specimen. If a person suffer from disease, either local or general, let the following remedy be tried. Take a magnet, impregnated with mummy, and mixed with rich earth...."[1001]

The medical community applied mummy in many ways, giving credibility to the notion that Middle Age Europeans can never be accused of lacking imagination. During the 1600's an odd treatment for wounds grew in popularity. Called "weapon salve" or "sympathy powder" it was an Unguentum Sympatheticum (sympathetic ointment) administered by Paracelsus and other physicians who swore to its efficacy in healing wounds inflicted by weapons. The remedy, according to occultist Herbert Stanley Redgrove, "Was peculiar. It was not, as one might expect, applied to the wound itself, but any article that might have blood from the wound upon it was either sprinkled with the Powder or else placed in a basin of water in which the Powder had been dissolved, and maintained at a temperate heat. Meanwhile, the wound was kept clean and cool."[1002]

Francis Bacon (1561-1626) writes of sympathetic cures as follows: —"It is constantly Received, and Avouched, that the *Anointing* of the *Weapon* that maketh the *Wound* wil heale the *Wound* it selfe. In this *Experiment* upon the

---

[998] Ibid., p. 169.
[999] Charles Mackay notes Paracelsus believed there were six kinds of mummies. He believed the 6th kind contained cells that emitted spiritual essence that could be captured. Paracelsus wore an amulet around his neck that he claimed held a spirit as hostage.
[1000] Many Dark Ages alchemists believed magnets were the mysterious philosopher's stone.
[1001] Charles Mackay, *Memoirs of Popular Extraordinary Delusions and the Madness of Crowds*, p. 263.
[1002] H. Stanley Redgrove, *Bygone Beliefs Being A Series of Excursions in the Byways of Thought*, p. 48.

Relation of *Men* of *Credit*, (though my selfe, as yet, am not fully inclined to beleeve it,) you shal note the *Points* following; First, the *Ointment*... is made of Divers *ingredients*; whereof the Strangest and Hardest to come by, are the *Mosse* upon the *Skull* of a *dead Man, Unburied*; And the *Fats* of a *Boare*, and a *Beare*, killed in the *Act* of *Generation*. These Two last I could easily suspect to be prescribed as a Starting Hole; That if the *Experiment* proved not, it mought be pretended, that the *Beasts* were not killed in due Time; For as for the *Mosse*, it is certain there is great Quantity of it in *Ireland*, upon Slain Bodies, laid on *Heaps, Unburied*. The other *Ingredients* are, the *Bloud- Stone* in *Powder*, and some other *Things*, which seeme to have a *Vertue* to *Stanch Bloud*; As also the *Mosse* hath.... Secondly, the same kind of *Ointment*, applied to the Hurt it selfe, worketh not the *Effect*; but onely applied to the *Weapon*....

Fourthly, it may be applied to the *Weapon*, though the *Party Hurt* be at a great *Distance*. Fifthly, it seemeth the *Imagination* of the Party, to be *Cured*, is not needfull to Concurre; For it may be done without the knowledge of the *Party Wounded*; And thus much hath been tried, that the *Ointment* (for *Experiments* sake,) hath been wiped off the *Weapon*, without the knowledge of the *Party Hurt*, and presently the *Party Hurt*, hath been in great *Rage* of *Paine*, till the Weapon was *Reannointed*. Sixthly, it is affirmed, that if you cannot get the *Weapon*, yet if you put an *Instrument* of *Iron*, or *Wood*, resembling the *Weapon*, into the *Wound*, whereby it bleedeth, the *Annointing* of that *Instrument* will serve, and work the *Effect*. This I doubt should be a Device, to keep this strange *Forme* of *Cure*, in Request, and Use; Because many times you cannot come by the *Weapon* it selve. Seventhly, the *Wound* be at first *Washed clean* with *White Wine* or the *Parties* own *Water*; And then bound up close in *Fine Linen* and no more *Dressing* renewed, till it be *whole*."[1003]

According to *Chronicles of Pharmacy*, the ointment called for the use of a human male who "died a violent death, one who had been hanged, preferably, and who had not been buried." There were other conditions involved in its preparation and application that supposedly made it an effective cure. They included preparing the potion in the autumn; keeping the potion in a closed glass vessel; and wetting the patient's bandages with the his own urine. Paracelsus' weapon salve recipe is as follows: "Take of moss growing on the head of a thief who has been hanged and left in the air; of real mummy, of human blood, still warm-of each, one ounce; of human suet [fat], two ounces; of linseed oil, turpentine, and Armenian bole-of each, two drachms. Mix all well in a mortar, and keep the salve in an oblong narrow urn."[1004] Mackay adds that: "With this salve the weapon, after being dipped in the blood from the wound, was to be carefully

---

[1003] Ibid., pp. 52-54.
[1004] Mackay, *Memoirs*, p. 264.

anointed, and then laid by in a cool place."

Mummy medicine was not only a treatment prescribed for humans. As I mention in Chapter 4 nobles frequently pampered their feathered pets, the hawks and falcons. So fond of their birds were they that physicians prescribed mummy to keep them healthy, too. According to *The Ornithology of Francis Willughby*, the nobleman: "Ought to carry into the field with him mummy in powder, with other medicines, for frequently the Hawk meets with many accidents, as bruises at encounters...."[1005] An additional recipe of meat powdered with mummy was prescribed for birds with poor livers.[1006]

Hawks and falcons were not the only animals fed with powdered mummy. Cumming reports: "In truth, the human form divine received small veneration from the philosophers of those days, when the bait most highly recommended for the luring of fish was a compound of man's fat, cat's fat, heron's fat, powdered mummy, assafoetida,[1007] and various oils. In The Angler's Yade Mecum, published in 1681, it is stated that man's fat for this purpose could readily be obtained from the London chirurgeons concerned in anatomy!"[1008]

With so many exotic preparations manufactured from mummy, it is not surprising that in time demand exceeded supply. Researchers state that when authentic mummy could not be found, freshly dead humans (this is an interesting oxymoron) became the preferred substitute. Some medical practitioners winced at the fakery. Noted alchemist Oswald Crollius was not one of them: "In his 'Royal Chemist' he gives a process for preparing one [a human corpse]. The [carcass] of a young man (some say a red-haired young man) who had been killed, that is, did not die of disease, and, it is to be presumed, had not been buried, was to lie in cold water in the air for twenty-four hours. The flesh was to be cut in pieces and sprinkled with myrrh and a little aloes. This was then to be soaked in spirit of wine and turpentine for twenty-four hours, hung up for twelve hours, again soaked in the spirit mixture for twenty-four hours, and finally hung- up in a dry place to dry. Mummies were principally recommended for consumption, wasting of flesh, ulcers, and various corruptions,"[1009] writes Wootton.

Despite Crollius' *thoughtful* instructions, inauthentic, freshly created replacement mummies disappointed and angered many physicians. According to several historians, including Pettigrew, in 1564 Guy De La Fontaine traveled to Egypt to meet with the principal supplier of mummies. There La Fontaine asked to inspect the supplier's stock of mummies:

[1005] John Ray, *The Ornithology of Francis Willughby*, p. 400.
[1006] Ibid., p. 432.
[1007] This is a Persian spice.
[1008] Gordon-Cumming, *Memories*, p. 473.
[1009] Wootton, *Pharmacy*, vol. 2, pp. 24-25.

"Several bodies heaped one on the other were speedily shown to him... all the bodies then before them, amounting to between thirty and forty, had been prepared by him during the last four years, and that they were the bodies of slaves or other persons indiscriminately collected... whether they had died of any horrible disease, such as leprosy, the small pox, or the plague... he cared not whence they came, whether they were old or young, male or female, or of what disease they had died, so long as he could obtain them, for that when embalmed no one could tell...."[1010]

Druggist Pomet railed against the deceptive use of these "white[1011] mummies" he said came from bodies that had drowned at sea, washed ashore, and sold as Egyptian mummies because they had "little or no virtue in them" unlike the black mummies. He writes: "I shall only advise such as buy, to chuse [sic] what is of a fine shining Black, not full of Bones or Dirt, of a good Smell, and which being burnt, does not stink of Pitch. This is reckon'd [sic] proper for Contusions, and to hinder the Blood from coagulating in the Body; but its greatest Use is for catching Fish."[1012]

Cumming relates the resourcefulness of apothecaries who were either unaware of or showed unconcern for the lack of virtue of "white mummies" attested to by Pomet. One managed to secure his own stash of mummies closer to home: "The apothecaries of England found an economical substitute in the bones of ancient Britons. Thus Dr. Toope of Oxford, writing in 1685, tells how, at the circles on Hakpen Hill, in Wiltshire, he had discovered a rare lot of human bones—skeletons—arranged in circles, with the feet towards the centre. He says, 'The bones were large and nearly rotten, but the teeth extream [sic] and wonderfully white.' Undisturbed by any qualms of reverence for the ancestors of his race, he adds: "I dug up many bushells [sic] with which I made a noble medicine!"[1013]

That medical professionals had no misgivings regarding slithering around the graves comes at no surprise to those of us familiar with the stories of hospitals in the United States employing grave robbers to steal the corpses of African-Americans from their final resting places.[1014]

> In the course of some studies for the history of the New York State Medical Society (New York, 1906) I found that nearly every one of the first half dozen presidents of the New York Academy of Medicine, which is not much more than sixty years old, had had body-snatching experiences when they were younger. Dr. Samuel Francis, the medico-historical writer, tells of a personal

---

[1010] Pettigrew, *A Mummies*, p. 8.
[1011] Authentic mummies are black in color.
[1012] Pomet, *Druggs*, p. 229.
[1013] Gordon-Cumming, *Memories*, p. 473.
[1014] Harriet A, Washington, *Medical Apartheid*, p. 122.

expedition across the ferry in the winter time, bringing a body from a Long Island graveyard. In order to avoid the constables on the Long Island side and the police on the New York side, because there had been a number of cases of body-snatching recently and the authorities were on the lookout, the corpse was placed sitting beside the physician who drove the wagon, with a cloak wrapped around it, as if it were a living person specially protected against the cold. Similar experiences were not unusual.[1015]

In fact, a widely held belief in the African-American community is that authorities designated separate burial sites for the races because it made locating the corpses belonging to African-Americans an easier task. The following story illustrates that two hundred years following Dr. Toope's grave-robbing expedition, the sordid remedies of European medieval physicians were alive and well, and that people knew from where to acquire the ingredients for making them:

Next appeared [on 15th February, 1890, before the Court at Hagen, in Westphalia] a servant, 70 years of age, named A. S(ander), of Wengern, on the serious charge of robbery of dead bodies, and desecration of graves. The accused has already been punished with ten years' imprisonment for a similar crime in 1873; according to the new legislation the maximum punishment is two years' imprisonment. The accused confesses that on the night of 6th December last year he went to the cemetery of the parish of Wengern, looked at the fresh graves, and dug up with a spade lying on the spot a child's grave, from which he then raised the little coffin, took it under his arm, and wandered off to his dwelling. He then hid the coffin under the hay on the house floor, and next day, after opening the coffin with a screw-driver, cut out of the thigh of the corpse a piece of flesh, which he laid on a wound he had had many years on his body. The deed of the accused is therefore, like the former one for which he was condemned, the result of a fearful superstition. S. says he got the recipe many years ago from an old doctor as a remedy for his wound. He even imagines, at least he said so in to-day's hearing of the case, that the remedy has done good. The little coffin was accidentally noticed by the employer of the accused on the ground beneath the hay, and thus the affair came to light. The accused was condemned to two years' imprisonment."[1016]

Renaissance era anatomist Andreas Vesalius [1514-64] studied at Paris, and is the noted father of western anatomy. Students studying under Vesalius, and Mundinus (Mondino di Liucci) prior to him often took corpses to classes with them for dissection. However, church authorities accused Vesalius of engaging in body-snatching expeditions of his own.

[1015] Walsh, *Old-Time Makers of Medicine*, pp. 223-24.
[1016] Strack, *Sacrifice*, pp. 92-93.

The many corpses on display at the French gibbets provided Vesalius with plenty of gross samples for his studies:

> From the outset Vesalius proved himself a master. In the search for knowledge he risked the most terrible dangers, and especially the charge of sacrilege, founded upon the teachings[1017] of the Church for ages... despite ecclesiastical censure, great opposition in his own profession, and popular fury, he studied his science by the only method that could give useful results. No peril daunted him. To secure material for his investigations, he haunted gibbets and charnel-houses, braving the fires of the Inquisition and the virus of the plague.[1018]

In any event, the medieval maniacs of the medical community loved their mummy, authentic or fake. Cumming describes the extremes to which they went to get their mummy: "So great was the demand for this ingredient, to lead to the establishment in Alexandria of a secret factory for converting all manner of dead bodies into such profitable articles of trade."[1019]

Pettigrew cites Ambrose Pare as one physician who attempted to step between doctors and their morbid medieval madness:

> Ambrose Pare has a chapter expressly upon " Mummie," under the division of Contusions and Gangrenes. He speaks of mummy as the means upon which most dependence was placed in his time; but he states that neither the physicians who prescribe mummy, nor the authors that have written of it, nor the apothecaries who sell it, know any thing of certainty respecting it.... — "This wicked kinde of drugge, doth nothing helpe the diseased, in that case, wherefore and wherein it is administered, as I have tried an hundred times, and as Thevet witnesses, he tryed in himselfe whenas hee tooke some thereof by the advice of a certaine Jewish physition in Egypt, from whence it is brought; but it also inferres many trouble some symptomes, as the paine of the heart or stomacke, vomiting, and stinke of the mouth. I, perswaded by these reasons, doe not onely myselfe prescribe any hereof to my patients, but also in consultations, endeavour what I may, that it bee not prescribed by others."[1020]

There was another outspoken voice of reason that tried to wrest the madness out of medieval medicine. Cumming writes: "Old Sir Thomas Browne, after enumerating the various diseases for which divers great doctors recommend mummy as an infallible remedy, protests against such unworthy use of the ancient heroes, and declares that to serve up Chamnes

---

[1017] According to White, the church forbade dissection, because they believed in the body's resurrection.
[1018] White, *Warfare*, vol. 2, p. 50.
[1019] Gordon-Cumming, *Memories*, pp. 472-73.
[1020] Pettigrew, *A Mummies*, pp. 10-11.

and Amosis in electuaries and pills, or that Cheops and Psammetichus should be weighed out as drugs, is dismal vampirism, more horrible than the feasts of the ghouls."[1021] Another author quotes Browne, too: "Sir Thomas Browne, in his Urn-burial, says of it: "The Egyptian mummies which Cambyses or time hath spared, avarice now consumeth. Mummie is become merchandise. Mizraim cures wounds, and Pharaoh is sold for balsams."[1022]

The following narrative justifies Browne's concerns. The story highlights the intentional consequences of mummy madness; the obscene callousness of Europeans; and the indifference to debasing human remains as medieval Europeans exercised their cannibalistic tendencies: "We are told by Abdallatif, a traveler of the twelfth century, who also records how one of his friends found in the tombs of [Giza] a jar carefully sealed, which he opened, and found it to contain such excellent honey that he could not resist eating a good deal of it, and was only checked in his feast by drawing out a hair, whereupon he investigated further, and found the body of an ancient Egyptian baby in good condition, and adorned with jewels. He does not record how he enjoyed that meal in retrospect. Imagine dining off the honeyed essence of a baby-Pharaoh!"[1023] Knowingly devouring the remains of babies, or celebrated folks, or anyone, really, is ghoulish... unless, of course, it is a cultural practice accepted as a normal activity by its members.

Europeans Believed Killers' Hands Could Cure

Despite the belief that the practice of consuming dead humans stopped when *real mummy* ran out, consider that people tend to cling to the familiar and to what they believe works. And cannibalism in Indo-European[1024] cultures goes back as far as their history, as we shall read shortly. Strack introduces readers to some very peculiar lyrics to a Russian folk song, "From a Russian folk-song, which in truth sounds like a survival of cannibalism, Löwenstimm, 120 sq. quotes the following passage: 'I bake pastry out of the hands, out of the feet, I forge a drinking-cup out of the mad head, I pour drinking-glasses out of his eyes, out of his blood I brew intoxicating beer, and out of his fat I mould candles.'"[1025] Though credited to the workings of witches, there are European folklore books filled with

---

[1021] Gordon-Cumming, "Strange Medicines." *The Nineteenth Century*, vol. 21, no. 119 (1887) p. 909.
[1022] Robert Fletcher, *The Witches' Pharmacopoeia*, p. 7.
[1023] Gordon-Cumming, "Strange Medicines." *The Nineteenth Century*, vol. 21, no. 119 (1887) p. 909.
[1024] Practically every source I read on European cannibalism reports on the Chinese and the proliferation of mummy medicines in their ancient physicians' bags.
[1025] Strack, *Sacrifice*, p. 107.

incantations that call for children's blood and body parts. Still, one has to wonder how much of that folklore either flowed out into the culture or arose from within. Also, Strack documents many stories from the late 19th century of Europeans grave-robbing for body parts.

> "Gifts were placed upon the graves, and the bones of a victorious general were scattered in the city in order to secure the presence and aid of his spirit."[1026]

Furthermore, we read earlier that hands and fingers held special powers. European folklorists tell us medieval executioners not only provided eager audiences with human fat, but that the hands of the executed were valuable assets for them to sell. As Schneider and White mention earlier, medieval medical practitioners believed in "the doctrine of *signatures*" and that their god visibly marked plants intended as cures: Enter the mandrake root, said to grow in the shape of a human body. Shrouded in European folklore, the mandrake has a biblical connection to Solomon and is an ingredient in aphrodisiacs and fertility drugs.

Worshippers placed the juice of mandrakes in a drink of the gods, according to a historian. Another traces its use to the ancient Egyptians whose word for the root translates to "arm" or "bracelet" signifying confirmation, says he. Whatever the case, this root plays an ancient and important role in medieval European superstitions, and as a healing agent and cure for illnesses. Also, named the "gallows plant" because it "thrives in the ground below the gibbet" where fat from the executed murderers' fat dripped, the mandrake "When drawn from the ground it emitted shrieks like the cries of a human being, and death or madness fell upon the rash experimenter. It was partly a plant and partly an evil spirit, and it may be well supposed that with all these qualities it was a choice ingredient for the witches' potions." [1027] Additionally, according to European folklore executed murderers carry the power collected from victims' blood into the next realm where it's used to aid persons on Earth.[1028] These beliefs convinced Europeans corpse hands of hanged criminals held powers of invincibility and invisibility. They called the severed hands of criminals "Hand of Glory:"

> Among my nurse's fearful stories about it was one relating to the curing of a

---

[1026] Paton, *Spiritism*, p. 103.

[1027] Fletcher, *Pharmacopoeia*, p. 21.

[1028] "In Sicily there is a kind of criminal worship of the most notorious felons and cut-throats, the belief being that men who had slain many victims carried into the other world an evil power which they had won by blood, and that murderers are even regarded as sainted, and miracles wrought by them!" M.J. Walhouse, "Folklore Parallels and Coincidences," Folk-Lore: A Quarterly Review Myth, Tradition, Institution, & Custom, vol. 8, no. 1 (1897) p. 199.

wen by the touch of the dead murder's hand, and she described most graphically the whole frightful scene: how a patient was taken under the gallows in a cart, and was helped up in order that she might reach the dead hand, and how she passed it three times over the wen and returned home cured. This practice has happily become extinct with the destruction of the gibbet; but the remedy of the dead hand is still sometimes resorted to. Not very long ago, in the neighboring village of Storrington, a young woman afflicted with goitre was taken by her friends to the side of an open coffin in order that the hand of the corpse might touch it thrice." It may be observed that they say in North Germany [1879] that tetters and warts disappear if touched by the hand of a corpse.[1029]

European Cannibalism Older Than Methuselah, as Common as Dirt

Recall that we have already learned that Anglo-Americans fondly collected the extremities of African-American men, women, and children after their hangings. Today, modern Europeans are routinely tried and convicted for practicing cannibalism. Additionally, the illegal harvesting of human body parts is still taking place around the world; a casual Internet search reveals locales where men practice their inhumanity toward men, women and children. Finally, Europeans still eat an ancient European dish served mostly during holidays. Blood pudding is a favorite delicacy in European countries, and as far as I know,[1030] the blood in this pudding comes from animals.

As I mentioned earlier, devouring human body parts to cure diseases began early in European history. Here in a rather lengthy complaint from Pliny the Elder, he informs us on the widely accepted ghoulish practice of including human body parts in therapeutic treatments:

Epileptic patients are in the habit of drinking the blood even of gladiators, draughts teeming with life, as it were; *a thing that, when we see it done by the wild beasts even, upon the same arena, inspires us with horror at the spectacle! And yet these persons, forsooth, consider it a most effectual cure for their disease, to quaff the warm, breathing, blood from man himself, and, as they apply their mouth to the wound,*

[1029] William Henderson, *Notes on the Folk-Lore of the Northern Counties of England and the Borders*, p. 154.

[1030] There is the 16th century tale written in *Shadows of Old Paris* of a barbershop near the gates of Paris. It was a convenient spot for travelers to catch a shave and haircut. It was also the spot where men were "last seen." Next door to the shop was a bakery famous for its scrumptious pastries. One day a dog ran into the shop and began sniffing at the floor. The barber kicked at the dog, shoving a mat aside. Beneath the mat was a trap door. When it was opened, the dog followed his nose to the corpse of his master. An investigation found more human remains, plus a passageway to the bakery. The barber is said to have confessed his crimes of turning "unshaven gentlemen into succulent pork-pies" with the help of the baker. See pp. 69-70.

to draw forth his very life; and this, though it is regarded as an act of impiety to apply the human lips to the wound even of a wild beast! Others there are, again, who *make the marrow of the leg-bones, and the brains of infants, the objects of their research!*

Among the Greek writers, too, there are not a few who have enlarged upon the distinctive flavours [sic] of each one of the visceral and members of the human body, pursuing their researches to the very parings of the nails! As though, forsooth, *it could possibly be accounted the pursuit of health for man to make himself a wild beast,* and so *deserve to contract disease from the very remedies he adopts for avoiding it.* Most righteously, by Hercules! if such attempts are all in vain, is he disappointed of his cure! *To examine human entrails is deemed an act of impiety of what then must it be to devour them?*

Say, Osthanes,[1031] "who was it that first devised these practices; for it is thee that I accuse, thou uprooter of all human laws, thou inventor of these monstrosities; devised, no doubt, with the view that mankind might not forget thy name! Who was it that first thought of devouring each member of the human body? By what conjectural motives was he induced? *What can possibly have been the origin of such a system of medicine as this? Who was it that thus made the very poisons less baneful than the antidotes prescribed for them?* Granted that barbarous and outlandish tribes first devised such practices, must the men of Greece, too, adopt these as arts of their own?

We read, for instance, in the memoirs of Democritus [c. 460 BCE], still extant, that for some diseases, the skull of a malefactor is most efficacious, while for the treatment of others, that of one who has been a friend or guest is required. Apollonius [c. 15-c. 100 CE], again, informs us in his waitings, *that the most effectual remedy for tooth-ache is to scarify the gums with the tooth of a man who has died a violent death;* and, according to Miletus, *human gall is a cure for cataract.* For epilepsy, Artemon has prescribed water drawn from a spring in the night, and drunk from the skull of a man who has been slain, and whose body remains unburnt. From the skull, too, of a man who had been hanged, Antaeus made pills that were to be an antidote to the bite of a mad dog. Even more than this, man has resorted to similar remedies for the cure of four-footed beasts even—*for tympanitis in oxen, for instance, the horns have been perforated, and human bones inserted; and when swine have been found to be diseased, fine wheat has been given them which has lain for a night in the spot where a human being has been slain or burnt!*[1032] (Italics added).

[1031] Osthanes was a Persian magus to Zoroaster. Osthanes was thought to be an alchemist, and early practitioner of magic.
[1032] Bostock and Riley, *Pliny's*, vol. 5, pp. 276-278.

13

IF WE ARE WHAT WE EAT, THEN....

For my flesh is meat indeed, and my blood is drink indeed. He that eateth my flesh, and drinketh my blood, dwelleth in me, and I in him. - John 6:55-56

I am the living bread which came down from heaven: if any man eat of this bread, he shall live for ever: and the bread that I will give is my flesh, which I will give for the life of the world." - John 6:51:

Council of Trent (16th century): CHAPTER IV. *On Transubstantiation. And because that Christ, our Redeemer, declared that which He offered under the species of bread to be truly His own body, therefore has it ever been a firm belief in the Church of God, and this holy Synod doth now declare it anew, that, by the consecration of the bread and of the wine, a conversion is made of the whole substance of the bread into the substance of the body of Christ our Lord, and of the whole substance of the wine into the substance of His blood; which conversion is, by the holy Catholic Church, suitably and properly called Transubstantiation.*[1033]

Is Christian Communion Actually a Celebration of European Cannibalism?

Note I became a Christian late last century. When I took that plunge, my decision was both embraced and ridiculed. Of course, my new pastor embraced it. He recognized my passion for learning and gifted me with a bible concordance and an entire set of biblical theology books that I devoured and put into practice during morning Sunday school lessons. One friend who ridiculed my conversion informed me that the Christian tradition of communion is an ancient ritual of cannibalism. I vehemently disagreed with his description of certain biblical passages after I consulted my newly acquired volumes that nowhere mentioned my friend's interpretation. However, I neglected to stretch my research beyond the confines of biblical literature. Had I done so, I would have discovered that cannibalism in Christianity is an age-old debate, still unresolved.

Years ago, I fully rejected Christian indoctrination - the ingestion of the spiritual teachings of hostile (to me and all African people) nations - though I did not disown my Christian vow until after I began research for this essay.

[1033] Donovan, *Catechism*.

Christianity's celebration of communion, the fellowship that indulges in eating the flesh and drinking the blood of the mythical Christ, takes on ominous overtones once one realizes that Europeans were long practitioners of cannibalism. One of my more appalling discoveries lies in the linguistics of communion. The Greek word for communion is /eukharistia/ or Eucharist. In English it means thanksgiving. During Thanksgiving we devour the first fruits of the harvest. Smith writes the following about the hoary communal tradition in which worshippers share a sacrificial animal:

> Nevertheless the slaughter of such a victim is permitted or required on solemn occasions, and all the tribesmen partake of its flesh, that they may thereby cement and seal their mystic unity with one another and with their god. In later times we find the conception current that any food which two men partake of together, so that the same substance enters into their flesh and blood, is enough to establish some sacred unity of life between them; but in ancient times this significance seems to be always attached to participation in the flesh of a sacrosanct victim, and the solemn mystery of its death is justified by the consideration that only in this way can the sacred cement be procured which creates or keeps alive a living bond of union between the worshippers and their god. This cement is nothing else than the actual life of the sacred and kindred animal, which is conceived as residing in its flesh, but especially in its blood, and so, in the sacred meal, is actually distributed among all the participants, each of whom incorporates a particle of it with his own individual life.[1034]

Here we learn that ancient communities shared sacrifices. Worshippers believed that maintaining contact with their god required an offering. So sacred was the victim's flesh that it gave the community grounds for continuing its relationship with their deity. But, only for a short time after which worshippers had to, once again, offer up another sacrifice. Smith records many vital points of ancient sacrificial offerings, two of which I include here: "The leading idea in the animal sacrifices of the Semites, as we shall see by and by, was not that of a gift made over to the god, but of an act of communion, in which the god and his worshippers unite by partaking together of the flesh and blood of a sacred victim..."[1035] and "We are led to conclude (1) that the libation of blood is a common Semitic practice, older than fire-sacrifices, and (2) that the libation of wine is in some sense an imitation of, and a surrogate for, the primitive blood-offering." [1036] Other historians have already validated that blood was substituted by wine.

[1034] Smith, *Lectures*, p. 313.
[1035] Ibid., pp. 226-27.
[1036] Ibid., p. 231.

Ritual Sacrifices of Humans Replaced by Animals: Communion Table and Altar Historically the Same

Some researchers believe that animal sacrifice actually replaced human sacrifice: "And when Asclepiades [d. 217 CE] states that every victim was originally regarded as a surrogate for a human sacrifice, he is confirmed in a remarkable way by the Elohistic account of the origin of burnt-sacrifice in Gen. xxii., where a ram is accepted in lieu of Isaac," writes Smith.[1037] Human sacrifices benefit the community at the cost of the victim, according to Smith who states that altar sacrifices of humans was a feature of Semitic rituals. "Indeed the shows of the gladiators were founded on human sacrifice,"[1038] Tertullian adds. And there are examples from the Old Testament where a seeming vengeful, and angry Christian deity demands that burnt offerings be made from the bones of pagan high priests. What is most especially interesting about the Christ myth is that historical evidence points to the sacrificial altar, and the communion table being one in the same. There is some history to the altar being first called a communion[1039] table in Indo-European history. Did the Jesus myth[1040] merely give structure to an ancient Indo-European tradition? Smith tells us, "The altar is above all things a hearth, and the burning of the sacrificial fat is the most solemn part of the service. This, however, is certainly not primitive; for even in the period of fire-sacrifice the Hebrew altar is called... 'the place of slaughter,' and in ancient times the victim was slain on or beside the altar..."[1041]

The table of shewbread has its closest parallel in the lectisternia of ancient heathenism, when a table laden with meats was spread beside the idol. Such tables were set in the great temple of Bel at Babylon, and, if any weight is to be given to the apocryphal story of Bel and the Dragon in the Greek Book of Daniel, it was popularly believed that the god actually consumed the meal provided for him, a superstition that might easily hold its ground by priestly connivance where the table was spread inside a temple.[1042]

[1037] Ibid., p. 309.
[1038] Dodgson, *Tertullian*, p. 204.
[1039] "Indeed, it is claimed, with a show of reason, that the very word (surqvnu) which was used for 'altar' in the Assyrian, was primarily the word for 'table'; that, in fact, what was later known as the 'altar' to the gods, was originally the table of communion between the gods and their worshipers. There seems to be a reference to this idea in the interchanged use of the words altar." *Covenant*, p. 167.
[1040] In the Jesus myth, communion takes place before his sacrifice. In many African-American Christian churches, the congregations quietly and reverently commune while the pastor prepares and anoints the sacrificial offering.
[1041] Smith, *Lectures*, p. 341.
[1042] Ibid. p. 225.

Strack researched assertions behind Jewish blood libel charges, but found cases of Christian cannibalism instead. In his book, he cites philosopher G. F. Daumer who did extensive research into the sacrificial elements of Christianity. Daumer, according to Strack, "Tried to prove that the characteristics of the Christian religion from its beginning to the end of the middle ages consisted in human sacrifices and cannibalism and the use of human blood."[1043] Daumer reveals the following disturbing stories of the Eucharist:

"When the holy office was celebrated, a Jew mingled among the crowd, as if he were a Christian, because he wanted to learn about the order of the Officium and the gift of the Communion. He there beholds how a little child is cut to pieces, limb by limb, in the hands of Basilius. He approached with the other communicants, and flesh was actually given him. Then he was also present at the handing of the cup, which was full of blood, and took part in drinking from it. Keeping some remains of both, he goes home and shows them to his wife. − /. 85 (Life of the Martyr S. George, "Acta Sanctorum," S3 April). A Saracen saw a priest kill and cut up a child, place the pieces in the paten, pour the blood into the cup, and eat one of the pieces and drink from the cup. − /. 118 sq., tells of the dissensions between the Dominicans and Franciscans in Bern 1507, after the Bernese Chronicle of Calonius Grönneirus, 1585, 615 sq., and Hottinger, 'Helvetische Kirchengeschichte,' Zurich, 1708 sq. Vol. II, 553 sq., 556 sq.: The Dominicans were alleged to have offered a consecrated wafer coloured with Christ's blood to Jezer, a tailor who had been received into their Order, whom they wanted to make their Saint. They are also said to 'have handed him a drink composed of ointment, Easter baptismal- water, Easter-taper wax, consecrated salt... and the hair and blood of a child.'− In the confession cited by Grönneirus 622 it is asserted the Dominicans had made use of Jew blood, and the eyebrows of a Jewish child. −There is more in Daumer- I., 36 sq., 73, 85 sq."[1044]

Clearly something is amiss in the Indo-European cultural paradigm with its far ranging experiences with cannibalism; the deuterocanonical book *Wisdom of Solomon* 12:5-7, (ca. 2nd or 1st century BCE) scolds them for practicing it: "For it was by thy will to destroy by the hands of our fathers both these old inhabitants of the holy land, whom thou hatedst [sic] for doing odious works of witchcrafts, and wicked sacrifices; And also those merciless murderers of children, and devourers of man's flesh, and the feasts of blood... and the parents, that killed with their own hands souls

---

[1043] Strack, *Sacrifice*, p. 33.
[1044] Ibid., pp. 33-34.

destitute of help...."[1045]

Long before Solomon's wisdom, Micah 3:3 (ca. 18th BCE) accuses the leaders of Israel of committing cannibalism. They receive a warning that because of it their cries for help will go unanswered. In Ezekiel 5:10 (593-571 BCE), the Christian god threatens the children of Jerusalem with intra-family cannibalism because they worshiped idolatry. There are many biblical verses that refer to cannibalism, making it clear that it was a familiar practice. Indeed, cannibalism is a long-standing custom for Europeans. Seven thousand years ago, Herxheim Germany may have been one focal point for the custom. Recently, archaeologists recovered human remains from graves that show customary signatures of having been consumed by other humans: teeth marks, and skinning among those cited. According to the archaeologists, these feasters of humans spared no one, including the very young, and fetuses. There are even suggestions that cannibals placed human parts on a roasting spit.[1046] Much farther back in time – 15,000 years ago – English graves depict a similar scene of cannibalism. There in Somerset's Gough's Cave, researchers discovered drinking vessels crafted from human skulls, as well as signs of ritualistic cannibalism.[1047] These findings perhaps prove how long Indo-Europeans[1048] have practiced cannibalism.

A disturbing revelation of cannibalism comes to us by way of 2 Kings 6:24 (ca. 590-560 BCE). A woman in Samaria, under siege by the king of Aram, appeals to the king of Israel for mercy. A second woman who desires to eat her son as a meal offering approaches her. In return for giving up her son, the second woman promises to serve her own son as a meal on the following day. The woman agrees and they both eat the first woman's son. But, when the next day arrives, the second woman breaks her promise by hiding her own son. Despite cannibalism's relatively high visibility in Christian canonical literature – the Wisdom of Solomon is part of the Septuagint, or Christian wisdom books – the European's practice in cannibalism remains mostly unknown.

Of course it makes sense that a people carry their traditions with them as they venture away from home. Such was the case in 17th century when European settlers relocated to the United States. Virginia colonists recorded multiple instances of cannibalism. When food went scarce, cannibalistic Europeans made supper of Indians and fellow colonists, sometimes even

---

[1045] William J. Deane, *The Book Of Wisdom: The Greek Text, The Latin Vulgate, and The Authorised English Version with an Introduction, Critical Apparatus and a Commentary*, p. 79.
[1046] Lewis Smith "Evidence of Mass Cannibalism Uncovered in Germany." *The Independent*. 6 Dec. 2009. Web. 26 Aug. 2014.
[1047] "Cannibalism at Gough's Cave." *Natural History Museum*. Web. 26 Aug. 2014.
[1048] Some Asian populations use(d) human body parts in their medicinal treatments, too.

disinterring them. In 1624 Captain John Smith records explicit details of recipes prepared from the bodies of Indians and family members during times of intense hunger.[1049] And, of course, filmmakers have produced shocking documentaries of the 19th century Anglo-Americans who survived by eating family members and companions on the trail to California after being trapped by snow. There are other examples of Europeans transporting[1050] their disturbing appetite for humans to other lands and cultures.

European Pre-Christian Gods Practiced Cannibalism, Too

Cultural myths give insight into a people's traditions, ethics and values. Their stories may be based on fact or can be fictional. According to Webster, while some Greek gods were personifications of natural phenomenon, he echoes the sentiments of Clement of Alexandria who writes that gods were "subject to every sort of human emotion."[1051] "The Greeks," writes Webster, "made their gods and goddesses after themselves. The Olympian divinities are really magnified men and women, subject to all human passions and appetites, but possessed of more than human power and endowed with immortality.... The gods, morally, were no better than their worshipers. They might be represented as deceitful, dissolute, and cruel but they could also be regarded as upholders of truth and virtue."[1052] In other words, gods simply reflected the fantasies of Europeans who desired to be super human; and those fantasies ran amok as Greeks and Romans worshipped gods who practiced cannibalism (and other questionable traditions). And though some of the gods loathed cannibalism, and punished those who participated in it... other gods celebrated it. Smith writes the following about the gods and their appetites for animal flesh:

> Homeric deities " feast on hecatombs," nay, particular Greek gods have special epithets designating them as the goat-eater, the ram-eater, the bull-eater, even "the cannibal," with allusion to human sacrifices. Among the Hebrews the conception that Jehovah eats the flesh of bulls and drinks the blood of goats, against that the author of Ps. 1. protests so strongly, was never eliminated from the ancient technical language of the priestly ritual, in which the *sacrifices are*

[1049] See: Lyon Gardiner Tyler, ed., *Narratives of Early Virginia 1606-1625* (New York: Charles Scribner's Sons,1907), p. 295.
[1050] Herodotus records the campaign of Cambyses against the Ethiopians. When his soldiers ran out of food they cast lots to determine which of them would become that night's feast. Disgusted with their behavior, Cambyses disbanded the group and quit the campaign. Rawlinson, vol. 2, pp. 73-74.
[1051] G. W. Butterworth, trans. *Clement of Alexandria*, p. 75.
[1052] Webster, *History*, p. 77.

called " *the food of the deity*.[1053] (Italics added).

Following is a brief list of human flesh eating gods. The Greek god Tantalus celebrated cannibalism. He arranged a feast for his fellow gods prepared from the body of his son, Pelops, who he killed, dismembered, and boiled. According to one version of the myth, this act displeased gods who punished Tantalus. Zeus' father Chronos (Kronos) ate his children to prevent one of them from occupying his throne; Zeus escapes only when his mother saves his life. Except for his heart, Dionysus, the infant son of Zeus, was either boiled or roasted and then eaten by the Titans. And Zeus devoured his wife, Metis, to stop his throne from being usurped. As mentioned earlier, Tertullian scolds the blood sacrifices made to Roman goddess of war, Bellona, and her successor alter-ego Ma-bellona: "In this age, in this country, blood from a wounded thigh, caught in the palm of the hand, and given to eat, sealeth those consecrated to Bellona."[1054] Another writer notes that the priests of Bellona "gashed their arms and legs and poured their blood upon the altar while sacrificing to her."[1055] Döllinger furnishes a long list of human sacrifices to Roman gods and reveals their connection to ritual magic:[1056]

> Every year, on the ides of May, twenty four shapes of men, made out of rushes, were thrown by the vestal virgins from the Sublician bridge into the Tiber. They were substitutes for the human victims once thrown into the stream, bound hand and foot, to Saturn.

> In the year 227 B.C., it was discovered from the Sibylline books that Gauls and Greeks were to make themselves masters of the city. To ward off this danger, a decree was passed that a man and woman of each of those two nations should be buried alive in the forum, and so should fulfil [sic] the prediction by being allowed to take that kind of possession of the city. It was done; and though Livy speaks of it as a thoroughly un-Roman sacrifice, yet it was often repeated.

> In times of violence and disturbance, the idea of a strange effectiveness in human sacrifice always returned upon the people. Once, when a tumult was raised by Caesar's soldiers in Rome, two of them were sacrificed to Mars by the pontiffs and the flamen martialis [high priest to the god of war, Mars] in the Campus Martius, and their heads were fixed upon the [sacred triangular] Regia, the same as in the sacrifice of the October[1057] horse. Besides this, the Romans

---

[1053] Smith, *Lectures*, p. 224.
[1054] Dodgson, *Tertullian*, p. 23.
[1055] Freese, *Minucius*, p. 83.
[1056] Döllinger, *Gentile*, pp. 85-87; pp. 214-15.
[1057] This October 15 festivity celebrated the end to Rome's military campaigns season, and likely was a purification ceremony for returning soldiers. This ritual sacrificed the right-

were familiar with the notion of offering human lives as victims of atonement for the dead; this was the object with which gladiatorial games had begun... The previously mentioned example of a sacrificial murder committed by the most distinguished Roman priests, in the heart of Rome, on Roman soldiers, shows how little custom was a restraint: and the time was that of the proscriptions, and of promiscuous butchery, in which citizen-blood was poured out like water, Sextus Pompeius, too, had men thrown alive into the sea along with horses, as an oblation to Neptune, at the time when his enemies' fleet was destroyed by a great storm. Caligula's having innocent men dressed out as victims, and then thrown down precipices, as an atonement for his life, was indeed the act of a bloodthirsty tyrant; but it shows what ideas were abroad.

The image of Jupiter Latiaris was annually sprinkled with human blood; that shed by the gladiators in the public games was used for the purpose. A priest caught the blood in a cup from the body of one who was just wounded, and threw it when still warm at the face of the image of the god. This was of regular occurrence still in the second and third centuries after Christ: Tatian, amongst many others, speaks of it as an eye-witness.

Wherever human sacrifice was offered, it was always either in direct connection with magic, or magical usages were coupled with it... The Romans had children sacrificed principally with this object of witchcraft... Pliny said of Nero that there was no lack of human blood in the magical incantations to which he had given himself up for a time. Catiline and the emperors Didius Julianas and Heliogabalus are all accused of child-sacrifice... The emperor Valerian ($3^{rd.}$ c. CE) was prevailed upon by an Egyptian magician to sacrifice the children of unhappy fathers, to disembowel new-born babes, and mangle God's creatures. The same expressions are used by Juvenal of the haruspex [entrails reader] of Commagene, who promised the lustful wife a lover or a rich inheritance.

There was a still more revolting custom, that of cutting the embryo child out of a living woman's womb, as did the tribune Pollentianus in order to conjure up the spirits whom he was curious to consult as to the successor of Valens. Maxentius did the same at Rome. After the death of the emperor Julian, a woman was found suspended by the hair and her body cut open in a temple at Carrse, which he had devoted to mysterious rites.

It is not surprising, then, that critics accused Christians of acting out Eucharist ceremonies, that we shall read about shortly. Some of my more surprising discoveries come from Europe's historical stories that find parallels in their myths. In the following passage Herodotus tells the tale of

---

hand side winning horse of a chariot race. The public cut off his head and placed it on a sacred site. They cut off the tail and poured blood from it on a sacred hearth. Farmers received the rest of the blood for their sacrificial offerings the following spring.

a king who ruthlessly punishes a trusted ally for disobeying an order:

> Harpagus [sic], on hearing this, made obeisance, and went home rejoicing to find that his obedience had turned out so fortunately, and that, instead of being punished, he was invited to a banquet given in honour of the happy occasion. The moment he reached home he called for his son, a youth of about thirteen, the only child of his parents, and bade him go to the palace, and do whatever Astyages should direct. Then, in the gladness of his heart, he went to his wife and told her all that had happened. Astyages, meanwhile, took the son of Harpagus, and slew him, after which he cut him in pieces, and roasted some portions before the fire, and boiled others; and when all were duly prepared, he kept them ready for use. The hour for the banquet came, and Harpagus appeared, and with him the other guests, and all sat down to the feast. Astyages and the rest of the guests had joints of meat served up to them; but on the table of Harpagus, nothing was placed except the flesh of his own son. This was all put before him, except the hands and feet and head, which were laid by themselves in a covered basket. When Harpagus. seemed to have eaten his fill, Astyages called out to him to know how he had enjoyed the repast. On his reply that he had enjoyed it excessively, they whose business it was brought him the basket, in which were the hands and feet and head of his son, and bade him open it, and take out what he pleased. Harpagus accordingly uncovered the basket, and saw within it the remains of his son. The sight, however, did not scare him, or rob him of his self-possession. Being asked by Astyages if he knew what beast's flesh it was that he had been eating, he answered that he knew very well, and that whatever the king did was agreeable. After this reply, he took with him such morsels of the flesh as were uneaten, and went home, intending, as I conceive, to collect the remains and bury them. Such was the mode in which Astyages punished Harpagus...."[1058]

Thyestean Feasts: Centuries-Long Accusations of Christian Cannibalism

Harpagos was a trusted Median general who lived during the 6th century BCE. His story provides further evidence that the story of cannibalism belongs to Indo-Europeans and is a very old one. The charges against early Christians of participating in Thyestean (Thyestian) Feasts was a 300 years long accusation. These feasts take their name from the Mycenaean myth of the god Thyestes. According to the myth, Thyestes had an affair with his brother's wife that raised questions about Atreus' sons' paternity. Also, his lover worked against her husband on behalf of Thyestes. Learning of their treachery, Atreus plotted his revenge against his brother. At a reconciliation dinner planned by Atreus, Thyestes filled his stomach with

---

[1058] Rawlinson, *Herodotus*, vol. 1, pp. 128-29.

food specially prepared in his honor. After dinner, Atreus' servants brought another platter out to the table. Upon lifting the lid, Thyestes discovered the hands and feet of his sons, the only parts of their bodies left uneaten by Thyestes.

The Christian's orgiastic Thyestean Feasts supposedly included eating bread dipped into the blood of sacrificed babies[1059] and incestuous acts performed between the parents and their children: fathers and their daughters, and mothers and their sons, perhaps. African-born Roman Marcus Cornelius Fronto (2nd century rhetorician and jurist) provides posterity with a vivid description of the feasts that he said were true and popularly known: "The 'Incestuous Banquets' of the Christians and about their banquet the facts are known: they are common talk everywhere: the speech of our fellow citizen from Cirta also bears witness to them: — 'On a regular day they come together for a feast with all their children and sisters and mothers, persons of both sexes and of every age. Then after much feasting, when the banquet has waxed hot and the passion of impure lust and drunkenness has been kindled in the company, a dog which has been tied to the standing lamp is incited to jump and bound up by a little cake thrown to it beyond its tether. The tell-tale light being by this means cast down and extinguished, the guests under cover of the shameless darkness embrace one another in their unspeakable concupiscence, as chance brings them together, and, if not in fact yet in guilt, all are alike incestuous, since whatever can result by the act of individuals is potentially desired by the wish of all."[1060] Tertullian flatly denies the charges writing, "Monsters of wickedness, we are accused of observing a holy rite in which we kill a little child and then eat it, in which after the feast we practise [sic] incest, the dogs-our pimps, forsooth, overturning the lights and getting us shamelessness of darkness for our impious lusts, This is what is constantly laid to our charge, and yet you take no pains to elicit the truth of what we have been so long accused."[1061] Other prominent Christian apologetics, like Minucius Felix, who argued that Fronto lacked evidence, vehemently denied the charges, too.

Despite modern Christians' denial that communion is a cannibalistic act, during Transubstantiation only the appearances of bread and wine remain intact. The Council of Trent has determined that their essences become the body and blood of the mythical Christ.

[1059] Dodgson, *Tertullian*, pp. 19-20.
[1060] C. R. Haines, trans., *The Correspondence of Marcus Cornelius Fronto with Marcus Aurelius Antoninus, Lucius Verus, Antoninus Pius, vol. 2* (London: William Heinemann, 1920), pp. 283-85.
[1061] Roberts and Donaldson, *Tertullian*, p. 67.

Council of Trent (16th century): CANON II. -If any one saith, that, in the sacred and holy sacrament of the Eucharist, the substance of the bread and wine remains conjointly with the body and blood of our Lord Jesus Christ, and denieth that wonderful and singular conversion of the whole substance of the bread into the Body, and of the whole substance of the wine into the Blood-the species Only of the bread and wine remaining-which conversion indeed the Catholic Church most aptly calls Transubstantiation; let him be anathema.[1062]

[1062] Donovan, *Catechism*.

14

MEDIEVAL TERRORISTS

The medieval blood sports of wars, games, massacres, slavery, the Inquisitions and the Crusades all coalesce around the theme of terrorism. For while there was no literacy to speak of, no art to muse over, nor scientific achievements to rally around,[1063] we have seen how mobs united around blood sports to vent everyday frustrations; to displace their own sufferings; to exercise their ego; or maybe simply to act out some fantasy or predilection. Whatever the case may have been, old and young alike engaged their creativity in a multiplicity of ways to humiliate, mutilate, obliterate, terrorize, punish and murder fellow citizens: "The inquisitorial courts of the church, and the governing bodies of the free cities of the Continent, appear to have rivaled each other in their inventions for inflicting the most exquisite degree of torment, in different manners calculated for each particular member of the human body, and so as to endure longest without leading to insensibility or death." [1064] Their dysfunctional social system, nurtured by beastly brutality, operated by identifying and then attacking "others," even when those "others" were none other than themselves.

Many people may have images of men only being subjected to inhumane treatment. But women, and even children, routinely found themselves standing before the court, as was the case during the witch trials that lasted for centuries. However, there were many times when cruel punishment was the remedy sought for engaging in ordinary crimes: "It is... difficult to believe that the mediaeval judges were actuated by any humane feelings, when we find that, in order to reconcile a respect for propriety with a clue compliance with the ends of justice, the punishment

---

[1063] Many African historians tell us that the industrial revolution could not have happened without the human and mineral resources from Africa that fueled it. Ludlow writes of the 11th and 12th centuries: "The industrial arts had been lost or had come to be entirely neglected after the barbaric conquest which swept away the Roman civilization, and during the centuries since there had been scarcely any attempt to revive them. The very faculty of invention seems to have become paralyzed by disuse." p. 11. Hallam writes that it was not until 1148 that Roger (Guiscard) of Sicily established a [royal court] silk factory at Palermo, that "gave perhaps the earliest impulse to the industry of Italy," *View, vol. 2*, p. 521. "Such times were necessarily marked by the narrow limitation and degradation of common life." Ludlow, p. 11.

[1064] Frederick W. Fairholt, *Miscellanea Graphica Representations of Ancient, Medieval, and Renaissance Remains*, p. 84.

of burying alive was resorted to for women, who could not with decency be hung up to the gibbets.[1065] In 1460, a woman named Pirate, accused of theft and of receiving stolen goods, was condemned by the Provost of Paris to be 'buried alive before the gallows,' and the sentence was literally carried out."[1066] Europeans punished their own children severely, too. Those narratives are tremendously disturbing. For centuries European sadists pacified their own populaces with terrorism, yet it remains a strong force for uniting Europeans and Anglo-Americans. To this day terrorism rallies them to support some rather despicable behaviors for some rather shady causes

The Mechanics of Torture

Bustling and vibrant European public squares that today accommodate gooey-eyed lovers, picturesque sidewalk cafes, artist's palettes and souvenir shops, a mere one or two centuries ago were gathering spots for maddened European crowds lusting for blood. Over the centuries millions of people willing crowded round to watch as magistrates arbitrarily cast humanity aside.

Thousands at a time cheered on as executioners crushed their neighbors' legs with sledge hammers; burned them to death; or placed them on what I call the *Wheel of Misfortune*,[1067] just three of possibly thousands of different torture techniques. While the first two techniques are fairly easily to visualize, Lacroix explains the workings of the wheel, "This torture, which does not date earlier than the days of Francis I. [d. 1547], is thus described: The victim was first tied on his back to two joists forming a St. Andrew's cross, each of his limbs being stretched out on its arms. Two places were hollowed out under each limb, about a foot apart, in order that the joints alone might touch the wood. The executioner then dealt a heavy blow over each hollow with a square iron bar, about two inches broad and rounded at the handle, thus breaking each limb in two places. To the eight blows required for this, the executioner generally added two or three on the chest, which were called *coups de grace*, and which ended this horrible execution. It was only after death that the broken body was placed on a wheel, which was turned round on a pivot. Sometimes, however, the sentence ordered that the condemned should be strangled before being broken, which was

---

[1065] Gallows.
[1066] Lacroix, *Manners*, p. 420.
[1067] The wheel's use on Africans is documented. In one case in South Africa: a man's body was "broken alive upon the wheel, after the flesh had been torn from his body, in eight different places, with red-hot pincers...." The torture lasted for 15 minutes. The man was accused of setting a house on fire. Pasfield Oliver, ed., *The Voyage of Francois Leguat*, vol. 2, (London: Hakluyt Society, 1891), p. 182.

done in such cases by the instantaneous twist of a rope round the neck."[1068]

Crowds lessened, one author says, only after nobility were no longer beheaded and "there were no more cries of agony to hear, and no more ashes carried away by the wind."[1069] In other words, the crowds departed once the *special effects* waned, though many still gathered to watch as ordinary citizens were physically violated. Bingham writes that the church and nobility held the European populace so tightly under control that the intellectuals[1070] of the day had no moral integrity to rail against what was so obviously an inhumane system from the time of its implementation until the 19th century. Sadly, when Europeans finally began speaking out against torture they did so only because torture proved ineffective in rendering truthful confessions. In fact, Ludlow informs us that, "The fact that questions involving the most sacred rights of the individual, such as the holding of property, the protection of the body from mutilation on the rack, the retaining of life, and the vindication of character, were not so much as brought to the court of intelligence and conscience argues the degradation of both these faculties."[1071]

The Terrorizing Torturing Punishments of the Papacy

Of course the church played a major role in torturing its own citizens. I wrote about Rome's Castle St. Angelo in an earlier chapter. It was there where many church officials faced their doom, along with church laity. Base violence from an institution that purports to wear the righteous robe of its most esteemed character passes beyond the borders of irony into a type of bizarre hypocrisy. But, some historians describe Pope Urban VI as one of the most violent clergymen of them all, which really says a lot considering the high level of depravity and wickedness of other popes. In the following passage, Story provides an account of Urbana's violence:

> He was a man of a very violent and vindictive character, and the prisons of St. Angelo were seldom empty. On one occasion, suspecting some of the Cardinals by whom he was surrounded of treachery, he here put them to the torture to extract confession; and while they were stretched on the rack, he recited composedly his breviary in the adjoining chamber, totally unmoved by the shrieks of anguish drawn from his suffering victims.[1072]

There was so much violence wrought at the papal castle that "Every now and then an arm, a hand, a foot, a head, a leg, or some part of a corpse,

---

[1068] Lacroix, *Manners*, p. 422.
[1069] Bingham, *Bastille*, vol. 1, p. 65.
[1070] Recall that the church stunted intellectual life.
[1071] Ludlow, *Crusades*, p. 18.
[1072] Story, "Castle St. Angelo and the Evil Eye," 351.

is nailed up on the wall of the Castle, to [announce] an execution performed; but this is so common that nobody pays attention to it, unless, indeed, it relate to a person of importance, or of some one engaged in a popular crime, — as was the case of Macrino di Castagno, who agreed with Bajazet to poison his brother Zemi in Rome, and, having been discovered, was executed, quartered, and nailed outside the wall."[1073]

The church employed its own papal executioner. One infamous hangman, Giovanni Battista Bugatti, lived during the 19th century. Bugatti murdered an estimated 500 people in the 60 years he held that *job*. His reign of terror ended in the 1860's. In 1864 the beloved author Charles Dickens observed the Bugatti execution of a young man of 26 years who had confessed to robbing a countess on a pilgrimage to Rome:

> On one Saturday morning, (the eighth of March) a man was beheaded here....
>
> It is very unusual to execute in Lent; but his crime being a very bad one, it was deemed advisable to make an example of him at that time, when great numbers of pilgrims were coming towards Rome, from all parts, for the Holy Week....
>
> The beheading was appointed for fourteen and a half o'clock, Roman time: or a quarter before nine in the forenoon....
>
> The scaffold was built. An untidy, unpainted, uncouth, crazy-looking thing of course: some seven feet high, perhaps: with a tall, gallows-shaped frame rising above it, in which was the knife, charged with a ponderous mass of iron, all ready to descend....
>
> He appeared on the platform, bare-footed; his hands bound; and with the collar and neck of his shirt, cut away, almost to the shoulder.... He immediately kneeled down, below the knife. His neck fitting into a hole, made for the purpose, in a cross plank, was shut down, by another plank above; exactly like the pillory. Immediately below him, was a leathern bag. And into it, his head rolled instantly.
>
> The executioner was holding it by the hair, and walking with it round the scaffold, showing it to the people, before one quite knew that the knife had fallen heavily, and with a rattling sound.
>
> When it had travelled round the four sides of the scaffold, it was set upon a pole in front—a little patch of black and white, for the long street to stare at, and the flies to settle on. The eyes were turned upward, as if he had avoided the sight of the leathern bag, and looked to the crucifix. Every tinge and hue of life had left it in that instant. It was dull, cold, and, wax. The body also.
>
> There was a great deal of blood. When we left the window, and went close up to the scaffold, it was very dirty; one of the two men who were throwing water over it, turning to help the other lift the body into a shell, picked his way as

---

[1073] Ibid., p. 608.

through mire. A strange appearance was the apparent annihilation of the neck. The head was taken off so close, that it seemed as if the knife had narrowly escaped crushing the jaw, or shaving off the ear; and the body looked as if there were nothing left above the shoulder.

Nobody cared, or was at all affected. There was no manifestation of disgust, or pity, or indignation, or sorrow... It was an ugly, filthy, careless, sickening spectacle; meaning nothing but butchery beyond the momentary interest, to the one wretched actor. Yes! Such a sight has one meaning and one warning. Let me not forget it. The speculators in the lottery, station themselves at favorable points for counting the gouts of blood that spurt out, here or there; and buy that number. It is pretty sure to have a run upon it.[1074]

During the 14th century popes resided in Palais des Papes in Avignon, the Palace of the Popes. Dickens describes it as "an impregnable fortress, a luxurious palace, a horrible prison, a place of torture, the court of the Inquisition: at one and the same time, a house of feasting, fighting, religion, and blood: gives to every stone in its huge form a fearful interest, and imparts new meaning to its incongruities." Like Castle St. Angelo, these chambers of horrors represented the obvious schizophrenia of church leaders who had given themselves permission to crucify opponents, real or imagined. Dickens tours the gruesome vaults of this palace led by a tour guide he refers to as "Goblin." The effect his ghastly surroundings have on him are clear:

The Chamber of Torture! And the roof was made of that shape to stifle the victim's cries!

Goblin is up, in the middle of the chamber, describing, with her sunburnt arms, a wheel of heavy blows. Thus it ran round! cries Goblin. Mash, mash, mash! An endless routine of heavy hammers. Mash, mash, mash! upon the sufferer's limbs. See the stone trough! says Goblin. For the water torture! Gurgle, swill, bloat, burst, for the Redeemer's honour! Suck the bloody rag, deep down into your unbelieving body, Heretic, at every breath you draw!

See! cries Goblin. There the furnace was. There they made the irons red-hot. Those holes supported the sharp stake, on which the tortured persons hung poised: dangling with their whole weight from the roof. "But;" and Goblin whispers this; "Monsieur' has heard of this tower? Yes? Let Monsieur look down, then!"

A cold air, laden with an earthy smell, falls upon the face of Monsieur; for she has opened, while speaking, a trap-door in the wall. Monsieur looks in. Downward to the bottom, upward to the top, of a steep, dark, lofty tower: very

---

[1074] Charles Dickens, *Pictures From Italy*, pp. 200-07.

dismal, very dark, very cold. The Executioner of the Inquisition, says Goblin, edging in her head to look down also, flung those who were past all further torturing, down here. "But look! does Monsieur see the black stains on the wall?" A glance, over his shoulder, at Goblin's keen eye, shows Monsieur - and would without the aid of the directing-key - where they are. " What are they?" " Blood!"

Goblin's finger is lifted; and she steals out again, into the Chapel of the Holy Office... She assembles us all, round a little trap-door in the floor, as round a grave. "Voila!" she darts down at the ring, and flings the door open with a crash, in her goblin energy, though it is no light weight." Voila les oubliettes! Voila les oubliettes! Subterranean! Frightful! Black! Terrible! Deadly! Les oubliettes de l'Inquisition!"

My blood ran cold, as I looked from Goblin, down into the vaults, where these forgotten creatures, with recollections of the world outside: of wives, friends, children, brothers: starved to death, and made the stones ring with their unavailing groans.[1075]

Europe's Macabre Chambers of Horrors

The real-life house of horrors in England's Tower of London is well known. It was where rats[1076] ripped the skin off of sleeping prisoners, and where Europeans inflicted other cruelties: "In the 18th century, it was a common practice in England to put prisoners in irons before they were tried, and Howard found prisoners 'chained down upon their backs on the floor, across which were several iron bars, with an iron collar with spikes about their necks, and a heavy iron bar over their legs.'"[1077] England had another penal institution called Newgate where torture included, "pressing to death, the boot, the rack, whipping, branding, mutilation, the pillory, the ducking stool, and fetters...."[1078] Concerning the type of pain inflicted by boot torture, Bingham informs us that such horror was wrought by this torture that spectators dreaded merely watching, "When any are to be struck in the boot it is done in the presence of the Council; and upon that occasion almost all offer to run away. The sight is so dreadful that, without an order restraining such a number to stay, the board would be forsaken. But the Duke of York, while he was in Scotland, was so far from withdrawing that he looked on the while with an unmoved indifference and with an attention as if he had been to look on some curious experiment. This gave a terrible idea of him to all that observe it, as of a

---

[1075] Dickens, *Pictures*, pp. 26-31.
[1076] Bingham, *Bastille*, vol. 1, pp. 72-73.
[1077] Ibid., p. 89.
[1078] Ibid., p. 91.

man that had no bowel or humanity in him."[1079]

Across the English Channel in France stood the infamous Bastille that began its service as a fortress, but devolved into use as a prison/dungeon.[1080] In the following quote, Bingham cites historian M. [François] Ravaisson who apparently archived Bastille documents: "Although there were many methods of torture, two[1081] only were used in the Bastille - that of 'water' and of the 'boot.' When the first was applied, the victim was tied down on a plank, and water was poured down his throat until his sufferings became intolerable. The manner in which the 'boot' was applied is tolerably well known."[1082] The next passage is an account of a man tortured by *boot*:

> Sir Walter Scott, in "Old Mortality," thus describes the torture of the "boot" applied to Macbriar:" The executioner, with the help of his assistants, enclosed the leg and knee within the tight iron boot, or case, and then, placing a wedge of the same metal between the knee and the edge of the machine, took a mallet in his hand, and stood waiting for further orders. A surgeon placed himself on the other side of the prisoner's chair and applied his thumb to the pulse in order to regulate the torture according to the strength of the patient. When these preparations were made, the President of the Council repeated with the same stern voice the question: ' When did you last see John Balfour of Burley? '
>
> "The prisoner, instead of replying, turned his eyes to heaven, as if imploring divine strength....
>
> "The Duke of Lauderdale glanced his eye around the Council, as if to collect his suffrages, and, judging from their mute signs, gave a nod to the executioner, whose mallet instantly descended on the wedge and forcing it between the knee and the iron boot, occasioned the most acute pain, as was evident from the flush which instantly took place on the brow and on the cheeks of the sufferer. The fellow then again raised his weapon and stood prepared to give a second blow.
>
> "'Will you yet say,' repeated the Duke, 'when and where you last parted from Balfour of Burley?'"
>
> "'You have my answer.'" said the sufferer resolutely, and the second blow fell. The third and fourth succeeded; but at the fifth, when a larger wedge had been introduced, the prisoner set up a scream of agony . . .
>
> "''He is gone,' said the surgeon; ' he has fainted, my lords, and human nature can endure no more.'" And when the unfortunate Macbriar was recalled to his

---

[1079] Ibid., p. 72.
[1080] Dungeons were damp, dark, crowded underground fortresses. See the chapter on Inquisitions for more details on dungeons.
[1081] Bingham notes the likelihood that torture devices had been dismantled earlier. *Bastille*, vol. 1.
[1082] Bingham, *Bastille*, vol.1, p. 63.

senses the Duke passed sentence of death upon him.[1083]

But, then again, executioners subjected their victims to extreme punishments. Bingham mentions three kinds of extreme penalties: the gibbet, the axe, and the stake: "It is some comfort to know, that 'when a prisoner was ordered to be burned.... the executioner, while pretending to arrange the faggots, managed to strangle the victim by tightening the iron collar by which he was attached to the stake. This was done *secretly so as not to disappoint* the spectators.'"[1084] (Italics added). When poisoning became fashionable in France, "an Act was passed defining it as high treason, and prescribing boiling to death as the penalty."[1085] The Bastille, though it was the first institution to fall to the bloody-thirsty mob at the beginning of the French Revolution, may not have been the worst prison in France.

Europeans Fine-tune Physical Torment to Elicit Confessions, True and False

Torture, according to Lacroix, "might be either previous or preparatory: previous, when it consisted of a torture which the condemned had to endure previous to capital punishment; and preparatory, when it was applied in order to elicit from the culprit an avowal of his crime, or of that of his accomplices."[1086] Persecutions, says he, could last as short as one hour or as long as five or six consecutive hours. Torture lasting for several hours that inflicted considerably more pain was *extraordinary,* a term that became familiar to many United States citizens when *extraordinary renditions*[1087] became routine during the presidencies of Anglo-Saxons Bill Clinton and George W. Bush. Executioners deprived victims of food for eight to ten 10 days before they began persecutions. And victims had all hair shaved from their bodies. It was normal to torture women ahead of men, and for sons to precede their fathers. This tactic sometimes successfully provoked confessions from victims waiting their turn.

One motive[1088] behind torture was to gain so-called confessions. In keeping with a social construct that covers over immoral acts with a thin veneer of legitimacy, Europeans made gaining confessions of supposed criminals a high priority. For those admissions of guilt made everything

---

[1083] Ibid., pp. 70-71.
[1084] Ibid., p. 63.
[1085] Ibid., p. 88.
[1086] Lacroix, *Manners*, p. 407.
[1087] Suspected terrorists were flown from the United States into client countries where they were subjected to the most brutal torture techniques.
[1088] Executioners were revered or reviled, depending on the location. Their pay came from the seized assets of victims; executioners were sometimes rewarded by "titles and privileges of nobility." Lacroix, p. 412.

that happened to the victim afterwards, i.e., death, forfeiture of property, and wealth, etc., *legal*. That was the case, too, with torture that resulted from Inquisitions. The church, desiring to keep its own hands blood stain-free, always had magistrates or hired executioners carry out the sentencing. It is perhaps unnecessary to point out that the victim's estate paid for his own execution. Oddly, Europeans considered torture as a *normal*, quaint function of "judicial machinery."[1089] Torturers devised special instruments to intensify the pain, too.

Tragically, Europeans have used their tools of torment, plus methods like water boarding, or quartering on captured Africans during antebellum South and more recently on *suspected* Muslim terrorists. (The torture techniques these demented terrorists applied to Egun is discussed more fully at the end of this chapter). While modern media have made us aware of water boarding techniques, many may not know that quartering during the Middle Ages included poking skin with red-hot pokers and cutting off hands and feet: "At Autun [France], after high boots made of spongy leather had been placed on the culprit's feet, he was tied on to a table near a large fire, and a quantity of boiling water was poured on the boots, which penetrated the leather, ate away the flesh, and even dissolved the bones of the victim,"[1090] observes Lacroix.

In other cases, these sadists compressed a prisoner's limbs or stretched them from their sockets, or injected vinegar, water, or oil into a victim's body. In other cases torturers placed dice under the sufferer's skin and hot eggs under their armpits. Still another torture included weighting a person's feet with two hundred pounds, lifting him to great heights and then dropping him again and again dislocating his bones. These examples are representative of an extensive list of European torture techniques. They do not include the most insane and cruelest techniques devised by Europeans. (Historians write that each town had its own deranged method for eliciting so-called confessions).[1091] However, presenting a full inventory and description of the horrors medieval Europeans inflicted on fellow humans goes beyond the scope[1092] of this essay, though it is information easily enough for one to acquire.

Sociopathic Europeans hung rotting corpses across the lands as reminders to passers-by of behaviors not tolerated in their already depraved, uncivilized society. They routinely placed whole corpses as well as torsos, legs, arms, and heads of the tortured dead on display in public areas. Travelers commonly witnessed bodies slowly withering away from

---

[1089] Bingham, *Bastille*, vol. 1, p. 66.
[1090] Lacroix, *Manners*, p. 408.
[1091] Confessions were, for the most part, information the torturer wanted confessed. Information did not have to be factual.
[1092] See Appendix C.

years of hanging from these gibbets. One prominent gibbet in Paris, the tiered Gibbet of Montfaucon, accommodated multiple corpses at once; its construction closely resembles a building frame. And while one day watching a group of children nearby playing beneath the Paris sun, a 20th century writer reflects on Montfaucon's ominous past: "Those children do not yet know that the sand with which they are amusing themselves, or that the earth out of which they are making mud pies, was reddened with the blood of many victims in former days. For it was on that spot that the Gibbet of Montfaucon was erected."[1093] Birds gathered by the thousands to pick at the flesh of the dead from these wide-open displays of tormented humans. But, birds were not the only ones picking at those tortured bones. Recall that the corpses on display at the French gibbets provided anatomist Andreas Vesalius with plenty of samples for his studies.

Europeans Use Perfected Torture Techniques on Africans

Given the Europeans' hostility toward each other, readers can understand how they readily butchered those most unlike them. In *The Story of Africa and Its Explorers*, Robert Brown writes that the Portuguese enslaved and robbed (the Africans) in the Lord's name; the British, says he, were salt water thieves. Brown recounts tales of terror inflicted on the Mombasa citizens during the 1500's by the Portuguese: "To this day the legends of Portuguese cruelty are vivid among the natives-tales of their creed treated with [contempt], their holy places defiled, and the arms of women hacked off to enable the inhuman robbers to obtain more easily the bangles with which they were ornamented. Tales of dignitaries tortured by having boiling lead poured on them until they revealed (or invented) plots, produced treasure or betrayed those who had any to produce are the stock traditions which, handed from father to son, have made 'Christian' a name of horror in many a quiet village along the Mohammedan strip of the African shore."[1094] The incredibly large numbers of disturbing stories that depict the violence inflicted by terrorist Europeans on Egun stagger the mind. As the above narrative states, amputations were characteristic of the extent to which Europeans, and their Black collaborators, ventured. But, again, there was no lack of imagination when it came to their brutality. From South Africa we have the following event unfold: "The Governor understanding a Negro Slave had committed a piece of Roguery in his Kitchen, he told him he would have him chastis'd. Now the way here to punish these sort of People when they were found in any fault, was to bind them naked to a Ladder, and scourge them with a Rod made of Reeds, with knots at the end. When they had made their Bodies all bloody, they were to

---

[1093] Henry Haynie, *Paris: Past and Present*, vol. 1, p. 355.
[1094] Robert Brown, *The Story of Africa and Its Explorers*, vol. 4, pp. 6-7.

be rubb'd with Pepper and vinegar."[1095]

Many readers know that Europeans casually raped Egun females (and sometimes men, too) on plantations. However, sexual abuse could occur wherever Europeans exercised control over their environment. In the following passage, Newton describes how European men rape African women and girls aboard slave ships destined for plantations, and calls the abuse normal:

> The enormities frequently committed in an African ship, though frequently flagrant, are little known *here*, and are considered *there*, only as matters of course. When the women and girls are taken aboard a ship, naked, trembling, terrified, perhaps almost exhausted with cold, fatigue, and hunger, they are often exposed to the wanton rudeness of white savages. The poor creatures cannot understand the language they hear, but the looks and manner of the speaker are sufficiently intelligible. In imagination, the prey is divided, upon the spot, and only reserved till opportunity offers. Where resistance or refusal, would be utterly in vain; even the solicitation of consent is seldom thought of. [1096]

One supposes that men unfeeling enough to rape their own females found it quite unnecessary to seek permission for sex from non-European women. Newton remarks, "Such is the treatment which I have known permitted, if not encouraged, in many of our ships-they have been abandoned, without restraint, to the lawless will of the first comer."[1097] Narratives of African imprisonment do not discuss the horrors inflicted upon our African children that included being tossed overboard by ship captains for crying, according to Newton. Blake tells us that ships heading for the Americas crowded with children below the age of 15 years were not unusual. The following narrative reveals the tragic story of an African newborn infant subjected to one psychopathic European's sickening abuse. What follows is a graphic eyewitness account of a Mr. Isaac Parker:

> There was a child, says he, on board, nine months old, which refused to eat, for which the captain took it up in his hand, and flogged it with a cat,[1098] saying, at the same time, "Damn you, I'll make you eat, or I'll kill you." The same child having swelled feet, the captain ordered them to be put into water, though the ship's cook told him it was too hot. This brought off the skin and nails. He then ordered sweet oil and cloths, which Isaac Parker himself applied to the feet; and as the child at mess time again refused to eat, the captain again took it up and flogged it, and tied a log of mango-wood eighteen or twenty inches long, and of

---

[1095] Oliver, *Leguat*, vol. 2, p. 181.
[1096] Newton, *Posthumous Works*, p. 239.
[1097] Ibid., p. 240.
[1098] A cat-o'-nine tail is a rope whip with knotted cords.

twelve or thirteen pounds weight, round its neck, as a punishment. He repeated the flogging for four days together at mess time. The last time after flogging it, he let it drop out of his hand, with the same expression as before, and accordingly in about three quarters of an hour the child died. He then called its mother to heave it overboard, and beat her for refusing. He however forced her to take it up, and go to the ship's side, where, holding her head on one side, to avoid the sight, she dropped her child overboard, after which she cried for many hours.[1099]

Sadly, that tragic scene is just one among millions.[1100] Europeans manifested their perfected torture techniques upon Egun in Africa. And they did it with the same amount of gusto and perverted imagination exhibited toward their own citizens, including the children.

[1099] Blake, *Slavery*, p. 132.
[1100] Many African-Americans are not aware that Anglo-Americans baited alligator traps with our babies in Florida.

15

EUROPEANS EXPORT TERRORISM TO AFRICA

Despite European highbrow pronouncements of exporting civilization to the brown and black countries, there was nothing at all civilized about the European world of bloodlust, torture, and chicanery that Egun entered into once snatched, shackled and led away from their mother Continent. Even those Egun who never strode upon the shores of Europe faced brutality on lands hijacked and looted by Europeans. To these locations they exported their deranged social traditions where Europeans, including their criminal class, relentlessly exercised them: "The system brought upon the lands to which the slaves were taken a terrible and perpetual punishment, which ought to have been foreseen, but was not, or at least was disregarded in the prospect of immediate gain,"[1101] observes the Euro-centered historian George McCall Theal in his book, *The Beginning of South African History*. In the Americas and the islands Egun became all too familiar with many of these madmen's medieval methods. And, as cited in the previous chapter on torture, Africans remaining on the Continent, described by more thoughtful Europeans as "patient, courteous, forgiving, loyal, courageous, jolly, incisive, logical, sociable, hospitable, creative and hard-working" experienced the "full of cruelty" European culture first-hand, too. In sorting out Europe's social paradigm it helps to understand just how all encompassing it is. Colonialism and slavery are two sides of the same coin. Our African sisters and brothers were negatively affected by restrictive European policies, too. The following passage speaks to how the kindness of South Africans was repaid by Europeans. The author, Olivier, remarks on the shameful habits of Europeans that they quickly and proudly revealed to Africans:

> The African has learnt a good deal about the seamy side of the white man. However uprightly and admirably he may have been dealt with by European missionaries, administrators and colonists, and whatever confidence and affection these may have won with him, it has never been possible for him to appraise the value and efficacy of the Christian religion, as the religion of the white man, quite so highly as the missionary and the administrator would have had him do.

[1101] George McCall Theal, *The Beginning of South African History*, p. 383.

And now he has seen the British Government publicly promise self-determination to African peoples in the Peace Settlement and, so far, ignore that promise, having indeed, even before it was made, assigned some of his territories by secret conventions as counters in a deal with its allies, directly in the face of the inhabitants' imploring petitions. While South Africans were giving their services, and their women at home their poor little contributions[1102] towards the task of the war, they have been experiencing the scandalous persecutions on the part of the dominant race in South Africa which Mr. Scully has set out with such indisputable authority in the Edinburgh Review for July, 1919, whilst others have experienced the injustice and cruelty with which coloured [sic] men have been dealt with in connection with riots at Liverpool and elsewhere. And with regard to that excess of animalism that so often is [snickeringly] imputed to them as a danger to white communities, they have encountered in our camps, our streets, our parks, and our Law Courts, abundant material- for at least a defensible judgment that white men and white women are fully as erotic as their own people and much more unrestrainedly and openly licentious.

Whilst, therefore, the white and the coloured [sic] peoples of our Commonwealth have been brought nearer together for co-operation by the increase of mutual recognition and appreciation, and the black man's appreciation of the military efficiency of the white has probably been enhanced, they have also been brought nearer together by the enlightening education and discipline which numbers of Africans have received, and by a certain amount of disillusionment of the latter as to the boasted superiorities of the white man. I do not wish to over-emphasize this factor, but it exists, and it will be a mistake to ignore it.[1103]

Europe Kills Millions Vowing to "Serve the Well-Being of the Native"

Belgian king, Leopold, whose inhumanity and outrageous greed promoted frightfully inhumane treatment of Africans, has been rightly condemned for his actions. However it is important to broaden the European narrative so that Leopold's brutality does not cloud over the tortuous practices employed by *all* the other imperialistic European countries making false claims of "saving" Africans. We know that Europeans committed genocide

---

[1102] During World War I South African women supported the effort: "In the Free State the enslaved coloured [sic] women spent their poor savings in the purchase of material which they worked by the light of the dim candles in their scanty hours of leisure, into garments for the distressed Belgian women and children." African men had left their homes and families to assist the Allies on the promise of greater freedom and better treatment upon their return. However when the men returned home, they found their jobs taken over by European men, and more restrictive laws in place. See: William Charles Scully, "The Colour Problem in South Africa," *The Edinburgh Review*, vol. 230, no. 469 (1919) p. 92.
[1103] Olivier, preface, pp. vii-ix.

against American Indians, but many do not realize that Europeans committed mass murder against Egun, too.

After centuries of wantonly murdering and stealing Africans and their resources a European-wide promise to cultivate good relations with Africans came during the 1885 Berlin Conference. The true objective of the Conference was to organize trade, recognize boundaries and divvy up African land (and resources) among the participating European nations, though these countries treacherously disguised their "mission" to the rest of the world as diplomacy. Participating nations to the Conference included: Belgium, Britain, France, Portugal, the Netherlands, Denmark, Austria-Hungary, Russia, Spain, Sweden-Norway, Denmark, and Italy. However, *African nations were excluded from participation in the conference.* Participants agreed that, "All the Powers exercising sovereign rights or influence in the aforesaid territories *bind themselves to watch over the preservation of the native tribes, and to care for the improvement of the conditions of their moral and material well-being,*"[1104] (Italics added).

Despite that agreement and its superior sounding proclamations of assisting Africans - yet providing further evidence that the European cultural paradigm papers over unethical policies with thin layers of western legality, stomach-turning brutality ensued. Instead of improving the moral and material welfare of Africans, Europeans carelessly, though intentionally erased established boundaries that shattered existing peace agreements; divvied up African nations; and stripped African nations of self-governance. Additionally, Europeans continued to mutilate, torture and murder millions of Africans. Harris reflects on the European's killer instinct unleashed on Egun, "However great the crime of slavery, cruelty and torture, whereby millions of Africans have perished, no bounds can be set to the monumental folly of the white races [sic] which has wiped out of existence millions of native [Africans]...."[1105]

Godard, quoted earlier in this essay on the sinisterness of imperialism sums up the shrewd motives of imperialists:

> For let there be no mistake about the matter. Although Imperialism does not promote the welfare of the nation; although it does not even add to the entire volume of trade; it does promote the sordid interest of certain classes, and enables them to appropriate a larger share of the produce; and it breeds an army of officials and parasites who are all interested in its maintenance and extension.[1106]

Every single one of those participating European nations gained

---

[1104] Edmund D. Morel, *King Leopold's Rule in Africa*, p. 6.
[1105] John H. Harris, *Africa: Slave Or Free?*, p. 25.
[1106] Godard, *Supremacy*, p. 110.

immense wealth from their African ventures.[1107] In the unsuitably named Congo *Free* State where Leopold placed ridiculously high quotas on Egun to perform the miserable task of collecting rubber – a back-breaking and time-consuming chore - it did not take long before African lands became untended and uncared for, or for Africans to begin to starve on acreage that for hundreds of thousands of years had secured their needs. Still, in 1905 the unrepentant hoarder Belgian Prime Minister Paul de Smet de Naeyer had the nerve to proclaim that, "[Africans] are not entitled to anything: What is given them is a veritable gratuity."[1108]

Egun Civil Despite Europe's Cruelties: "African Savagery" Meme is Projection of European Behavior and Traditions

It should be clear that Europeans assisting in black (or brown) nation building is akin to monkeys serving meals at a formal dinner: in both scenarios the result is havoc. The only difference, perhaps, is that monkeys might make an honorable attempt. Commenting on the negative influence of Europeans and Anglo-Americans on Africans, Harris worries about, "the absorption of the white man's vices [that] at the same time destroys in the native some of the most attractive features of the African race."[1109] Scully observes that the pressures stemming from regressive European policies had not (thus far) negatively affected African morals: "That the natives have not evolved a definite criminal class is, under the circumstances, marvellous [sic]. That such a class will be evolved in the near future is certain.... In the mines and cities the native, cut off from family life and from the salutary influence exercised by contact with his clan, loses his ethical basis. In a large number of cases he takes to drink, and forms casual connexions [sic] with women of his class. And yet, wonderful to relate, he remains law-abiding and responsive to sympathetic treatment. One strange peculiarity of the native is his power of moral resilience. A European who has once made a bad false step seldom or never fully recovers his self-respect. No doubt society is largely responsible for this. But with the native it is quite different; under sympathetic treatment an habitual criminal will

---

[1107] Belgium grabbed the Congo Basin, along with France. The British grabbed 355,000 sq. miles in the west; 960,000 sq. miles in the south and south-center; and 1,255,000 sq. miles in the east. France grabbed western Sudan and Madagascar. Portugal grabbed 850,000 sq. miles on the west (Angola) and east coasts, plus islands. The Netherlands, Denmark, Austria-Hungary, Russia, and Spain grabbed 200,000 sq. miles in the western Sahara, and Canaries. Sweden-Norway, Denmark, and Italy grabbed (600,000 sq. miles) the southeastern coasts of the Red Sea, southern Somaliland and a preponderant interest in Abyssinia (Ethiopia). Germany's settlement in Africa, according to Johnston, was not solely the outcome of the Berlin agreement. They grabbed 800,000 sq. miles on the west, south-west and east coasts.
[1108] Morel, *Leopold's Rule*, p. 58.
[1109] Harris, *Africa*, p. 183.

become quite trustworthy."[1110]

Early Europeans were incapable of advancing other cultures given their tumultuous medieval social construct that swirled with outrageous levels of violence, corruption, social inequality, brutal justice and a host of other problems. And except for their ability to read a few biblical passages here and there, Europeans were dreadfully illiterate and uneducated. To top it off, Europe experienced enormous public health issues[1111] and they failed to properly feed and adequately sustain their own populations.

What's more, charges leveled against supposedly culturally undeveloped Egun prove deceptive and incredulous, especially in light of African oral history and documentations of early African visitors, and when placed beside European practices and social standards of the same period. Moreover, European accusations of wild and savage Africans in the face of their own wild and savage traditions, and their charges of witchcraft - given their medical practitioners' commitment to "dead humans" medicines and witchy medical spells, fall flat once prudently scrutinized. Research even crushes their claims of naked[1112] Africans: Some classical Africans took pride in their nudity, believing that clothing hid things, such as the truth:[1113] Based on the wisdom of this ancient tradition, African

---

[1110] William Charles Scully, "The Colour Problem in South Africa," *The Edinburgh Review*, vol. 230, no. 469 (1919) pp. 81-82.

[1111] The following accounts of later plagues are found in White, *Warfare*, vol. 2: "The most sober accounts of travellers in the Spanish Peninsula until a recent period are sometimes irresistibly comic in their pictures of people insisting on maintaining arrangements more filthy than any which would be permitted in an American backwoods camp... The outbreaks of cholera in recent years have done some little to bring in better sanitary measures." p. 81. "The great plague of London in 1665, which swept off more than a hundred thousand people from the city. The attempts at meeting it by sanitary measures were few and poor; the medical system of the time was still largely tinctured by superstitions resulting from mediaeval modes of thought; hence that plague was generally attributed to the Divine wrath caused by 'the prophaning [sic] of the Sabbath.' p. 83. "Noteworthy is the plague at Marseilles near the beginning of the last century [18th]. The chronicles of its sway are ghastly. They speak of great heaps of the unburied dead in the public places, 'forming pestilential volcanoes': of plague-stricken men and women in delirium wandering naked through the streets; of churches and shrines thronged with great crowds shrieking for mercy; of other crowds flinging themselves into the wildest debauchery; of robber bands assassinating the dying and plundering the dead; of three thousand neglected children collected in one hospital and then left to die; and of the death-roll numbering at last fifty thousand out of a population of less than ninety thousand. p. 86.

[1112] Shackling people is unacceptable and indefensible. Enslaving people for superficial reasons, such as their clothing or tattooing, etc., is more troubling. Africa is brutally hot in places. Egun had developed different sensibilities than Europeans who shielded their own bodies from their hostile climate. However, note that not all African nations lacked clothing. Many customarily wore natural fabrics, such as cotton and silk.

[1113] Basil Davidson, *The African Genius*, p. 72. (I will add here that Africans dressed differently from each other. That some tribes went naked is perfectly okay. Feeling shame for the human body is a European custom, not an African one).

families living beneath the searing Sun on the Continent ought to have been more suspicious of the woolens-wrapped, bible toting, smiling and hand waving Europeans. The next passage makes this abundantly clear:

> Within two centuries after the suppression of slavery in Europe, the Portuguese, in close imitation of those piracies which we have mentioned as existing in the uncivilized ages of the world, made their descents upon Africa, and committing depredations upon the coast, first carried the wretched inhabitants into slavery. This practice, thus inconsiderable in its commencement, soon became general, and *we find most of the maritime Christian nations of Europe following the piratical example.* Thus did the Europeans, to their eternal infamy, *revive a custom, which their own ancestors had so lately exploded from a consciousness of its impiety.* The unfortunate *Africans fled from the coast, and sought in the interior part of the country a retreat from the persecution of their invaders. But the Europeans still pursued them entered their rivers, sailed up into the heart of the country, surprised the Africans in their recesses, and carried them into slavery.* The next step which the Europeans found it necessary to take, was that of *settling in the country of securing themselves by fortified posts; of changing their system of force into that of pretended liberality; and of opening, by every species of bribery and corruption, a communication with the natives.* Accordingly they erected their forts and factories; landed their merchandize [sic], and *endeavored by a peaceable deportment, by presents, and by every appearance of [charity], to allure the attachment and confidence of the Africans.* The Portuguese erected their first fort in 1481, about forty years after Alonzo Gonzales had pointed out to his countrymen, as *articles of commerce,* the southern Africans.
>
> The *scheme* succeeded. *An intercourse took place between the Europeans and Africans, attended with a confidence highly favorable to the views of ambition and avarice. In order to render this intercourse permanent as well as lucrative, the Europeans paid their court to the African chiefs, and a treaty of peace and commerce was concluded, in which it was agreed that the kings, on their part, should sentence prisoners of war, and convicts, to European servitude; and that the Europeans should in return supply them with the luxuries of the north.* Thus were laid the foundations of that nefarious commerce....[1114] (Italics added).

The Portuguese Oppress an African King and a Nation

No, Europeans were not the wizened sages of the ages who had acquired the necessary scholarship that would benefit other cultures. But, they had mastered manipulation; and they harbored strong appetites for domination and greed. Because making war was always an option within their social construct, Europeans regularly deployed it to satisfy their cravings for people and resources. The next few paragraphs look at the Mwenemutapa

---

[1114] Blake, *Slavery,* pp. 22-23.

(Zimbabwean) Empire. This ancient civilization has an Afristory as rich as its lands, but experienced the ravages of Europeans after her king refused to allow the Portuguese to indulge their greed on that precious land.

In 1628 Mwenemutapa King Kapranzine, son of Gasilusere, warred with the Portuguese traders and other Christians. A coalition identified by Theal as consisting of mostly Bantu, Batonga, plus some "mixed breeds," assisted the "few" Portuguese in their effort. They managed to hold off the king. After a few more rounds of fighting, Manuza, the king's relative whom for years had been tutored by a Dominican and therefore "inclined toward Christianity," declared himself king at their bidding. Afterwards, he successfully pushed Kapranzine to the country's outskirts. With Kapranzine out of the way, the Portuguese signed a treaty with King Manuza on May 24, 1629. Excerpts appear below:[1115]

> First that this kingdom is delivered to him in the name of the king of Portugal, our lord, of whom he shall acknowledge himself to be a vassal, since he gives him the kingdom taken by his subjects because of the treachery he committed against our lord the king, breaking the faith and word of brothers in arms, killing his ambassador, and robbing and killing the merchants who were in his land selling their merchandise under his faith and word; and he shall recognise all the captains who shall come to the fortress of Mozambique, and those empowered by them.
>
> That he, the said king, shall allow all the religious of whatever order who may be in his zimbahe [sic] to build churches and in all the other lands in his dominions, and to make Christians all those who desire to receive holy baptism, without opposition from any one; treating the said religious as holy persons, to whom great respect is due.
>
> He shall treat with great respect the captain of Masapa, and shall give places for the *meamocuros* [meetings] he may wish to make in his kingdom; *he shall consult with him concerning war and any other novel events which may arise,* and *he shall have leave to come to the zimbahe as often as he pleases without being obliged to make a present, and his servants the same;* and those whom the king sends to the coast or to the captain of Masapa shall not require presents, nor shall they demand them, and to the captain of Masapa he shall give the usual lands, and at the market of Loanze he shall give him the land which belonged to the Inhama....
>
> Throughout all his kingdom *he shall allow as many mines to be sought for and opened as the Portuguese like, without ordering them to be closed, as this will be a source of great profit to the king and the merchants,* and *his lands will become very rich.*
>
> He shall be obliged to inquire throughout the kingdom where there is silver, and to make it known to the captain of Masapa, that he may inform the

---

[1115] George McCall Theal, *Records of Southeastern Africa*, vol. 5, pp. 290-92.

governor; and if his Majesty sends miners they shall be allowed to seek and dig for it freely throughout his territories. (Italics added).

The treaty includes mandatory deportation of Moors and seizure of their valuables and property, annexation of lands, and forbids harboring fugitive slaves. Treaties of this nature usually provided a small monthly stipend to the African king or Chief. Though I did not find those words expressly written in the treaty signed by Manuza, I would be surprised if a tiny allowance was not a condition. In any event, once Manuza signed the treaty Kapranzine made further attempts to retake his empire. Again the Portuguese enlisted and armed Bantu and other Africans who were at war with Kapranzine's coalition members. Fighting raged on and on.

On the march to their last battle European medieval mania gripped Manuza when he claimed to see a brilliant cross glowing in the sky. The priest at his side said the vision was identical to Constantine's and proclaimed their upcoming clash with Kapranzine a "holy war." Ultimately Kapranzine's lost the war. His final defeat - mostly at the hands of fellow Africans, was full of dire consequences: Manuza kept the throne; Africans had slaughtered tens of thousands of other Africans; and Europeans took women and children as "booty." Theal makes it clear that "mixed breeds, half-castes" and volunteering Europeans had helped Manuza only because they wanted to keep their trading enterprises operating profitably. He goes on to mention that Portugal introduced feudalism into South-eastern Africa by granting prazos "great estates" to Europeans who expected Bantu to work the land for free. Regarding the Bantu and other people in the country, Theal adds: "In general they were found to be faithful. [Portuguese control] gave them what they needed: someone to think for them, someone to direct and to look after them."[1116]

Christian Missionaries Gain Riches in Africa, Egun Lose Their Homes, Their Hope and Their Future

While it is generally understood that European kings, queens and their business partners grew crazy rich from exploiting African resources, few people realize that Africa made the church wealthy, too. The Dominican Order provides a fitting example. As holders of prazos, Theal reports that during the mid 17th century, Dominicans had 9 places of worship, but only 6 missionaries in the field. Africans, who had bought the European propaganda, watched as family and neighbors surrendered to dismay and apathy. Many Africans joined the Order hoping to control their country's affairs. Or perhaps they thought, they, rather than Europeans, would have *some* control over the fates of Africans. It cannot have taken long for the

---

[1116] Theal, *Beginning*, pp. 383-84.

Dominicans to disabuse them of their *lofty* ideas. And in the ruins of devastated African lives, Dominicans, according to Theal, spent most of their time trading and growing rich. They centered their ambitions on exploiting African resources and talents, too.

Adam Hochschild's *Leopold's Ghost* provides modern audiences with reasons why many priests traveled to Africa. *Leopold's Ghost* is largely about the evils that king inflicted on Africans, but informs readers of the un-priestly enterprises of European clergy there, a subject not often discussed. But we can reflect on the *Portuguese-instigated* struggle between Africans that allowed them to continue to rape the Continent of people and resources. In addition to filling their money bags, the Dominicans "took great pains to instruct" African children in Christianity: It was as important a clerical mission as any to train the young minds to betray their own kind and to peacefully accept their own subjugation. In fact, Theal reports that Manuza's successor embraced his African culture, before rejecting it and accepting Christianity instead. He, like his predecessor, had allowed the Dominicans to rewire his brain while they *educated him*.

Throughout the Continent, Europeans successfully cloaked their nefarious goals within the pious robes of Christianity to push their agenda of "commodifying and controlling resources" aka materialism in Africa and around the globe, oblivious to the needs of anyone - save themselves - whether any one liked it or not. Indeed.

The Past is Always Present in Our Lives

Why is the story of medieval Europe even important today? The misery of medieval Europe is alive within today's culture. The sons and daughters of the parents who lived through the medieval upheaval have exported a culture of wars, violence, poverty, hunger, suicide, slavery, deceptive business practices, market manipulation, etc., along with them to the new (to Europeans) world. Consider, for example, the early days of New York City and the aptly named Wild West. It's all here. When we turn on our flat screens we passively watch the mania play out in programs popular only because they display uncountable scenes of gore; or we fasten our attention to settings of carnage in first-person video games. Our bodies bump and grind to its disturbing lyrics; and we read bedtime stories to our children from books filled with it. Chariot racing became car racing. Pain-filled, though far less deadly, sports are still with us disguised as hockey, football, and extreme boxing; and the theatre (movies) is still bawdy causing consternation among some segments of the population. European and Anglo-Saxon "princes" make endless warfare while they exercise the medieval "shock and awe" strategy against native populations.

The so-called war and gun tourism industries taking root within the borders of the United States has made *blowing things up* in places like Las

Vegas and Florida leading tourist attractions; and the indefensible and wicked use of torture are but a few cultural crumbs that are found on the short, and narrow trail to medieval-ville. Besides, history is prologue, what's past is present; strategically placed genetic and savory cultural morsels easily lure disorientated stragglers back into the medieval fold. Such is the case with visual tribal cues supplied by a Euro-centered entertainment media that normalize violent, and disturbing behaviors. Other medieval traditions wait in a sort of stasis for the right opportunity for reintroduction into the broader culture.

And then there is this: In 1910, Stanford University president writes about the bloodlines of a nation: "Equally true is it that the present character of a nation is made by its past history. Those who are alive to-day are the resultants of the stream of heredity as modified by the [fluctuations] through which the nation has passed. The blood of the nation flows in the veins of those who survive."[1117] Jordan's book reads mostly like a rant and instruction manual for eugenicists. Still, we understand better today that genetic memory is significant and that genetic cells absorb traumatic (shocking) incidents and pass them on generationally.

Cultural identity is another consideration: "What is called modern history is in reality the formation of a new cycle of culture, connected in several stages of its development with the perishing or perished civilization of the Mediterranean states, as this was connected with the primitive civilization of the Indo-Germania stock, but destined, like the earlier cycle, to traverse an orbit of its own,"[1118] Mommsen reasons. It is not so easy a thing to dismiss the misdeeds of blood ancestors with a casual shrug of the shoulders that attempts to hide the European identity within an American one. What's more, Anglo-Americans who connect African-Americans to our past cannot rationally deny their own past connections to Europe, especially those who continue to munch on the sweet fruits growing from trees planted by their ancestors - but watered with Egun's blood. In other words, Europeans and Anglo-Americans cannot inherit their ancestors' assets without inheriting those liabilities, too. This, in fact, is a long-established tradition of Europe's social construct as Timothy Dwight, Yale College president from 1795-1817 acknowledges:

> Our parents and ancestors have brought their [Africans] parents, or ancestors, in the course of a most [wicked] traffic, from their native country; and made them slaves... It is in vain to alledge [sic], that our ancestors brought them hither, and not we. As well might a son, who inherited an ample patrimony, refuse to pay a debt, because it was contracted by his father. We inherit our ample patrimony with all its incumbrances [sic]; and are bound to pay the debts

---

[1117] David Starr Jordan, *The Blood of The Nation*, p. 8.
[1118] Mommsen, *Rome*, vol. 1. p. 24.

of our ancestors. *This* debt, particularly, we are bound to discharge....[1119]

That is because the deeds of the fathers were for the direct benefit of the sons. Finally, Anglo-Americans cannot insist that African-Americans "get over it" while they continue their ancestors' depraved policies that make living while Black a criminal act; this includes flooding the African-Maafan community with unethical laws and schemes that lock us into prisons, as well as economic poverty. African-Maafans cannot get over events that are still on going: The past is ever present with us.

But, many medieval traditions are kept alive today by unsuspecting African-Americans who carry them forward unaware, psychologically and metaphysically, that these foreign traditions that honor the sacraments, and blood rituals of European ancestry also strangle the African brain.

Indo-Europeans Conjure Religious Theories to Overthrow African Supremacy

Of course, one cannot speak of blood rituals without mentioning Christianity, a topic that I did not originally intend to focus so much of this essay on though well over half of the book documents malicious activities stemming from European religious practices. I explored wherever their information carried me. In this case, western culture laid the Christian foundation; it makes sense that a European religion incorporates the early traditions of Europeans. The European cultural leaders sought to rule the world; it was their intention that the Christian religion displace classical African customs, and that the fake religiosity of European church could wield enormous power throughout the world:

> In many ways, indeed, the Church was comparable to the Roman Empire of old, whose territorial and administrative organization it had taken over and whose official language, Latin, it still maintained in its services, records, and literature. Both were international in character. Every one recognized the pope as every one had worshiped the emperor. The Church had its legal system and courts.... Its missionaries and crusaders on the frontiers of Christendom were like the ancient legionaries on the Roman borders. Its monasteries were scattered over the face of the land as thickly as had been the Roman military camps and colonies. Its secular clergy corresponded to the administrative bureaucracy of the Empire. And at the head and center of it all, watching over the whole world, interfering in everything, exercising temporal as well as spiritual power, receiving reports and questions and appeals from all quarters, and reserving to himself the settlement of all questions in the last resort, sat Innocent III with an authority quite comparable to that of a Trajan or a

---

[1119] Timothy Dwight, *The Charitable Blessed*, pp. 20, 22.

Diocletian.[1120]

It can hardly be a coincidence that early Christian father Origen's 3rd century biblical interpretation links Ham's curse to the "discoloration"[1121] of African skin. The Hebrew's Rabbah Genesis, collected sometime during the 4th century CE is similarly interpreted, but accuses Ham of other despicable behaviors:

> R. Berekiah said: Noah grieved very much in the Ark that he had no young son to wait on him, and declared, 'When I go out I will beget a young son to do this for me.' But when Ham acted thus to him, he exclaimed, 'You have prevented me from begetting a young son to serve me, therefore that man [your son] will be a servant to his brethren!' R. Huna said in R. Joseph's name: [Noah declared], 'You have prevented me from begetting a fourth son, therefore I curse your fourth son.' R. Huna also said in R. Joseph's name: You have prevented me from doing something in the dark [sc. Cohabitation], therefore your seed will be ugly and dark-skinned. R. Hiyya said: Ham and the dog copulated in the Ark, therefore Ham came forth black-skinned while the dog publicly exposes its copulation. R. Levi said: This may be compared to one who minted his own coinage in the very palace of the king, whereupon the king ordered: I decree that his effigy be defaced and his coinage cancelled. Similarly, Ham and the dog copulated in the Ark and were punished.[1122]

In the ancient Arabian version of the Noah story, the pale-skinned (?) Ham's wife births babies with black skin. In this creation story recited by an influential Jewish convert to Islam, Ham completely rejects his black-skinned offspring. It appears that rabbis may have had more than a little influence on early creation theories made up about Africans. Polygenist/anthropologist Paul Topinard (d. 1911) points to ancient church councils that sought to make separate creation stories for Africans and Europeans. He remarks, "In the early centuries AD, when Christianity was looking for its seat, the Rabbis of Babylon and the Emperor Julian defended the doctrine of multiple creations, for white and black; a council discussed whether the Ethiopians descended from Adam, and the opposition making progress Augustine intervened in his City of God in 415, declaring that none could doubt true that all men regardless of color, shape, size or language, were not out of the same protoplasm."[1123] Among polygenism's (the debunked theory that different ethnicities had different original

---

[1120] Thorndike, *Europe*, p. 435.
[1121] See Origen's Genesis Homily 16. Here discoloration is intended to mean "stain" or "blackness."
[1122] H. Freedman and Maurice Simon, trans., *Midrash Rabbah Genesis*, vol.1, (Genesis. London: Soncino, 1939), p. 293.
[1123] Paul Topinard, "De La Notion De Race," *Revue Anthropologie*, ser 2 (1879): 589-90.

parents) many propositions is, of course, that Europeans preceded Africans in creation. Still, the skin curse discussion is a curious one since, ironically, the bible considers that skin whitening (leprosy) is the curse, not blackness. Regardless, it is small wonder that we of African descent face tremendous challenges in today's world where whole populations have been seized by the social construct of the world's minority population with its outrageous orthodoxy that teeters upon the disrepute and humiliation of an entire culture. Ever since Indo-Europeans gained control over the world's resources, Earth's original people have become a despised people. One has to wonder why that it is the case: Just what horrible things have Africans done in the world?

16

AFRICAN FIRSTS: INTRODUCING SOME AFRICAN SOCIAL CUSTOMS

Egun spent tens of thousands of years testing methods to get our act together. By the time new-worlder Europeans came around, Egun were coasting:

Before people spoke Greek or French, they spoke !Kung. Before costly cosmetics, there was red ochre; before Audrey dreamed of diamonds, or women went gaga for sequined gowns, Africans adorned themselves with shell beads and stitched together the first clothing. Before beds had cozy mattresses, before consummate cuisine was French, or fashionable footwear was Italian, these concepts were all African innovations and are listed among Africa's firsts. Before Sylvia conjured Spooks or doctors doodled on chalkboards, Africans discerned Spirits and Sangomas healed with herbs. Before perfumeries counted to 5, pharmacies patented their first drug or Van Gogh sketched his first scene, these products were African originals created by Africans first.

Africans Develop a Sturdy Constitution: Feudalism is not an African Tradition

African Maafans may wonder whether the Medieval Ages was a phenomenon exclusive to Europeans. Feudalism, according to Diop,[1124] could never be a feature of classical African societies. He writes that African political structures established pretty much around the Continent did not lend themselves to such a regressive system and mentions several policies that hindered its genesis: A strong tradition of matriarchy [1125] and matrilineal societies; the lack of individual land ownership, plus abundant natural resources; and the lack of barbarian invasions (the Sahara slowed Arab attacks into interior Africa) are listed. Additionally, early Africans had developed a sturdy social Constitution that guided kings who had to abide by the wishes of the people as African scholar, Egun Chancellor Williams points out. In his writings, Diodorus (1st c. BCE) seems to admire aspects of the ancient culture of KMT and its justice system. He writes the following about Thebes: "There were many statues of wood, representing the pleaders and spectators, looking upon the

---

[1124] Cheikh Anta Diop, *Pre-Colonial Black Africa*, pp. 99-103.
[1125] Concerning the world's so-called *oldest profession*, it's unlikely that matrilineal and matriarchal societies such as existed in classical Africa supported a system that objectified and exploited women. However, ancient Christian leaders and scientists frequently demonized women.

judges that gave judgment. In the middle sat the chief justice with the image of truth hanging about his neck, with his eyes closed, having many books lying before him. This signified that a judge ought not to take any bribes, but ought only to regard the truth and merits of the cause."[1126]

Diodorus includes much information on the laws[1127] of KMT. Here are a few he describes as being "remarkable for their antiquity or strange and different from all others"[1128] (numbered according to Diodorus):

1. And in the first place, those were to die who were guilty of perjury being such as committed the two greatest crimes; that is, impiety towards the gods [Nature], and violation of faith and truth, the strongest bond of human society.

2. If any upon the road saw a man likely to be killed, or to be violently assaulted, and did not rescue him, if he were able, he was to die for it. And if in truth he were not able to defend him, yet he was bound to discover the thieves, and to prosecute them in a due course of law. If he neglected this, he was, according to the law, to be scourged with a certain number of stripes, and to be kept without food for three days together.

3. False accusers were to suffer the same punishment as those who they falsely accused were to have undergone, if they had afterwards been convicted of the offense.

4. All the Egyptians were enjoined to give in their names in writing, to the governors of the provinces, shewing how and by what means they got their livelihood. He that gave a false account in such case or if it appeared he lived by robbery, or any other unjust course, he was to die; which law it is said Solon brought over out of Egypt into Athens.

5. He that willfully killed a freeman; nay, a very bond slave, was by the law to die; thereby designing to restrain men from wicked actions, as having no respect to the state and condition of the person suffering, but to the advised act of the offender; and by this care of slaves, men learned that freemen were much less to be destroyed.

6. Parents that killed their children, were not to die, but were forced for three days and nights together to hug them continually in their arms, and had a guard all the while over them, to see they did it; for they thought it not fit that they should die, who gave life to their children; but rather that men should be deterred from such attempts! by a punishment that seemed attended with

---

[1126] Booth, *Diodorus*, p. 54.
[1127] Greeks, such as Solon and Pythagoras, exported some laws of KMT to Greece where they were adapted to their own populations.
[1128] Booth, *Diodorus*, pp. 79-82.

sorrow and repentance.

7. But for parricides, they provided a most severe kind of punishment: for those that were convicted of this offense, were laid upon thorns, and burnt alive, after they had first mangled the members of their bodies with sharp canes, piecemeal, about the bigness of a man's thumb. For they counted it the most wicked act that man could be guilty of, to take away the lives of them from whom they had their own.

9. These are the capital laws which are chiefly worthy of praise and commendation; as to others, those concerning military affairs, provided that soldiers who ran away from their colours [sic], or mutinied, though they should not die, yet should be otherwise punished with the utmost disgrace imaginable; but if they afterwards wipe off their disgrace by their valour [sic], they are restored to their former post and trust. By thus inflicting of a punishment more grievous than deaths the lawgiver designed that all should look upon disgrace and infamy as the greatest of evils: besides it was judged, that those who were put to death, could never be further serviceable to the common wealth; but such as were degraded only, (through a desire to repair their reputation), might be very useful, and do much service in time to come.

10. Such as revealed the secrets of the army to the enemy, were to have their tongues cut out.

11. They that coined false and adulterated money, or contrived false weights, or counterfeited seals; and scriveners or clerks that forged deeds, or razed public records, or produced any forged contracts, were to have both their hands cut off, that every one might suffer in that part wherewith he had offended in such a manner as not to be repaired, during their life; and that others, warned by so severe a punishment, might be deterred from the commission of the like offense.

12. In relation to women, the laws were very severe: for he that committed a rape upon a free woman, was to have his privy members cut off; for they judged that three most heinous offenses were included in that one vile act, that is, wrong, defilement, and bastardy.

13. In case of adultery, the man was to have a thousand lashes with rods, and the woman her *nose* cut off. For it was looked upon very fit that *the adulteress that tricked up herself to allure men to wantonness, should be punished in that part where her charms chiefly lay.* [Italics added].

14. They say that [Bakenranef] made the laws concerning merchandise. As to these, it was a law, that if a man borrowed money, and the lender had no writing to shew for it, and the other denied It upon hit oath, he should be quit of the debt; to that end, therefore, in the first place, they were to sacrifice to the

gods, as men making con science, and tender and scrupulous in taking of an oath. For it being clear and evident, that he that swears often again and again, at last loses his credit; every man to prevent that mischief, will be very cautious of being brought to an oath. Moreover, the lawgiver had this design, that by grounding a man's credit and reputation wholly upon the integrity of his life and conversation, every one would be induced to honest and virtuous actions, lest he should be despised as a man of no credit or worth. Besides, it was judged a most unjust thing, not to believe him upon his oath, in that matter relating to his contract, to whom credit was given in the self-same thing, without an oath before.

15. For those that lent money by contract in writing, it was not lawful to take usury above what would double the stock; and that payment should be made only out of the debtor's goods; but his body was not to be liable in any wise to imprisonment: and those were counted the debtor's goods, which he had either earned by his labour, or had been bestowed upon him by the just proprietors....

16. There is a very remarkable law among the Egyptians, concerning theft. Those that enter into the list of thieves, are to give in their names to one who is their chief and head, and whatever they steal, they engage to bring to him. They that have lost any things are to set down in writing every particular, and bring it to him, and set forth the day, hour, and place, when and where they lost their goods. Every thing being thus readily found out, after the things stolen are valued, the true owner is to pay a fourth part of the value, and so receive his goods again. For being it was not possible to restrain all from thieving, the lawmaker found out a way that all might be restored, except a small proportion for redemption.

Much earlier written creeds exist in ancient Africa. The Instructions of Ptah-hotep, also called the Maxims of Ptah-hotep (ca. 2400 BCE), are among the oldest recordings of principles in ancient Africa. These creeds describe what it takes to gain and sustain good character, a necessary contribution to social stability. The creeds established over 4000 years ago, long before Europeans introduced African Egun to their bible, remain relevant. Compare[1129] the bible - a book that encourages war, slavery, and slaughter as long as *god's warriors* are administering *his* justice, with Ptah-hotep's principles. Ptah-hotep gives great insight into the culture of ancient Africans by way of his guiding principles. These principles highlight the stability Egun sought as they attempted to balance their behaviors, not only with the laws of nature, but with their fellow Africans, as well. The translator of Ptah-hotep's papyrus, Battiscombe Gunn, in 1918 notes that.

[1129] More relevant comparisons can be made between the 42 Laws of Ma'at and the European bible where examples of cultural shadowing are evidenced.

It is as fresh and readable as in the year after it was written... our moralist, by advancing counsels of perfection for every contingency, has left us a faithful record of his age. The veil of five-and a- half thousand years is rent, and we are met with a vivid and a fascinating picture of the domestic and social life of the ' Old Kingdom.' We read of the wife, who must be treated kindly at all costs; the genial generosity of the rich man, and the scowling boor, a thorn in the side of his friends and relations, the laughing-stock of all men; the unquenchable talkers of every station in life, who argue high, who argue low, who also argue round about them, as common as now in the East, and the trusted councillor [sic], weighing every word; the obstinate ignoramus who sees everything inverted, listening open-mouthed to the disjointed gossip of those near him, and the scholar, conversing freely with learned and unlearned alike, recognising [sic] that, measured against the infinite possibilities of knowledge and skill, we are all much of the same stature; the master of the estate or province, treated with infinite respect by his subordinates in rank and wealth, and the paid servants that are never satisfied, who leave after presents have been made them; the hard-working clerk who casts accounts all day, and the tradesmen who will perhaps give you credit when money is dear, if you have previously made friends of them; the well-bred diner-out, lightly passing on his favourite [sic] dish, contenting himself with plain fare, and the gourmand [big eater] who visits his friends at mealtimes, departing only when the larder is entirely exhausted.[1130]

People have not changed. Attitudes and personalities that existed yesteryear are with us today perhaps making many ancient solutions relevant. Following are principles (numbered according to the papyrus) excerpted from the instructions of Ptah-hotep:[1131]

5. If thou be a leader, as one directing the conduct of the multitude, endeavour [sic] always to be gracious, that thine own conduct be without defect. Great is Truth, appointing a straight path; never hath it been overthrown since the reign of Osiris. One that oversteppeth the laws shall be punished. Overstepping is by the covetous man....

6. Cause not fear among men....

8. If thou be an emissary sent from one noble to another, be exact after the manner of him that sent thee, give his message even as he hath said it. Beware of making enmity by thy words, setting one noble against the other by perverting truth. Overstep it not, neither repeat that which any man, be he prince or peasant, saith in opening the heart; it is abhorrent to the soul.

[1130] Battiscombe Gunn, trans., *The Wisdom of the East: The Instruction of Ptah-hotep and the Instruction of Ke'Gemni: The Oldest Books in the World*, (London: John Murray, 1918), pp. 26-27.
[1131] Ibid., pp. 43-56.

20. Be not covetous as touching shares, in seizing that which is not thine own property. Be not covetous toward thy neighbours [sic]....

21. If thou wouldest be wise, provide for thine house, and love thy wife that is in thine arms. Fill her stomach, clothe her back; oil is the remedy of her limbs. Gladden her heart during thy lifetime, for she is an estate profitable unto its lord. Be not harsh, for gentleness mastereth her more than strength. Give (?) to her that for which she sigheth and that toward which her eye looketh; so shalt thou keep her in thine house....

25. If thou be powerful, make thyself to be honoured [sic] for knowledge and for gentleness. Speak with authority, that is, not as if following injunctions, for he that is humble (when highly placed) falleth into errors. Exalt not thine heart, that it be not brought low. Be not silent, but beware of interruption and of answering words with heat. Put it far from thee; control thyself. The wrathful heart speaketh fiery words; it darteth out at the man of peace that approacheth, stopping his path....

34. Let thy face be bright what time thou livest. That which goeth into the storehouse must come out therefrom; and bread is to be shared. He that is grasping in entertainment shall himself have an empty belly; he that causeth strife cometh himself to sorrow. Take not such an one for thy companion. It is a man's kindly acts that are remembered of him in the years after his life.

35. Know well thy merchants; for when thine affairs are in evil case, thy good repute among thy friends is a channel [?] which is filled. It is more important than the dignities of a man; and the wealth of one passeth to another. The good repute of a man's son is a glory unto him; and a good character is for remembrance.

36. Correct chiefly; instruct conformably [therewith]. Vice must be drawn out, that virtue may remain. Nor is this a matter of misfortune, for one that is a gainsayer becometh a strife-maker.

From the Instruction of Ke'Gemni:

4. If a man be lacking in good fellowship, no speech hath any influence over him. He is sour of face toward the glad-hearted that are kindly to him; he is a grief unto his mother and his friends; and all men [cry], 'Let thy name be known; thou art silent in thy mouth when thou art addressed!'[1132]

"Valley of Dreams": Europeans Describe Africa to Other Europeans

Europeans have for centuries described Africa in ways that induced

---

[1132] Ibid., p. 63.

African-Maafans to experience feelings of shame towards their motherland. European media have flooded our collective consciousness with foul images of seemingly crazed Africans living amidst dense, tangled and tortuous underbrush of the "Dark Continent." In the late 19th century French author Felix Dubois traveled to Tomboutou. In the following passages he describes Africa as he beheld her during his journeys[1133] there:[1134]

> Life in the bush means flocks of guinea-fowls running about in the thickets, and coveys of young partridges that rise, careless of sportsmen, from under your horse's very hoofs. It means strange, intoxicating scents that suddenly envelop you, and leave you as suddenly as they came; and a delirium of sunsets passionately colouring [sic] a sky that was monotonously colourless [sic] the moment before. And nights! One night we encamped in the huts surrounding a village square, and my men lighted huge fires in the open air. The gleams from their flames carved a vault of red and gold upon the darkness, and under this arch a fantastic ballet took place. The wings of bats, illuminated from below, made streaks of light upon the night, like the trails of falling stars, and were distantly encircled with satellites of fire flies. But I can only give a tenth part, and that feebly, of the unexpected sights and sensations I enjoyed. You cannot taste life's choicest morsels reclining in an arm-chair.
>
> The road from Dioubaba to Bannnaku cuts from east to west across the massive Foota Jallon range that separates the basin of the Senegal from that of the Niger. It is full of pictures recalling the Forest of Fontainebleau, and is so abundantly watered that you fall asleep every night to the sound of some gurgling cascade or waterfall.
>
> You see the colonial life coming and going upon it from day to day; and it also reflects the retrospective image of the life that rolled along the great European highways before the days of coaches.
>
> So far the country has been pleasantly varied, recalling somewhat of Switzerland without giving an equal impression of fertility; but in the next and

---

[1133] Dubois journeyed through Africa by canoe. Harris calls it, one delight of African travels: "Despite the mosquitos in the evening and the "midges" by the million during the day, insidious but venomous attacks at all hours by the tsetse fly, and miasma all the time, the joy of whirling hour after hour through the rushing waters to the continuous "dip, dip" of forty paddlers, and the rhythmic song of the "coach" and the even beat of the "tom-tom," is an experience only possible in primitive Africa. This delight to the white man spells for the African an unbroken strain of eight hours' paddling for days on end, which dwarfs to pigmy proportions the relatively comfortable exercise of the Oxford and Cambridge boat race. The assumption of "laziness" in the African is generally due to a lofty superiority not unrelated to ignorance." Harris, *Africa*, p. 10.
[1134] Dubois, *Timbuctoo*, pp. 8-36.

last twenty-five miles of the road springs and rivulets multiply at every step. Agriculture, interspersed with charming glimpses of silvery water, spreads over uninterrupted fields for the rest of the way. The villages cluster closer together, and are more densely populated. In a delightful valley of the great Kati mountains a stream tumbles along between two rocky ledges, which start suddenly aside and spread into a fan, to disappear upon the distant banks of the Niger.

'There is the Djoliba,' says my historical servant, as calmly as if he were announcing 'Dinner is served.' It is an impressive spectacle from the height of the road that still clings to the hill. A vast horizon lies at my feet bathed in the splendours of a tropical sunset, and down there, in a plain of gold and green and red, shines a silver trail bordered by a line of darkness. There it is, a mere vapour [sic], the dream of a river in a valley of dreams, and the dark line is the hills by which it flows, almost invisibly. 'God is great' as they say here. There is no disillusion, as is so often the case in the realisation [sic] of the unknown. I can scarcely take my eyes from the serenely majestic panorama that is spread before me. And now come what may! I remount my horse and urge him to a gallop along the road, bordered by trees, that stretches across the plain. A postern stops me, bearing a placard on which is written in white letters on black, like the name of a railway station: Bammaku.

An equally unexpected vision awaits the traveller beyond Lake Debo; and it is now a landscape from Normandy or England that is disclosed to eyes stupefied by such an apparition in the heart of tropical Africa. Great meadows of a moist, intense green are bordered by park-like woods. So vivid is the impression that you are *disappointed not to see the turrets and battlements* of a Lancashire manor, or the slated roofs of some Chateau of the Eure, rising from their midst. The superb troops of humped cattle, large and sleek, scarcely dispel this northern illusion. All this changes after Sarafara, and it is now the tangle of a tropical forest that defiles before my yacht, now some Eastern scene that I have already witnessed in Egypt or Syria. Palm-trees, slenderly erect, dominate a scanty vegetation containing the melancholy green of the olive - trees of Palestine, and thickets of low bushes that recall the fig-trees of Judaea. (Italics added).

It would be ungrateful if among all these pictures, pale images as they are of hours of enchantment, I forgot to include the twilights and nights upon the Niger. The moments of sunset upon the river are those the greatest intensity of life. The canoes multiply near the villages bringing the fruit of the field to buildings to which the people will flock for to-morrow's market. The ferry-boat causes the river to resound with gay chatter and laughter, the bleating of sheep, and the clucking of frightened poultry.

No wonder classical African wisdom rejects squirreling away segments of land for selfish reasons. Such majesty must not be commodified, nor its view restricted. In tens of thousands of years of our existence, not one single African man or woman felt morally capable of taking sole ownership of such breathtaking magnificence, splendor provided for everyone's enjoyment:[1135]

> The European conception of the commercial ownership of land is totally alien to primitive native thought; a century ago almost any of the tribes in Africa would have looked upon the sale of tribal lands as an act of the most revolting kind. Land to the primitive African is one of three component parts of African social and economic life—sun, water, land, represent to the native mind not three elements, but a single element, the supreme object of which is the provision of human sustenance. This machinery is so interdependent that the primitive African would be as horrified at the alienation and sale of land as of water or sun. It thus follows that the ownership of land is nowhere vested in the individual but in the whole race inhabiting a particular area, whilst every member of the tribe possesses as much right to the usage of adequate land as he does to the usage of an adequate share of the warmth of the sun or a draught of water from the local spring.
>
> It may be assumed that such tribal ownership precludes immigrant settlers—it does nothing of the kind! *-It precludes monopoly, it shuts out self-interest it is true*, but there are adequate means by which any man, no matter of what race, creed or colour [sic], may obtain secure title to occupancy right of adequate land. The immigrant entering tribal areas would be confronted not with a question as to what land he requires and at what price, but with the initial question of whether or not he is a fit and proper person to become part of the tribal order; If it is decided that the immigrant is a suitable person to enter the community, the allotment of land follows as naturally as the gift of a wife, for the African believes it to be the first duty of man to multiply and replenish the earth.
>
> Over the greater part of *Africa this primitive conception has been shattered by the influx of the white races — exploitation and the concessionaire have done their fell work of goading the native to rebellion and then confiscating his land rights;* in some parts a hybrid system, partly European and partly African, has taken the place of the old one.... (Italics added).

Despite the countless bottles of booze[1136] Europeans supplied to African Chiefs they exploited, the selling of and acquisition of ancestral land to Europeans was illegal because Chiefs did not hold exclusive title to them. Traditionally and spiritually, the lands *belong* to Egun. That condition *has*

[1135] Harris, *Africa*, pp. 107-09.
[1136] "Strong liquors, such as brandy, rum, or English spirits... being an article much in demand, so that without it scarcely a single slave can be purchased, it is always on hand." Newton, *Posthumous Works*, p. 233.

not changed. Returning to Dubois, who seems to have been an opinionated and a not so easy traveling companion for Africans, often remarks on the individuals he encounters. A few of them have been reproduced below:[1137]

> The old men, with wrinkled skins and white hair and eyebrows, were my favourite historians. They could recall to me the past prosperity and great commerce of the Valley of the Niger. They told me of the desolating conquerors and disastrous wars of the present century; of Cheikou Ahmadou, the fanatic [Muslim] Foulbe king, who changed the prosperity of former days to misery. Timbuctoo was the most frequent subject of my questions. It was the home of their youthful memories, and they would speak of it enthusiastically, and with laughter — much laughter — at the recollections of their gay life there, the lively frolics which sweetened their labours, and the especially vivid remembrance of the bewitching beauty of the ladies of Timbuctoo. In the villages of the Bosoa the Niger formed the basis of our conversation. They would narrate to me the legends and the life and being of the giant.
>
> [Niger River] waters were now blue as the Mediterranean, now grey as the North Sea, and now again they were apparelled [sic] in the green of the great ocean; while Venus Anadiomenes in black sported upon its banks. If these latter were not smilingly coiling their tresses, it was only because their hair was short and greased with butter. Failing this poetic occupation, they were engaged inalternately [sic] scrubbing their cooking utensils and washing their children in the splashing wave. Art, however, lost nothing by that, for, in their constantly changing attitudes, their perfect nudity only served to call attention to their marvellously [sic] sculptured torsos and their bronze skins, touched into gold by the brightness of the sunshine.

And in describing the merchandise sold inside Djenné, Dubois gives us insight into African beauty secrets: "Antimony [black powder, kuhl, an ingredient in make-up], used by the negresses to darken the orbits of their eyes and increase their brilliancy — the blonde among them (for there are fair negresses) using it to darken their complexions."[1138] It is essential to ask each other why Europeans have invested so much time and energy in propagandizing Africa and her people so negatively, yet cannot stay away themselves.

Literacy in Africa Long Before White Europe Develops

Africans being illiterate and ignorant are two such lies finally put to rest by revelations that aside from Mdu Ntr, many ancient African scripts exist including proto-Saharan, Vai, Nsibidi, and Meroitic. One African scholar

---

[1137] Dubois, *Timbuctoo*, pp. 36-37; p. 25.
[1138] Ibid., p. 166.

has successfully connected the Igbo language to Ogam (also spelled Ogham), an ancient script written on stones in Ireland. Nor is it ever mentioned that most Africans living today are polyglots, meaning they have mastered communicating in multiple languages. One expression of African literacy is found in the once great Tomboutou (Timbuctoo), home to the distinguished learning center that gained prominence under African dynastic rule. Students from around the Continent and the world studied with some of Africa's finest educators. Here Dubois reflects on these African professors and their students:[1139]

> The scholars of Timbuctoo [sic] yielded in nothing to the saints and their miracles. During their sojourns in the foreign universities of Fez, Tunis, and Cairo, 'they astounded the most learned men of Islam by their erudition.' That these negroes were on a level with the Arabian savants is proved by the fact that they were installed as professors in Morocco and Egypt. In contrast to this we find that the Arabs were not always equal to the requirements of Sankore [sic]. 'A celebrated jurist of Hedjaz (Arabia), arriving in Timbuctoo [sic] with the intention of teaching, found the town full of Sudanese scholars. Observing them to be his superiors in knowledge, he withdrew to Fez, where he succeeded in obtaining employment.'
>
> It would be superfluous to insist that these learned men must have possessed marvellous [sic] libraries, for their catalogues are mentioned by the Sudanese authors. Religious, judicial, and grammatical works occupy the first place.
>
> Works on law are represented by the doctrines of the sect of Iman Malek....
>
> Poetry and works of imagination are not lacking, nor compositions of a kind peculiar to Arabian literature; such as the Hariri and Hamadani. I found a copy of the Choke of Marvels, composed at Mossul by the learned Abu Abdallah ben Abderrahim of Grenada in the year 1160. The historical and geographical works of Morocco, Tunis, and Egypt were well known in Timbuctoo (Ibn Batouba being often quoted), and the pure....
>
> Sciences were represented by books on astronomy and medicine.
>
> Amongst other trades, the city made a speciality of manuscripts. 'Books sell very well there,' said Leon the African, 'and a greater profit is to be made out of them than out of any other merchandise.' The learned doctors were, to use an expression which may appear strange when applied to negroes, bibliophiles. In the best sense of the word, be it understood; they had no mania for collecting uncut books and bindings, but were true lovers of books. We see them 'searching with a real passion for volumes they did not possess,' and making copies when they were too poor to buy what they wanted. They would in this manner collect from seven hundred to two thousand volumes; and in marked contrast to the miserly book-lovers of our day, these bibliophiles experienced a

---

[1139] Ibid., pp. 285-88.

real joy in sharing their most precious manuscripts with others.

The libraries of Timbuctoo were sadly reduced by the pillage of the Foulbes [mainly Muslim] and Toucouleurs [mainly Muslim]. At the present time the marabuts and kadis are best provided, but every wealthy inhabitant prides himself upon the possession of a few books. He does not often read them, it is true, but he likes to show them, which, to him, is almost as good. In spite of this I found it very difficult to procure any books.

African children and their parents were as invested in education as their teachers:[1140]

From the masters we will turn to the pupils. These flocked to the city from all sides, from the desert, Morocco, and all parts of the Sudan. Jenne and the secondary intellectual circles, such as Tindirma, Dia, Sa, Korienza, etc., served as preparatory schools for Timbuctoo. The sons of the Songhoi kings quitted the palaces of Gao, and the children of the Touaregs deserted their great tents to receive an education at the University of Sankoré. The Tarik mentions this interesting fact: 'One of the Askia, Mohammed Bankouri, collected an army with which to dispute the supreme power with a king proclaimed at Gao. Pausing at Timbuctoo, and having conversed with the Grand Kadi, he requested him to write a letter to his rival, saying that he, Bankouri, renounced the throne that he might follow the life of a student in this city of books.' Side by side with princes and sons of chieftains came poor wretches, eager for knowledge, who were supported by the dignitaries of the town, and by those merchants who liked to play the *role* of Maecenas.

The student or *Taliba* arrives armed with the groundwork of instruction; some small marabut of his native country having taught him to read and write. It is a picture one constantly sees in the Sudan. In the shade before the schoolmaster's house, a collection of children are gathered together in the coolest corner. Arranged in circles and sitting on their heels, they repeat verses of the Koran in chorus, following the inflections, marking the pauses, and imitating the tone indicated to them. They learn to form the Arabic characters by copying a page of the holy book on the wooden tablets which take the place of the too costly paper. From time to time the tablet is washed and set in the sun to dry, after which it is again ready for use.

Reading and writing being accomplished, the master delivers a grammatical and exegetical explanation of the text. He either takes the words one by one, or grouped in sentences, and discourses on the rules of syntax, explains the meaning of the passage, and adds some religious or historical reflections. When the entire Koran has been gone through, the parents, who have offered weekly presents of cowries or in kind, make a final and more extensive present to the professor, and invite him to a little *fete* given to their friends and acquaintances.

[1140] Ibid., pp. 292-94.

The young man is now prepared for the reading of works of greater importance of another kind....

Thus prepared, the *Taliba* sets out for Timbuctoo, and there he usually studies under several masters, each of whom makes a speciality of elucidating some particular work. He goes from one to another, according to their merits or the dictates of his own fancy. The lessons are given under the arcades of the mosque of Sankore, or in the court or gardens of the teacher's house.

The branches of instruction were many and various. The theologians commented upon and analysed [sic] the great sacred books, and taught rhetoric, logic, eloquence, and diction in order to prepare the student to spread abroad the words of God and maintain controversies. The jurist expounded the law according to the Malakite dogmas, and the stylists taught the art of writing 'in ornamental terms.' Others professed grammar, prosody, philology, astronomy, and ethnography; and others again were 'very versed in the traditions, biographies, annals, and histories of mankind.' Mathematics do not appear to have formed a special course; and as for medicine, the grossest empiricism was mingled with the hygienic principles of the therapeutic Arab. A certain sheik is shown curing a toothache 'with a little earth from his garden,' and, worse than that, 'a great personage having been attacked by leprosy, doctors came from all parts of Africa to prescribe for him. One of them said, 'He can only be cured by eating the heart of a young man.' The emir instantly ordered one to be killed, but it did no good, and the great personage died of his disease....'

The students, having completed their education, receive a diploma or licence to teach. They are now marabuts in their turn, and all the liberal careers of the Sudan are open to them. They can enter the mosques and become imans or preachers in some small town, or they can aspire to the position of kadi, or assistant-kadi, in their own country. Some adopt the careers of their masters and found fresh families of sheiks.

Moral Codes of Africa

Traditional African family life was harmonious, and stable. The following quote comes from the 1913 South African Commission and provides a great deal of insight into the moral code of traditional Africans: *"They have always had a social system and institutions which, with all their defects, have also a side which exercises a considerable influence for good. Loyalty to the Chief and to the Tribe has always been the mainspring of native morality. The responsibility of the tribe and the family for the offences [sic] of its members was a recognized factor, which imposed upon every member of it a personal obligation in the prevention of crime, and caused him to be directly interested in the observance of the law."*[1141]

[1141] Harris, *Africa*, pp. 166-67.

(Italics added). European invaders who looked at Africa through some bogus Christian filter beat Egun about the head over the evils of polygamy, while they conveniently and hypocritically ignored polygamous marriage arrangements of major biblical characters. And though polygamous (polyandrous) unions were not a consistent custom across Africa, it obviously served a purpose where instituted: traditional Africans implemented time-tested policies that made sense, and that *benefitted all*. Surprisingly, Harris cites a few advantages of polygamy that I gladly share:[1142]

> "Under the African marriage system," he says, " there are no ' women of the under world,' no ' slaves of the abyss.' *Every woman is above ground, protected and sheltered.*
>
> "Again: we are told by English periodicals that there are a little over five millions of unmarried women in Great Britain and the number is increasing. It is stated also that in the City of London alone there are 80,000 professional outcasts.
>
> "We are quite sure that there are not so many unmarried women in the whole of Africa between the Atlantic and the Red Sea and from the Cape to the Mediterranean.
>
> "Now, if polygamy has done nothing else it has saved and is saving Africa from all these evils. Is this nothing to be thankful for? We are not confronted by those frightful evils, which in Europe and America are the despair of the guardians of pubic order and the reformers of public morals.
>
> "Africa solved the marriage question for herself thousands of years ago. It has needed no revision and no amendment, because founded upon the law of Nature and not upon the dictum of any ecclesiastical hierarchy. Europe is still grappling with the problem,[1143] and finds that not only is her solution unsatisfactory, but out of it have grown other difficult questions. 'There is not one social question,' said Gambetta, 'there are social questions....'
>
> "The marriage laws of Europe have proved disastrous in the equatorial regions of the globe...."

Matrilineal systems of classical Africa made certain that the needs of women were properly cared for. The African-Maafan community can regain power by introducing some ancestral customs into our communities that hold individuals accountable for their actions against community members, thereby strengthening communal ties. The ancient technique of "sex without penetration" practiced by some groups might be beneficial.

[1142] Ibid., pp. 159-61.
[1143] While the divorce rate in the United States is roughly 53%, in some European countries the number is higher peaking at a stunning 70% in Belgium.

Another custom to consider is age-group initiations for our children that would establish common causes and interrupt violent gang activity; If African-Maafans do not assist our own children to properly develop into adulthood, no one else will. We can research and adopt (and adapt, if necessary) other time-tested practices from Egun that structure our families with sensible customs that feel comfortable to our psyches.

Africans Use "Honors System." Hurt by Lack of Trust Ask, "What! Do You Think I am a White Man?"

Turning now to war and violence, African scholar Chancellor Williams, whose book *The Destruction of Black Civilization* takes a comprehensive look at the traditions and history of African nations, describes ones that employed scare tactics in their efforts to ward off violence.[1144] Basil Davidson, author of *The African Genius*, speaks of the overriding importance of social stability among families. He confirms that many nations went to great lengths to avoid warring with others. But, if fighting was unavoidable looting the defeated and vanquished group's village afterward was offensive to Africans.[1145] Both of these researchers did extensive study of African social structures on the Continent. Of course, Middle Ages Europeans went to great lengths to shatter the peace of Africa. They increased tensions by redrawing established ancestral boundaries and trading/selling guns to only some. These tactics fueled tensions and created a power imbalance. Europeans destroyed Africa and her people *partly* because of their insatiable greed. On the matter of trade, Africans believed in honest trading. Herodotus describes the way ancient African countrymen conducted business:

> We have the same authority of the Carthaginians to affirm, that beyond the columns of Hercules [the Straits of Gibraltar] there is a country inhabited by a people with whom they have had commercial intercourse. It is their custom, on arriving among them, to unload their vessels, and dispose their goods along the shore! This done, they again embark, and make a great smoke from on board. The natives, seeing this, come down immediately to the shore, and placing a quantity of gold by way of exchange for the merchandize (sic), retire. The Carthaginians then land a second time, and if they think the gold equivalent, they take it and depart; if not, they again go on board their vessels. The inhabitants return and add more gold, till the crews are satisfied. The whole is conducted with the strictest integrity, for neither will the one touch the gold till they have left an adequate value in merchandize, nor will the other remove the

---

[1144] Chancellor Williams, *The Destruction of Black Civilization*, p. 164.
[1145] Davidson, *Genius*, p. 75.

goods till the Carthaginians have taken away the gold.[1146]

Herodotus' translator discloses that Moors carried on a similar "honor's system" in trading with supposedly "barbarous nations" along the River Niger adding, "They transact their exchange without seeing one another, or without the least instance of dishonesty or perfidiousness on either side." Cited as a witness to these types of transactions in 1721 is a naval officer: "The method of trading in some of these parts is very extraordinary, for they do not see the persons they trade with, but passing over a little river, leave their salt at the accustomed place, and retire. Then the people take the salt, and put into the same pot as much gold as they judge it worth, which if the Moors approve of, they take it away; otherwise they set the pot on edge, and retire again, and afterwards find either more gold or their salt returned."[1147] Other leaders employed weights and standards. There are stories of kings with weights made of gold, so important honest measurements were to them.

Newton describes accounts of the many ways Europeans dealt with Africans despite their fair, honest and open trade policies:

Accustomed thus to despise, insult, and injure the slaves on board [ships], it may be expected that the conduct of many of our people to the natives, with whom they trade, is, as far as circumstances admit, very similar; and it is so. *They are considered as a people to be robbed and spoiled with impunity. Every art is employed to deceive or wrong them. And he who has most in address in this way, has most to boast of.*

Not an article that is capable of diminution or adulteration is delivered genuine, or entire. The spirits are lowered by water. False heads are put into kegs that contain the gunpowder; so that, though the keg appears large, there is no more powder in it, than in a much smaller. The linen and cotton cloths are opened, and two or three yards, according to the length of the piece, cut off, not from the end, but out of the middle, where it is not so readily noticed.

The natives are cheated, in the number, weight, measure, or quality of what they purchase, in every possible way: and, by habit and emulation, a marvelous dexterity is acquired in these practices. And thus the natives in their turn, in proportion to their commerce with the Europeans, and (I am sorry to add) particularly with the English, become jealous, insidious, and revengeful.[1148] (Italics added).

While there were Chiefs who refused to do business with the European cheaters until they made group-wide apologies first, Newton explains that Europeans who deceived Africans faced threats of war, until amends were

---

[1146] William Beloe, trans., *Herodotus*, vol. 3. (London: Leigh & S. Sotheby, 1806), pp. 107-08.
[1147] Beloe, *Herodotus*, p. 109.
[1148] Newton, *Posthumous Works*, pp. 240-41.

made:

> *For so far their vindictive temper is restrained by their ideas of justice, they will not, often, revenge an injury received from a Liverpool ship, upon one belonging to Bristol or London.*
>
> *They will usually wait with patience the arrival of one, which, they suppose, by her sailing from the same place, has some connection with that which used them ill....*
>
> For, with a few exceptions, the English and the Africans, reciprocally, consider each other as consummate villains, who are always watching opportunities to do mischief. In short, we have, *I fear too deservedly, a very unfavourable character upon the coast. When I have charged a black with unfairness and dishonesty, he has answered, if able to clear himself, with an air of disdain, "What! Do you think I am a white man?"* [1149] (Italics added).

But, I would be remiss if I closed this section without stating that Europeans did not like to hear the word "no" from Africans when it came to making trades and doing business. Nor was it unusual for Europeans to launch attacks against nations and Chiefs who refused to do business with them.

Africans Choose Their Leaders, Evict Narcissists From Village

Researchers state that classical Africans selected their leaders, a custom very much unlike early European systems. Williams writes that Africans once had true democracy; the Chiefs were beholden to the people. Self-serving Chiefs were quickly dismissed. Sometimes dismissed Chiefs faced exile from their village and had to suffer having the story of their misdeeds spread far and wide.[1150] Herodotus provides an anecdote on the way ancient Ethiopians chose their leaders, "[They]... are said to be the tallest and handsomest men in the whole world. In their customs they differ greatly from the rest of mankind, and particularly in the way they choose their kings; for they find out the man who is the tallest of all the citizens, and of strength equal to his height, and appoint him to rule over them."[1151] As an aside, Herodotus tells us, too, that the Ethiopians had their own fountain of youth that allowed them to live to 120 years; he describes the dressing and burial of their dead in crystal coffins. And as caretakers of land that belonged to Egun, they passed it along the mother's line.

Much has been written about the self-rule of individual traditional African communities situated within more powerful nations. Newton provides us with an 18th century view of the Sherbro, an African people

---

[1149] Ibid., p. 241.
[1150] Williams, *Destruction*, pp. 96-98.
[1151] Rawlinson, *Herodotus*, vol. 2, p. 69.

that settled along the Sierra Leone coast:

> The Sherbro people live much in the patriarchal way. An old man usually presides in each town, whose authority depends more on his years, than on his possessions: and he, who is called the king, is not easily distinguished, either by state or wealth, from the rest. But the different districts, which seem to be, in many respects independent of each other, are incorporated, and united, by means of an institution which pervades them all, and is called the Purrow. The persons of this order, who are very numerous, seem, very much, to resemble the Druids, who once presided in our island.[1152]

Newton further describes the Purrow as having "legislative and executive authority." Sherbro laws that Newton says, "in the main are wise and good" forbade them from shedding another person's blood; punished some forms of theft with servitude (not European-structured slavery); and allowed a harmed individual to seek damages until he was satisfied:

> So that, if a rich man seduces the wife of a poor man, he has it in his power to change places with him; for he may send for every article in his house, one by one, till he says, "I have enough." The only alternative, is personal slavery [servitude]."[1153]

"Your Money or Your Life" is Not an African Tradition: African Healing

As for medicines, Egun had the help of nature in curing ailments. Known as healers, Sangoma, Ithwasa, Musawo, etc., depending on the nation, these Africans became skillful physicians who after studying nature and human anatomy for tens of thousands of years learned to effectively use tree juices, barks, roots, plants, etc., for healing. (It was not unheard of for Africans to place animal blood in our diet, or in spiritual ceremonies). Natural cures healed major and minor aches and pains; cured diseases; healed wounds; and addressed psychological issues caused by spiritual discontent. Perfumes and insecticides came from plants, too. As did soaps. Egun were a clean people and had several techniques to wash dirt away. One was to harvest plants containing ingredients that lather when rubbed or mixed with water. Another is described by a European who journeyed across South Africa during the 1790's and recommends its exportation to Great Britain: "Canna... is that plant from the ashes of which almost all the soap, that is used in the colony is made. These ashes when carefully burnt and collected, are a pure white caustic alkalai a solution of which, mixed up with the oily fat of the large broad tails of the sheep of the colony, and boiled slowly for five or six days takes the constituency and the quality of

---

[1152] Newton, *Posthumous Works*, p. 243.
[1153] Ibid. p. 244.

an excellent soap... besides serving the colony, for the whole consumption of Great Britain...."[1154] Our strong, beautiful and naturally bright white teeth represent the high level of dental hygiene used by Egun.

Western Pharmaceuticals Make Millions Adopting African Medicines

Classical African treatments for illnesses were routinely mocked by invading Europeans but upon examining this essay readers understand a bit more why that was the case: Obviously, Dark, Medieval and Renaissance era Europeans falsely believed their science proved the effectiveness of cures utilizing human body parts. In fact, despite that unenlightened persons, or racists — sometimes they are the same — mock our traditional medical practices, pharmaceutical[1155] companies quietly steal into Africa to study the ancient traditions of Sangoma,[1156] and to extract Africa's natural resources.[1157] Western companies make billions[1158] of dollars from traditional medicines derived from our homeland while many African and African-Maafans not only lack health insurance, but also often cannot afford the high cost of medicines. (Many African citizens remain poor despite the vast resources that continue to grow the wealth of European countries and swell the personal pockets of African leaders who have dark skin, but use "a white man's brain" to join in the schemes of Europeans to exploit their own people and stall African progress. Certain African-Americans who grow rich in the United States while their constituencies and congregations languish in poverty can be similarly denounced). Additionally, one of the more fatal holdovers from medieval Europe is the lack of universal healthcare. When some Anglo-Americans argue against universal healthcare, they are tapping into some very ancient genetic coding:

> Physicians are described as wearing expensive robes of silk with trimmings of fur. "Physic" in *Piers Plowman* wears a hood richly trimmed with fur, and gold buttons on his cloak. They demanded large fees and received them. In other cases a man might choose whether to purchase or to do without; but in illness there was left him only the highwayman's choice, "Your money or your life."

[1154] John Barrow, *An Account of Travels into the Interior of Southern Africa*, pp. 91-92.
[1155] Priya Shetty. "Integrating modern and traditional medicine: Facts and figures." *SciDevNet*. 30 June 2010. Web. 22, Aug. 2014.
[1156] Western psychologists quietly study the effectiveness of Sangoma healing practices.
[1157] Donald E. Bierer, Thomas J. Carlson, and Steven R. King. "Network Science: Shaman Pharmaceuticals: Integrating Indigenous Knowledge, Tropical Medicinal Plants, Medicine, Modern Science and Reciprocity into a Novel Drug Discovery Approach." *Shaman Pharmaceuticals, Inc.* Web. 12 May 2014.
[1158] "Herbal/Traditional Products in South Africa." *Euromonitor International*. March 2014. Web. 12 June 2014.

Poor folk had not the money necessary to buy their lives of these great doctors, and therefore they went with their ailments to the barber. He was permitted by law to apply plasters and ointments to wounds that did not threaten to become dangerous, and often to give simple remedies. In most diseases, the first treatment was to bleed the patient, and the barber's pole of to-day is a reminder of the custom.

Traditional Africans Take From the Land Only What's Needed

Concerning the vast natural resources in the African land of plenty, early Europeans write of their surprise at finding low hanging, delicious fruit everywhere. Likewise, they marvel at the gold and silver routinely found scattered upon the ground. Seeing *precious metals* randomly strewn across the Earth may sound strange to our 21st century ears, but Egun tempered their desires. (Also, many African nations traded with Cowry shells, kola nuts, copper, etc. Gold was used in ornamentation (jewelry, utensils, weapons, etc.) and traded with Asian, Arabian and European countries).

A 19th century Anglo-American *missionary* to West Africa, Mungo Park, notes the bounties available for export including gold, ivory, and honey. He writes about other local products such as cotton, indigo and tobacco that Africans produce: "But of all these (which can only be obtained by cultivation and labour) the natives raise sufficient only for their own immediate use; nor, under the present system of their laws, manners, trade, and government, can any thing farther be expected from them.... *Nothing is wanting to this end but example to enlighten the minds of the natives, and instruction to enable them to direct their industry to proper objects*.... Much more did I lament, *that a people, of manners and dispositions so gentle and benevolent,* should either be left, as they now are, immersed in the gross and uncomfortable blindness of pagan superstition, *or permitted to become converts to a system of bigotry and fanaticism, which, without enlightening the mind, often debases the heart.*"[1159] (Italics added).

Park's thoughts are notable for several reasons including that Africans took from the land only what they needed and when they needed to. However, Park's cultural frame of reference is so finely tuned toward greed he misses learning a valuable African lesson altogether: Take only what you need. In his covetous mind the fault lies with African "paganism." Park's goal is to "direct their industry to proper objects" that will likely make him and others like him very rich men, while at the same time subjugate the African body, and mind to the European agenda.

[1159] Mungo Park, *Testimony in favour of the possibility of Civilizing the Africans*, The African Repository and Colonial Journal, vol.4, no.1 (1829) pp. 76-77.

An Introduction to a Few Sturdy Civilizations Egun Developed

Egun were an astute people who found benefit in erecting sound civilizations with healthy people of good mind and character; Encouraging Africans to develop both these aspects led to stable and secure societies for everyone. Innovative Africans designed the original pattern for what a successful culture should look like and then spread that wisdom around the globe. In 1906, Flora Shaw, mentioned earlier, shares her opinion on enterprising Africans after studying the cultural history of Sudan and Nigeria:

> When the history of Negroland [sic] comes to be written in detail, it may be found that the kingdoms lying towards the eastern end of the Soudan [sic] were the home of races who inspired, rather than of races who received, the traditions of civilisation [sic] for us with the name of ancient Egypt. For they cover on either side of the Upper Nile, between the latitudes of 10° and 17°, territories[1160] in which are found monuments more ancient than the oldest Egyptian monuments. If this should prove to be the case, and the civilised [sic] world be forced to recognise [sic] in a black people the fount of its original enlightenment, it may happen that we shall have to revise entirely our view of the black races, and regard those who now exist as the *decadent representatives of an almost forgotten era, rather than as the embryonic possibility of an era yet to come.*[1161] (Italics added).

Modern researches into ancient African societies prove Africans had established advanced civilizations and accomplished great achievements in Africa, dispelling earlier European anti-Africa myths and propaganda. In fact, when the Europeans sailed the seas to the rest of the world for the first time during the early 1400's, they became witnesses to successful African civilizations that had existed for thousands of years. Returning to Dubois, he expresses shock to see Djenné, a place he narcissistically describes in all appearances as "a real town in the European sense of the word.... Here are true houses; not primitive shelters crowned with roofs that are either flat or in the shape of an inverted funnel. Streets too; not seed-plots[1162] of buildings amongst which one wanders by paths that serpentine more than the most serpentining serpent."[1163]

[1160] Parts of the Sudan were flooded in 1970 to make way for the Aswan Dam that submerged many Nubian structures and artifacts.
[1161] Shaw, *Tropical*, pp. 17-18.
[1162] Africans copied nature in designing their homes and villages. See Ron Eglash's "African Fractals: Modern Computing and Indigenous Design," a fascinating book on the complex math behind classical African structures. Fractal, the term used to describe the nature-inspired African design concept first entered European languages during the 1970's.
[1163] Dubois, *Timbuctoo*, pp. 83- 84.

If we refer to the antique bas-reliefs which reproduce the principal features of the ancient Egyptian habitations, and to the works of the orientalists [sic], we shall find they agree in every particular with the buildings of Jenne [sic]. 'The private houses were simple, and were not constructed of stone nor granite, as were the temples and palaces, but of rough bricks. The walls were plastered within and without, and enclosed a suite of rooms which were not uniformly disposed, but were divided according to the taste of the proprietor. They consisted of a ground floor and a second floor surmounted by a terrace. The approaches to the wealthiest houses were adorned with pylons and obelisks. The summits and angles of the clay walls were finished by a kind of framework of reeds held together by transverse bands. The roof was flat, and formed by placing planks across the length and breadth of the house; branches and rushes were strewn upon them, and the whole was covered by a thin layer of earth reduced to the consistency of mud. This covering slightly projected from all sides of the wall.'

The same methods of construction are pursued in the buildings of Jenne [sic]; all these details are to be found, with others that are veritably stupefying when seen in the heart of a negro country. A system of baked pipes is established in every dwelling to carry away the household water, and latrines, with perfectly constructed drainage, are established on all the terraces. The survival, through all those ages, of this method of building is due, not only to the fact that the town has never been destroyed, but also to the great durability of the houses.[1164]

In addition to a host of researchers who confess that advanced African civilizations were obvious to ancient travelers, there are reports from archaeologist Leo Frobenius. He writes of 15th century Europeans shocked to see well-planned streets and prosperous industries. In other words, there were well-organized, constitutional governments in place throughout the Continent. Moreover, some Africans loved to dress stylishly, a tradition that Diodorus opines came to us by way of the Kemetan leader Narmer.

Arab travelers and historians recorded their impressions of parts of West Africa. One, Ibn Khaldún, writes this about Ghana:

> "When the conquests of the West (by the Arabs) was completed, and merchants began to penetrate into the interior, they saw no nation of the Blacks so mighty as Ghánah, which... is divided into two parts, standing on both banks of the Nile, and ranks among the largest and most populous cities of the world."[1165]

Ghana was rich and formidable. During the 12th century the king is recorded as living in a fortified castle with glass windows. It was elaborately decorated with pictures and sculptures. The king is said to have held court surrounded by men bearing gold encrusted weaponry.

[1164] Ibid., pp. 151-52.
[1165] William Desborough Cooley, *The Negroland of the Arabs*, p. 61.

In keeping with an ancient African custom, travelers to 14th century Mali could only enter the central city by permission. According to Shaw, Arab traveler Ibn Battuta impressed by the immense wealth displayed by Mansa Musa during his sojourn to Egypt a few years earlier sought and was granted permission to visit "Negroland." A distinguished group, including "men of letters, lawyers, jurisconsults and a judge" greeted Battuta in Mali, according to Shaw.

Fourteenth century Mali was indeed impressive. The Sultan held court with the utmost ceremony and splendor. Political, judicial and social life was highly organized with schools present in most towns. There was an impressive military divided into combat units. Like many Africans, the people of Mali dressed in silks and decorated their bodies with gold and silver ornaments. In this passage Battuta highly praises the people of Mali, applauding them for their embrace of civility and justice:

> "Of all people," he thinks that "the blacks are those who most detest injustice. Their Sultan never forgives any one who has been guilty of it." He also praises the "complete and general safety which is enjoyed in the country. Neither those who travel nor those who remain at home have anything to fear from brigands, thieves, or violent persons." "The blacks do not," he says, " confiscate the goods of white men who die in the country, even though it may be a question of immense treasure. On the contrary, their goods are always placed in charge of some white man, trusted by the community, until those who have a right to them can apply and take possession of them."[1166]

Being a Muslim country meant Malians, unfortunately, felt little kinship towards non-Muslims and conducted vicious raids on African villages in search of slave labor, though Battuta writes that slaves were not mistreated.

Also, we have the refreshing autobiography of Olaudah Equiano. Born in 1745, he was son to a village Chief in the Benin Empire. Equiano's glimpse into African life before slave raiders snatched him from his family's compound forever banishes the European's oft-painted negative portrayals of Africans as man-eating, always drum-beating, fetish-bearing dwarfs. Equiano mentions a bountiful land that left his community wanting for little, and introduces readers to African traditions of ancestor-veneration, wedding customs, and living arrangements. No one was idle and there were no beggars because everyone worked together to sustain the community. It was not all work, either. Equiano remembers a home filled with poets, musicians and dancers who used graceful body movements to tell stories. Citizens dressed simply and women adorned their arms and legs with gold.

[1166] Shaw, *Tropical*, p. 144.

Another description of Benin [Ile-Ibinu, later named Ubini],[1167] comes from Captain Alan Boisragon who gives a brief history of her from 16th century eyewitness accounts. He writes, "From a Dutch account written a few years later it appears to have been quite a magnificent city. The narrator talks of entering the city on horseback through a gate where there was a very thick high earthen bulwark, with a deep broad ditch, which, however, was dry and full of trees. Later writers speak of Ubini being surrounded by a high wall... of an enormous broad street running through the city, and other great streets running off it-so long that it was impossible to see the end of them. He also gives a description of the King's Court, which seems to have been very grand...."[1168] Ubini's capital city fell under siege to British troops who burned and looted her in 1897. The founding of Ubini extends to a time well before the Common Era. Citizens of Ubini (1440-1897) were known for their incredibly exquisite art and iron casting.

As part of Egun's many achievements, creative and inventive Africans learned to cultivate palm trees so that they produced leaves from which delicate threads were harvested. These velvety threads were woven into fine damask and brocade patterns often worn by the king. Also, Africans harvested tree barks to weave durable netting and waterproof tents.

Yet, despite these and other displays of sophistication and organization Europeans showed no hesitation in disrupting African lifestyles. Educating our African minds to the progress achieved in Africa and comparing it to Europe's social, moral and emotional development of the same period will give us a better understanding of the considerable challenges that Africa's enormous natural resources and talented and gifted people presented to the European cultural and social paradigm.

[1167] "Eweka was sent to the town as king. He bought a slave named Ubini; when he died he buried him near him, and told all the world that whoever came and asked the name of this country should be told *Ubini* or *Aiye*. So the Benin people became very plenty." Charles Hercules Read and Ormonde Maddock Dalton, *Antiquities of the City of Benin and West Africa*, p. 5.
[1168] Boisragon, *Benin*, pp. 8-9.

17

AFRICANS FACE TROUBLE IN EUROPE'S PARADIGM

In 1802 during Haiti's battle for independence: "Battle after battle was fought, and all the resources of European military skill were opposed to the furious onsets of the negro masses. All was in vain: before October, the negroes, under the command of [Jean-Jacques] Dessalines [d. 1806] and [Henri] Christophe [d. 1820], had driven the French out of Fort Dauphin, Fort de Paix, and other important positions."[1169] Toussaint L'Ouverture [d. 1803], Dessalines, Christophe, together with hundreds of thousands of Africans, championed the cause for a free Haiti. After these Africans fought for and won their freedom, commerce and prosperity increased on the island. Both L'Ouverture and Dessalines: "Laid the foundation of a new state with the foresight of a mind that could discern what would decay and what would endure. St. Domingo [Haiti] rose from its ashes; the reign of law and justice was established; those who had been slaves were now citizens. Religion again reared her altars; and on the sites of ruins were built new edifices.... In consequence of these arrangements, a most surprising change took place: the plantations were again covered with crops; the sugar-houses and distilleries were re-built; the export trade began to revive; and the population, orderly and well-behaved, began to increase.

"In addition to these external evidences of good government, the island exhibited those finer evidences which consist in mental culture and the civilization of manners. Schools were established, and books became common articles in the cottages of the negro laborers. Music and the theatre were encouraged; and public worship was conducted with all the usual pomp of the Romish church. The whites, the mulattoes, and the blacks mingled in the same society, and exchanged with each other all the courtesies of civilized intercourse."[1170] The years following Haiti's hard won independence filled Haitians with hope and great expectations for the future. Africans were expert at empire building, and Toussaint along with his many followers laid a strong foundation to erect just such a one. But, danger was at hand. One European researcher warns readers, "Should they adhere to the basis on which they have founded their proceedings, and remain unmolested by European powers, they may arrive at the most

---

[1169] Blake, *Slavery*, p. 277.
[1170] Ibid., pp. 272-73.

enviable state of grandeur and felicity...."[1171] Unfortunately, Haitians were molested by powers, both foreign and domestic. Napoleon led the charge. Determined to stop the progress and "successes of the Africans" of Haiti, he ordered the arrest and imprisonment of Toussaint; the great African warrior who led the successful charge against the French would never see Haiti again. Later, the French government shackled Haitians with an outrageously enormous debt for *depriving them of profits* from slave labor. The French government backed up their demands for those reparations with gunships.

Napoleon's desires to hold back African progress mirrors those of the FBI's whose goal was "to prevent the rise of a leader who might unify and electrify... and prevent the growth of [Black nationalist] groups among America's youths."[1172]

Such regressive attitudes might fall under the heading of genetic inadequacy felt by minority Europeans/Anglos living in a world dominated with people of color.[1173] Highly esteemed German philosopher Arthur Schopenhauer describes the concept this way, "I may here express my opinion in passing that the white colour [sic] of the skin is not natural to man, but that by nature he has a black or brown skin... that consequently a white man has never originally sprung from the womb of nature, and that thus there is no such thing as a white race, much as this is talked of, but every white man is a faded or bleached one... Therefore in sexual love nature strives to return to dark hair and brown eyes as the primitive [prime, first] type; but the white colour [sic] of the skin has become a second nature...."[1174] There is plenty to fear, and admire in the color to which nature defaults.[1175] The fear for some is in the all-consuming dominance of blackness, while for others admiration comes from understanding all the embryonic possibilities that exist within that realm of blackness.

Those who may wish to reject that concept might take a close look at the European pattern of destroying established brown and black societies in an act that I call de-storying. Because in de-storying cultures invaders attempt to remove all traces of the indigenous story in order to replace it with a European one. Or as the stories of Rig-Veda demonstrate, Europeans obscure their ugly deeds in mystical legends of gods conquering ungodly people. So, accounts that should serve as reminders of heinous crimes

---

[1171] Marcus Rainsford, An Historical Account of the Black Empire of Hayti, p. 360.
[1172] "The Federal Bureau of Investigation," C. Sullivan, *FBI Memorandum*, February 29, 1968.
[1173] The idea of genetic annihilation is explained in The Isis Papers: The Keys To The Colors, Dr. Frances Cress Welsing, Preface vi.
[1174] Arthur Schopenhauer, *The World As Will And Idea*, p. 358.
[1175] Looking beneath the surface (of the earth), and beyond this planet (in the ether) reveals the realm of black's dominion.

against humanity instead become mythical delusions or *adventures* of supposedly great explorers. Enter the Cristoforo Colombo (Columbus) fantasy play. It is only after centuries of disinformation that *his* story reveals the heinous cruelties meted out to native peoples by Colombo and his men, though now storytellers distort Colombo's acts as atypical. They do not disclose that Colombo and his men's belligerent behaviors were normal for medieval Europeans of that era. The fact is that during 15th century Italy, "nothing was cheaper than human life" when hunting dogs were "tearing human bodies."[1176] That was the case with Giovanni Maria (d. 1412) who attacked his own citizens with vicious dogs, and forbade them to utter the words, peace and war.[1177] On the other hand, the personal accounts of the tribal people Colombo slaughtered are forever lost, as are the great history of the Indus Valley citizens, and the narratives of some of the great civilizations of Africa.

As a play on the phrase American exceptional-ism, I use the term American (self) deception-ism. For here is where self-deception - an invisible fortification that blinds the collective mind of the domineering culture in the United States - makes its stand. Anglo-Americans can not fathom that ancestral Europeans were acting as barbarian invaders forcing their way into Africa,[1178] nor do they consider the obvious gross irony of a system that implements vile inhumane practices in order to supposedly *save* others. (In fact, they tell themselves slavery was gentle. Recall the croaking frogs story from an earlier chapter).

Any discourse on colonialism and its accompanying *strange institution* argues that Africans possessed inferior customs/standards of living; whatever happened had to happen so that the daily lives of Africans improved, they tell themselves. The self-deception opened the door to payment[1179] of reparations to criminal slave holders (aka kidnappers) making them - rather than Africans forcefully removed from their homes, and forced to labor without pay - de jure *victims of a system of their own creation and management*. On the other hand, the sufferers of the brutal structure became detested outcasts. The promise of partial reparation, revoked.

[1176] Burckhardt, *Renaissance*, p. 14.
[1177] Dogs were used against African-Americans chanting peace slogans in 20th century United States, and those seeking freedom much earlier.
[1178] During their colonization of North America, Europeans believed that pestilences killing Indians were "attributed in a notable work of that period to the Divine purpose of clearing New England for the heralds of the gospel; on the other hand, plagues which destroyed the white population were attributed by the same authority to devils and witches " White, *Warfare*, vol. 2, p. 85.
[1179] It is preposterous that Haitians, who had fought for and won their freedom, made payment to Europeans. Reparations were extorted from them with the help of 500 French canons aimed at the tiny island in the name of former slaveholders.

The deceptive narrative reaches its illogical conclusion once Europeans and Anglo-Americans portray these same tortured Africans as violent, perpetrators of crimes and as lazy, unintelligent people who lack the ability to care for themselves, despite that they spent hundreds of years bearing the personal burdens of Europeans; despite that Egun played the largest part in growing and sustaining their economies; and despite that African labor and resources made Europeans, and Anglo-Americans the wealthiest people on this planet - the frameworks of Wall Street and the stock market were constructed from the bones of long-ago dead Africans; and despite that it was Europeans who perpetrated crimes against Africans: The hunter (Europeans/Anglos) is always the hero of his own story, no matter how unlikely - or bizarre - the narrative.

Expanding on the words of a social activist, brown, black and yellow countries where the Europeans landed and transgressed need independent crime scene investigators. Godard, mentioned earlier in this essay, informs us that, "the truth that all the talk about the ultimate good of conquered races proceeds from pure self-deception, whereby we conceal the fact that we are merely pursuing our own interests, or gratifying our own passions, or asserting our own supremacy. There is only one logical basis for Imperialism and that is found in the doctrine of the superior person, the doctrine of the divine right, the doctrine of the chosen nation; in short, the doctrine, by whatsoever name known, of which the foundation is inequality."[1180]

It should be unnecessary to add that people convalescing in such a state of madness are unable to grasp real events, or relate them coherently. Nor are they able to confront the white washing of a social construct that not only subjects them too, but also stunts their emotional development.

Owning Our African Past

The story of events that transpired in Africa belongs to Egun. It was always our story to tell, because invaders broke into our homes. After a burglary takes place in the United States, the police ask the residents for details of the transgression before they begin their search for criminals. When we tell our Afristory we control the scenes, actions and dialogue of the characters. We can tell the world what we were doing before Europeans invaded our homes. We can tell the world how the invasion negatively affected our children and us. We can humanize Egun and share their tears. Then we can stop feeling shame for what Europeans *did to them*, and by extension, what they did to us. Events on the Continent did not occur because of African cultures, but because of European ones.

However, if we continue to allow Europeans to focus the story on *"those*

[1180] Godard, *Racial Supremacy*, p. 58.

savage Africans" we will never consider the cruelty acted out against Egun as having any significance. Furthermore, the Europeans' crimes against humanity will continue to escape review, and they will reject responsibility for their actions. Their cultural construct will continue to ignore the reality that chaos (a lack of balance) is not only unproductive, but is unsustainable; unchecked gluttony is not sustainable, as its goal is to consume everything regardless of the consequences. Closing the present paradigm, that makes Europeans the focus, and opening an African one begins the long journey of seeking competent answers to legitimate questions. We can draw critical conclusions from our questions, then decide whether we want to take part in their chaotic pattern, relegated to the role of dark-skinned Caucasians; a socially-engineered people (no doubt who also lack any historical cultural heritage) who think and act as they do, only with darker hue, as Johnston predicted in 1903. Or we can decide to join together with African Maafans and continental Africans to begin to build a better world for our children.

> We should flatly reject the European definition that measures human development by the size of guns, cigars, classical music, or whether or not one uses a dinner fork, etc., while conveniently ignoring human dignity as the most important element of civilization. It is dangerous to let materialism outrank humanity on a scale held in balance by Nature.

Those who would give Europeans a pass by suggesting that past actions are indicative of an era when rules (and people) were different coddle actors whose poor practices and behaviors toward humanity should never be tolerated that. Regardless of the era it is unacceptable to excuse or shrug away practices that negate or diminish people. Indicting bad practices from the past ensures they do not continue into the present and future; but they must first be recognized, and acknowledged.

Why Africans Feel Shame When Europeans Feel None: Exposing a Few of Europe's Tricks of the Trade

I do not want to form an impression that Africans were saintly citizens who never did any wrong. (Though Williams indicates that traditional Africans were a relatively peaceful, sedentary people). Africans may not have behaved in the most honorable fashion every time, overtime. That is not the point. The point is that we were never the people Europeans told us we were then, nor are we who their media tell us we are now. We did not do the things they accused us of doing. And, even if we committed all the atrocities Europeans accused us of committing, they did not have the moral authority to "fix us." Africans are no worse than Europeans and Europeans are no better than Africans. Europe's horrific practices in the world yesterday and today re-enforces this reality. They were not the people they told us they were, either. Nor are they who they tell us they are now. Those skeletons that are pushed to the back of Europe's collective closet are real human ones. This is the powerful take away of this essay, a truth that many of us can open ourselves to and embrace. Already, we have luxurious remnants of a functional, healthy ancient culture that we can dress ourselves up in, but first we have to shed the rags our present paradigm has forced upon us. In the year 2015 African-Americans celebrate 150 years since Egun fought for and won freedom that had been our birthright from Nature the moment the Sun shone its radiance on the beautiful blue-black skin of the original African man, and woman. Yet, chains bind the minds of far too many of us. The words of Harry H. Johnston reverberate from the past, and stay as relevant today as they were 110 years ago:

> *Paganism will disappear. The continent will soon be divided between nominal Christians, and nominal Muhammadans....* The Arab and the Hamite for religious reasons may strive again and again to shake off the Christian yoke, but I strongly doubt whether there will be any universal mutiny of the black man against the white. --- The negro has no idea of racial affinity. He *will equally ally himself to the white or to the yellow races in order to subdue his fellow black, or to regain his freedom from the domination of another negro tribe.* There may be here and there a revolt against the white rule in such and such a state; but *the diverse civilizations under which the African will be trained, and the different languages he will be taught to talk, will be sufficient to make him as dissimilar in each national development as the white man has become in Europe.* And just as it would need some amazing and stupendous event to cause all Asia to rise -as one man against the invasion of Europe, *so it is difficult to conceive that the black man will eventually form one united negro people demanding autonomy, and putting an end to the control of the white man, and to the immigration, settlement, and intercourse of superior races from Europe and Asia.*[1181] (Italics added).

Johnston's predictions were much more than wishful thinking on his part. Medieval documents show evidence of practical methods employed by European agents that manipulated the circumstances, hearts and minds of Egun. The manual *Guide Pratique de l'Européen dans l'Afrique Occidentale (1902)* contains many such techniques. The guide encourages French citizens living part-time and permanently on the Continent to have sex with African women.[1182] Several reasons are given for this advice: maintaining good hygiene and decreasing boredom and alcoholism are some of the more mundane ones listed. More nefarious reasons include the belief that sexual liaisons with daughters of Chiefs strengthen relations between Africans and Europeans, and ease European management of the

---

[1181] Harry H. Johnston, *A History of the Colonization of Africa By Alien Races*, pp. 283-84.
[1182] Louis Barot,, *Guide Pratique de l'Européen dans l'Afrique Occidentale*, pp. 528-31.

African territories (probably giving Europeans access to secret African rituals, plans, alliances, etc.).

This *bedroom diplomacy,* according to the guide, had successfully led to "white weddings," and treaty ratifications. The children from these unions and their ability to adapt to the hot African climate seem to have been of great importance to the overall scheme. As they matured, these offspring of European fathers received slightly better treatment than full-blooded Africans. Europe's leaders expected these children as adults to align their interests with Europe and to work on its behalf to subjugate the African populations. This scheme, along with a few others listed below, was successful in securing Europe's domination over Africans. However, as full of guile as the French plot is, it is not an original one. Williams notes that European men have a long, successful history of mingling sexually[1183] with African women as a way of infiltrating the indigenous African cultures for the strategic purposes of securing leadership positions and gaining power. In fact, in their journals European men brag of the ease with which they have sexual intercourse with African women in exchange for cheap trinkets and without marital bonding. This is said to have been the situation in 1913 South Africa:

> The percentage of unmarried white men outside missionary circles who cohabit with African womanhood is deplorably high—probably more than 90 per cent. The races differ but little so far as the practice is concerned, but continental nationalities live this life openly with the one redeeming feature that, generally speaking, the coloured [sic] offspring is cared for and educated. The Britisher lives the life, brings forth, and then, wherever practicable, abandons the children, the only redeeming feature in his case being that the Britisher is, generally speaking, so thoroughly ashamed of himself that everything is done to cover up his shame....
>
> The African has an extraordinarily logical mind, and is now questioning why his women folk should be debauched by white men whereas such grave penalties are attached to sexual relationship between the African and white women....
>
> It is not difficult to picture that indignant Chief before the Natal Commissioner, who, in vehement and passionate language, suiting gesture to words with dramatic effect, asked; "What are these white things, which their girls were bringing home on their backs in such numbers What did the Government mean by allowing their girls to bear so many white children? Did they want to breed muledrivers? (in allusion to the fact that men of mixed race invariably drive Government conveyances.)"[1184]

[1183] Williams, *Destruction,* pp. 71-79.
[1184] Harris, *Africa,* pp. 163-66.

Colorism is a psychological disease that manifests itself broadly within the African and African-Maafan communities. Europeans were clearly obsessed with the various hues of Africans as their journals contain a vast assortment of physical descriptions of Africans. From Egun's sometimes 'yellow' or 'tan' skin tone Europeans assumed particular clans descended from or once mixed with Asian races. Europeans especially noted complexions of babies born to African women and European fathers. Africans whose physical features closely approximated Europeans (pale skin, beak-like nose) were automatically deemed higher functioning and civilized. Europeans treated these children less harshly. Africans with dark skin and broad, flat noses experienced oppression. The socially engineered enmity between the Hutu and Tutsi clans is an example of the types of problems the weapon of division can incite once Africans have allowed Europeans to distract us from unity. Colorism is very much a part of social politics of the United States according to the article, *Lighter Skin Reduces Prison Time Among Black Women,* authored by The Sentencing Project.

Brutal laws and imprisonment: Regressive laws implemented to restrict fair competition and designed to dispirit Africans. Unfair laws of the United States like sentencing disparity laws and poll taxes are well known. The Supreme Court of the United State's recent ruling that gutted voting rights is the Anglo-American's shot across the bow of their intentions to return us to the issues of "the good ole days." The South African government employed similarly unfair laws designed to negatively affect Africans socially, physically, psychologically, and economically. The phenomena of police shootings gripping the African-American communities compels me to include examples of old South African laws to show how closely that system mirrored antebellum South; but I include others because of their similarity to practices and events current within the United States. Europeans and Anglos found a formula that worked against Africans and so they worked it across African populations:

> The laws relating to natives and coloured [sic] people in the Transvaal are so severe that they cannot be carried out — except sporadically. It is impossible for such people to exist in any town or village without continually violating some often preposterous law or regulation having the force of law. But the police are familiar with these laws, and thus have endless opportunities of working off grudges or levying blackmail. These police are either Dutchmen of the ' poor white ' class — a class often physically and mentally below the native — or else big, brawny Zulus, who cannot speak the language of the Transvaal natives.[1185]
>
> A special law relating to Cape Town and Port Elizabeth has been passed, which provides that no native who is not a registered voter can sleep in either of these

---

[1185] William Charles Scully, "The Colour Problem in South Africa," *The Edinburgh Review*, vol. 230, no. 469 (1919) p. 85.

cities except a domestic servant on his master's premises. Locations with sheet-iron huts have been established in the environs, but these are disgracefully overcrowded — as many as sixteen people sometimes sleeping in one small room. It is in fact impossible for all the natives employed at the docks, or in handling merchandise, or at other unskilled labour, to be accommodated in the locations referred to. Nevertheless natives are continually arrested for breaking a law which it is a physical impossibility for them to obey. Yet the very existence of the communities involved depends upon the labour of these natives. If the latter were to be eliminated, all business would stop as inevitably as would a watch with a broken spring.[1186]

Some of the municipal regulations in force are grotesquely oppressive. For instance, no girl of the age of sixteen is permitted to live, even with her parents, in a location unless she be in European service. In the Free State there is a law in force — common to all municipal areas — under which all females over the age of sixteen have to take out passes, for which a substantial charge is made. The police are in the habit of making domiciliary visits, and bitter complaints are made regarding their treatment of girls approaching the taxable age. The municipal locations are unspeakably wretched places, as a rule. The miserable huts are built upon small plots, and are thus huddled grievously together. Yet in many of these locations any native found outside the door of his hut after nine o'clock P.M. is liable to arrest, fine, and imprisonment. Section 33 of the municipal regulations for the town of Reitz reads as follows :— *'Every resident in the location shall be obliged to report immediately to the Town Clerk the arrival of any strange native whose apparent intention is to remain for twenty-four hours, and shall point out where such strange native is staying.'*[1187]

On the 24th October 1916 a native girl, named Sanna, was alleged to have deserted from her master, an Englishman. A native policeman was sent to her home to arrest her. The ordinary procedure would have been to issue a summons. The girl's father, when told that the girl was to be brought before a special justice of the peace — a class of official usually both ignorant and prejudiced — refused to permit the girl to go, stating at the same time his willingness to convey her himself to be tried before the resident magistrate of the district. The policeman departed and returned with the girl's master and another man, all three carrying firearms. The girl, her father and mother and another man were the only ones at the kraal. The armed party shot the girl's father dead with a rifle bullet, wounded the girl severely in the back and thighs with shot, beat her mother unmercifully with the butt of a rifle, and broke a gun-stock over the second man. The three braves were tried before the circuit court and acquitted.[1188]

[1186] Ibid., pp. 80-81.
[1187] Ibid., p. 83.
[1188] Ibid., p. 80.

The conditions under which the natives live in the locations established in the environs of the towns of the Cape Province—and, in fact, of South Africa generally—are most pitiful. There is no fixity of tenure, and the plots allotted are preposterously small. The inhabitants are heavily taxed, but the taxes are not spent for their benefit. Utter squalor and discomfort usually reign. At places such as Port Elizabeth, Grahamstown, and Somerset East, while the European death-rate is about 14 per 1000, that of the natives is in the neighbourhood [sic] of 70. There is no possibility of social or intellectual advancement. Municipal officers administer the local bye-laws [sic] fitfully, often reviving some long dormant regulation, of the existence of which the natives were unaware. During an outbreak of typhus fever in Queenstown, Cape Province, in 1917, sick people were pulled out of bed, and their bedding, after being soaked in disinfecting liquid, was thrown back at them, wet.[1189]

On the 30th January 1913 two natives, a man and a woman, left the farm 'Lowlands', in the Ladybrand district of the Free State, with eleven head of cattle and thirty-eight sheep in their possession. Their destination was Basutoland. As they did not arrive at their home, a search was instituted by their friends. The stock was traced to one, P--, a Boer, who was known to be in financial difficulties. He had sold some of the stock, and with the proceeds satisfied a judgment against him, in which a writ had been taken out. In P-- 's maize field two skeletons were found, with bullets in the skulls. These bullets corresponded with a revolver found in P-- 's possession. P-- was tried before the circuit court at Bloemfontein in the following September, and acquitted by a jury of Englishmen. The verdict was hailed with the wildest enthusiasm, the accused being carried out of court on the shoulders of his admirers. In the following April P--was tried before the circuit court at Ficksburg for theft of the stock, found guilty, and sentenced to three years' imprisonment with hard labour.[1190]

To stifle African independence Europeans displaced them from their ancestral lands, reserving the most productive acreages for European invaders. The use of malicious schemes to push Africans into surrendering to the European status quo had the side effect of forcing many Africans into employment in servile positions on plantations where owners demanded they wear European clothing. One proposal to the East African Native Labour Commission suggested: "Making the native wear European clothes, in order to buy which he will be compelled to seek work from the whites."[1191] Another unscrupulous person proposed that: "If the Reserves were cut down sufficiently, it would undoubtedly have the effect of turning off a large number of natives, who would be made to work for their

---

[1189] Ibid., p. 81.
[1190] Ibid., pp. 79-80.
[1191] Harris, *Africa*, p. 125.

living."¹¹⁹² And the next proposal sought to fill stolen plantations with black labor: "If the policy was to be continued that every native was to be a land holder of a sufficient area on which to establish himself, then the question of obtaining a satisfactory labour supply would never be settled."¹¹⁹³

Another tactic Europeans employed was to *ply Africans with booze*, mentioned earlier: "There is no comparison between European distilled spirits and the native drinks of Africa. Irish and Scotch whiskies and gin contain from 45 to 60 per cent, of alcohol; put a match to them and they burn with scorching flame! The foaming wines of the Raphia, Borassus and Oil palms possess, according to Sir Harry Johnston, only 2 to 3 per cent, of alcohol, whilst millet and maize beers seldom exceed 2 per cent. As Sir Harry Johnston so characteristically remarks: 'The native fermented drinks might make people quarrelsome, but they do not make them mad.'"¹¹⁹⁴ Olaudah confirms that the citizens of his country were unfamiliar with "strong or spirituous liquors" and drank palm wine. There is documentation of the burdens European alcohol place on African-Maafans, though Europeans and Anglos generally deny that strong alcohol similarly affects them: "Is the premise sound that the white man is capable of the necessary self-control? Of course it is not, the argument is both absurd and dishonest."¹¹⁹⁵

Seasoning was another practical method Europeans implemented. They employed this technique to break the Spirit of Egun, making them more compliant, and less willing to revolt.¹¹⁹⁶ "Seasoning" supposedly prepared Africans for the brutal life on the plantation. It took the form of psychological manipulation, and beatings. Africans, with their own broken Spirits, meted out punishment. Given the cannibalistic history of Europeans, the practice of "seasoning" Africans takes on much broader, and more ominous tones.

The infamous Henry M. Stanley boasts of the need to *take blood oaths with African leaders*, a tradition one historian claims Africans adopted from Arabs. Stanley used the seriousness of that tradition to gain African trust (gain safe passage through territories), steal land, and lay the foundations for commercial enterprise that enriched Europe. The weight that oath bore can be measured by one African's binding words, as recorded by Stanley: "If either of you break this brotherhood now established between you, may the lion devour him, the serpent poison him, bitterness be in his food, his friends desert him, his gun burst in his hands and wound him, and

---

¹¹⁹² Ibid.
¹¹⁹³ Ibid., p. 126
¹¹⁹⁴ Ibid., p. 148.
¹¹⁹⁵ Ibid., p. 152.
¹¹⁹⁶ Plantation revolts were common. Africans escaped, sometimes killing Europeans in the process, then set up their own communities in South America and the West Indies.

everything that is bad do wrong to him until death."[1197] And though African Chiefs may have had good intentions in signing treaties, it was not unusual for Stanley's assistants to take blood oaths in his place. Lies and exaggerations to achieve European goals were not uncommon, either.

And of course, storytelling and messaging tops the list of insidious practices Europeans and Anglos employ to "keep us in our place." As a reminder – traditionally - European narratives take advantage of events to guide the listener's emotions that will achieve specific social results. To this end, character assassination, whereby critics' motives or credibility is challenged in order to derail their charges and disinformation campaigns are utilized. Both tricks - character assassination and disinformation campaigns - are just two of a myriad of propagandistic tools Europeans and Anglos employ as they attempt to smear our perception and sway our opinions. A good truism to combat these distortions is: "If their lips are moving, they are lying to you." This is a mental prompt for remembering that all forms of European/Anglo media from TV to radio to Internet are worthy of scrutiny. This criticism applies across the board to all professional TV script readers, no matter their ethnicity. (Script readers may speak with authority, however they do not set news policy, nor do they write their own scripts). Initially remaining skeptical of European and Anglo *news* gives us time to research their claims on our own from reliable, independent sources. Another tactic is to ask the rhetorical question: "Do I believe them or my own lying eyes?" This question directs us to trust our own observations more than the storyteller's. As I wrote earlier, we will never see the prison bars until we stop focusing on the monkey.

Another leading stealthy and insidious technique used to separate Africans from their traditions is, of course, *converting*[1198] *Africans to foreign religions*. Both Christianity and Islam continue to plague and divide the people living on the African Continent as Africans foolishly engage in millenniums-old blood feuds between Europeans and Arabs, and take up arms against other Africans. Africans defend customs, practices, ideologies and doctrines that have nothing to do with their original African ancestry:[1199] In his observation of the effects of Christianity and Islam on certain Africans, Harris writes: "Family bonds are equally threatened by Christianity [and Islam]… [that] trains the child, whether deliberately or otherwise, to look upon his parents as living a life of sin, thus introducing a

---

[1197] Henry M. Stanley, *Through the Dark Continent*, p. 493.
[1198] Williams, *Destruction*, pp. 56-58.
[1199] Even if, as some insist, Christianity and Islam have foundations in Africa, their connection to African customs has weakened to the point of disrupting traditional African values. *Hatred of women is not an African value.* That concept comes to us by way of a male-centered construct.

subversive element into the household."[1200] And although the author opines that Islam does not demand worshippers commit "race suicide" as he believes Christianity does, I submit that both religions require that their members practice foreign customs, therefore rejecting their own African culture. As Africans engage in maintaining power structures that call for the death of the African psyche, they destroy their own African heritage and mind in the process. Though some traditional spiritual practices of Africans long ago blended with Christian ones the following quote from Harris, himself a Christian missionary, is on the mark: "It will be noted that the word "pagan" is seldom used [in his book], for the reason that the author regards the African as a deeply religious man, and that in certain respects [traditional] African worship appears to go deeper and is not less pure than the general religious atmosphere of so-called civilized races. It is therefore essential to consider the beliefs of the African as a basis upon which it is possible to erect a stable faith."[1201] At least we can all agree on the wisdom of adopting customs, traditions, and practices that have our best interests in mind, and that *result in better circumstances for all Africans*, rather than welcome one that "has taught men to believe that the vilest spirit may be washed white, with the atoning blood of the purest, offered up as a bribe to an avenging God. "[1202]

A Person is a Person because there are People: Building an African Future

African-Americans have an unsettling skill for stepping in-between the European/Anglo-American's idealization of reality and the real world that shields them from experiencing hurt feelings and shedding "white tears."[1203] But, we should not seek to soothe the feelings of others at the expense of our own survival.

However, the European's greatest strategy relies on the dependability of the African psyche. In other words, we tend to be our own worst enemy. We participate in traditions that keep a dysfunctional system functioning; we allow Europeans and Anglos to train our brains so that we carry forward their goal to devalue our lives; and we are not always the loudest cheerleaders for our own history, or backers of our own causes; nor have we put into action long-term plans for dealing with our issues. We allow

---

[1200] Harris, *Africa*, p. 158.
[1201] Ibid., p. 202.
[1202] Gerald Massey, *The Historical Jesus and Mythical Christ*, p. 25.
[1203] So-called white tears refer to Europeans/Anglo Americans who become upset as their lily white washed reality hits a bump in the road. The social paradigm of so-called white supremacy does not prepare White folks for reality beyond the one that the system has created for them; when the ideology fails, many will strike out angrily and violently.

self-appointed men to stand before us as "leaders." And instead of them acting as traditional African Chiefs who set an agenda subject to our approval, they grow their own wealth while pretending to address our concerns. In the meantime many African-Americans continue to suffer mightily from the effects of racism.

Some African-Americans try to avoid the issues of Black America by walking a well-trodden road that puts as much territory as possible between them and African people and customs. These *sidesteppers*, the "I'm not African," Africans firmly believe that by side-stepping black America and its issues Europeans/Anglos will see them as Americans who are not *too* terribly *black*. Meanwhile regardless of wealth, clothes, or public stature (the material trappings that validate the status of Europeans and Anglos) the "Black people are dangerous" meme applies to sidesteppers who are treated suspiciously, too. Ultimately, side-steppers become the only ones completely satisfied that they are not being *too* terribly black.

Here is where I shake my head as I reluctantly acknowledge that although Europeans and Anglo-Americans victimized Africans and African-Maafans the world over, they effectively flipped the script. European storytellers identified African-Maafans as lazy, murderous, dishonest, dirty, cheating, thieving, lustful, uneducated, illiterate barbarians who routinely ate other humans; Every single shameful habit of Dark, Medieval and Renaissance era Europeans, as recorded by their own historians, was projected onto us. And it all stuck. European and Anglo-American media teaches children to dance to our music, but to beware our presence, though *their* ancestors placed our Egun in shackles and tortured them; and though it was Whites who collected in groups to hang innocent African-Americans from trees; and it was *their* ancestors who – apparently carrying forward traditions and patterns set by even earlier ancestors - burned down thriving Black-built American cities, such as Tulsa and Rosewood. No matter how much we dress like Europeans, how well we speak their Indo-European languages, how well we think like Europeans, Black equals dangerous. One apt response to our social muddle might be found in the words of my mother who always told me: "You might as well do want you want. People will think what they want about you anyway." (Of course, my mother was not suggesting that I do anything morally wrong, but was encouraging me to stand for what is morally right, an action that in the western culture can bring great distress).

Returning briefly to the story of Mwenemutapan King Kapranzine, only Bantu know the kind of lies the Portuguese spoke that convinced them to fight the king, resulting in their own subjugation. The following passages are important for many reasons, but especially for their clarity in revealing a few European methods that tempted Africans to exploit other Africans: (1) "Sir George Young found slaves to be procured by war, by crimes, real or imputed, by kidnapping, which is called *panyaring*, and a fourth mode was the inhabitants of one village seizing those of another weaker village, and selling them to the ships.... (2) Mr. Falconbridge was assured by the Rev. Philip Quakoo, chaplain at Capo Coast Castle, on the Gold Coast, that the greatest number of slaves were made by kidnapping. He has heard that the men on this part of the coast, dress up and employ women, to entice young men, that they may be convicted of adultery and sold.... (3) Mr. Falconbridge thinks crimes are falsely imputed, for the sake of selling the accused.... (4) Mr. Town observes, that the intercourse of the Africans with the Europeans, has improved them in roguery, to plunder and steal, and pick up one another to sell. Dr. Trotter asking a black trader, what they made of their slaves when the French and English were at war, was answered, that when ships ceased to come, slaves ceased to be taken....

"Mr. Wadstrom says, the king Barbesin, while he, Mr. Wadstrom, was at Joal, was unwilling to pillage his subjects, but he was excited to it by means of a constant intoxication, kept up by the French and mulattoes of the embassy, who generally agreed every morning on taking this method to effect their purpose. When sober, he always expressed a reluctance to harrass [sic] his people. Mr. Wadstrom also heard the king hold the same language on different days, and yet he afterwards ordered the pillage to be executed. Mr. Wadstrom has no doubt, but that he also pillages in other parts of his dominions, since it is the custom of the mulatto merchants (as both they and the French officers declare) when they want slaves, to go to the kings, and excite them to pillages which are usually practiced on all that part of the coast.

"The French Senegal company, also, in order to obtain their complement of slaves, had recourse to their usual method on similar occasions, namely, of bribing the Moors, and supplying them with arms and ammunition, to seize king Dalmammy's subjects.... (5) Mr. Dalrymple understood it common for European traders to advance goods to chiefs, to induce them to seize their subjects or neighbors. Not one of the mulatto traders at Goree ever thought of denying it.... Mr. Bowman having settled at the head of Scassus river, informed the king, and others, that he was come to reside as a trader, and that his orders were, to supply them with powder and ball, and encourage them to go to war.[1204] They answered, they would go to war in two or three days. By this time they came to the factory,[1205] said they were going to war, and wanted powder, ball, rum and tobacco.... When these were given them, they went off to the number of from twenty-five to thirty, and in six or seven days, a part of them returned with three slaves....

[1204] Blake explains that "wars" mean pirates going on kidnapping expeditions for Africans. They set villages on fire and caught those running for safety.
[1205] Factories, reinforced trading posts, warehoused kidnapped Africans.

"(6) Mr. Morley owns, with shame, that he has made the natives drunk, in order to buy a good man or woman slave, to whom he found them attached. He has seen this done by others. Captain Hildebrand, commanding a sloop of Mr. Brue's, bought one of the wives of a man, whom he had previously made drunk, and who wished to redeem her, when sober next day, as did the person he (Mr. Morley) bought the man of, but neither of them was given up. He supposes they would have given a third more than the price paid, to have redeemed them.... (7) Mr. Brae had two hostages, kings' sons, for payment for arms, and all kinds of military stores, which he had supplied to the two kings, who were at war with each other, to procure slaves for at least six or seven ships, then lying in the road....

"(8) Mr. J. Parker has known presents made by the captains, to the black traders, to induce them to bring slaves. Captain Colley in particular gave them some pieces of cannon, which he himself saw landed.... It was proposed to [General Rooke] by three captains of English slave ships, lying under the fort of Goree, to kidnap a hundred, or a hundred and fifty, men, women and children, king Darnel's subjects, who had come to Goree in consequence of the friendly intercourse between him and Damel.... They said such things had been done by a former governor...."[1206]

When We Stand on Truth We Trample Lies and Rise to Meet our Destiny.

Africans conspiring with Europeans to disrupt African lives was an unfortunate practice at least as far back as *his* story goes. I suppose now is a good time to reveal that Origen, Tertullian, Lactantius and Augustine are all African born men who wielded great influence in the early Roman world. Though Origen was not likely what we might today call a "brother." Still, these "African-born" men had much to do with undermining their own African customs. (Because nothing is new under the Sun, some African-Americans often side with Anglo-Americans against other African-Americans even when it comes to obvious injustices such as police brutality, unequal enforcement of laws and voting rights issues).

Europeans use the African's inclinations towards patience, fairness, and forgiveness against us, too. The European can depend on an African psyche that patiently forgives injustices and leans towards civility in response to aggressive and violent treatment. This spirit while laudable puts us at a distinct disadvantage in the face of cultural forces that demonstrates cunning ability to divide, conquer and propagandize. Even in Haiti after the French slaughtered thousands of innocent Blacks and ordered dogs to sniff down retreating Africans, this scene plays out: "On the departure of

---

[1206] Blake, *Slavery*, pp. 112-20.

the French, Dessalines, Christophe, and the other generals proclaimed the independence of the island 'in the name of the blacks and the people of color.' At the same time they invited the return of all whites who had taken no part in the war; but, added they, 'if any of those who imagined they would restore slavery return hither, they shall meet with nothing but chains and deportation.'"[1207] Currently, Anglo-American abuses of African Maafans play out daily in regressive laws, severe punishments, and violent behaviors towards our men, women, and children.

Despite what European/Anglo-American media tells us, take a look around the world. African-Maafans are a patient, peace-loving people. Furthermore, we are all in this together no matter how we self-identify: San, Moor, British, Igbo, Khoekhoe, European, African-American, Afri-Caribbean (including Dominicans), Bantu, Dravidian, Brazilian, Hutu, etc. When far too many pale-skinned Europeans and Anglo-Americans see one of us, they see "an other," a Black person fully distinct from them. How do African-Maafans sufficiently cope with this European cultural construct? What do African-Maafans and Africans do to mitigate or redirect a seemingly unbalanced European culture that targets our children, women and men? What are appropriate responses to a culture that systematically uses brutality against mostly non-violent cultures, and then culturally conditions its members to accept a system as benign that devalues human life? How do we as a people prevent Europeans from continuing to manipulate us individually and collectively?

It is in our best interest to discuss these and other questions. However, as with all abusive relationships, mistreatment ends at the beginning of the abused person's discovery of her/his self-worth. Learning to embrace our African identity, as well as adopting Egun traditions is just the first hurdle we climb on the road to freshening up our African psyche. We rise above another barrier once we stop perceiving the European paradigm as a normal construct for humanity as well as the most advanced. We triumph psychologically once we stop expecting and begging the people who manufactured our predicament to destroy the culture that succeeds from abusing us. Instead, we can turn toward one another (and to those who embrace our struggle) for relief and solutions.

Consider, too, that our current paradigm is the culmination of two thousand years of white domination… the product of Europe's best minds. See the greed, the hoarders, the child and adult slavery, the men who hate women and children, the poverty, the anti-intellectualism, the wars, the diseases, the hunger, the homelessness, the pollution, the racism, the oppression, the prison industrial complex, the bombs, the terrorism, the murders and the destruction; this global madness is the best Europeans

---

[1207] Blake, *Slavery*, p. 277.

have to offer the world. And if what we are witnessing is not their best, then we must ask, "What are they waiting for?"

But we can also ask ourselves that very same question? What are *we* waiting for? Considering the social upheaval of the past 2000 years, quite frankly, if African-Maafans want to live in a political paradise, we will have to build that empire for ourselves. But, then again, we have built empires - including this American one – many times over. As the African population explodes we will necessarily step forward with leadership. Will Africans offer the world the traditions learned at the feet of Europeans or will we value customs from Egun that might help make the world a better place to live for everyone?

In closing, I would like to impart to readers that this essay, though challenging and demanding, was not a labor of love for me, but rather a joyful endeavor in pursuit of truth and clarity. I deliver it with much love from my African self to my African brothers and sisters the world over. I dream that the information presented here inspires us to stand courageously, boldly and proudly for Africa, and for our African identity. Regardless of the challenges we face as Africans and African-Maafans, we can learn to use the strengths of African Egun to empower ourselves.

It is within *knowing* that wisdom blossoms, and change occurs.

Perhaps some hard-hearted pleader may suggest, that [rape] would indeed be cruel, in Europe: but the African women are negroes, savages, who have no idea of the nicer sensations which obtain among civilized people. I dare contradict them in the strongest terms. I have lived long, and conversed much, amongst these supposed savages. I have often slept in their towns, in a house filled with goods for trade, with no door than a mat; in that security, which no man in his senses would expect in this civilized nation, especially in this metropolis [Philadelphia], without the precaution of having strong doors, strongly locked and bolted. And with regard to the women, in Sherbro, where I was most acquainted, I have seen many instances of modesty, and even delicacy, which would not disgrace an English woman.[1208]

When we stand firmly on truth, we trample lies and rise to meet our destiny.

Htp,
Sheshet Kemet

"The most potent weapon in the hands of the oppressor is the mind of the oppressed." – Stephen Biko African Activist, 1971

[1208] Newton, *Posthumous Works*, p. 240.

MEDIEVAL MASSACRES

Massacres occurred wherever warlords - commonly called popes, kings, queens and princes - ruled, or aspired to rule. It is possible that not all massacres that occurred during the Middle Ages have been recorded. Below are a handful of cited massacres. This much-abbreviated list of white on white crimes does not include the vast number of massacres or other atrocities medieval and Renaissance era Europeans committed against Africans, or other people of color. Extensive lists of European massacres can be found on the Internet:

- After the Paris Massacres of 1408 and 1418, children dragged bodies through the streets like dolls. Four thousand people were murdered in 1418 when the people rose up against Constable d'Armagnac.

- The Rhineland Massacres of the Jews during the First Crusade of 1190.

- William the Conqueror slaughters 100,000 people in 1069.

- Viking Massacre (979-1016), Anglo-Saxon king ordered all the Danish Vikings within his realm be killed.

- St. Bartholomew Massacre.

- Battle of Visby, 1361. Danish king sent troops to subdue Swedish countrymen. Nearly 2000 countrymen and peasants killed.

- Crusaders massacre an est. 60,000 in French city of Languedoc, 1209.

- Capua citizens slain in a massacre of 1501 on the orders of Cesare Borgia, son to Pope Alexander VI. Described thusly by Rafael Sabatini: "The invader butchered every human thing he came upon, indiscriminant [sic] of age or sex, and the blood of some four thousand victims flowed through the streets of Capua like water after a thundershower. That sack of Capua is one of the most horrid pages in the horrid history of sacks. You will find full details in d'Auton's chronicle, if you have a mind for such horrors."

- The Friulian Revolt of 1511 against clergy and nobility.

- Peasants' War, 1525. Thousands of peasants killed.

APPENDIX A

SELECTED PASSAGES FROM THE JEW AND HUMAN SACRIFICE

I became quite ill literally during the reading of certain material associated with this essay. Many writers give graphic details of blood rituals used by their European forebears. Though this is an essay that attempts to bring to light the corrupt actions of Indo-Europeans over the centuries at the same time they shamed Egun, my challenge was to inform readers while limiting the shock value associated with that information. Still, it is valuable information for African-Americans to have, especially when the wrong click on the computer keyboard can lead us into some very seamy websites where the content suggests that remnants of early European ages remain with us in this so-called modern world.

Warning: Some material presented in these appendices is very disturbing. Children should not be allowed to read the material contained within Appendices A, B, C, D without parental supervision.

Any material presented in these pages should constitute only the beginning of research.

From the Bibliography of the Jew and Human Sacrifice

"In Book v., the 'Animal science,' is a 20-page section devoted to man. It begins p. 31: 'The natural apothecary articles. These are taken either from the still living body, and are: The hairs, the nails, the spittle, the ear-wax, the sweat, the milk, the menstrual blood, the after-birth, 'the urine, the excrement, the semen, the blood, testicles, worms, the lice, the skin that surrounds the head of the foetus. Or from parts of the dead body, such are: The whole corpse, the skin, the fat, the bones, skulls, the pulp of skulls, the brain, the gall, the heart.'—P. 33: 'If you then ask, whether one can safely use inwardly the menstrual blood? This we can answer with a Yes. Take a cloth, steep it well in the menstrual blood, let it dry; when you wish to use it, draw the same with squill vinegar out of the cloth which one can fitly employ to promote the woman's monthly flux. The linen cloth soaked in such blood and dried is laid externally on erysipelas or also on other swellings and pains; pre-eminently it quiets the pains of Podagra. It has cured tertian fever when such a cloth has been merely hung on the neck. The maidens prepare their love-potions from it, after which commonly ensues delirium or madness.'" -The Jew and Human Sacrifice, pp. 27-28.

Blood Ritual

"G. F. Daumer, in a book, which though extravagant in its conclusions, displays wide reading and keen perception, 'Geheimnisse des christlichen Alterthums,' Hamburg, 1847, 2 volumes, tried to prove that the characteristics of the Christian religion from its inception to the end of the middle ages consisted in human sacrifices and cannibalism and the use of human blood. I give here some of Daumer's examples in attempted proof of his position. One may gather from them what persons with vividly excited imaginations thought they saw, and how strongly realistic impressions were held admissible as facts, especially in more remote times:

Amphilochius in the 'Life of Basilius' (Herib. Rosweidi Vitae patrum [Antwerp, 1615], I., 156; " Leben der Vdter," Augsburg, 1704, 739): When the holy office was celebrated, a Jew mingled among the crowd, as if he were a Christian, because he wanted to learn about the order of the Officimn and the gift of the Communion. He there beholds how a little child is cut to pieces, limb by limb, in the hands of Basilius. He approached with the other communicants, and flesh was actually given him. Then he was also present at the handing of the cup, which was full of blood, and took part in drinking from it. Keeping some remains of both, he goes home and shows them to his wife. −/., 85 (Life of the Martyr S. George, "Acta Sanctorum," S3 April). A Saracen saw a priest kill and cut up a child, place the pieces in the paten, pour the blood into the cup, and eat one of the pieces and drink from the cup. −/., 118 sq. tells of the dissensions between the Dominicans and Franciscans in Bern 1507, after the Bernese Chronicle of Calonius Grönneirus, 1585, 615 sq., and Hottinger, "Helvetische Kirchengeschichte," Zurich, 1708 sq.. Vol. II., 553 sq., 556 sq. : The Dominicans were alleged to have offered a consecrated wafer coloured with Christ's blood to Jezer, a tailor who had been received into their Order, whom they wanted to make their Saint. They are also said to "have handed him a drink composed of ointment, Easter baptismal- water, Easter-taper wax, consecrated salt... and the hair and blood of a child."− In the confession cited by Grönneirus 622 it is asserted the Dominicans had made use of Jew blood, and the eyebrows of a Jewish child. −There is more in Daumer-I., 36 sq., 73, 85 sq.

"In the middle ages, appearances of Christ at Holy Communion in the form of a child or a lamb are not infrequently mentioned, vide e.g., Paschasius. Radbertus, 'De corpore et sanguine Christi,' 14; Germanus in Edm. Martene, 'Thesaurus novus Anecdotorum,' V. (Paris, 1717), 96, 95. In fact, the fantasy required a small body, which should find a place at the table or altar. Berthold von Regensburg, the great popular preacher of the 13th century, says in reply to the question, Why Christ, as he is present at Holy Communion, does not let Himself be seen in it: 'Who would like a little child to have his little head, or his little hands, or his little feet bitten off?' ('Predigten,' published by F. Pfeiffer, II., Vienna, 1880, 270.)." -The Jew and Human Sacrifice, pp. 33-34.

"**Epiphanius xxvi., 5, describes as follows the conduct of the so-called**

Gnostics: After the common meal they turn to free concubitus. Next, men and women take semen virile in their hands and speak to the All-Father: 'We bring Thee this gift as the body of Christ.' They eat thereof, and say, 'This is the body of Christ and the Passover meal.' Likewise they take sanguinem menstruum: 'This is the blood of Christ.' If a woman has become pregnant they triturate [grind] the embryo, mix the mass with honey, pepper and herbs, and taste the dish at their gathering with the finger, which dish is esteemed the perfect Passover meal.

"The contents of these documents are so revolting that one would be glad to agree with H. Usener, 'Das Weihnachtsfest,' Bonn, 1889, 110, and others, who contest their credibility. Epiphanius, the chief witness, they say, lived too long after the occurrences (he died, at the age of about 100, in 403 a.d.). But he appeals, xxvi. 17, 18, to the oral information of credible men, to original writings of the Gnostics, and to personal intercourse which, as a quite young man, he had with these Gnostics.

"Nevertheless, I hold with R. Seeberg it is very probable that the account of the use of the embryo, which is found only in Epiphanius, should be considered unhistorical. After all, Epiphanius was credulous enough to say about even the Montanists, that they employed in their sacrifices the blood of a child, whose body they had pierced with needles, xlviii. 14. The first part, however, of Epiphanius's last description is not merely confirmed by the remarks of Clement of Alexandria and Irenaeus, but also by two Gnostic writings which have only recently become known. Firstly, the Gnostic writing which was written in Egypt in Greek at the end of the third century a.d., but preserved only in Coptic, 'Pistis Sophia . . .'" -The Jew and Human Sacrifice, pp. 35-36.

"Remarkable parallels are reported in Russian sects. Sectarianism in Russia, the Raskol, falls into two big groups: the Popowzy and the Bespopowzy ("the priestless"). The latter think the end of the world is near, and the dominion of Antichrist has already begun. Many of them made it their duty to dispatch the innocent souls of the newly born to heaven; others believed they were doing their friends and relations a service of love, if they kept them from dying a natural death. It not infrequently happened that whole families, even villages, united to offer themselves to God as a living sacrifice. The peasant Chodkin (under Alexander II.) persuaded some twenty persons to die with him of hunger in the forests of Perm." -The Jew and Human Sacrifice, pp. 37-38.

"The mystic sects of the Chlysty ('scourgers') and the Skopzy ('castrates'), which stand in close relations to one another, do not belong to the real Raskol. The gatherings of the Chlysty, or, as they are called, Ljudi Boshii ('God-men'), are outwardly comparable to those of the well-known 'dancing dervishes' in Cairo and Stamboul. Whilst most Chlysty use only water and black bread for the celebration of the Holy Communion, some of them, according to more than one witness {Leroy-Beaulieu, 450, cites Philaret's 'History of the Russian Church,' Liwanow's 'Raskolniki I Ostroshniki,' Renzki's 'Ljudi Boshii I Skopzy,') used the flesh and blood of a new-born child, and particularly of the first boy, who might be expected from a 'holy virgin' chosen to be the 'mother of God,' after the ecstatic and obscene ceremonies following upon her selection. If a girl was born, she in turn became a holy virgin; but if a boy 'Christosik' ('little Christ') he was sacrificed on the eighth day after his birth. The communion bread was renewed by a mixture of his heart and blood with flour and honey. That was called communicating with the blood of the lamb. Others, as is conjectured, communicated with the yet warm blood of the little Jesus." - The Jew and Human Sacrifice, p. 39.

"**Von Haxthausen, I., 349, mentions another way by** which the Skopzys and Chlystys produced the materials for the solemnizing of their Communion: A **virgin of fifteen,** who has been persuaded by great promises, has her left breast severed, whilst she sits in a tub with warm water. The breast is cut into small pieces on a dish, which are consumed by all the members of the congregation present. Then the girl in the tub is lifted on to an altar standing near, and the whole congregation dances wildly around it and sings at the same time…. My above-mentioned clerk made the acquaintance of several such girls, who were then always worshipped like saints, and says that at nineteen to twenty they looked as if they were fifty to sixty; these also usually died before thirty. One, however, was married, and had two children." -The Jew and Human Sacrifice, pp. 39-40.

"**The following events are to be considered as relapses into heathendom or as survivals from heathen times.** About two hundred versts (kms.) from Kasan is the village of Stary-Multan, whose inhabitants belong to the Russian Orthodox Church, with a church and a priest. Owing to bad harvests, famine and typhus visited them in 1892, and there was a fear of cholera. They began to doubt whether their way of worshipping God was the right [way]. They thought they must appease the supernatural powers by sacrifice. Animal sacrifices helped nothing. Whereupon a sage of the village received the revelation that a 'two-legged' sacrifice (kurban) was required, that is, a human sacrifice. There lived in the village a man from another district, so that he was without relations and friends in the place itself. This unfortunate man, on 4th (16th) May, 1892, was dragged into the Town Hall, stripped there, and hung up by his feet to the ceiling, and then fifteen persons with knives began to stab at his naked body. The blood streaming from the wounds was carefully caught in vessels, cooked and drunk by the sacrificers. The lungs and heart were also consumed. The village magistrate, the peasant-born policeman, and the chief elder of the church took part in the ceremony. The people were so convinced of the righteousness of their action that they did not take the least pains to conceal the murder. So it soon came to the knowledge of the authorities. After two and a half years the trial came to an end, and the perpetrators of the ritual murder were condemned to many years' [sic] hard labour. (Urquell, 1897, 118 sq., after the Freies Blatt, Vienna, 13 Jan., 1895, No. 145)." -The Jew and Human Sacrifice, pp. 40-41.

"**Government of Minsk, district of Nowogrud. In** 1831 the country people, during a cholera epidemic, wanted to bury a priest alive; he only saved himself by begging his parishioners for a respite, in order to prepare for death. In August, 1855, the inhabitants of the village of Okopowitschi, in a similar epidemic, on the advice of an army surgeon Kosakowitsch, pushed an old woman, Lucia Manjkow, alive, as a sacrifice, into a pit, in which there were already corpses, and then quickly heaped earth upon it. In August, 1871, the inhabitants of the village of Torkatschi wanted to inflict the same fate on an invalid peasant woman; her husband and son-in-law came only just in time to the rescue; it is said that another woman who was ill, and by herself, was then sacrificed alive. The whole of the village authorities shared the conviction that they could save themselves from the cholera by the burying of a living person. In the Turuchan district, government Jenissei, a peasant P., by descent a Russian, buried alive, in 1861, a girl akin to him in order to save himself and his family from a prevalent epidemic disease by the sacrifice {Löwenstimm, 12-14)." -The Jew and Human Sacrifice, p. 41.

"**A woman, living in the Madras Presidency, was said to be possessed of the devil, and therefore barren.** Her father accordingly asked advice of an exorciser, who declared a human sacrifice needful. So one evening the father, the exorcist, and five or six other men met together, and after a religious ceremony sent for the victim determined on. Without suspecting any evil, he came and was forthwith given so much spirituous drink, that he became unconscious. They then cut off his head and offered his blood mingled with rice to the Deity as a sacrifice; the corpse they cut in pieces and threw in a reservoir. The murderers, who were soon discovered, made a frank confession." (L. Fuld, Neve Freie Presse, Vienna, 4 May, 1888, No. 8510, reproduced from an English medical journal)." -The Jew and Human Sacrifice, p. 42.

Blood of Executed Persons: Hangman's Rope

"**The celebrated fairy story-teller [Hans Christian?] Andersen describes in his autobiography an execution which he witnessed** at Skelskor in 1823: 'I saw a poor sick man, whom his superstitious parents made drink a cup of the blood of the executed person, that he might be healed of epilepsy; after which they ran with him in wild career till he sank to the ground.'" -The Jew and Human Sacrifice, pp. 70-71.

"On 6th June, 1755, K. G. Zeibig, who when drunk had murdered a man, was beheaded on the Rabenstein at Dresden. . . . Before the execution two foremen of the tailor fraternity at Dresden begged the Prime Minister, Count Heinr. v. Brühl, on behalf of their brother member, Joh. Ge. Wiedemann, who suffered severely from epilepsy, that the same be allowed to drink the blood of the murderer for his restoration to health. An entry in the register announces that Brühl assented to the request, and also that Wiedemann, after drinking the blood of the individual beheaded, 'ran off.' Th. Distel, 'Neues Archiv für Sächsische Geschichte u. Alterthumskunde,' IX. [Dresden, 1888] 160, rightly adds 'It is remarkable in this connection that even the highest official should have granted the request for the drinking of such human blood, and thus simply promoted crass superstition.'" -The Jew and Human Sacrifice, p. 71.

"'Carl Lehmann, 'Chronik der freien Bergstadt Schneeberg' III. (Schneeberg, 1840), 299 describes the execution at Zwickau of the murderer Karl Heinr. Friedrich on 15th Dec, 1823 (Cf. inf. ch. 12). He says at the end: 'And with our own eyes we saw how a pot full of the blood of the executed man was drunk dry by various persons, and how these persons, mostly children, were driven with blows from whips to run at utmost speed over the field.'" -The Jew and Human Sacrifice, p. 71.

"'When a criminal is executed, some of his blood must be obtained in a piece of linen. Bakers and brewers must dip such a rag into their dough and their beer, merchants and innkeepers into the broached brandy barrels, then they get a large number of customers; horse-owners must rub in their horses with it, that they may become sleek and shiny. The power of the blood, however, only extends to the third member (general).' — The story of 'Der Sündenfinger,' well known in Stolp, in its essential point (v. Urds-Brunnen VI. [1888-9], 76 sq.) amounts to this: A merchant in Stolp had concealed in the spirit cask a finger of an executed person. In consequence of which customers flocked to him in crowds, and the business flourished. The ostler denounced his master, who was severely punished, and the finger taken away from him. After fulfilling his term of prison the merchant had no luck any more; the customers remained away.

"'Preussen,' Frischbier 24: 'Skinners' families preserve the blood of executed people as a magic remedy.' 106: 'The finger or blood of an executed person brings luck into house and into business (Dönhoffstadt). If such a finger be put in the stables, the horses thrive well (Ermland). — As is evident from the Report on the Conitz witch-trial in 1623 ('Preussiche Provinzial-Blätter' II., 133 sq.), in former times not only were the fingers and *other limbs of corpses hanging on* the gallows lucky,* but also gallows-

---

*Pliny informs us that rope from a used cross was similarly used for healing: "So, too, in cases of quartan fever, they take a fragment of a nail from a cross, or else a piece of a halter

chains and gallows-nails; they helped to good beer brewing and sale of beer, quickened manual work, made horses indefatigable, etc.' Cf. also Tettau and Temme. 265. — Mannhardt 49 : 'A good many [executioners and skinners] keep the blood of the executed as a magic specific.'" -The Jew and Human Sacrifice, p. 73.

"**After Andreas Hofer had been executed in 1810,** some soldiers, among them Müller, the subsequent Director of Prisons in Vienna during the fifties, banded together to get hold of a limb of his body, because they regarded such as an amulet. They were, however, caught and punished (communicated by Prof. G. Wolf, of Vienna).

"'Shanghai, 15 July. (East-As. Lloyd). In Foochow at the beginning of the month, occurred the execution of a pirate. After the criminal had been made a head shorter, the executioner opened the corpse with his sword, tore out the liver and distributed it in pieces among his assistants. The fact is that the liver of persons who have been hurried into the beyond by the executioner's sword is deemed a radical cure for various illnesses, especially consumption.'" (Voss. Zeitung, 26 Aug., 1892, No. 397). -The Jew and Human Sacrifice, p. 74.

"'**The corpse-hand. Pliny, 'N. H.' xxviii. 4, 11; 'Stroking with the hand of a person who has died early is supposed to cure goître,** glandular swellings near the ear, and throat complaints; nevertheless, a good many think this can be effected by any corpse's hand, provided only the dead person be of the same sex, and the thing is done with the left hand upturned.'" -The Jew and Human Sacrifice, p. 80.

Blood-superstition among Criminals and its Consequences

"'Oldenburg,' Strackerjan, I.,100: '**The finger of an unborn child is useful to thieves** by keeping the dwellers asleep in a house into which they have penetrated; it is simply laid on the table (Vechta).—The saying goes in Wardenburg that robbers and murderers cut open the bellies of pregnant women, and make candles of the fingers of the unicorn children. When these candles are lit, they allow no sleeper to wake up as long as they burn. The candles can only be extinguished by dipping them in sweet milk.'" -The Jew and Human Sacrifice, p. 105.

"'Preussen,' Lemke (East Prussia), I., 114: '**Human fat' yields a light** which is useful to thieves. 'Many a one murders a man simply for the purpose of making a candle out of his fat'—at least so everybody says—

---

that has been used for crucifixion, and, after wrapping it in wool, attach it to the patient's neck; taking care, the moment he has recovered, to conceal it in some hole to which the light of the sun cannot penetrate." Bostock and Riley, *Pliny's*, vol. 5, p. 293.

whether it's true, it is impossible for me to tell. Such a candle is supposed to be the best thing a thief can have. But when they've lit it, they must hold it under the soles and under the noses of the sleepers; then the sleepers don't wake till the thieves are away. Such light can be put out neither in water nor in brandy, nor by kicks; such light can only go out in milk." -The Jew and Human Sacrifice, p. 106.

"**Montanus, 'Die deutschen Volksfeste, Volksbräuche** und deutscher Volksglaube,' Iserlohn, 1858, 130 sq. : 'This peculiar superstition of illumination with a child's limbs seems to hang together with folkbeliefs [sic] about will-o'-the-wisps. Thieves are said to have also wrought very powerful magic results, pertinent to their night work, with the hearts of new-born or innocent children as well as with their blood, and even with children cut out of their mothers' wombs, which superstition has then demonstrably had as a consequence several murders of innocent children and of wives about to become mothers.—The following incident put together from the documents of investigation may serve for the explanation and significance of a superstition even now prevailing among the masses. . . .'" -The Jew and Human Sacrifice, p. 110.

"**Lammert, 84 : 'A horrible example of superstition about the magic power of unborn children** is afforded in more recent times by Hundssattler, who was executed in the middle of last century at Bayreuth. He was under the delusion that a man could fly if he ate nine hearts of new-born children. With this object he had already butchered, cut up, and eaten the still throbbing, warm hearts of eight pregnant women (Meissner, 'Skizz.' xiii., 107). The Nuremberg reports* of 1577 and 1601 are lamentable for a similar reason.'

*"The Nuremberg executioner, Meister Frank, broke on the wheel in 1577, at Bamberg, a murderer who had cut open three pregnant women; in 1601 he executed a monster at Nuremberg, who had slain 20 persons, among them also several pregnant women, 'whom he afterwards cut open, cut the children's hands off, and made little candles of them for burglary....' Nuremberg, 1801" -The Jew and Human Sacrifice, pp. 111-12.

APPENDIX B

SELECTED PASSAGES FROM THE BLOOD COVENANT

I became quite literally ill during the reading of certain material associated with this essay. Many writers give graphic details of blood rituals used by their European forebears. Though this is an essay that attempts to bring to light the corrupt actions of Indo-Europeans over the centuries at the same time they shamed Egun, my challenge was to inform readers while limiting the shock value associated with that information. Still, it is valuable information for African-Americans to have, especially when the wrong click on the computer keyboard can lead us into some very seamy websites where the content suggests that remnants of early European ages remain with us in this so-called modern world.

Warning: Some material presented in these appendices is very disturbing. Children should not be allowed to read the material contained within Appendices A, B, C, D without parental supervision.

Any material presented in these pages should constitute only the beginning of research.

The Primitive Rite Itself

"... **the Arabic words for friendship, for affection, for blood, and for leech,** or blood-sucker, are but variations from a common root. 'Alaqa means 'to love,' 'to adhere,' 'to feed.' 'Alaq, in the singular, means 'love,' 'friendship,' 'attachment,' 'blood.' As the plural of 'alaqa, 'alaq means 'leeches,' or 'blood-suckers.' The truest friend clings like a leech, and draws blood in order to the sharing thereby of his friend's life and nature." -The Blood Covenant, p. 8.

Amys and Amylion

"This belief in the **life-bringing power of baths of blood** to the death-smitten lepers, was continued into the Middle Ages; and that it finally 'received a check from an opinion gradually gaining ground, that only the blood of those would be efficacious, who offered themselves freely and voluntarily for a beloved sufferer.'" -The Blood Covenant, p. 117.

The Royal Blood

"The inspiring power of blood is a thought that runs all through the

early Norseland legends. Thus, Kvaser, according to the Scandinavian mythology, was a being created by the gods with preternatural intelligence. Kvaser traversed the world, teaching men wisdom; but he was treacherously murdered by the dwarfs Fjalar and Gala. The dwarfs let Kvaser's blood run into two cups and a kettle. 'The name of the kettle is Odroerer, and the names of the cups are Son and Bodn. By mixing up his blood with honey, they composed a drink of such surpassing excellence, that whoever partakes of it acquires the gift of song.' And that was the origin of poetry in the world; although there have been a good many imitations of the real article since that day." -The Blood Covenant, pp. 139-40.

"**So, again, in the Elder Edda, the hero Sigurd killed** Fafner, at the instigation of Fafner's brother Regin. Regin cut out the heart of his brother, and gave it to Sigurd to roast, while he drank the blood of the murdered one. Touching the bleeding heart with his fingers, and then putting his fingers into his mouth, Sigurd found that he was now able to understand the voice of birds; and thenceforward he was a hero inspired. Afterwards he gave his bride, Gudrun, 'to eat of the remnant of Fafnir's [sic] heart; so she grew wise and great-hearted.'" -The Blood Covenant, p. 140.

"'**The Taurobolium of the ancients was,**' as we are told, 'a ceremony in which the high-priest of Cybele was consecrated; and might be called a **baptism of blood**, which they conceived imparted a spiritual new birth to the liberated spirit. . . The high-priest about to be inaugurated was introduced into a dark excavated apartment, adorned with a long silken robe, and a crown of gold. Above this apartment [which would seem to have represented a place of burial] was a floor perforated in a thousand places with holes like a sieve, through which the blood of a sacred bull, slaughtered for the purpose, descended in a copious torrent upon the inclosed priest, who received the purifying [or re-vivifying] stream on every part of his dress, rejoicing to bathe with the bloody shower his hands, his cheeks, and even to bedew his lips and his tongue with it [thereby tasting it and so securing the assimilation of its imparted life]. When all the blood had run from the throat of the immolated bull, the carcass of the victim was removed, and the priest issued forth from the cavity, a spectacle ghastly and horrible, his head and vestments being covered with blood, and clotted drops of it adhering to his venerable beard. As soon as the pontifex appeared before the assembled multitude the air was rent with congratulatory shouts; so pure and so sanctified, however, was he now esteemed that they dared not approach his person, but beheld him at a distance with awe and veneration.'

"Here seems to be the idea of a burial of the old life, and of a new birth into the higher nature represented by the substitute blood; as that idea appears in the Norseland method, of entering into the blood-covenant under the lifted sod. It also appears to represent the receiving of new life by the bath of blood." -The Blood Covenant, pp. 362-63.

Supplement

"Poseidonios tells of the custom, among the primitive German peoples, of opening 'the veins upon their foreheads, and mixing the flowing blood with their drink,' as their method of entering into the blood-covenant. A trace of this primitive custom would seem to be found in a still extant method of making brotherhood among the students in German universities. Bayard Taylor describes this ceremony as he observed it at Heidelberg, in 1846. When new students are to be made 'Burschen' (or fellows), while at the same time the bands of brotherhood are to be kept fresh and sacred among those who are already banded together in their student life, the 'consecration song' of the Landesvater is sung with mutual beer-drinking and cap-piercing. The ceremony includes the striking of glasses together, as held in the right hand before drinking; the crossing of swords, as held in the lefthand; the piercing of each one's cap with a sword (the caps of all who take part in the ceremony being successively strung upon the two swords of those who conduct it); the exchanging of the cap-laden swords between those leaders, the return of each pierced cap to its owner; the resting of the ends of the crossed swords on the heads, covered by the pierced caps, of each pair participating in turn in the ceremony; with the singing in concert of the song of consecration...." -The Blood Covenant, pp. 366-67.

APPENDIX C

SELECTED PASSAGES FROM MANNERS, CUSTOMS, AND DRESS

I became quite literally ill during the reading of certain material associated with this essay. Many writers give graphic details of blood rituals used by their European forebears. Though this is an essay that attempts to bring to light the corrupt actions of Indo-Europeans over the centuries at the same time they shamed Egun, my challenge was to inform readers while limiting the shock value associated with that information. Still, it is valuable information for African-Americans to have, especially when the wrong click on the computer keyboard can lead us into some very seamy websites where the content suggests that remnants of early European ages remain with us in this so-called modern world.

Warning: Some material presented in these appendices is very disturbing. Children should not be allowed to read the material contained within Appendices A, B, C, D without parental supervision.

Any material presented in these pages should constitute only the beginning of research.

Punishments

"**Every country had special customs as to the manner of applying torture**....

"At Avignon, the ordinary torture consisted in hanging the accused by the wrists, with a heavy iron ball at each foot; for the extraordinary torture, which was then much in use in Italy under the name of reglia, the body was stretched horizontally by means of ropes passing through rings riveted into the wall, and attached to the four limbs, the only support given to the culprit being the point of a stake cut in a diamond shape, which just touched the end of the back-bone. A doctor and a surgeon were always present, feeling the pulse at the temples of the patient, so as to be able to judge of the moment when he could not any longer bear the pain. At that moment he was untied, hot fomentations were used to revive him, restoratives were administered, and, as soon as he had recovered a little strength, lie was again put to the torture, which went on thus for six consecutive hours.

"In Paris, for a long- time, the water torture was in use; this was the most easily borne, and the least dangerous. A person undergoing it was tied to a board which was supported horizontally on two trestles. By means of a horn, acting as a funnel, and whilst his nose was being pinched, so as to force him to swallow, they slowly poured four coquemars (about nine pints) of water into his mouth ; this was for the ordinary torture. For the extraordinary, double that quantity was poured in (Fig. 341). When the torture was ended, the victim was untied, 'and taken to be warmed in the kitchen,' says the old text.

"At a later period, the brodequins were preferred. For this torture, the victim was placed in a .sitting posture on a massive bench, with strong narrow boards fixed inside and outside of each leg, which were tightly bound together with strong rope; wedges were then driven in between the centre boards with a mallet; four wedges in the ordinary and eight in the extraordinary torture. Not unfrequently [sic] during the latter operation the bones of the legs were literally burst.

"The brodequins which were often used for ordinary torture were stockings of parchment, into which it was easy enough to get the feet when it was wet, but which, on being held near the fire, shrunk so considerably that it caused insufferable agony to the wearer." -Manners, Customs and Dress During the Middle Ages and During the Renaissance Period, pp. 408-10.

"When a criminal had been condemned to be burnt, a stake was erected on the spot specially designed for the execution, and round it a pile was prepared, composed of alternate layers of straw and wood, and rising to about the height of a man. Care was taken to leave a free space round the stake for the victim, and also a passage by which to lead him to Having been stripped of his clothes, and dressed in a shirt smeared with sulphur, he had to walk to the centre of the pile through a narrow opening, and was then tightly bound to the stake with ropes and chains. After this, faggots and straw were thrown into the empty space through which he had passed to the stake, until he was entirely covered by them; the pile was then fired on all sides at once....

"They were not satisfied with burning the living, they also delivered to the flames the bodies of those who had died a natural death before their execution could be carried out, as if an anticipated death should not be allowed to save them from the punishment which they had deserved. It also happened in certain cases, where a person's guilt was only proved after his decease, that his body was disinterred, and carried to the stake to be burnt." -Manners, Customs and Dress During the Middle Ages and During the Renaissance Period, p. 416.

"The tire which surrounded the young heroine [Joan of Arc] on all sides had reached her and no doubt suffocated her, although sufficient time had not elapsed for it to consume her body, a part of the blazing wood was withdrawn,' in order to remove any doubts from the people," and when the crowd had satisfied themselves by seeing her in the middle of the pile, " chained to the post and quite dead, the executioner replaced the fire . . . ." - Manners, Customs and Dress During the Middle Ages and During the Renaissance Period, p. 417.

"**The sentence of punishment by fire did not absolutely imply death at the stake,** for there was a punishment of this description which was specially reserved for base coiners, and which consisted in hurling the criminals into a cauldron of scalding water or oil.

"We must include in the category of punishment by fire certain penalties, which were, so to speak, but the preliminaries of a more severe punishment, such as the sulphur-fire, in which the hands of parricides, or of criminals accused of high treason, were burned. We must also add various punishments which, if they did not involve death, were none the less cruel, such as the red-hot brazier, *bassin ardent*, which was passed backwards and forwards before the eyes of the culprit, until they were destroyed by the scorching heat; and the process of branding various marks on the flesh, as an ineffaceable stigma, the use of which has been continued to the present day.

"In certain countries decapitation was performed with an axe; but in France, it was carried out usually by means of a two-handed sword or glave [sic] of justice, which was furnished to the executioner for that purpose. We find it recorded that in 1476, sixty sous parisis were paid to the executioner of Paris 'for having bought a large espée à feuille,' used for beheading the condemned, and 'for having the old sword done up, which was damaged, and had become notched whilst carrying out the sentence of justice upon Messire Louis de Luxembourg.'" - Manners, Customs and Dress During the Middle Ages and During the Renaissance Period, pp. 417-18.

"**Quartering may in truth be considered the most horrible penalty invented by judicial cruelty.** This punishment really dates from the remotest ages, but it was scarcely ever inflicted in more modern times, except on regicides, who were looked upon as having committed the worst of crimes. In almost all cases, the victim had previously to undergo various accessory tortures sometimes his right hand was cut off, and the mutilated stump was burnt in a cauldron of sulphur; sometimes his arms, thighs, or breasts were lacerated with redhot pincers, and hot oil, pitch, or molten lead was poured into the wounds.

"After these horrible preliminaries, a rope was attached to each of the limbs of the criminal, one being bound round each leg from the foot to the knee, and round each arm from the wrist to the elbow. These ropes were then fastened to four bars, to each of which, a strong- horse was harnessed, as if for towing a barge. These horses were first made to give short jerks; and when the agony had elicited heartrending cries from the unfortunate man, who felt his limbs being dislocated without being broken, the four horses were all suddenly urged on with the whip in different directions, and thus all the limbs were strained at one moment. If the tendons and ligaments still resisted the combined efforts of the four horses, the executioner assisted, and made several cuts with a hatchet on each joint. When at last—for this horrible torture often lasted several hours—each horse had drawn out a limb, they were collected and placed near the hideous trunk, which often still showed signs of life, and the whole were burned together. Sometimes the sentence was, that the body should be hung to the gibbet, and that the limbs should be displayed on the gates of the town, or sent to four principal towns in the extremities of the kingdom. When this was done, 'an inscription was placed on each of the limbs, which stated the reason of its being thus exposed.'" -Manners, Customs and Dress During the Middle Ages and During the Renaissance Period, pp. 420-22.

"**The accounts of the city of Paris prove that the expense of executions was more heavy** than that of the maintenance of the gibbet, a fact easy to be understood if one recalls to mind the frequency of capital sentences during the Middle Ages. Montfaucon was used not only for executions, but also for exposing corpses which were brought there from various places of execution in every part of the country. The mutilated remains of criminals who had been boiled, quartered, or beheaded, were also hung there, enclosed in sacks of leather or wicker-work. They often remained hanging for a considerable time, as in the case of Pierre des Essarts, who had been beheaded in 1413, and whose remains were handed over to his family for Christian burial after having hung on Montfaucon for three years." -Manners, Customs and Dress During the Middle Ages and During the Renaissance Period, p. 424.

"**Hanging to Music.** (A Minstrel condemned to the Gallows obtained permission that one of his companions should accompany him to his execution, and play his favourite instrument on the ladder of the Gallows.) Bruges, about 1490." -Manners, Customs and Dress During the Middle Ages and During the Renaissance Period, p. 425.

"**The Pain of the Cross, specially employed against the Jews;** the Arquebasade, which was well adapted for carrying out prompt justice on soldiers; the Chatouillement, which resulted in death after the most intense tortures; the Pal, flaying alive, and, lastly, drowning, a kind of death frequently employed in France. Hence the common expression, gens de sac et de corde, which was derived from the sack into which persons were tied who were condemned to die by immersion." -Manners, Customs and Dress During the Middle Ages and During the Renaissance Period, p. 427.

"**From various reliable sources we learn that there was a place in the Grand Chatelet [one of the most ancient prisons in Paris**, called the Chausse d'Hypocras, in which the prisoners had their feet continually in water, and where they could neither stand up nor lie down; and a cell, called Fin d'aise, which was a horrible receptacle of filth, vermin, and reptiles; as to the Fosse, no staircase being attached to it, the prisoners were lowered down into it by means of a rope and pulley. By the law of 1425, the gaoler was not permitted to put more than two or three persons in the same bed. He was bound to give " bread and water" to the poor prisoners who had no means of subsistence; and, lastly, he was enjoined " to keep the large stone basin, which was on the pavement, full of water, so that prisoners might get it whenever they wished." In order to defray his expenses, he levied on the prisoners various charges for attendance and for bedding, and he was authorised [sic] to detain in prison any person who failed to pay him. The power of compelling payment of these charges continued even after a judge's order for the release of a prisoner had been issued." -Manners, Customs and Dress During the Middle Ages and During the Renaissance Period, pp. 430-31.

"**The subterranean cells of the Bastille did not differ much from those of the Chatelet.** There were several, the bottoms of which were formed like a sugar-loaf upside down, thus neither allowing the prisoner to stand up, nor even to adopt a. tolerable position sitting or lying down. It was in these that King Louis XL, who seemed to have a partiality for filthy dungeons, placed the two young sons of the Duke de Nemours (beheaded in 1477), ordering, besides, that they should be taken out twice a week and beaten with birch rods, and, as a supreme measure of atrocity, he had one of their teeth extracted every three months. It was Louis XL, too, who, in [1470's], ordered the famous iron cage to be erected in one of the towers of the Bastille, in which Guillaume, Bishop of Verdun, was incarcerated for fourteen years." -Manners, Customs and Dress During the Middle Ages and During the Renaissance Period, p. 431.

"**The Chateau de Loches also possessed one of these cages, which received the name of Cage de Balue, because the Cardinal Jean de la Balue was imprisoned in it.** Philippe de Commines, in his " Meruoires," declares that he himself had a taste of it for eight months. Before the invention of cages, Louis XL ordered very heavy chains to he made, which were fastened to the feet of the prisoners, and attached to large iron balls...." -Manners, Customs and Dress During the Middle Ages and During the Renaissance Period, p. 432.

APPENDIX D

SELECTED PASSAGES FROM CHRONICLES OF PHARMACY, v.2

I became quite literally ill during the reading of certain material associated with this essay. Many writers give graphic details of blood rituals used by their European forebears. Though this is an essay that attempts to bring to light the corrupt actions of Indo-Europeans over the centuries at the same time they shamed Egun, my challenge was to inform readers while limiting the shock value associated with that information. Still, it is valuable information for African-Americans to have, especially when the, wrong click on the computer keyboard can lead us into some very seamy websites where the content suggests that remnants of early European ages remain with us in this so-called modern world.

Warning: Some material presented in these appendices is very disturbing. Children should not be allowed to read the material contained within Appendices A, B, C, D without parental supervision.

Any material presented in these pages should constitute only the beginning of research.

Animals in Pharmacy

"**Pigeons were cut in half** while they were alive and applied to the feet of patients. Pepys alludes two or three times to this and always as an indication that the case is nearly hopeless. The Queen of Charles II was one of the instances." -Chronicles of Pharmacy v.2, pp. 10-11.

"**Oil of Puppies was made by cutting up two newly** born ones and boiling them in a varnished pot for twelve hours with one pound of live earthworms. Very good for strengthening the nerves, for sciatica, and for paralysis, says Lemery. The gall of a black puppy, says Schroder, cures epilepsy to a wonder. It had to be prepared with vinegar. Ambrose Paré says he got a recipe from a famous surgeon at Turin for a balm with which he treated gun-shot wounds with extraordinary success. It was to boil young whelps just born with earthworms, Venice turpentine, and oil of lilies." -Chronicles of Pharmacy v.2, p. 11.

"**Swallows, hedgehogs, toads, and frogs were prepared b**y cutting their throats and leaving the blood to dry on them. They were then baked in a close vessel well covered." -Chronicles of Pharmacy v.2, p. 11.

"**Snails were made into a cough syrup by hanging** them in a bag with sugar and catching the droppings." -Chronicles of Pharmacy v.2, p. 11.

"He recommends the brain of a hare roasted to help children to breed their teeth; a dead mouse, dried and powdered, one whole one to be taken each morning for three consecutive days, for diabetes; grasshoppers for colic; and hedge-sparrows salted for stone." - Chronicles of Pharmacy v.2, p. 12.

"The cat has been largely used in medicine. Galen recommends the head of a black cat to be burned in a glazed vessel, and the ashes to be used in diseases of the eye, including cataract. Pliny says that the faeces of this animal mixed with mustard cured ulcers in the head. Sylvius prescribed cats' flesh for haemorrhoids and lumbago. In Lemery's 'Pharmacopoeia' a cat ointment is ordered. It was to be made from a newly born kitten cut up into small pieces in a pot varnished with crushed earthworms. Cats' faeces were employed in the eighteenth century as an application for baldness, and cat's skin was recommended to be worn over the stomach for strengthening the digestion." -Chronicles of Pharmacy v.2, p. 13.

"Spiders have been often employed in medicine. A live spider rolled up in butter and swallowed as a pill was a seventeenth century cure for jaundice. Spiders taste like nuts, says Lalande. Galen recommended spiders' eggs mixed with oil of nard for toothache. Elias Ashmole in his 'Diary' (1681) writes: 'I took early in the morning a good dose of elixir and hung three spiders about my neck, and they drove my ague away. Deo gratias.'" -Chronicles of Pharmacy v.2, p. 14.

SELECTED BIBLIOGRAPHY

Achilli, Giacinto. *Dealings with the Inquisition; or, Papal Rome, Her Priests, and Her Jesuits, With Important Disclosures.* London: Arthur Hall, Virtue & Co., 1851.
Anderson, James H. *Riddles of Prehistoric Times.* New York: Broadway, 1911.
Ani, Marimba. *Yurugu; An Afrikan-Centered Critique of European Cultural Thought and Behavior.* Washington DC: Nkonimo Publishing, 2007.
Bacon, Roger. *The Cure of Old Age, and the Preservation of Youth.* Translated by Richard Browne. London, 1683.
Badham, Charles, trans. *Juvenal.* New York: Harper & Bros., 1837.
Bailey, Cyril. "Roman Religion." *Encyclopaedia Britannica,* 1911.
Barker, W. H., and William Rees. *The Making of Europe: A Geographical Treatment of the Historical Development of Europe.* London: A. & C. Ltd., 1920.
Barot, Louis. *Guide Pratique de l' Europeen dans l'Afrique Occidentale.* Paris, 1902.
Barrow, John. *An Account of Travels into the Interior of South Africa.* New York: G. F. Hopkins, 1802.
Beazley, C. Raymond. *A Notebook of Mediaeval History, A. D. 323-1453.* Oxford: Clarendon, 1917.
Belloc, Hilaire. *Paris.* London: Methuen & Co., 1902.
Bingham, Denis Arthur. *The Bastille.* Vol. 1. New York: James Pott & Co., 1901.
Blake, William O., ed. *The History of Slavery and the Slave Trade. Ancient and Modern.* Columbus: H. Miller, 1859.
Boisragon, Alan. *The Benin Massacre.* London: Methuen & Co., 1897.
Bombast, Aureolus Philippus Theophrastus. *The Hermetic and Alchemical Writings of Aureolus Philipus Theophrastus.* Translated by Arthur Edward Waite. Vol. 1. London: James Elliot & Co., 1894.
Booth, George. *The Historical Library of Diodorus the Sicilian, In Fifteen Books.* London: M'Dowall, 1814.
Bostock, John, and H. T. Riley, trans. *Pliny's Natural History Remedies Derived From Man.* Vol. 5. London: Henry G. Bohn, 1856.
Bostock, John, and H. T. Riley, trans. *The Natural History of Pliny.* Vol. 3. London: Henry G. Bohn.
Boutell, Charles. "Cross." *Encyclopaedia Britannica,* 1888, 9th ed.
Brehaut, Ernest. *An Encyclopedist of the Dark Ages: Isidore of Seville.* New York: Longmans, Green, & Co., 1912.
Brown, Robert. *The Story of Africa and its Explorers.* Vol. 4. London: Cassell & Co. Ltd., 1895.
Brownlow, Canon. "Roman Slavery and Medieval Serfdom." *The Month, A Catholic Magazine and Review* 68 (1890): 203-04.
Burckhardt, Jacob. *The Civilisation of the Renaissance in Italy.* Translated by S.G.C. Middlemore. London: George Allen & Unwin Ltd., 1921.
Bury, John Bagnell. *The Cambridge Medieval History.* 2 vols. New York: Macmillan Co., 1911.
Butterworth, G. W., trans. *Clement of Alexandria.* Cambridge: Harvard University Press, 1919.
Campbell, Thomas. *Life and Times of Petrarch With Notices of Boccacio.* 2 vols. London: Henry Colburn, 1843.
Cary, Earnest, trans. *The Roman Antiquities of Dionysius of Halicarnassus.* Vol. 1. Cambridge: Harvard University Press, 1937.

Castle, Marie-Louise Egerton. "Petrarch at Naples." *The Treasury* (G. J. Palmer & Sons) 11 (1908): 555.

Chambers, Edmund Kerchever. *The Mediaeval Stage.* Vol. 1. Oxford: University Press, 1903.

Church, Alfred John, and William Jackson Brodribb, trans. *Pliny's Letters.* Edinburgh: William Blackwood & Sons, 1872.

Church, Alfred John, and William Jackson Brodribb, trans. *The Agricola and Germany of Tacitus, and the Dialogue on Oratory.* London: Macmillan & Co., 1885.

Church, Alfred John, and William Jackson Brodribb, trans. *The Annals of Tacitus.* London: Macmillan & Co., 1906.

Churchward, Albert. *The Signs and Symbols of Primordial Man, The Evolutions of Religious Doctrines From the Eschatology of the Ancient Egyptians.* 2nd Edition. London: George Allen & Co., Ltd., 1913.

Clayton, A. C. *The Rig-Veda and Vedic Religion.* London: Christian Literature Society for India, 1913.

Cooley, William Desborough. *The Negroland of the Arabs Examined and Explained.* London: J. Arrowsmith, 1841.

Coulton, G. G. *A Medieval Garner, Human Documents from the Four Centuries Preceding the Reformation.* London: Constable & Co., 1910.

Cox, George, and Eustace Hinton Jones. *Popular Romances of the Middle Ages.* New York: Henry Holt & Co., 1886.

Cumont, Franz. *The Mysteries of Mithra.* Translated by Thomas J. McCormack. Chicago: Open Court, 1903.

Dallas, Alex R. "A Day in the Dungeons of the Inquisition at Rome." *The Gospel Magazine and Protestant Beacon,* 1858: 163.

Davis, H. W. Carless. *Medieval Europe.* London: Williams & Northgate, 1915.

Davis, William Stearns. *Readings in Ancient HIstory: Greece and the East.* Boston: Allyn & Bacon, 1912.

De Azurara, Gomes Eannes. *The Chronicle of Discovery and Conquest of Guinea.* 2 vols. London: Hakluyt Society, 1896.

Deane, William J. *The Book of Wisdom.* Oxford: Clarendon, 1881.

Dearmer, Percy. "Faith and Healing." Edited by Anthony Deane. *The Treasury* (G. J. Palmer & Sons) 11 (April-September): 155-56.

Dickens, Charles. *Pictures From Italy.* London: Bradbury & Evans, Whitefriars, 1846.

Dickson, WIlliam P., trans. *The History of Rome by Theodor Mommsen.* Vol. 4. New York: Charles Scribnser's Sons , 1895.

Dickson, WIlliam P., trans. *The History of Rome by Theodor Mommsen.* 2 vols. New York: Charles Scribner's Sons, 1887.

Diop, Cheikh Anta. *Precolonial Black Africa.* Translated by Harold Salemson. Chicago: Lawrence Hill Books, 1987.

—. *The African Origin of Civilization: Myth or Reality.* New York: Hill, 1974.

Dobschutz, E. Von. "Charms and Amulets (Christian)." *Encyclopaedia of Religion and Ethics,* 1908.

Dods, Marcus, trans. *The City of God.* Edinburgh: T. & T. Clark, 1872.

Dollinger, John I. *The Gentile and the Jew in the Courts of the Temple of Christ: An Introduction to the History of Christianity.* Translated by N. Darnell. Vol. 2. London: Longman, Green, Longman, Roberts & Green, 1862.

Donovan, J. *The Catechism of the Council of Trent.* Baltimore: Lucas Brothers, 1829.

Du Chaillu, Paul. *The Viking Age.* New York: Charles Scribner's Sons, 1890.

Dubois, Felix. *Timbuctoo The Mysterious.* Translated by Diana White. London: William Heinemann, 1897.

Duruy, Victor. *The History of Rome and the Roman People.* Translated by M. Ripley and W. J. Clarke. Boston: C. F. Jewett, 1883.

Duval, G. *Shadows of Old Paris*. London: Francis Griffiths, 1910.
Dwight, Timothy. *The Charitable Blessed. A Sermon Preached in the First Church in New Haven*. Sidney's Press, 1810.
Elliot, James Sands. *Outlines of Greek and Roman Medicine*. New York: William Wood & Co., 1914.
Encyclopaedia Britannica. "Circus." 1910, 11th ed.
Encyclopaedia Britannica. "Hecato of Rhodes." 1910, 11th ed.
Equiano, Olaudah. *The Interesting Narrative of the Life of Olaudah Equiano, or Gustavus Vassa, the African, Written by Himself*. London: Olaudah Equiano, 1789.
Fairholt, Frederick W. *Miscellanea Graphica Representations of Ancient, Medieval, and Renaissance Remains*. London: Chapman and Hill, Piccadilly, 1857.
Fallow, Thomas Macall. "Cross and Crucifixion." *Encyclopaedia Britannica*, 1910, 11th ed.
Flaccus, Quintus Horatius. *The Works of Quintus Horatius Flaccus*. London: Longman, Brown, Green & Longmans, 1844.
Fletcher, Robert. *The Witches' Pharmacopoeia*. Baltimore: Friedenwald Co., 1896.
Fletcher, William D., trans. *The Works of Lactantius*. Edinburgh: T. & T. Clark, 1871.
Forester, Thomas. *The Chronicle of Florence Worcester*. London: Henry G. Bohn, 1854.
Freedman, H., and Maurice Simon, trans. *Midrash Rabbah Genesis*. London: Soncino, 1939.
Freese, J. H., trans. *The Octavius of Minucius Felix*. New York: Macmillan Co., 1919.
Galvao, Antonio. *The Discoveries of the World*. Edited by Rchard Hakluyt. London: Hakluyt Society, 1862.
Gasquet, Francis Aidan. *The Great Pestilence (A.D. 1348-9) Now Commonly Known as the Black Death*. London: Simpkin Marshall, Hamilton, Kent & Co., Ltd., 1893.
Gaye, Selina. "Sketches From Hungarian History." *The Monthly Packet of Evening Readings* 19 (1875): 323-24.
Gibbon, Edward. *The Decline and Fall of the Roman Empire*. New York: Peter Fenelon Collier & Son, 1900.
Giles, John Allen. *The Anglo-Saxon Chronicle*. London: G. Bell & Sons, 1914.
—. *William of Malmesbury's Chronicle of the Kings of England*. London: Henry G. Bohn, 1847.
Godard, John George. *Racial Supremacy Being Studies in Imperialism*. Edinburgh: Geo. A. Morton, 1905.
Goodwin, William W., ed. *Plutarch's Morals*. Boston: Little, Brown, & Co., 1878.
Gordon-Cumming, Constance Frederica. *Memories With Illustrations*. Edinburgh: William Blackwood & Sons, 1904.
Gordon-Cumming, Constance Frederica. "Strange Medicines." *The Nineteenth Century* 21 (1887): 908-09.
Gregorovius, Ferdinand. *History of the City of Rome in the Middle Ages*. Translated by Annie Hamilton. 4 vols. London: George Bell & Sons, 1894.
Greive, James, trans. *A. Corn Celsus of Medicine*. Edinburgh: Dickson & Co., 1814.
Gunn, Battiscombe, trans. *The Wisdom of the East; The Instruction of Ptah-hotep and the Instruction of Ke'Gemni*. London: John Murray, 1918.
Gunst, Frans Christiaan. *Martyrs*. San Francisco: S. N., 1870.
Gwynn, John. *Commentary on the Apocalypse, Acts, and Epistles, of Dionysius Barasalibi: Hippolytus and His Heads Against Caius*. 2005. http://www.tertullian.org.
Haines, C. R., trans. *The Correspondence of Marcus Cornelius Fronto*. Massachusetts: Harvard University Press, 1919.
Hallam, Henry. *History of Europe During the Middle Ages*. Vol. 1. New York: Colonial, 1899.
—. *View of the State of Europe During the Middle Ages*. 2 vols. New York: A. C. Armstrong & Son, 1880.
Harris, John H. *Africa: Slave Or Free?* London: Student Christian Movement, 1919.
Hartland, E. Sydney. "The Cult of Executed Criminals at Palermo." *Folk-Lore: A Quarterly Review Myth, Tradition, Institution & Custom* 21 (1910): 176.
Hauck, Albert. "Relics." *Encyclopaedia Britannica*, 1911, 11th ed.

Haynie, Henry. *Paris: Past and Present.* Vol. 1. New York: Frederick A. Stokes Cp., 1902.

Hilliard III, Asa G. "The Meaning of KMT (Ancient Egypt) History for Contemporary African American Experience." 11 (1992).

Hodgkin, Thomas. *Italy and Her Invaders.* 2 vols. Oxford: Clarendon, 1892.

Holland, Philemon, trans. *Pliny's Natural History in Thirty-Seven Books.* 2 vols. London: George Barclay, 1847.

Howe, Samuel Burnett. *Essentials in Early European History.* 4th Edition. New York: Longman's, Green, and Co., 1912.

Indicopleustes, Cosmas. *The Christian Topography of Cosmas Indicopleustes.* Edited by E. O. Winstedt. Cambridge: University Press, 1909.

James I, King of England. *Daemonologie, in forme of a dialogie.* Edinburgh, 1597.

James, George G. M. *Stolen Legacy: Greek Philosophy is Stolen Egyptian Philosophy.* New Jersey: Africa World Press, 1992.

Jennings, Hargrave. *Phallism: A Description of the Worship of Lingam Yoni.* London, 1892.

Johnston, Harry Hamilton. *A History of Colonization of Africa by Alien Races...With Eight Maps, etc.* Cambridge: University Press, 1905.

Jones, Alonzo Trevier. *The Great Empires of Prophecy from Babylon to the Fall of Rome.* Battle Creek: Review and Herald, 1898.

Jordan, David Starr. *The Blood of the Nation: A Study of the Decay of Race Through the Survivial of the Unfit.* Boston: American Unitarian Association, 1910.

Knight, Charles. *Charles Knight's Popular History of England.* Vol. 1. London: Bradbury, Evans & Co., 1862.

Krey, August C. *The First Crusade: The Accounts of Eyewitnesses and Participants.* Princeton: Princeton University Press, 1921.

Kurze, Friedrich, and Johann Martin Lappenberg, trans. *Thietmari Merseburgensis Episcopi Chronicon.* Hannoverae: Impensis Bibliopolii Hahniani, 1889.

Lacroix, Paul. *Manners, Customs, and Dress During the Middle Ages and During the Renaissance Period.* New York: D. Appleton & Co., 1874.

Lake, Krisopp. "Christmas." *Encyclopaedia of Religion and Ethics,* 1910.

Lang, A. "Method and Minotaur." *Folk-Lore: A Quarterly Review Myth, Tradition, Institution, & Custom* 21 (1910): 142.

Lea, Henry Charles. *A History of the Inquisition of the Middle Ages.* New York: Harper & Harper Brothers, 1887.

Lean, Stuckey Vincent. *Lean's Collectnea.* Vol. 3. Bristol: J. W. Arrowsmith, 1903.

Lechner, P. Peter. *The Life and Times of St. Benedict: Patriarch of the Monks of the West.* London: Burns and Oates, 1900.

Leeper, Alexander, trans. *Thirteen Satires of Juvenal.* London: Macmillan & Co., Ltd., 1902.

Livius, Titus. *Livy.* Translated by B. O. Foster. London: William Heinemann, 1919.

Ludlow, James M. *The Age of the Crusades.* New York: Christian Literature Co., 1896.

Lugira, Aloysius M. *World Religions, African Traditional Religion.* 3rd Edition. New York: Chelsea House, 2009.

Macaulay, G. C. *The Chronicles of Froissart.* Translated by John Bourchier. London: Macmillan and Co., Ltd., 1913.

Machiavelli, Niccolo. *Discourses on the First Decade of Titus Livius.* Translated by Ninian Hill Thomson. London: Kegan Paul, Trench & Co,, 1883.

Mackay, Charles. *Memoirs of Extraordinary Popular Delusions and the Madness of Crowds.* 2nd Edition. London: George Rutledge & Sons, 1869.

Madden, R. R. *The Life and Martyrdom of Savonarola the Christian hero of the Fifteenth Century.* Vol. 2. London: Thomas Chuiley Newby, 1853.

Magie, David, trans. *The Scriptores Historiae Augustae.* Vol. 3. Massachusetts: Harvard University Press, 1921.

Massey, Gerald. *The Historical Jesus and Mythical Christ.* London: Villa Bordighiera, 1880.

Mawer, Allen. *The Vikings.* London: Cambridge University Press, 1913.
McMurdo, Allen. *Portugal from the Reign of D. Diniz to the Reign of D. Alfonso V.* London: Sampson Low, Marston, Searle, & Rivington, 1889.
Michelet, Jules. *La Sociere: The Witch of the Middle Ages.* Translated by L. J. Trotter. London: Simpkin, Marshall & Co., 1863.
Middleton, John Henry, and Henry Stuart Jones. "Rome, Places of Amusement." *Encyclopaedia Britannica*, 1911, 11th ed.
Mierow, Charles Christopher. *The Gothic History of Jordanes.* Princeton: Princeton University Press, 1915.
Miles, Clement A. *A Christmas in Ritual and Tradition, Christian and Pagan.* London: T. Fisher Unwin, 1912.
Miller, Beaupre, ed. *Through Fairy Halls of My BookHouse.* Chicago: The BookHouse for Children, 1920.
Montesquieu, Charles. *The Persian Letters.* London: Atheneum, 1897.
Montgomery, James. *Journal of Arabic and Islamic Studies: Ibn Fadlan and the Rusiyyah.*
Morel, Edmund D. *King Leopold's Rule in Africa.* London: William Heinemann, 1904.
Murphy, Arthur, trans. *The Works of Sallust.* London: James Carpenetr and J. Cuthell and P. Martin, 1807.
Myers, Phillip Van Ness. *Outlines of Ancient History.* Boston: Ginn & Co., 1887.
Newton, John. *The Posthumous Works of the Late John Newton.* Vol. 2. Philadelphia: W. W. Woodward.
Olivier, Pasfield, ed. *The Voyage of Francois Leguat.* Vol. 2. London: Hakluyt Society, 1891.
Oman, Charles. *A History of the Art of War, From the Fourth to the Fourteenth Century.* New York: G. P. Putnam's Sons, 1898.
Ozanam, A. Frederic. *History of Civilization in the Fifth Century.* Translated by Ashley C. Glyn. Vol. 1. London: W. H. Allen, 1868.
Park, Mungo. "Testimony in Favour of the Possibility of Civilizing the Africans." *The African Repository and Colonial Journal* 4 (1829): 76-77.
Paton, Lewis Bayles. *Spiritism and the Cult of the Dead in Antiquity.* New York: Macmillan Co., 1921.
Peacock, Mabel. "Executed Criminals and Folk-Medicine." *Folk-Lore: A Quarterly Review Myth, Tradition, Institution & Custom* 7 (1896): 270-76.
Pelham, Henry Francis, and Henry Stuart Jones. "Rome, Republic; Rome, Empire." *Encyclopaedia Britannica*, 1911, 11th ed.
Peloubet, Francis Nathan, trans. *The Holy Bible Containing the Old and New Testaments.* Philadelphia: A. J. Holman & Co., 1920.
Pettigrew, Thomas Joseph. *A History of Egyptian Mummies and an Account of the Worship and Embalming of the Sacred Animals of the Egyptians.* London: Longman, Rees, Orme, Brown, Green, and Longman, Paternoster Row, 1834.
Phyfe, William Henry P. *Five Thousand Facts and Fancies: A Cyclopaedia of Important, Curious, Quaint and Unique Information in History, Literature, Science, Art, and Nature.* New York: G. P. Putnam's Sons, 1901.
Plaisted, David. *Estimates of the Number Killed in the Middle Ages and Later.* 2006. http://www.cs.unc.edu/~plaisted/estimates.html.
Plato. *The Dialogues of Plato.* Translated by Benjamin Jowett. New York: Charles Scribner's Sons, 1871.
—. *The Dialogues of Plato.* Translated by Benjamin Jowett. New York: Charles Scribner's Sons, 1871.
—. *The Dialogues of Plato.* Translated by Benjamin Jowett. New York: Charles Scribner's Sons, 1871.
—. *The Dialogues of Plato.* Translated by Benjamin Jowett. New York: Charles Scribner's Sons, 1871.
Pomet, Pierre. *A Compleat History of Druggs.* 3rd Edition. London: J. & J. Bonwicke, R. Wilkin,

S. Birt, T. Ward, and E. Wickfleed, 1737.
Purchas, Samuel. *Hakluytus Posthumous or Purchase his Pilgrimes.* Vol. 13. Glasgow: MacLehose, 1906.
Rainsford, Marcus. *An Historical Account of the Black Empire of Hayti.* James Cundee, Ivy-Lane, Paternoster-Row, 1805.
Ramsay, George, trans. *The Histories of Tacitus.* London: John Murray, 1915.
Rawlinson, George, trans. *The History of Herodotus.* 2 vols. New York: Tandy-Thomas Co., 1909.
Ray, John, trans. *The Ornithology of Francis Willughby.* London: A. C. for John Martyn, 1678.
Read, Charles Hercules, and Ormonde Maddock Dalton. *Antiquities of the City of Benin and from the Other Parts of West Africa.* London: Longman & Co., 1899.
Redgrove, H. Stanley. *Bygone Beliefs Being A Series of Excursions in the Byways of Thought.* London: William Rider & Son, Ltd., 1920.
Roberts, Alexander, and James Donaldson, trans. *The Writings of Tertullian.* Vol. 1. Edinburgh: T. & T. Clark, 1869.
Robinson, James Harvey. *Readings in European History.* Vol. 1. Boston: Ginn & Co., 1904.
Rule, William Harris. *History of the Inquisition.* Vol. 1. London: Hamilton, Adams & Co., 1874.
S., G. F. "Ancient Kingdoms of the Soudan." *The Church Missionary Review* (Church Missionary Society) 58 (January 1907).
Sabatini, Rafael. *The Life of Cesare Borgia.* 1914.
Salvanius. *On the Government of God.* Translated by Eva M. Sanford. New York: Columbia University Press, 1930.
Sayce, A. H., trans. *The Ancient Empires of the East, Herodotus.* London: Macmillan & Co., 1883.
Schneider, Albert. "Some Ancient Therapeutics." *Merck's Archives,* 1901: 255-58.
Schopenhauer, Arthur. *The World as Will and Idea.* Translated by R. B. Haldane and J. Kemp. London: Trubner & Co., Lugate Hill, 1886.
Scully, William Charles. "The Colour Problem in South Africa." *The Edinburgh Review* 230 (1919): 78-92.
Seneca, Lucius Annaeus. *L. Annaeus Seneca Minor Dialogues Together With the Dialogue on Clemency.* Translated by Aubrey Stewart. London: George Bell & Sons, 1889.
—. *Morals of a Happy Life, Benefits, Anger, and Clemency.* Translated by Roger L'Estrange. Chicago: Belford, Clarke, & Co., 1882.
Shaw, Flora. *A Tropical Dependency.* London: J. Nisbet & Co., 1905.
Sinclair, Upton. *The Book of Life.* Chicago: The Paine Book Co., 1922.
Sinding, Paul C. *History of Scandinavia.* 2nd Edition. New York: Pudney & Russell, 1859.
—. *The Scandinavian Races: The Northmen; The Sea-Kings and Vikings.* New York: Paul C. Sinding, 1875.
Smith, Horatio, and Samuel Woodworth. *Festivals, Games, and Amusements Ancient and Modern.* New York: J. & J. Harper, 1831.
Smith, W. Robertson. *Lectures on the Religion of the Semites.* London: Adam and Charles Black, 1894.
Stanley, Henry M. *Through the Dark Continent.* Vol. 1. New York: Harper & Brothers, 1879.
Store, Francis. "Games, Classical." *Encyclopaedia Britannica,* 1910, 11th ed.
Story, William W. "Castle St. Angelo and the Evil Eye." *Blackwood's Edinburgh Magazine* 109 (1871): 351.
Story, William W. "Castle St. Angelo and the Evil Eye." *Blackwood's Edinburgh Magazine* 108 (1870): 755-56.
Story, William W. "Castle St. Angelo and the Evil Eye." *Blackwood's Edinburgh Magazine* 110 (1871): 604-08.
Strabo. *The Geography of Strabo.* Translated by W. Falconer. London: Henry G. Bohn, 1857.
Strack, Herman L. *The Jew and Human Sacrifice-Human Blood and Jewish Ritual.* New York:

Bloch, 1909.
Tacitus, C. Cornelius. *A Treatise on the Situation, Manners, and Inhabitants of Germany and the Life of Agricola*. Translated by John Aiken. Cambridge: W. Grant, 1823.
Tappan, Eva March. *When Knights Were Bold*. Boston: Houghton Mifflin Co., 1911.
Theal, George McCall. *Records of Southeastern Africa*. Vol. 5. London: William Clowes & Son, 1901.
—. *The Beginning of South African History*. London: T. Fisher Unwin, 1902.
Thorndike, Lynn. *The History of Medieval Europe*. Boston: Houghton Mifflin Co., 1917.
Timpson, Thomas. *The Inquisition Revealed*. London: Aylott and Jones, Paternoster Row, 1851.
Topinard, Paul. "De La Notion De Race." *Revue Anthropologie*, 1879: 589-90.
Trumbull, H. Clay. *The Blood Covenant*. 2nd Edition. Philadelphia: John D. Wattles, 1893.
Turberville, Arthur Stanley. *Mediaeval Heresy & the Inquisition*. London: Crosby Lockwood & Son, 1920.
Tyler, Lyon Gardiner, ed. *Narratives of Early Virginia 1606-1625*. New York: Charles Scribner's Sons, 1907.
Vitalis, Odericus. *The Ecclesiastical History of England and Normandy*. Translated by Thomas Forester. 2 vols. London: Henry G. Bohn, 1853.
Volney, C. F. *Ruins, Or, Meditation On the Revolutions of Empires: and the Law of Nature*. Translated by Peter Eckler. New York: Peter Eckler, 1890.
Von Andel, M. A. "Adeps Hominis: A Relic of Prehistory Therapy." *The American Journal of Pharmacy* 94 (1922): 655-71.
Von Klein, Carl Heinrich. *The Medical Features of the Papyrus Ebers*. Chicago: American Medical Association, 1905.
Walhouse, M. J. "Folklore Parallels and Coincidences." *Folk-Lore: A Quarterly Review Myth, Tradition, Institution, & Custom* 8 (1897): 199.
Walsh, James J. *Medieval Medicine*. London: A. & C. Black, Ltd., 1920.
—. *Old-Time Makers of Medicine*. New York: Fordham University Press.
Warfield, Benjamin B. *Counterfeit Miracles*. New York: Charles Scribner's Sons, 1918.
Washington, Harriet A. *A Medical Apartheid: The Dark History of Medical Experimentation on Black Americans from Colonial Times to the Present*. New York: Harlem Moon, 2006.
Watson, Alfred Edward Thomas. "Horse-Racing (Great Britain)." *Encyclopaedia Britannica*, 1910, 11th ed.
Webster, Hutton. *Early European History*. Boston: D. C. Heath & Co., 1917.
Weeks, John H. *Among the Primitive BaKongo*. London: Seeley, Service & Co., Ltd., 1914.
Welsing, Frances Cress. *The Isis (Yssis) Papers*. Chicago: Third World Press, 1991.
White, Andrew Dickson. *A History of the Warfare of Science With Theology in Christendom*. New York: Appleton & Co. , 1896.
Williams, Chancellor. *The Destruction of Black Civilization*. Chicago: Third World Press, 1987.
Williamson, James A. *The Foundation and Growth of the British Empire*. London: Macmillan & Co., 1916.
Wilson, William, trans. *The Writings of Clement of Alexandria*. Vol. 2. Edinburgh: T & T Clark, 1869.
Withington, E. "Roger Bacon and Medicine." In *In Roger Bacon Essays*, edited by A. G. Little. Oxford: Clarendon, 1914.
Wootton, A. C. *Chronicles of Pharmacy*. London: Macmillan & Co., Ltd., 1920.
Young, Charles. *Harald: First of the Vikings*. New York: Thomas Y. Crowell Co., 1911.
Zinn, Howard. *A People's History of the United States*. New York: HarperCollins Publishers, 1999.

www.ingramcontent.com/pod-product-compliance
Lightning Source LLC
Chambersburg PA
CBHW021758220426
43662CB00006B/113